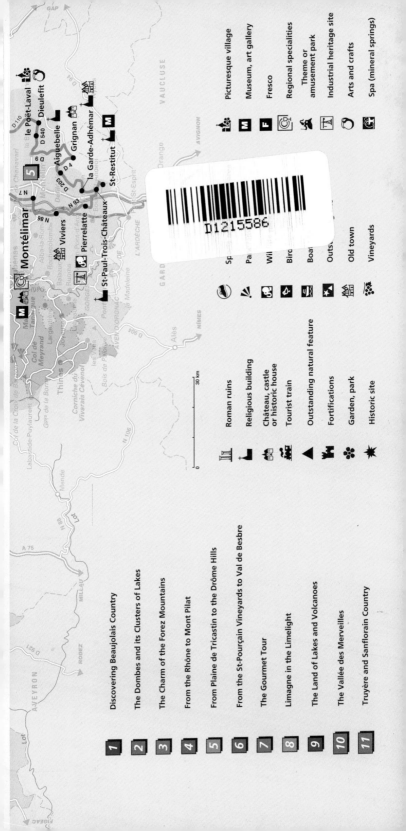

Legend / Tour list:

1. Discovering Beaujolais Country
2. The Dombes and its Clusters of Lakes
3. The Charm of the Forez Mountains
4. From the Rhône to Mont Pilat
5. From Plaine de Tricastin to the Drôme Hills
6. From the St-Pourçain Vineyards to Val de Besbre
7. The Gourmet Tour
8. Limagne in the Limelight
9. The Land of Lakes and Volcanoes
10. The Vallée des Merveilles
11. Truyère and Sanflorain Country

Roman ruins
Religious building
Château, castle or historic house
Tourist train
Outstanding natural feature
Fortifications
Garden, park
Historic site

Sp
Pa
Wil
Bird
Boat
Outs
Old town
Vineyards

Picturesque village
Museum, art gallery
Fresco
Regional specialities
Theme or amusement park
Industrial heritage site
Arts and crafts
Spa (mineral springs)

AUVERGNE
RHÔNE VALLEY

Editorial Director   Cynthia Clayton Ochterbeck

THE GREEN GUIDE AUVERGNE RHÔNE VALLEY

Editor   Jonathan P. Gilbert
Principal Writer   Terry Marsh
Production Manager   Natasha G. George
Cartography   Alain Baldet, Michelle Cana, Peter Wrenn
Photo Editor   Lydia Strong, Yoshimi Kanazawa
Proofreader   Alison Coupe, Rachel Mills
Layout & Design   John Higginbottom, Natasha G. George
Cover Design   Laurent Muller, Ute Weber

Contact Us: The Green Guide
                              Michelin Maps and Guides
                              One Parkway South
                              Greenville, SC 29615
                              USA
                              www.michelintravel.com
                              michelin.guides@us.michelin.com

                              Michelin Maps and Guides
                              Hannay House
                              39 Clarendon Road
                              Watford, Herts WD17 1JA
                              UK
                              ☎ (01923) 205 240
                              www.ViaMichelin.com
                              travelpubsales@uk.michelin.com

Special Sales: For information regarding bulk sales,
                              customized editions and premium sales,
                              please contact our Customer Service
                              Departments:
                              USA   1-800-432-6277
                              UK   (01923) 205 240
                              Canada 1-800-361-8236

Note to the Reader
While every effort is made to ensure that all information printed in this guide is correct and up-to-date, Michelin Apa Publications Ltd. accepts no liability for any direct, indirect or consequential losses howsoever caused so far as such can be excluded by law.

One Team…
A Commitment to Quality

There's just one reason our team is dedicated to producing quality travel publications—you, our reader.

Throughout our guides we offer **practical information**, **touring tips** and **suggestions** for finding the best places for a break.

Michelin driving tours help you hit the highlights and quickly absorb the best of the region. Our descriptive **walking tours** make you your own guide, armed with directions, maps and expert information.

We scout out the attractions, classify them with **star ratings**, and describe in detail what you will find when you visit them.

Michelin maps featured throughout the guide offer vibrant, detailed and easy-to-follow outlines of everything from close-up museum plans to international maps.

Places to stay and eat are always a big part of travel, so we research **hotels and restaurants** that we think convey the essence of the destination and arrange them by geographic area and price. We walk you through the best shopping districts and point you towards the host of entertainment and recreation possibilities available.

We **test**, **retest**, **check and recheck** to make sure that our guidebooks are truly just that: a personalized guide to help you make the most of your visit. And if you still want a speaking guide, we list local tour guides who will lead you on all the boat, bus, guided, historical, culinary, and other tours you shouldn't miss.

In short, we remove the guesswork involved with travel. After all, we want you to enjoy exploring with Michelin as much as we do.

The Michelin Green Guide Team

PLANNING YOUR TRIP

INTRODUCTION TO AUVERGNE RHÔNE VALLEY

J. Damase/MICHELIN

CONTENTS

DISCOVERING THE SIGHTS OF THE AUVERGNE

HOW TO USE THIS GUIDE

PLANNING YOUR TRIP

The blue-tabbed PLANNING YOUR TRIP section at the front of the guide gives you **ideas for your trip** and **practical information** to help you organize it. You'll find tours, a host of breaks in the great outdoors, a calendar of events, information on shopping, sightseeing, kids' activities and more.

INTRODUCTION

The orange-tabbed INTRODUCTION section explores **Nature** from the mineral springs to the volcanic landscape. The **History** section spans from the Neolithic to the Vichy government. The **Art and Culture** section covers architecture, art, literature, traditions and folklore, while **The Region Today** delves into the modern Auvergne.

DISCOVERING

The green-tabbed DISCOVERING section features the Auvergne's Principal Sights,

Sidebars

Throughout the guide you will find peach-colored text boxes (like this one), with lively anecdotes, detailed history, and background information.

arranged alphabetically, featuring the most interesting local **Sights**, **Walking Tours**, nearby **Excursions**, and detailed **DrivingTours**.

🛈 Contact information, ⬿ admission charges, 🕐 hours of operation, and a host of other **visitor information** is given wherever possible. Admission prices shown are normally for a single adult.

STAR RATINGS★★★

Michelin has given star ratings for more than 100 years. If you're pressed for time, we recommend you visit the ★★★, or ★★ sights first:

★★★ Highly recommended
★★ Recommended
★ Interesting

Address Books - Where to Stay, Eat and more...

WHERE TO STAY

We've made a selection of hotels and arranged them by price category to fit all budgets (👜 see the Legend on the cover flap for an explanation of the price categories). For the most part, we've selected accommodations based on their unique regional quality, their regional feel, as it were.

👜 See the back of the guide for an index to where to stay.

👜 See the red-cover Michelin Guide France for more addresses.

WHERE TO EAT

We thought you'd like to know the popular eating spots in the Auvergne. So, we selected restaurants that capture the regional experience. We're not rating the quality of the food per se; as we did with the hotels, we selected restaurants for many towns and villages, categorized by price to appeal to all wallets.

👜 See the back of the guide for an index to where to eat.

👜 See the red-cover Michelin Guide France for more addresses.

MAPS

- 🔿 **Principal Sights map** and **Driving Tours Map** on the cover.
- 🔿 Detailed maps for **major cities** and **villages**, including **driving tour maps** and larger-scale maps for **walking tours**.

All maps in this guide are oriented north, unless otherwise indicated by a directional arrow. The term "Local Map" refers to a map within the chapter or Tourism Region. A complete list of the maps found in the guide appears at the back of this book, along with a comprehensive index.

See the map Legend at the back of the guide for an explanation of map symbols.

> 😊 **A Bit of Advice** 😊
>
> Green advice boxes found in this guide contain practical tips and handy information relevant to the sight in the DISCOVERING section.

ORIENT PANELS

Vital statistics are given for each principal sight in the DISCOVERING section:

- 🛈 **Information:** Tourist Office/Sight contact details.
- ▶ **Orient Yourself:** Geographic location of the sight with reference to surrounding boroughs, towns and roads.
- 🅿 **Parking:** Where to park.
- 🔿 **Don't Miss:** Unmissable things to do.
- 🕐 **Organising Your Time:** Tips on organising your stay; what to see first, how long to spend there, crowd avoidance, market days and more.
- Kids **Especially for Kids:** Sights of particular interest to children.
- 👍 **Also See:** Nearby PRINCIPAL SIGHTS featured elsewhere in the guide.

SYMBOLS

Spa	**Spa Facilities**	👣	**Tours**
Kids	**Interesting for Children**	🅿	**On-site Parking**
👍	**Also See**	▶	**Directions**
🛈	**Tourist Information**	✕	**On-site eating Facilities**
🕐	**Hours of Operation**	⚠	**Camping Facilities**
🕘	**Periods of Closure**	⚐	**Beaches**
☞	**Closed to the Public**	🍵	**Breakfast Included**
👛	**Entry Fees**	😊	**A Bit of Advice**
🚫	**Credit Cards not Accepted**	😟	**Warning**
♿	**Wheelchair Accessible**		

Contact – Addresses, phone numbers, opening hours and prices published in this guide are accurate at the time of press. We welcome corrections and suggestions that may assist us in preparing the next edition. Please send your comments to:

UK
Michelin Maps and Guides
Hannay House
39 Clarendon Road
Watford, Herts WD17 1JA
travelpubsales@uk.michelin.com
www.michelin.co.uk

USA
Michelin Maps and Guides
Editorial Department
P.O. Box 19001
Greenville, SC 29602-9001
michelin.guides@us.michelin.com
www.michelintravel.com

Chaine des Puys with the Puy de
Dôme in the background
©Marc Legendre/istockphoto.com

MICHELIN DRIVING TOURS

Local Drives

The following is a selection of the Driving Tours in the Discovering section:

- **Beaujolais vineyards**
  See BEAUJOLAIS. Villefranche-sur-Saône to St-Amour-Bellevue. 98km/61mi – 5hr. The road climbs through the vineyards of Beaujolais and crosses a granite escarpment before descending to the Saône.

- **Monts du Cantal**
  See MONTS DU CANTAL. The Route du Lioran from Aurillac. 55km/34mi – 4hr. This agreeable drive makes the most of the Cère and Alagnon valleys.

- **A mini tour of the volcanoes**
  See CLERMONT-FERRAND. A half-day tour of the volcanoes around Clermont-Ferrand. 35km/21mi. Visit the Plateau de Chanturgue and the spectacular Puy de Dôme.

- **Alpine Pastures of Le Cézallier**
  See CONDAT. From the Rhue Gorge to gentiane country. 80km/50mi – allow one day. Waterfalls, gorges and wild flowers.

- **The Land of Stone Roofs**
  See CRÉMIEU. A tour of the Île Crémieu. 60km/37mi – 3hr. Cliffs, lakes, stone roofs, standing stones and country houses.

- **The Dombes lakes**
  See La DOMBES. A round trip of 99km/61mi from Villars-les-Dombes – a full day. Myriad lakes and ways.

- **The Puy Mountain range**
  See MONTS DÔME. 120km/75mi – allow a full day. Visit the volcanoes and byways of the Monts Dôme.

- **The Monts de Forez**
  *See MONTS DU FOREZ. A full day tour in the Parc Naturel Régional Livradois-Forez. From Boën via the Col de Béal – vineyards, chateaux and rugged scenery.

- **Discover Lauze country**
  See LAC d'ISSARLÈS. Lac d'Issarlès to the Loire's source and rural architecture.

- **Approaching the Livradois**
  See ISSOIRE. 45km/28mi round trip – 2hr. Issoire to the Château de Parentignat and beyond.

- **The Dauphiné d'Auvergne**
  See ISSOIRE. 60km/37mi – half a day. SW of Issoire between the Cézallier and the Allier valley.

- **The Upper Velay valley**
  See GORGES DE LA LOIRE. Gerbier-de-Jonc to Le Puy-en-Velay. 115km/71mi. Explore the gorges of the Loire valley.

- **Monts du Lyonnais**
  See LYON. From Lyon to St Étienne. 128km/80mi – allow a full day. Explore the hills to the south-west of Lyon.

- **Along the left bank of the Loire**
  See MONISTROL-SUR-LOIRE. From Le Monistrol-sur-Loire. 30km/19mi – half a day. Visit medieval castles and the valley of the Ance.

- **Explore Le Pilat**
  See LE PILAT. From St Étienne to Condrieu. 89km/56mi – half a day, or more to explore St Étienne. An agreeable way to discover the delights of the Parc Naturel Régional du Pilat.

- **The valley of the Borne**
  See Le PUY-EN-VELAY. A half-day round trip of 60km/37mi. From Le Puy-en-Velay along the Borne river.

- **Discover Les Combrailles**
  See RIOM. From Riom a round trip of 75km/47mi – allow half a day. Gorges, lakes and chateaux.

- **Limagne Bourbonnaise**
  See VICHY. From St Pourçain-sur-Sioule. 75km/47mi – allow half a day. Visit medieval villages, manor houses and Romanesque churches.

- **Explore the Sancy Range**
  See MASSIF du SANCY. From Le Mont-Dore. 85km/53mi, round trip – allow a full day. One of the most picturesque areas in the Auvergne.

Regional Drives

See the Driving Tours map on the front cover flap.

1 BEAUJOLAIS COUNTRY

Round tour of 129km/80mi leaving from Villefranche-sur-Saône.
This tour of the sun-drenched slopes of Beaujolais naturally starts from Villefranche-sur-Saône, seen by many as the capital of the famous Beaujolais *appellation*.
The former walled city of Belleville is now an important wine-making centre, but it has kept many vestiges of its 12C church, notably an interesting series of capitals. Corcelles Château boasts a fine 17C vat whose aromas will make your head spin! The "Hameau du Vin" and its "station" set up in Romanèche-Thorins form a small museum that pays tribute to the noble traditions that have governed the art of wine making throughout the centuries, and the adjoining safari park will delight young children. In Beaujolais each vineyard has developed its own peculiarities: the Fleurie grapes yield a young, lively wine, whereas the Villié-Morgon bottles are usually for laying down.
A great many *crus* can be found in Beaujeu, a town wholly devoted to the commerce of wine. After pausing to admire the stunning panorama stretching from Mont Brouilly to the Saône plain, pay a visit to the Salles-Arbuissonnas-en-Beaujolais Priory, dating back to the 10C.
The two châteaux of Montmelas-St-Sorlin and Jarnioux are your next stop, leading to the quaint village of Oingt, perched on a hillside and crowned by a tower.
Driving through the Bagnols vineyards, you reach Châtillon and its 12C stronghold. In St-Jean-des-Vignes, the Museum of Geology explains the origins of the topography which characterises the Beaujolais region and which has produced its unique *terroir*. The tour ends with the village of Chazay-d'Arzergues, from where you can return to Villefranche via Anse.

J. Damase/MICHELIN

The village of Oingt

2 THE DOMBES AND ITS CLUSTERS OF LAKES

Round tour of 155km/96.5mi leaving from Lyon.
Leaving from Lyon, a city that has successfully taken up the challenges of modern life while preserving its historical legacy, this tour is a charming nature trail dotted with ancient monuments. Stop to admire the medieval towers of Rochetaillée Château and then press on to Ars, famous for its bishop who was canonised in 1925 and who is the patron saint of all parish bishops. After visiting Ambérieux-en-Dombes, another town with religious associations awaits you: Châtillon-sur-Chalaronne, where St Vincent de Paul founded the first brotherhood of charity and where you can visit the Apothicairerie. The tour then takes you to the Romanesque church in St-Paul-de-Varax and the 19C Notre-Dame-des-Domes Abbey, which was instrumental in draining the surrounding plains. The bird sanctuary in Villars-les-Dombes is the perfect spot for a family outing, and the brick castle in Le Montellier is an impressive sight indeed. The hilltop village of Pérouges, circled by ancient ramparts and crossed by winding streets, is often used as a backdrop for historical films. Finally, after a halt in Montluel, you can return to the city of Lyon and its many attractions.

S. Sauvignier/MICHELIN

Lavaudieu

③ THE CHARM OF THE FOREZ MOUNTAINS

*Round tour of 200km/124mi
leaving from Roanne*

The region, generally referred to as Forez, comprises a range of mountains, a series of plains, a natural park and a web of meandering roads. This tour begins in Roanne, a Roman city today known for its textile and food-processing industries. After a short drive through vineyards producing a lively rosé wine, you reach pretty Ambierle with its old Cluniac priory, Flamboyant Gothic church and museum devoted to traditional costumes and lore. The fortified village of St-Haon-le-Châtel features some interesting Renaissance houses and the nearby Tache Dam, which dominates the local vineyards, is the starting point for charming country walks across the Monts de la Madeleine. Driving down the Gorges Roannaises de la Loire, you come to St-Maurice-sur-Loire, where the church apse boasts remarkable 13C frescoes and the keep commands a fine panorama of the gorges. Also steeped in history are the two towns of St-Germain-Laval and Pommiers and their intricate network of cobbled alleys. After visiting the Château de la Vigne et du Vin in Boën, drop by the fortress in Sail-sous-Couzan and feast your eyes on the Forez plain. Château de la Bastie-

d'Urfé was once the residence of the famed writer Honoré d'Urfé, whose romantic novel *L'Astrée* set a new literary trend in early-17C France. A more austere atmosphere permeates the 14C church in Champdieu and the old convent of Montbrison, dominated by its 18C dome and circled by stone ramparts. Although the living quarters within the castle was destroyed by a fire in the 18C, Montrond-les-Bains is a pleasant fortified city whose spa is ideal for treating diabetes and other disorders. After a breath of fresh air, strolling through the bird sanctuary at the Écopôle du Forez, resume your history lesson by exploring the ancient city of Feurs and visiting its Gallo-Roman Museum of Archaeology. The medieval hamlet of Villerest has a curious museum retracing the history of fire and its domestic uses through the ages. The Loire gorges cutting across the rocky plains leads you back to Roanne, where the tour can be nicely concluded with a boat ride.

④ FROM THE RHÔNE TO MONT PILAT

*Round tour of 170km/105.6mi
leaving from St-Étienne*

The tour begins in St-Étienne, a city with deep-rooted traditions that has kept abreast of the times, and houses an admirable Museum of Modern Art. Your journey then takes you to St-Chamond, the site of a factory producing armoured vehicles, Rive-de-Gier and St-Genis-Laval. You approach Lyon via the antique city of Oullins. As for the modern metropolis, frequently dubbed France's second capital, it offers a host of museums, cafés, restaurants and historical monuments. Further on, you reach Vienne, yet another Roman city, whose Jazz Festival enjoys a prestigious reputation. At your next stop, Condrieu, take a seat on the sunny quays and sip a glass of *viognier*, the local white wine, as you watch boats gliding into port. After visiting Pélussin and its museum, do not miss the stunning vista afforded by the Crêt de l'Œillon, extending over the Rhône Valley and Crêt de la

Perdrix. For a sweeping panorama, try the viewing table on the Pics du Mézenc. If weather conditions are favourable, why not tackle one of the skiing slopes at Le Bessat or venture down the formidable gully appropriately named "Chasm of Hell"? Round off the tour with a pleasant drive back to St-Étienne and a visit to the famous confectioner Weiss, whose chocolates will literally melt in your mouth.

5 FROM PLAINE DE TRICASTIN TO THE DRÔME HILLS

Round tour of 210km/130mi
leaving from Montélimar
The starting-point of this tour is Montélimar, world famous for its delicious nougat topped with chopped hazelnuts and almonds! But the city is also a popular tourist destination, and has many attractions, including the Miniature Museum.

The former episcopal town of Viviers leads to the Plaine du Tricastin, where Pierrelatte, encircled by three mountainous ranges, is home to a nuclear power plant, not to mention a crocodile farm. In St-Paul-Trois-Châteaux, make a point of visiting the cathedral and the Maison de la Truffe. For a change of scene, after admiring the church in St-Restitut, take time to check out the wine cellars at Le Cellier des Dauphins. History lovers will appreciate the White Penitents' Chapel in La Garde-Adhémar and the abbey church at Notre-Dame-d'Aiguebelle. You drive through a series of charming villages, including La Bégude-de-Mézenc, Le Poët-Laval, a medieval gem housing a former commandery, and Dieulefit, a bustling city dedicated to local arts and crafts. After leaving Soyons, you head for the Saoû Forest nestling at the foot of a sheer cliff face and offering pleasantly shaded walks.

Or you may prefer to seek refuge in the keep at Crest. Finally, your drive back to nougat country introduces you to the pretty towns of Marsanne and Mirmande.

6 ST-POURÇAIN VINEYARDS TO VAL DE BESBRE

Round tour of 160km/99.5mi
leaving from St-Pourçain
The vineyards around St-Pourçain yield a lively, fragrant white wine stored in local cellars which it is your duty to taste…in moderation! The more academic visitors will enjoy studying the numerous medieval frescoes that enliven the tiny churches dotted around St-Pourçain; the murals at Le Saulcet deserve special mention. After your exertions at the sports and leisure park in Le Pal, follow the course of the River Besbre, which guides you to Thoury and its pink-sandstone castle, to Jaligny and its Renaissance château, and finally to Lapalisse, a popular place among anglers for its waters teeming with trout and carp.

7 THE GOURMET TOUR

Round tour of 250km/155mi
leaving from Ambert
This tour pays tribute to Fourme d'Ambert, a deliciously smooth blue cheese made with cow's milk that is typical of the region. Made around Ambert and on the Forez heights, this delicacy is presented in the shape of a large circular slab speckled with blue and is lesser known but more subtle than the traditional Roquefort cheese. The nearby town of Thiers is the coun-

Lac Chambon

try's leading knife manufacturer and you will be ideally equipped to carve a generous slice of Fourme d'Ambert and savour it along the banks of the River Dore.

8 LIMAGNE IN THE LIMELIGHT

Round tour of 250km/155mi leaving from Clermont-Ferrand
After leaving Clermont-Ferrand, the bustling yet discreet capital of the Auvergne, you will encounter the curious lava flows of Volvic stone where the famous mineral water has its source. Your next stop is Billom, where a pleasant climate combines with a fine morning mist and a soft light reminiscent of the great Impressionist works. This stunning landscape is enhanced by the golden sunflower fields contrasting with the brown earthy plains, overshadowed by the volcanic range looming above the horizon.

9 THE LAND OF LAKES AND VOLCANOES

Round tour of 415km/258mi leaving from Le Mont-Dore
Whatever your reasons for visiting the Auvergne, you can but succumb to the charm of Puy de Sancy, the highest peak towering above central France. The Dore mountain range and Pays des Couzes form a natural setting of outstanding beauty, enclosing a cluster of deep blue lakes with shimmering waters (Guéry, Servière, Aydat, Godivelle, Chambon). The surrounding villages too are worthy of note: Montpeyroux and its colony of artists and craftsmen; St-Nectaire, where the local cow's milk cheese is matured on a bed of rye; Besse and its Alpine skiing resort; lastly Orcival, graced with a fine Romanesque basilica.

10 THE VALLÉE DES MERVEILLES

Round tour of 335km/208mi leaving from Brioude
Before setting out on this tour, pay a visit to the Basilique St-Julien in Bri-

oude and admire the intricate carvings adorning the Romanesque east end. Following the peaceful, lazy meanderings of the Sénouire, you discover the abbeys of Lavaudieu and La Chaise-Dieu, where the chancel houses early splendid 16C tapestries from Brussels and Arras.
The Allier, on the other hand, is an impetuous river whose waters swell between Monistrol and Lavoûte-Chilhac. While the more adventurous tourists engage in a spot of canoeing or rafting, ramblers and cyclists can pause to admire the Romanesque church of Chanteuges and the flower-decked streets in St-Arcons.
The pretty painted churches dotted around the Haut-Allier region have earned it the name of "Vallée des Merveilles" (Valley of Wonders). As you continue on the tour, you come upon the Puy-en-Velay, one of the most extraordinary and unforgettable sites in France, sitting like a crown on the landscape it dominates.

11 TRUYÈRE AND SANFLORAIN COUNTRY

Round tour of 270km/168mi leaving from St-Flour
St-Flour, the starting-point of the tour, is perched on a basaltic plateau that faces south. You will be charmed by the landscapes around Les Margerides and by the chaotic course of the Truyère, which has carved sharp chasms between the Cantal and Aveyron. After reaching Pierrefort and tucking into a tasty *aligot* consisting of mashed potatoes seasoned with garlic and Cantal cheese, you can pay a visit to the spa resort of Chaudes-Aigues. From the fine medieval castle of Pesteils, perched on its rocky outcrop, drive up to Plomb du Cantal, the highest summit of the range, where you will be greeted by a calm, soothing atmosphere and a sweeping expanse of lush countryside.

WHEN AND WHERE TO GO

When to Go

The region covered by this guide presents a great variety of climatic conditions in all seasons. Spring weather is unpredictable: there may be heavy snowfall at higher altitudes while at the same time the valleys are fragrant with fruit blossom. In late spring, the Auvergne is outstandingly beautiful, as melting snow swells the rivers. The summer months are generally sunny and warm. The Ardèche Gorges are especially popular in July and August, when many small craft take to the water.

Along the Rhône, the weather in autumn is usually mild, but in other regions (like the Cévennes) heavy rains are likely to fall. The colours in the Puys, Livradois and Dombes regions are especially vibrant at this time of year. Winter brings snow to the high peaks, where it can cover the ground for several months, closing off mountain passes to traffic. The wind in the region of the volcanoes of Auvergne can be intense. But south of Valence and in the southern part of the Cantal region, the climate is milder, and winter skies are usually clear thanks to winds blowing up from the Mediterranean. The city of Lyon seems to have a climate all its own: summers are hot and sticky, with thick morning mists, and in the winter a mist seems to hang overhead all day. Spring and autumn are the best times to visit the city, as the weather is usually clearer then.

WEATHER FORECAST

For **Météo-France** (national weather bureau, www.meteo.fr) reports in French, dial 3250, then select from the recorded choices (0.34€/min).

For **departmental forecasts** dial ☎08 92 68 02... followed by the number of the *département*: Ain 01; Allier 03; Ardèche 04; Cantal 15; Drôme 26; Haute-Loire 43; Isère 38; Loire 42; Puy-de-Dôme 63; Rhône 69).

Mountain weather forecast:
☎08 92 68 04 04; for information about snow cover and avalanche risk, ☎08 92 68 10 20.

Weather forecast for microlights and light aircraft ☎08 92 68 10 14. Information is also available on www.meteo.fr.

Themed Tours

HISTORY

Routes historiques are signposted local itineraries following an architectural and historical theme, accompanied by an explanatory booklet, available from local tourist offices.
The **Route historique des châteaux d'Auvergne** takes in a selection of the best castles in the region: imposing ruined fortresses as well as elegant manor houses; some of these house exhibitions, organise concerts and sports events; others offer bed-and-breakfast accommodation or are open late in the evening to enable visitors to appreciate their fascinating atmosphere. There are six itineraries: Bourbonnais, Limagnes, Volcans, Livradois-Forez, Montagnes cantaliennes and Haute-Loire. ⚑Route historique des châteaux d'Auvergne, 17 rue des Minimes, 63000 Clermont-Ferrand ☎04 73 19 12 16; www.route-chateaux-auvergne.org.

On the way to Santiago de Compostela – Pilgrims on their way to pay homage to the relics of St James have been going through the Auvergne since the Middle Ages. Two itineraries converge on Le Puy-en-Velay: one from Lyon via St-Ferréol and Monistrol-sur-Loire, the other from Cluny via Pommiers and Montbrison. Beyond Le Puy, the via podiensis

(GR 65) leads to Roncevaux and the Spanish border (28 days on foot).

ARCHITECTURAL HERITAGE

Viaducts – The introduction of railways in this mountainous region meant the construction of several impressive viaducts spanning the Truyère, the Sioule, the Allier and the Besbre rivers. Six of these are now listed among the region's historic monuments: Garabit and Barajol (Cantal), La Récoumène (Haute-Loire), Les Fades (Puy-de-Dôme), Neuvial and Rouzat (Allier).

TRADITIONS AND NATURE

The **Route des jardins du Massif Central** links 27 botanical gardens dedicated to the preservation and promotion of the Massif Central's vegetation. ⓘLe Jardin pour la Terre, 63220 Arlanc ☎04 73 65 00 71; www.jardinsmassifcentral.com.

The **Route des métiers en Livradois-Forez** winds its way across the Parc naturel regional du Livradois-Forez, linking authentic workshops where ancient crafts are perpetuated: Maison des Couteliers (cutlers' workshop) in Thiers, Maison du Verre (glass workshop) in Puy-Guillaume, Moulin Richard-de-Bas (traditional mill) and Musée de la Fourme (cheese museum) in Ambert. ⓘParc naturel regional du Livradois-Forez, Masion du Parc, 63880 Saint-Gervais-sous-Meymont ☎04 73 95 57 57; www.parc-livradois-forez.org; Route des Metiers ☎06 30 95 07 28; www.routedesmetiers.com.

The **Route des Villes d'Eaux** links the region's numerous spas. ⓘLa Route des Villes d'Eaux, 8 avenue Anatole-France, 63130 Royat ☎04 73 34 72 80; www.villesdeaux.com.

The **Route des Fromages** is a gourmet tour of the main farming areas producing the best cheeses the Auvergne has to offer: Saint-Nectaire, Fourme d'Ambert, Bleu d'Auvergne, Cantal and Salers. ⓘAssociation des fromages d'Auvergne, 52 avenue des Pupilles-de-la-Nation, 15000 Aurillac ☎04 71 48 66 15; www.fromages-aoc-auvergne.com.

WINE-TASTING

Côtes d'Auvergne (Puy-de-Dôme) – Some 1 240ha/3 064 acres produce five different wines: Madargue, Châteaugay and Chanturgue north of Clermont-Ferrand, Corent and Boudes south of Clermont- Ferrand. The Fédération viticole du Puy-de-Dôme, place de la Mairie, 63340 Boudes ☎04 73 96 49 00, proposes a Route des Vins divided into three itineraries exploring the Riomois, Clermontois and Lembronnais areas.

Saint-Pourçain (Allier) – This is one of the oldest wine-growing areas in France; destroyed by phylloxera at the end of the 19C, the vines have been gradually replanted and the vineyards now cover 600ha/1 483 acres. ⓘOffice de Tourisme en Pays Saint-Pourcinois, 29 Rue Marcelin Berthelot, 03500 Saint-Pourcain ☎04 70 45 32 73; www.tourismesaintpourcinois.com.

The following centres provide information about wine-growing in the Rhône Valley:

Beaujolais – Le Pays Beaujolais (bookings of tours and accommodation, guides/interpreters), contact the Maison du tourisme, 96 rue de la Sous-Préfecture, 69400 Villefranche-sur-Saône, ☎04 74 07 27 50; www.beaujolais.com.

Côtes-du-Rhône – You can browse at www.vins-rhone.com or contact the Maison des vins de Tournon (16 avenue du Maréchal-Foch, 07300 Tournon ☎04 75 07 91 50) and the Maison des vins d'Avignon (6 rue des Trois-Faucons, 84024 Avignon ☎04 90 27 24 00) to obtain a list of cellars, wine-tour itineraries etc.

Tourist Trains

These offer the opportunity of discovering some spectacular scenery, away from busy modern communications routes. Contacts include:

Chemin de Fer du Vivarais, Avenue de la gare, 07300 Tournon-sur-Rhone-Ardeche ☎04 78 28 83 34; www.ardeche-train.com. Three viaducts, two tunnels and spectacular views.

Chemin de Fer du Haut-Rhône, Office du tourisme, 1 rue du Rhone, 38390 Montalieu Vercieu ☎04 74 88 48 56; www.paysdelapierre.org. 50min steam-train journey between Montalieu and the Pont de Sault-Brenaz.

Chemin de Fer Touristique du Velay, Office de Tourisme de Tence ☎04 71 59 81 99. Several daily trips between Tence and Ste-Agrève along the Lignon Valley (mid-July to end of August).

Chemin de Fer Touristique d'Anse, Association Voie de 38cm, 8 avenue de la Libération, 69480 Anse ☎04 74 60 26 01; runs from Easter to the last Sunday in October on Sundays, holidays (also Saturdays from June to September) in the afternoon.

Train touristique des Monts du Lyonnais, RN 89, La Giraudière, 69690 Brussieu ☎04 74 70 90 64 (reservations); www.monts-du-lyonnais.org. Exhibition of railway stock in Ste-Foy-l'Argentière station (end of the line). In addition, a steam train (Hobby 69) runs on Sundays from June to September.

Train touristique de l'Ardèche méridionale, Viaduc 07, Gare de Vogué, 07200 Vogué ☎04 75 37 03 52. Picturesque 14km/8.7mi journey from Vogüé to St-Jean-le-Centenier.

Train de la découverte du Livradois-Forez, Several possibilities along the Dore Valley between Courpière and La Chaise-Dieu via Ambert. AGRIVAP "train touristique", La Gare, 63600 Ambert ☎04 73 82 43 88.

Train touristique des Gorges de l'Allier, Magnificent unspoilt landscapes unfold on this journey between Langeac and Langogne. The train runs through 53 tunnels and negotiates steep slopes and tricky bends. Office du tourisme des Gorges de l'Allier, Place Aristide Briand 43300 Langeac ☎04 71 77 05 41.

Le Train touristique Garabit, Guided tour from Aurillac via Le Lioran, Murat and the Garabit viaduct where the train stops for a while. Office de Tourisme du Pays de Saint-Flour, 17 bis, pl Armes 15100 Saint Flour ☎04 71 60 22 50.

Autorail touristique Gentiane Express, A fine journey through the summer pastures of the famous Salers cattle, from Bort-les-Orgues to Lugarde via Riom-ès-Montagne and the Barajol viaduct. Daily in July and August, Sundays and holidays from mid April to September ▯Office du tourisme de Bort-les-Orgues ☎05 55 96 02 49, or Office du tourisme du Pays Gentiane (Riom-ès-Montagnes) ☎04 71 78 07 37.

Aerial Views

For an aerial view of the region either as passenger or pilot, try one of the following.

Hot-air balloons
Contact local tourist offices, or:

France Montgolfière, 24, rue Nationale, 41400 Montrichard ☎02 54 32 20 48; www.franceballoons.com.

Objectif Montgolfière, 14, rue de Bellevue, Le Mas, 63970 Aydat ☎04 73 60 11 90; www. objectif-montgolfiere.com.

Quatre Vents,
Aéronaute Montrodeix 63870
Orcines ☎04 73 62 29 30; flight
over the Chaîne des Puys or the
Sancy mountain range.

Montgolfière club du Velay,
Pouzols, 43200 St-Jeures
☎04 71 65 47 89.

Les Montgolfières d'Annonay,
BP 111, 07102 Annonay Cedex
☎04 75 67 57 56.

Centre aérostatique de l'Ardèche,
RN 82, 07430 St Clair
☎04 75 33 71 30.

**L'Association des Montgolfières en
Velay**, 55 avenue des Champs-
Élysées, Chadrac, 43770 le Puy-en-
Velay ☎04 71 02 73 18.

Light aircraft and gliders

Aéro-club d'Auvergne,
Avenue Youri Gagarine,
63000 Clermont-Ferrand
☎04 73 92 00 56.

Aéro-club Pierre-Herbaud,
Aérodrome d'Issoire, BP 33, 63501
Issoire Cedex ☎04 73 89 16 62;
http://perso.orange.fr/acph/.

Aéro-club du Livradois,
Le Poyet, 63600 Ambert
☎04 73 82 01 64.

Up, up and away

J. Damase/MICHELIN

Helicopters

Héli Volcan, Aérodrome d'Issoire,
63500 Issoire ☎04 73 55 03 60;
www.helivolcan.com.

**Aéroport de Clermont-Ferrand-
Aulnat**, 63510 Aulnat
☎04 73 62 70 67.

Microlights

Aéro-club Combrailles,
École de pilotage, 63640 St-Priest-
des-Champs ☎04 73 86 84 52.

Auvergne ULM,
Aréo Club et École de pilotage,
Prouilbat, 63310 Riom
☎04 73 68 69 22.

Air libre, vallée verte, place de l'Office
de tourisme, 63710 St-Nectaire
☎04 73 88 57 95; flights over the
Massif du Sancy.

Eco-Tourism

RIVER AND CANAL CRUISING

Self-skippered holidays
Boats can be hired in Port-sur-Saône,
Gray, St-Jean-de-Losne and Roanne to
explore the Saône and the Rhône from
Corre to Port-St-Louis-du-Rhône. The
main harbours on the way are Lyon,
Les Roches-de-Condrieu and Valence
l'Épervière; a basic service is available
in St-Germain-au-Mont-d'Or, Tournon-
sur-Rhône, Viviers and Avignon.
In the Lyon region, a series of moor-
ing places along the Saône enables
visitors to enjoy the surrounding area.
Information is available from **Bureau
de la Plaisance**, 2 rue de la Quaran-
taine, 69321 Lyon Cedex 05 ☎04 72
56 59 28.
The stretch of canal between Roanne
and Briennon offers a pleasant journey
with several locks along the way;
contact **Marins d'Eau Douce**, Port de
Plaisance de Briennon 42720 ☎04 77
69 92 92. www.elphicom.com/
lesmarinsdeaudouce/.

Cruises

A few companies organise boat trips along the Rhône, the Isère and canals in the Loire region.

Aquaviva organise one-week cruises from March to November between Châlon-sur-Saône and Avignon. Information and bookings ☎01 45 75 52 60 (Paris number).

Naviginter offer cruises and boat trips along the Rhône and Saône rivers; information and bookings, 13 bis quai Rambaud, 69002 Lyon ☎04 78 42 96 81.

NATURE PARKS AND RESERVES

Parks

The region described in this guide includes four regional nature parks:

Parc naturel régional des Volcans d'Auvergne (&see Parc naturel régional des VOLCANS D'AUVERGNE) Château Montlosier 63970 Aydat ☎04 73 65 64 00; www.parc-volcans-auvergne.com.

Parc naturel régional Livradois-Forez (&see Monts du FOREZ). For information, contact the Maison du Parc, BP 17, 63880 St-Gervais-sous-Meymont ☎04 73 95 57 57; www.parc-livradois-forez.org.

Parc naturel regional du Pilat (&see Le PILAT). For information, contact the Maison du Parc, Moulin de Virieu, 42410 Pélussin ☎04 74 87 52 00; www.parc-naturel-pilat.fr.

Parc naturel régional des Monts d'Ardèche (&see AUBENAS). This is the most recently created of the four parks. Apply to PNR des Monts d'Ardèche, La Prade, BP3, 07560 Montpezat-sous-Bauzon ☎04 75 94 35 20; www.parc-monts-ardeche.fr.

Nature reserves and nature-discovery centres

The following organise activities on the theme of nature:

Vallée de Chaudefour,
Maison de la Réserve naturelle de la Vallée de Chaudefour, Parc naturel regional des Volcans d'Auvergne, 63790 Chambon-sur-Lac ☎04 73 88 68 80; www.grandevallee.com – guided tours (dogs are not allowed, even on a leash).

Sagnes de la Godivelle,
63850 La Godivelle ☎04 73 65 64 00 or 04 73 71 78 12 (2–6pm, Jul–Aug, last two weekends in Jun and first two weekends in Sept).

Val d'Allier,
Outings are organised by the Ligue pour la Protection des Oiseaux. Espace Nature du Val d'Allier, 8–12 boulevard de Nomazy, 03000 Moulins ☎04 70 44 46 29.

Centre permanent d'initiatives pour l'Environnement,
avenue Nicolas-Rambourg, Tronçais, 03360 St-Bonnet-Tronçais ☎04 70 06 14 69.

Office national des Forêts,
Les Portes d'Avermes, 03000 Avermes ☎04 70 46 82 00; www.onf.fr. Rambles through Tronçais Forest.

Espace Nature du Val d'Allier,
&see address above.

DONKEYS AND HORSE-DRAWN CARAVANS

How about a **walk with a donkey** for company and to amuse the children? Contact the **Fédération Nationale Ânes et Randonnées** (FNAR): www.ane-et-rando.com, or the **Comité Départemental du Tourisme** in Privas at ☎04 75 64 04 66, for the list of places where donkeys may be hired.

Horse-drawn caravans, complete with bunk beds and kitchen facilities, may be hired in some areas to follow a planned itinerary; contact the Parc naturel régional du Pilat ☎04 74 87 52 00 or local tourist offices.

KNOW BEFORE YOU GO

Useful Websites

www.franceguide.com
The French Government Tourist Office site has practical information and links to more specific guidance. The site includes information on everything you need to know about France.

www.FranceKeys.com
This site has practical information covering all the regions, with links to tourist offices and related sites.

www.franceway.com
An on-line magazine which focuses on culture and heritage. For each region, there are also suggestions for activities and practical information on where to stay and how to get there.

www.fr-holidaystore.co.uk
This website offers links to companies offering ferry tickets, car rentals, hotels and tours.

www.visiteurope.com
The European Travel Commission provides useful information on travelling to and around 30 European countries, and includes links to commercial services, rail schedules, weather reports and more.

www.holidayfrance.org.uk
The Association of British Travel Organisers in France has created this tidy site, which covers just about everything.

www.justfrance.com
This website offers detailed information on French culture, history, business, education, media, etc., useful travel information, as well as links to commercial sites. Notably, there is information about disabled access.

www.ambafrance-us.org
The French Embassy in the USA has a website providing basic information (geography, demographics, history),
a news digest and business-related information. It offers special pages for children, and pages devoted to culture, language study and travel, and you can reach other selected French sites (regions, cities, ministries) with a hypertext link.

Tourist Offices

ABROAD

For information and assistance in planning a trip to France travellers should apply to the official French Tourist Office in their own country:

Australia – New Zealand
 Sydney – Level 13, 25 Bligh Street, 2000 NSW, Sydney
 ☎+61 (0)2 9231 5244.
 http://au.franceguide.com.

Canada
 Montreal – 1800 Avenue McGill College, Suite 1010, Montreal H3A 3J6 ☎ (514) 288 2026.
 http://ca-uk.franceguide.com

Eire
 Dublin – No office ☎+15 60 235 235 (Irish information line).
 http://ie.franceguide.com.

South Africa
 3rd Floor, Village Walk, Office Tower, cnr Maude and Rivonia, Sandton ☎+27 (0) 11 523 82 92.
 http://za.franceguide.com.

United Kingdom
 Lincoln House, 300 High Holborn, London WC1V 7JH ☎09068 244 123. www.franceguide.com.

United States
 http://us.franceguide.com
 New York – 825 Third Avenue, 29th Floor (entrance on 50th Street), New York, NY 10022 ☎1 (514) 288 1904.

Chicago – Consulate General of France, 205 North Michigan Avenue, Suite 3770, Chicago, IL 60601 ☎1 (312) 327 0290.
Los Angeles – 9454 Wilshire Boulevard, Suite 210, Los Angeles, CA 90212 ☎1 (310) 271 6665.

IN THE AUVERGNE

Visitors will find more precise information through the network of tourist offices in France. The addresses and telephone numbers of local tourist offices, called *syndicats d'initiative* in smaller towns, are listed after the symbol 🄸 in the introductions to individual sights. Addresses for regional and departmental tourist offices covered in this guide are listed below:

Tourism Offices:
    Regional: Comité Régional du Tourisme (CRT)
    Departmental: Comité Départemental du Tourisme (CDT)

Comité Régional de Développement Touristique d'Auvergne (CRT)
Parc Technologique Clermont-Ferrand La Pardieu, 7 allée Pierre de Fermat, 63178 AUBIÈRE ☎0 810 827 828. www.auvergne-tourisme.info.

Comité Régional du Tourisme de la Vallée du Rhône (CRT) – 104 route de Paris, 69260 Charbonnières-les-Bains ☎04 72 59 21 59. www.crt-rhonealpes.fr.

Ain (CRT) – 34 rue du Général-Delestraint, BP 78, 01002 Bourg-en-Bresse Cedex ☎04 74 32 31 30. www.ain-tourisme.com.

Ardèche (CRT) – 4 cours du Palais, BP 221, 07002 Privas Cedex ☎04 75 64 04 66. www.ardeche-tourisme.com.

Drôme (CRT) – 8 rue Baudin, 26005 Valence. ☎04 750 82 19 26. www.drometourisme.com.

Isère (CRT) – 14 rue de la République, BP227, 38019 Grenoble Cedex ☎04 76 54 34 36. www.isere-tourisme.com.

Loire (CRT) – 5 place Jean-Jaurès, 42021 St-Étienne Cedex 1 ☎04 77 43 59 14. www.cg42.fr.

Rhône (CRT) – 35 rue St-Jean, BP 5009, 69245 Cedex 05 ☎04 72 61 78 90. www.rhonetourisme.com.

Allier (CDT) – Pavillon des Marronniers, Parc de Bellevue, BP 65, 03402 Yzeure Cedex ☎04 70 46 81 50. www.allier-tourisme.com.

Cantal (CDT) – 36, rue de Sistrières, 15000 Aurillac ☎0826 96 15 15. www.cantal-tourisme.fr.

Haute-Loire (CDT) – 1 place Monseignuer de Galard, BP 332, 43012 Le Puy-en-Velay Cedex ☎04 71 07 41 54. www.mididelauvergne.com.

Puy-de-Dôme (CDT) – Place de la Bourse, 63038 Clermont-Ferrand Cedex 1 ☎04 73 42 22 50. www.planetepuydedome.com.

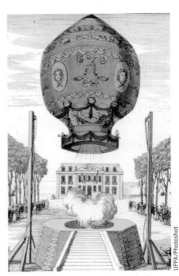

The Montgolfier Brothers' hot-air balloon

UPPA/Photoshot

Fourteen towns and areas, labelled **Villes et Pays d'Art et d'Histoire** by the Ministry of Culture, are mentioned in this guide (Clermont-Ferrand, the Dauphiné d'Auvergne, the Forez, the Haut-Allier, Lyon, Montluçon, Moulins, Paladru-Les-Trois-Vals Lake, Le Puy-en-Velay, Riom, Saint-Étienne, Valence and Vienne).

They are particularly active in promoting their architectural and cultural heritage and offer guided tours by highly qualified guides as well as activities for 6 to 12-year-olds. More information is available from local tourist offices and from www.vpah.culture.fr.

International Visitors

FOREIGN EMBASSIES AND CONSULATES

Australia – 4 rue Jean-Rey, 75015 Paris ☎01 40 59 33 00. www.france.embassy.gov.au.

Canada – 35 avenue Montaigne, 75008 Paris ☎01 44 43 29 00. www.amb-canada.fr.

Eire – 4 rue Rude, 75016 Paris ☎01 44 17 67 00. www.embassyofireland.fr.

New Zealand – 7 ter rue Léonard-de-Vinci, 75016 Paris ☎01 45 01 43 43. www.nzembassy.com.

South Africa – 59 quai d'Orsay, 75007 Paris ☎01 53 59 23 23. www.afriquesud.net.

UK– 35 rue du Faubourg St-Honoré, 75383 Paris ☎01 44 51 31 00. www.britishembassy.gov.uk.

USA – 2 avenue Gabriel, 75008 Paris ☎01 43 12 22 22. www.amb-usa.fr.

DOCUMENTS

Passport – Nationals of countries within the European Union entering France need only a national identity card (although most airlines require passports). Nationals of other countries must be in possession of a valid national **passport**.

Visa – No **entry visa** is required for Canadian, US or Australian citizens travelling as tourists and staying less than 90 days, except for students planning to study in France. If you think you may need a visa, apply to your local French Consulate.

General passport information is available by phone toll-free from the Federal Information Center ☎800-688-9889. US passport application forms can be downloaded from http://travel.state.gov.

CUSTOMS

In Britain, go to the Customs Office (UK) website at www.hmrc.gov.uk for information on allowances, travel safety tips, and to consult and download documents and guides.

Residents from a Member State of the **European Union** are not restricted with regard to goods for private use, but the recommended allowances for alcoholic beverages and tobacco are as follows:

There are no customs formalities for holidaymakers bringing their caravans into France for a stay of less than

Spirits (whisky, gin, vodka etc)	10 litres
Fortified wines (vermouth, port etc)	10 litres
Wine (not more than 60 sparkling)	90 litres
Beer	110 litres
Cigarettes	800
Cigarillos	400
Cigars	200
Smoking tobacco	1 kg

six months. No customs document is necessary for pleasure boats and outboard motors for a stay of less than six months, but the registration certificate should be kept on board.

The **US Customs Service** offers a publication *Know Before You Go* for US citizens to consult and download at www.customs.ustreas.gov (click on 'Travel').

Australians will find customs information at www.customs.gov.au.

For **New Zealanders**, "Advice for Travellers" is at www.customs.govt.nz.

HEALTH

First aid, medical advice and chemists' night service rota are available from chemists/drugstores (*pharmacie*) identified by a green cross sign. You should take out comprehensive insurance coverage as patients receiving medical treatment in French hospitals or clinics must pay the bill.

Nationals of non-EU countries should check with their insurance companies about policy limitations. All prescription drugs should be clearly labelled; it is essential that you carry the prescription.

British and Irish citizens should apply **before travelling** for a European Health Insurance Card, which entitles the holder to urgent treatment for accident or unexpected illness in EU countries.

British citizens apply online to www.dh.gov.uk/travellers, telephone ☎0845 606 2030, or pick up an application at a post office.
Irish citizens should consult www.ehic.ie.

Americans and **Canadians** concerned about travel and health can contact the International Association for Medical Assistance to Travelers, which can also provide details of English-speaking doctors in different parts of France: www.iamat.org ☎*for the US* (716) 754-4883; *for Canada* (416) 652-0137 or (519) 836-0102.

Useful Numbers
The American Hospital of Paris is open 24hr for emergencies as well as consultations, with English-speaking staff, at 63 boulevard Victor-Hugo, 92200 Neuilly-sur-Seine, ☎01 46 41 25 25.

The Hertford British Hospital is just outside Paris at 3 rue Barbès, 92300 Levallois-Perret ☎01 46 39 22 22. www.british-hospital.org.

Accessibility

The sights described in this guide that are easily accessible to people of reduced mobility are indicated in the *Admission times and charges* section by the symbol &.
Since 2001, the designation **Tourisme at Handicap** has applied to a thousand sites accessible to the disabled: go to **www.franceguide.com**. The principal French source for information on facilities is the **Association des Paralysés de France**, www.apf.asso.fr.
On TGV and Corail trains operated by the national railway (SNCF), there are special wheelchair slots in 1st class carriages available to holders of 2nd-class tickets. On Eurostar and Thalys, special rates are available for accompanying adults. All airports are equipped to receive physically disabled passengers.
Web-surfers can find information for slow walkers, mature travellers and others with special needs at **www.access-able.com**.
For information on museum access for the disabled contact La Direction, *Les Musées de France,* Service Accueil des Publics Spécifiques, 6 rue des Pyramides, 75041 Paris Cedex 1 ☎01 40 15 80 72.
The **Michelin Guide France** and the **Michelin Camping France** indicate hotels and campsites with facilities suitable for physically less able people.

GETTING THERE AND GETTING AROUND

By Air

It is very easy to arrange air travel to one of Paris' two airports (Roissy-Charles-de-Gaulle to the north, and Orly to the south). There are also regular flights from the UK and the US to **Lyon-Saint-Exupéry** airport, which is linked to the city centre by a regular shuttle service. Contact airline companies and travel agents for details of package tour flights with a rail link-up or Fly-Drive schemes.

Visitors arriving in **Paris** who wish to reach the city centre or a train station may use public transportation or reserve space on the **Airport Shuttle** (for Roissy-Charles-de-Gaulle ☎01 45 38 55 72, for Orly ☎01 43 21 06 78).

By Ship

There are numerous **cross-Channel services** (passenger and car ferries) from the United Kingdom and Ireland, as well as the rail Shuttle through the Channel Tunnel (**Le Shuttle-Eurotunnel**, ☎08705 35 35 35. www.eurotunnel.com).

To choose the most suitable route between your port of arrival and your destination use the Michelin Tourist and Motoring Atlas France, Michelin map 726 (which gives travel times and mileages) or Michelin maps from the 1:200 000 series (with the orange cover). For details apply to travel agencies or to:

P & O Ferries
Channel House, Channel View Road, Dover CT17 9JT ☎08716 645 645 (UK dialling), or 0825 120 156 (in France). www.poferries.com. Service between Dover and Calais.

Norfolk Line
Norfolk House, Eastern Docks, Dover, Kent CT16 1JA ☎0870 870 10 20 (in the UK), 03 28 59 01 01 (in France). www.norfolkline.com. Service between Dover and Dunkerque.

Brittany Ferries
Millbay Docks, Plymouth, Devon PL1 3EW ☎0871 244 0744 (in the UK), 825 828 828 (in France), www.brittanyferries.com. Services from Portsmouth, Poole and Plymouth.

Seafrance
Whitfield Court, Honeywood Close, Whitfield, Kent CT16 3PX. ☎0871 663 2546. www.seafrance.com. Services between Dover and Calais.

By Train

Eurostar, composed of British, French and Belgian railways operates a high-speed passenger service between **London** (St Pancras) and **Paris** (Gare du Nord) with up to 16 trains daily. **Eurailpass**, **Flexipass**, **Eurailpass Youth**, **EurailDrive Pass** and **Saverpass** are travel passes which may be purchased by residents of countries outside the European Union. In the US, contact your travel agent or **Rail Europe** 2100 Central Ave. Boulder, CO, 80301 ☎1-800-4-EURAIL or **Europrail International** ☎1 888 667 9731. If you are a European resident, you can buy an individual country pass, if you are not a resident of the country where you plan to use it.

All rail services throughout France can be arranged through **RailEurope** in the UK: Rail Europe House, 34 Tower View, Kings Hill, West Malling, Kent ME19 4ED. Telephone 08448 484 064; www.raileurope.co.uk.

There are numerous **discounts** available when you purchase your tickets in France, from 25–50% below the regular rate. These include discounts for using senior cards and youth cards, group rates and seasonal promotions. There are a limited number of discount seats available during peak travel times, and the best discounts are available for travel during off-peak periods.

Tickets must be validated *(composter)* by using the orange automatic date-stamping machines at the platform entrance (failure to do so may result in a fine).

The French railway company SNCF operates a **telephone information, reservation and prepayment service in English** from 7am to 10pm (French time). In France call ☎08 36 35 35 39 (when calling from outside France, drop the initial 0 and replace with 33).

Gare de Lyon-Perrache

By Coach/Bus

www.eurolines.com is the international website with information about travelling all over Europe by coach (bus).

From the **UK** telephone ☎08717 71 71 71 for travel advice and ticket information.

A **Disabled Persons Travel Helpline** is available on 08717 818179.
A **textphone** is provided for customers who are deaf or hard of hearing on 0121 455 0086.

By Car

DRIVING IN FRANCE

The area covered in this guide is easily reached by main motorways and national routes. **Michelin map 726** indicates the main itineraries as well as alternate routes for avoiding heavy traffic during busy holiday periods, and gives estimated travel times. **Michelin map 723** is a detailed atlas of French motorways, indicating tolls, rest areas and services along the route; it includes a table for calculating distances and times. The latest Michelin route-planning service is available on Internet, **www.Via Michelin.com.** Travellers can calcu-

late a precise route using such options as shortest route, route avoiding toll roads, Michelin-recommended route and gain access to tourist information (hotels, restaurants, attractions). The service is available on a pay-per-route basis or by subscription.

The roads are very busy during holiday periods (particularly weekends in July and August) and, to avoid traffic congestion it is advisable to follow the recommended secondary routes (signposted as *Bison Futé – itinéraires bis*). The motorway network includes rest areas *(aires de repos)* and petrol stations *(stations-service),* usually with restaurant and shopping complexes attached, about every 40km/25mi; long-distance drivers have no excuse not to stop for a rest.

DOCUMENTS

Driving licence – Travellers from other European Union countries and North America can drive in France with a valid national or home-state driving licence. An **international driving licence** is useful because the information on it appears in nine languages (bear in mind that traffic officers are empowered to fine motorists). A permit is available from the **National Automobile Club**, 1151 East Hillsdale Boulevard, Foster City, CA 94404 ☎650-294-7000 or **national-autoclub.com**; or contact your local branch of the **American Automobile Association.**

Registration papers

For the vehicle, it is necessary to have the registration papers (logbook) and a nationality plate of an approved size.

Insurance

Certain motoring organisations (AA, RAC, AAA) offer accident insurance and breakdown service schemes for members. Check with your current insurance company for coverage while abroad. Because French autoroutes are privately owned, your European Breakdown Cover service does not extend to breakdowns on the autoroute – you must use the emergency telephones, or drive off the autoroute before calling your breakdown service.

HIGHWAY CODE

In France the minimum driving age is 18. Traffic drives on the right. All passengers must wear **seat belts.** Children under the age of 10 must ride in the back seat. Headlights must be switched on in poor visibility and at night; side-lights may be used only when the vehicle is stationary.

In the case of a **breakdown,** a red warning triangle or hazard warning lights are obligatory. In the absence of stop signs at intersections, cars must **give way to the right.** Traffic on main roads outside built-up areas (priority indicated by a yellow diamond sign) and on roundabouts has right of way. Vehicles must stop when the lights turn red at road junctions and may filter to the right only when indicated by an amber arrow.

The regulations on **drinking and driving** (limited to 0.50g/l) and **speeding** are strictly enforced – usually by an on-the-spot fine and/or confiscation of the vehicle.

Speed limits

Although liable to modification, these are as follows:

- toll motorways (autoroutes) 130kph/80mph (110kph/68mph when raining);

- dual carriageways and motorways without tolls 110kph/68mph (100kph/62mph when raining);
- other roads 90kph/56mph (80kph/50mph when raining) and in towns 50kph/31mph;
- outside lane on motorways during daylight, on level ground and with good visibility – minimum speed limit of 80kph/50mph.

Parking regulations

In built-up areas there are zones where parking is either restricted or subject to a charge; tickets should be obtained from nearby ticket machines (horodateurs – small change necessary) and displayed inside the windscreen on the driver's side; failure to display may result in a fine, or towing away and impoundment. Other parking areas in town may require you to take a ticket when passing through a barrier. To exit, you must pay the parking fee (usually there is a machine located by the exit – sortie) and insert the paid-up card in another machine which will lift the exit gate.

Tolls

In France, most motorway sections are subject to a toll (péage). You can pay in cash or with a Visa or Mastercard.

Petrol (US: gas)

French service stations dispense: sans plomb 98 (super unleaded 98), sans plomb 95 (super unleaded 95), diesel/gazole (diesel) and GPL (LPG). Prices are listed on signboards on the motorways; it is usually cheaper to fill up after leaving the motorway at the large hypermarkets on the outskirts of towns.

CAR RENTAL

There are car rental agencies at airports, railway stations and in all large towns throughout France. European cars have manual transmission; automatic cars are available only if an advance reservation is made. Drivers must be over 21; between ages 21–25, drivers are required to pay an extra daily fee; some companies allow drivers under 23 only if the reservation has been made through a travel agent. It is relatively expensive to hire a car in France. There are many on-line services that will look for the best prices on car rental around the globe. **Nova** can be contacted at www.rentacar-worldwide.com or ☎0800 018 6682 (freephone UK) or ☎+44 28 4272 8189 (calling from outside the UK).

A Baron's Limousine ☎01 45 30 21 21 provides cars and drivers (English-speaking drivers available), www.barons-limousines.com.

Worldwide Motorhome Rentals offers fully equipped campervans for rent: www.mhrww.com or call (US

toll-free) US ☎888-519-8969; outside the US ☎530-389-8316.

All of the firms listed below have Internet sites for reservations and information. From within France, you can call the following numbers:

Avis: ☎08 20 05 05 05
Europcar: ☎08 25 82 54 57
Budget France: ☎08 25 00 35 64
Hertz France: ☎01 47 03 49 12
SIXT-Eurorent: ☎08 20 00 74 98
National-CITER: ☎01 45 22 77 91

WHERE TO STAY AND EAT

Where to Stay

FINDING A HOTEL

Turn to the Address Books throughout *Discovering the Sights* for descriptions and prices of typical places to stay and eat with local flair. The Legend on the cover flap explains the symbols and abbreviations used in these sections. Use the **Map of Places to Stay** on pages 32–33 to identify recommended places for overnight stops. For an even greater selection, use the red-cover **Michelin Guide France,** with its famously reliable star-rating system and hundreds of establishments all over France. Book ahead to ensure that you get the accommodation you want, not only during the tourist season, but throughout the year, as many towns fill up during trade fairs, arts festivals etc. Some places require an advance deposit or a reconfirmation. Reconfirming is especially important if you plan to arrive after 6pm.

For further assistance, **Loisirs Accueil** is a booking service that has offices in some French *départements* – contact the tourist offices listed above for further information .

A guide to good-value, family-run hotels, **Logis et Auberges de France,** is available from the French tourist office, as are lists of other kinds of accommodation such as hotel-châteaux, bed-and-breakfasts etc.

Relais et Châteaux provides information on booking in luxury hotels with character: 15 rue Galvani, 75017 Paris, ☎01 45 72 90 00, www.relaischateaux.com.

Economy Chain Hotels

If you need a place to stop en route, these can be useful, as they are inexpensive and generally located near the main road. While breakfast is available, there may not be a restaurant; rooms are small, with a television and bathroom. Central reservation numbers:

♦ **Akena** ☎01 69 84 85 17
♦ **Best Hotel** ☎03 28 27 46 69, www.besthotel.fr.
♦ **Mister Bed** ☎01 46 14 38 00
♦ **Villages Hôtel** ☎03 80 60 92 70

Many chains have on-line reservations: www.etaphotel.com; www.ibishotel. com, www.bestwestern.fr.

RENTING A COTTAGE, BED AND BREAKFAST

Rural accommodation

The **Maison des Gîtes de France** is an information service on self-catering accommodation in France. *Gîtes* usually take the form of a cottage or apartment decorated in the local style where visitors can make themselves at home, or bed and breakfast accommodation *(chambres d'hôtes)* which consists of a room and breakfast at a reasonable price.

Contact the Gîtes de France office in Paris: 59 rue St-Lazare, 75439 Paris Cedex 09, ☎01 49 70 75 75, www.gites-de-france.com, or their representative in the UK, ♿**Brittany Ferries.** The Internet site **www. gites-de-france.fr** has a good English version. From the site, you can order catalogues for different regions illustrated with photographs of the properties, as well as specialised catalogues (bed and breakfasts, chalets in skiing areas, farm stays etc). You can also contact the local tourist offices, which may have lists of available properties and local bed and breakfast establishments.

The Fédération Française des Stations Vertes de Vacances,

6 rue Ranfer-de-Bretenières, BP 71698, 21016 Dijon Cedex ☎03 80 54 10 50 www.stationsvertes.com, is able to provide details of accommodation, leisure facilities and natural attractions in rural locations selected for their tranquillity.

Ramblers

Ramblers can consult the guide entitled *Gîtes d'étape et refuges* by A and S Mouraret (Rando-Éditions, BP 24, 65421 Ibos, ☎05 62 90 09 90. www.gites-refuges.com).

HOSTELS, CAMPING

To obtain an International Youth Hostel Federation card (there is no age requirement), you should contact the IYHF in your own country:

♦ UK ☎01727 324170, International Youth Hostel Federation, 2nd Floor, Gate House, Fretherne Road, Welwyn Garden City, Herts AL8 6RD. There is a booking service on the Internet (www.iyhf.org), which you may use to reserve rooms as early as six months in advance..
♦ US ☎202 783 6161. www.hiusa.org.
♦ Canada ☎613 273 7884. www.hihostels.ca
♦ Australia ☎61 2 9565 1669, www.yha.com.au

The main youth hostel association *(Auberges de Jeunesse)* in France is the **Ligue Française pour les Auberges de la Jeunesse** (67 rue Vergniaud, 75013 Paris, ☎01 44 16 78 78. www. auberges-de-jeunesse.com).

There are numerous officially graded **campsites** with varying standards of facilities throughout the Rhône Valley. The **Michelin Camping France** guide lists a selection of campsites. The area is very popular with campers in the summer months, so it is wise to reserve in advance.

Where to Eat

Turn to the Address Books throughout *Discovering the Sights* for descriptions and prices of selected places to eat in the different locations covered in this guide. The Legend on the cover flap explains the symbols and abbreviations used in these sections.

Use **The Michelin Guide France**, with its hundreds of establishments all over France, for an even greater choice. If you would like to experience a meal in a highly rated restaurant from the Red Guide, be sure to book ahead! In the countryside, restaurants usually serve lunch between noon and 2pm and dinner between 7.30pm and 10pm. It is not always easy to find something in between those two meal times, as the "non-stop" restaurant is a rarity in the provinces. However, a hungry traveller can usually get a sandwich in a café, and ordinary hot dishes may be available in a *brasserie*.

Among places in the Auvergne region that have been awarded the special distinction of *site remarquable du goût* are Billom (for its particularly fine pink garlic), St-Nectaire (for its soft cheese made from cow's milk), Salers (for its firm cheese similar to Cantal); www.sitesremarquablesdugout.com.

Bottles of Côte Rôtie

A TYPICAL FRENCH MENU

La Carte	The Menu

Entrées	**Starters**
Crudités	Raw vegetables
Terrine de lapin	Rabbit terrine (pâté)
Frisée aux lardons	Curly lettuce with diced bacon
Escargots	Snails
Salade au crottin de Chavignol	Goat's cheese salad
Potage	Soup, broth

Plats (Viandes)	**Main Courses (Meat)**
Bavette à l'échalote	Sirloin with shallots
Faux filet au poivre	Steak in a pepper sauce
Pavé de rumsteck	Thick rump steak
Côtelettes d'agneau	Lamb cutlets
Filet mignon de porc	Pork fillet
Blanquette de veau	Veal stew in a cream sauce
Nos viandes sont garnies	Meat dishes are served with vegetables

Plats (Poissons, Volaille)	**Main Courses (Fish, Fowl)**
Filets de sole	Sole fillets
Dorade aux herbes	Sea bream with herbs
Saumon grillé	Grilled salmon
Truite meunière	Trout fried in butter
Magret de canard	Breast fillet of duck
Poulet rôti	Roast chicken

Fromage	**Cheese**
Fromage de chèvre	Goat's cheese
Fromage maigre	Low-fat cheese
Fromage à pâte dure	Hard cheese
Fromage à pâte molle	Soft cheese
Fromage râpé	Grated cheese

Desserts	**Desserts**
Tarte aux pommes	Apple tart
Crème caramel	Warm baked custard with caramel sauce
Mousse au chocolat	Chocolate mousse
Sorbet: trois parfums	Sorbet: choose 3 flavours

Boissons	**Beverages**
Bière	Beer
Eau minérale (gazeuse)	(Sparkling) mineral water
Une carafe d'eau	Tap water (no charge)
Vin rouge, vin blanc, rosé	Red wine, white wine, rosé
Jus de fruit	Fruit juice

Menu Enfant	**Children's Menu**
Jambon	Ham
Steak haché	Minced beef
Frites	French fries
Purée	Mashed potatoes

Well-done, medium, rare, raw = **bien cuit, à point, saignant, cru.**

Lyonnaise food

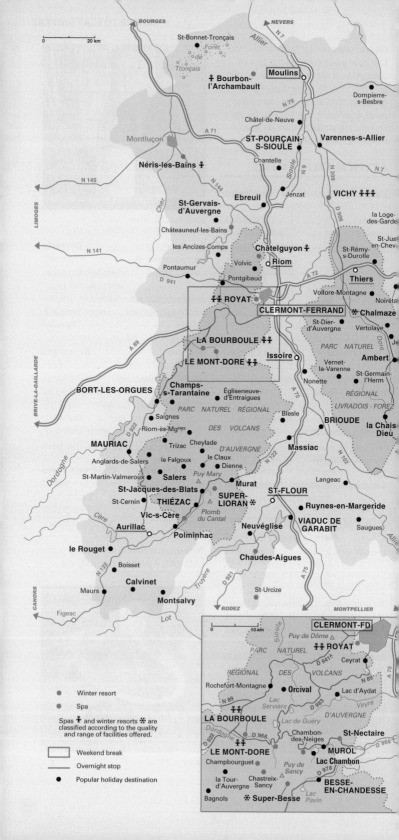

Places to stay

WHAT TO SEE AND DO

Outdoor Fun

CYCLING AND MOUNTAIN BIKING

Tourist offices should be able to provide lists of local firms which hire bicycles and mountain bikes (*vélos tout terrain,* or VTT). Some SNCF (the French National Railway Company) stations organise bike rentals, and mountain bikes can be hired in season from information points within the Pilat park. A leaflet giving details is available from railway stations. Local tourist offices also have details of suggested cycle and mountain bike routes.

Useful information can be obtained from the **Fédération Française de Cyclotourisme**, 12 rue Louis-Bertrand, 94200 Ivry-sur-Seine ☎01 56 20 88 88. www.ffct.org. You can also apply to the **Fédération Française de Cyclisme,** 5 rue de Rome, 93561 Rosny-sous-Bois Cedex ☎01 49 35 69 24. www.ffc.fr. This organisation publishes a guide listing 45 000km/28 000mi marked mountain-bike tracks.

CAVING

Comité départemental de spéléologie, route d'Enval, 63200 St-Genès-l'Enfant ☎04 73 38 71 29.

FISHING

The abundance of rivers, streams and lakes provides anglers with many opportunities to catch salmon, trout, perch, tench or carp; whatever the site, however, it is necessary to be affiliated to a fishing association and to abide by fishing regulations. Daily fishing permits are available in certain areas. Contact the local tourist office or apply to the local fishing federations or fishing tackle stores.

Useful Addresses

Conseil supérieur de la pêche, 134 avenue Malakoff, 75016 Paris ☎01 45 02 20 20.

Allier – Fédération de pêche et de protection du milieu aquatique, 8 rue de la Ronde, 03500 St-Pourçain-sur-Sioule ☎04 70 45 42 90.

Cantal – Fédération départementale de pêche et de protection du milieu aquatique, 14 allée du Vialenc, 15000 Aurillac ☎04 71 48 19 25. Association Cantal Pêche, Moulin du Blaud, 15100 Roffiac ☎04 71 60 75 75 or 04 71 46 22 00. www.cdt-cantal.fr. Cantal Pêche publishes a free brochure full of useful advice on fishing and accommodation in this *département*.

Haute-Loire – Fédération de pêche et de protection du milieu aquatique, 32 rue Henri-Chas, Le Val-Vert, 43000 Le Puy-en-Velay ☎04 71 09 09 44.

Loire – Fédération de la Loire pour la Pêche et la Protection du Milieu Aquatique, 14 allée de l'Europe, 42480 La Fouillouse ☎04 77 02 20 00.

Puy-de-Dôme – Fédération de pêche et de protection du milieu aquatique, Site de Marmilhat Sud, 63370 Lempdes ☎04 73 92 56 29. The federation's annual publication, *Le Pêcheur du Puy-de-Dôme,* includes a map of rivers and lakes.

Rhône – Fédération de pêche, Le Norly, 42 chemin Moulin-Carron, 69130 Écully ☎04 72 18 01 80. www.rhonepechenature.org.

GOLF

For locations, addresses and telephone numbers of golf courses in France, consult the map *Golfs, Les Par-*

cours Français published by Éditions Plein-Sud based on Michelin map 989.

Fédération française de golf, 68 rue Anatole-France, 92309 Levallois-Perret Cedex ☎01 41 49 77 00. www.ffgolf.org.

HANG-GLIDING AND PARAGLIDING

The Auvergne mountains and the Massif du Mézenc in the Ardèche offer exceptional opportunities practising hang-gliding and paragliding.

Ligue Auvergne de vol libre, 4 chemin des Garennes, 63960 Veyre-Monton ☎04 73 69 72 00.

École Ailes Libres Auvergne Limousin, 63730 Les Martres de Veyre ☎04 73 39 72 72 or 06 87 79 42 74. Departures are from the Camping de La Font Bleix.

Archipel Volcans, route de Clermont, 63122 Laschamps ☎04 73 62 15 15; www.archipel-volcans.com; other facilities include hot-air ballooning, rambling, snowshoeing, mountain biking etc.

Quatre Vents, rue de la Tonne à Montrodeix, 63870 Orcines ☎04 73 62 29 30; flight over the Chaîne des Puys or the Sancy mountain.range

Para l'Aile, 13 rue des Alouettes, 63800 Cournon-d'Auvergne ☎04 73 84 45 00 or 06 80 08 25 41.

Vol Can, Centre Espace Volcan, Route du Col de Moreno, Laschamps, 63122 St-Genès-Champanelle ☎04 73 62 26 00. www.espacevolcan.fr.

Mont-Dore Parapente, Club de Parapente du Mont Dore, contact the tourist office.

Delta Auvergne, La Fougedoire, 63600 Ambert ☎04 73 82 91 41 or 06 80 40 07 00. www.delta-auvergne.com.

Barbule, École ardéchoise de parapente, 07140 Les Vans ☎04 75 39 36 67. www.parapente-fr.com/barbule.

Acro d'Aile, Association de parapente; contact M. Jobard ☎06 88 16 82 57.

WALKING

Exploring the region on foot is an enchanting way of discovering the landscape and the life of the countryside. Many long-distance footpaths *(Sentiers de Grande Randonnée* or "GR") cover the area described in this guide. Short-distance paths *(Sentiers de Petite Randonnée* or "PR") and medium-distance paths offer walks ranging from a few hours to a couple of days. A collection of *Topo-Guides* showing the routes and the time needed, details of access points, accommodation and places of interest en route for footpaths throughout France is published by the **Fédération Française de la Randonnée Pédestre**, 14 rue Riquet, 75019 Paris ☎01 44 89 93 90; some of the guides have been translated into English and are available in many bookshops in the region. You can also order the catalogue of 170 publications through the Internet at the association's site **www.ffrandonnee.fr** (in French).

Useful Addresses

Comité départemental de randonnée pédestre de l'Allier, Centre Éric Tabarly, 03300 Cusset ☎04 70 96 00 26. The Comité publishes a *Topo-guide* of the Montagne Bourbonnaise area.

Comité départemental de randonnée pédestre du Cantal, Maison des Sports, 15000 Aurillac ☎04 71 63 75 29.

Comité départemental de randonnée pédestre de la Haute-Loire, La Croisée des chemins, 23 rue Boucherie-Basse, 43000 Le Puy-en-Velay ☎04 71 04 15 95 or 06 08 50 84 80. www.lacroiseedeschemins.com.

Scaling a frozen waterfall, Sancy

S. Sauvignier/MICHELIN

Comité départemental de randonnée pédestre du Puy-de-Dôme, Résidence des Lycées, 70 avenue des Paulines, 63000 Clermont-Ferrand Cedex ☎04 73 91 94 01.

Chamina, 5 rue Pierre-le-Vénérable, 63057 Clermont-Ferrand Cedex 1 ☎04 73 92 81 44; www.chamina.com. This association promotes rambling and mountain biking throughout the Massif Central region and the western slopes of the Rhône Valley.

Play It Safe

Safety first is the rule for everyone when it comes to exploring the mountains as a climber, skier or walker. The risk associated with avalanches, mud slides, falling rocks, bad weather, fog, glacially cold waters, the dangers of becoming lost or miscalculating distances, should not be underestimated. **Avalanches** occur naturally when the upper layer of snow is unstable, in particular after heavy snowfalls, and may be set off by the passage of numerous skiers or hikers over a precise spot. A scale of risk, from 1 to 5, has been developed and is posted daily at resorts and the base of hiking trails. It is important to consult this *Bulletin Neige et Avalanche* (BNA) before setting off on any expeditions cross-country or hors-piste.

Lightning storms are often preceded by sudden gusts of wind, and put climbers and walkers in danger. In the event, avoid high ground, and do not move along a ridge top; do not seek shelter under overhanging rocks, isolated trees in otherwise open areas, at the entrance to caves or other openings in the rocks, or in the proximity of metal fences or gates. An automobile is a good refuge.

KARTING

Commission régionale de karting, 15 rue Cheval, 63100 Clermont-Ferrand ☎04 73 23 35 26.

Kartingliss, 11 rue Louis-Blériot, 63800 Cournon-d'Auvergne ☎04 73 84 27 41. www.kartingliss.fr.

Concept Kart Indoor, 98 avenue de Chazeuil, 03150 Varennes-sur-Allier ☎04 70 45 61 61.

RIDING TOURS

For information about riding holidays, contact the **Comité national de tourisme équestre,** 9 boulevard Macdonald 75019 Paris ☎01 53 26 15 50, which publishes the annual handbook *Cheval Nature, l'Officiel du tourisme équestre en France,* giving details of selected riding stables and equestrian establishments throughout France. At regional level, contact:

Association régionale du tourisme équestre d'Auvergne (ARTE), Roland Renaglia, 63420 Apchat ☎04 73 71 84 30.

Comité regional des sports équestres d'Auvergne, 46 boulevard Pasteur, 63000 Clermont-Ferrand ☎04 73 34 86 06.

Association Rhône-Alpes pour le tourisme équestre, Maison du tourisme, 14 rue de la République, BP 227, 38019 Grenoble Cedex ☎04 76 44 56 18.

ROCK-CLIMBING

There are numerous opportunities to tackle cliff faces in the Auvergne region. Information can be obtained from the **Club Alpin Français** (section Auvergne), 3 rue Maréchal-Joffre, 63000 Clermont-Ferrand ☎04 73 90 81 62, or the **Comité Départemental de la Fédération Française de la Montagne et de l'Escalade**, 22ter impasse Bonnabaud, 63000 Clermont-Ferrand ☎04 73 29 24 71.
In January and February, some winter sports resorts offer an introduction to scaling frozen waterfalls:

Club alpin français du Haut-Cantal, 3 place du Monument, 15400 Riom-ès-Montagnes ☎04 71 78 14 63.

Le Mont-Dore: contact the Peloton de Gendarmerie de Montagne (mountain squad of the Gendarmerie Nationale), rue des Chasseurs Alpins, 63240 Le Mont-Dore ☎04 73 65 04 06.

SKIING

The Auvergne region is well equipped for the practice of Alpine skiing with three important resorts: Mont-Dore (&see MONT-DORE), Super-Besse (&see BESSE-EN-CHANDESSE) and Super-Lioran (&see Le LIORAN), where the **Ski Pass Massif Central** can be used. It is also ideal for those who prefer cross-country skiing as there is an extensive network of tracks spread over twelve main ski areas.

The Massif du Pilat and the high plateaux of the Ardèche are also suitable for cross-country skiing and ski touring. In addition, **summer skiing** and **sledging** are popular summer activities in Le Mont-Dore, Super-Besse and Picherande; information is available from tourist offices.

Useful Addresses

General information – Contact **Ski France**, an association of winter sports resorts, for their annual publications *Guide Pratique Hiver/Été* and *Guide des Tarifs* (both free), 61 boulevard Haussmann, 75008 Paris ☎01 47 42 23 32.

Other useful contacts include:

Montagne Auvergne, Centre Couthon-Delille, 23 place Delille, 63000 Clermont-Ferrand ☎04 73 90 23 14.

Association de gestion du domaine nordique des crêtes du Forez, Mairie, 63480 Vertolaye ☎04 73 95 20 64.

Domaine Lioran-Haute Planèze, Col de Prat de Bouc, 15300 Albepierre-Bredons ☎04 71 73 32 13; www.cantal-nature.com.

École de ski français de Super-Besse, 1 ronde de Vassivière, 63610 Super-Besse ☎04 73 79 61 75.

Snow-cover information – The following provide up-to-date information about snow conditions in the various ski areas.

Alpine skiing

©Steven Tilston/istockphoto.com

Domaine nordique des crêtes du Forez: ☎04 73 95 20 61.
Super-Besse: ☎04 73 79 62 92.
Zone nordique du Mézenc: ☎04 71 08 34 33.
Stations du massif du Pilat: ☎04 77 20 43 43.
Stations des monts du Forez: ☎04 77 24 83 11.

Useful Websites

The regional tourist office site – **www.crt-auvergne.com** – has information on ski resorts and conditions. Another site for information and reservations is **www.skifrance.fr**, including all the latest updates on snow conditions in French resorts (some sites also list available accommodation).
www.super-besse.com offers the possibility of visualising the resort's weather conditions in real time via several webcams.

WATERSPORTS

Natural and artificial lakes offer a wide choice of possibilities for the practice of various water sports: rowing, windsurfing, water skiing, canoeing, kayaking, rafting and canyoning.

Canoeing and kayaking

Discover the region from the swirling waters of the Ardèche, the Sornin or the Allier: information on suitable spots for canoeing from the Fédération **Française de Canoë-Kayak, 87** Quai de la Marne, BP 58, 94344 Joinville-le-Pont ☎01 45 11 08 50; www.ffcanoe.asso.fr. Map of French waterways available.

Rafting and canyoning

Rafting is the easiest of these freshwater sports, since it involves going down rivers in inflatable craft steered by an instructor; special equipment is provided.

Canyoning is a technique for bodysurfing down narrow gorges and over falls, as though on a giant water slide. This sport requires protection: wear a wet suit and a helmet.

Information from **AN Rafting Haut-Allier**, Le Bourg, 43580 Monistrol-d'Allier ☎04 71 57 23 90.

Rowing

Club aviron Vichy, 3 avenue de la Croix-St-Martin, 03200 Vichy ☎04 70 32 36 52; leisure activities and competitions.

Activities for Children   Kids

Sights of particular interest to children are indicated with a Kids *symbol.*

The Auvergne region of France has a lot to offer children, from having fun with water in amusement parks such as the Parc aquatique d'Ambert (☎04 73 82 14 23), the Centre aquatique de Chamalières (☎04 73 29 78 78) or Iloa in Thiers (☎04 73 80 14 90 or 04 73 80 88 80), to visiting zoos, châteaux, museums and sights of special interest. *see also Tourist trains and Eco-tourism.*
Children are welcome everywhere in France; the French are very much family-oriented. It is quite commonplace to see well-behaved children dining in restaurants in the early evening. Moreover, France is a wonderful destination to bring babies, toddlers, in fact, children of all ages.
Most attractions, parks, museums and buildings offer reduced rates for children, with very young children often going free.

Useful Websites

A useful sources of ideas is **www.france4families.com**, which contains a lot of general information and tips. There are also other useful websites, like **www.takethefamily.com**, which has tips and destination guides, and **www.babygoes2.com**, which contains pages of information to help parents travelling with small children. **www.tinytotsaway.com** allows you to order in advance all the things you would normally pack, from nappies to particular brands of baby food, which they then buy and ship to your hotel/destination, to be there as you arrive.

When you get there

Many of the local tourist office websites have pages dedicated to what children can do, and it is useful to consult those for your destination. But, when you are in France, don't be afraid of visiting the tourist office to see if there is anything happening during your stay, like a local festival, concert or celebration.

Spas and Mineral Springs

SPAS OF THE AUVERGNE

There are dozens of spas in France, ranging from up-market spa resort hotels to charming small spa villages that have relaxed visitors since the days of the Ancient Romans. The Auvergne and Rhone Alpes are no exception.

The thalassotherapy, balneotherapy and thermal spring centres of the Auvergne are renowned for their professional treatments and warm welcome. Thermal spa waters from the volcanoes have therapeutic virtues that were appreciated by the Romans. Nowadays, spas offer care adapted to various ailments. Water cures exploit the riches of water from natural springs. You drink it and bathe in it, and each spring has its own peculiar properties that might help slimming, help breathing problems or soothe physical or psychological ailments. Throughout the region, spas combine the benefits of fresh water with very fashionable and sometimes bizarre treatments: a chocolate body wrap, a body rub with black soap, a hot stone massage…

Flowing out of the immense natural filter formed by the volcanoes of Auvergne, mineral springs swell out of the ground at locations whose names have become famous brands of mineral or spring waters: Volvic, Châteauneuf, Sainte-Marguerite,

Mont-Dore, Vichy, Saint-Yorre and Arvie will all find a place at your table or in a restaurant, not to mention less well-known brands like La Cantaline, La Tessièroise, Renlaigue, Chateldon or Hydroxydase.

RESORTS

The region has many spa resorts:

Bourbon-l'Archambault‡
  see BOURBON-L'ARCHAMBAULT
La Bourboule‡‡
  see LA BOURBOULE
Châteauneuf-les-Bains
  see gorges de la SIOULE
Châtelguyon‡
  see RIOM, Châtelguyon
Chaudes-Aigues
  see ST FLOUR, Chaudes-Aigues
Le Mont-Dore
  see LE MONT-DORE
Montrond-les-Bains‡
  see MONTBRISON
Néris-les-Bains‡
  see MONTLUÇON
Neyrac-les-Bains‡
  see AUBENAS
Royat-Chamalières‡‡
  see CLERMONT-FERRAND, Royat
St-Nectaire‡
  see ST-NECTAIRE
Vals-les-Bains‡‡
  see AUBENAS, Vals-les-Bains
Vichy‡‡‡
  see VICHY

INFORMATION

You can obtain brochures and information by contacting the following:

Chaîne thermale du soleil,
  32 avenue de l'Opéra, 75002 Paris ☎01 44 71 37 00; www.sante-eau.com.
Union Nationale des Établissements Thermaux, 1 rue Cels, 75014 Paris ☎01 53 91 05 75; www.france-thermale.org.
Auvergne thermale, 8 avenue Anatole-France, 63130 Royat ☎04 73 34 72 80.

Shopping

Remember that people travelling to the USA cannot import plant products or fresh food, including fruit, cheeses and nuts. It is permitted to carry tinned products or preserves.

FAIRS AND MARKETS

Traditional fairs – These offer visitors an opportunity to witness long-standing local customs; the most colourful ones are listed below.

- **Tournon-sur-Rhône**, 29 August: onion fair
- **St-Sorlin-en-Valloire**, 1st Sat in September: foal fair
- **Claveyson**, 11 November: truffle fair
- **Chénelette**, 11 November: goat and cattle fair
- **Romans-sur-Isère**, from the last Sat in September to the 1st Sun in October: Dauphiné Fair

Markets – The most important fruit and vegetable market in the Rhône Valley takes place in **Pont-de-l'Isère** daily except Sundays from May to September, on Mondays, Wednesdays and Fridays the rest of the year. Other markets in the Rhône Valley:

- **Bourg-de-Péage:** Thu morning
- **Hauterives:** Tue morning
- **Romans-sur-Isère:** Tue, Fri and Sun mornings
- **Ruoms:** Fri morning
- **St-Donat-sur-l'Herbasse:** Mon morning

- **St-Rambert-d'Albon:** Fri morning
- **Tain-l'Hermitage:** Sat
- **Les Vans:** Sat morning; a traditional handicraft market livens up the town's historic centre between 6 and 10pm on Tue in July and August.
- **Villeneuve-de-Berg:** Wed morning; activities are organised on Tue evenings throughout July and during the first fortnight of August.

LOCAL SPECIALITIES

Beaujolais and **Côtes-du-Rhône** wines go well with local cheeses such as **Picodon**, made from goat's milk, or **St-Marcellin**, made from a subtle mixture of goat's and cow's milk. You may be tempted by a pair of fine **shoes** from Romans-sur-Isère, once the capital of the shoe industry (visit the interesting local museum), or by a hand-painted silk scarf or tie from Lyon, or even by **woollen clothes** from the local manufacture in St-Pierreville (Eyrieux Valley).
If you are looking for ideas, visit the **Marché de la Création** (painting, sculpture, pottery…) which takes place in Lyon along quai Romain Rolland on Sunday mornings or the **Marché de l'Artisanat** (handicraft) which takes place along quai Fulchiron, also on Sunday mornings.

Books

Speak the Culture – (Thoroughgood Publishing, 2008). A general guidebook that shows you where to go in France and what to say when you get there, reasoning that through exploring the people and their lifestyles you will achieve an intimate understanding of France and its people.

Walks in Volcano Country – Alan Castle (Cicerone Press). Routes in the Auvergne and Velay of southern central France, including the 10–15 day traverse of the High Auvergne, or the 100-mile

© José Nicolas/World Pictures/Photoshot

Producing picodon

walk in the gentle hill country around Le Puy.

Mourjou: The Life and Food of an Auvergne village – *Peter Graham, (Prospect Books, 2003).*
The author explores the traditions, folklore and gastronomy of the Auvergne, discovering the rhythms of its rustic life, the warmth of its people and their passion for food.

Summer days in Auvergne – *Herbert de Kantzow (Adamant Media Corporation, 2004).*
A descriptive account of the author's travels in France and the Auvergne, originally published in 1875.

Portrait of the Auvergne – *Peter Gorham (Robert Hale, 1975).*
There are few places in France where past and present mingle so naturally. Yet the true wealth of the Auvergne remains in its countryside...

Exiles – *Anita Burgh (Orion Publishing, 2001).*
A work of fiction continuing the story of Kate Howard, a successful writer, who for the past three years has lived happily with her lover Stewart and her daughter Lucy in an old farmhouse in the wilderness of the Auvergne. The novel explores what happens when her son arrives, and the outside world begins to affect her French haven.

Films

The **Auvergne Film Commission** is a collaboration of directors who make films in the beautiful landscapes of the Auvergne. Among these are:

7 years – *(Bruno Todeschini, Valérie Donzelli and Cyril Troley, 2005).*
Maïté is married to Vincent who has just been sentenced to seven years in prison. The only intimacy left to them lies in the prison's visiting rooms.
Twice a week, she picks up his laundry, washes it, irons it, and brings it back to him…

The Singer – *(Cecile de France, Gérard Depardieu, Mathieu Amalric, 2005)*
Alain is a fifty-year-old singer at popular balls who also performs before factory committees and at inaugurations. He has dyed hair and is famous throughout Clermont-Ferrand. Singing was his whole life until he became acquainted with Marion, a young woman…

Crimson Rivers 2: Angels of the Apocalypse – *(Jean Reno, Benoît Magimel, Camille Natta, 2003)*
Chief Niemans is investigating a series of ritual murders: The victims are crucified. He teams up with young officer Reda. Together with a specialist on Christian mythology they uncover a mysterious group called "Angels of the Apocalypse".

To be and to have – *(2001)*
There are still, almost everywhere in France, single-classroom schools that bring together, under the same schoolteacher, all the children from the same village, from nursery age to their last year of primary education. Whether their individual members are withdrawn or outgoing, these assorted little groups share everyday life, for the best and for the worst. It was in one of these schools, somewhere in the heart of the Auvergne, that this film was shot.

Bon Voyage – *(2002, with Isabelle Adjani, Virginie Ledoyen, Yvan Attal, Gregori Derangère)*
At the start of World War II, the fate of the free world hangs in the balance at the Hotel Splendide in Bordeaux. Cabinet members, journalists, physicists, and spies of all persuasions gather to escape the Nazi occupation of Paris.

CALENDAR OF EVENTS

JANUARY

Villefranche-sur-Saône
Fête des Conscrits. ☎04 74 07 27 40; www.villefranche.net

FEBRUARY

Clermont-Ferrand
International Short-Film Festival. ☎04 73 91 65 73
Le Mont Dore - La Bourboule
Festival of Jazz.
☎04 73 65 20 21 (Mont Dore)
☎04 73 65 57 71 (La Bourboule)

MARCH

Clermont-Ferrand
"Vidéoformes": International video and multimedia art festival.
☎04 73 17 02 17
Auvergne
"Chamineige": trek across the Cévennes from La Margeride to Mont Aigoual, on cross-country skis, mountain bikes and on foot.
☎04 73 31 20 32.
Lyon
International Fair. ☎04 72 22 33 37

MAUNDY THURSDAY

Le Puy-en-Velay
Torchlight procession of the White Penitents in hooded robes in the streets around the cathedral.
☎04 71 09 38 41

MAY

Vichy
Une Saison en Eté: theatre, classical music, opera, variety shows at the Vichy Opera House from May to October. ☎04 70 30 50 30; www.ville-vichy.fr
Allanche
Fete de l'Estive ☎04 71 20 48 43

EVE OF ASCENSION DAY

Orcival
Pilgrimage in honour of the Virgin Mary: torchlight procession and midnight mass.

WHITSUN

Lyon
International French Bowls Tournament (Tournoi Bouliste).
☎04 78 37 16 10

SUNDAY FOLLOWING 15 MAY

Clermont-Ferrand
Feast of Our Lady of the Port ending with an afternoon procession through the old town.

FRENCH MOTHERS' DAY WEEKEND (LAST SUNDAY IN MAY) – ON EVEN YEARS

Villerest
Medieval Festival: procession and tour of ramparts. ☎04 77 69 69 67

JUNE

Clermont-Ferrand
Medieval Festival in Montferrand.
☎04 73 23 19 29
Vic-le-Comte
Celtrad: Celtic music festival.
☎04 73 69 02 12

Street theatre festival in Aurillac

J. Damase/MICHELIN

FRIDAY NEAREST TO 24 JUNE

Villefranche-sur-Saône
Midsummer Night: bonfires,
singers, illuminations.
☎04 74 65 04 48

JULY

Forez
Concerts of classical music in
churches and castles of the Forez
region. ☎04 73 51 55 67
Auvergne
Thermathlon du Sancy: fun trek
along the Route des Villes d'Eaux
of the Massif Central (moun-
tain biking, walking, canoeing,
archery…). ☎04 73 31 20 32
Montélimar
Festival "Voix et Guitares du
Monde" and international guitar
competition. ☎04 75 00 77 55;
www.festivalvoixetguitares.com
Orcines
Open Golf des Volcans: International golf championship (last
week of the month). ☎04 73 62
15 51. www.golfdesvolcans.com
Issoire
International Folklore Festival.
☎04 73 89 92 85
Ambert
Festival de Folklore ☎04 73 82 14
49. www.livradoue-dansaire.com
Royat
Festival VOLCADIVA – song
festival, concerts and recitals
☎04 73 29 74 70.
Vollore
Festival des Concerts de Vollore – classical music, jazz and
'musique tzigane' ☎04 73 51 55
67. www.letransfo.fr
Le Puy-en-Velay
Festival de Musiques Vocales
☎06 72 58 27 67.
Gannat
Cultures du Monde: world folklore
festival. ☎04 70 90 12 67.
www.gannat.com.

JULY–AUGUST

Saint-Agrève (grange de Clavières)
International Art Festival (music,

art photography, painting).
☎04 75 30 22 43

AUGUST

La Font-Sainte, Cheylade
Pilgrimage of young shepherds
who gather for a procession and
the "shepherds' meal".
La Chaise-Dieu
International Music Festival. ☎04
71 09 48 28. www.chaise-dieu.com
Aurillac
International Street Theatre
Festival. ☎04 71 45 47 45.
www.aurillac.net
St-Pourçain-sur-Sioule
Wine Festival. ☎04 70 45 32 73
Mont Brouilly
Wine-producers' pilgrimage to
Brouilly Chapel. ☎04 74 66 82 19

SEPTEMBER

Ravel
Pottery market (3rd weekend).
☎04 73 68 44 74

SEPTEMBER–DECEMBER

Beaujolais, Coteaux du Rhône
and du Forez
Grape Harvest and Wine Festivals
in the wine-growing regions.

OCTOBER

Montbrison
Fourme Cheese Festival;
procession of flower-decked floats.
☎04 77 96 18 18
Clermont-Ferrand
International Jazz Festival. ☎04 73
93 70 83. www.jazzentete.com

9–11 NOVEMBER

Le Puy-en-Velay
International Hot-Air Balloon Rally.
☎04 71 02 73 18

8 DECEMBER

Lyon
Festival of Light. ☎04 72 10 30 30

BASIC INFORMATION

Business Hours

Most of the larger **shops** are open Mondays to Saturdays from 9am to 6.30 or 7.30pm. Smaller, individual shops may close during the lunch hour. Food shops – grocers, wine merchants and bakeries – are generally open from 7am to 6.30 or 7.30pm; some open on Sunday mornings. Many food shops close between noon and 2pm and on Mondays. Bakery and pastry shops sometimes close on Wednesdays. Hypermarkets usually stay open without a break from 9am until 9pm or even later.

Although business hours vary from branch to branch, **banks** are usually open from 9am to noon and 2pm to 5pm and are closed either on Mondays or Saturdays. Banks close early on the day before a bank holiday.

Post offices open Mondays to Fridays, 8am to 7pm, Saturdays, 8am to noon. National museums and art galleries are closed on Tuesdays; municipal museums are generally closed on Mondays.

Communications

TELEPHONE

Most public phones in France use prepaid phone cards *(télécartes)*, rather than coins. Some telephone booths accept credit cards (Visa, Mastercard/Eurocard).

Télécartes (50 or 120 units) can be bought in post offices, branches of France Télécom, *bureaux de tabac* (cafés that sell cigarettes) and newsagents and can be used to make calls in France and abroad.

Calls can be received at phone boxes where the blue bell sign is shown; the phone will not ring, so keep your eye on the little message screen.

NATIONAL CALLS

French telephone numbers have 10 digits. Paris and Paris region numbers begin with 01; 02 in north-west France; 03 in north-east France; 04 in south-east France and Corsica; 05 in south-west France.

INTERNATIONAL CALLS

To call France from abroad, dial the country code (33) + 9-digit number (omit the initial 0). When calling abroad from France dial 00, then dial the country code followed by the area code and the number you require.

International dialling codes (00 + code):

Australia	☎ 61
New Zealand	☎ 64
Canada	☎ 1
United Kingdom	☎ 44
Eire	☎ 353
United States	☎ 1

International Information: 32 12
International operator: 31 23
Local directory assistance: 12
Toll-free numbers in France begin with 0 800.

MOBILE PHONES

Dual- or tri-band mobile phones will work almost anywhere In France, but at international roaming rates. If you are staying for an extended period you might consider renting a mobile phone locally.

A.L.T. Rent A Phone	☎ 01 48 00 06 06, E-mail altlocjve.fr
Rent a Cell Express	☎ 01 53 93 78 00, Fax 01 53 93 78 09
Ellinas Phone Rental	☎ 01 47 20 70 00

AT&T	☎ 0-800 99 00 11
Sprint	☎ 0-800 99 00 87
Canada Direct	☎ 0-800 99 00 16

INTERNET

The internet is widely available throughout France, and most major hotels offer a WiFi service (charged). Compared to other countries there are few 'Internet cafés', although these are increasing. There is unlikely to be widespread internet availability in rural parts of the Auvergne.

MINITEL

Minitel is a 'Videotex' online service accessible through the telephone lines, and is considered one of the world's most successful pre-Internet online services. It was launched in France in 1982 by the PTT (Poste, Téléphone et Télécommunications. It is still widely in evidence in France, but has lost ground to the internet.

Electricity

In France the electric current is 220 volts. Circular two-pin plugs are the rule. Adapters and converters (for hairdryers, for example) should be bought before you leave home; they are on sale in most airports. If you have a rechargeable device (video camera, portable computer, battery recharger), read the instructions carefully or contact the manufacturer or retailer. Sometimes these items only require a plug adapter, in other cases you must use a voltage converter as well or risk ruining your device.

Emergencies

Police	☎**17**
Paramedics (SAMU)	☎**15**
Fire (Pompiers)	☎**18**
European Emergency Call	☎**112**

Yellow post box

Mail/Post

Smaller branch post offices often close at lunchtime between noon and 2pm and in the afternoon at 4pm.
Stamps are also available from newsagents and tobacconists.
Stamp collectors should ask for *timbres de collection* in any post office.
Poste Restante (General Delivery) mail should be addressed as follows: Name, Poste Restante, Poste Centrale, post code of the *département* followed by town name, France. The Michelin Guide France gives local post codes.

Money

Along with most EU countries, France uses the Euro (€). There are no restrictions on the amount of currency visitors can take into France. Visitors carrying a lot of cash are advised to complete a currency declaration form on arrival, because there are restrictions on currency export.

BANKS

&*See Business Hours for opening times.*
A passport is necessary as identification when cashing travellers cheques in banks. Commission charges vary and hotels usually charge more than banks for cashing cheques.

American Express ☎ 01 47 77 72 00
Visa ☎ 0 800 901 179
MasterCard/Eurocard ☎ 0 800 901 387
Diners Club ☎ 0 810 314 519

CREDIT AND DEBIT CARDS

The most economical way to obtain cash in France is by using **ATM machines** to get money directly from your bank account (with a debit card), or you can use your credit card to get a cash advance. Be sure to remember your PIN number, you will need it to use cash dispensers and to pay with your card in shops, restaurants etc. Code pads are numeric. Visa is the most widely accepted credit card, followed by Mastercard; other credit and debit cards are also accepted in some cash machines. American Express is more often accepted in premium establishments. Most places post signs indicating which card they accept; if you don't see such a sign and want to pay with a card, ask before ordering or making a selection. Cards are widely accepted in shops, hypermarkets, hotels and restaurants, at toll booths and in petrol stations.
Before you leave home, check with the bank that issued your card for emergency replacement procedures.
Carry your card number and emergency phone numbers separate from your wallet and handbag; leave a copy of this information with someone you can easily reach. It is also a good idea to notify your credit card bank that you will be using the card in a foreign country. You must report any loss or theft of credit cards or travellers cheques to the local police who will issue you with a certificate (useful proof to show the issuing company).

PRICES AND TIPS

Since a service charge is automatically included in the prices of meals and accommodation in France, it is not necessary to tip in restaurants and hotels. However, if the service in a restaurant is especially good or if you have enjoyed a fine meal, an extra tip (this is the *pourboire,* rather than the *service)* will be appreciated. Usually 2 to 4€ is enough, but if the bill is big (a large party or a luxury restaurant), it is not uncommon to leave more.

Restaurants usually charge for meals in two ways: a menu that is a fixed-price menu with 2 or 3 courses, sometimes a small jug (*pichet*) of wine, all for a stated price, or à la carte, the more expensive way, with each course ordered separately.

Cafés have very different prices, depending on where they are located. The price of a drink or a coffee is cheaper if you stand at the counter (*comptoir*) than if you sit down (*salle*), and sometimes it is even more expensive if you sit outdoors (*terrasse*).

Public Holidays

Public services, museums and other monuments may be closed or may vary their hours of admission on public holidays:
National museums and art galleries are closed on Tuesdays; municipal museums are generally closed on Mondays. In addition to the usual

1 January	New Year's Day (Jour de l'An)
	Easter Day and Easter Monday (Pâques)
1 May	May Day (Fête du Travail)
8 May	VE Day (Anniversaire 1945)
Thurs 40 days after Easter	Ascension Day (Ascension)
7th Sun-Mon after Easter	Whit Sunday and Monday (Pentecôte)
14 July	France's National Day (Fête Nationale)
15 August	Assumption (Assomption)
1 November	All Saints' Day (Toussaint)
11 November	Armistice Day (Armistice 1918)
25 December	Christmas Day (Noël)

school holidays at Christmas and in the spring and summer, there are long mid-term breaks in February and early November.

Reduced Rates

Significant discounts are available for senior citizens, students, young people under the age of 25, teachers, and groups for public transportation, museums and monuments and for some leisure activities such as the cinema (at certain times of day). Bring student or senior cards with you, and bring along some extra passport-size photos for discount travel cards.

The **International Student Travel Confederation** (www.isic.org), is a confederation of travel companies worldwide that specialise in providing flexible travel arrangements for students, young people (under 26) and teachers.

The ISTC network includes over 5000 Student and Youth Travel Offices in 102 countries worldwide. These offices offer a wide range of services, including international identity cards, inexpensive, flexible airfares and travel tickets, travel insurance, work and study abroad programmes, accommodation, tours and much more.

Smoking

Since the beginning of 2008, smoking has been forbidden in all public places in France, especially bars, restaurants, railway stations and airports.

Taxes

There is a Value Added Tax in France *(TVA)* at a standard rate of 19.6% on almost every purchase (33% for luxury goods, 5.5% for food). However, non-European visitors who spend more than 175€ (2008) in any one participating store may get the VAT amount refunded. Usually, you fill out a form at the store, showing your passport. Upon leaving the country, you submit all forms to customs for approval

©Marilyn Nieves/istockphoto.com

(they may want to see the goods, so if possible don't pack them in checked luggage). The refund is usually paid directly into your bank or credit card account, or it can be sent by mail.

Big department stores that cater to tourists provide special services to help you; be sure to mention that you plan to seek a refund before you pay for goods (no refund is possible for tax on services). If you are visiting two or more countries within the European Union, you submit the forms only on departure from the last EU country. The refund is worth while for those visitors who would like to buy fashions, furniture or other expensive items, but remember, the minimum amount must be spent in a single shop but not necessarily on the same day.

Time

France is 1hr ahead of Greenwich Mean Time (GMT). France goes on daylight-saving time from the last Sunday in March to the last Sunday in October. In France "am" and "pm" are not used, but the 24-hour clock is widely applied.

When it is **noon in France,** it is
3am in Los Angeles
6am in New York
11am in Dublin
11am in London
7pm in Perth (6pm in summer)
9pm in Sydney (8pm in summer
11pm in Auckland (10pm in summer)

USEFUL WORDS & PHRASES

Here are some French words you may see on local maps or road signs

SIGHTS

abbaye	abbey
beffroi	belfry
chapelle	chapel
château	castle
cimetière	cemetery
cloître	cloisters
cour	courtyard
couvent	convent
écluse	lock (canal)
église	church
fontaine	fountain
halle	covered market
jardin	garden
mairie	town hall
maison	house
marché	market
monastère	monastery
moulin	windmill
musée	museum
parc	park
place	square
pont	bridge
port	port/harbour
porte	gateway
quai	quay
remparts	ramparts
rue	street
statue	statue
tour	tower

NATURAL SITES

abîme	chasm
aven	swallow-hole
barrage	dam
belvédère	viewpoint
cascade	waterfall
col	pass
corniche	ledge
côte	coast, hillside
forêt	forest
grotte	cave
lac	lake
plage	beach
rivière	river
ruisseau	stream
signal	beacon

source	spring
vallée	valley

Here are a few French translations for things you might need to say

SHOPPING

bank	la banque
baker's	la boulangerie
big	grand
butcher's	la boucherie
chemist's/drugstore	la pharmacie
closed	fermé
cough syrup	du sirop pour la toux
throat lozenges	des pastilles pour la gorge
entrance	l'entrée
exit	la sortie
fishmonger's	la poissonnerie
grocer's	l'épicerie
newsagent, bookshop	la librairie
open	ouvert
post office	la poste
shop	le magasin
small	petit
stamps	des timbres

ON THE ROAD

car park	le parking
driving licence	le permis de conduire
(to the) east	(à l') est
garage (for repairs)	le garage
(to the) left	(à) gauche
motorway/highway	l'autoroute
(to the) north	(au) nord
petrol/gas	l'essence
petrol/gas station	la station essence
(to the) right	(à) droite
(to the) south	(au) sud
straight ahead	tout droit
toll	le péage
traffic lights	le feu tricolore
tyre	le pneu
(to the) west	(à l') ouest

On national and departmental roads, there are often roundabouts (traffic circles) just outside the towns, which serve to slow traffic down. At a French roundabout (**rond point**), you are likely to see signs pointing to **Centre Ville** (city centre) or to other towns (the French use towns as directional indicators, rather than cardinal points). You are also likely to see a sign for **Toutes Directions** (all directions – this is often the bypass road to avoid going through the town) or **Autres Directions** (other directions – in other words, any place that isn't indicated on one of the other signs on the roundabout!).

50	cinquante
60	soixante
70	soixante-dix
80	quatre-vingt
90	quatre-vingt-dix
100	cent
1000	mille

TIME

today	aujourd'hui
tomorrow	demain
yesterday	hier
winter	hiver
spring	printemps
summer	été
autumn/fall	automne
week	semaine
Monday	lundi
Tuesday	mardi
Wednesday	mercredi
Thursday	jeudi
Friday	vendredi
Saturday	samedi
Sunday	dimanche

NUMBERS

0	zéro
1	un(e)
2	deux
3	trois
4	quatre
5	cinq
6	six
7	sept
8	huit
9	neuf
10	dix
11	onze
12	douze
13	treize
14	quatorze
15	quinze
16	seize
17	dix-sept
18	dix-huit
19	dix-neuf
20	vingt
30	trente
40	quarante

A FEW USEFUL PHRASES

Hello/good morning	**Bonjour**
Goodbye	**Au revoir**
Thank you	**Merci**
Excuse me	**Excusez-moi**
Yes/no	**Oui/non**
Sorry!	**Pardon!**
Why?	**Pourquoi?**
When?	**Quand?**
Please	**S'il vous plaît**
Do you speak English?	**Parlez-vous anglais?**
I don't understand.	**Je ne comprends pas**
Please talk more slowly	**Parlez plus lentement, s'il vous plaît**
Where is …?	**Où est...?**
When does the ... leave?	**À quelle heure part...?**
When does the ... arrive?	**À quelle heure arrive...?**
When does the museum open?	**À quelle heure ouvre le musée?**
When does the film/show start?	**À quelle heure commence le film/le spectacle?**
When is breakfast served?	**À quelle heure sert-on le petit-déjeuner?**
How much does it cost?	**Combien est-ce que cela coûte?**
Where can I buy an English paper?	**Où puis-je acheter un journal en anglais?**
Where is the nearest petrol station/gas station?	**Où se trouve la station essence la plus proche?**
Where can I change traveller's cheques?	**Où puis-je échanger des traveller's cheques?**
Where are the toilets?	**Où sont les toilettes?**
Can I pay with a credit card?	**Est-ce que je peux payer avec ma carte bancaire?**

Côte-Rôtie vineyards
J. Damase/MICHELIN

NATURE

The name **Auvergne** conjures up visions of a superb natural environment of outstanding beauty, a rugged landscape of mountain ranges and volcanoes, and lakes and springs in the heart of France. The area has been less accessible from the rest of France since time immemorial because of a lack of roads or railways. The local people are proud and austere, and agriculture remains a primary industry.

The **Rhône Valley,** on the other hand, is long and wide. It is an important through route for road and rail, a region of different cultures, and an area at the forefront of industrial progress, destined to play an increasingly important role within Europe in the future. The region is dominated by Lyon, the second largest city in France, with a lively cultural life, museums, a new opera house and a long-standing tradition of good food.

Rhône Valley

THE RHÔNE CORRIDOR

La Dombes – This is a clay plateau dotted with lakes which ends in the fairly sheer **"côtières"** of the Saône to the west and the Rhône to the south. In the north, the plateau runs into Bresse. The waters of the melting glacier in the Rhône valley dug shallow dips into the surface of the land and left moraines, an accumulation of debris swept along by the glacier, on the edge of the dips. It is on these **poypes** or slight rises that the villages were built. The **Dombes** is now a charming area of tranquil countryside, with lines of trees, countless birds, and calm lakes reflecting the sky above.

Lower Dauphiné

The countryside in Lower Dauphiné is a succession of stony plateaux, plains and hills.

The Île Crémieu is a limestone plateau separated from the Jura to the north by the Rhône and to the west by an unusual cliff. The water that infiltrated the soil created a series of caves, the best-known of which are the Grottes de la Balme.

The **Balmes area** west of Vienne is partially covered in vineyards. It consists of granite and shale hills separated from Mont Pilat by the Rhône. It extends into the **Terres Froides plateau** which is slashed into strips by narrow valleys filled with fields of vegetables.

The **Bonnevaux and Chambaran plateaux** are vast expanses of woodland stretching south from Vienne and almost totally devoid of human habitation.

The wide fertile **Bièvre and Valloire plains** specialise in cereal crops. They indicate the course once followed by the Isère, but abandoned after the ice receded.

The **Isère Valley** itself opens out onto the Valence plateau; its well-cultivated terraces covered with walnut groves.

The Valence and Tricastin areas

From Tain to the Donzère gorge, the Rhône Valley widens to the east of the river, forming a patchwork of plains until it reaches the foothills of the Préalpes.

The **Valence plain** consists of a series of alluvial terraces built in steps. Its irrigated fields and its climate are a foretaste of the south of France and the Mediterranean. It was here that the "Tree of Gold," the mulberry, was first planted in the 17C and provided the local inhabitants with a reasonable living from the cultivation of silkworms. Nowadays, the many orchards have maintained the old-fashioned appearance of the countryside in which hedgerows abound.

The **Montélimar basin,** south of the Cruas gorge, is similar to but narrower than the Valence plain; olive trees grow on the south-facing slopes.

The **Tricastin area,** crossed by the Lauzon and the Lez, is a succession of arid hills covered with vineyards and

Suspension bridge over the Rhône at Tournon

olive trees. Its old villages perched on defensive sites form remarkable lookout posts.

THE EDGE OF THE MASSIF CENTRAL

The Massif Central ends to the east in a scarp slope high above the Rhône valley. It is a formidable precipice consisting of a mountain range that was broken down, raised up then overturned by the after-effects of Alpine folding. It has been severely eroded by the rivers, forming narrow gorges.

The Beaujolais region
To the north, the upper Beaujolais is a mountainous zone of mainly granite soil. Tributaries of the Saône run down its steep slopes from west to east. The Lower Beaujolais, to the south, is formed of sedimentary soils. These soil types include a limestone that is almost ochre in colour and has earned the area the nickname 'Land of Golden Stone'.
Economically, there is a clear demarcation of this region east to west, between the escarpment *(La Côte)* overlooking the Saône Valley in the east, the wine-producing region, and the hills *(La Montagne)* or hinterland to the west, in which forests, crop-farming and industry predominate.

The Lyonnais area
Set between the St-Étienne basin and the city of Lyon, the plateau is dotted with high grassy hills, pine forests, beech woods and orchards. The Mont-d'Or is a rugged area (highest peak: Mont Verdun, altitude 625m/2 031ft). The Lyonnais area owes its uniform appearance to the industries that have existed here for centuries. It ends in the Fourvière hill, the superb promontory that stands high above the confluence of the Saône and Rhône and the vast city of Lyon.

Forez and Roannais
In the **Forez mountains,** fields and meadows cover the slopes up to an altitude of 1 000m/3 250ft. Above them are oases of beech and pine forest, providing raw material for sawmills. In summer, animals are taken up to graze on the scrubby mountain tops (on the land called the Hautes Chaumes) rising to the Pierre-sur-Haute moors. At the foot of the mountains is the water-logged Forez plain crossed by the River Loire. This is dotted with volcanic hillocks where castle and church ruins are found. The **Roanne basin** is a fertile rural area specialising in animal husbandry and is overlooked, to the west, by the vine-covered slopes of the Madeleine mountain range.

Mont Pilat and the St-Étienne basin
Mont Pilat is a forest-clad pyramid with something of a mountainous air, rising above the surrounding dales. Its peaks are topped with granite boulders known as *chirats,* which form splendid observa-

tion platforms. The St-Étienne basin at the foot of the mountain follows the outline of the coalfield that stretches from the Loire to the Rhône, and contains a string of factories, in stark contrast to the pastures on the slopes of Mont Pilat and the Lyonnais mountain range.

The Vivarais area

This forms the largest part of the eastern edge of the Massif Central. Huge basalt-lava flows running down from the Velay area, shale ridges, and widespread erosion make this a bizarre landscape of strange natural features.

The **Upper Vivarais** reaches from Mont Pilat and the Velay area to the Rhône valley. People here earn a living from cattle farming and cutting timber in the pine forests. Nearer the banks of the Rhône, there are fruit trees and vineyards. The **Vivarais cévenol** (lying within the Cévennes range) runs from the Upper Allier valley to the Aubenas basin. To the west, the "uplands" are strongly characterised by volcanoes. They are covered in pine, beech and meadow. From Lablachère and Privas to the Rhône valley, the **Lower Vivarais** is a limestone area with a succession of basins and plateaux in which scrub, olive trees, almond trees, blackberry bushes and vines provide a foretaste of a more southerly environment.

To the north it is separated from the **Upper Vivarais** by the Coiron plateau and its black basalt cliffs. The unusual features of the vast plains *(planèzes)* grazed by flocks of sheep are the **dikes** and **necks** (pinnacles), the most famous of which is the one in Rochemaure. The limestone Gras plateau forms a stretch of whitish stone, with swallowholes, deep narrow gullies and rocks shaped like ruined buildings.

Auvergne

Granite and volcanic mountains

In the region to the east, the climate is hard and the landscape rugged. From north to south, the **Madeleine** mountain range, **Forez and Livradois areas** consist of valleys, rounded hilltops, forest plateaux and pastures on which

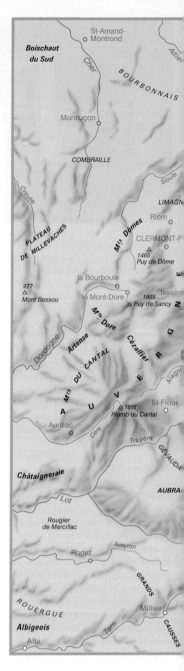

flocks of sheep graze. The area is covered with forests that provide timber. Further south, the **Velay area** is a succession of vast basalt plateaux lying at altitudes of more than 1 000m/3 250ft beneath skies that are a foretaste of the Riviera. Dotted

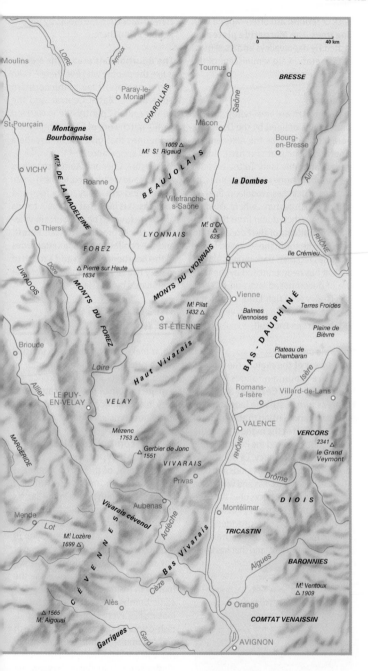

across the countryside are **outcrops of rock** formed by lava. Crops are generally so rare that the basin around Le Puy, which is irrigated by the Loire, looks almost like an oasis. The mountains in the **Devès area** form one vast plateau where lava flows are covered with pasture and fields of barley or lentils. Along the watershed between the Loire and Allier basins are deep lakes in volcanic craters. The *planèze* (sloping plateau) is dotted with cinder cones consisting of black or reddish ash often capped with pine trees. The **Margeride plateau** is gashed by deep valleys and its climate and vegetation are reminiscent of the Forez mountains.

Limagnes

The *limagnes* are low-lying, fertile, sunny plains drained by the Dore and, more particularly, by the Allier and its tributaries. The plains consist almost entirely of arable land. To the east are the "poor Limagnes" or "Varennes," a hilly area of marshes, woodland, fields of crops and lush pastures where alluvium has been washed down from the crystalline mountains of the Forez area. To the west, the soil in the so-called fertile Limagnes region is dark brown, almost black. It has been enriched by the mixture of decomposed lava and volcanic ash. This is very rich land, producing tobacco, wheat, sugar beet, vegetable and seed crops and fruit.

Volcanic uplands

To the west of the region, the **Dômes** and **Dore** mountain ranges and the mountains in the **Cézallier** and **Cantal** areas form a striking landscape of extinct volcanoes rising to an altitude of 1 885m/6 126ft at the highest peak, the Puy de Sancy. Around the Puy de Dôme, Puy Mary, Puy de Sancy, La Bourboule and St-Nectaire, forests, woods and pastures alternate with lakes and waterfalls. The **Artense,** which backs onto the Dore mountain range, is a rocky plateau worn away by glaciers; it now provides grazing land for sheep and cattle. The cultivated areas represent land that has been

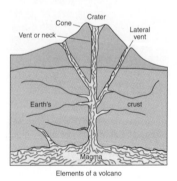

Elements of a volcano

Elements of a volcano

clawed back from the moors by the few people living there.

The Bourbonnais area – The scenery is like the people who live there – calm and temperate. It marks the northern edge of the Massif Central, and the gently rolling countryside is covered with a patchwork of fields hemmed in by hedges that give the landscape a wooded appearance.

The Besbre, Cher and Aumance valleys are wide and well drained, forming open, fertile areas crossed by major road and rail links. It is here that the main towns are to be found. The St-Pourçain vineyards, the impressive Tronçais Forest, and the conifers on the mountainsides in the Bourbonnais area add a touch of variety to a landscape that is otherwise dominated by grassland.

THE VOLCANOES OF THE AUVERGNE

What makes the Auvergne so unusual is the presence of a large number of volcanoes which, although extinct, are a major feature of the landscape. They vary in appearance depending on their formation, type and age.

Inverse composite volcanoes (Stromboli-type)

In the depths of the earth, magma is subjected to enormous pressure and infiltrates through cracks in the Earth's crust (*see diagram*). When the pressure becomes too great, there is an explosion accompanied by a sudden eruption of incandescent matter. A huge column of gas, smoke and vapour rises into the sky, spreading out like a parasol, while the matter in fusion (spindle-shaped volcanic bombs, gas-swollen pozzolana looking like a very lightweight, dark reddish-coloured stone) falls back to earth and accumulates around the mouth of the volcano, gradually building up a **cinder cone.** At the top is a **crater.** The most typical of all can be seen on the Puy des Goules and the Pariou.

When the pressure inside the Earth's crust decreases and the matter thrown up by the eruption is more fluid, lava flows are created, running from the

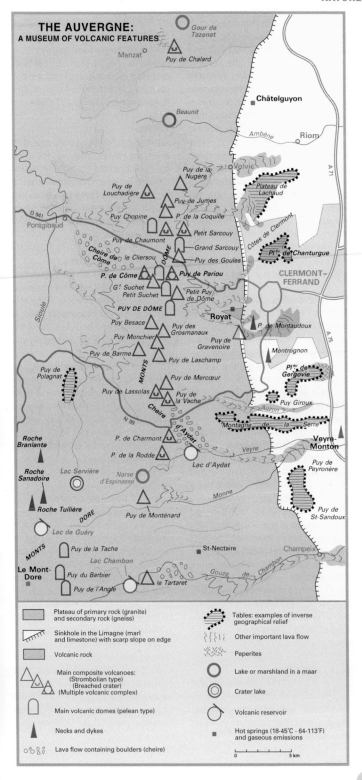

THE AUVERGNE:
A MUSEUM OF VOLCANIC FEATURES

Gour de Tazenat

Manzat

Puy de Chalard

Châtelguyon

Beaunit

Ambène

Riom

A 71

Volvic

Puy de la Nugère

Puy de Louchadière

Puy de Jumes

Plateau de Lachaud

P. de la Coquille

Côtes de Clermont

D 941

Puy Chopine

Pontgibaud

Puy de Chaumont

le Cliersou

Petit Sarcouy

Grand Sarcouy

Puy des Goules

Pl.eu de Chanturgue

Cheire de Côme

P. de Côme

DÔME

Gd Suchet
Petit Suchet

Puy de Pariou

CLERMONT-FERRAND

Petit Puy de Dôme

PUY DE DÔME

Royat

Sioule

Puy Besace

Puy Monchier

Puy de Barme

Puy des Grosmanaux

Puy de Gravenoire

P. de Montaudoux

A 75

Montrognon

MONTS

Puy de Laschamp

Puy de Polagnat

Puy de Mercœur

Pl.eu de Gergovie

Puy de Lassolas

Puy de la Vache

Puy Giroux

Auzon

Cheire d'Aydat

N 89

Montagne de la Serre

Roche Branlante

P. de Charmont

Veyre-Monton

P. de la Rodde

Lac d'Aydat

Veyre

Lac Servière

Puy de Peyronère

Roche Sanadoire

Narse d'Espinasse

Monne

Roche Tuilière

DORE

Puy de Monténard

Puy de St-Sandoux

Lac de Guéry

MONTS

Puy de la Tache

St-Nectaire

Champeix

Lac Chambon

Le Mont-Dore

Puy du Barbier

Gouze de Chambon

Puy de l'Angle

le Tartaret

	Plateau of primary rock (granite) and secondary rock (gneiss)		Tables: examples of inverse geographical relief
	Sinkhole in the Limagne (marl and limestone) with scarp slope on edge		Other important lava flow
	Volcanic rock		Peperites
	Main composite volcanoes: (Strombolian type) (Breached crater) (Multiple volcanic complex)		Lake or marshland in a maar
	Main volcanic domes (pelean type)		Crater lake
	Necks and dykes		Volcanic reservoir
	Lava flow containing boulders (cheire)		Hot springs (18-45°C - 64-113°F) and gaseous emissions

0   5 km

crater or down the mountainsides. Depending on the type of rock, these **lava flows** *(cheires)* may cool to form a fairly smooth surface or, alternatively, be rough and full of boulders. When the mass of lava is very thick, it contracts as it cools, breaking into prisms or columns (very much like organ pipes, hence their French name *orgues)* such as those in Bort-les-Orgues or Murat.

Sometimes a lava flow or an explosion carries away a piece of the volcanic cone, as it did in the Puy de Louchardière or the Puy de la Vache; in this case, the crater is described as **breached** and is shaped like a half-funnel. In the Pariou and the Puy de Dôme, a new cinder cone was formed inside the crater of an older volcano. This led to the formation of a **multiple volcanic complex.**

Volcanic domes (Mount Pelée-type composite volcano)

Sometimes, the volcanic eruption throws up a lava paste which solidifies upon contact with the ground. It then forms a dome with steep sides but has no crater at the summit. The Puy de Dôme is a good example of this type of volcano.

Volcanoes with planèzes

When the Cantal volcano was active more than 9 million years ago, it would have been a formidable sight: it had a circumference of 60km/37mi and rose to an altitude of 3 000m/9 750ft. Formed by a succession of layers of lava and ash, it was dissected by erosion which cut its sides into **planèzes** (sloping plateaux) with a tip pointing towards the centre of the volcano.

The Dore mountain range, which is younger than the Cantal volcano (2–3.5 million years), also consists of successions of layers of lava and ash but the *planèzes* are less well-developed.

Necks and dikes

Scattered across the Limagne in total disorder are volcanic systems which penetrated, and were consolidated within, a mass of sedimentary rock that has since been worn away.

All that remain are a few spurs of rock called necks or ridges known as dikes, which no longer have their covering of soil. The Puy de Monton near Veyre, and Montrognon near Ceyrat, are typical necks. Montaudoux to the south of Royat is a good example of a dike.

Tables

Ancient lava flows originally spread out across the valleys, protecting the underlying soil from the erosion that cleared the area between rivers and caused an inversion relief. These lava flows now jut out above the surrounding countryside, forming tables like the Gergovie and Polignac plateaux.

Lahars and Peperites

Volcanic eruptions are often accompanied by torrential rain and enormous emissions of water vapour. They then cause *lahars* (an Indonesian word) or flows of mud and boulders that move at astonishing speed, destroying everything in their path.

The Pardines plateau near Issoire owes its existence to this type of phenomenon. South of Clermont-Ferrand, some of the small plateaux and hillocks in the Limagne area consist of rock formations created by underwater volcanic eruptions. Their "peppery" appearance is due to the mixing of lava and sediment from the bed of the lake.

Lakes of volcanic origin

The volcanoes have given the landscape of the Auvergne a very particular relief and magnificent stretches of water that reflect the surrounding countryside. In some places, a lava flow closed off a valley, holding back the waters of a river; examples of this are the Aydat and Guéry lakes (the latter was also formed by the action of glaciers).

In other places, a volcano erupted in the middle of a valley, blocking it with its cone, as was the case in Chambon and Montcineyre. Still elsewhere, subsidence caused by underground volcanic activity was filled with run-off water (Lake Chauvet). *Maars* are lakes which were formed in craters (Lake Servière).

J. Damase/MICHELIN

Lac de Servière

The volcanoes of the Auvergne at present

The volcanoes are now well preserved depending on their age and the hardness of their rocks. The **Dômes** mountain range, with its 80 volcanoes that became extinct around 7 000 years ago, has a strikingly fresh-looking relief. The **Dore** mountain range is older and has a more fragmented appearance. The lava flows on Sancy, Aiguiller and Banne d'Ordanche are heaped up to a height of more than 1 000m/3 280ft but water, snow and glaciers have worn away the sides. With its 60km/37mi circumference and altitude of 3 000m/9 750ft, the **Cantal volcano** was even more impressive in its day. The landscapes today are only a fraction of the original; it is difficult to imagine the initial size of the range.

Auvergne's Mineral Springs

Whether naturally carbonated or still, water is one of the main sources of wealth in the Auvergne and it has been exploited here since antiquity. Puy-de-Dôme and the Vichy basin alone account for a third of French mineral springs.

Origins

Ordinary springs are created by water that seeps into permeable land and eventually meets an impermeable layer down which it runs. When the imperme-able layer rises to the surface, the water follows suit. **Mineral springs** are either springs of infiltrated water or springs rising from the depths of the Earth's crust. In this case, substances or gases that have therapeutic properties are added naturally to the water as it flows underground. The adjective **"thermal"** is used more accurately to describe springs with water at a temperature of at least 35°C/95°F when it comes out of the ground: Vichy water, for instance, has a temperature of 66°C/150°F and the water in Chaudes-Aigues rises to as much as 82°C/179.6°F.

Resurgent springs

The water in these springs only flows at intervals, for example every eight hours. The column of water rising from the depths of the Earth is subjected, at some point along its course, to a very high increase in temperature. The steam produced at this point acquires sufficient pressure to project the upper part of the column of water above the surface of the ground. The projection is interrupted for as long as it takes to heat a second column, then the whole process begins again. This type of spring can be found in Bellerive, near Vichy.

Properties of thermal springs

When thermal water rises to the surface, it gives off a very low level of radioactiv-ity which stimulates the human organ-

Mineral spring (iron), Vallée de Chaudefour

S. Sauvignier/MICHELIN

ism. However, the water is very unstable and deteriorates as soon as it comes out of the ground. This is why it is important to take the water where it rises to the surface and why spa towns were built. The composition of water varies depending on the type of rocks through which it passes.

People visit Vichy to treat disorders of the digestive system, Royat for heart and arterial disease, Châtelguyon for intestinal problems, Le Mont-Dore for asthma, La Bourboule for respiratory diseases, St-Nectaire for liver complaints, etc. Spa towns declined in popularity after the Second World War, but are enjoying a revival. The medical aspect of "taking the waters" has been maintained, but people also come to keep fit, enjoy a round of golf, a day at the races, or a night at the opera.

Mineral water, a boom industry

The French drink more mineral water than any other nationality. This is why the Auvergne is so popular – it has everything they could ask for. Bottling has required the development of modern techniques, for water is one of the most difficult commodities to package. It is, though, a source of employment for small towns such as Volvic which has become famous not only in France but far beyond its borders.

Flora and Fauna

RHÔNE VALLEY

The Rhône Valley is not only a major road and rail route and intersection of geographical areas, it also combines differing natural environments which have resulted in a variety of flora and fauna. Almost 3 000 species of plant, some 60 wild mammals and more than 200 birds have been observed in the forests, plains and lakes. The Pilat Regional Nature Park alone boasts some 90 species of bird.

Flora

In addition to the plants ordinarily found in the centre of France, the area also has mountain plants which have come down from the Alps and the Jura, and Mediterranean plants that have spread from the south. Because of this, it is possible to find, in the mountains in the Forez area for example, gentians, monkshood, or the superb martagon (or Turk's Cap) lily. This is a very rare plant, a hardy annual growing to a height of 30–80cm/12–30in or even, on occasions, to more than 1.10m/3ft 6in, with clusters of reddish-orange flowers spotted with black growing on a tall stem. Nor is it unusual, on the lower plateaux and hillsides in the Saône and Rhône valleys, to see evergreen oak, Montpellier aphyllantes, lavender, purple orchid or other varieties of orchid growing in the month of April on dry grasslands.

Fauna

Just like flora, Mediterranean species of fauna are found in the Rhône valley as the northernmost habitats are sited in the Rhône basin. Among them is the Provençal field mouse, a tiny rodent, and the mouse-eared bat. Deer are adaptable creatures and occur throughout the region in forested areas. The Rhône valley is a major point along migratory routes followed by **birds** between Northern Europe and the Mediterranean. The banks of the Saône and Rhône are full of larks, buntings, quail, plovers and curlews. But it is the lakes of the **Dombes** that boast the largest numbers of birds. Birds from all over the world can be seen at the bird sanctuary in Villars-les-Dombes where toucans and parrots rub shoulders with rare species such as the black-tailed godwit, or the corncrake, an endangered species.

The wels, the largest freshwater fish

Before it was introduced into France in the second half of the 19C by fish farmers, this species of large catfish was found mainly in the waters of the Caspian Sea and the River Danube. Those living in the Rhône and Saône can, in rare cases, grow to a length of 3m/10ft and weigh some 100kg/220lb (14st). It feeds on bream, moorhens, ducks and rats; to kill its prey, it grabs their paws and drags them down to the river-bed until they drown. This little aquatic monster is however short-sighted and dislikes the light, so it waits until nightfall before seeking to catch its food; it is therefore unlikely to be seen, except perhaps on a dinner plate as it is becoming increasingly popular with fishermen.

Beavers of the Île du Beurre

The beaver is a hard-working animal, cutting, felling and nibbling branches of trees in order to build dams and dikes. These days, though, lodges are no longer built because beavers have changed their habits and they now live in burrows dug into the river banks. They are particularly fond of the banks of the Île du Beurre (in old French, *beurre* meant beaver). This island to the south of Lyon is the last place in France in which beavers live in the wild and, because of this, it has been covered by a preservation order since 1988.

AUVERGNE

The Auvergne has a diverse landscape, with extensive forest and peat bog, each area with a particular flora and fauna.

Vegetation at different altitudes

Forests in the Auvergne grow in specific tiers. The hillsides are covered with pedunculate oak on clay soil and sessile oak on better-drained ground. On the mountains there are beech and pine although conifer predominates in cold, damp areas. The beech is the most common tree in the Auvergne and grows to a height of 30–40m/97–130ft after 150 to 300 years. It is easily recognisable for its smooth, grey bark and leaf colouring – red in winter and soft green in spring. Natural pine groves cover the driest hillsides like those in Upper Loire.

The **moors** of the Margeride area often mark the abandonment of pastures or farmland. In fact, moorland precedes the stage at which land is overrun by forest. Ferns, calluna, gorse, myrtle and redcurrants grow here. Gradually, however, the forest takes over, with birch, hazelnut and pine being the first trees to appear.

The **mountain pastures** higher than 1 000m/3 280ft provide a natural environment for species that have been observed here for centuries, such as the three-coloured violet, the scented wild pansy, the red-purple saw-wort (used to produce a yellow dye), and globe flower. The gentian, a delightful yellow flower, is used to make the liqueur that bears its name; other species of gentian produce blue flowers.

The **subalpine stage** of vegetation begins at altitudes greater than 1 400–1 500m/4 600–5 000ft; plant life varies depending on the exposure of the slopes. Calluna and myrtle grow on moorland, and ground-cover plants on grassland, rocks and scree. It is here, from May to July, that the spring anemone blooms, a rare plant with delicately indented leaves and flowers with huge white petals tinged with purple. Mountain arnica, a downy plant with yellow flowers, is used to make creams that prevent bruising. The blue carnation, which is actually a very unusual bluish green in colour, can be seen in tufts only a few inches high on the peaks in the Dore and Cantal mountain ranges.

Peat bogs

Peat bogs are natural environments created by an accumulation of organic matter in damp areas. There are a number of features which lead to the formation of peat bogs, such as a break in a slope along the course of streams, or cold springs as in the mountains of Cantal. They also tend to form on valley floors, along meanders and streams like those in the Upper Forez area, in the bases of volcanic craters, or over-deepening caused by glacial erosion as in the Margeride, Forez and Artense regions. *Maars* (lakes in the bottom of craters) can also be overrun by vegetation, as can be seen in the Devès range and the Velay.

Peat is formed from a range of spongy mosses, which ensure photosynthesis and store water. These mosses retain up to 30 times their dry weight of water. The bogs are exceptional because some have survived for more than 5 000 years and have developed a unique form of plant and animal life.

Carnivorous plants like the sundew and drosera, which suffer from nitrogen deficiency, have adapted to this environment. They capture small insects by secreting a sticky substance.

The animals are also extraordinary. There are flies and mosquitoes which, because they have had to adapt to cold environments in which they cannot fly, have no wings. Common frogs live on land and only enter the water to spawn.

The odyssey of the salmon

Born in a river, the salmon stays in the area where it was born for two years before letting the river carry it down to the sea tail-first, during the period known as downstream migration. At this stage its scales turn white.

Certain salmon travel as far as Greenland. Here, they grow and acquire their more familiar appearance – it is the shrimps on which they feed that give them their "salmon pink" colouring.

Two years later the salmon swims up the Loire to return to its spawning grounds in Allier or Upper Loire, in particular around Brioude which is famous as the "salmon's paradise", a trip that can take several months. When the fish arrives, it is exhausted and very thin, because it has had to overcome a number of obstacles, quite apart from the fact that it does not feed in rivers.

The female burrows into the gravel on the river bed with her tail and lays the eggs that the male covers with his milt. The salmon then usually die, although sometimes a salmon survives to make the journey twice.

In the Auvergne, the salmon is the subject of many anecdotal tales. One recounts how, at the turn of the 19C when the railway line was being built through the Allier gorge, the workmen went on strike because they had nothing to eat – nothing, that is, but salmon!

REGIONAL NATURE PARKS

The Auvergne-Rhône Valley region includes four regional nature parks, described in the Sights section of this guide (see AUBENAS, Monts du FOREZ, Le PILAT and Parc naturel regional des VOLCANS D'AUVERGNE).

Gentian on the shores of Lac de Guéry

HISTORY

Time Line

BC PREHISTORY

7500–
2800 **Neolithic Era: Stone Age.** Volcanoes in the Puys range cease to erupt. Farmer-stock breeders settle in the Rhône Valley and the Massif Central, leaving some 50 dolmens and 20 or more menhirs.

c 180–700 — Bronze Age. Human settlements become denser and the Rhône valley is the major amber and tin route. The Celts settle in Gaul. The Helvians settle on the right bank of the Rhône, the Allobroges on the left and the Arverni in the Auvergne.

Arverni domination of the Auvergne – The main expansion of the Celtic people occurred during the 5C BC, probably as a result of the push southwards by Germanic tribes fleeing the rigorous climate of Northern Europe. Little is known about them; they had no written literature and were divided into different peoples in accordance with criteria that have remained mysterious. What *is* known is that the Celts in Gaul, like the **Allobroges** in Lugdunum (Lyon), were subject to the authority of the **Arverni** in the Massif Central. They traded with their own coinage. In order to ensure the submission of other peoples, their sovereigns acted as demagogues. King Luern, who reigned in the 2C, was famous for his gifts of gold. Rome, worried by his power, launched a campaign against his son, Bituit, who died in battle with Roman forces near Bollène in 121 BC. The Roman legions settled in Vienne, the capital of the Allobroges. The Arverni monarchy was no more. The great Celtic families took power and, thereafter, were forced to share it with the Aedui of Burgundy who were allied to Rome.

43 Lyon founded soon after Caesar's conquest of Gaul by one of his lieutenants, Munatius Plancus. Roman settlers arrive and build houses on the hillsides above the banks of the Saône.

27 Lyon, capital of the Gauls (Aquitaine, Lyon area, Belgium); the Rome and Augustus Altar is built on the hill at La Croix-Rousse.

AD
1C Preachers come to spread the gospel in the Auvergne and the Rhône valley.

177 Marcus Aurelius instigates persecution. Christians are martyred in Lyon.

280 Emperor Probus removes the monopoly on sales of wine in Gaul previously enjoyed by the people of Lyon. This marks the start of Lyon's decline and, during the reign of Diocletian (284–305), the city is nothing more than the capital of the Lyon province.

406 After the invasion of the Vandals, the emperor introduces a federation of barbarian states in Gaul with the Visigoths in the Auvergne and the Burgundians on the left bank of the Rhône.

Vercingetorix, a chief of the Arverni, who led Gauls' unsuccessful war against Julius Caesar's army

J. Damase/MICHELIN

Sidonius Apollinaris stands up to the Visigoths – Sidonius Apollinaris was born in Lyon in AD 432 to a wealthy family of senators; later, his father-in-law, Avitus, was one of the last emperors of the Western world. Sidonius remained in Rome after the death of Avitus in AD 456 and wrote tributes to the emperors. His poetry pleased them and when he returned to the Auvergne, he was elected Bishop of Clermont.

Euric, King of the Visigoths, who already owned a large part of Aquitaine, threatened the Auvergne. Sidonius headed the resistance and withstood a siege lasting several years in the walled town of Clermont. Eventually the province was transferred to the barbarians in exchange for Provence, and Sidonius went into exile. Twenty years later, the province passed into the hands of the Franks after the Battle of Vouillé.

5C–9C	Founding of the first abbeys – in Lyon, Vienne, Romans, in the Vivarais, the Lyonnais and the Velay.
761–767	Pepin the Short attempts to gain power over the noblemen of the Auvergne by means of military expeditions.
800	Charlemagne is crowned.
843	Treaty of Verdun. Charlemagne's empire is divided into three kingdoms (West, Central, and East). The Auvergne is ruled by Charles the Bald (West Francia); the Rhône Valley by Lothair I (Lotharingia).
9C–10C	Power is actually held by the many castle owners, all of them difficult to control. Safe on their feudal mottes, they war against their neighbours, devastate the countryside, attack churches and pillage monasteries.
951	The first pilgrimage to Santiago de Compostela starts from Le Puy-en-Velay.
999	Gerbert, a former monk from Aurillac, is elected to the papacy as Sylvester II.

He is the first French Pope and he occupies the papal throne at the end of the first millennium.

1095	Pope Urban II preaches the First Crusade in Clermont.

The wave of popular faith aroused by his call arrives just at the right time to channel the warring energies of the turbulent feudal lords.

The Pope has a chance to gauge the vitality of the Church in the Auvergne. The Gregorian Reform purges the parishes by removing the power of the layman. The influence of a few of the great monasteries begins to spread.

The counts of Albon, who come from Vienne, extend their territory; their lands, stretching from the Rhône to the Alps, become known as Dauphiné.

11C–12C	Founding of new abbeys in the Vivarais area.

Royal intervention in the Auvergne – Divided between their position as vassals to the King of France and their allegiance to the Duke of Aquitaine, the great lords of the Auvergne failed to come to an agreement that would enable them to set up their own State. These feuding lords of mixed loyalties governed large estates with no clearly defined borders, which eventually enabled the sovereign to annex sections of the region little by little over the 12C and 13C; first Riom and the Limagne, then Montferrand and the area subsequently known as Dauphiné and finally Lower Auvergne.

13C–14C	The development of towns leads to the granting of numerous municipal charters. Royal authority gains a foothold and is strengthened in Auvergne and the Rhône Valley:
1210	Philip Augustus annexes the Auvergne to his kingdom.

1292	Nomination of a royal "guardian" in Lyon.
1307	The so-called "Philippine" conventions strengthen Philip the Fair's hold on Lyon.
1308	The Bishop of Viviers recognises royal sovereignty.
1349	Dauphiné is annexed to France as the States of Dauphiné.
1229	The Treaty of Paris ends the Albigensian Crusade and the influence of the counts of Toulouse in the Vivarais area.
1241–71	The Auvergne is part of the appanage with which Alphonse of Poitiers, St Louis' brother, is endowed. He dies childless and the region is returned to the royal estate.
1262	Marriage of St Louis' son, Philip, to Isabella of Aragon in Clermont.
1337–1453	— Hundred Years War.
1348	The Black Death ravages France.
1360	The Auvergne becomes a duchy and is given to John the Good's son, Jean, Duc de Berry.
15C	The first firearms are made in St-Étienne.
1416–25	The Auvergne and the Bourbonnais region are united for 100 years under the authority of the House of Bourbon.
1419	The first fairs in Lyon, instituted by the heir to the throne, the future Charles VII, make the town one of the largest warehouses in the world.
1450	Charles VII grants Lyon a monopoly on the sale of silk throughout the kingdom.

Auvergne, held in appanage by Jean de Berry – The sovereign's hold on the Auvergne took it out of the sphere of influence of Southern France. It was divided in two with the creation of a bailiwick in the mountainous region corresponding to Upper Auvergne. The Church proceeded to follow suit, setting up the bishopric of St-Flour.

While the Bourbons continued to increase their power, with a barony that was raised to a duchy in 1327 (the Bourbonnais area), the Auvergne was granted in appanage to Jean, Duc de Berry in 1360.

War and epidemics combined with the heavy fiscal pressures imposed by a spendthrift lord.

In order to circumvent the rules on land held in appanage, Jean de Berry transferred the Duchy of Auvergne to his son-in-law, the Duke of Bourbon, an action which the monarchy, by then in a weakened position, was obliged to accept formally in 1425.

The Bourbons were then at the head of a huge feudal State which continued to exist until the Constable of Bourbon's treachery in 1527.

1473	The first book is printed in Lyon by Barthélemy Buyer.
1494	The start of the Italian Campaign. Charles VIII brings his court to Lyon. The bank in Lyon enjoys a period of rapid development.
1527	After the Constable of Bourbon's treachery, the Auvergne and the Bourbonnais region are confiscated by François I.
1528	The Reformation is preached in Annonay.
1536	A silk-making factory is opened in Lyon.
1546	The first Reform Church is opened in the Lyon area.
1562	Protestants led by Baron des Adrets ransack the Rhône Valley and Forez area.
1572	After the St Bartholomew's Day Massacre, the Auvergne enters a period of chaos. Bloody battles are won in turn by the Huguenots, the royal army, and members of the Catholic League.
1598	Promulgation of the Edict of Nantes which grants freedom of conscience to the Protestants along with

limited rights to hold church services, and gives them political equality.

The Reformation and the Wars of Religion – In 1525, the Reformation spread right across the Cévennes and the Rhône valley, through the Vivarais area and along the Durance valley. The Auvergne, perhaps partially because of the mountainous lie of the land, was little concerned by the Reformed Religion, except in Issoire and the papermaking areas of Ambert and Aurillac.

The local people were attracted to Calvinist ideas, which allied with their taste for independence. The concepts were spread by craftsmen in the villages, carders and silk merchants travelling to Montpellier via Le Puy-en-Velay and Alès. The ideas were also spread by shoemakers whose shops, like the tanneries, served as centres of propaganda. By 1550–60, the Reformed Religion had conquered the locality. Property belonging to the Catholic Church was sold and, by the end of the century, Mass was no longer being celebrated.

However, Catholics and Protestants were soon to engage in conflict. Eight wars, fought over a period of almost three decades, coincided with a time of political instability. Interspersed with ceasefires and edicts aimed at pacifying both sides, they never totally appeased the people's passion. In 1562 the murder of a group of Protestants in Champagne led to the Huguenot uprising, and Catholic resistance was led by the Parliament of Toulouse. The conflict was particularly bitter in the Dauphiné and Vivarais regions where the warring factions laid waste to entire towns and committed massacres. The Baron des Adrets captured the main towns in Dauphiné, where he was the leader of the Huguenot movement, before moving on to decimate the Rhône valley with his troops and marching to the Forez area where he took Montbrison. After the tragic St Bartholomew's Day massacre (24th August 1572), the conflict took on a more political character and, paradoxically, led to forms of cooperation between Huguenots and Catholics in the face of royal authority and power.

Peace was not re-established until the Edict of Nantes was signed.

1629   Siege and destruction of Privas by the king's troops. Richelieu orders the dismantling of fortresses.

17C   Counter-Reformation: founding of many convents.

1643   Accession of Louis XIV.

1685   Revocation of the Edict of Nantes. The dragoons sweep through the Vivarais area, ill-treating and killing people.

1704   First edition of the Trévoux Dictionary by the Jesuits in reaction against the Age of Enlightenment.

1783   First public ascent by the Montgolfier brothers in a hot-air balloon.

Auvergne's finest hours – Although the aristocracy in the Auvergne was careful not to become involved in the Fronde Revolt against the monarchy, the king brought the hand of royal justice to bear on the region in order to ensure its submission for all time.

In September 1665, Louis XIV sent commissioners to the Auvergne, to provide a display of royal authority. The return to law and order included the repression of often tyrannical behaviour and excessive violence used by the local nobility to stamp out revolt among the country people. In the Auvergne as elsewhere, rural uprisings had resulted from the constraints imposed by a central authority that had not yet acquired its finality.

The Court heard 1 360 cases and passed 692 sentences, of which 450 were handed down by default for the suspects had fled as soon as the first of the 23 executions was carried out. Thereafter, offenders were sentenced in their absence and effigies were hung in their place.

This simulation of justice "without any spilling of blood" **(Esprit Fléchier)** nevertheless allowed for the return of a large amount of property and the destruction of castles that had been spared by Richelieu 40 years earlier. The authority of the State and royal justice could be felt by all throughout France. The magistrates tried to remedy abuses of the system by drawing up regulations on statute labour, weights and measures. The **Intendants** began to check the titles held by the nobility and laid the foundations for a fiscal reform in order to share the burden of taxation more fairly.

1789	Start of the French Revolution. 14th July: capture of the Bastille Prison. France is subdivided into *départements*.
1790	The first town council is set up in Lyon.
1793	A Resistance movement is set up in Lyon to fight the Convention: the town is subject to vicious reprisals as a result. In the Auvergne, **Georges Couthon**, a member of the Committee of Public Salvation, orders the demolition of bell-towers in the Auvergne on grounds of equality. Non-juring priests seek refuge in the mountains.
Early 19C	Mining begins in the coalfields around St-Étienne.
1804	The Jacquard loom is invented.
1820	Silk production becomes a boom industry in the Vivarais area.
1825	The Seguin brothers build the first suspension bridge over the Rhône.
1832	The St-Étienne-Lyon railway line is inaugurated. Barbier and Daubrée open a factory in Clermont and begin working with rubber; this is the pioneer of the future Michelin group.
1831–34	Silk workers revolt in Lyon.
1850	Pebrine, a disease that attacks silkworms, causes a crisis in the silk industry. There is a sudden sharp drop in the number of silkworm farms.
1855	The railway is extended as far as Clermont.
1870–71	The Fall of the Second Empire; the Third Republic is founded.
1880	Phylloxera destroys half of the vineyards in Ardèche. Orchards are planted in the Rhône and Eyrieux valleys.
1889	Phylloxera devastates the vineyards in the Limagne.
Late 19C	The chemical industry is set up in Lyon and metalworking sees a period of expansion.
1895	The cinematograph is invented by the Lumière brothers in Lyon.

The birth of the cinematograph – In 1882 a photographer from Besançon named Antoine Lumière opened a workshop in a shed in Lyon and began to produce dry silver bromine plates to a formula that he had invented himself. Within four years he had sold over one million plates under the brand name *Étiquette bleue*. The former photographer's two sons, Louis and Auguste **Lumière**, worked with their father on a new device; the equipment, invented in 1895 and exhibited in Lyon in June 1896, was to be known as the cinematograph.
The general public, after initial indifference, rushed to see the first 10 films – short farces whose humour has withstood the test of time. The first film, *Workers Leaving the Lumière Factory* was followed by *The Arrival of a Train in the Station, The Gardener* (including the famous scene of the gardener being doused with water from the garden hose) and *Baby Food*.

1939–45 Second World War.
1940 Vichy becomes the capital of occupied France.

The Vichy government – The armistice signed in Compiègne on 22 June 1940 marked the defeat of France, which was divided into two zones – the North was occupied by Nazi Germany and the South was declared a free zone. Parliament, tolling the death knell of the Third Republic, vested all power in **Maréchal**

J. Damase/MICHELIN

The Lumière brothers

Pétain, the victor of Verdun in 1916. The choice of a seat for the new government fell on the prosperous spa town of Vichy (see VICHY).

1942–44	Lyon is the centre of the French Resistance Movement.
1944	Battles are fought in the Rhône valley and in the Cantal (Mont Mouchet) as part of the liberation of France. The Germans blow up the bridges over the Rhône.

Lyon, a centre of the Resistance Movement – Lyon, a city in the southern zone, found itself near the demarcation line after the signing of the armistice in 1940. Countless Parisians sought refuge here and initially it became the intellectual and patriotic heart of France. The city was one of the major centres for the printing of literature, posters, and journals, many more popular with readers than the press that supported Vichy.

Important Resistance actions were carried out in Lyon, but they were badly organised until the arrival of **Jean Moulin**, sent by General de Gaulle; the various groups then joined together in 1943 to form the *Mouvements Unis de la Résistance* (Unified Resistance Movements). Moulin set up an administrative structure for the Resistance, organising services that were common to all the

networks and a secret army operating in the south of France and the Rhône Valley. Georges Bidault, who took over after Moulin's arrest, created the *Forces Françaises de l'Intérieur* (FFI).

1946	Start of the Fourth Republic.
1957	The Treaty of Rome leads to the setting up of the EEC.
1958	Birth of the Fifth Republic.
1969	Georges Pompidou, who was born in Cantal, is elected President of the Republic.
1972	The Auvergne and Rhône-Alpes regions are created.
1974	Valéry Giscard d'Estaing, Mayor of Chamalières (Puy-de-Dôme), elected President of the Republic.
1981	The first high-speed train service (TGV) runs between Paris and Lyon (journey time: 2hr 40min).
1986	**Superphénix**, Europe's first fast-breeder reactor to operate on an industrial scale, is brought into service in Creys-et-Pusignieu (Isère).
1989	Completion of the motorway link (A 71) between Clermont-Ferrand and Paris (Orléans).
1993	The EU introduces the Single Market.

1996	Lyon's hosting of the G7 summit confirms the city's international role.
2000	Clermont-Auvergne International Airport is inaugurated.
2002	Opening of **VULCANIA**, located in the heart of the Puy range, Vulcania, the European Volcano Park, plunges you deep into the world of volcanoes and the earth sciences. www.vulcania.com
2006	The La Chaise Dieu International Festival's 40th anniversary. Founded by Georges Cziffra in 1966, the Festival is one of France's leading sacred and classical music festivals. www.chaise-dieu.com.
2008	Olypique Lyonnais become French football ligue 1's most consecutive winners (2002–2008).

Famous Local Figures

THE RHÔNE VALLEY – A LAND OF INNOVATORS

Few regions in France have given the country so many scientists and engineers – the engineer Marc **Seguin** (steam boiler), the physicis André-Marie **Ampère** (electrodynamics), the physiologist Claude **Bernard** and cinematographers the **Lumière** brothers.

The Montgolfier brothers and the first flight – In the years before the French Revolution, the brothers Joseph and Étienne de Montgolfier became famous by achieving the first flights in a hot-air balloon.

Tirelessly continuing research into a gas that was lighter than air, Joseph completed his first experiment with a taffeta envelope filled with hot air. His brother joined him in his research and they launched their first aerostat on place des Cordeliers in Annonay on 4 June 1783. It was so successful that Louis XVI asked them to repeat it in his presence, and so it was that, on 19 September of that same year, the first "manned" flight took place in Versailles, under the control of Étienne and in the presence of the amazed royal family and Court. Attached beneath the balloon was a latticework cage containing the first passengers – a cockerel, a duck and a sheep. In just a few minutes, the **Réveillon** bearing the king's cipher on a blue background rose into the air and then came to rest in Vaucresson woods.

One month later, at the Château de la Muette in Paris, Marquis d'Arlandes and Pilâtre de Rozier completed the first human flight in a hot-air balloon.

The trials and tribulations of an inventor: Jacquard and the weaving loom – Jacquard was born in Lyon in 1752. His father, a small-time material manufacturer, employed his son to work the cords that operate the complicated machinery used to form the pattern in silk.

After his father's death, Jacquard tried to set up a fabric factory, but his lack of commercial experience and the experiments he undertook to try and perfect the weaving of the fabric left him financially ruined. In 1793 he enlisted with a military regiment. On returning to Lyon, he worked for a manufacturer. He spent his nights working on the design of a new loom and on a machine to manufacture fishing nets. He registered his first patent in 1801. The officers of the Republic were looking for inventors and so Jacquard was brought to Paris where he earned a salary of 3 000 francs. At the newly created **Conservatoire**, he perfected a machine invented by a man from Grenoble named Vaucanson, who had already installed a new type of mill in Aubenas.

In 1804 Jacquard returned to Lyon to complete work on the loom with which his name has remained linked ever since. In place of the ropes and pedals that required the work of six people, Jacquard substituted a simple mechanism based on perforated cards laid on the loom to define the pattern. A single worker, in place of five in earlier times, could make the most complicated fabrics as easily as plain cloth. In a town that

*Ciselé velvet
(Lyon, Second Empire)*

*Embroidery
(France, Régence period)*

*Silk and linen brocatelle
(Lyon, 1867)*

*Silk lampas
(France, early 18C)*

*Embroidered satin
(France, late 19C)*

*Corded figured silk
(France, 18C)*

had 20 000 looms, tens of thousands of workers found themselves under threat of losing their jobs. They immediately protested against the new loom which deprived them of work. Despite this, Jacquard convinced them of the utility of his invention. By decreasing the production costs, it would be possible to withstand foreign competition and increase sales. Manufacturers set an example and, in 1812, several Jacquard looms were brought into service in Lyon. The experiment worked so well that the name is still in use today.

Thimonnier, the unfortunate inventor of the sewing machine – Unlike Jacquard, Thimonnier did not have the good fortune to see his invention being used in his native country. His father was a dyer from Lyon who had fled the town and its upheavals during the French Revolution. In 1795 the family settled in Amplepuis where the young Thimonnier was apprenticed to a tailor.

In 1822 he left the region to set up in business as a tailor near St-Étienne. Haunted by the idea of sewing clothes mechanically, and taking inspiration from the hooks used by embroiderers in the Lyonnais mountain range, he built a wooden and metal device that would produce chain stitch – the first sewing machine.

To register a patent, the inventor entered a partnership with Auguste Ferrand, a teacher at the Miners' School in St-Étienne. An application was filed on 13 April 1830 in the names of both partners. Thimonnier then left St-Étienne for Paris where the first mechanical sewing shop soon saw the light of day.

There, 80 sewing machines produced goods six times quicker than manual workers, arousing the hatred of Parisian tailors who feared that their profession was on the point of ruin. On the night of 20 to 21 January 1831, 200 workers employed in the sewing and tailoring business ransacked the Parisian workshop. Thimonnier was ruined and he returned to Amplepuis where, in order to feed his large family, he again began work as a tailor. In 1834 he was back in Paris but nobody was interested in mechanical sewing. Two years later,

utterly destitute, he travelled south again on foot, carrying his machine on his back and using it to pay for his board and lodging on the way.

Worn out by 30 years of work and struggle, Thimonnier died at the age of 64 – without seeing the extraordinary success enjoyed by the sewing machine.

LEADING LIGHTS FROM THE AUVERGNE

538–594 – **Gregory of Tours** (born in Clermont-Ferrand), churchman and historian

938–1003 – **Gerbert d'Aurillac,** theologian and scholar who went on to become Pope Sylvester II

1555–1623 – **Henri de La Tour d'Auvergne**, Marshal of France under Henri IV and Calvinist leader

1623–1662 – **Blaise Pascal** (Clermont-Ferrand), academic, writer and philosopher

1652–1719 – **Michel Rolle** (Ambert), mathematician and author of a treaty of algebra

1757–1834 – **Marquis de La Fayette** (Chavaniac), general and politician

1851–1914 – **Fernand Forest** (Clermont-Ferrand), inventor (four-stroke engine)

1853–1929 – **André Messager** (Montluçon), composer

1853–1931 and

1859–1940 – **André** and **Édouard Michelin** (Clermont-Ferrand), industrialists (rubber tyres and tourist publications)

1884–1932 – **Albert Londres** (Vichy), journalist and writer

1911–1974 – **Georges Pompidou,** politician and President of the French Republic (1969–74)

b 1926 – **Valéry Giscard d'Estaing,** politician and President of the French Republic (1974–81)

ART AND CULTURE

Architecture and Art

RELIGIOUS ARCHITECTURE

VALENCE – Ground plan of St-Appollinaire Cathedral (12C)

The Romanesque cathedral in Valence has undergone many changes, and was much damaged during the Wars of Religion. Renovation and rebuilding efforts, mainly carried out in the 17C and 19C, generally respected the original plans and appearance of the cathedral.

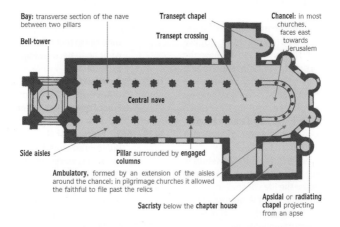

Bay: transverse section of the nave between two pillars

Bell-tower

Transept chapel

Transept crossing

Chancel: in most churches, faces east towards Jerusalem

Central nave

Side aisles

Pillar surrounded by **engaged columns**

Ambulatory, formed by an extension of the aisles around the chancel; in pilgrimage churches it allowed the faithful to file past the relics

Sacristy below the **chapter house**

Apsidal or **radiating chapel** projecting from an apse

LA GARDE-ADHÉMAR – Cross-section of St-Michel Church (12C)

Restored during the 19C, this small Romanesque church illustrates the major developments of Romanesque art in the 12C. It is one of the few churches of the period to have a double apse.

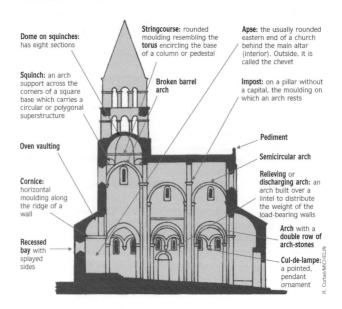

Dome on squinches: has eight sections

Squinch: an arch support across the corners of a square base which carries a circular or polygonal superstructure

Oven vaulting

Cornice: horizontal moulding along the ridge of a wall

Recessed bay with splayed sides

Stringcourse: rounded moulding resembling the **torus** encircling the base of a column or pedestal

Broken barrel arch

Apse: the usually rounded eastern end of a church behind the main altar (interior). Outside, it is called the chevet

Impost: on a pillar without a capital, the moulding on which an arch rests

Pediment

Semicircular arch

Relieving or **discharging arch:** an arch built over a lintel to distribute the weight of the load-bearing walls

Arch with a **double row of arch-stones**

Cul-de-lampe: a pointed, pendant ornament

R. Corbel/MICHELIN

ORCIVAL – Notre-Dame Basilica (12C)

Most of the churches in Auvergne are in the Romanesque style, and belong to a school of design which developed in the 11C and 12C, which has a number of unique characteristics.

Relieving or **discharging arch:** an arch built over a lintel to distribute the weight of the load-bearing walls

Two-storey, **octagonal bell-tower**

Geminated bays: occur in pairs

Bays: occurring in groups of two, three, four, etc

Transept

Rounded hip roof covering the chevet

Gable-wall

Semicircular bay

Sloping hip roof

Apsidal chapel or **radiating chapel**

Modillion: a horizontal bracket or console; here the decorative scrolling recalls wood shavings

Cornice with checkerboard pattern

Buttress: masonry structure bonded to and projecting from the wall, which gives stability

Chevet: the graceful fall of tiered roofs is the most distinctive and attractive feature of churches in Auvergne

R. Corbel/MICHELIN

CLERMONT-FERRAND – Notre-Dame-du-Port Basilica (11C and 12C)

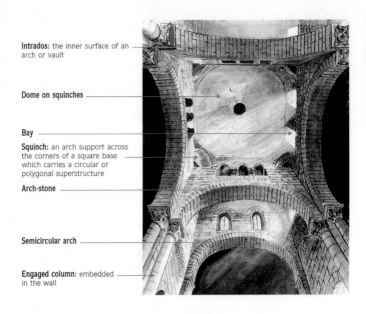

Intrados: the inner surface of an arch or vault

Dome on squinches

Bay

Squinch: an arch support across the corners of a square base which carries a circular or polygonal superstructure

Arch-stone

Semicircular arch

Engaged column: embedded in the wall

ISSOIRE – St-Austremoine Abbey (12C)

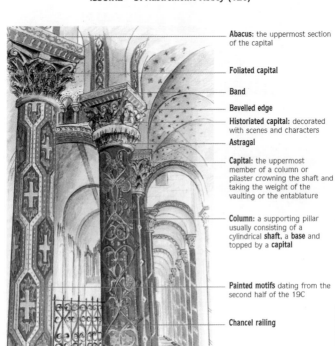

Abacus: the uppermost section of the capital

Foliated capital

Band

Bevelled edge

Historiated capital: decorated with scenes and characters

Astragal

Capital: the uppermost member of a column or pilaster crowning the shaft and taking the weight of the vaulting or the entablature

Column: a supporting pillar usually consisting of a cylindrical **shaft**, a **base** and topped by a **capital**

Painted motifs dating from the second half of the 19C

Chancel railing

R. Corbel/MICHELIN

LE PUY-EN-VELAY – Doorway of St-Michel Chapel (12C)

Seeming to rise out of the rock below it, this chapel has been called the "eighth wonder of the world". Eastern influences are apparent in the polychrome motifs and geometric designs.

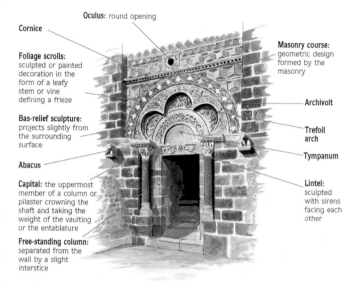

Oculus: round opening

Cornice

Foliage scrolls: sculpted or painted decoration in the form of a leafy stem or vine defining a frieze

Bas-relief sculpture: projects slightly from the surrounding surface

Abacus

Capital: the uppermost member of a column or pilaster crowning the shaft and taking the weight of the vaulting or the entablature

Free-standing column: separated from the wall by a slight interstice

Masonry course: geometric design formed by the masonry

Archivolt

Trefoil arch

Tympanum

Lintel: sculpted with sirens facing each other

CRUAS – Former Abbey (11C to 13C)

This beautiful abbey, typical of the Vivarais region, has managed to withstand the ravages of time. As research continues, new discoveries have brought to light architectural marvels from the Carolingian and Romanesque periods.

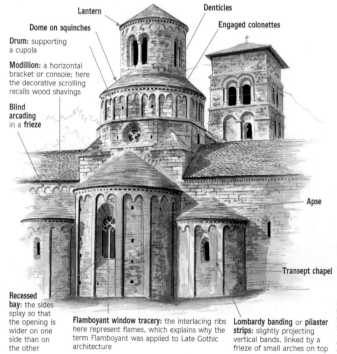

Lantern

Dome on squinches

Drum: supporting a cupola

Modillion: a horizontal bracket or console; here the decorative scrolling recalls wood shavings

Blind arcading in a **frieze**

Denticles

Engaged colonettes

Apse

Transept chapel

Recessed bay: the sides splay so that the opening is wider on one side than on the other

Flamboyant window tracery: the interlacing ribs here represent flames, which explains why the term Flamboyant was applied to Late Gothic architecture

Lombardy banding or **pilaster strips:** slightly projecting vertical bands, linked by a frieze of small arches on top

R. Corbel/MICHELIN

MILITARY ARCHITECTURE

TOURNEMIRE – Château d'Anjony (15C)

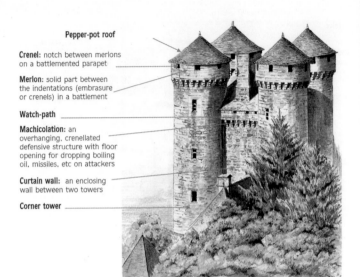

Pepper-pot roof

Crenel: notch between merlons on a battlemented parapet

Merlon: solid part between the indentations (embrasure or crenels) in a battlement

Watch-path

Machicolation: an overhanging, crenellated defensive structure with floor opening for dropping boiling oil, missiles, etc on attackers

Curtain wall: an enclosing wall between two towers

Corner tower

ST-POURÇAIN-SUR-BESBRE
Fortified gate of Thoury Château (15C)

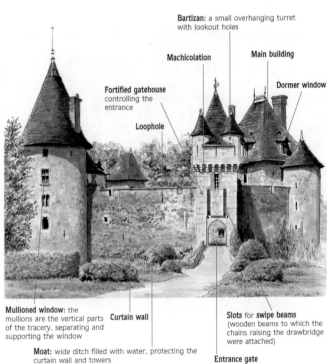

Bartizan: a small overhanging turret with lookout holes

Machicolation

Main building

Fortified gatehouse controlling the entrance

Dormer window

Loophole

Mullioned window: the mullions are the vertical parts of the tracery, separating and supporting the window

Curtain wall

Slots for **swipe beams** (wooden beams to which the chains raising the drawbridge were attached)

Moat: wide ditch filled with water, protecting the curtain wall and towers

Entrance gate

R. Corbel/MICHELIN

CIVIL ARCHITECTURE

MARCY-L'ÉTOILE – Château de Lacroix-Laval (17C – 18C)

Renovated under the guidance of Soufflot in the 18C, this château was ransacked from cellar to attic during the French Revolution. It has since been restored several times, but has kept the classic façade typical of family manor houses in the 18C.

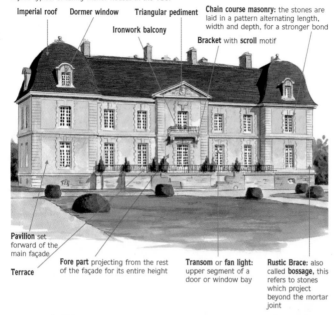

Imperial roof

Dormer window

Triangular pediment

Ironwork balcony

Chain course masonry: the stones are laid in a pattern alternating length, width and depth, for a stronger bond

Bracket with **scroll** motif

Pavilion set forward of the main façade

Terrace

Fore part projecting from the rest of the façade for its entire height

Transom or **fan light:** upper segment of a door or window bay

Rustic Brace: also called **bossage,** this refers to stones which project beyond the mortar joint

INDUSTRIAL ARCHITECTURE

LYON – Halle Tony-Garnier (1914)

The covered market is a display of technical prowess: the 18000m^2/193 750sq ft area stands without interior pillars. Designed by local architect Tony Garnier, it now serves for cultural events and trade fairs, and remains a landmark of contemporary architecture.

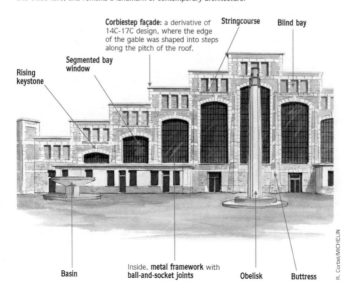

Corbiestep façade: a derivative of 14C-17C design, where the edge of the gable was shaped into steps along the pitch of the roof.

Stringcourse

Blind bay

Segmented bay window

Rising keystone

Basin

Inside, **metal framework** with **ball-and-socket joints**

Obelisk

Buttress

R. Corbel/MICHELIN

SPA-RESORT ARCHITECTURE

LE MONT-DORE – Caesar's spring gallery (1890 and 1935-38)

The design expresses the architectural eclecticism typical of spa towns. The inspiration can be traced to the Roman baths of Antiquity; the high ceilings and ornate decoration lend grandeur. The distinctive Romanesque style of Auvergne creates an atmosphere reminiscent of an opulent temple.

Transverse arch: semicircular, with **arch-stones** in an alternating white (limestone) and grey (andesite) pattern, typical of the Romanesque style in Auvergne

Cabochons in yellow glass

Entablature and **capitals** stucco moulding

Tympanum with **fresco** (Roman baths of Mont-Dore)

Coffered barrel vault

Colonnade of **engaged columns**

Claustra: a slab of stone or terracotta pierced in a geometric pattern, forming a bay

Aedicula: a niche in the form of a **tabernacle**, from which Caesar's spring flows

Floor laid with **tile** and **glass bricks**

Grand arcade with false transom (fan light)

R. Corbel/MICHELIN

ROMAN ARCHITECTURE IN THE RHÔNE VALLEY

By the 1C, the region had become the starting point for the conquest of Germany and Lyon was the capital of Gaul. In the 2C, major road building and town planning work was undertaken in Vienne and Lyon, then at the height of their power. However, the fires, pillaging and devastations by the Barbarians, coupled with the later destruction during the Middle Ages destroyed the remains of the old civilisation.

From 1922 in Vienne and 1933 in Lyon, archaeologists began to uncover groups of buildings, in particular small theatres adjacent to smaller buildings or odeons. Some of the buildings are still being unearthed and large areas remain to be explored, in particular in St-Romain-en-Gal on the right bank of the Rhône where part of a residential district has been uncovered.

Theatres

These consisted of tiers of seats ending in a colonnade known as the **cavea**, an orchestra pit, a dais used by dignitaries and a raised stage *(scena)*. The actors performed in front of a wall with doors in it through which they made their entrances. Behind the wall at the back of the stage were the richly decorated, actors' dressing rooms and the stores. Beyond that was a portico opening onto gardens where the actors walked before entering the stage. Spectators could stroll there during intervals or take shelter from the rain.

Temples

A closed sanctuary contained the effigy of a god or the emperor, and an open vestibule. They were partially or totally surrounded by a colonnade. The Temple of Augustus and Livia in Vienne is one of the best preserved anywhere.

Roman baths

Roman baths were public and free of charge. They were not only public baths but also fitness centres, meeting places and a place for games and entertainment. Romans had acquired extensive knowledge concerning water supplies and heating. Water was brought to the baths by an aqueduct, stored in tanks then piped through a system of lead and mortar ducts. Waste water was carried away through a sewage system. The water and rooms were heated by a system of hearths and hypocausts in the basement. The hot air obtained by the burning of coal and wood circulated through a conduit built into the walls. The buildings were vast, sumptuous and luxurious. There were columns and capitals decorated with vivid colours, mosaic facing on the walls, marble floors and wall coverings, richly coffered ceilings, and frescoes and statues like those found in the remains of the Roman baths in Ste-Colombe near Vienne.

Amphitheatres

Shows were staged in the arena, usually oval in shape. There were fights between wild beasts or gladiators, and people sentenced to death were executed. Around the arena were tiers of seats for the audience. Lyon, the official centre for the worship of Rome in Gaul, had its own amphitheatre.

Circus

The circus attracted crowds of people who enjoyed watching chariot racing. In the middle of the track was a long rectangular construction – the **spina** – marked at each end by huge, semicircular stones. The horses and drivers wore the colours of the rival factions organising the competitions. Built partly of timber, the circus was, despite its impressive size, particularly vulnerable to destruction.

Aqueducts

On the plateau to the south-west of Lyon stand well-preserved sections of aqueduct (Arches de Chaponost, *see LYON: Monts du Lyonnais*). Aqueducts were one of the essential features of any town. The tall arches built to maintain the level of the pipes were monuments in their own right. Indeed, the aqueduct, more than any other construction, is a striking illustration of the building skills of the Romans who attached very great importance to the quality of the water supplied to their towns and cities.

Decorative arts

The large, delicately coloured mosaics found in Lyon (circus games, Bacchus etc) prove that mosaic makers were particularly active in Lyon. The medallions that decorated the sides of vases were made by potters from Lyon and Vienne who excelled in illustrations of scenes from mythology or everyday life.

RELIGIOUS ARCHITECTURE

The Romanesque period

There is no Romanesque School inherent to the Rhône valley since the region, situated as it is at the junction of countless roads, was influenced by artists from Italy, Burgundy, Provence – and the Auvergne. In the Auvergne a Romanesque School developed which is considered one of the most unusual in the history of the architecture of the Western world, giving the churches an air of similarity that is immediately apparent. It originated in the 11C. After the great invasions and the establishment of the Capetian kingdom, the Auvergne enjoyed a period of prosperity. The local people undertook land clearance, acquiring new areas of land and instigating new building projects. In the 11C this movement was amplified by the Gregorian Reform and the desire on the part of men of the Church for independence from lay authorities. Gradu-

ally, countless churches and chapels were built across the countryside and, even today, they reveal something of the soul of the Auvergne and its people, for they are all built with an economic use of resources and an immense simplicity. This is what gives the architecture its strength.

The churches in Clermont-Ferrand (Notre-Dame-du-Port), Issoire, Orcival, St-Nectaire and St-Saturnin are just some of the finest examples of this Romanesque style in which the beauty is both austere and logical.

An unusual school

It developed in the 11C and 12C within the large diocese of Clermont. The churches, often small but always beautifully proportioned, give an impression of being much bigger than they actually are. Paul Bourget describes the appearance of these churches, powerful and rugged as those who created them: "Seen from the east end, especially with the tight semicircle of chapels huddled up against the mass of the main building, these churches give a striking impression of aplomb and unity".

Volcanic building materials

In Limagne, arkose, a yellowish metamorphic sandstone, was used until the 13C. Volcanic lava stone was first used for bonding beneath load-bearing arches, in the upper sections of buildings which did not support the weight of the vaulting and to which they added a touch of colour. In the 13C improvements to the quality of tools made it possible to cut the hard blocks of lava stone and developments in stone-cutting techniques made it the commonest building material available.

Great churches in Lower Auvergne

The layout of the churches slowly changed to meet new needs arising out of pilgrimages. The basic layout is the one seen in Clermont Cathedral, which was consecrated in AD 946 and was the first one to have an ambulatory and radiating chapels. Today, all that remains is the crypt. Yet it took a period of trial and error (churches in Ennezat, Glaine-Mon-

Nave of Notre-Dame-du-Port, Clermont-Ferrand

J. Damase/MICHELIN

taigut) to achieve the perfection of the 12C buildings.

Exterior features

West Front – Exposed to the weather and almost devoid of decoration, the west front – which includes a porch – forms a stark contrast to the east end because of its austerity. In some cases, it is topped by a central bell-tower and two side towers.

Bell-towers – Two-storey, traceried, octagonal bell-towers were a source of light, emerging from the mass of the building around the dome. They stood high above the chancel and ambulatory. In Auvergne, there are a large number of bell-cotes (clocher à peigne) – gable walls with openings in which the bells are hung in one or two tiers.

Side walls – The windows in the side aisles are built inside enormous load-bearing arches that support the walls. Beneath these arches, the stone often has a decorative role through its colour or layout. Above them is the line of the clerestory in which the windows are linked by arcading.

East end – The magnificent layout of the various levels at the east end is the most beautiful and most characteristic part of the Auvergne churches. This master-piece of austerity counterbalances the thrust from the octagonal bell-tower. It stands like a carefully combined pyramid, giving an impression of harmony and security through the perfection of each of its elements and the regularity of the design.

Interior

The nave is often stark; the only decorative features are the capitals and they are not immediately apparent because most of these buildings are very dark. Huge arches support the gallery and the weight of the bell-tower if it has been built above the west front.

Nave and vaulting – The wide naves lined with side aisles providing extra support were designed to cater for large numbers of pilgrims.

Heavy Romanesque barrel vaulting replaced roof rafters which were too susceptible to fire and which, between the 5C and 11C, led to the loss of many churches.

Chancel – This part of the church was reserved for the clergy and the celebration of Mass. By raising it up a few steps and lowering the vaulting, perspective made it appear larger than it actually was. It was here that sculptors gave free rein to their talent and the beautifully designed carved capitals in the chancel are often the finest in the church.
In large churches, the chancel included a straight bay.
Behind it was a semicircle around which tall columns, set out in such a way as to avoid blocking the light, extended into small raised arches forming a sort of crown.

Ambulatory – In large churches, an ambulatory extended beyond the side aisles and skirted the chancel. An even number of radiating chapels formed a crown around the ambulatory so that, on major feast days, several Masses could be celebrated simultaneously. The chapels were separated from each other by windows.

Transept and dome – The construction of the transept posed a difficult problem for architects; they had to design large ribbed vaulting capable of supporting the entire weight of the central bell-tower and which was formed by the interpenetration of the vaulting in the nave and the arms of the transept.

Crypt – Beneath the chancel in large churches, there is often a crypt laid out like the church above it. The chancel in the crypt, like the one in the upper church, is flanked by an ambulatory decorated with radiating chapels. The crypt never extends westwards beyond the transept.

Decorative features

Capitals – The capitals are magnificently carved with fanciful scenes. Most of them are to be found around the chancel. Many artists introduced

Virgin Mary in Majesty, Issoire

J. Damase/MICHELIN

an entire portrait gallery of figures: figures from Antiquity rub shoulders with eagles, mermaids, centaurs, minotaurs, telamones, snakes, genies, figures from the Orient, griffons and birds drinking out of a chalice. Beside them are the heroes of medieval epics, the founders of the church, knights in armour dating from the period of the First Crusade and local saints.

Statues of the Virgin Mary in Majesty and statue-reliquaries – Worship of the Blessed Virgin Mary has always been an important part of religion in the Auvergne for, in Celtic countries, the Christian religion was grafted onto worship of a mother-goddess.

The Gothic Period

Gothic architecture came from the north and took some time to spread further south. It reached Lyon in the early 13C but the Rhône Valley has none of the great churches of which Northern France is so proud and it continued to be subject to the influence of the south as is evident in the width of the buildings and the horizontal line of the roofs.

The Auvergne, strong in its own Romanesque School, resisted change for a long time. Not until the language of Northern France, *langue d'oïl,* was introduced in place of the Southern French *langue d'oc,* after the province had been conquered by Philip Augustus, did the Rayonnant Gothic style gain a foothold on the rebellious region, to the detriment of the sources of inspiration from further south which had been predominant until that time. This change of style marked the seizure of the province by the Capetians. There were, though, two main currents in the architectural style – Northern French Gothic and Languedoc Gothic.

Northern French Gothic

Clermont Cathedral, dating from the 13C and 14C, is only very vaguely reminiscent of the great buildings of the Paris basin and not until the 19C was Gothic architecture introduced into its west front and spires designed by the architect Viollet-le-Duc. Lava stone from Volvic, a building material that was too hard to be carved but which architects liked for its strength, resistance and permanence, gave the cathedral an austerity that even the sun cannot brighten up. The roofs on the chapels and side aisles consist of stone slabs forming a terrace beneath the flying buttresses, a very unusual design that was totally unknown in the north of France.

The same stylistic movement can be seen in the Ste-Chapelle in Riom.

Languedoc Gothic

Characterised by a wide nave devoid of side aisles, side chapels inserted between the piers and the absence of flying buttresses, this was the commonest style in the area. The abbey church at La Chaise-Dieu, a masterpiece of monastic architecture, is a fine example, as are other churches commissioned by the mendicant orders such as the Marthuret Church in Riom or Notre-Dame-des-Neiges in Aurillac.

Painting

A vast selection of medieval painting has been preserved within the Auvergne. The frescoes in the church of St-Julien in Brioude, for instance, date from the 12C; there is the 13C representation of the legend of St George in one of the ambulatory chapels in Clermont Cathedral, and the 14C Assumption and Coronation of the Virgin Mary in Billom. From the 15C are the Last Judgement in Issoire, St George Slaying the Dragon in Ébreuil,

Château de Cordès (13C–15C)

the Dance of Death in La Chaise-Dieu, and the frescoes in Ennezat. The triptych painted on wood by the Maître de Moulins is one of the last masterpieces of Gothic painting in France.

MILITARY AND CIVIL ARCHITECTURE

Defensive castles

During the days of the feudal system, the country was dotted with castles; by building fortresses, lords, viscounts and barons could display their power and authority compared to that of the king. This is why there are so many castles, with outlines that adapt to the shape of the rock beneath them. From the 13C, they were subject to successive attacks by the troops under Philip Augustus, who conquered 120 of them from 1210 onwards, to destruction during the Hundred Years War and, at the end of the conflict, to destruction by villagers who, at enormous cost, succeeded in routing the mercenaries and captains who were using them as a source of building material for their own houses.

The gentler architecture of the Renaissance

The influence of the Italian Renaissance travelled to Northern France via the Rhône corridor and in the 15C it slowly penetrated the Auvergne where a certain taste for well-being made itself apparent after the end of the war. The fortresses were turned into charming residences in which ornamentation supplanted systems of defence, even if, in the Auvergne, the austerity of the building in lava stone remained intact. Numerous castles were bought up by gentlemen of the robe or members of the middle classes who had recently acquired wealth through trade.

Town planning during the Classical period

In Lyon this manifested itself in a new form of town planning, which can be seen mainly in the 17C Terreaux district around the town hall. In the 18C, a new concept of urban layout was introduced, based on speculation. The main feature of these areas is place Bellecour, laid out during the reign of Louis XIV and flanked by Louis XVI residences.

The 19C and the architecture of the Auvergne spas: a fantasy world

In the spa towns of the 19C, "taking the waters" was not a new idea but it was during this period that it became fashionable. On the pretext of taking the waters and enjoying a rest, members of high society, and those with power or money, flocked to spa towns. Their visits were an opportunity to lead an active social life and it was this that governed the architectural style. In the centre of the town were the pump rooms, a veritable palace to which the architects paid particular attention; around them were the park and springs built to resemble Ancient Greek or Roman temples. The casino and the luxury hotels were decorated with an exuberance that was almost Baroque. In the streets of the town, troubadour-style castles stood next to Venetian palaces, and Henri IV residences rubbed shoulders with Art Nouveau mansions.

The history of this architecture, designed for enjoyment and pleasure, is a history of intermingling. The eclectic mix was the result of ideas by the most fashionable urban architects of the day combined with those of the architects of the Auvergne who were inspired by a long tradition based on Early Romanesque architecture and the volcanic and granite rocks available locally; these ideas were also influenced by the mixture of water and a natural environment with a town of stone, including its culture and its social events. Even the railway stations were not forgotten, since they provided the first impression for visitors who had just arrived. The result was a luxurious style of architecture full of exuberance and voluptuousness in the dream world constituted by the resorts in the heart of the Auvergne.

The new opera house in Lyon, a fine example of 20C architecture

Throughout the 19C and 20C Lyon was considered an ideal place for architectural experiments. In 1825 iron suspension bridges were built over the Rhône, using new techniques. In 1896 the basilica on Fourvière hill was completed in a Byzantine-cum-medieval style.

In the 1970s, with a view to the launch of the high-speed train service which would bring Lyon to within 2hr of Paris, a major development was begun in the La Part-Dieu district: a new business centre that was to take the city to the forefront of Europe's business world. In 1993 the latest architectural feat was completed; the old opera house designed in 1831 had to be renovated and it was **Jean Nouvel** who took up the gauntlet. All that remains of the old building are the four walls and an old foyer decorated with gold leaf and stucco work.

Traditional Rural Housing

Over the centuries, changes in rural housing have kept pace with changes in agricultural work. Housing has also been subject to the influence of neighbouring regions and new building techniques.

AUVERGNE

Roofs

Owing to its geographical situation the Auvergne is in contact with two civilisations, "the Northern French one in which roofs are built with a 45° slope and flat tiles, and that of the Mediterranean basin in which the roofs have a slope of 30° and rounded tiles" (Max Derruau). In the mountains, thatch is replaced by slate or corrugated iron. The most attractive roofs are those made of stone slabs called lauzes that look like gigantic tortoise shells. They can only be mounted on a steeply sloping roof with a very strong set of rafters. On the plains, the old round tiles and rows of guttering once common in the countryside are beginning to lose ground in the face of competition from more stable mass-produced tiles.

Housing in the Limagne

The houses with upper storeys, which belong to wine-growers or farmers specialising in mixed agriculture, are commonplace in the old villages huddling on the hillsides. The ground floor is used for work (stables, cellars) and the upper floor is the house, reached by an outside flight of steps leading to a balcony sheltered by a porch roof.

Housing in the mountains

These houses are sturdy buildings, constructed from large blocks of basalt. The heavy roofs extend below the top of the walls. The single building contains both dwelling and byre side by side. They always face south, and are sheltered from bad weather by the haybarn. Doors and windows are narrow and the roof drops down to the ground at the rear of the building. In the Upper Livradois area, the house is raised and is separate from the farm buildings.

From Beaujolais to Lower Vavarais

House in the Beaujolais region

Farm and dovecote on Dombes plateau

Jasserie: summer farmstead in the Forez mountains

House in Lower Dauphiné

Farm in the Mézenc range

House in Lower Vivarais

R. Corbel/MICHELIN

Housing in the Velay area

Houses in this area are unusual as their walls are made of ashlar, with a predominance of grey or dark-red lava stone in volcanic areas, light-coloured granite in areas of older soil, and yellow arkose in areas of sedimentary rock. The blocks of stone are cemented together using a mortar that is often mixed with pozzolana, a reddish volcanic gravel. In the villages, a bell turret indicates the village hall (assemblée) or "maison de la béate."

Shepherds' and cowherds' huts

A buron is a squat, stone-roofed temporary dwelling high up in the mountains, used by cowherds during periods of trans-humance.

This was where the cheese and butter was made which the cantalès, or master of the buron, then sent down to the valleys from time to time. A small number of these huts are still in use. In the Livradois and Forez areas, and on the slopes of Mont Pilat, there are "jasseries" or "mountain farms" used during the summer months. Solidly built of stone with thatched roofs, they consist of a living room, a byre and a cheese cellar below.

RHÔNE VALLEY

Housing in the Forez and Lyonnais areas

Houses in the Forez area are farmsteads enclosed by high walls around a central courtyard. The walls are often made of rows of stones set at a slant. In the Dombes area, the farmhouses are elongated and have an upper storey. External pebbledash protects the walls made of terracotta bricks or cob.

Housing in the Rhône Valley

On the **Valence and Montélimar plains,** the walls often have no doors or windows on the north side since this is where the mistral wind blows. Additional protection is often provided by a row of thuyas, cypress and plane trees. Large, isolated farmsteads consist of a group of buildings around a walled courtyard, and their external walls, devoid of doors or windows, make them look like fortresses.

Housing in Lower Dauphiné

Between Bourbe and Isère, pebbles or **"rolled stones"** were often used as a building material because they were commonplace in this area of moraine and alluvial deposits. The stones are assembled end on, on a bed of mortar, and the angle changes from one level to the next. In some areas (eg Morestel and Creys) there is a style of roofing that has been imported from the Préalpes: **crowstepped or corbie-stepped gabling.**

Housing in the Upper Vivarais area

On the edges of the Velay area, along the Mézenc range and on the high plateaux above the upper reaches of the Ardèche and Eyrieux, the houses are low and squat with stone-slabbed roofs, seeming almost weighed down by this shell designed to withstand bad weather. On the St-Agrève plateau, the granite farmhouses have an upper storey and bedrooms next to the hayloft.

Housing in the Lower Vivarais area

Houses here have an upper storey and are built in a square, like southern French houses. The gently sloping roofs have half-round tiles. At the top of the wall, between wall and roof, there is typically a double or triple row of guttering made with fragments of tiles mounted in mortar. The south-facing wall is often decorated with a trellis.

Literary Life

THE LANGUAGE

Like all the regions in France the Auvergne has its own language, which has undergone continual development since the days of Antiquity. This means that the borders of the area in which the dialect of the Auvergne is spoken do not correspond to the historical and administrative borders of the province. Auvergnat, the dialect of the Auvergne, which is considered to be similar to North Occitan, is said to have developed from a Medio-Roman language used in the part of central France occupied by the Romans and which gradually died out in the face of competition from *oïl*, the language of northern France. The dialect spoken in and around Aurillac is closer to the Guyennais dialect spoken in the south-west of France (Aquitaine), which was under English domination for a considerable time, but it has nevertheless been influenced by Auvergnat.

A FEW GREAT WRITERS FROM THE AUVERGNE

Local writers have brought fame to a few of the Auvergne's prelates among them Sidonius Apollinaris, Gerbert (10C) and Massillon who gave Louis XIV's funeral oration in the 18C. The Auvergne also had poets such as Théodore de Banville (1823–91) who founded the Parnassian School of Poetry and philosophers such as Pierre Teilhard de Chardin (1881–1955). In the 20C, Henri Pourrat and the chronicler Alexandre Vialatte have both described their native land, each in his own style. Of all the Auvergne authors, the best-known is Blaise Pascal, though Gregory of Tours, the medieval chronicler, is almost equally important.

Gregory of Tours

He was born c 583 in Clermont-Ferrand into a rich family of Senators. He spent most of his life in Tours, to which he was appointed Bishop in 573, yet he never forgot the place of his birth. His *History of the Franks* which retraces the reigns of the Merovingian kings and their ancestors is one of the main sources of historical information about the Auvergne during the Dark Ages.

Gregory of Tours was not only concerned with the Auvergne. His work covers the whole of Gaul and is one of the only sources of information about that time. Indeed, it is the first historical work concerning the kingdom of the Franks that has survived to this day.

Blaise Pascal

It was in 1623 that Pascal, undoubtedly the most famous native of the Auvergne, was born in Clermont-Ferrand. His mother died when he was three years old and it was his father, President of the Court of Aids (forerunner of the Customs

Blaise Pascal

J. Damase/MICHELIN

& Excise) in Clermont, who brought him up. In 1631 Pascal senior came to Paris to devote all his time to his son who was already showing signs of extraordinary intelligence. Châteaubriand described him as a "terrifying genius." At the age of 11 he wrote a treatise on sound and, at 19, he invented his first mathematical machine to assist him in his calculations. In 1646 Pascal entered Port-Royal, the abbey where he wrote his treatises on Physics and Philosophy. He then left the abbey to lead a life among high society where he discovered that "the heart has its reasons which reason ignores." It was at this time that he wrote his *Discourse on the Passions of Love*. Soon, though, he began to suffer from the "emptiness" of his life. In 1664 he survived a carriage accident and believed that this was a sign from on high. He retired to Port-Royal, which he was never again to leave, and continued his writings. It was because his memory played tricks on him that he began noting his *Thoughts*, with a view to writing an *Apology of the Christian Religion*. This was his most famous work, but was never completed. Pascal died in 1662, at the age of 39.

THE REGION TODAY

Government

Decision-making in France was once highly centralised, each *département* headed by a government-appointed prefect, in addition to a locally elected general council (*conseil général*). But in 1982, the national government decided to decentralise authority by devolving a range of administrative and fiscal powers to local level. Regional councils were elected for the first time in 1986.

Administrative units with a local government consist of 36 779 communes, headed by a municipal council and a mayor, grouped in 96 *départements*, headed by a *conseil général* and its president, grouped in 22 regions, headed by a regional council and its president. The centre of administration of a département is called a *préfecture* (prefecture) or *chef-lieu de département*, which is usually geographically central to the départment.

The *conseil général* as an institution was created in 1790 by the French Revolution in each of the newly created departments (they were suppressed from 1942 to 1944). A *conseiller général* (effectively a local councillor) must be at least 21 years old and either live or pay taxes in locality from which he or she is elected.

The *conseil général* discusses and passes laws on matters that concern the department; it is administratively responsible for departmental employees and land, manages subsidised housing, public transportation, and school subsidies, and contributes to public facilities. The council meets at least three times a year and elects its president for a term of three years, who presides over its 'permanent commission', usually up to 10 other departmental councillors. The *conseil général* has accrued new powers in the course of the political decentralisation that has occurred in France during the past thirty years.

Different levels of administration have different duties, and shared responsibility is common; for instance, in the field of education, *communes* run public elementary schools, while *départements* run public junior high schools and regions run public high schools, but only for the building and upkeep of buildings; curricula and teaching personnel are supplied by the national Ministry of Education.

In the Auvergne, the *départements* are Allier, Cantal, Haute Loire and Puy-de-Dôme. The population of the Auvergne is a little over 1.3 million; one of the least populated regions in the whole of Europe.

Economy

INDUSTRY

Industry came into being in the 16C with the introduction of silk working around Lyon, paid for by the capital earned from fairs. Later, the coalfields in the area were a major factor leading to the expansion of industry. Once the seams had been worked out, the energy supply was provided by the hydroelectric plants and, since the 1970s and 1980s, by the nuclear power plants along the Rhône Valley. Around Clermont-Ferrand the major industry is tyre making.

Metal working

After the gradual shut-down of the coal mines in the area around St-Étienne, the metalworking sector began to specialise in the production of steels, rare metals, fissile products for use in the nuclear industry, and smelting, a sector that benefits from the high demand for moulded components (boiler-making, pipes). The region along the Rhône ranks second to the Paris basin in the field of mechanical engineering (machine tools, precision engineering, car manufacture). Electrical and electronic engineering are well represented with companies producing high-voltage equipment, communications equipment and domestic appliances. Until the 19C, tin and copper were the two main materials used in the Auvergne.

Textiles

After the silk workers' revolts in 1831 and 1834 in the streets and alleyways of Lyon, the textile industry relocated to villages and manufacturers distributed the jobs (weaving and dyeing) to a rural work force. This was the so-called outworker system which still functions today. The importance of silk has decreased greatly in the face of competition from man-made fibres but the weaving of silky fabrics made of a combination of fibres and threads of all types has remained famous. The new products have remained faithful to the innovation and tasteful designs which won Lyon its reputation for silks.

The production and weaving of man-made textiles is carried out in Valence (nylon and polyester) and Roanne (viscose). The industry has many offshoots like dyeing and dressing, and clothing (ready-to-wear, sportswear, lingerie, hosiery, curtains, net curtains, ribbons, elastic, lace).

Chemicals

A major chemical industry developed in Lyon in order to meet the needs of the textile industry. It was here that one of Europe's petrochemical centres was established.

In Feyzin, there is a large oil refinery and the Institut Français du Pétrole has set up its largest research centre here. The region currently leads the field in certain areas of the chemical industry, notably fungicides, paint, varnish and, especially, pharmaceuticals.

Additional industries

Other industrial activities in the region include tyre making, food processing (dairy products, pork meat products, health foods), shoemaking, cabinet-making, quarrying (Volvic), and mineral-water bottling (Vichy, Volvic) as well as the production of building materials, glass, wires, cables, leather, paper, jewellery, tobacco and enamelled lava (signposts, viewing tables). Thiers is one of France's major cutlery-making centres. Traditionally, industry in the Auvergne has centred around specialist crafts, production frequently operating on a cottage-industry scale, such as copper-

Sparkling water from Vichy

J. Damase/MICHELIN

smithing (Cantal), lacemaking (Velay) and papermaking (Livradois).

Administration offices (local authority and government offices etc) and tourism also play an important part in the local economy; traditional industries (eg cheese-making) no longer do any more than "top it up".

Harnessing the Rhône

Important works upstream and downstream of Lyon, completed during the second half of the 20C, have offered this highly industrialised region the possibility of tapping the power resources of the mighty Rhône (16 billion kWh are produced yearly). At the same time, a series of canals provide a total of 330km/205mi of navigable waterways between Lyon and the sea.

AGRICULTURE

The Auvergne is first and foremost a rural area, in marked contrast to the Rhône valley, where industry predominates. Life on farms experienced profound change during the 20C: the introduction of motor vehicles, and the destruction of hedgerows which ended the subdivision of properties into small fields. In many places, the traditional landscape of fields and narrow lanes lined with walnut trees has given way to one of wide, open fields. Farmers, who are decreasing in number, have also had to comply with the milk quotas imposed on them by the EU; despite these difficulties, animal breeding and crop farming remain an important part of the economy of the region.

Stock breeding

The high plateaux and mountains are popular with cattle breeders and, to a lesser extent, sheep farmers. The pastures on the slopes of the Dômes and Dore mountain ranges provide grazing land for the **Salers** breed of cattle (of which it is said that its fiery red coat turns pale if it leaves the basalt areas of Cantal), the French black and white Friesian, and the Montbéliarde.

Towards the middle of May the animals leave their byres and, for the five months of summer, live on the mountain pastures which are now fenced so that there is no need for a herdsman to be in attendance. In days gone by, cowherds had a squat, low summer hut called a *buron,* built to withstand the wind.

The **fairs** give visitors an opportunity to enjoy the busiest moments of rural life. They are held in most of the centrally situated localities and in other places that lie in the heart of the stock-breeding areas. The largest fairs are held in late summer and in autumn.

Crops – In the Auvergne, wheat, barley and oats have traditionally been grown on the fertile black soil of the Limagnes, and now also sugar beet, tobacco, sunflowers and fodder or maize crops from selected strains of seeds.

At the southern end of the Rhône valley the dampness and cold of maritime or continental climates gives way to the heat and radiant skies of the south of France – almond and olive trees and a few mulberry bushes can be seen in the countryside.

The natural environment here is both crop- and farmer-friendly. The land is fertile and easy to irrigate; the soil is light and siliceous; well-sheltered corries and dales benefit from the spring sunshine.

Orchards

It was in 1880 that fruit production took over from wine, after the vineyards had been blighted by phylloxera. The long, fruit-producing season, made possible by careful selection of varieties and the differences in exposure or altitude, enable the orchards in the Rhône valley to produce one-third of all French fruit. Every type of fruit can be found here – raspberries, redcurrants and blackcurrants in Isère, sweet chestnuts in Ardèche, cherries, apricots, apples and pears and, in particular, peaches, the fruit that has made the Eyrieux Valley famous.

Vineyards

The vineyards in the Rhône valley, which were already popular in Roman times, underwent massive expansion after the crisis in the silkworm-breeding industry in the mid-19C. Today, the vineyards cover more than 150 000ha/579sq mi, one-third of which produces high-quality wines. The best are the **Côtes du Rhône.** Châteauneuf-du-Pape, St-Joseph, Crozes-Hermitage, Hermitage, Côte-Rôtie, Château-Grillet and Condrieu are wines that age well, and have brought the area its reputation for excellence. With an annual output of 3.5 million hectolitres of *appellations contrôlées*, the Rhône valley vineyards account for 15% of the total French production of fine wines.

The vineyards stretch for 200km/124mi producing a variety of wines thanks to the **types of vines** selected: Marsanne and Viognier for the whites, Syrah and Grenache for the reds. The wines also vary depending on the different types of soil on which the vines are planted – the crumbly granite of the gorges, and the sands, pebbles or marl that predominate in alluvial plains. There are climatic dif-

Côtes du Rhone wines

J. Damase/MICHELIN

ferences in the basins and, finally, the terraces that climb the hillsides between this area and the Alps face in different directions.

Further north, the vineyards of the **Beaujolais** – which are usually grouped with those of neighbouring Burgundy in wine guides – produce wines which go very well indeed with the traditional cuisine of Lyon, where they are to be found in every local brasserie or *bouchon*. The third Thursday in November is a 'red letter' day locally (and further afield, now that the reputation of Beaujolais wines has spread abroad!) as it marks *l'arrivée du beaujolais nouveau*, or the release for sale to the public of the latest Beaujolais vintage *(vin primeur)*. For further details on Beaujolais wines, ☙ *see BEAUJOLAIS*. The limestone hillsides to each side of the Limagnes used to be covered with vineyards. Nowadays, some of the wines fall within the all-enveloping name Côtes d'Auvergne, among them Châtaugay, Corent, Boudes and St-Pourçain.

Traditions in the Auvergne

Because of the isolated nature of much of the Auvergne countryside, many ancient traditions have survived; today, the inhabitants are doing their utmost to preserve the special character of this region and the cultural heritage.

Fêtes and festivals

Many of the old customs are upheld on the most important occasions. Bonfires are still lit on the mountain tops to celebrate the summer solstice (Feast of St John), and local fêtes have kept up the tradition of the music and songs played to young girls by the young men of the village. There has also been a revival of country festivals to celebrate haymaking, cheesemaking, harvesting, grape harvests, etc.

Costume

Today every folk group has its own interpretation of traditional costume. The men wear the *biaude,* a voluminous dark blue smock over a pair of coarse black trousers, with a brightly coloured scarf, a wide-brimmed, black felt hat and the clogs or hob-nailed boots that are so vital when tapping out the dance rhythm.

The women are dressed in long, waisted, multicoloured dresses with an embroidered apron and a headdress that varies depending on the region.

The bourrée

This dance dates back a long time but it has been synonymous with the Auvergne since the 18C. The *bourrée* enacts the chasing of a coquettish young girl by an enterprising young man, whom she alternately runs away from and then beckons to.

S. Sauvignier/MICHELIN

La Bourrée

Processions and pilgrimages

Worship of the Virgin Mary is very important in the Auvergne. Countless churches and chapels have been dedicated to her. Indeed, the statues of the Virgin Mary in the Auvergne are among the oldest in France.

Processions and pilgrimages in honour of the Blessed Virgin remain very much alive and are quite spectacular. The processions to Notre-Dame-du-Port (Clermont-Ferrand) or Orcival, and the pilgrimages to Mauriac and Thiézac in Cantal and to Marsat and Monton in Puy-de-Dôme are the most popular.

Food and Drink

The Rhône valley abounds in good food because it is situated at the heart of various regions containing an outstanding wealth of local produce. Bresse is famous for its poultry, the Charolais area produces beef, the Dombes region abounds in game, the lakes of Savoy teem with fish and the Forez and Rhône valleys specialise in fruit.

The Auvergne, a rugged area of countryside, is not the place for complex, sophisticated cuisine; it specialises in family cooking – and plenty of it.

LYON

In the 19C silk workers ate, like their employers, in small family-run restaurants; there was no snobbery in Lyon when it came to good food. The dishes served were based on cheap cuts of meat and offal, but the food was plentiful and tasty. Diners could eat sausages, potted pork, black sausage, pigs' trotters, knuckle of veal and other stewed meats.

The tradition of good food remains unchanged. Today, local specialities include spicy saveloy sausage with truffles and pistachio nuts, pigs' trotters and tails, cardoons with marrow bone jelly, pork brawn in vinaigrette, and gently stewed tripe. Other dishes include braised, stuffed trout, fish in Burgundy wine, poultry – especially chicken cooked in stock with thin slivers of truffle inserted between the skin and the meat, and chicken in cream.

Forez

Hunting, shooting, fishing and stock breeding provide the basic ingredients for a delicate, tasty type of cooking. Among the local dishes are crayfish and trout from the River Lignon, or poultry and meat of outstanding quality. Also on offer may be a local form of pork pie, a dish of duck, a delicious local ham, Feurs sausage or, in the autumn, game pâté, sometimes even woodcock.

Vivarais

Food here is rustic; this is the land of chestnuts and wild mushrooms such as St George's agaric and boletus. Among the filling, tasty specialities are partridge with cabbage, thrush with grapes, chicken cooked in a bladder, chicken with crayfish, goose and turkey with chestnuts, hare with *poivrade* (a highly seasoned sauce), and pork meat products from Ardèche. During the summer, the cherries, apricots, peaches, pears, plums and apples are among the finest such fruits found anywhere in France.

Lower Dauphiné

The Rhône valley area of Lower Dauphiné marks the transition between the Lyonnais area and Provence. This is the land of *gratin dauphinois*, veal with leeks, *pognes* (brioches, a sort of sweet bread) in Romans and Valence, cheese from St-Marcellin, Grignan-style braised beef and the inimitable Montélimar nougat.

No "fast food" here

J. Damase/MICHELIN

AUVERGNE

The food in the Auvergne has traditionally been farm cooking, and as a result it has been accused of lacking any appreciable local specialities; this criticism is, happily, totally unfounded. The people of the Auvergne have taken great national specialities and adapted them to suit local taste so that, in the Auvergne, food is rich and sometimes heavy but it is always extremely good.

Meat and fish

The *coq au vin* (chicken stew) is delicious, especially when flavoured with a good wine. The *tripoux* from Aurillac, St-Flour and Chaudes-Aigues are wonderful, too. There is ham from Maurs, local sausages, trout from mountain streams, eels from the Dore, and salmon from the Allier.

Vegetables

The *truffade* from Aurillac is a smooth blend of fresh Tomme cheese and mashed potatoes; seasoned with garlic in Chaudes-Aigues and Aubrac, it is called *aligot*. Potato paté, a light pastry browned in the oven with a lot of fresh cream and potatoes, is one of the specialities of the Montluçon and Gannat area. Morel mushrooms are cooked with cream and used to fill omelettes and stuff poultry. Peas from the Planèze and green lentils from Le Puy are well-known to gourmets.

Cheeses

This is one of the region's main specialities. The round, flat St-Nectaire is a delight when well matured. There is also Fourme d'Ambert and Fourme de Montbrison, a blue cheese with an orange-tinted rind, Bleu d'Auvergne and Cantal. These are the best-known of the local cheeses but there is in addition Murol, a variant of St-Nectaire, or the garlic-flavoured Gaperon, made on the plains and shaped like a rounded cone.

Locally, the cheese usually known as Cantal is called Fourme, named after the wooden mould (or form) used to hold it together. This word gave the French language the word *formage* (forming) which later became *fromage* (cheese). It

Some cheeses of the Auvergne: (left to right) Cantal, Bleu d'Auvergne, Fourme d'Ambert, St-Nectaire

takes the milk of 20 to 30 cows to make a 40kg/88lb Cantal cheese.

WINES

The Auvergne still boasts a few wines like the famous St-Pourçain that can be left to age for up to four years, or Côtes d'Auvergne wines (Châteaugay and Corent), known since Roman times. But the best wine-growing areas are to be found in the Rhône valley, where Beaujolais and Côtes du Rhône are produced.

Côtes du Rhône

The vineyards on the Côtes du Rhône are thought to be the oldest in France, founded on vine stock introduced by the Greeks several centuries BC. They stretch along both banks of the river like a narrow ribbon, producing wines whose quality and balance are guaranteed by a skilful blend of varieties of grape. The reds should be consumed slightly cool, the whites well chilled. Château-Condrieu and Château-Grillet are among the greatest of all French white wines. If drunk young, they are a marvellous accompaniment to a crayfish gratin. Cornas was much appreciated by Charlemagne. Further south, where the valley enters Provence, the vineyards produce the warm, friendly Châteauneuf-du-Pape, Gigondas, the sweet, suave and flavoursome Muscat from Beaumes-de-Venise and, on the other bank of the Rhône, the rosés from Tavel and the reds and rosés from Lirac and Chusclan.

East end of the old abbey in Issoire
S. Sauvignier/MICHELIN

AIGUEPERSE

POPULATION 2,505

MICHELIN MAPS 326: G-6

This charming town at the heart of the Limagne is circled by avenues that have replaced the former ramparts. The Hôtel de Ville (town hall) is housed in a 17C convent building; note the three jack o' the clocks who chime the hours.

- **Information:** Office Culturel Nord Limagne, 196 Grande Rue, 63260 Aigueperse. ☎04 73 63 72 70. www.aigueperse.net.
- ▶ **Orient Yourself:** Aigueperse is 34km/21mi NNE of Clermont Ferrand.
- **Also See:** CLERMONT FERRAND, VICHY.

Driving Tour

Discovering La Limagne

70km/43.5mi – allow 3hr.
This itinerary runs across the Limagne, a vast fertile plain extending north of Clermont-Ferrand towards the Bourbonnais region.

- ▶ *Leave Aigueperse to the N: D 151 leads to the Butte de Montpensier, 4km/2.5mi further on.*

Butte de Montpensier

Montpensier "Hill" is a typical volcanic neck. From it, there is a fine view over the Limagne plain. A fortress once stood on the hilltop and it was here that King Louis VIII, the father of St Louis, died in 1226 on his return from the Albigensian Crusade. The castle was razed to the ground on the orders of Richelieu in the 17C.

- ▶ *Continue along D 151 to crossroads, then take D 93 on the right.*

Château d'Effiat★

6km/3.7mi NE of Aigueperse.
&. ☞Guided tours Jul–Aug daily except Mon, 2pm–7pm. ☞6€. ☎04 73 63 66 76.
On the Vichy-Aigueperse road stands the Château d'Effiat, a fine Louis XIII building of considerable historic and architectural interest.

- ▶ *Take D 93 and drive to Bas-et-Lezat, then take D 63.*

Villeneuve-les-Cerfs

A picturesque **dovecote**★ stands in a meadow at the entrance to the village.

- ▶ *Continue along D 63 until you reach the intersection with D 1093 and turn right.*

Limagne plain

J. Damase/MICHELIN

Maringues

This large village of Gallo-Roman origin, a busy agricultural trading centre, stands along the recently canalised Morge. Until the mid-19C, wool and leather working were the traditional local activities: around 1850 there were 60 tanneries operating along the river.

▶ *Leave to the SW and take D 224, heading for Riom.*

Ennezat

Ennezat, a large farming village on the Limagne plain lies near marshes in a landscape of vast, geometrical fields separated by drainage ditches and rows of aspen trees and willows. The former collegiate **church**★ is a mix of 11C Auvergne Romanesque and 13C Gothic styles.

▶ *Leave Ennezat and follow the diverted route to Vichy on D 210.*

Thuret

A 13C keep dominates the village.

▶ *Leave Thuret on D 211 and drive to Sardon. Enter Sardon on D 51, then, on leaving the town, turn left onto D 122 to the junction with D 985. Turn right onto D 985 to St-Myon.*

St-Myon

There is a small Romanesque church here with a fine stone-slabbed roof.

▶ *Continue along D 223 to the E.*

Artonne

The village retains numerous sections of its medieval town wall. St Martin of Tours came here to pray at the tomb of St Vitaline.

🥾 **Coteau du Puy St-Jean,** *500m/547yd.* A nature discovery trail leads to a viewpoint overlooking the village.

Traditional dovecote

S. Sauvignier/MICHELIN

▶ *Drive NW out of Artonne and turn right onto D 22 towards St-Agoulin then follow D 12.*

Château de la Roche

🕐*Open Jul–mid Sept daily except Tue 2.30pm–5.30pm, Sun and public holidays 3pm–5.30pm.* ⬤7€. ☎04 73 63 65 81.
This medieval manor, slightly altered in the 16C, was the fief of the vassal families of the dukes of Bourbon.
It was elevated to a castellany by Charles III, the rebel commander-in-chief of the French armies, for Jean de L'Hospital, his doctor. The illustrious **Michel de L'Hospital** was born at La Roche, which he was given as a dowry in 1537.

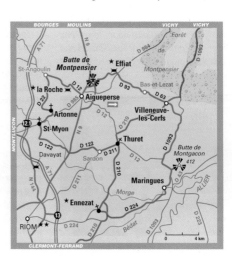

AMBERT

POPULATION 7,500
MICHELIN MAP 326: J-9

The small, seemingly-isolated town of Ambert lies in the middle of a low, wide plain between the Livradois and Forez mountains. Ambert is a centre of diversified economic activity (including the manufacture of braiding) and the ideal starting point of excursions across the surrounding high pastures. Ambert's origins are obscure but the town began to make its name in the 15C, when the paper industry here came into its own; in the 16C the area had more than 300 mills.

- 🛈 **Information:** 4 pl. de l'Hôtel-de-Ville, 63600 AMBERT. ☎04 73 82 61 90. www.tourisme.fr/office-de-tourisme/ambert.htm.
- ▶ **Orient Yourself:** At the heart of the Livradois-Forez, 77km/48mi from Clermont Ferrand and 79km/49mi from St-Étienne.
- 🕐 **Organising Your Time:** Half a day to explore; market Thursday morning.
- 👣 **Also See:** CLERMONT FERRAND, ST-ÉTIENNE, THIERS.

Sights

Église St-Jean★
Place St-Jean.
The church of St-Jean is a typical example of flamboyant Gothic architecture, except for the upper part of the tower and a chapel which both date from the Renaissance.

Hôtel de ville
Boulevard Henri IV.
An unusual routunda made famous by Jules Romains' *Copains* novel.

Maison de la Fourme et du Fromage
🕐*Open Jul–Aug guided tours (1hr) 9am–7pm; Sept 9am–noon, 2pm–7pm; Apr–Jun daily except Mon 9am–noon, 2pm–7pm; Oct–Nov and Feb–Mar Tue, Thu, Fri and Sat 9am–noon, 2pm–7pm.* ⊜*5€.* ☎*04 73 82 49 23.*

Hôtel de ville

This museum devoted to cheesemaking is housed in a 15C building. Guided tours describe the manufacture of **fourme d'ambert,** the delicious local blue cheese.

Musée de la Machine Agricole et à Vapeur [Kids]
👪🕐*Open mid-Apr–mid Oct: 2pm–6pm (Jul and Aug 10am–12.30pm, 2pm–6.30pm).* 🕐*Closed mid-Dec–mid Jan).* ⊜*5.20€, children 3.50€.* ☎*04 73 82 60 42.* http://agrivap.free.fr.
This museum installed in a former saw mill boasts a large collection of steam-powered machines from the early 20C.

Livradois-Forez tourist train★
[Kids] *Jul–Aug Tue, Thu, Sun, leaves at 2.15pm, arrives back 6.30pm.* ⊜*14€ (children 11€) return.* ☎*04 73 82 43 88.*
In the summer, a panoramic tourist train travels along the Dore Valley via Ambert, through typical landscapes of the Livradois-Forez Regional Park.

Parc Zoologique du Bouy [Kids]
8.5km/5mi S on D906; right on D 56 to Champetières.
🕐*Open Feb–Nov 10am–6pm (Oct–Nov Wed, Sat, Sun).* 🕐*Closed Dec–Jan.* ⊜*8€ (children 4€).* ☎*04 73 82 13 29.*
Many species of animal, whose habits and characteristics are explained on information panels, live here in semi-liberty: birds, monkeys, lions, lynx,

jackals, hyenas, wolves, kangaroos, camels, bison, white deer, emus etc.

Driving Tours

Le Val Lagat *60km/37mi*

⚓ *See THIERS for tour map (route* **3** *).*

▶ *Leave Ambert E along D 966, heading towards Montbrison.*

Musée de l'école 1900

In Saint-Martin-des-Olmes. ◷*Open Jun–Sept 9am–noon, 2pm–7pm.* ⊛*5€ (children 3€).* ☎*04 73 72 66 80.* The village school, dating from the 1880s and closed in 1989, houses this interesting school museum which recreates the atmosphere of a classroom at the turn of the 20C.

▶ *Turn back and take the first road on the right.*

Moulin Richard-de-Bas★

On D 57. ◷*Open daily all year, 9.30am–12.30pm, 2pm–6pm (Jul–Aug 9.30am–7pm).* ◷*Closed 1 Jan and 25 Dec.* ⊛*6.50€ (children 4€).* ☎*04 73 82 03 11. www.richard debas.com.* Old houses and paper mills, still surmounted by pine stretchers on which paper or printed sheets were hung to dry, are evidence of the industrial importance of the Lagat Valley which, for several centuries, was one of the main papermaking centres in France. Today, Richard-de-Bas is the only remaining mill in activity producing 400 to 500 sheets daily.

▶ *Turn around and, at Valeyre, turn right onto D 67.*

🚶 A discovery trail, **Le Chemin des Papetiers,** starts from Valeyre and runs along the steep mule track followed by rag-pickers.

Cirque de Valcivières

This attractive cirque shelters several hamlets on its stream-strewn slopes and among the fields. Turn right onto D 106 and up to Col des Supeyres.

Col des Supeyres

1,336m/4,481ft. This pass on the eastern edge of the Livradois-Forez Nature Park is surrounded by a landscape of badly-drained mountain pastures, without a soul in sight.

Un colporteur et des jasseries

🚶 From Col des Supeyres, walk through high pastures along a discovery trail, following in the footsteps of pedlars of bygone days.

Jasserie du Coq-Noir

◷🍽*Open daily Jul–Aug except Thu 1pm–6pm.* ⊛*3.50€ (children 2.50€).* ☎*04 73 95 47 06. www.coq-noir.fr.* This former summer farm offers valuable insight into mountain farming, roof thatching and cheesemaking. A snack of milk rye bread and Fourme (local cheese) is available.

▶ *Return to Col des Supeyres and Valcivières.*

After Valcivières the route follows a rock-strewn ravine to emerge above the Ambert plain and then descends the lower slopes of the Forez mountains.

▶ *D 66, then D 906 back to Ambert.*

Livradois to the Dore
100km/62mi round tour

▶ *Leave Ambert W along D 996, for St-Amand-Roche-Savine. The Le Monestier/St-Amand road takes you past a small castle, the* **Domaine Nobles des Escures** *(⊶).*

St-Amand-Roche-Savine
Every summer, this charming hamlet nestling amid the Livradois heights welcomes many visitors, especially during the lively rock festival.

▶ *Drive N; 1km/0.5mi after St-Amand, turn right onto D 87, then D 65.*

Cunlhat
Pretty trading community formerly specialised in woolmaking, surrounded by lush wooded vegetation.

▶ *Leave Cunlhat to the S and drive along D 105 to St-Eloy-la-Glacière; turn left after entering the village.*

La ferme des Bois Noirs
⏱*Open Easter-end Oct 2pm–7pm Sat, Sun and public holidays (daily, mid-Jun–mid Sept).* ◉*5€.* ☎*04 73 72 13 47.*
Unaltered since it was built in 1763, this farmhouse illustrates the life and work of a peasant family in the Livradois region, a poor mountainous area where men had to take on seasonal work to supplement the meagre income the family derived from farming.

▶ *Drive back to St-Eloy and turn left onto D 105 to Fournols.*

Fournols
This small summer resort boasts several fine old mansions.

▶ *D 37 will lead to St-Germain-l'Herm.*

St-Germain-l'Herm
Summer holiday resort offering a wide range of activities.

▶ *Follow D 999 and turn right onto D 999A; drive through St-Bonnet-le-Chastel, and continue to Novacelles.*

Novacelles
You will enjoy visiting this small village tucked away in a valley watered by the Dollore.

▶ *Take D 105 to St-Sauveur-la-Sagne, then D 38 along the Dore gorges. Turn right onto D 907.*

La Chaise-Dieu
♿*See La CHAISE-DIEU.*

▶ *Drive N out of La Chaise-Dieu along D 906 then turn right onto D 202.*

Dore-l'Église
The village, situated at the confluence of the Dore and Dorette, has a 12C church which underwent alterations in the 15C. To the left of the church is a **Gallo-Roman memorial.**

▶ *Take D 906 N.*

Arlanc
The small market town is hemmed in between Forez and the Livradois mountains. The **Musée de la Dentelle** (🛈☎04 73 95 00 03. www.arlanc.com/musee_dentelle.htm) is housed in the vaulted cellars of the town hall.

Jardin pour la Terre
⏱*Open daily, May–Sept 2pm–7pm.* ◉*6€.* ☎*04 73 95 00 71. www.arlanc.com.*
This garden retraces the history of small trees and shrubberies from all five continents and their adjustment to European climatic conditions.

Marsac-en-Livradois
On the square to the south of the church stands the old White Penitents' Chapel. It houses the **Musée des Pénitents Blancs du Livradois** (♿⏱*open Jul–Aug guided tours (45min) 10am–noon, 3pm–7pm;* ☎*04 73 95 60 08; www.cc-livradois. fr/marsac/penitent),* a museum bursting with memorabilia relating to this brotherhood.

▶ *Go back to Ambert on D 906.*

ANNONAY

POPULATION 17,522
MICHELIN MAP 331: K-2

Annonay is located in a deep cleft of the Vivarais plateau, at the confluence of the River Deûme and River Cance. In the Middle Ages, the exceptional quality of the water here encouraged a leather and wool industry to be established which then flourished. Being one of the first towns to uphold the principles of the Reformation, Annonay suffered greatly during the Wars of Religion. In the 17C, however, following the establishment in the town of the Johannot and Montgolfier families' paperworks, Annonay began to prosper once again.

- **Information:** Pl. des Cordeliers, 07100 ANNONAY. ☎ 04 75 33 24 51. www.ot-annonay.fr.
- **Orient Yourself:** Almost directly south of Lyon and north of Valence.
- **Don't Miss:** The Old Town.
- **Organising Your Time:** Spend at least half a day to a day relaxing here.
- **Also See:** ST-ÉTIENNE, MONTÉLIMAR, VALENCE.

A Bit of History

The native city of the Montgolfier brothers, Annonay was also the home of one of their descendants, **Marc Seguin** (1786–1875), the engineer who improved the steam boiler.

Observing that hot air rises, the **Montgolfier brothers** decided to harness this energy. On 4 June 1783, in the presence of the States General of the Vivarais area, they launched a **balloon** of 769m³/27,157cu ft. The strips forming the balloon itself were made of packaging fabric and paper, held together by some 1,800 buttons. Rising in nine and a half minutes to a maximum height of 1,000–2,000m or 3,250–6,500ft (according to different eyewitness accounts) the balloon remained in the air for half an hour and finally landed more than 2km/1mi from its launch site. This feat is commemorated by an obelisk at the roundabout in avenue Marc-Seguin and a plaque on place des Cordeliers, where the experiment was conducted.

Walking Tour

Old Town

The old quarter on the hills overlooking the two rivers is currently benefiting from a major restoration project.

▶ Begin from place de la Libération.

On this square stands a statue of the Montgolfier brothers, erected in 1883.

▶ Turn onto rue Boissy-d'Anglas.

Chapelle de Trachin

This Gothic chapel is all that remains of a priory founded in 1320 by Guy Trachin, a wealthy resident of Annonay.

▶ From the bottom of place de la Liberté turn onto Montée du Château.

Fortified Gates (R)

Montée du Château forms a steep incline up to the old machicolated gate; a sec-

Reconstitution of the first flight

Address Book

For coin ranges, see the cover flap.

WHERE TO STAY

⊜⊜ **Hôtel D'Ay** – *Gourdan golf course, 6.5km/4mi N of Annonay. ☎04 75 67 01 00. www.domainestclair.fr. 35 rms. ☐10€. Restaurant⊜⊜.* A modern hotel on an 18-hole golf course. Well-equipped spacious rooms.

⊜ **Chambre d'hôte La Désirade** – *07340 St-Désirat, 15km/9mi E of Annonay. ☎04 75 34 21 88. http://ph.meunier. free.fr. Closed Christmas and 1 Jan.*

6 rms. Amid grapevines and trees, this renovated 19C house has pleasant rooms giving onto a courtyard, or park and vineyard.

WHERE TO EAT

⊜⊜ **Restaurant La Moustache Gourmande** – *Le Village, 07430 St-Clair, 3.5km/2mi from Annonay. ☎04 75 67 01 81. Closed Feb school holidays, 15 days in Sept and Wed.* This restaurant in a charming village has a fine selection of sea food dishes.

ond gate also survives, at the end of rue de Bourgville.

▶ *Rue Montgolfier leads to the bridge.*

Pont Montgolfier

Upstream, the view is of the humpback **Valgelas bridge** (14C) and the convent of Ste-Marie (16C). Downstream, the Deûme flows into the **Défilé des Fouines,** a dark, narrow rocky gorge.

▶ *Walk to Valgelas bridge and follow Voûtes Soubise, a vaulted passageway, to the steps of rue Barville. Turn right onto rue de Deûme and continue to avenue de l'Europe.*

Avenue de l'Europe partly covers the Deûme. From the intersection with rue de la Valette there is a **view** west over the **Tour des Martyrs** (12C–13C), the last remnant of the old ramparts.

Place de la Liberté

This square located in the centre of the old town becomes a bustling hub of trade on market days *(Wednesdays and Saturdays).* The square is graced by a statue of Marc Seguin.

Rue Franki-Kramer

Annonay's old high street, like the nearby place Grenette and place Mayol, is flanked by picturesque 16C, 17C and 18C houses.

▶ *Walk through place Grenette and return to rue Franki-Kramer.*

Museums

Musée des Papeteries Canson et Montgolfier (M¹)

2.5km/1.5mi NE. *Vidalon, BP 139, 07100 ANNONAY. ⏱Wed and Sun 2.30pm–6pm. ⊜4.50. ☎04 75 69 89 20.*
This museum, in the house where the Montgolfier brothers were born, retraces the history of the local paperworks.

Musée Vivarois César-Filhol (M²)

⏱*Open Jul–Aug 2.30pm–6pm; Sept–Jun Wed, Sat–Sun 2.30pm–6pm.* ⏱*Closed 14 Jul, 15 Aug, public holidays. ⊜3€. ☎04 75 67 67 93. www.mairie-annonay.fr.*
This ancient royal bailiwick dating from 1700 contains interesting collections on old Annonay, its famous citizens and the folklore of the Vivarois area.

Excursions

Safari-Parc de Peaugres★ 🄺🄸🄳🅂

⏱*Open Jul–Aug 9.30am–7pm; mid-Feb–Mar and Sept–mid Nov 10am–5pm; Apr–Jun 9.30am–6.30pm.* ⏱*Closed mid-Nov–mid Feb. ⊜17.50€ (children 14€). ☎04 75 33 00 32. www.safari-peaugres.com.*
Located at the foot of the Pilat massif, this nature reserve is home to 400 mammals, 300 birds and around 60 reptiles.

Boulieu

5km/3mi to the N on avenue de l'Europe.
Former fortified village with square ramparts flanking the main street.

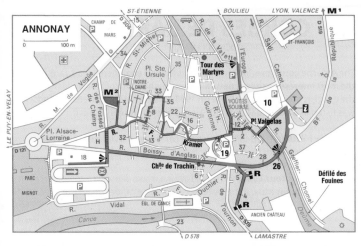

ANNONAY		Cordeliers Pl. des	10	Montgolfier Pont	26
		Deûme R. de	12	Montgolfier R.	28
Barville. R.	2	Épiphanie R.	13	Poterne R. de la	32
Bechetoille R. J.-B.	3	Frachon R. E.	15	Réforme R. de la	33
Boissy-d'Anglas R.		Grenette Pl.	16	St-Étienne R.	34
Bourgville R. de	4	Libération Pl. de la	18	Ste-Marie R.	35
Château Montée du	5	Liberté Pl. de la	19	Valgelas R.	37
Clocher R. du	6	Mayol Pl.	22		
Consuls R. des	8	Meyzonnier R.	23		

Musée des Papeteries		Musée vivarois		Portes fortifiées	R
Canson et Montgolfier	M¹	César-Filhol	M²		

Musée de l'Alambic★

St-Désirat (13km E); from Davézieux, follow D 82 for 7km; turn left onto a small road to St-Désirat. ⏰*Open daily, 8am–noon, 2pm–6.30pm (Jul–Aug 8am–7pm) (Sat–Sun and public holidays 10am).* ⏰*Closed 1 Jan and 25 Dec.* ⊛*No charge.* ☎*0810 000 148. www.jeangauthier.com.*
This museum within the Gauthier distillery, recalls the life of distillers.

Driving Tour

Ay and Cance valleys

Round tour of 48km/29mi – allow 2hr.

▶ *Leave Annonay by rue de Tournon to the S heading for Lamastre.*

Quintenas-le-Peyron

The village is dominated by the 14C belfry of its Romanesque church.

▶ *In Quintenas, on the right, facing the church, follow directions for St-Romain-d'Ay.*

The narrow road meanders through the countryside, affording pretty views of the Haut-Vivarais.

▶ *Leave the church of St-Romain on your left and drive to D 6; turn left. After 90m/100yd, on the right, a steep road leads to Notre-Dame-d'Ay.*

Notre-Dame-d'Ay

This modest sanctuary perched on top of a rocky outcrop is a popular place of pilgrimage.

▶ *Turn back, turn right onto D 6, then take D 221 to Sarras. In Sarras, turn left onto N 86 and after 2km/1mi, before the bridge spanning the River Cance, turn left onto D 270.*

The corniche road follows the steep banks of the Cance Valley, carpeted with oak trees. The **Roche Péréandre**★ looms majestically.

▶ *Proceed along D 270, then D 371 until you reach Annonay.*

GORGES DE L'ARDÈCHE ★★★

MICHELIN MAPS 331: I-7 TO J-8

The Ardèche gorge, overlooked by an audaciously engineered road, ranks among the most impressive sites of natural beauty in the south of France; a large part of the gorge is now a nature reserve. In 1993, this exceptional stretch of landscape was listed as a major national site (Grand Site d'Intérêt National).

▶ **Orient Yourself:** It is difficult to get a complete overview of the gorges, but the view from the panoramic road is as good as any.

🕭 **Don't Miss:** The Pont d'Arc.

🕐 **Organising Your Time:** You should allow a whole day to do a complete circuit.

▦ **Especially for kids:** If the water is calm, take a canoe trip on the river.

🕭 **Also see:** Aven d'ORGNAC.

A Bit of History

Spates and Droughts – In the upper valley the Ardèche cuts a steep downhill course, but it is in the lower valley that the more interesting formations are to be seen. Here the river has carved a passage through the limestone of the plateau, already undermined by subterranean streams. The Ardèche's tributaries flowing down from the mountain accentuate its sporadic yet typically Mediterranean flow. During the autumn spates, when the river's volume can increase dramatically, there is a tremendous convergence of flood waters at Vallon-Pont-d'Arc. The strength of these erratic flood waters is such that the river pushes the flow of the Rhône eastwards and deposits alluvial debris in its river bed. In 1890, the force of the Ardèche spate was so strong that it cut right across the course of the Rhône and broke through the Lauzon dike on the opposite bank.

Driving Tours

① Route Panoramique

38km/24mi starting from Vallon-Pont-d'Arc – allow half a day.
The D 290 overlooks the gorge from the clifftops at the edge of the Gras plateau, giving views from the many look-out points (belvédères) along the way.

Vallon-Pont-d'Arc

This town is the departure point for boat trips down the gorge. Southeast of the town, on the slope of a hill, stand the ruins of Vieux Vallon Castle, a reminder of the old medieval village here.

Exposition Grotte Chauvet-Pont-d'Arc

At the end of 1994, a set of cave paintings was discovered on the site of the Combe-d'Arc in the Ardèche gorge. Part of a vast network of underground galleries, the cave (Grotte Chauvet) features numerous prehistoric red and black paintings of some 400 animals, including horse, mammoth, bear, woolly rhinoceros, cat and auroch; figures of a hyena and an owl are also portrayed, which is exceptionally rare. Initial studies of the art date them to about 30,000 years before present. The number, quality and originality of the paintings place the cave on a par with the Cosquer cave east of Marseille and the Lascaux cave in the Dordogne, in terms of the importance of their contribution to the study of prehistory worldwide.

▶ *Head S for Pont-d'Arc on D 290.*

The road skirts the ruins of **Vieux Vallon Castle** and after crossing the Ibie, comes to the Ardèche. On the left is the **Grotte des Tunnels**, a cave through which an underground torrent once ran, and then **Grotte des Huguenots** (🕐 open mid-Jun–Aug 10am–7pm; ⌾4€; ☎04 75 88 06 71), which houses an exhibition on speleology, prehistory and the history of the Huguenot population of the southern Vivarais region.

J. Damase/MICHELIN

Pont-d'Arc

Pont-d'Arc★★

🏃 At one time the river skirted this promontory and the arch would have been just a gully through which underground waters drained. General erosion and the river wore away the land around the arch, and then the river itself, during some particularly large spate, abandoned its old meander to slip through the passage. Beyond Pont-d'Arc the landscape becomes more impressive. The river follows a series of gentle curves, interspersed with rapids, at the bottom of a deserted gorge. After Chames the road veers round to the left at the bottom of Tiourre Valley which forms an impressive, rocky **cirque**★ before reaching the edge of the plateau.

Belvédère du Serre de Tourre★★

Poised almost vertically above the Ardèche, this viewpoint offers a superb **view** of the meander known as the **Pas du Mousse**, with the ruins of the 16C Château d'Ebbo clearly visible on the rocky promontory.

Belvédères de Gaud★★

There is a fine view of the upstream sweep of the Gaud meander and the turrets of its small 19C castle.

Belvédères d'Autridge★

To reach the two viewpoints, take the panoramic curve. The needle of rock known as Aiguille de Morsanne soars up from the Ardèche like a ship's prow.

Belvédères de Gournier★★

These viewpoints are well situated, high above the Ardèche. Below, the Gournier farm lies in ruins in a meadow beside the river.

▸ *Continue to the Marzal chasm along the road across the Gras plateau (D 590).*

Aven de Marzal★

Interior temperature 14°C/57°F; 743 steps. The chasm is a natural well, and leads to caves rich in stalagmites, stalactites and other limestone formations.

You can also visit the **Musée du Monde Souterrain** (♿🕐 *open Apr–Sept 10am–6pm; Mar, Oct and Nov Sun and public holidays 2pm–6pm.* ☎*04 75 55 14 82*), a museum devoted to the history of speleology in France. The **Zoo Préhistorique** (♿🕐 *open Apr–Sept daily, 10am–6pm; Mar and Oct–Nov Sun, public and school holidays, 1pm–5.30pm.* ☎*8€.* ☎*04 75 55 14 82*) is laid out along a shaded route displaying life-size reproductions of extinct animals that lived from the Primary to the Quaternary Era.

▸ *D 201 leads to Bidon.*

Bidon

This tiny village boasts a **Musée de la Vie** (♿🕐*open Apr–mid Nov 10am–6pm.* 🕐*closed the rest of the year.* ☎*6€.* ☎*04 75 04 08 79*) illustrating the evolution of the universe.

Address Book

PRACTICAL INFORMATION

A FRAGILE ENVIRONMENT

The Ardèche Nature Reserve is a conservation area, so every effort should be made to protect its ecosystem. In particular, visitors must not light a fire, leave behind rubbish, pick plants or stray from the signposted footpaths. Picnicking is possible all along the way. Camping or bivouacking are prohibited outside authorised camp sites *(see overnight stops below)*.

DOWNRIVER BY BOAT OR CANOE

The whole trip (starting upriver from Pont d'Arc) means covering a distance of 30km/18.6mi; however, it is possible to shorten the distance to 24km/15mi by starting from Chames. If you feel like a boat trip without any physical exertion, contact the Confrérie des Bateliers de l'Ardèche (information and bookings available at the tourist office in Vallon). The river can be explored by canoe year-round, although the best time is in May, June (except weekends) and September (daily); during the cold season (October to April), canoeists should wear a waterproof and isothermal suit. Depending on the season and the water level, it is wise to allow six to nine hours to complete the trip (departures are not allowed after 6pm). There are a few difficult passages (rapids) which require a good canoeing technique; in addition, it is essential to be able to swim. Life jackets must be worn by participants and heavy fines are applied to those who do not comply with regulations; these are available from hiring companies, town halls, tourist offices and gendarmeries (police stations in country areas).

Canoe hire – Some 50 hiring companies, based in Vallon-Pont-d'Arc, Salavas, Ruoms, St-Martin, St-Remèze, propose unaccompanied and guided trips lasting one or two days for an average price of 35€ (one day) or 45€ (two days without accommodation) per person (children under 7 years of age are not allowed on these trips). A list of hiring companies is available from tourist offices in Ruoms (rue Alphonse-Daudet, 07120 Ruoms, ☎04 75 93 91 90), Vallon-Pont-d'Arc (Cité administrative, 07150 Vallon-Pont-d'Arc, ☎04 75 88 04 01) and St-Martin-d'Ardèche (place de l'Église, 07700 St-Martin-d'Ardèche, ☎04 75 98 70 91). For unaccompanied trips, it is necessary to book an overnight stop from central booking offices located in the above-mentioned tourist offices.

Overnight stops – Overnight stops along the gorge are allowed in two places only: Aire Naturelle de Gaud and Aire Naturelle de Gournier; 6€ or 8€ (under a tent). Longer stays are possible at two camp sites: Camping des Templiers (naturism, ☎04 75 04 28 58) and Camping des Grottes de St-Marcel (☎04 75 04 14 65).

FOLLOWING THE GORGE ON FOOT

Before embarking upon a walk along the gorge, remember to check the weather forecast and signs indicating daily water levels to be sure of being able to cross the fords safely.

Allow two days for the 21km/13mi hike from Chames (starting point just beyond the village in a bend; two information panels, parking area below the road). Start early in the morning, wear adequate walking shoes, take 2l of water (it gets very hot in the middle of the day), some food, a first-aid kit and a pair of sandals for crossing the fords. Apart from the two fords, there are a few difficult passages, but all are equipped with handrails.

A topoguide, *Les Gorges de l'Ardèche et leurs plateaux* (no 2, Gilbert de Cochet) is published by the Syndicat Intercommunal des Gorges de l'Ardèche et de leur Région Naturelle (SIGARN ☎04 75 98 77 31).

J. Damase/MICHELIN

For coin ranges, see the legend on the cover flap.

WHERE TO STAY

Hôtel Le Clos des Bruyères – *Rte des Gorges, 07150 Vallon-Pont-d'Arc. ☎04 75 37 18 85. www.closdesbruyeres. fr. Closed Oct–Mar.* **P**. *32 rms.* ⚏*8€.* The road through the gorges of the Ardèche is magnificent, but the curves can be awfully tiresome. Take a break in this regional-style house whose arcades open onto the summer pool. Rooms with a balcony or on the ground floor. Seafood served in the restaurant with a terrace.

Camping Le Provençal – *1.5km/0.9mi SE of Vallon-Pont-d'Arc. ☎04 75 88 00 48. Open 12 Apr–20 Sept. Reservations recommended. 200 sites. Food service.* Beyond its pretty, flowery entrance, this elongated terrain stretches to the banks of the Ardèche. The sites are well defined and shaded. An agreeable place to stay, with its children's playground, attractive pool and tennis court.

WHERE TO EAT

L'Auberge Sarrasine – *R. de la Fontaine, 30760 Aiguèze. ☎04 66 50 94 20. Closed Tue.* While meandering through the ancient village alleys, you'll come across this small restaurant taking up three vaulted rooms dating from the 11C. The chef does a fine job of marrying the flavours of Provence with different spices.

▶ *Return to the La Madeleine junction.*

This is the **Haute Corniche★★★**, the most outstanding section of the drive, offering views of the gorge from a series of viewpoints in quick succession.

Belvédère de la Madeleine★

From here there is an imposing view of the Madeleine "fortress" a rocky outcrop blocking the view of the rest of the gorge downstream. These are the highest cliffs of the entire gorge.
🚶From the parking area, a stony footpath leads through dense vegetation to the Belvédère de la Cathédrale (*see below*).

Grotte de la Madeleine★ Kids
🕐*Open Jul–Aug 9am–7pm; Mar–Jun and Sept 10am–6pm; Oct 10am–5pm.* ⚏*7.50€ (children: 4.50€). ☎04 75 04 22 20. www.grottemadeleine.com.*
This cave was carved by an underground river which once drained part of the Gras plateau. Enter through the Grotte Obscure, then follow a tunnel hewn out of the rock (*steep stairway*) which leads to the Salle du Chaos, a vast chamber divided into two by columns coming down from the cave roof.

La Haute Corniche

J. Damase/MICHELIN

Belvédère de la Cathédrale★★

This look-out point gives an unparalleled view of one of the most fascinating natural sights along the gorge: an immense jagged rock known as the "Cathedral," whose rocky spires rise sheer above the river.

Balcon des Templiers

From the "Templars' Balcony" there are striking views of a tight loop in the river, cut deep into the magnificent surrounding rock walls.

Belvédère de la Maladrerie

From here there is a good view of the "Cathedral" rock upstream.

Belvédère de la Coutelle

This viewpoint overlooks the Ardèche. To the right is the end of the Garn ramparts; to the left, along the axis of the gorge, are the Castelviel rocks.

Grotte de St-Marcel★

Guided tours (1hr): Jul–Aug 10am–7pm; mid-Mar–Jun and Sept 10am–6pm; Oct–mid Nov 10am–5pm. 8€ (Children 4.50€). English tours Mon, Tue, 10.30am. 04 75 04 38 07.

A tunnel dug through the rock leads into chambers and passageways lined with stalagmites and stalactites.

Belvédère du Colombier★

From here, there is a view over a meander enclosed by walls of rock. The road follows a loop along a dry valley, skirts the Dona Vierna promontory and makes a long detour along the Louby Valley.

Belvédère du Ranc-Pointu★★

This viewpoint at the mouth of the Louby Valley overlooks the last meander of the Ardèche.

From here the landscape changes dramatically on the way down to St-Martin: the bare defile gives way to a cultivated valley which opens out as it gets nearer the Rhône. On the opposite bank, the village of **Aiguèze** (see below) can be seen clinging to a rocky crest.

St-Martin-d'Ardèche

This is the first settlement since Vallon and a haunt of anglers, walkers and canoeists.

▸ Cross the river via the narrow suspension bridge then turn left onto D 901 and right again onto D 180.

Aiguèze

This medieval village crowns the last clifftops along the gorge.

The 14C fort has a watch-path which offers **views**★ of the mouth of the gorge, with Mont Ventoux in the distance and the suspension bridge linking Aiguèze to St-Martin-d'Ardèche in the foreground.

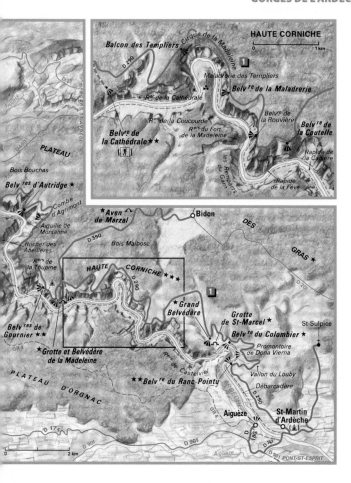

2 Plateau d'Orgnac

45km/28mi itinerary starting from Aven d'Orgnac. 🕐 *see Aven d'ORGNAC.*

Following the Ardèche Gorges★★★

By boat or canoe

After a long, calm stretch, the river flows into a bend and enters the gorge. The impressive Rapide du Charlemagne comes just before the natural arch of Pont-d'Arc. After passing the Saleyron cliffs, the river forms rapids before reaching the Gaud meander and cirque. Rapids alternate with smooth-flowing stretches beneath impressive cliffs. After negotiating the boulders of the Toupine de Gournier, the Rocher de la Cathédrale looms into sight in the distance. Just before you actually pass this rock, the river takes you past a natural opening into La Madeleine cave.

Downriver from the strange-looking Coucourde rock (Provençal for "crane") and the Castelvieil cliff, the opening of St-Marcel cave appears on the left and, as you round a bend, the Dona Vierna promontory and the Belvédère du Ranc-Pointu can be seen. The cliffs melt away as the valley finally widens out, overlooked by the tower of Aiguèze on the edge of the rocky outcrop to the right.

On foot

Two-day walking tour with an overnight stop at the Gournier bivouac (booking essential). A chance to spot the rare Bonelli's eagle who reigns supreme over the gorge.

AUBENAS

POPULATION 11,018
MICHELIN MAP 331: I-6

Aubenas stands in an impressive **setting**★, perched on a spur of rock overlooking the Ardèche. The roads hugging the Coiron cliffs to the east reveal a wonderful **view** of the valley below. Aubenas is known for its candied chestnuts and jam.

- **Information:** 4 blvd Gambetta, 07200 ☎04 75 89 02 03. www.aubenas.fr.
- ▶ **Orient Yourself:** Aubenas is 40km/25mi west of Montélimar.
- 🅿 **Parking:** There are numerous car parks in the centre of town.
- 🕓 **Organising Your Time:** Allow half a day for a relaxed stroll around town.
- 👶 **Also See:** MONTÉLIMAR.

A Bit of History

Following the bitter winter of 1669–70 which killed all the local olive trees, rumours of new taxes fuelled deep-seated dissatisfaction. On 30 April 1670 a farm inspector was stoned in Aubenas; the ringleader of the attackers was thrown into prison, but the rioters, led by a country squire from La Chapelle-sous-Aubenas, **Antoine du Roure**, effected his release the very next day. While the governor of Languedoc played for time by holding negotiations, Roure's men captured Aubenas. Towards the end of July, the rebels fought the royal army at Lavilledieu. The peasants were massacred, and Roure was subsequently executed in Montpellier. Aubenas and La Chapelle were condemned to pay heavy fines as a reflection of royal wrath.

Sights

Château

👀Guided tours (1hr 30min) Jul–Aug 11am, 2pm, 3pm, 4pm and 5pm; Jun and Sept Tue–Sat, 10.30am, 2.30pm; Oct–May Tue, Thu, Fri and Sat, 2pm. 🚫Closed public holidays. 💶5€. ☎04 75 87 81 11. www.aubenas.fr.
The oldest parts of this fine building date from the 12C. The castle was enlarged by a succession of families.

Dôme St-Benoît

♿🕓Open Jul–Aug: guided tours at 5pm from Tourist Office. ☎04 75 87 81 11.

This hexagonal building is the former Benedictine chapel of Aubenas (17C–18C).

Old houses

The 16C "House of Gargoyles" stands opposite the château; its tall polygonal turret is decorated with magnificent gargoyles. There is a charming 16C staircase-turret in the courtyard of the "Maison de Castrevieille" on place Parmentier; handsome town houses line rue Jourdan.

Excursion

Jastres Panorama★

7.5km/4.5mi SE via N 102. 4km/2.5mi beyond the bridge spanning the Ardèche, turn left on the access road to an industrial estate. After 200m/220yd, turn right onto a tarred road. After 1km/0.6mi turn left on a rocky uphill road. Park at the top.
🚶The edge of the plateau was the site of a prehistoric settlement. Where the road ends, the view encompasses the entire Lower Ardèche, the Aubenas valley, and the Coiron range to the north-east.

Driving Tours

Défilés de l'Ardèche★

44km/27mi

- ▶ Take D 104 from Aubenas to St-Étienne-de-Fontbellon, then turn left onto D 579.

Address Book

🕯 *For coin ranges, see the legend on the cover flap.*

WHERE TO STAY

🍽 **Hôtel Ibis** – *Rte de Montélimar.* ☎*04 75 35 44 45.* 🅿. *43 rms.* ⊟*6€.* *Restaurant* 🍽. On the edge of town going towards Montélimar, this chain hotel holds no surprises: modern, clean rooms. The dining room bay windows look out over the pool.

🍽 **Camping Le Chamadou** – Mas de Chaussy, *07120 Balazuc, 3.5km/2.1mi E of Balazuc.* ☎*04 75 37 00 56. www.camping-le-chamadou.com. Open Apr–15 Sept. Reservations advised in summer. 86 sites. Food service.* This little spot in the countryside is very well maintained, the only thing that's missing is a bit of shade. Simple comfort; pool, mini-golf, fishing pond and bungalows.

🍽 **Chambre d'hôte Le Mas de Mazan** – *07200 Mercuer, 5km/3mi NW of Aubenas via D 104 and D 435.* ☎*04 75 35 41 88. http://perso.orange.fr/masde mazan.* 🚭. *5 rms.* This couple welcomes guests to their farm with warmth and enthusiasm. Delighted to share their passion for the region and open the doors of their typically Cévenole farm to visitors, they'll make sure your stay in the area is a memorable one. Simple decor and congenial ambience.

WHERE TO EAT

🍽 **Le Fournil** – *34 r. du 4-Septembre.* ☎*04 75 93 58 68. Closed Feb, Nov and Christmas school holidays, 22 Jun–9 Jul, Sun and Mon.* This old house welcomes diners onto its patio when the weather is good. There or in the dining room, you'll be able to choose between several appetizing fixed-price menus that highlight regional specialities.

The light-filled Ardèche valley forms a wide dip stretching to the basin of the Lower Chassezac in the west. The river flows through fertile basins. Here the road runs close to the river, in between orchards and vineyards.

Vogüé

The village of ancient, arch-spanned streets dominated by a castle is built against a cliff overlooking the Ardèche. The vast 16C **château** (🕐 *open mid-Jun–mid Sept daily 10.30am–6.30pm; Apr–mid Jun Thu–Sun and public holidays 2pm–6pm; mid-Sept–Oct Sat–Sun and public holidays 2pm–6pm;* ⊟*4€;* ☎*04 75 37 01 95; www.chateaudevogue.net*), which still belongs to the Vogüé family, replaced the original medieval fortress and now houses exhibitions on the Vivarais region.

▶ *Head back S to D 1, then D 401 on the left to Rochecolombe.*

Rochecolombe★

The medieval village of Rochecolombe occupies a secluded **site**★ overlooking a stream rising from a limestone corrie. There are in fact two villages of Rochecolombe: the upper one is the first one, reached by road, with houses clustered around a church. From the square in the upper village, turn left onto a road down to a bridge across the stream.

▶ *Park a little further along, just before a bend, and follow the footpath down to the water's edge.*

On the right stands the **medieval village**, at the foot of the ruins of a square tower and the bell-tower of a Romanesque chapel. At the bottom of the corrie, enclosed by limestone cliffs with

Vogüé

J. Damase/MICHELIN

wild scrub clinging to their ledges, are two **Vauclusian springs.**

▶ *Return towards Vogüé on D 579; left on D 114 after crossing the Ardèche.*

In Lanas, the road crosses the river by a narrow bridge, offering a view of the Auzon confluence with the Ardèche.

▶ *In St-Maurice-d'Ardèche turn right onto D 579, then right onto D 294 just after the station in Balazuc.*

Balazuc★

This once-fortified village is perched above a secluded gorge. Cross the bridge to the opposite bank for a good view of the village, and the remains of its watchtowers.

▶ *During the summer season, leave the car in the car park before entering the village.*

Like many villages in the Lower Vivarais area, Balazuc was founded by a Saracen colony in the 8C and 9C. It now makes a pleasant place for a stroll, particularly in the old streets up to the castle.
🚶For a pleasant walk downstream along the banks of the Ardèche, take the dirt track to the left of the bridge at the foot of the village. Here the river flows through a narrow passage between walls of rock.

▶ *Take D 104 to Uzer; on reaching Bellevue, follow D 4 to Ruoms.*

The entrance to the Ligne gorge is marked by a narrow rocky passage. A beautiful **view** unfolds upstream of the Ardèche at the confluence of the two rivers. The Ligne gorge is followed by the **Défilé de Ruoms★**, alongside which the road passes through picturesque tunnels in the rock.

▶ *Take the bridge on the left to Ruoms.*

Ruoms

The walled centre of this town lies within a quadrilateral of ramparts flanked by seven round towers.

▶ *Leave Ruoms on D 579, heading towards Vallon. On the right bank of the Ardèche, take a winding road making its way up the mountain.*

Rocher de Sampzon

🚶Leave the car in the car park down from the church of Sampzon and go to the summit on the tarmac road, then on the path level with the platform.
From the top, the **panorama**★★ encompasses the Vallon basin, the Orgnac plateau and the River Ardèche.

Labeaume

West of Ruoms *(D 245)* lies Labeaume, at the edge of a gorge with arcaded streets and galleried houses.

Gorges de La Beaume★

The walk along the left bank of the river is most pleasant, offering pretty views of the shimmering waters and the sculpted limestone cliffs.

Montagne and Haute Vallée de l'Ardèche★

▶ *Leave Aubenas N along D 104, which becomes the N 102. Take the D 578.*

Vals-les-Bains♨♨

www.vals-les-bains.com.
This spa resort lies at the bottom of the deeply-encased Volane valley. About 145 springs rise here and many of these have been exploited since 1600 though the town only became popular as a spa resort in the mid-19C.
The waters here are cold (13°C/55°F) and rich in sodium bicarbonate. Mainly used for drinking (several million bottles are exported from Vals each year) it has a settling effect on the stomach and at the same time a stimulating effect on the liver.
The waters are recommended for treating diabetes and nutrient deficiencies and may be taken in showers, baths and massages as well as taken orally.

Intermittent Spring

This spring gushes from the middle of the park at the southern end of town. It rises to a height of 8m/26ft every six hours (*11.30am, 5.30pm in summer, 10.30am, 4.30pm in winter*).

Rocher des Combes

2km/1.2mi E via a road alongside the hospital – 15min on foot there and back.

From the viewing table there is a good view over the surrounding mountains.

▶ *Return to the N 102 and follow the upper Ardèche valley to Pont-de-Labeaume; turn right onto D 536 towards Montpezat-sous-Bauzon.*

Parc naturel regional des Monts d'Ardèche

La Prade, BP 3, 07560 Montpezat-sous-Bauzon ☎ 04 75 94 35 20. www.parc-monts-ardeche.fr.

Founded on the initiative of local chestnut growers, this nature park comprises 132 municipalities committed to the protection of the natural and cultural heritage of the Monts d'Ardèche.

Montpezat-sous-Bauzon

The old village has given its name to an electrical complex set up in 1954, consisting of several dams designed to collect the waters coming from the upper Loire Valley and its tributaries.

Église Notre-Dame-de-Prévenchère

The interior of this 12C–13C church is characterised by four short naves featuring Romanesque or Gothic vaulting. Driving back towards Montpezat, you encounter the **town** with its narrow main street flanked by old granite houses built in the mountain style: curved façades, with low porches resting on round arches.

▶ *Take D 536 for Suc de Bauzon until you reach D 110. Turn left to go to St-Cirgues-en-Montagne. Then take D 239 S heading towards Mazan-l'Abbaye.*

Mazan-l'Abbaye★

In a clearing of Mazan Forest, this 12C abbey was the first Cistercian sanctuary built in the province of Languedoc.

Forêt de Mazan★

Small waterfalls, moss-covered rocks and wild blueberries and raspberries provide a charming backdrop to a walk through the lush undergrowth.

▶ *Continue along D 239, which leads to Col de la Chavade and the start of the Ardèche Valley.*

Col de la Chavade

This pass marks the watershed between the Atlantic Ocean and the Mediterranean. N 102 between Le Puy and Viviers follows the traditional route from the Velay area to the Rhône valley. Just over a mile beyond the pass, the road crosses the Ardèche. This hilly drive offers beautiful views down the valley.

The harshness of this valley is softened by a few sunny orchards surrounding the villages, by rambling plants on house fronts and retaining walls, and by humpback bridges used by travellers in the Middle Ages. Adding to the interest of the drive, the road passes the ruins of feudal castles: **Château des Montlaur** upstream from Mayres, the tall round tower of **Château de Chadenac** downstream of Mayres.

Thueyts★

This small town surrounded by orchards lies on a basalt flow, the remains of an ancient volcanic eruption. A **way-marked footpath**★ (*1hr 30min return; follow the red arrows*) leads along the edge of the lava flow.

Pont de Neyrac

J. Damase/MICHELIN

Just upstream from the Pont du Diable, the Ardèche flows through a narrow gorge, making an interesting **scene**★ against the dark backdrop of the basalt cliffs. Two sets of steps – the **Échelle du Roi** *(narrow, steep and slippery)* and the **Échelle de la Reine** *(easier, allow an extra 30min return)* – lead up to the top of the basalt cliffs, affording pretty views of the river valley.

Neyrac-les-Bains ☩
This small spa town backs onto the slopes of the Soulhiol volcano. In the Middle Ages its bicarbonated hot springs were thought to cure leprosy.

▶ *At the exit of Pont-de-Labeaume turn left following signs to Notre-Dame de Niègles; the road drops into a valley before reaching a plateau. Park the car down on the right.*

Notre-Dame de Niègles
The church stands on a hill overlooking the river. Little remains of the original 10C building.
The road back to Pont-de-Labeaume commands pleasant views of the medieval fortress of Ventadour.

Château de Ventadour
🕐*Open Jul–Sept guided tours (45min) 9am–noon, 2pm–7pm, Sat–Sun 3pm–7pm.* ⊗3€. ☎04 75 38 00 92. www. chateau.ventadour.free.fr.
Partly demolished and abandoned, this imposing medieval fortress would have eventually disappeared without the valiant efforts of Pierre Pottier and his wife, who since 1969, have undertaken to restore it.

Village of Ucel

▶ *N 102 and then D 104 lead back to Aubenas.*

Vallée de la Volane and Vallée de la Bourges★★

A round trip of 69km/43mi makes the most of the countryside surrounding Vals-les-Bains, taking in the hill village of **Antraigues-sur-Volane** which focuses on a shaded square popular with *boules* players.
Most of the villages through these valleys offer fine views both of mountains and valleys. **Mézilhac** is a case in point standing on the sill between the Eyrieux and Ardèche valleys, from where there is a **view**★ to the Gerbier de Jonc peak and the Mézenc range. On the way to Burzet, a stop to admire the **Cascade du Ray-Pic**★★ is justified. 🚶A path leads to the foot of these falls, where the river gushes between overhanging walls of basalt in an austere landscape at the bottom of a ravine.
Burzet is renowned for its annual procession to a calvary overlooking the village. The return to Vals-les-Bains via St-Pierre-de-Colombier, Juvinas and D 243, takes a pretty little road through the Bézorges valley.

Col de l'Escrinet★

The **Col de L'Escrinet** provides access to both the south of Ardèche and the Plateau du Coiron. A round tour of 85km/53mi from Vals-les-Bains visits the ancient village of **Ucel** built in a circle on a hilltop overlooking the River Ardèche. The **Château de Boulogne**★ was originally a fortress, on a spur between two ravines, but was transformed over the centuries into a sumptuous residence. Pourchères is typical of many villages here, which focus on their church. Here it dates from the 12C and is built on a slope. The highest summit on the plateau is the **Crête de Blandine** on the way to Freysenet, although it is somewhat marred by the presence of a television transmitter. There is an agreeable return route from the Col de l'Escrinet via St-Private and Ucel.

AURILLAC★

POPULATION 30,551

MICHELIN MAP 330: C-5 – LOCAL MAP SEE MONTS DU CANTAL

Aurillac, the business and tourist capital of Upper Auvergne, is a modern town that has sprung up around an old neighbourhood with narrow, winding streets.

- **Information:** 7 due des Carmes, 15000 AURILLAC. ☎04 71 48 46 58. www.iaurillac.com.
- **Orient Yourself:** At the southern edge of Cantal, Aurillac is directly SW from Clermont-Ferrand.
- **Parking:** There are numerous parking places in the centre of town.
- **Don't Miss:** A tour of the old town; plan from tourist office.
- **Organising Your Time:** Allow half a day for a tour of the old town, or a full day if you want the bigger picture.
- **Also See:** ST-FLOUR.

A Bit of History

Gerbert, the first French Pope (10C–11C) – Aurillac's Gallo-Roman origins were brought to light by the discovery of a 1C temple (Rue Jacques-Prévert, reached from avenue Milhaud). In the 9C St Gerald, Count of Auvergne, built an abbey, laying the foundations for the city's future prosperity; this abbey gave Christianity its first French Pope. Gerbert, a shepherd from the Aurillac area, attracted the attention of the monks of St-Géraud, who quickly taught this unusually bright student everything they knew. After completing his studies at the abbey, Gerbert left for Spain where he studied medicine and mathematics at the Moorish universities. He built the first pendulum clock, invented an astrolabe for sailors and improved the church organ. In AD 999 he became Pope under the name Sylvester II. He was the "Pope of the Millennium," who managed to impose the "Truce of God" – whereby hostilities were suspended on certain days and during certain seasons – on the feudal classes.

Gold-washers – According to Gerbert's contemporaries, his knowledge smacked of witchcraft. The gold flakes found in the River Jordanne were popularly ascribed to his spells.

Aurillac

J. Damase/MICHELIN

Address Book

For coin ranges, see the legend on the cover flap.

WHERE TO STAY

Chambre d'hôte de Barathe – Barathe, 15130 Giou-de-Mamou, 7km/ 4.2mi E of Aurillac via N 122 and D 58. ☎04 71 64 61 72. 🗶. *Reservations required.* 5 rms. The windows of this fine old house built in 1777 open onto a superb landscape and the irresistible sound of cowbells tinkling in the distance.

Grand Hôtel de Bordeaux – 2 av. de la République. ☎04 71 48 01 84. 32 rms. 🗶10€. On a corner of place du Square, this elegant, early 20C hotel has a glass awning above the entrance.

WHERE TO EAT

A QUICK BITE

Le Bouchon Fromager – 3 pl. du Buis. ☎04 71 48 07 80. Mon–Sat noon–2pm, 7pm–11pm. 🗶. Both wine bar and cheese restaurant, this inviting, rustic eatery is often packed with patrons enjoying a fine wine served by the glass and the delicious cuisine of the Cantal.

A LEISURELY MEAL

Poivre et Sel – 4 r. du 14-Juillet. ☎04 71 64 20 20. Mon–Sat noon-2.30pm, 7pm–11pm. Closed 2 wks in Feb and 1 wk in Nov. *Reservations recommended.* Hesitating between local fare and traditional French cuisine? This small restaurant can satisfy every whim thanks to well-prepared dishes made from fresh ingredients.

La Reine Margot – 19 r. G.-de-Veyre. ☎04 71 48 26 46. Closed Sat and Sun lunch, Sun and Mon evening. A restaurant in a small street downtown. The main, 1950s-style dining room is decorated with painted woodwork illustrating the life of Queen Margot.

La Belle Époque – 15130 Sansac-de-Marmiesse, 7km/4.2mi W of Aurillac via N122 and D153. ☎04 71 62 87 87. Daily Apr–Oct. A restaurant set in an old, secluded house in the countryside. The smart interior design features murals depicting the 1920s, fine furniture and nicely set tables.

SHOPPING

Distillerie Louis-Couderc – 14 r. Victor-Hugo. ☎04 71 48 01 50. www.distillerie-couderc.com. Tue–Sat 9am–noon, 2pm–7pm. Closed public holidays. Founded in 1908, the Couderc distillery sells a wide variety of regional products made from gentian root, chestnut cream and berries.

Parapluies Piganiol – 28 r. des Forgerons. ☎04 71 43 05 51. Tue–Sat 9am–noon, 2pm–7pm, Mon 2pm–7pm in Aug and Dec. Closed public holidays. Piganiol have been manufacturing umbrellas in Aurillac since 1884.

La Poterie du Don – Le Don, 15120 Montsalvy, 9km/5.4mi SW of Montsalvy via D 19 and D 119. ☎04 71 49 95 65. 9am–noon, 2pm–6.30pm except Oct–Mar, closed Sat except holidays. Nigel and Suzy Atkins, potters who specialise in salt-glazed stoneware, create utilitarian and decorative pieces that are all the rage.

The gold industry was born, but remained fairly primitive: flakes of gold were collected by holding a fleece in the water to trap them.

Baron des Adrets (16C) – The people of Aurillac remained at odds with their lord, the abbot, but eventually managed to obtain administrative autonomy, as the consuls' residence (Maison Consulaire) proves.

The town was flourishing when it became involved in the Wars of Religion. In 1561 the governor ordered the slaughter of the large local Protestant population. They were avenged eight years later by the Baron des Adrets, a Protestant leader notorious for his brutality. His men began by swooping down on the monasteries on the outskirts of the town, burning or flaying the monks alive. On the night of 6 September 1569 the Huguenots blew up the town gate and burst their way in on the slumbering citizens, who were caught unawares and so put up minimal resistance.

From lace to umbrellas – Aubenas was struggling to recover from these events for many years until Colbert founded a laceworks which doubled as a gold and silver smithy. This entrepreneur also encouraged other industries, such as boiler-making and tanning, which have since declined.

Modern Aurillac's economy is based on agriculture and the manufacture of furniture, cheese, plastics and umbrellas.

Walking Tour

Old Town

Place St-Géraud (D)
The Romanesque façade with arcades and colonettes opposite the church entrance probably belonged to a pilgrims' hospice. The colonial house on the left dates from the late 15C.

Église St-Géraud
This old abbey church was founded in the late 9C by Count Gerald and became a stopover for pilgrims on their way to Santiago de Compostela.

▶ *Walk down rue du Monastère and rue des Forgerons and turn right onto rue Victor-Hugo.*

On reaching the 19C Hôtel de Ville, follow rue Vermenouze to place d'Aurinques. The **Chapelle d'Aurinques,** built at the end of the 16C in a tower in the city wall, was completed in the 19C.

▶ *Follow rue de la Coste.*

No 7 in rue de Noailles, on the right, has a **Renaissance courtyard (B)** *(access through cours de Noailles).*

▶ *Return to rue de la Coste.*

4 rue du Consulat has a staircase tower.

Maison Consulaire
This Renaissance building has been restored and turned into an exhibition hall. Note the sculptures adorning the door on rue de la Coste.

▶ *Continue to place Gerbert and the* **Musée de Cire** (history of Aurillac).

View of the Jordanne
The old houses along the River Jordanne can be seen from a spot near Pont Rouge (Red Bridge) and Cours d'Angoulême.

Volcanic Landscape

Château St-Étienne
The castle keep dates from the 13C; the rest of the buildings date mostly from the late 19C. The upper terrace offers a magnificent view of the Jordanne Valley and the Cantal mountains.

Musée des Volcans★   Kids
Open Jan–mid-Jun and mid-Sept–end Dec Tue–Sat 2pm–6pm; mid-Jun–mid Sept Mon–Sat 10am–6.30pm (Sun 2pm–6pm). Closed Easter Mon, 1 May, 14 Jul, 11 Nov, 22 to 25 Dec, 29 Dec–1 Jan. 4€ (under-18s no charge). 04 71 48 07 00.
The Volcano Museum includes four large rooms offering interactive models, multimedia terminals and video films to explain volcanic phenomena.

Carmes District

Place du Square
South of the old town, the Carmes district, with its large shaded park, is a haven of peace and quiet.

Palais de Justice (J)
Open daily except Sat–Sun 8.30am–noon, 1.30pm–5pm. Closed public holidays. No charge. 04 71 45 59 59.
The Assizes Chamber in the law courts contains three 17C Flemish tapestries.

Église Notre-Dame-des-Neiges or Notre-Dame-des-Cordeliers
Open daily except Sat–Sun.
This chapel, once part of a 14C Franciscan monastery, was rebuilt in the 17C. A chapel on the left contains a widely revered **Black Virgin** from the 18C.

Jardin des Carmes
Once part of a monastery, this pleasant garden gives access to an arts centre.

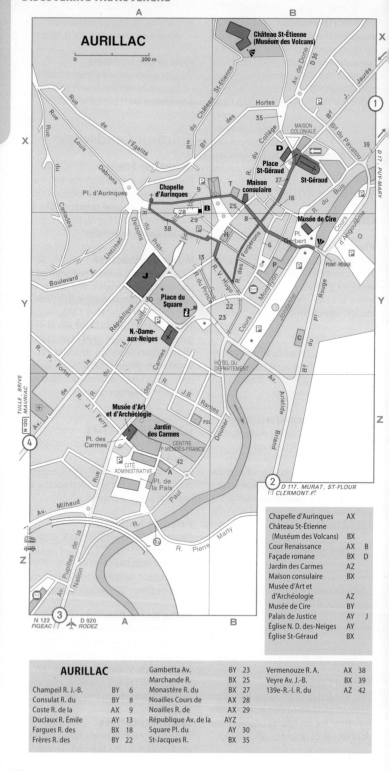

AURILLAC

0 —— 200 m

Chapelle d'Aurinques	AX	
Château St-Étienne		
(Muséum des Volcans)	BX	
Cour Renaissance	AX	B
Façade romane	BX	D
Jardin des Carmes	AZ	
Maison consulaire	BX	
Musée d'Art et		
d'Archéologie	AZ	
Musée de Cire	BY	
Palais de Justice	AY	J
Église N. D. des-Neiges	AY	
Église St-Géraud	BX	

AURILLAC

			Gambetta Av.	BY	23	Vermenouze R. A.	AX	38
			Marchande R.	BX	25	Veyre Av. J.-B.	BX	39
Champeil R. J.-B.	BY	6	Monastère R. du	BX	27	139e-R.-I. R. du	AZ	42
Consulat R. du	BY	8	Noailles Cours de	AX	28			
Coste R. de la	AX	9	Noailles R. de	AX	29			
Duclaux R. Émile	AY	13	République Av. de la	AYZ				
Fargues R. des	BX	18	Square Pl. du	AY	30			
Frères R. des	BY	22	St-Jacques R.	BX	35			

Musée d'Art et d'Archéologie

Centre Pierre Mendès France,
37 rue des carmes.

&🕐*Open Feb–Oct daily except Sun and Mon 10am–noon, 2pm–6pm (Jul and Aug daily 10am–noon, 2pm–6pm, Sun 2pm–6pm). 🕐Closed public holidays and 25 May.* ✑2.50€. ☎04 71 45 46 10.
The Art and Archaeology Museum is housed in the former Visitandines Convent (17C) which, after the Revolution, was used as a stud farm before being recently turned into an arts centre.

Les Écuries

&🕐*Open daily except Sun 1.30pm–6.30pm (last admission 6pm).* ☎04 71 45 46 08.
A museum annexe in the former stables houses contemporary art exhibitions (painting, sculpture and photography).

Driving Tours

The Cère to the Maronne

100km/62mi – allow one day
Nearby dams, rivers and gorges.

▶ *Leave Aurillac on N 122 heading towards Figeac.*

Sansac-de-Marmiesse

A restored barn on the outskirts of the village houses the town hall and the **Maison du Bâtiy** (🕐*daily except Sat–Sun and public holidays: 10am–noon, 2pm–5pm;* ✑*no charge;* ☎04 71 47 74 75), a local museum illustrating the 13 different areas which make up the Cantal region with their specific types of rural housing and traditions.

▶ *Continue along N 122 then turn right onto D 64 to Viescamp and on to the dam on the River Cère.*

Barrage de St-Étienne-Cantalès★

An imposing dam resembling a vault contains the waters of the River Cère. The view is enhanced by the charming sight of small islets, peninsulas and jagged coastlines.

▶ *D 207, then D 7 lead to Laroquebrou, a pretty village on the banks of the Cère.*

Laroquebrou

Small municipality located at the entrance to the Cère gorges, dominated by an isolated outcrop bearing a statue of the Virgin Mary and the ruins of the **castle** (🕐*open mid-Jul–mid Aug 10am–noon, 3pm–7pm;* 🕐*closed 1st Sun in Aug.* ✑2€; ☎04 71 46 07 97), once home to the Lords of Montal.

▶ *Follow D 653 that cuts across N 120 at Pont d'Orgon, then take D 2 for 15km/9mi. Turn right onto D 302 and continue until you reach the Enchanet dam spanning the Maronne, a tributary of the Dordogne.*

Barrage d'Enchanet★

Its elegant silhouette is set against the backdrop of the Maronne gorges. D 61 offers a good overall view of the dam and its peaceful waters.

▶ *D 442 leads to St-Santin-Cantalès. Continue on D 52 and go back to Aurillac via St-Victor.*

Chestnut Grove Country

100km/62mi
This round tour through "La Châtaigneraie Cantalienne" offers an interesting insight into local chestnut land, with long plateaux, luxuriant valleys and typical architecture.

▶ *South of Aurillac, drive through Arpajon-sur-Cère and onto D 6 (2km/1.2mi).*

Arpajon-sur-Cère, Arboretum   [Kids]

🕐*8am–8pm.* ✑*No charge.* ☎04 71 43 27 72.
Enjoy a pleasant stroll through gardens of different styles including the Devil's garden, the pond, the maple grove, the oak grove… *Guided tours in summer (including tasting), themed weekends in spring and autumn.*

▶ *Return to Arpajon-sur-Cère, turn right onto D 58, which leads to Conros.*

Château de Conros

🕐*Open Jul–Aug: 2pm–6pm.* ✑6€. ☎04 71 63 50 27. www.chateau-conros.com.

Château de Conros

On a spur of rock high above a meander of the River Cère stands the massive medieval keep that once belonged to the Astorgs, lords of Aurillac. Over the centuries it has been transformed into a majestic residence.

▸ *Continue along D 58 to the intersection with D 17, turn left and drive 12km/7.5mi; D 66 leads to Marcolès (3km/1.9mi).*

Marcolès

In this restored medieval city, characteristic narrow lanes stem from rue Longue closed off by an elegant 15C **porch**. West of the village, D 64 leads to the **Rochers de Faulat** (1.5km/0.9mi) where several megaliths stand on a mound planted with oak trees.

▸ *Take D 64, then D 17 and follow the banks of the River Rance.*

Entraygues

Small village featuring a château typical of the area with its pepper-pot roofs.

▸ *Go on driving until you reach Maurs.*

Maurs

Maurs is situated to the south-west of the mountains in Cantal on a hill beside the River Rance, and is the main town in the **La Châtaigneraie** area. The granite plateau is almost entirely covered with undulating moorland and gashed by green valleys where most of the local population lives.

In Maurs, which still has the circular layout dating back to the days when it was a fortress, there is a definite air of Southern France; this is the start of the "Cantal Riviera" with its flowers and vineyards, thus explaining why Maurs has been dubbed the "Nice of Cantal." The **Benedictine abbey** in Maurs, founded in the 10C, no doubt gave rise to the development of the village.

By the late Middle Ages, Maurs had become one of the six "good towns" in Upper Auvergne and the seat of a provostship. It suffered during the Wars of Religion: captured and recaptured by the Huguenots in 1568 and 1583, it was pillaged and ransacked; in 1643 peasant rebels from the Rouergue sought refuge here and the King's troops were forced to intervene.

The **church** (*Guided tours available, ask at the tourist office; ☎04 71 46 73 72*), dating from the 14C, is preceded by a carved doorway (15C-16C); inside there is a nave but no side aisles as in most churches in southern France.

▸ *Follow D 663 towards Decazeville then D 28 to Mourjou.*

Mourjou _{Kids}

The convivial **Maison de la Châtaigne** (♿🕐 *open Jun–Aug daily except Sat 2pm–6pm (Jul–Aug 10.30am); Apr–May public holidays 2pm–6pm; ⊝5€ (children 2.50€); ☎04 71 49 98 00; www.mourjou.com*) retraces the use of chestnuts through the ages.

▸ *Follow D 28 to Calvinet, then take D 19 and drive 15km/9mi to Montsalvy.*

Montsalvy

Nestling on the Plateau de la Châtaigneraie, this once fortified town has kept several of its original gates. The church features a Romanesque nave, Gothic vaulting (15C), and a 15C **wooden Christ.** Near the church stand the **ruins** of the former abbey: the cloisters, the chapter-house, and the 14C refectory which has now been restored.

▸ *Come back to Aurillac on D 920.*

BEAUJOLAIS★★

MICHELIN MAP 327 : F-2/4/4, G-2/3/4, H-2/3/4

According to an old French saying, Lyon is fed by three rivers, the Rhône, the Saône and… the Beaujolais. It is true that the Beaujolais is renowned both within and beyond French borders largely as a wine-growing region, but although this industry makes a substantial contribution to local economy, it is by no means the region's only source of income.

▶ **Orient Yourself:** The Beaujolais region lies northwest of Lyon and west of the Saone, roughly between Villefrance and Macon.
◉ **Don't Miss:** The 15C Chateau de Corcelles, built to defend the Burgundy border.
◉ **Organising Your Time:** Visit Villefranche-sur-Saône first, but allow two days to tour the region.
◉ **Also see:** La DOMBES, LYON, Le MONT-DORE.

A Bit of History

Beaujolais owes its name to the aristocratic **Beaujeu** family, at the height of their power from the 9C to the 11C. In 1400, Édouard de Beaujeu gave his estate to the House of Bourbon-Montpensier, one of whose members, Pierre de Bourbon, married Louis XI's daughter. The Beaujolais passed briefly into the hands of the Crown under François I, who confiscated it among other territories from the Connétable de Bourbon as punishment for his negative attitude towards his monarch, but by 1560, the Bourbon-Montpensiers had been reinstated as landlords. Anne-Marie-Louise d'Orléans, Duchesse de Montpensier, who was known as **"La Grande Mademoiselle"** (renowned for her love affairs and active support of the Roman Catholic Fronde movement), bequeathed the Beaujolais to the House of Orléans, who remained its owners until the Revolution.

A Bit of Geography

The Beaujolais is a mountain range which stretches between the Loire and Rhône valleys, on the line where the Atlantic and Mediterranean watersheds meet. The Beaujolais is best described as hilly, rather than mountainous. Its distinguishing features are numerous mountain plateaux crisscrossed by narrow sinuous valleys. To the east the land drops sharply to the Saône, whereas to

Village of Theizé in the Beaujolais

©Olivier Lebrat/istockphoto.com

the west it slopes gently away. The cliffs formed by the subsidence of the Saône river bed are home to the vineyards of the "Côte Beaujolaise," whereas the rest of the region forms "La Montagne."

La Montagne – a region of picturesque hills, valleys, and landscapes as varied as they are appealing. The upper slopes of the mountains are carpeted with broom and pines; lower down there are stands of oak separated by wide clearings.

Beaujolais Wine

Beaujolais vineyards and the wine they produce have secured the region's reputation far beyond the borders of France. Unlike most other red wines, Beaujolais is best drunk young, served slightly chilled.

The vine has been cultivated here since Roman times. Today, the vineyards stretch from Mâcon in the north to the Azergues valley in the south. A single grape variety – Gamay – is used to produce the light and fruity red Beaujolais wines with their characters determined by the soil in which the grapes were grown. Beaujolais vineyards are divided into two areas of production.

Coteaux de Beaujolais

North of Villefranche, the soil is granitic and perfect for the Gamay vine. This is the region of **Beaujolais-Villages**: Moulin-à-Vent, Fleurie, Morgon, Chiroubles, Juliénas, Chénas, Côte de Brouilly, Brouilly, St-Amour and Régnié.

Cloisters in Salles

Pays des Pierres Dorées

Between Villefranche and the Azergues valley the soil is composed more of sedimentary rocks which alter the flavour of the wine. The wines here are "Beaujolais" and "Beaujolais Supérieur".

Driving Tours

Beaujolais Vineyards★

1 Villefranche-sur-Saône to St-Amour-Bellevue *98km/61mi – allow 5hr*

The road winds its way through the vineyards, at first climbing the granite escarpments, then dropping down towards the Saône valley.

▶ *Leave Villefranche on D 504, take D 19 on the right, then D 44 on the left.*

Montmelas-St-Sorlin

Drive round to the north of the feudal castle, which was restored in the 19C by Dupasquier, a student of Viollet-le-Duc.

▶ *Carry on from Montmelas as far as Col de St-Bonnet. From the pass, a track leads off to the right to the St-Bonnet beacon.*

Signal de St-Bonnet

From the east end of the chapel there is a view of Montmelas in the foreground, set against the hills and vineyards of the Beaujolais and beyond them the Saône valley.

▶ *From the pass, take D 20 on the right.*

St-Julien

This pretty little wine-growing village is the birthplace of the doctor **Claude Bernard** (1813–78). The **Musée Claude-Bernard** (☉*open daily except Mon and Tue, Apr–Sept 10am–noon, 2pm–6pm (Oct–Feb 5pm);* ☉*closed Mar, 1 Jan 1 May, 25 Dec;* ✆5€; ☎04 74 67 51 44) recalls his work in the field of physiology, in particular on the absorption of fats and sugars by the liver.

Address Book

For coin ranges, see the legend on the cover flap.

WHERE TO STAY

Chambre d'hôte Domaine des Quarante Écus – *Les Vergers, 69430 Lantignié, 4km/2.4mi E of Beaujeu via D 78.* ☎04 74 04 85 80. *5 rms.* This vineyard is named after *arbre aux quarante écus* (the tree of forty coins – Ginkgo biloba) planted in front.

Chambre d'hôte M. et Mme Bonnot – *Le bourg, 69430 Les Ardillats, 5km/3mi NW of Beaujeu via D 37.* ☎04 74 04 80 20. *Closed Jan.* *5 rms. Meals.* A most enjoyable stopover offering delicious meals and an attractive wine cellar dedicated to Beaujolais.

Hôtel Les Vignes – *Rte de St-Amour, 69840 Juliénas.* ☎04 74 04 43 70. *www.hoteldesvignes.com. Closed 7–22 Feb, 21–28 Dec and Sun from Dec–Mar.* ☐. *22 rms.* ☐9€. On the St-Amour road leading out of Juliénas, this house is set in the heart of the Beaujolais.

Chambre d'hôte Domaine de La Grosse Pierre – *69115 Chiroubles.* ☎04 74 69 12 17. *www.chiroubles-passot.com. Closed Dec and Jan. 5 rms.* The perfect address for a total immersion halt in the heart of the Beaujolais region.

WHERE TO EAT

Le Coq à Juliénas – *Pl. du Marché, 69840 Juliénas.* ☎04 74 04 41 98. *www. coq-julienas.com. Closed 22 Dec–22 Jan and Wed.* The cock is the king of wine country - or at least of this stylish establishment on the Place de Juliénas.

Christian Mabeau – *69460 Odenas, 15km/9mi NW of Villefranche via D 43.* ☎04 74 03 41 79. *Closed 2–12 Jan, 30 Aug–12 Sept, Sun evening and Mon except public holidays.* Located in the heart of the village of Odenas. Pleasant dining room and fixed-price menus.

SHOPPING

In wine-growing regions such as the Beaujolais, many wine-producers offer tours of their cellars, enabling visitors to discover different vintages through tastings and knowledgeable explanations. Some of these cellars are famous – those of Château de la Chaize (108m/354ft long!), Clochemerle and Villié-Morgon, for example.

La Maison des Beaujolais – *441 avenue de l'Europe, 69220 St-Jean-d'Ardières.* ☎04 74 66 16 46. *www.lamaisondes beaujolais.com. Daily 11am–9pm, summer 'til 10pm. Closed Christmas school holidays.* The sign tells the name of the game: this establishment is dedicated to Beaujolais wines.

Caveau des Beaujolais-villages – *Pl. de l'Hôtel-de-Ville, 69430 Beaujeu.* ☎04 74 04 81 18. *May–Nov 10.30am–1pm, 2pm–7.30pm. Closed 3 wks in Jan.* The handsome bust of Bacchus points the way to this cellar in the lower floor of the Marius-Audin museum.

Moulin à Huile – *29 rue des Écharmeaux, 69430 Beaujeu.* ☎04 74 69 28 06. *Mon–Sat 8.30am–noon, 2.30pm–7pm. Closed 1–8 Jan and public holidays.* The big old millstone of this 19C oil mill still crushes nuts (walnuts, filberts, pine nuts…) and seeds to make the most flavourful virgin oils imaginable. Visits and tastings.

▶ Take D 19 as far as Salles.

Salles-Arbuissonnas-en-Beaujolais

The monks of Cluny founded a **priory** in Salles in the 10C. This was taken over by nuns of the Benedictine Order in the 14C, who ran it until they were replaced by "aristocratic" canonesses in the 18C.

▶ From Salles, take D 35, then D 49E to the right.

Vaux-en-Beaujolais

This wine-growing village and the ribaldry of its wine-tippling inhabitants in the 1920s inspired **Gabriel Chevalier**(1895–1969) to write his satirical novel Clochemerle.

▶ Carry on along D 49E through Le Perréon and then D 62 to Charentay.

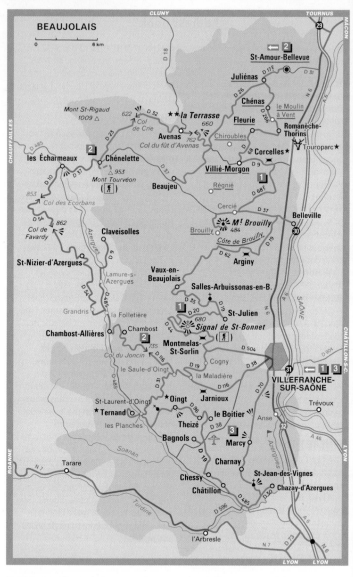

On the map above, the wine-producing area is shown in green – Names of grands crus are underlined in red.

The unusual shape of the Château d'Arginy comes into sight 1km/0.6mi east of Charentay.

Château d'Arginy

All that remains of the castle is the great red-brick tower known as the Tour d'Alchimie: some say it was used by the Knights Templar to hide their treasure.

▶ Follow D 68, turn left onto D 19, then right onto D 37 to Belleville.

Belleville

This old fortified town at the crossroads of communications routes is now a centre of wine-production and industry (manufacture of agricultural machinery).

The **Hôtel-Dieu** (&⃝*guided tours (1hr): Aug–Sept daily except Mon and Tue, 10am–4pm; Apr–Jul and Oct–Nov daily except Sun-Tue, 10am–4pm.* ⃝*closed*

Villié-Morgon vineyards

public holidays. ∞*5€.* ☎*04 74 66 44 67),* built in the 18C to replace the old hospital, was in use for the care of the sick until 1991. Beyond Cercié *(carry on along D 37),* the road skirts Mont Brouilly.

▷ *Those wishing to climb Mont Brouilly should take D 43, turn left onto D 43E, then 100m/110yd further on take the road signposted "La Côte de Brouilly" again to the left.*

Mont Brouilly

Côte de Brouilly, a fruity wine with a fragrant bouquet, comes from the grapes harvested on the sunny slopes of Mont Brouilly.

From the esplanade, there is a marvellous **view**★ of the vineyards, the Beaujolais hills, the Saône valley and the Dombes region.

▷ *Return to Cercié. On leaving the village turn left onto D 68E towards the old village of Corcelles, then continue onto D 9 to the left.*

Château de Corcelles★

♿ ◷ *Open Mar–Nov 10am–noon, 2.30pm–6.30pm; Dec–Feb 10am–noon, 2.30pm–5.30pm.* ◷*Closed Sun and public holidays.* ☎*04 74 66 00 24.*
This fortress was built in the 15C to protect the border between Burgundy and Beaujolais. Above the entrance to the keep is the family coat of arms of Madeleine de Ragny. The inner court-

yard is surrounded by Renaissance arcades and contains a fountain with an ornate piece of 15C wrought-iron work on top.

▷ *Rejoin D 9 to the right.*

The road goes through vineyards of famous *grands crus* of the Beaujolais.

Villié-Morgon

Unusually for Beaujolais wines, the wine produced in Villié-Morgon matures well. It has a particularly fruity taste because of the broken up schist soil in which the vines are cultivated.

▷ *Leave Villié-Morgon N on D 68.*

Fleurie

Fleurie wines are best drunk young.

▷ *In Fleurie take D 32 E; left on D 186.*

Romanèche-Thorins

The famous Moulin-à-Vent wine is produced here and in the neighbouring village of Chénas. There is a wine museum located in the railway station – **Le Hameau en Beaujolais**★ (◷*open Apr–Oct 9am–7pm; Nov–Dec and Feb–Mar 10am–6pm;* ◷*closed 2 weeks in Jan, 25 Dec;* ∞*13–16€;* ☎*03 85 35 22 22; www.hameauduvin.com).* The **Musée du Compagnonnage Guillon** (◷*open Jan–May and Oct–Dec 2pm–6pm, Jun–Sept 10am–6pm;* ◷*closed*

1 May, 15 Dec–1 Jan; ☞4€, no charge 1st Sunday in the month; ☎03 85 35 22 02) displays exhibits from the days of itinerant craftsmen; there are particularly fine examples of their work.

▶ *At the Maison-Blanche crossroads on N 6, take D 466B, leading to St-Romain-des-Îles.*

Parc Zoologique et d'Attractions Touroparc★ [Kids]

&♿ ⓘ*Open daily Jun–Aug 9.30pm–7pm; mid-Jan–Feb 1.30pm–5.30pm; Mar–May and Sept–mid Nov 9.30am–6pm. ☞10–16.50€. ☎03 85 35 51 53. www. touroparc.com.*
In a delightfully verdant setting dotted with ochre buildings, this zoo and breeding centre presents birds and animals from the five continents.

▶ *Rejoin D 266, which goes through the hamlet of Moulin-à-Vent, to D 68.*

Chénas

Home of robust, top quality Moulin-à-Vent and the lighter Chénas.

Juliénas

The strong wines from this locality can still be tasted in the **Cellier de la Vieille Église** (♿ⓘ*open all year, daily, 9.45am–noon, 2.30pm–6.30pm; ⓘclosed 1–15 Jan, mid-Feb–Mar; ☎04 74 04 42 98)*, tasting cellars in an old church converted for the purpose.

▶ *Drive on to St-Amour-Bellevue.*

St-Amour-Bellevue

This village at the northerly tip of the Beaujolais produces dark-red wines with plenty of body, and high quality white wines.

Mountain Tour★

[2] **St-Amour-Bellevue to Villefranche sur-Saône**
134km/83mi – allow 6hr

This pretty drive continues from **St-Amour-Bellevue**, through vine-clad hills to dark pine forests, then drops to the Azergues valley.

▶ *From Juliénas, take D 26 uphill, going through two passes.*

Beaujeu

The capital of the Beaujolais lies amid vine-covered hillsides.

Les Sources du Beaujolais

♿ⓘ*Open Mar–Dec daily except Tue, 10am–12.30pm, 2pm–6pm (Sun and public holidays 10am–12.30pm, 3pm–6pm; Jul–Aug daily until 7pm). ⓘClosed 25 Dec, Jan–Feb. ☞6€. ☎04 74 69 20 56. www. beaujeu.com.*
This wine centre is devoted to the development of the Beaujolais area.

Musée Marius-Audin

ⓘ*Open May–Sept daily 9.30am–12.30pm, 2.30pm–6pm (Jul–Aug, 7pm); Mar–Apr and Oct–Nov daily except Mon and Tue, 10am–noon, 2.30pm–6pm. ⓘClosed Dec–Feb. ☞2€. ☎04 74 69 22 88. www. beaujeu.com.*
Audin (1872–1951) was a printer from Beaujeu who founded this museum of traditional folk art in 1942.

▶ *Follow D 26 and D 18 to La Terrasse.*

La Terrasse★★

The **view** from a bend in D 18 after Col du Fût d'Avenas covers the Saône valley, Bresse plateaus, Jura peaks and Alps.

Avenas

The Roman road from Lyon to Autun once passed through this village.

▶ *Take D 18E, then D 32.*

Shortly before the pass (Col de Crie), there is a beautiful view north down the Grosne Orientale valley. As the road carries on downhill, it passes Mont St-Rigaud, the highest peak in the region.

Chénelette

This small village lies in a charming wooded setting. The **Tourvéon** towers above it. This summit was once the site of the great fortress of Ganelon who betrayed Charlemagne's army, bringing about its defeat and the death of Roland at Roncevaux.

Les Écharmeaux

This summer resort is set against a back-drop of pine forests and meadows. From Les Écharmeaux, follow D 10 towards Ranchal. It crosses the Aillets pass and, after a stretch through forest, the Écorbans pass. Between Ranchal and St-Nizier-d'Azergues, D 54 affords **views**★ of the Azergues valley.

St-Nizier-d'Azergues

This small town occupies a pleasant site above the Azergues Valley. The pretty road carries on to Grandris.

▶ *After Grandris, turn left onto D 504 as far as La Folletière, then left again on D 485 along the upper valley of the Azergues and through Lamure-sur-Azergues. In Le Gravier, turn right onto D 9.*

Claveisolles

This little village is well known for its plantations of coniferous trees. In the 19C, the Comte du Sablon introduced Douglas firs from America.

▶ *Drive back to D 485 and turn left to Chambost-Allières.*

Chambost-Allières

This is an amalgamation of two very different villages: Allières in the valley, a busy place with lots of passing traffic; and **Chambost,** a rural hamlet above the valley.

The road from Chambost-Allières to Cogny via Le Saule-d'Oingt makes a **pretty drive**★★. It climbs to the Joncin pass and then runs along the ridge, offering a **view**★ of the Alps.

▶ *In Le Saule-d'Oingt, turn left onto D 31, then left again onto D 19.*

As the road drops down to the valley, the view stretches over the Saône valley, the Bresse region and the Jura foothills.

▶ *D 504 leads back to Villefranche.*

Le Pays Des Pierres Dorées★★

3 Round tour from Villefranche-sur-Saône
59km/37mi

This trip explores the **Pays des Pierres Dorées** which owes its name to the pretty ochre-coloured local stone used to build farmsteads, castles and whole villages in the region.

▶ *From Villefranche, take D 70 S.*

Marcy

Outside this market town stands a **telegraph tower** (⏰*open Mar–Nov Sun. 2.30pm–6pm (Nov closing time 5pm);* ☎*04 74 67 02 21 (town hall);* ⏰*closed Dec–Feb;* ✆*2€)* built by Claude Chappe in 1799. The original semaphore mechanism was used to transmit messages until 1850.

Charnay

This small fortified town at the top of a hill still has the remains of its original citadel.

▶ *Take a narrow road heading S from Charnay to St-Jean-des-Vignes.*

St-Jean-des-Vignes

There is a good view of the countryside around Lyon from the small church perched on a hillside.

Espace Pierres Folles

⏰*Open Mar–Nov 10am–12.30pm, 2pm–6pm (Wed, Sat–Sun and public holidays 2.30pm–6pm).* ✆*5€.* ☎*04 78 43 69 20. www.espace-pierres-folles.fr.*
A museum founded to reflect the presence of a number of important geological sites in this area.

▶ *Rejoin D 30 to reach Chazay-d'Azergues.*

Chazay-d'Azergues

All that remains of the fortified town overlooking the Azergues is the belfry, a few 15C and 16C houses and a town gateway known as the Porte de Babouin after a juggler who, disguised as a bear, rescued his feudal lord's wife and young daughter from a blazing tower, for which he was rewarded with the daughter's hand in marriage.

▶ *Take D 30 as far as Lozanne, then D 485 to Châtillon.*

Châtillon

A fortress built in the 12C and 13C to protect the mouth of the Azergues valley towers masterfully over this village. The **Chapelle St-Barthélemy** (⏰*open mid-Apr–Oct Sun and public holidays, 2.30pm–6pm; ☎04 78 43 92 66)*, originally part of the fortress itself, was extended in the 15C by Geoffroy de Balzac.

▶ *Carry on along D 485.*

Chessy

Near Chessy, a rich seam of copper which belonged to Jacques Cœur was once mined. The ore obtained was known as **chessylite** and was a variety of azurite with a beautiful blue glint to it, highly prized by collectors.

▶ *Take D 19 to Bagnols.*

Bagnols

In this village is a 15C castle converted into a hotel. There are pretty 15C–16C houses on the village square.

▶ *Go back to D 19 and follow it to the left.*

Le Boitier

As you leave this hamlet, the road takes you past Clos de la Platière, which belonged to the Rolands, who became famous during the Revolution. **Mme Roland de la Platière** stands out from her contemporaries as a cultured, well-educated woman who forged close connections with the politicians of her age. However, she made no secret of her antipathy towards Danton and Robespierre and paid for this in 1793 by being sent to the guillotine.

Theizé

This village, characteristic of the Pierres Dorées area, has two churches and two castles. The main tourist attraction is the **Site de Rochebonne** in the upper part of the village, which includes the former chapel and the château.

Oingt★

All that remains of the once mighty fortress here is the Porte de Nizy, the gateway at the entrance to the village. Narrow streets lined with beautiful houses lead to the church, an old castle chapel dating from the 14C. From the top of the **tower** (🛈 ☎04 74 71 21 24. *www.oingt.com)* there is a view of the Lyonnais and Beaujolais hills and the Azergues valley.

▶ *Carry on along D 96.*

In **St-Laurent-d'Oingt**, note the church with a porch.

▶ *At the junction with D 485, turn right.*

On the left stands the old fortified town of Ternand.

Ternand★

Ternand retains some of its earlier fortifications, such as the keep and the watch-path, from which there is a good view of the Tarare hills and the Azergues valley.

▶ *Turn back through Les Planches and follow D 31.*

The pass **road**★★ over **Col du Saule-d'Oingt** is very pretty. Picturesque farmsteads on the hillside overlook meadows below.

▶ *At La Maladière turn right towards Jarnioux.*

Jarnioux

The **castle** (⏰*open early Jul and mid-Aug–Sept Mon, Wed, Fri; 2pm–6pm, Tue and Thu 9am–noon;* ⏰*closed rest of year, 14 Jul, and 15 Aug;* ⬤4€; ☎04 74 03 80 85)*, built between the 15C and 17C, has six towers and includes a particularly charming Renaissance section.

▶ *Take D 116 and D 38 back to Villefranche.*

BESSE-EN-CHANDESSE★

POPULATION 1,672
MICHELIN MAP 326: E-9

With its old houses and fortifications, Besse is a picturesque and charming town, and the beauty of its surroundings makes it a popular place to stay. The town is the setting for a biological research centre specialising in the study of regional flora and fauna, which was set up by the Faculty of Science of Clermont-Ferrand University.

🛈 **Information:** Pl. du Dr-Alfred-Pipet, 63610 BESSE-EN-CHANDESSE. ☎04 73 79 52 84.

▶ **Orient Yourself:** Besse lies mid-way between Aurillac and Mauriac, in the south-west of Cantal.

🔎 **Don't Miss:** A tour of the Old Town.

🕒 **Organising Your Time:** Allow half a day.

🖉 **Also See:** AURILLAC, ST-FLOUR, MASSIF DU SANCY.

Old Town

Houses with picturesque corbelled turrets line the narrow streets of the old town.

Rue des Boucheries★

This is a quaint street with black houses made of lava stone. Note the 15C shops and **Queen Margot's House** (15C), on the corner with rue Mercière. According to local legend, Marguerite de Valois lived in this house. Its Gothic doorway, surmounted by a coat of arms, opens onto a beautiful spiral staircase.

Town Gate★

Corner of rue de l'Abbé and Le Petit Mèze. In the 16C this gate, which is protected by a barbican, was adapted to the use of fire arms. The belfry was added at a later date.

Château du Bailli

These remains of the outer town wall are visible from the road *(northwest)* behind the church.

Additional Sights

Musée du Ski

Rue de la Boucherie. ⏱*Open school holidays: 9am–noon, 2pm–7pm.* ⊜*3€.* ☎*04 73 79 57 30. www.sancy.com.*

This Skiing Museum is the first of its kind in France. Among the displays are 30 different pairs of skis, a 1925 bobsleigh, ski boots and shoes, and a pair of 1910 skates. Prints and photographs show Besse at the turn of the 20C.

Maison de l'Eau et de la Pêche

Rue de la Boucherie, Besse-en-Chandesse. 🚻⏱*Open mid-Jun–mid Sept, daily except Sat 10am–noon, 2pm–7pm (last admission 1hr before closing).* ⏱*Closed 1 Jan and 25 Dec.* ⊜*4€.* ☎*04 73 79 55 52.* Located on the banks of the Couze de Pavin, this house contains an exhibition centre displaying local aquatic species, equipped with videofilms, microscopes, models, computer terminals.

Excursions

Super-Besse❋

6km/3.7mi West.

Super-Besse – a high-altitude outpost of Besse – is first and foremost promoted as a winter sports resort, but it is also popular in summer because of its quiet, peaceful surroundings.

There are a variety of chalets and holiday residences available. The vast, south-facing ski slopes are reached by ski lift; additional facilities include a skating rink and a swimming pool.

Ski area

This resort, developed at the foot of Puy de la Perdrix, has south-facing ski slopes, drag-lifts, chair-lifts, and a gondola leading to 27 Alpine-ski runs (seven green, six blue, eleven red and three black runs). The ski pass sold on location gives access to the Mont-Dore skiing area (*see Le MONT-DORE*).

In summer, the nearby lake can be used for swimming, canoeing and windsurfing. The area is ideal for walking.

Puy Ferrand

15min by cable-car, then 45min on foot there and back from Super-Besse.

The cable-car for Perdrix leaves from the Biche corrie and ends at the peak of Puy de la Perdrix. Follow the crest to the summit of Puy Ferrand, which offers a **view**★★ of the Dore mountain range, the lakes and Chaudefour Valley.

Lac Pavin★★

4.5km/3mi SW of Besse via D 149, which is a one-way road, joining up with D 978 from Besse to Condat, or via the "Fraux road" S of Besse which connects Besse to Pavin via a pasture-covered mountain.

The Fraux parking area offers a lovely **view**★ of the lake. This lake surrounded by forests and superb rocks, is one of the most beautiful in the Auvergne.

In the past, it was said that the old town of Besse was swallowed up by the lake as a divine punishment, and that throwing a stone into it would unleash terrific storms; this is why it is called Pavin, from the Latin *pavens* meaning dreadful.

A gentle path offers a very pleasant stroll around the lake (about 45min on foot).

Puy de Montchal★★

The summit overlooking Lac Pavin offers a magnificent **panorama**★★ – to the northwest, the Dore mountain range; to the north, the Dômes mountain range, clustered around Puy de Dôme; further to the east, the Couzes and Comté valleys; to the northeast and east, the Livradois and Forez mountains and to the southeast, in the far distance, the Chaise-Dieu plateau and Velay mountains.

Lac de Montcineyre

8km/5mi SW along D 36. Skirt Lac de Bourdouze and, 1km/0.6mi further on, follow a path on the right (1km/0.6mi).

Crescent-shaped Montcineyre Lake owes its existence to the wooded Puy Montcineyre, which dams the valley. Follow the lakeshore along the foot of the volcano for an attractive view of the Massif du Sancy (*see Massif du SANCY*).

Lac Pavin

J. Damase/MICHELIN

Address Book

⏳*For coin ranges, see the legend on the cover flap.*

WHERE TO STAY/WHERE TO EAT

⊖⊖ **Le Levant** – *20 r. de l'Abbé-Blot, 63610 Besse & St Anastaise. ☎04 73 79 50 17 (closed Wed).* How do you like your trout? With cabbage, wild mushrooms or lentils? Or would you prefer a different regional dish? There's plenty of choice here, served in a decor that seems to be firmly grounded in the 1970s.

⊖⊖ **Auberge du Lac Pavin** – *Au Lac Pavin, 4km/2.4mi W of Besse via D 149. ☎04 73 79 62 79. www.lac-pavin. com. Closed 1 Nov–20 Dec.* The fish – char, among others – served in this restaurant once lived in the alpine lake that you see from the dining room. The owner, who is also the chef, prepares simple dishes from fresh ingredients. A few modest rooms have views of the lake.

⊖⊖ **Hostellerie du Beffroy** – *26 rue Abbé Blot. ☎04 73 79 50 08. www.lebeffroy.com. Closed 4 Nov–26 Dec, Mon and Tue except in Jul–Aug and Feb, Wed lunch in Jul–Aug. Reservations required Sun.* ⏛*10€. Meals*⊖⊖. This handsome 15C

building in the village centre used to be the guardhouse. The gourmet fare is served in a charming dining room with white-draped tables and old wooden beams.

⊖⊖ **Ferme-auberge La Voûte** – *8 r.de la Mastre, 63320 Clémensat, 5km/3mi S of Champeix via D 28. ☎04 73 71 10 82. Open Sun lunch and Sat, evenings Jul–Aug except Sun and Mon.* ⏛*. Reservations required.* A very popular farm-inn nestling in a small village. The vaulted dining room is often crowded with savvy diners enjoying fare from the farm, local recipes or savoury Auvergnat specialities (to be ordered ahead). Spacious, refurbished bedrooms.

⊖⊖ **Auberge du Point de Vue** – *Trossange, 63610 St-Pierre-Colamine, 7km/4.2mi NW of Besse via D 978 and D 619. ☎04 73 96 31 45. Closed Jan, Mon, Tue evening and Wed evening except school holidays. Reservations recommended.* The view from the terrace of this aptly named inn is breathtaking. Whether you dine al fresco in the summer or by the fireplace in the winter, local cuisine is the mainstay here, chosen à la carte or from one of the hearty fixed-price menus.

Driving Tour

The Couze Valleys
65km/40mi – allow 1–2 days.

Leaving from Besse, take D 633, a charming corniche road offering interesting views of the Couze de Pavin Valley and the Courgoul gorges. It becomes D 619 after crossing Trossagne.

▶ *Turn right onto the narrow road running above the Grottes de Jonas.*

Grottes de Jonas
🕐*Open Feb–Oct and Christmas school holidays: guided tours (50min).* 💶*6.20€ (children 4.70€). ☎04 73 88 57 98. www. grottedejonas.com.*
The most rudimentary of these manmade caves carved out of the volcanic tufa in a cliff were doubtless inhabited

in prehistoric times. Over the centuries their descendants also made use of them; in the Middle Ages a chapel – its vaulting still bears traces of **frescoes** dating from 1100 – and a fortress were built in the caves. The tower of the fortress contains a spiral staircase with 80 or so steps carved into the rock; it leads up to apartments laid out over several floors.

▶ *Return to Le Cheix and turn right onto D 978 then right again onto D 621.*

Cheminée de Fée de Cotteuges
Before reaching the hamlet, turn right onto the Bedeaux track.
🚶This path leads through a wood to an earth pillar standing among excavations. This interesting geological formation, known as the **"Fairy's Chimney"**

Fairy's Chimney

is a clay column topped by a block of hard rock.

Beyond Cotteuges the road crosses one of the *cheires* (lava flows) that are a characteristic feature of this area. Further on, high above to the left of the road, stand a number of superb sheer-sided rocks.

▶ *Continue along D 621.*

Saurier

This is an old fortified village. Left of the road crossing the River Couze there is an attractive view of the old bridge

and its chapel. The valley narrows again and basalt rocks can be seen on the hillsides.

▶ *Take D 26 towards Issoire.*

St-Floret★

First of all, take a look at Chastel plateau, probably the original site of the village. The **Église du Chastel** (🕐*open mid-Jun–mid Sept: guided tours daily except Tue and Wed 2pm–6pm; mid-Sept–mid Jun apply to the town hall (Mon and Thu 2pm–7pm);* ☎*04 73 71 10 39*) is built on a promontory overlooking the Couze de Pavin. Near the church are the remains of a Merovingian graveyard (tombs dug into the rock, ossuary). The **château**, located in the village of St-Floret itself, was built in the 13C and modified a century later. Large 14C **frescoes**★ depicting episodes from a tale of chivalry (Tristan) decorate the walls in the lower chamber.

▶ *After the church, turn left onto D 28, which will take you to Champeix.*

Champeix

This village stands between hillsides once carpeted with vineyards. The ruins of the old medieval castle, the "Marchidial," stand high above the village on a sheer-sided spur of rock.

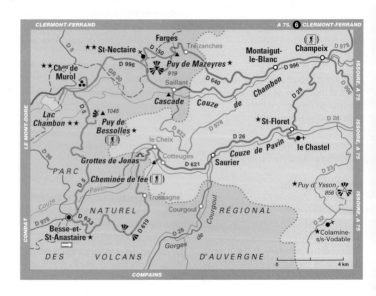

Site du Marchidial

Can be reached on foot starting from the bridge; access by car: follow D 28 towards St-Floret; after 1km/0.6mi, turn right towards the college.

In the upper part of Champeix, this district owes its name to the markets and fairs which used to take place on the plateau during the Middle Ages. A narrow lane running east leads to the ruins of the former medieval fortress offering a fine view.

▶ *Leave Champeix heading W towards St-Nectaire on D 996.*

Montaigut-le-Blanc

The village lies in the shadow of its ruined castle. Its somewhat Mediterranean appearance – houses with flat roofs and rounded tiles, terraced vineyards, and fruit trees at the head of the valley – heralds the Limagne plateau.

▶ *Carry on along D 996 for another mile or so. Turn right onto D 640. Just after Treizanches, turn left onto D 150.*

Farges

This hamlet is home to an interesting group of **troglodytic houses** (open May–Sept and school holidays 10am–noon, 2pm–6pm (Jul and Aug 10am–6pm); closed Oct–Apr; 6€; 04 73 88 52 25), hollowed out of the white tufa, which date from the Middle Ages. Visitors may also like to discover more about the maturing process of St-Nectaire cheese, in a cellar where this takes place.

The traditional method of making St-Nectaire can be viewed at **Ferme Bellonte** (open 8.30am–10.30am, 5.30pm–7pm (cows milked at 7.45am, 5pm). 04 73 88 52 25).

A little further on from Farges, a quarry comes into sight to the right of the road. The powdery white rock extracted here is pumice stone, evidence of the tremendous volcanic eruptions that shook this region millions of years ago.

▶ *Carry on along D 150, then turn left.*

Puy de Mazeyres★

From the hilltop, there is a beautiful **panorama** of the Dore mountain range.

▶ *Rejoin D 150.*

St-Nectaire★★

see ST-NECTAIRE.

▶ *From St-Nectaire-le-Bas, take D 996 for Champeix, as far as Saillant.*

Cascade de Saillant

In this village the river tumbles over a basalt outcrop, forming a waterfall.

▶ *Return to St-Nectaire and take D 996 towards Le Mont-Dore.*

Château de Murol★★

Open Apr–Jun and Sept–Oct daily, 10am–12.30pm, 1.30pm–6.30pm; Jul–Aug Wed–Sat, 10am–7pm; Nov–Mar Sat, Sun, public and school holidays, 2pm–5pm. Closed 14 Jul. 8€. 04 73 88 67 11. www.chateaudemurol.com.

It was a descendant of the lords of Murol, Guillaume de Sam, an erudite baron and patron of the arts, who completed the original, inner fortress by building the keep, the second chapel and the eastern buildings. The castle, after passing into the hands of the powerful D'Estaing family in the 15C, was lavishly ornamented and, at the beginning of the following century, encircled by a huge curtain wall flanked with towers.

Murol emerged victorious from a siege during the time of the Catholic League. Peril having been averted, Jean d'Estaing foresook his vast abode and built the charming pavilion at the foot of the inner castle. Abandoned some time afterwards, Murol was spared by Richelieu because of the D'Estaing family's influence at court. After being used as a prison for some time, it became a robbers' hideout during the Revolution. During the 19C it fell into ruin and the inhabitants of the region came here looking for building stone.

In recent years, extensive alterations have been made to the castle. Guided tours and colourful evening shows are organised by the *Compagnons de*

Gabriel to provide an authentic medieval atmosphere. Visitors pass through the outer curtain wall through a fortified gatehouse on the southside, passing the Murol tower on the right.

The Renaissance Pavilion (**1**) stands in the outer courtyard (the windows provide an attractive view of the Capitaine tower).

To the north is the inner castle (Château Central), its walls rising above a thick basalt base. Next to the keep, connected to a tower of smaller dimensions by a curtain wall, are the chapels. The first (**2**) was built in the 13C; the second (**3**) in the 15C, and though of greater proportions is less graceful. A stepped ramp leads up to an elegant door (**4**) decorated with the Murol and Gaspard d'Estaing coats of arms. In the inner courtyard, note the gallery once surmounted by the Knights' Hall followed by the guard-room.

Take the spiral stairway of the Chautignat tower up to the terrace from which there is a very beautiful **panorama**★ of Murol, the Couze Valley, Lake Chambon, the Dore mountain range and Tartaret volcano. The watch-path leads to the Châtelaine tower (note the 16C door **5**). Next come the kitchen, the bakery and its outbuildings (**6**). The adjacent rooms (**7**) were living quarters.

▶ *On leaving the castle, walk down to the village, cross the road and walk through a gate leading into the Parc Municipal.*

Parc municipal du Prélong

Once part of a private estate (the house now contains the Musée des Peintres de l'école de Murols), the park boasts a beautiful collection of azaleas, rhododendrons and camellias. The French-style garden has alleyways lined with box trees leading to the rose-garden, offering a striking contrast with the English-style park. At the entrance stands the **Chaumière** (◔*open daily 3pm–6pm*) which houses a small archaeological collection (Gallo-Roman finds excavated locally).

Musée des Peintres de l'école de Murols

◔*Open Jun–Oct daily 10am–noon, 2pm –6pm; Nov–May Sat–Sun and school holidays except Tue, 2pm–6pm.* ◔*Closed 1 Jan, 1 May, 25 Dec.* ◔*4€.* ☏*04 73 88 60 06. www.musee-murol.net.*

At the turn of the 20C, some 50 landscape painters found inspiration in and around the village. Gathered round Abbé Boudal, who was the initiator of this artistic movement, and Charenton

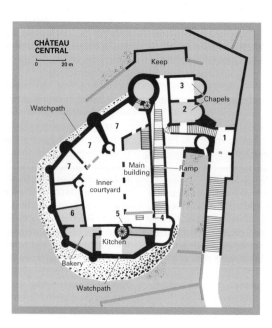

J. Damase/MICHELIN

Lac Chambon

who was its leader, this group of artists was close to two contemporary trends, Impressionism and Fauvism. The permanent collection is displayed in five rooms and another room is reserved for temporary exhibitions.

▸ *Leave Murol on D 996, then turn left at the junction with D 5.*

The road runs along the slopes of the Tartaret volcano. Note to the left, in a tiny quarry, the volcanic cinders which make up the cone.

Lac Chambon★★

The lake was formed by the Tartaret volcano, which erupted in the middle of the Couze Valley and stemmed the flow of water. It is a vast but fairly shallow lake lying in a very attractive setting. It is dotted with tiny islands and has an extremely jagged shoreline, except on the north, and to the south-east where there is a large beach.

To the north of the lake is a slender rocky peak known as the **Saut de la Pucelle** (Maiden's Leap) which is all that remains of the ancient **Dent du Marais** volcano.

The village of Chambon-sur-Lac lies at the end of the Couze de Chaudefour, in a mountainous area to the west of the lake, and consists of a group of houses huddling round the church.

The tiny skiing resort of **Chambon-des-Neiges**✳ (Chambon 1200 and Chambon 1400) lies high above the Chaudefour Valley (◖ *see Massif du SANCY*). The resort is equipped with snow-making facilities; it has a number of pistes designed for both Alpine and cross-country skiing.

▸ *Return to Murol and turn right onto D 5 towards Besse-en-Chandesse. After 2km/1.2mi turn right onto D 619, then after about 100m/ 110yd turn left.*

Puy de Bessolles★

This peak is one of the best look-out points in the Couzes region, giving an impressive view of the Dore mountain range and Lake Chambon.

🚶 *Follow the footpath signposted Plateau de Bessolles–Panorama. Allow 45min on foot to get to the viewpoint and back, and 2hr to follow the footpath right round the plateau (signposted in yellow).*

▸ *Go back to Besse-en-Chandesse via D 5.*

BILLOM★

POPULATION 4,246

MICHELIN MAP 326: H-8

Billom is situated on the Limagne plain at the foot of the Livradois mountains. It flourished in the Middle Ages and had a university before Clermont-Ferrand. This university, transformed in the 16C, became the first Jesuit college and was well-known throughout the Auvergne.

- **Information:** 13 r. Carnot, 63160 BILLOM. ☎04 73 68 39 85. www.billom.com.
- ▶ **Orient Yourself:** Billom lies 27km/17mi SE of Clermont-Ferrand.
- 🅿 **Parking:** Parking is limited in the centre of town.
- **Don't Miss:** A walk around the Medieval district.
- ⏱ **Organizing Your Time:** 2–3 hours would suffice, but stay for lunch.
- **Also See:** CLERMONT-FERRAND.

A Bit of History

During the Reign of Terror in the wake of the French Revolution, Couthon, a member of the Convention, issued a famous edict ordering the demolition of all belfries in the province on the basis that they were "contrary to equality"; this was how the church of St-Cerneuf lost its elegant little tower.

Modern Billom plies a wide variety of economic activities: sawmills, wood veneering, car body workshops, industrial brush and ironware works. Cultivation of the regional speciality, garlic, is declining, but many companies continue to store and sort fresh garlic for consumption or to process it for pharmaceuticals, powders and garlic paste.

Walking Tour

Medieval District

From the Hôtel de Ville follow quai de la Terraille to place du Creux-du-Marché, surrounded by old houses. Cross Pont du Marché-aux-Grains: three troughs and gutters hewn out of Volvic stone are visible on the parapet on the right – they were used to measure grain.

Walking up rue de l'Étézon, note the 16C belfry on the right and the 16C **Maison du Bailli** at the top of the street.

▶ *Turn left, and walk past the former trade tribunal to place des Écoles.*

Maison du Chapitre

This 15C mansion, known as the chapterhouse, was part of the medieval university and was used as a prison during the Revolution.

Porte de l'Évéché

This gateway into the medieval town marked the first line of fortifications.

Église St-Cerneuf★

This Gothic church was erected over an old Romanesque church from which a crypt★ remains.

Address Book

For coin ranges, see the cover flap.

WHERE TO EAT

Auberge du Ver Luisant – 63910 Bouzel - 12km/7.2mi NW of Billom via D 229 and D 10. ☎04 73 62 93 83. closed 1–6 Jan, 15 Aug–9 Sept, Wed evening, Sun evening and Mon. The dining room of this village restaurant set in former stables has handsome wooden beams and a mezzanine.

Le Paris – 6 r. des Lucioles, 63520 St-Dier-d'Auvergne, 16km/9.6mi SE of Billom via D 997. ☎04 73 70 80 67. Closed Jan, Sun evening and Tue except Jul–Aug. Reservation recommended. Locals are quite fond of this simple, inviting village inn with an outdoor terrace used as soon as the weather warms up.

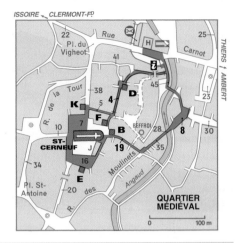

▶ *Turn right on leaving the church, and turn left onto rue Pertuybout.*

Maison de l'Échevin

The entrance to this 16C alderman's house features an attractive staircase tower and a well with its wheel.

Rue des Boucheries

This narrow street paved with pointed stones is flanked by medieval houses including the **Maison du Doyen** which has a beautiful basket-handle arch over its window and a Renaissance staircase, and the 15C **Maison du Boucher** which has stone walls on one side, half-timbered walls on the other and two overhanging upper floors.

Driving Tours

Val d'Allier

50km/31mi – allow 3hr.

▶ *Leave Billom along D 997 towards Pont-du-Château and turn left onto D 81.*

Chas

This old fortified village has kept its gateway and turret and its Romanesque church, fronted by a Renaissance porch and a pretty fountain.

Chauriat

Located north of the Comté, this small wine-growing village stands out because of its two churches. The deconsecrated **Église Ste-Marie** was built in Merovingian times. The **Église St-Julien** is characteristic of the Auvergnat Romanesque style.

▶ *Drive to Pont-du-Château along D 4.*

Pont-du-Château

For a long time this strategically important town was fortified: it was the location of the only bridge spanning the River Allier between Moulins and Brioude. During the 19C Pont-du-Château was a busy port loading up goods for Paris; this history is recalled in the **Musée Pierre-Mondanel** (◷ *open Jul–Aug guided tours (1hr) 10am–noon, 2pm–6pm, Sat–Sun 2pm–6pm; Sept–Jun by appointment;* ✆ *2.50€ (museum and castle: 3€);* ☎*04 73 83 73 98)*, housed in the kitchens of an old château. It uses models of boats among the exhibits to tell of river fishing life of a mariner.

▶ *Leave Pont-du-Château to the S and take D 1 heading towards Vic-le-Comte.*

The road meanders along the banks of the River Allier, offering pretty views of the mountain ranges.

Hills locally known as Turlurons

J. Damase/MICHELIN

▶ *Turn left onto D 117, which crosses Mirefleurs. Follow a steep slope towards the road to Bosséol.*

Château de Busséol
See VIC-LE-COMTE.

▶ *Continue along D 117, then D 301 towards St-Julien-de-Coppel.*

Drive up through Notre-Dame-des-Roches, a small chapel perched on a rock, for a view of Billom country.

▶ *Continue on D 118 to see the ruins of Coppel Tower; just before La Beauté, turn left. D 14 will take you back to Billom through the lush Angaud valley.*

Livradois Châteaux
45km/28mi – allow 3hr.

This route provides lovely views of the first Livradois summits and gives access to the main strongholds in the Pays de St-Dier.

Château de Montmorin
Open 1–15 Jun and 15 Jul–31 Aug, daily, 2pm–6pm (last tour at 5pm). 5€ (6–12-year-olds 2.50€). 04 73 68 30 94.
This former citadel used to consist of a keep flanked by round towers; it now lies largely in ruins. Several rooms in the main building have been turned into a museum.

▶ *Take D 337, then D 338 towards St-Dier-d'Auvergne, then Fayet-le-Château.*

St-Dier-d'Auvergne
The 12C **church** here was fortified in the 15C; it has a buttressed west front with arcading.

▶ *Drive 5km/3mi to the S on D 997.*

Les Martinanches
Nestling at the bottom of a valley and surrounded by a moat is a **castle** (*Open Easter-Nov; guided tours, 2pm–6.30pm, except Sat of Jul and Aug (Sun, public holidays, 2pm–6pm); 5.50€; 04 73 70 81 98; www.chateau-des-martinanches.com*), built originally in the 11C but altered in the 15C and the 19C. Inside there are beamed ceilings, fine porcelain and earthenware, and period furniture.

Château de Mauzun
The mighty fortress standing on a spur of basalt rock, once the property of the bishops of Clermont-Ferrand, offers a fine panoramic view of the Limagne plain. Although still in ruins, the castle retains its two defensive walls and 20 towers.

▶ *Take D 20 to Neuville, then D 152 and D 229 back to Billom.*

BORT-LES-ORGUES

POPULATION 3,534
MICHELIN MAP 330: Q-3

Situated in pleasant surroundings in the Dordogne Valley, Bort owes its fame to the celebrated basalt columns which overlook it and to its enormous dam. The town, straddling the boundary between the former territories of the Arverni and Lemovici tribes, flourished in the Middle Ages. Charles VII granted it the right to build a town wall, of which a few ruins survive.

- **Information:** Pl. Marmontel, 19110 BORT-LES-ORGUES. ☎05 55 96 02 49. www.bort-artense.com.
- **Orient Yourself:** Bort lies SW of Clermont-Ferrand along the A89.
- **Parking:** Limited parking areas in the centre of town.
- **Don't Miss:** The famous Orgues de Bort.
- **Also See:** AURILLAC, CLERMONT-FERRAND, MAURIAC, MURAT, SALERS.

Sights

Barrage de Bort★★

The dam's sheer size makes it a showcase of hydroelectric production. Its reservoir is partly filled by water from the Rhue, a tributary of the Dordogne. The road running along the top of the dam (390m/425yd long) overlooks the reservoir upstream dotted with **cruisers** (⊙*May–Sept: boat trip (1hr) Château de Val/DordogneValley; Jul–mid-Sept: boat trip (1hr) Bort dam/château de Val 11am, 2pm–5pm;* ⊛*8€ return).* A **tourist itinerary** *(apply to the Tourist office,* ☎*05 55 96 02 49)* can be followed, starting from the foot of the dam on the west bank between the hamlet of Les Granges and Bort's tanning and leather works.

Church

The extremely simple architecture of Bort's church (12C and 15C) highlights a few fine works of art including modern stained-glass windows. A 17C priory stands by the church.

Cascade du Saut de la Saule

Leave Bort on D 922 towards Mauriac and turn left onto the road running up to the clinic. Follow the path across the Rhue, then turn left and follow the river.
The path soon reaches a little gorge where pebbles caught by the waters have formed so-called "giant's cauldrons." Walk on to the outcrop beyond, which overlooks the Saut de la Saule; here the Rhue crosses a threshold of rock 5–6m/16–20ft high.

Barrage de Bort

©koakoo/Wikimedia Commons

Address Book

⏱For coin ranges, see the cover flap.

WHERE TO STAY

⊜⊜ **Le Rider** – *Av. de la Gare.*
☎05 55 96 00 47. www.lerider.com.
*Closed 28 Jun–6 Jul and 15 Dec–4 Jan.
24 rms. ⊡5€. Restaurant⊜. Meals
are taken in a dining room-veranda
with wrought-iron furniture and an
original trompe-l'œil fresco depicting a
house front and an imaginary country
landscape.*

⊜ **Camping Municipal de la Siauve**
*– 15270 Lanobre, 3.5km/2.2mi N of Bort-
les-Orgues via D 922 and secondary road.
☎04 71 40 31 85. Open 31 May–14 Sept.
Reservations recommended. 220 sites.*
Located on the edge of the lake in a
beautiful natural environment, this is
the perfect camp site for a stimulating
out-of-doors holiday. Choose among
beach activities, fishing and sight-see-
ing on foot or by bicycle. Chalets and
cabins for rent.

Driving Tours

Orgues de Bort★
Round trip of 15km/9mi – allow 2hr.

▶ *Leave Bort on D 979 towards Limoges; then, turn uphill on D 127.*

As the road climbs, there is a beautiful
view of the Rhue Valley on the left.

▶ *Just after the last houses in Chan-
tery, park and turn right onto some
steps leading directly to the foot of
the columnar basalt–signposted
"Grottes des Orgues."*

These impressive columns extend for
2km/1mi and vary in height from 80 to
100m/260 to 330ft.

▶ *Return to D 127 and, 2km/1.2mi
further on, turn right onto a road
(signposted) which leads to a car
park near the television transmitter.
Park and walk to a viewing table
from which there is a different view
of the columnar basalt on the right.*

🚶The vast **panorama**★★ extends over
the Dordogne valley, the Artense and
Cantal regions and the Dore mountains.
To the south-west lies Lake Madic, relic
of an earlier course of the Dordogne.

▶ *Return to the car and follow
D 127 for another 500m/0.3mi:
here a path on the left leads to a
rocky outcrop.*

From here there is a panoramic view
over Puy de Sancy, the mountains of
Cantal, the Dordogne and its tributaries, the Monédières range and the Millevaches plateau.

On the way back to Bort, D 979 provides
a view of the charming **Château de
Pierrefitte** *(right)* and a splendid view
of the Bort reservoir.

The Artense
85km/53mi

The Artense, a granite plateau south-
west of the Dore mountain range, is cut
across by the Tarentaine, a tributary of
the Rhue which rises from Puy de Sancy.
The plateau was once covered with vast
glaciers that gave this region its highly
unusual appearance of varied relief
with peaks separated by small basins
that are now lakes, peat bogs or marshy
grasslands.

In a landscape typical of the Auvergne,
the Artense is graced by charming
copses, but the region was long known
for the poverty of its soil. The marshes
are gradually being drained, making it
possible to breed red Salers cattle, more
and more frequently sharing their pastures with black-and-white Friesians.
Most of the milk produced by these
cattle is used to make Cantal cheese
and particularly the local blue cheese,
Bleu d'Auvergne.

▶ *Leave Bort to the E on D 979. As it
climbs the hillside, the road provides
wonderful views of the columnar
basalt around Bort.*

Champs-sur-Tarentaine-Marchal

This holiday resort is huddled in a wooded valley near the confluence of the Rhue and Tarentaine.

▷ *Leave Champs-sur-Tarentaine-Marchal N along D 49 towards Lanobre and turn immediately right onto D 22, a pretty road winding across the plateau.*

Barrage and Lac de Lastioulles

This huge arch-dam is part of the hydro-electric works along the upper Tarentaine. An outdoor leisure park has been laid out in pleasant surroundings, on the north side of the reservoir.

▷ *Drive though St-Genès-Champespe and follow D 614 towards Issoire. As you come out of the village, take D 30 on the right.*

Lac de la Landie

This lake is surrounded by peaceful meadows and woodlands.

▷ *Rejoin D 614 then take D 203 on the right to Lac Chauvet.*

Lac Chauvet

See Massif du SANCY.

La Tour-d'Auvergne

See Massif du SANCY.

▷ *Drive SW out of La Tour-d'Auvergne along D 47.*

The road to Bagnols passes the foot of the tumultuous Pont de la Pierre water-fall on the left.

Bagnols

This village lies in the Tialle Valley, an undulating region of meadows and copses. Beyond Cros, the road winds down into the Tialle Valley.

▷ *Shortly after entering the Cantal département, turn left onto D 922.*

Château de Val★

Open mid-Jun–mid Sept daily 10am–noon, 2pm–6.30pm; rest of year daily except Tue 10am–noon, 2pm–5.30pm. 5€. Closed mid-Oct–Feb. ☎04 71 40 30 20. www.chateau-de-val.com.

Since the reservoir at Bort became functional, the **setting**★★ in which Château de Val stands is very picturesque. Walk a little way to the left for a charming view of the château, which dates from the 15C. The exterior, with its quaint pepper-pot towers, is evocative of the elegance of the period the château was built.

▷ *Turn back. At the crossroads take D 922 on the right to get back to Bort.*

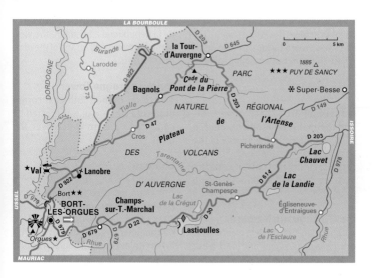

BOURBON-L'ARCHAMBAULT⚑

POPULATION 2,564
MICHELIN MAP 326: F-3

The name of this little town serves as a reminder of the Celtic god, Borvo, protector of thermal springs. The spring water has been appreciated since the days of Roman settlement here; it comes out of the ground at a temperature of 55°C/131°F and is recommended for the treatment of rheumatism, paralysis and functional rehabilitation. The town is overlooked by the ruins of its feudal castle.

🛈 **Information:** 1 pl. de l'Hôtel de Ville, 03160 BOURBON-L'ARCHAMBAULT. ☏04 70 67 09 79. www.ot-bourbon.com.
▶ **Orient Yourself:** Bourbon lies north of Clermont Ferrand, accessible along the A 71.
🅿 **Parking:** Gare Routière on Av Charles Louis Philippe or at the covered market.
🕓 **Organising Your Time:** Half a day will suffice, although a stay for lunch would make a relaxed day.
♿ **Also See:** MOULINS, MONTLUCON.

A Bit of History

Distinguished visitors – The waters at Bourbon, brought back into fashion by Gaston of Orléans, Louis XIII's brother, attracted many famous figures of the 17C, including Madame de Montespan, Louis XIV's favourite mistress who died here in disgrace in 1707.

For 30 years, Charles-Maurice de Talleyrand-Périgord (1754–1838), Prince of Bénévent and France's Minister of Foreign Affairs, visited Bourbon-l'Archambault every August to take the waters, which he considered the best guarantee of good health. His private swimming pool commemorates his visits in its name, "The Prince's Bath." His suite was visited by local personalities whose company he thoroughly enjoyed.

Spa Resort

Nouveau Parc

The thermal establishment, built in 1885, is situated in the middle of the park, together with the casino. The thermal establishment contains ceramics from the Parvilliers workshops, dating from 1885.

Musée Augustin Bernard

🕓 *Open Mar–Oct, Tue–Fri, guided visits at 2.30pm and 4.30pm, from the Office of Tourism.* ⊚*3€.* ☏*04 70 67 09 79.*

This museum, founded in 1937, is housed in the former pump rooms, also known as the "King's House," built by Gaston of Orléans in the town centre. The first floor includes a reconstruction of a local home and there are regional headdresses and costumes on display. Farm implements testify to the region's rural past.

Église St-Georges

Unaccompanied visits daily; guided tours Mon 2.30pm–5.30pm. ☏*04 70 67 03 44.*

This church was erected in the 12C, altered and enlarged in the 15C and again in the 19C.

Walk down to the town centre along rue de la République and admire the view of the fortified old town and of the ruins of its fortress.

Quiquengrogne Tower

This tower in the south-east corner of the old castle wall was erected by Louis II in order to watch over the town.

Château

🕓 *Open Feb–mid-Nov guided tours (1hr 15min, last departure 30min before closing) 2pm–6pm (mid-Jun–mid-Sept 10am–7pm).* ⊚*6€.* ☏*04 70 67 02 30.*

🚶In summer it is advisable to walk up to the castle. Louis II of Bourbon turned Bourbon castle into a princely residence, but the destruction wrought in the Revolution left nothing but three towers.

Driving Tour

Bocage Bourbonnais
Round trip of 45km/28mi – allow 2hr.

▶ *Leave Bourbon-l'Archambault heading N on D 1 towards Nevers.*

The Bocage Bourbonnais is a pleasantly undulating region, crisscrossed by hedges and dotted with forest groves which thrive in the heavy, clayey soil otherwise unsuited for farming.

▶ *Take D 135 towards Ygrande.*

Les Vignes
This hamlet is the home of the **Musée Émile-Guillaumin** (🕒*open May–Oct, 3pm–6pm, Thu, Sat, Sun and public holidays (Jul–Aug 3pm–6pm, Wed–Sun and public holidays); ⊖3€; ☎04 70 66 37 90; http://musee-emile-guillaumin. planet-allier.com).* This farmer-writer (1873–1951) chronicled the joys and griefs of the tenant farmers of the Bourbonnais area.

▶ *Drive SW from Les Vignes on D 953.*

Église d'Ygrande
The 12C church boasts one of the most beautiful stone spires in the region.

▶ *Leave Ygrande SE along D 192. In St-Aubin-le-Monial, turn left on D 492. At the crossroads, turn right onto D 18. Drive through Gipcy and turn right onto D 11. Continue to Meillers. Then leave on D 18. After the crossroads with D 11, turn right onto D 58.*

Église d'Autry-Issards
The main entrance to the **church** is topped by a signed lintel.

▶ *Drive NE out of Autry-Issards along D 58 which leads to St-Menoux.*

Église de St-Menoux★
At the heart of a peaceful village lying between Bourbon-l'Archambault and Moulins, stands one of the loveliest churches in the Bourbonnais. The present **church** was erected during the second half of the 12C, on the site of a 10C sanctuary built in honour of Menulphus, a Breton bishop, who died in the village in the 7C.

▶ *Continue along D 58.*

Église d'Agonges
Pretty church carved in pink sandstone. The friezes on the façade are decorated with animal motifs and the interior features figurative capitals.

▶ *Leave to the NW and drive on D 252 for 4km/2.5mi, heading for Franchesse, then turn left. D 139 will take you back to Bourbon.*

LA BOURBOULE⚕⚕

POPULATION 2,043
MICHELIN MAP 326: D-9

La Bourboule, located at an altitude of 852m/2,800ft in the lush valley of the Upper Dordogne, enjoys a climate with few seasonal variations. This well-known spa and rest resort offers many facilities for children. The town is situated at the confluence of the Dordogne which, at this point, is no more than a mountain stream 12km/7.5mi from its source, and the Vendeix, a tributary which also takes its source in the Sancy range. The resort's pump rooms, casino, town hall and gardens line the banks of the two rivers, which are crossed by a dozen or so bridges and footbridges.

- 🛈 **Information:** 15 pl. de la République, 63150 La BOURBOULE. ☎04 73 65 57 71. www.bourboule.com.
- ▶ **Orient Yourself:** La Bourboule isn't especially large and the best way to get a feel for the place is on foot (☝see Walking Tour). The more energetic can walk up to La Banne d'Ordanche (1hr return) for a splendid view over the valley and the town.
- 🅿 **Parking:** Opposite the Parc Fenestre, on Ave Agis Ledru.
- 🕐 **Organising Your Time:** Take a ride in the little tourist train, and then explore the town on foot before wandering off up the valley sides.
- 🚸 **Especially for Kids:** Parc Fenestre, a splendid wooded park with children's play area (☝see Parc Fenestre).

The Spa Resort

La Bourboule's first spa was opened in 1821. At the time, its cabins were closed off with serge curtains, revealing the bathers at the whim of the wind. The bathing water was used by several patients in turn, and water for the showers was pumped manually by an elderly peasant. In 1854 Thénard the chemist discovered arsenic in the waters of La Bourboule: when the news spread, every house-owner in the town promptly began exploring his property in the hope of finding his own spring and each person did his utmost to excavate faster and pump harder than his neighbour. Today, the town's springs are managed by the Société Thermale de La Bourboule and the Compagnie des Eaux Minérales. There are two springs in La Bourboule – a hot spring at Choussy-Perrière (60°C/140°F), and a cold spring at Fenêstre (19°C/66°F). Their waters contain metalloid arsenic and are used to treat respiratory dis-

---

Address Book

☝For coin ranges, see the legend on the cover flap.

WHERE TO STAY

🍽🍽 **L' Aviation** – R. de Metz. ☎04 73 81 32 32. aviation@nat.fr. Closed 1 Oct– 19 Dec. 41 rms. ⌕7€. Restaurant🍽🍽. Parc Fenêstre, a few steps from this 1900s gable-ended dwelling, is a nice place for your morning jog. The hotel's practical rooms can be a bit outmoded but are neat and tidy. Simple cuisine. Indoor pool and fitness room.

RECREATION

In summer, the La-Bourboule-Charlannes complex organises guided mountain-bike excursions (110km/68mi of marked tracks). Those who prefer rambling have a wide choice of itineraries crisscrossing the Massif du Sancy along some 670km/416mi of way-marked paths. In winter the Charlannes plateau becomes a cross-country skiing area (58km/36mi of tracks); the École du Ski Français (ESF) organises ski tours.

eases and dermatoses using techniques such as inhalations, sprays and electro-sprays, baths and showers. Treatment is available in two spa centres: **Choussy** and **Grands Thermes** (*Open May–Sept: guided tours (1hr) Tue and Fri at 5.30pm (Jul and Aug daily except Sun at 5.30pm); Apr Wed at 5.30pm; book in the morning at the thermal establishment shop; ⌖1€; ☎04 73 81 41 00).*

The resort has all the facilities of a major spa town including tennis courts, stables, a swimming pool, an amusement park etc.

Parc Fenestre★
<small>Kids</small>

Access to the park is free: Apr–Jun, 2p–6pm; Jul–Aug 2pm–7pm. The Little Train: Jul–Aug 10am–noon, 2pm–7pm; Apr–Jun and Sept, 3pm–7pm. Closed Oct–Christmas school holidays. ⌖5€ (Children 3€). ☎04 73 81 14 60. www. parcfenestre.com.

This splendid wooded park – partly planted with sequoias – is a charming place for outings and relaxation.

The children's play area consists of wide expanses of lawn and outdoor games. An additional attraction is the cable-car linking the park with the **Charlannes plateau.**

Walking Tour

A pleasant walk round the town will give you an opportunity to admire the Victorian-style architecture of the hotels and to understand how the city developed at the foot of the Roche des Fées. Near the church, a convincing pastiche of Romanesque art, you can see the **Maison Rozier** and its imposing balcony *(Boulevard Georges-Clemenceau),* the Grands Thermes, the former town hall, now a chocolate factory called the Marquise de Sévigné, and the casino, a listed, entirely renovated building.

Parc Fenestre★ – *See above.*

Roche des Fées

1hr on foot there and back.
Take the footpath from place G.-Lacoste.
This granite "Fairy Rock" rises some 50m/162ft above the spa and provides an attractive view of the town and its surroundings.

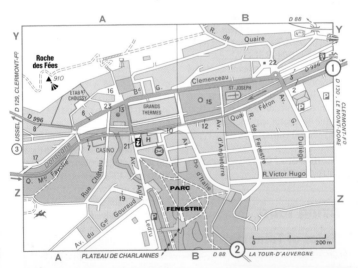

La Banne d'Ordanche

Visit

St-Sauves-d'Auvergne

4km/2.5mi NW along D 996. This village, situated on the north bank of the Dordogne, houses an interesting museum for children of all ages.

Le Monde Merveilleux du Train et de la Miniature [Kids]

Open daily, Easter-Nov 10am–noon, 2pm–6.30pm; the rest of the year: 2.30pm–6pm. Closed Dec–Mar. 4.50€ (Children 3.50€). ☎04 73 81 13 72.
This museum on three levels contains collections of toys and models (cars and lorries). There is a train diorama as well as the reconstruction of a typical village from the Auvergne, with miniatures picturing ancient crafts.

Le Mont-Dore♯♯

See Le MONT-DORE.

Driving Tours

1 Tales of Toinette

10km/7mi N of La Bourboule.

▶ *Leave the town on D 88.*

Murat-le-Quaire

A rocky spur, once the site of a castle, marks the entrance to this village. There is a look-out point on the spur with a pretty view of the upper section of the Dordogne valley. Besides its role as a rural holiday destination, Murat-le-Quaire hosts a Bread Festival every other year (odd numbers) as part of its campaign to preserve local tradition.

▶ *From the church, take D 609 towards La Banne d'Ordanche, as far as the school.*

Scénomusée La Toinette et Julien★

Open all year, daily, 10am–noon, 2pm–6pm (Easter-Aug, 7pm). 5.60€, Julien: 4.40€, combined ticket: 7.80€. ☎04 73 81 12 28. www.toinette.com.
A gateway opens into a large courtyard in which the town hall and the museum are to be found.
The museum contains an account of rural life through the seasons in the Dore mountain range region of the Auvergne during the 19C, presented through the eyes of a local woman of that period, Toinette Chaumard.
Beyond the belvedere lies the **Grange de Julien**, a barn where Toinette's young son returns from his travels and reflects on the future prospects of rural life in the area.

▶ *Carry on along D 609 past a lake, then follow it uphill round a series of hairpin bends with pleasant views, to the end of the road.*

La Banne d'Ordanche★★

1hr.

🚶 From the car park a steep footpath leads uphill to a viewing table. La Banne d'Ordanche (in the dialect of the Auvergne *banne* means "horn") rises from a grassy hillock. From the top of this basalt outcrop – the remains of the central chimney of an old volcano – there is a **wide view**★★ of the Dordogne valley, the Puy de Sancy range, Puy de l'Angle, the Dômes mountain range and the Limousin.

2 Tour of Waterfalls

3km/2mi – allow 4hr.

▶ Leave La Bourboule on D 130 along the Dordogne towards Le Mont-Dore. 1.5km/0.9mi after the swimming pool a track leads off opposite the Mont-Dore water company building (left of the road). Leave the car.

🚶 *Take the GR 30 footpath to the right. Go past a farm and uphill into the forest. After 15min walk, take a path to the right that cuts downhill.*

Cascade de la Vernière★

The Vernière waterfall is formed by a large volcanic rock which obstructs the bed of the Cliergue.

▶ Return to the path and turn onto the track leading to the Plat à Barbe refreshment kiosk. Here it is possible to go down a stepped path (potentially dangerous) to a platform constructed opposite the Plat à Barbe waterfall.

Cascade du Plat à Barbe★

This waterfall owes its name (literally "shaving dish") to the dip worn in the rock by its waters.

3 The Brigand's Den

4km/2.5mi trip – allow 4hr.

▶ Leave La Bourboule to the S on D 88 towards La Tour-d'Auvergne. 3.5km/2.3mi on past Parc Fenêstre,

turn right and leave the car at Vendeix-Haut.

Roche Vendeix★

Access along a footpath off D 88 by an inn. 30min on foot there and back.

🚶 This rock of basalt carries the ruins of a castle which was re-fortified in the 14C by **Aimerigot Marcheix**, an infamous local brigand eventually caught by the king's men in 1390; he was taken to Paris and beheaded and quartered.

4 Woodland to Valley

7km/4.5mi trip – allow 1hr.

▶ Leave La Bourboule to the W on D 129 towards La Tour-d'Auvergne via Col de la Sœur. About 500m/0.3mi after crossing the Dordogne, beyond a crossroads, leave the car and take a footpath branching off to the right.

Lac du Barrage

30min on foot there and back.

🚶 This delightful path runs through Charlet woods to the dam whose reservoir stretches for 1km/0.6mi along the Dordogne valley.

▶ Continue along D 129 and, 3km/1.9mi further on, turn left onto D 610.

Plateau de Charlannes

The beautiful Charlannes plateau is popular with spa patients for its restful scenery; it offers views of the Dore and Cantal mountains.

BRIOUDE★★

POPULATION 6,820
MICHELIN MAP 331: C-2

Brioude is a small, bustling town situated on a terrace overlooking the lush Allier plain.

- 🛈 **Information:** Le Dotenné, Pl. Lafayette, 43100 BRIOUDE. ☎04 71 74 97 49. www.ot-brioude.fr.
- ▶ **Orient Yourself:** Brioude is southeast from Clermont Ferrand, and accessible via the A 75.
- 🅿 **Parking:** Limited parking in the town centre.
- 😊 **Don't Miss:** The town walk is especially agreeable.
- 🕐 **Organising Your Time:** A relaxing half day would be sufficient, including lunch.
- 🕑 **Also See:** LAVAUDIEU, LE PUY EN VELAY.

A Bit of History

A saint, and a bandit from the Alps – Legend has it that a tribune of the Roman Legion named Julian, who was born in the Vienne region and was converted to Christianity, sought refuge in Brioude and was martyred in the year AD 304.

Pilgrims flocked to Brioude to pray at St Julian's tomb, particularly during the time of St Gregory of Tours (6C).

From the 9C onwards, the God-fearing town was subject to the authority of the canon-counts of St-Julien and remained so until the French Revolution, which put an end to their aristocratic tyranny.

Folk tales in Brioude still make reference to Mandrin, the notorious smuggler from Dauphiné. On 26 August 1754 he entered the town with a band of armed men, sought out the manager of the warehouse where tobacco was stored and taxed (the Farmers General held a monopoly on the sale of tobacco) and made the unfortunate man purchase a large batch of contraband Nicotine grass at an excessively high price. Mandrin then withdrew, while the people of Brioude turned a blind eye for they were delighted at the trick played on a system which they hated. The victim, however, never recovered from the shock; he died eight days later.

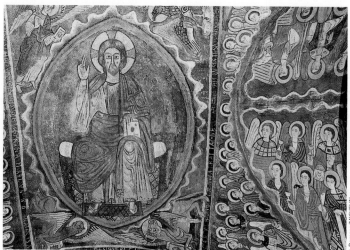

Frescoes in the Basilique St-Julien

J. Damase/MICHELIN

Basilique
St-Julien★★

St Julian's Basilica is the largest Romanesque church in the area, a "vast stone-built shrine standing over a famous tomb" (Bernard Craplet). It is typical of the Romanesque style seen in the Auvergne with its tiered east end and varying colours of masonry, though it differs in other respects – the portals are topped with smooth or carved coving or zigzag moulding instead of the traditional string-course of billet moulding. The ornamentation at the east end is also noticeably Burgundian in style.

Exterior

Building began on the church as it stands today with the narthex in 1060, and was completed in 1180 (chancel and east end). Its nave was raised and given rib vaulting in 1259, but the west front and square bell-tower above it were rebuilt in the 19C, as was the octagonal bell-tower above the transept crossing.

The fine concentric layout of the **east end**★★ makes this the most remarkable part of the building. It is one of the last examples of Romanesque architecture in the Auvergne.

The side **porches**★ with their groin vaulting constitute the oldest part of the church. They have an unusual appearance, the result of their use as chapels during the 16C and the inclusion of a gallery over the top.

Interior

The nave is particularly striking for its size and the warm hues of the red sandstone walls and pillars. The pebble **pavement**★ dating from the 16C in the nave and from the pre-Romanesque era in the fifth bay in the centre, was uncovered, together with the small crypt beneath the chancel, following restoration and excavation.

The church contains a large number of **capitals**★★ embellished with acanthus leaves, narrative scenes or themes commonplace in Auvergne churches.

The basilica contains a number of **altarpieces** and old **statues** that are worthy of note. The walls and pillars in the first bays, the ambulatory and the north gallery above the narthex still contain traces of 12C and 13C **paintings**★, which are surprising for their diversity, "modernism" and spirited representations of human figures. Turn to the right on entering the basilica to see:

(**1**) (south aisle) 14C statue of Christ the Leper (Crucifix), carved in wood with canvas backing, brought here from the former leper hospital in La Bajesse, near Brioude.

(**2**) (south aisle) 14C statue of Virgin Mary in childbirth in wood.

(**3**) (south aisle) 14C statue of Madonna with Bird carved in lava stone.

(**4**) (5th bay, south pillar) capital of Christ surrounded by the Evangelists.

(**5**) (first pillars of transept) carved corbels of heads of royal figures.

(**6**) (chancel) carved altarpiece (17C) behind the High Altar.

(**7**) (chancel, north pillar) capital depicting the Holy Women.

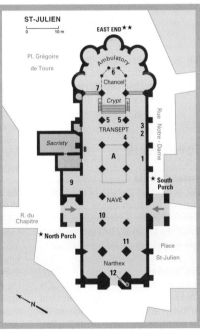

149

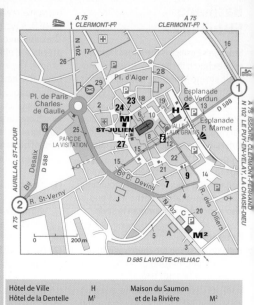

(**8**) (north aisle) 14C gilt wooden statue of the Madonna with Bird.

(**9**) (Chapel of the Cross) altarpiece attributed to 17C sculptor Vaneau.

(**10**) (3rd bay, north pillar) two capitals of groups of soldiers around a wounded soldier or prisoner.

(**11**) (south pillar in narthex) capital of the Punishment of the Moneylender; painting of a woman in profile, with an enlarged eye.

(**12**) (St Michael's Chapel) – in the south gallery of the narthex (access by a spiral staircase with 30 steps) – 12C frescoes; capital depicting donkeys playing musical instruments.

Town Walk

Hôtel de Ville

This is built on the site of the former castle of the canon-counts of St-Julien. There is a fine view over the Brioude section of the Limagne plain and the Livradois range from the adjacent terrace.

Old houses

In the district around the basilica is a network of narrow streets with old buildings and remarkable façades. To the north, on the corner of rue Talairat:

17C mansion with turrets and carved door; rue du 4-Septembre: no 29, Lace Centre (see below); no 25, 16C shop with arcades; no 22, 15C building known as **Mandrin's House**; place St-Julien: 15C half-timbered house; south of the basilica: no 21 rue de la Tour d'Auvergne, 18C mansion; place Eugène-Gilbert, Romanesque house with turret.

Hôtel de la Dentelle

○Open Apr–Oct Mon–Fri, 10am–noon, 2pm–6pm, Sat, 3pm–6pm. ○Closed Sun and public holidays. ☞4.50€. ☎04 71 74 80 02. www.hoteldeladentelle.com. The centre, housed in the 15C former residence of the counts of Brioude, contains collections of lacework and lacemaking equipment as well as a workshop where lacemakers can be seen at work.

Maison du Saumon et de la Rivière

♿○Open Apr–Sept Mon–Sat 10am–noon, 2pm–6pm (Jul–Aug, daily, 10am–7pm); Feb–Mar and Oct–Dec, 2pm–6pm. Sun, 2pm–6pm. ○Closed Jan. ☞5€. ☎04 71 74 91 43.

The Atlantic salmon, which reaches the spawning grounds of the Upper Allier at the end of its 800km/500mi journey upstream, is part and parcel of Brioude's history. Before learning about the importance of salmon fishing in the Brioude area in bygone days, you can see over 30 local species of river wildlife. But the main attraction is the "salmon river," a curved length of glass where migratory fish swim in simulated currents.

Excursion

Ardes-sur-Couze

34km NW of Brioude.

This old fortified town, once capital of the Duchy of Mercœur, has a 15C **church** in front of which there is a cross dating from the same period. Inside the church, the gilt-wood high altar (17C) features eight sculpture groups depicting the Passion. Near the chancel a strange carved wooden bas-relief adorns the shrine of St Hubert. Opposite the pulpit, there is a 16C stone **Pietà,** and the chapel at the back of the church contains a 15C lectern. 🖪 *Pl. de la Fontaine, 63420 ARDES, ☎04 73 71 80 39.*

The **Musée des Vieux Métiers** (*☺open Jun–mid Sept 10am–noon, 2pm–7pm; ⊸3€; ☎04 73 71 81 41*) shows exhibits relating to traditional crafts in the area, mainly used during the 19C.

🖼 The **Parc Animalier du Cézallier** (*☺Open Apr–Sept daily 10am–7pm; Oct–Mar Sun 2pm–dusk; ⊸8€ (children: 5€); ☎04 73 71 82 86; www.zoo-cezallier.com*, is a cross between a traditional zoo and a safari park. A great many animals of all types can be seen in relative freedom.

Driving Tours

Haut-Allier and Sénouire Valley★★

120km/75mi – allow one day.

▸ *Leave Brioude to the E on N 102, heading for Puy-en-Velay.*

Vieille-Brioude

An impressive winepress dating from 1873 stands in place de la Croix, testifying to the town's important wine-growing activities in the past. A whole network of cellars and galleries was dug

through the rocky spur on which Vieille-Brioude is perched.

Musée-jardin de la Vigne

☺Open mid-Jun–mid Sept 9am–7pm. ☎04 71 50 90 18.

Located at one end of the town, the Romanesque church stands in the middle of a garden where flowers grow next to herbs and medicinal plants.

▸ *In Vieille-Brioude, turn right onto D 585, which follows the Upper Valley of the Allier to Lavoûte-Chilhac.*

St-Ilpize

This medieval town, clinging to a basalt rock and towering above the River Allier, is crowned by the ruins of a castle. The defensive walls enclose a 14C **chapel.**

▸ *Rejoin D 585; turn right onto D 144.*

Église de Blassac

The church is built on a flow of basalt. Its chancel contains a set of 14C frescoes.

▸ *Rejoin D 585.*

Lavoûte-Chilhac

This village stands on the banks of the Allier, which washes up against the walls of the houses. It has an elegant 11C bridge, restored in the 15C, and a Gothic **church** (*☺open daily 9am–6pm*) surrounded by the buildings of an 18C Benedictine abbey.

Maison des Oiseaux du Haut-Allier

☺Open Jul–Aug Sun-Fri, 10am–noon, 2.30pm–6.30pm; Jun and Sept Wed and Sun 2.30pm–6pm; May Sun, 2.30pm–6pm. ☺Closed Sat. ⊸5€. ☎04 71 77 43 52.

This information centre of the Ligue pour la Protection des Oiseaux (LPO, Society for the Protection of Birds) presents the bird population of the Gorges de l'Allier and organises nature trails in season.

▸ *Rejoin D 585, which at this point hugs a meander in the Allier, giving a good view of the countryside.*

WHERE TO STAY

⊖⊖ **Ermitage St-Vincent** – *Pl. de l'Église, 43100 Vieille-Brioude.* ☎*04 71 50 96 47. Closed Dec–Jan.* ⌷. *5 rms. Meals*⊖⊖. Large, comfortable bedrooms, a garden bursting with flowers along the burbling river.

⊖⊖ **Sophie Pougheon Chambre d'hôte** – *Le Prieuré, 43100 Lamothe.* ☎*04 71 76 44 61.* ⌷. *5 rms.* Built on the heights above Brioude, this ancient priory, part of which was built in the 12C, offers a superb panoramic view of the town and surrounding landscape.

WHERE TO EAT

⊖ **Pons** – *7 r. d'Assas, Brioude.* ☎*04 71 50 00 03. Closed 16–24 Jun, 10 Nov–10 Dec, Sun evening, Tue evening and Mon. Reservations recommended.* The local population patronises this restaurant next to the Basilique St-Julien for its friendly atmosphere and regional cooking.

⊖ **Le Beffroi** – *R. du Vallat, Ardes-sur-Couze.* ☎*04 73 71 85 76. Closed Sat Sept–Easter.* As you drive through the village, this 'belfry' is easy to miss. Regional cuisine is served in two dining rooms whose vast bay windows look out on the garden.

SHOPPING

Cave Saint-Julien – *17 r. du Commerce.* ☎*04 71 74 90 18.* Wines from all corners of France garnish the shelves of this shop under a vaulted ceiling, along with bottles of champagne, other alcoholic beverages and 50-odd kinds of tea. The irresistible smell of Guatamalan or Mexican coffee beans being roasted wafts into the first part of the shop where Valette foie gras and Velay preserves surround an impressive display of dried mushrooms.

Gilles Guinet – *10 r. du Commerce.* ☎*04 71 50 12 47.* Vanilla bavaroise, nougatine, caramelised pears (*le Manon*) and la tarte dentellière vie for attention in the pastryshop, unless your tastes lean toward the family speciality, *la bombe au miel* (iced honey bombe).

Église de St-Cirgues

🕐*Open daily 9am–6pm.*
Inside, the two bays and the splays of the windows in the chancel are covered with interesting frescoes.

▶ *Carry on along D 585.*

Église d'Aubazat

This village in a pleasant setting has a church with a Pietà and wooden statues representing an Entombment (15C).

▶ *Rejoin D 585 for a further 500m/ 550yd, and at the crossroads turn right onto D 41, and then right again onto D 16.*

Église d'Arlet

This hamlet at the bottom of the Cronce valley has a Romanesque church.

Chilhac

Small village built on a terrace of columnar basalt. Its **Musée Paléontologique** (🕐*open daily, Easter-Jun and Sept–Oct 3pm–7pm; Jul–Aug 10am–noon, 3pm–7pm;* 🕐*closed Nov–Easter;* ⊜*5€;* ☎*04 71 77 47 26*) presents artefacts uncovered on local excavation sites since 1960.

Église de Peyrusses

Guided tours Wed 2pm–6pm. ☎*04 71 77 17 35.* This church contains a Virgin Mary in Majesty and splendid – if somewhat faded – frescoes.

▶ *Follow D 585 through Reilhac.*

Langeac

This busy little town lies in a cultivated "corridor" at the downstream end of the Allier gorge. One or two old houses are still to be seen along its streets.

▶ *Leave Langeac S along D 585.*

Église de Chanteuges

This attractive Romanesque church belonged to a local abbey which used to be the summer residence of the abbots of La Chaise-Dieu.

▶ *Turn right under a bridge, onto D 30.*

Pébrac

After running along the pretty little valley of the Desges between pine-covered slopes, the road brings you to this quiet hillside village with red-roofed houses and the ruins of an 11C **abbey**, which underwent extensive alteration in the 15C. Beautiful carved capitals have survived from the Romanesque era, one of which shows two large heads vomiting serpents.

▶ *Return to the intersection with D 585 and carry on along D 30, crossing to the opposite bank of the Allier.*

St-Arcons-d'Allier

The **church** has a very classic Romanesque nave with basalt columns. Its arcades are roofed by sturdy relief arches. The **Musée du Fer Blanc** (🕐*open Jul–Aug daily 3pm–7pm; ⊚4€; ☎04 71 74 02 04 (town hall)*) displays miscellaneous items made of tinplate: religious objects, lamps, moulds etc.

▶ *Cross the River Allier, drive through St-Arcons and take D 302 to Saugues. Turn left onto D 590, heading for Langeac. When you reach the locality called "Héraud," turn right.*

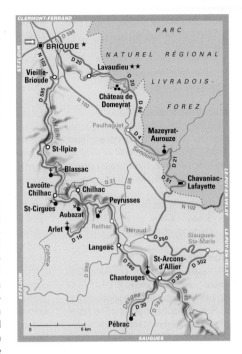

Château de Chavaniac-Lafayette

🕐*Open Apr–mid Nov daily except Tue 10am–noon, 2pm–6pm (Jul and Aug daily 9am–6pm). ⊚6€. ☎04 71 77 50 32. www.chateau-lafayette.com.*

The residence where Marie-Joseph-Gilbert, **Marquis de La Fayette**, was born on 6 September 1757, stands on one of the final outcrops of the Livradois area above the Allier valley; the history of Franco-American relations is more important here, however, than any archaeological feature.

The audio-guided tour leads visitors from room to room: a general biographical exhibition provides an introduction to the visit; next comes the kitchen where La Fayette's childhood is evoked, then the treasure room where personal objects and letters are displayed; this leads to the bedroom where he was born… his marriage is mentioned and the Grande Galerie recalls the ideas of the Age of Enlightenment; this is followed by a film on La Fayette's stay in America.

The grounds are graced by a pretty rose garden and three lakes.

▶ *Leave Chavaniac to the W on D 51; at the first crossroads, turn right onto D 21, then take D 4.*

Mazeyrat-Aurouze

This village has a lovely **church** (○ *open Mon and Thu 2pm–6pm by appointment. Apply to the town hall;* ☎*04 71 76 82 70)* built in pink stone, with frescoes depicting the lives of monks and peasants.

▶ *Go back to Brioude via the Sénouire Valley, by taking D 4 to Paulhaguet, then D 56.*

Domeyrat

The **castle** (○ *open Apr–Oct, daily, 10am –noon, 2pm–5pm;* ◎*5€;* ☎*04 71 76 69 12)* ruins dominating the Sénouire and its Romanesque bridge are a fine example of medieval military architecture. Dismantled in 1795, it still towers proudly above the River Sénouire spanned by the five-arches of a Romanesque bridge.

▶ *Continue along D 20, then D 203.*

Lavaudieu★★ – ○ *see LAVAUDIEU.*

▶ *Return to Brioude on D 20. Excursions.*

Valleys of the Cézallier
55km/34mi – about 3hr.

This round tour of the Cézallier (departing from Ardes) is linked to that of the Couze de Pavin and Couze de Chambon (○ *see BESSE-EN-CHANDESSE*) via the Gorges de Courgoul between Saurier and Valbeleix.

The valley of the Couze d'Ardes, a tiny tributary of the Allier, is known as the **Rentières d'Ardes**. The river cuts deeply into the Cézallier plateaux, forming a narrow furrow with valley sides carpeted with greenery. The circuit takes you through the village of **Brion,** overlooked by some very striking basalt columns. Not far from **Compains** is the spot where the Couze de Valbeleix rises; the river is most probably fed by the waters of Montcineyre Lake.

The valley of the **Couze de Valbeleix** forms an almost perfect U-shaped cross-section. Further on, tiny hanging glacial cirques on the west bank of the Couze give an idea of the depth of the ice which filled this valley 10,000 years ago.

To reach **Plateau de la Chavade**★ the road climbs up through the heart of a beech grove. From La Roche Nité there is a superb **view**★★ of the volcanic mountain ranges of the Cézallier and Dore mountain range, in which lava flows were truncated 10,000 years ago by gigantic tongues of ice.

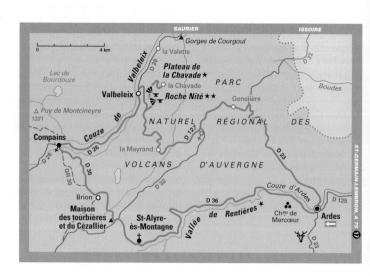

MONTS DU CANTAL★★★

MICHELIN MAP 330 : D-3 TO E-5

The mountains of Cantal, formed by the largest extinct volcano in France, embrace the most magnificent scenery in the Auvergne. Several of the peaks rise to more than 1,700m/5,580ft. Some, like the Puy Griou, are jagged; others, such as Puy Mary, are pyramid-shaped. The highest summit, Plomb du Cantal, is rounded and soars to a height of 1,855m/6,085ft. From the mountain heartlands, deep, picturesque valleys fan out, providing easy access for visitors.

▶ **Orient Yourself:** This is very much walking country without any clearly defined centres of habitation.
☺ **Don't Miss:** The Puy Mary, not the highest, but a superb vantage point.
🕐 **Organising Your Time:** Realistically you need to spend a few days here.
🐾 **Also See:** AURILLAC, MURAT, SALERS.

A Bit of Geography

The Etna of the Auvergne – The volcano in Cantal reached an altitude of 3,000m/9,840ft, and included a number of vents from which flowed viscous lava that solidified into needles, or the more fluid lava that spread out all round the volcano over an area 70km/44mi in diameter.

Effects of erosion – Glaciers formed in Cantal during the Quaternary Era. Their slow but powerful action wore down the summit of the mountain, uncovering the lava plugs that filled the vents, digging out corries that later became the valleys, and giving the mountain range the appearance it has today.

Dairy industry – The entire range was once covered by forest. Gradually, land was cleared and today it has disappeared in all but the entrance to a few valleys. Thanks to the basalt content of the lava, which produces a better quality pasture, Cantal has become best-known as a pastoral region.

Driving Tours

1 Route du Lioran★★
55km/34mi – about 4hr.
This itinerary follows the Cère and Alagnon valleys.

Aurillac★ – *see AURILLAC.*

▶ *Leave Aurillac E along D 117.*

The villages along the road have picturesque houses with hipped roofs that are typical of this area. The road then runs into the wide, attractive Cère Valley.

Polminhac
The houses in the village huddle round the foot of Pesteils Castle.

Château de Pesteils
see VIC-SUR-CÈRE.

Vic-sur-Cère★
see VIC-SUR-CÈRE.

Pas de Cère★★
45min on foot there and back.
The footpath leads off N 122, 3km/2mi upstream from Vic-sur-Cère.
🚶The path crosses a small meadow, then runs down through the woods to the Cère, which flows between high, narrow walls of rock.

Cascade de la Roucolle
From here, there is a wonderful view of the Roucolle waterfall and the Cère gorge.

Thiézac – *see VIC-SUR-CÈRE.*

Pas de Compaing★
High above the road on the left are tall cliffs from which, in rainy weather or when the snow melts, drops the superb **Malbec waterfall** (*it is inadvisable to*

Address Book

For coin ranges, see the legend on the cover flap.

WHERE TO EAT

Buron de la Brèche de Rolland – Col d'Eylac, 15300 Lavigerie, 7km/4.2mi N of Lavigerie via D 680. ☎04 71 20 81 43. Open May–1 Nov, daily 6.30am–10pm. 🍴. This small inn offers breathtaking views. Dishes include local delicatessen, *truffade*, stuffed cabbage, *pounti*…

RECREATION

Parapente Puy-Mary – 15400 Le-Claux. ☎04 71 78 95 21. www.parapente-puy-mary.com. Apr–Oct. Professionals introduce you to paragliding.

Mountain guides – Bureau des accompagnateurs, le Caylat, 15590 Lascelle. ☎04 71 47 97 20. www.cantal-randonnee.com. On foot or bike, benefit from the knowledge of the licensed guides.

---

park immediately below the cliffs because of the risk of a rockfall).

A short distance further on, the valley narrows and the road runs along the hilltop high above the deep gorge known as Pas de Compaing. Further on, the road enters the St-Jacques-des-Blats basin and the view extends to the end of the Cère valley, with the conical outline of Puy Griou to the left.

St-Jacques-des-Blats

This is an ideal centre for walking.

Col de Cère★

The D 67 skirting the Lioran road tunnel crosses the watershed separating the Dordogne basin into which flows the Cère, and the Loire basin into which flows the Alagnon. Just below the pass, the impressive pyramidal outline of Puy Griou can be seen to the left, in the distance. Beyond the wide Cère valley is the narrow Alagnon valley made darker by the pine forests lining it.

Le Lioran and Super-Lioran★
See Le LIORAN.

Gorges de l'Alagnon★
See St-FLOUR.

Beyond the **Pierre-Taillade bridge** which carries N 122 across a narrow stream fanning out in its course, the valley widens but the scenery is more sombre than in the Cère valley.

A few miles beyond Laveissière, the road runs along the foot of the handsome **Château d'Anterroches**, then

the basalt rocks above Murat come into view.

2 Pas de Peyrol★★

80km/50mi

This itinerary runs through "Puys" country along the Impradine, Mars and Maronne valleys. *D 680 which crosses the Peyrol pass is usually blocked by snow from November to June.*

Murat★ – *See MURAT.*

▶ *Leave Murat NW on D 680.*

As the road begins to climb, Plomb du Cantal, Puy de Peyre-Arse and Puy Griou come into view, one after the other, to the left. The road then skirts the foot of Chastel rock and runs down from Entremont pass offering views of the Dore mountain range in the distance and Puy Mary on the left.

After Dienne, as the road climbs up towards the Peyrol pass, it clings to the sheer sides of Puy Mary and provides **views**★★ over the Impradine and Rhue de Cheylade valleys, the Dore mountain range and the Cézallier area.

Pas de Peyrol★★

This is the highest mountain pass in the Massif Central. In the foreground, there is a view of the wooded Falgoux corrie overlooked by the Roc d'Auzière.

Puy Mary★★★

A steep footpath follows the north-west ridge of the mountain. From the summit there is a breathtaking view of

J. Damase/MICHELIN

The ridge along the top of the Puy Mary

Cantal's gigantic extinct volcano and a superb **view** over the crystalline plateaux that form the base of the volcanic area of the Auvergne. In the foreground is a striking view of the gigantic fan formed by the valleys radiating out from the centre of this natural water tower, separated by massive ridges with altitudes that decrease in the distance.

Rural life varies with the altitude across this countryside divided by deep corries. In the depths of the valleys near the villages are fields of crops and meadows. In the lesser exposed areas are birch woods followed by beeches half way up the slopes and conifers.

At higher altitudes are the alpine pastures dotted with burons (the huts once lived in by shepherds during the summer, where they made cheese) surrounded by ash trees. The drive down from Pas de Peyrol affords splendid views over the Mars Valley.

Cirque du Falgoux★★

The Mars valley starts here, as the river gouges out a course for itself along the foot of Puy Mary.

▶ *Head NW along D 12.*

Vallée du Mars★

The road follows the valley, in which there is a striking contrast between the shaded slopes, covered in woodland but devoid of houses, and the sunny slopes carpeted with meadows and trees, and dotted with houses. In the **Gorge de St-Vincent**★ the valley narrows.

To the left of the road beyond the gorge is the **Château de Chanterelle,** a fortified residence dating from the 17C with later restoration.

▶ *Return to D 680 (or drive to Salers on D 212 – follow signs to Anglards – and D 22).*

At the pass known as Col de Néronne, the road moves to the other side of the hill and overlooks the wide, glacial Maronne valley far below.

Puy Violent★

Walkers will enjoy Puy Violent, leaving from St-Paul-de-Salers.

▶ *Go to Vielmur and turn left. Follow a narrow shepherd's lane which leads beyond the Croix des Vachers.*

The walk to the top of the mountain (2hr 30min return) affords a lovely panorama, namely of the Maronne valley.

③ Crest Road★★
60km/38mi.

This itinerary takes over from the previous one and runs along the Aspre and Doire valleys.

The road up to Col de Legal is usually blocked by snow from December to April.

Salers★★ – ⟨see SALERS.

▶ *Leave Salers on D 35 E.*

Running along the western slopes of Cantal's ancient volcano, the road crosses a few of the valleys which fan out from the heart of the range. It hairpins down into the Maronne valley then crosses the river and enters the Aspre valley. The traces left by the ancient glaciers that formed these valleys are obvious, even today. On the hillsides, are huge boulders, carried there by the ice and now left lying scattered.

Fontanges

To the right, at the entrance to the village, is a **chapel** dug into a mass of volcanic rock; entry is through a wrought-iron door set between colonnettes and archivolts. The **castle,** which now lies in ruins, once belonged to the family of Louis XIV's mistress.

▶ *Continue o D 35 along the Aspre.*

Col de Legal

From this pass there is a view in the distance over the Limousin plateau.

▶ *At Col de Bruel turn right onto D 60 to Tournemire.*

Tournemire – ⟨see TOURNEMIRE.

Château d'Anjony★
⟨see TOURNEMIRE.

▶ *Turn back and take D 35 to the right.*

Beyond the Croix de Cheules, D 35, which is called the **Route des Crêtes★★** (Crest Road) follows the long ridge that separates the Authre and Jordanne valleys, and the journey provides some very attractive views of them.

▶ *After 6km/4mi, turn right onto D 58 to Marmanhac.*

Château de Sédaiges

Sédaiges, rebuilt in the 15C and modified in the 18C and 19C, is neo-Gothic. The furnishings and decor reflect the lifestyle of a 19C aristocratic family.

▶ *Return to the Route des Crêtes, D 35.*

As the road slopes down towards Aurillac, the broad plain at the edge of the town can be seen stretching away, whereas to the left there is a magnificent view of the Jordanne valley.

Aurillac★ – ⟨see AURILLAC.

④ **Vallée de la Jordanne★★**

25km/15mi

Pas de Peyrol★★ – ⟨see above.

▶ *Leave the pass on D 17 S.*

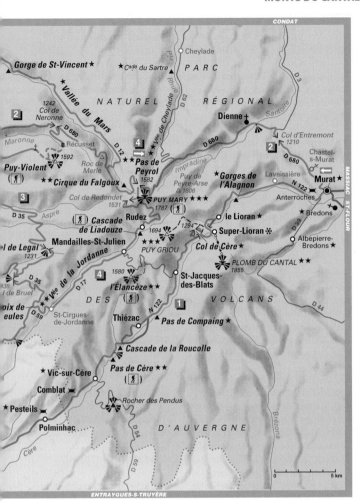

The cliffroad overlooks the superb Falgoux corrie where the River Mars rises. Beyond Redondet pass there is a view of Plomb du Cantal before the road runs into the Jordanne valley.

Rudez
Huddled together, the village houses cling to the mountain slopes in order to leave the valley floor free for pasture.

Vallée de la Jordanne★★
The slopes that flank this picturesque valley are lush and green, carpeted with meadows screened by clumps of trees. Here and there are a few rocky escarpments dotted with caves.

Cascade de Liadouze
🚶The waterfall drops over a threshold of rock into a narrow gorge.

Mandailles
This village, lying in picturesque surroundings, is the starting point of numerous rambles.

▶ *Turn right onto D59.*

The road crosses the Jordanne then wends its way up the hillside.

Croix de Cheules
The crossroads marks the start of the Crest Road.

MONTS DU CÉZALLIER★

MICHELIN MAP 326 : E-10 TO G-11

The Cézallier range is situated between the Dore mountain range and the mountains of Cantal; it consists of a succession of granite plateaux lying at an altitude of more than 1,200m/3,940ft, which were covered with a layer of basalt during the Tertiary Era.

▶ **Orient Yourself:** Lying south of Clermont-Ferrand, and accessible by A 75.
◐ **Organising Your Time:** This is a region for leisurely exploration; allow as much time as you can, certainly a day to enjoy the tours.
◖ **Also See:** CLERMONT FERRAND, CONDAT, ISSOIRE, ST-FLOUR.

A Bit of History

The volcanoes, from which the flows spread out all over the area, have neither cones nor craters. Indeed, they scarcely even jut out from above the surrounding countryside because the lava produced by the eruptions was very fluid and did not build up around the vents of the volcano. On the eastern side in particular the plateaux are gashed by impressive valleys.

The Cézallier range is one vast area of pasture dotted with former shepherd's huts (*burons*) and a few villages with huge barns and byres, and fountains made out of old drinking troughs. Here, in the summer months, thousands of heads of cattle graze on the plateaux. The local people supplement their income by digging up gentian roots, used in the production of an alcoholic drink.

Despite its lack of hotels and places to stay, the Cézallier area is popular with those who enjoy wide open spaces, solitude and fresh air, and also with winter sports enthusiasts, especially cross-country skiers since the lie of the land is ideal for this sport. Downhill skiing is also catered for, although facilities are, as yet, limited. The area is part of a regional park, the Parc Naturel Régional des Volcans d'Auvergne. Two trips are described below; the first leads through the "mountains" and the second follows the valley which plunges down to the River Alagnon to the east of the range.

Driving Tours

1 Alpine Pastures
90km/56mi – about 5hr.

Condat – ◖*see CONDAT.*

▶ *Leave Condat S on D 679 towards Allanche.*

The road skirts a stretch of water that is a recent reconstruction of a lake originally built in the 12C by monks.

High pastures of the Cézallier

Abbaye de Féniers

The Cistercian abbey founded in the late 12C was rebuilt in 1686 and closed during the French Revolution. The buildings were partially destroyed by fire in 1872; only a few vestiges of the abbey, cloisters and church have survived.

▶ *Turn right onto D 16.*

The road to St-Bonnet-de-Condat runs down into the Santoire Valley and through a wooded **gorge.**

▶ *In St-Bonnet-de-Condat; left on D 36.*

Marcenat

This is a modest winter sports resort which has also specialised in the production and selling of local cheese. One local curiosity is the **Maison de la Foudre** (🕐open Jul–Aug 10.30am–noon, 2.15pm–6pm; Jun and Sept 2.15pm–5.30pm; mid-Apr–May Sat–Sun and public holidays 3pm–5pm; ✎5€; ☎04 71 78 85 00), an exhibition of photographs of thunder and lightning taken during violent storms by an enthusiastic meteorologist.

Beyond Marcenat there are some superb views to the left of the road, over the Cézallier range.

Les Prades

Columnar basalt. From the summit, there is a delightful view of Landeyrat and the upper Allanche valley cutting into the planèze.

▶ *Turn left off D 679 onto D 39 then D 23. Both roads cross the plateau.*

Apcher

A short distance to the west of this village, an attractive waterfall drops down from the edge of the plateau.

▶ *On leaving Anzat-le-Luguet, leave D 23 and turn left onto D 271.*

Parrot

Small winter sports resort.

Signal du Luguet★

1hr 30min on foot there and back from Parrot. Climb up to the summit across

the meadows slightly to the left of the ski lift.

🚶The wooded summit scarcely stands out above the plateaux. From it there is a vast **panoramic view**★ over the Dore mountain range and the mountains of Cantal.

▶ *Continue along D 721 to Boutaresse then turn right onto D 724.*

The road twists and turns through picturesque scenery.

St-Alyre-ès-Montagne

On a rise near the small village is the south-facing church overlooking superb countryside nestled in the shadow of Mount Gamet. The church is unusual for the primitive carvings on its tympanum and the billet-moulding on the east end.

▶ *Leave St-Alyre W along D 36; 3km/ 1.9mi further on, turn left onto D 32.*

La Godivelle

This is a typical Cézallier hamlet with sturdy granite houses and a large, round fountain. Its other main feature is its geographical location, between a crater lake, the Lac d'En Haut (Upper Lake), and another, peaty lake, the Lac d'En Bas (Lower Lake), the haunt of countless migratory birds.

Ramble

🚶*3hr 30min there and back, starting from La Godivelle; follow the yellow markings; keep dogs on a leash.*
Walk across the peat bogs and high pastures as far as Jassy and return to La Godivelle via the lakes of Saint-Alyre and En-Bas.

▶ *Drive N out of La Godivelle along D 32, then 3km/1.9mi further on, turn right onto D 26.*

Col de la Chaumoune

Near this mountain pass are several conifer plantations.

▶ *Turn left onto D 30 and, 6km/ 3.7mi further on, turn left again onto D 978.*

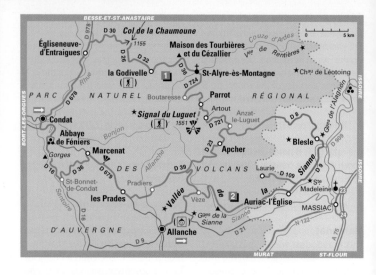

Égliseneuve-d'Entraigues

This small summer holiday resort has a Romanesque church, but do not miss the regional Cheese Museum housed inside a barn. The **Maison des Fromages** (⏱ *open mid-Jun–mid Sept 2pm–6pm (Jul–Aug 10am–12.30pm, 2.30pm–7pm)*; ✆4€; ☎04 73 71 92 01) is of interest to those wishing to find out about the history and production of St-Nectaire, Cantal, Bleu d'Auvergne, Fourme d'Ambert.

▶ *D 678 leads back to Condat along the lovely Rhue Valley.*

2 Vallée de la Sianne

50km/31mi – about 1hr 30min

Allanche

Winter sports resort. The west end of the old town still has a few remnants of its ramparts. The **church** (⏱ *open daily except Sun afternoon 9am–noon, 3pm–6pm*) contains Renaissance stalls, a painting on wood from the Flemish School and a moving Pietà carved in stone.

Rail-biking

Pedal away along disused tracks between Allanche and Lugarde or Neussargues aboard a kind of pedalo! *(Ask at the tourist office).*

▶ *Head E from Allanche on D 9 towards Chavanon.*

Between Allanche and Vèze, the road crosses the Cézallier's great alpine meadows and then, at the top of the rise, the mountains of Cantal come into view. The cliffroad subsequently runs down to the **Gorges de la Sianne**★, providing some fine views of the ravine on the way. The hillsides are covered with forest. Beyond several gorges where huge boulders jut out from above both banks of the river, the valley widens out, becoming less sombre, and fruit trees appear.

Auriac-l'Église

This village is attractively situated to the right of the road.
Lovers of Romanesque art will enjoy a detour via Laurie where the church houses a wooden statue of the Virgin Mary.

▶ *Turn right onto D 8.*

Blesle★

⏱*See ST-FLOUR.*

▶ *Return to Allanche via the Bellan Valley, Anzat-le-Luguet, and D 23, which will take you back to Vèze.*

You can also pursue your route towards Massiac and the Alagnon gorges ((⏱see ST-FLOUR).

LA CHAISE-DIEU★★

POPULATION 772
MICHELIN MAP 331: E-2
40KM/25MI NE OF LE PUY-EN-VELAY

Set amid lush green countryside with gently-rolling hills, the vast buildings and ornate architectural style of the famous abbey of La Chaise-Dieu come as a magnificent surprise. The abbey derives its name from the Latin "Casa Dei," meaning "the House of God." A renowned music festival takes place at the end of August in the abbey church and Cziffra Hall.

▯ **Information:** Pl. de la Mairie, 43160 La CHAISE-DIEU, ☎04 71 00 01 16. www.la-chaise-dieu.info.

▶ **Orient Yourself:** La Chaise-Dieu is all about its abbey, so the best way to orient yourself is to wander the maze of streets and see how the abbey would have dominated the original community here.

☺ **Don't Miss:** The old houses in the narrow streets adjacent to the place de l'Eglise.

🕓 **Organising Your Time:** Explore first, and then spend some time in the abbey, especially the cloisters; allow at least half a day.

A Bit of History

Foundation of the abbey – In 1043 Robert de Turlande, a former canon from Brioude, withdrew with a few companions to this desolate plateau. He was soon joined by increasing numbers of followers and founded a monastery under the Benedictine Rule for which, in 1052, he obtained the Pope's protection. Its success continued to grow to the extent that, at Robert's death in 1067, the monastery had 300 monks and 49 priories (including a convent, in Lavaudieu).

Increasing numbers of priories continued to be founded as far away as Italy and Spain (250 altogether) and this, taken with the flow of gifts and scope of its spiritual influence, made La Chaise-Dieu the third most important French monastic order in the mid-12C.

The Abbot was all-powerful. He was accountable to nobody but the Pope and, every year, he convened the Chapter General. In the 12C and 13C the abbots maintained the Order's independence and kept alive the spirit in which the abbey had been founded, thereby avoiding the excesses which weakened the great abbey at Cluny.

Papacy of Clement VI – The situation suddenly deteriorated in the early 14C, when the abbot's authority was undermined and several priories broke away from the mother-house. The election, however, in Avignon, of Pope Clement VI – one of the abbey's former novices and monks – brought a halt to this decline. The Pope had the church rebuilt as it is today between 1344 and 1352 to designs by an architect from Southern France named Hugues Morel. The Pope's nephew, Gregory XI, completed the building (last three bays in the nave and the abbey buildings).

In the early years of the 16C, Jacques de St-Nectaire gave the abbey a dazzling set of tapestries.

Contemporary rebirth – After centuries of decline, the abbey finally attracted attention in the early years of the 20C; yet it was not completely restored until after the Second World War. In 1965 the pianist **Georges Cziffra** fell in love with the abbey, and founded a festival of religious music in aid of the restoration project. Repair work on the great organ was begun in 1977 and not finished until 1995. The Festival de la Chaise-Dieu continues to make a name for itself as one of the main festivals of its type in France.

Église Abbatiale St-Robert

Abbey

Église Abbatiale St-Robert★★

ⓘ *Open May–Oct: daily, 9am–noon, 2pm–7pm; Nov–Apr: daily except Sun morning, 10am–noon, 2pm–5pm. Closed Jan, Mon in Dec and Feb, 25 Dec and 1 Jan.* ≈5€. ☎04 71 00 06 06. www.la-chaise-dieu.info.

Solidly built of granite, the church gives an impression of grandeur and austerity which seem to reflect the personality of its founder, Clement VI.

West Front

The architecture of the west front is military in style. It overlooks a sloping

Chancel

L'office de tourisme de la Chaise-Dieu

square decorated with a 17C fountain and is flanked by two towers, neither of which is very high. The portal, including a pier embellished with a statue of St Robert, was damaged by the Huguenots in 1562. The small house concealing the base of the south tower is said to have been used by Cardinal de Rohan.

Nave and side aisles

The interior has a vast nave roofed with flattened vaulting and is flanked by side aisles of the same height. Five radiating chapels open directly off the chancel. A 15C rood screen (**1**) breaks up the perspective and seems to reduce the height of the nave. At the top of it is a fine statue of Christ (1603) with, at the foot of the Cross, two wooden statues representing the Virgin Mary and St John (15C). The superb **organ loft**★ (**2**) facing it dates from the 17C.

Chancel★★

The chancel is surrounded by 144 oak **choir stalls**★★ (**3**) dating from the 15C, decorated with particularly fine carvings depicting a wide range of subjects. Above the enclosure are exquisite **tapestries**★★★ (**4**) from Arras and Brussels, made of wool, linen and silk, and dating from the early 16C. The subjects are drawn from the Old and New Testaments and illustrate the theme of Salvation copied from the Poor Man's Bible that was so commonplace in the Middle

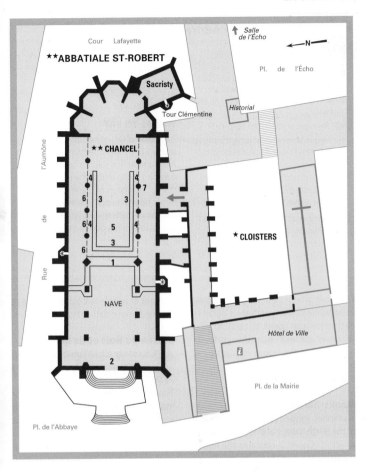

Ages. They are accompanied by legends written in Gothic script.

In the middle of the chancel is Clement VI's tomb (**5**). The Pope had it made during his own lifetime and carved by Pierre Roye, Jean David and Jean de Sanholis. It was originally surrounded by 44 statues representing members of the Pope's family. The Protestants damaged the tomb and all that now remains is the recumbent statue on a black marble slab. The north aisle features the famous fresco of the **Dance of Death**★ (**6**) (2m/6ft 6in high and 26m/85ft long): the three panels juxtapose the great and famous of this world and the dead; the dead are shown inviting the living to dance with them, a reminder of what lies before them. The fresco depicts the powerful to the left, the wealthy in the middle and the craftsmen to the right.

This theme was frequently depicted in the 15C, yet never before has it been treated with such realism and such a sense of movement. It was here that the composer **Arthur Honegger** (1892–1955) drew the inspiration, in 1938, for his work *The Dance of the Dead*, an oratorio with a libretto by Paul Claudel. In the south aisle lies the mutilated tomb of Abbot Renaud de Montclar (**7**) dating from the 14C; it still has its decoration of carved cherubs.

Cloisters★

The cloisters were built at the end of the 14C. Only two galleries have survived to the present day; one of them has an upper storey which was used as a library. Beyond the cloisters is a square: on the left-hand side, the second flight of steps into the hospice leads to the Echo

Address Book

For coin ranges, see the cover flap.

WHERE TO STAY

Écho et Abbaye – *Pl. de l'Écho. 04 71 00 00 45. Closed 12 Nov–26 Mar and Wed except Jul–Aug. 10 rms. 9€. Restaurant .* The haunt of numerous luminaries during the music festival, this tranquil hotel behind the abbey has comfortable, well-maintained bedrooms, some with a view of the cloisters. The restaurant serves regional dishes in a pleasant setting.

Chambre d'hôte La Jacquerolle – *R. Marchédial. 04 71 00 07 52. 4 rms. Meals.* Set in the lower part of the village, this handsome house built of local stone has a dining room furnished in period pieces with a stunning granite fireplace on the first floor. Guest rooms are as welcoming as they are comfortable.

WHERE TO EAT

Le Lion d'Or – *Av. de la Gare. 04 71 00 01 58. Closed Jan–Feb.* A restaurant in a traditional Auvergnat dwelling at the end of the town's main street. The generous, carefully prepared fare is served on plates shaped like their contents – quite the original touch! The reasonable prices add to the appeal.

Chamber where two people standing in opposite corners with their backs to each other can speak to each other in whispers and hear each other perfectly. It is said that the layout was designed in the Middle Ages to enable lepers to attend Confession.

Monks' library

This sober, vaulted room follows the line of the north gallery of the cloisters upon which it is built. It contains the abbey **treasury**, in which there are magnificent Brussels tapestries on display, as well as a 17C ivory statue of Christ, Clement VI's broken ring and various valuable pieces of church plate.

The Town

Historial de la Chaise-Dieu

Open Jul–mid Sept daily 9am–noon, 2pm–7pm; mid-Apr–Jun Sat–Sun 10am–noon, 2pm–5pm (Jun, daily except Mon). 2.50€. 04 71 00 06 99. www.la-chaise-dieu.info.

This gallery has been turned into a Waxworks Museum with displays illustrating the abbey's finest hours.

Historical houses

In the narrow streets adjacent to place de l'Église are a number of interesting houses with medieval façades. At the bottom of rue de la Côte is La Cloze, a fortified house dating from the 15C.

Musée du Bois et de la Forêt

Open May–Oct 10am–noon, 2.30pm–6pm. Closed Nov–Apr. 3€. 04 71 00 10 35.

Timber is still the area's main source of income and a local resident has opened a small museum explaining the different stages in the exploitation of forests.

Walks

Sentier du Serpent d'Or

2hr there and back.

Starting from La Chaise-Dieu *(next to the village hall),* this Serpent's Lane, named after the golden, meandering waters of the Sénouire, will take you down to the banks of the river, passing through Breuil Forest.

Signal de St-Claude

1km/0.6mi E.

Beyond the railway bridge, turn right onto the path that leads to the summit some 600m/660yd further on.

Fine panoramic view of Pierre sur Haute, the mountains in the Forez and Lyon areas, Mont Pilat, the Cévennes, the mountains of Cantal and the Dore mountain range.

CHARROUX★

POPULATION 330

MICHELIN MAP 326: F-5 – 15KM/9.3MI N OF GANNAT

Charroux is built on a hilltop and was one of the 19 castellanies of the Barony of Bourbon. The old houses, built of dressed stone and ornamented with carved mouldings, have been restored and make the village particularly attractive.

- **Information:** Maison de Tourisme ☎04 70 56 87 71. www.charroux.com.
- ▶ **Orient Yourself:** Charroux en Bourbonnais (to be precise) is just 10 minutes from the exit of the A71, mid-way between Montluçon (N) and Clermont Ferrand (S).
- **Organising Your Time:** Leave plenty of time for the driving tour.
- **Also See:** MONTLUÇON, CLERMONT FERRAND.

Walking Tour

Church

This fortified 12C building was once part of the town walls. The belfry rises above the transept crossing but its pyramid-shaped spire has been truncated.

▶ *Leave via the north aisle.*

On the square there is a **medieval house** with an overhanging upper storey. On the left stands the belfry, a square tower once used as a watchtower.

Rue de la Poulaillerie

An old stone well stands in the centre of this picturesque cobbled street.

Musée de Charroux et de son Canton

Open May–Jun Sat, Sun, 2.30pm–6.30pm; Jul–Aug daily except Tue, 2.30pm–6.30pm. ☜3.50€. ☎04 70 56 81 65. www.charroux.com.

This Regional History Museum is set up in a house with a façade decorated with carvings of animal heads, figures and nailhead moulding; objects and documents provide an insight into the history of the Charroux area. Downstairs there is a display of objects from the Roman era, along with Gothic and Renaissance sculptures, in addition to an exhibition on locally crafted fireplaces. Jambs, mantelpieces and photographs of different designs illustrate the dexterity of Charroux's stone cutters. One room contains a reconstruction of the workshop of Jean-Baptiste Cailhe-Decante, a highly reputed 19C maker of stringed instruments and hurdy-gurdies.

Porte d'Orient

The **East Gate** was one of the bastions in the town wall. The defensive system is still visible today.

Viewpoint

A circular platform surrounded by a low wall in the shade of an oak tree offers a view over the adjacent countryside.

Driving Tour 60km/37mi

▶ *Leave Charroux to the W and follow D 35 for 2km/1mi, then turn right onto D 68. After crossing the motorway, take D 183 on the left.*

Veauce

Nestling in a large shaded park, the **castle** (☜Guided tours (30min) daily except Tue 10.30am–noon, 2.30pm–6.30pm. ☜5€. ☎04 70 58 53 27), built 9C–15C,

Landscape of the Bourbonnais

is perched on top of a rocky outcrop dominating the River Veauce.

▶ *Leave Veauce to the N on D 118, then D 987. At Croix des Bois, take D 284 on the right.*

Forêt des Colettes
This forest planted with beech, oak and pine is dominated by the Signal de la Bosse situated near the intersection of D 998 and D 987 *(turn right).*

▶ *After crossing Coutansouze, take D 68 on the right.*

Bellenaves
This village has a fine Romanesque church.

▶ *Leave Bellenaves to the N on D 43.*

Chantelle
On a steep promontory stands a Benedictine abbey, built on the ruins of a former castle and monastery. The nuns who live here produce home-made soaps and eaux de toilette that can be purchased on the premises.

▶ *Take Grand-Rue (D 987) to rue Anne-de-Beaujeu, which leads to the Abbaye St-Vincent.*

The **conventual church** dates from the Romanesque era. Only the nave (attractive capitals) is open to the public. On leaving the convent, go to the nearby terrace to enjoy the view of the Bouble gorges, dominated by the Chantelle rooftops. It is possible to reach the shaded banks of the river by following the former castle moat.

▶ *Leave Chantelle to the E on D 987. After 6km/4mi, take D 115 on the right.*

Château de Chareil
◷*Open mid-Jun–mid Sept daily except Mon, 10am–noon, 2pm–6pm.* ◷*Closed rest of year.* ⊜*3€.* ☏*04 70 56 94 28.*
This former stronghold, restored in the 16C, is owned by the State. Part of the exterior has recently been restored (the doorway, the terrace and the 19C well). The interior is notable for its two imposing Renaissance fireplaces and its 16C **mural paintings**★ in shades of brown, representing mythological themes (Mars, Venus, Cupid, legend of Adonis).

▶ *Go back to D 987, heading for Chantelle, then take D 115 on the left and proceed to Ussel-d'Allier.*

Ussel-d'Allier
Leave Ussel on D 223. A dirt track to the left of the road leads to a raised viewing table. From there, you can admire a panorama of the Bourbon countryside.

▶ *Return to D 223.*

Église d'Étroussat

The church boasts a series of 14 modern **stained-glass windows**★ attributed to the master glassworker Frédérique Duran.

▶ *Leave Étroussat to the S on D 35 and drive back to Charroux.*

Excursions

Gannat

13km/8.7mi S. 🅸 *Pl. des Anciens-de-l'AFN, 03800 GANNAT,* ☎*04 70 90 17 78* lies
This ancient town on the edge of the Limagne plain and the granite base below the mountains of the Auvergne, on the threshold of the "Gateway to Occitania", the point of contact between two old forms of French language – *langue d'oc* and *langue d'oïl*. The area is important archaeologically, and digs have uncovered rhinoceros skeletons thought to be at least 23 million years old, together with the remains of crocodiles and fossilised birds.

World Culture Festival – Every summer Gannat is filled with the sounds of traditional folk dancers, musicians and singers who come here to take part in an international cultural event which resounds with colour and excitement.

Église Ste-Croix

Traces of the original Romanesque church are still visible. The church was rebuilt in the Gothic period and underwent minor alterations over the years.

Castle

The 12C fortress, dismantled in 1566, was used as a prison from 1833 to 1967. The castle has tall 14C walls flanked by corner towers.

Musée Municipal

🕐 *Open May–Oct daily except Tue 2pm–6pm (Jul and Aug 10am–noon, 2pm–6pm).* ⊛*5€.* ☎*04 70 90 00 50.*
The old warders' apartments and the prison cells now house the municipal museum. Among the items on display are 14C-18C parchments from the town's

Gospel book

J. Damase/MICHELIN

archives, 12C wrought-iron grilles, restored statues, votive images) and a beautiful **Gospel Book**★ with illuminations on vellum.

Jenzat

6km/3.7mi SE on D 42.
The late-11C **church** here is decorated with 15C paintings in tempera which are known as "Frescoes by the Masters of Jenzat." The **Maison du Luthier** (♿🕐*open Jun–Sept Sun-Mon, 2.30pm–6.30pm (Jul–Aug daily, Mon–Thu).* ⊛*4€.* ☎*04 70 56 81 78)* contains a museum on the craft of making musical instruments, in particular hurdy-gurdies – Jenzat was said to be the European capital in this respect in the 19C.

Église de Biozat

18km/11.1mi SE.
This beautiful, Romanesque **church** is typical of the Limagne area with its barrel-vaulted nave, half-barrel vaulting in the side aisles, dome over squinches and a number of interesting capitals.

▶ *From here you can drive 4km/2.5mi to Effiat and join up with the Limagne discovery trail (🕐see AIGUEPERSE).*

CLERMONT-FERRAND★★

POPULATION 137,140
MICHELIN MAP 326: F-8

Clermont-Ferrand is the natural capital of the Auvergne. The city centre is built on a slight rise, all that remains of a volcanic cone. The old houses built of volcanic rock in the "Black Town" huddle in the shade of the cathedral. Over the past 30 years or so, Clermont's urban landscape has undergone major changes. New developments include the **Jaude** (a vast shopping complex), the **St-Pierre** district (new covered market), the **Fontgiève** district (law courts, residential buildings), and place du 1er-Mai (sculpture by Étienne Martin), all of which combine contemporary architecture with an older urban environment. In 2006, a new urban tramway was inaugurated, the first phase in a transport revival of the city, and the first tram system in France to use bi-directional pneumatic tyres.

For visitors arriving from the Pontgibaud direction, there is a good general **view**★★ of the town from a **bend** on D 941^A. From left to right, the nearby heights of the Côtes de Clermont and Chanturgue plateau give an indication of the original level of the Limagne plain prior to the major period of erosion. Opposite the platform lies the city itself, dominated by its black cathedral. In the distance, beyond the Allier valley, are the mountains of the Livradois area. To the right are the Comté volcanoes, Gergovie plateau and Montrognon rock. Avenue Thermale runs along a hilltop north of Royat. From it there are more superb **views**★ over the town of Clermont and the surrounding area.

- 🛈 **Information:** Pl. de la Victoire, 63000 CLERMONT-FERRAND. ☎04 73 98 65 00. www.clermont-fd.com.
- ▸ **Orient Yourself:** Most of the bars, brasseries, theatres, pubs and restaurants are downtown, mainly around the place de Jaude.
- 🅿 **Parking:** Parking (charge) is available at a number of locations around the edge of the city centre. It is often better to park on the edge of the *centre ville* and walk in.
- 😊 **Don't Miss:** The place de Jaude; this is the focal point for everything that's 'happening' in Clermont-Ferrand.
- 🕐 **Organising Your Time:** The place de Jaude is a good place to start, to get a feel for the city, before going on to explore more widely.
- **Kids Especially for Kids:** Visit the Espace Massif Central, or Vulcania.
- 👣 **Also See:** ISSOIRE, THIERS, PUY DE DÔME.

Clermont-Ferrand by night

J. Damase/MICHELIN

A Bit of History

From Nemessos to Clermont-Ferrand
– The Arverni oppidum (settlement) of Nemessos was built on the site of the rise now occupied by the cathedral. Its name, meaning "wooded rise" or "sacred wood," is a reminder that the spot was used by the Druids as a place of worship. Gradually, over the course of the 1C AD, Druidic rites were abandoned.

A new settlement slowly grew up at the junction of several roads below the original town and, in honour of Caesar Augustus, its name was added on to that of the Roman Emperor. Augustonemetum had several major public buildings and a large number of private residences. An aqueduct brought water from the Villars valley to the summit of the rise where it was distributed to the various urban districts from a water tower.

At its height, in the 2C, the town underwent fairly large-scale expansion and its population rose to between 15,000 and 30,000 inhabitants. An ancient description indicates that it was "well-planted with vineyards, full of people, busy with traffic and trade and much given to pomp."

During the early Middle Ages the town sank into decline. It suffered a number of destructive sieges at the hands of the Franks, the Saracens and the Vikings. It was in the 8C that the name "Clermont" was first applied to the fortress destroyed by Pepin the Short in AD 761.

In the 10C the town entered a period of economic revival. Bishop Étienne II had a new cathedral built, the population increased, the town grew beyond the old town walls and there were no less than 34 churches and chapels inside and outside the walls.

For centuries the episcopal town of Clermont was rivalled by Montferrand, the count's stronghold, and later by Riom, the seat of the Court of Appeal. Clermont finally won the day and, in 1630, Montferrand merged with its neighbour to form the conurbation known as Clermont-Ferrand.

Blaise Pascal, a man of genius – A few years earlier, the great writer and philosopher **Blaise Pascal** (1623–62) was born in the town. Pascal was not only very gifted in the Arts, but he was also a brilliant scientist with an enormous talent for mathematics and physics. When he was 12, it became obvious that he had outstanding natural ability in geometry. At the age of 16, he amazed the philosopher Descartes with an essay on conic sections. Two years later, he invented a calculator. The "wheelbarrow" or "vinaigrette," a two-wheeled sedan chair, was also one of his inventions. It was Pascal, too, who had the idea of the "five *sous* coach service" travelling a fixed route and leaving at regular intervals. The coaches were an immediate success and they paved the way for the Parisian omnibus service. It was Pascal again, with his brother-in-law Périer, who proved the weight of air following an experiment at Le Puy-en-Velay.

Tyre town – It is perhaps surprising that Clermont, situated in the heart of the Auvergne far from the harbours through which rubber and cotton were imported and well away from the major wire-mills, became the leading centre of tyre production in France and, indeed, one of the industry's leading operators worldwide. The story behind this, however, is one of quite humble origins.

In the heyday of Romanticism, c 1830, a former solicitor named Aristide Barbier, who had lost three-quarters of his personal fortune as a result of the difficult financial climate, set up in partnership with his cousin, Edouard Daubrée, a captain in the King's Light Cavalry who had resigned his commission in order to open a small farm machinery factory on the banks of the River Tiretaine. In order to amuse her children, Madame Daubrée, niece of the Scottish chemist **Charles Macintosh** (1766–1843) who had discovered that rubber dissolves in petroleum, made a few rubber balls as she had seen her uncle do. The balls proved so popular that Barbier and Daubrée began mass-producing them. Soon, the factory diversified its output to include other items made of rubber, such as hoses and belts. However, after a period of prosperity, it fell into decline. In 1886 Barbier's grandsons, the **Michelin brothers** (André and, later, Édouard), took over the works. These two crea-

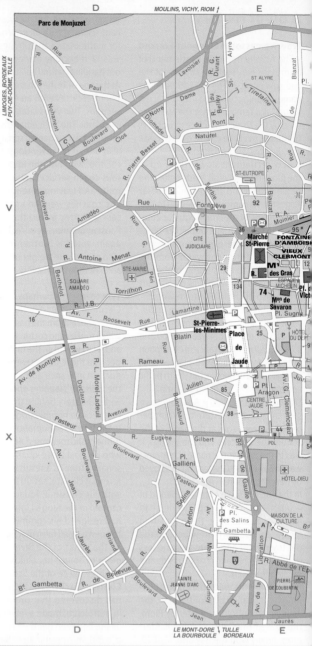

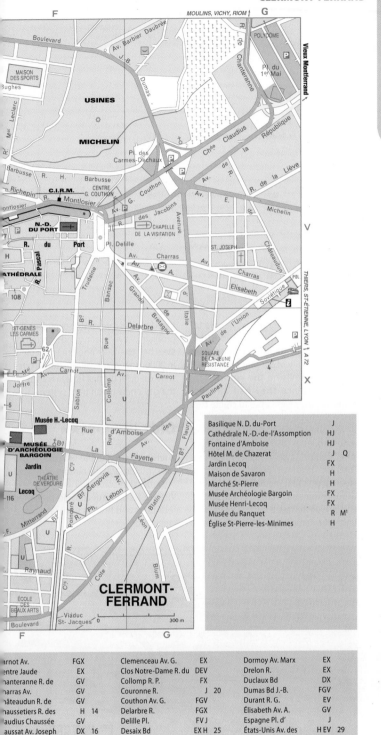

Basilique N. D. du-Port	J	
Cathédrale N.-D.-de-l'Assomption	HJ	
Fontaine d'Amboise	HJ	
Hôtel M. de Chazerat	J	Q
Jardin Lecoq	FX	
Maison de Savaron	H	
Marché St-Pierre	H	
Musée Archéologie Bargoin	FX	
Musée Henri-Lecoq	FX	
Musée du Ranquet	R	M¹
Église St-Pierre-les-Minimes	H	

tive geniuses were the first people to apply scientific methods to industrial production. By meeting clients' real needs, carefully observing reality and constantly revising the knowledge and experience they had already acquired, they were able to create the first detachable bicycle tyre (1891). This development was followed by tyres for automobiles in 1895 and the low-pressure "Confort" tyre in 1923. In 1937 the "Métalic" tyre was introduced, with a steel carcass that made lorries a viable proposition as a method of transport, and in 1946 the radial-ply tyre (marketed under the name "X" in 1949) which com-bined a radial carcass that overcame the problem of overheating and a triangular steel belt to ensure good road-holding. In 2006, pneumatic, bi-directional tyres were used, for the first time in France, on the city's new urban tram system.

Old Clermont★★

A leisurely stroll in the old district will take you through the narrow alleys laid out around the cathedral and place de la Victoire, featuring quaint, old-fashioned fountains and houses with lava stone courtyards.

PARIS-BORDEAUX 1895

Iʳᵉ VOITURE sur PNEUS MICHELIN

MICHELIN

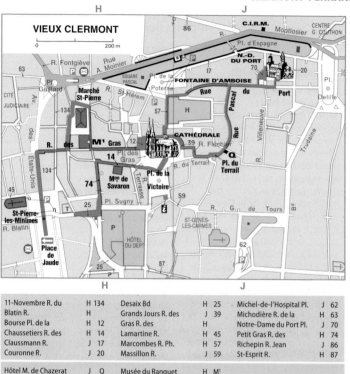

Place de Jaude

The ancient origins of the name of this square remain a subject of controversy. Two Renaissance documents use the name *platea galli* –"rooster square," since in local dialect the word for cockerel is *jô* or *jau*. The square is therefore thought to have been a poultry market. Another explanation links the origin of the word *jaude* to the name of a suburb of Clermont, known in the Gallic language as *Vasso Galate*. While *wasso* or *vasso* is said to be the name of a Gallic divinity, *galate* is merely a local name which has evolved over the years into *galde* or *gialde* (10C), *jalde* (12C) and, finally, *jaude*.

Place de Jaude is the centre of life in Clermont. It is bordered trees and surrounded by department stores, cinemas and, on the south side, by the **Centre Jaude,** a vast shopping complex.

Église St-Pierre-les-Minimes

Open daily except Sun. This vast domed church building in the Classical style has fine wood panelling in the chancel.

▶ *Walk down avenue des États-Unis then turn right onto rue des Gras.*

Rue des Gras

A flight of steps used to lead from here right up to the cathedral. At **no 28**, note the straight flight of steps, gallery and balcony dating from the 17C. **No 22** has two entrances opening onto small inner courtyards. One of them, dating from the 15C, is carved with a man's head; the other is topped by a lintel on which angel musicians are shown surrounding a young woman.

▶ *Take the second street on the left.*

Marché St-Pierre

This market is situated at the heart of an old district that has been renovated, and stands on the site of a Romanesque church. It is a bustling centre on which narrow, picturesque shopping streets such as rue de la Boucherie converge.

▶ *Return to rue des Gras then, at place de la Bourse, turn left onto rue Ph.-*

Address Book

For coin ranges, see the cover flap.

CLERMONT-FERRAND

WHERE TO STAY

Dav'Hôtel Jaude – *10 r. des Minimes.* ☎04 73 93 31 49. 28 rms. ⬜6€. This modern hotel within walking distance of the cathedral is located in a tranquil side street a few steps from the old quarter.

Hôtel Albert-Élisabeth – *37 av. Albert-Élisabeth.* ☎04 73 92 47 41. 38 rms. ⬜6€. A small hotel near the train.

Radio – *43 av. Pierre-Curie. 63400 Chamalières.* ☎04 73 30 87 83. *Closed 2–25 Jan and 5–14 Nov.* 🅿. 26 rms. ⬜10€. *Restaurant*⬜⬜. Drawing its inspiration from the very beginnings of the radio era, this hotel has a 1930s decoration scheme.

Hostellerie St-Martin – *63170 Pérignat-lès-Sarliève. 8km/5mi S of Clermont via N 9 then D 978.* ☎04 73 79 81 00. 🅿. 34 rms. ⬜9€. *Restaurant*⬜⬜. A former Cistercian abbey dating from the 14C, this hotel nestled in a grand park at the foot of the Gergovia plateau is pleasant indeed.

WHERE TO EAT

Le Bougnat – *29 r. des Chaussetiers.* ☎04 73 36 36 98. *Closed Jul, Mon lunch and Sun.* In the old part of the city near the cathedral, here's a pleasant if basic restaurant with a rural flair.

Aux Délices de la Treille – *33 r. de la Treille.* ☎04 73 91 26 90. ⬜. *Reservations required.* This restaurant nestled in a small street downtown is quite a discovery!

Le Chardonnay – *1 pl. Philippe-Marcombes.* ☎04 73 90 18 28. *Closed Sat lunch and Sun. Reservations required evenings.* The generous bistro style and the easy-going ambience make for a very enjoyable meal.

ON THE TOWN

Bars, *brasseries*, movie theatres, *crêperies*, pubs, restaurants and tea rooms are where you'll find most of the lively goings-on in neighbourhoods downtown. Many of these are concentrated around the Place de Jaude or near the cathedral, as well as Place Sugny, Rue Fontgiève and Place Gaillard.

THEATRE AND ENTERTAINMENT

Contemporary music concerts are held in the Maison des Sports (Place des Bughes). Classical music is generally performed in the Maison des Congrès (blvd Gergovia), where the Orchestre d'Auvergne plays. The auditorium of the Conservatory, the amphitheatre of the Faculty of Law and some churches accommodate chamber music recitals. The 'Rock au Maximum' Festival, early July, is tailor-made to please those who like it LOUD.

Plays are regularly staged at the Opéra Municipal (blvd Desaix) or at the Maison des Congrès.

La Maison du Tourisme serves as both tourist office and convention headquarters. It also houses a Massif Central wing and a Romanesque Art exhibit English language headsets available.

Le 15ème Avenue – *15 r. des Petits-Gras.* ☎04 73 37 27 28. *Fri–Sat 10pm–4am. Closed mid-Jul–early Sept.* The city's one and only jazz address, this cellar club has unsurprisingly become the rendezvous of Clermont's swing, hot and free jazz fans. Concerts weekends.

Le Zénith – *Plaine de la Sarilève 63800 Cournon d'Auvergne. Reservations on-line at www.fnac.com, or contact the Tourist office in Clermont.* The inaugural concert in December 2003 featured Johnny Hallyday, The patriarch of French rock n' roll. The hall seats 8,500 and the first year's schedule included pop stars and big entertainment spectaculars.

SHOPPING

Marché couvert-espace St-Pierre – *Pl. St-Pierre.* ☎04 73 31 27 88. *Mon–Sat 7am–7.30pm.* This covered food market features a few stands selling regional products (cheese, delicatessen). Chocolate lovers will melt for the pascaline (dark, raspberry flavoured chocolate) and the volcania (truffle), made by hand at the Trianon, 26 rue du 11-Novembre.

LEISURE ACTIVITIES

Espace Massif Central – *place de la Victoire, Maison du Tourisme.* This place is the Massif Central's showcase, where the different areas, cultures and traditions are represented in an exhibition and information centre with a rich reference department (topoguides, maps, books, CDs, and Internet terminals), that is also a lively meeting place.

SIT BACK AND RELAX

Gormen's café – 79 av. Édouard-Michelin. ☏04 73 90 65 65. Tue–Sat 8pm–2am, Sun, Mon for a post-match celebration; exceptional occasions: 3 or 4am. Closed mid-Jul–mid-Aug. Located in what used to be a garage, this hip bar is the rendez-vous of students and rugbymen.

La Perdrix – 14 r. Terrasse. ☏04 73 91 21 35. Sept–Jun Mon 5pm–2am, Tue–Sat noon-2am; Jul–Aug Mon–Sat 6pm–2am. For nearly thirty years, this bar right in the heart of the historic quarter between cathedral and prefecture has been setting the pace of old city nights. Intimate vaulted cellar downstairs.

Le Suffren – **48 pl. de Jaude** ☏04 73 93 40 97. Daily 7.30am–1.30am. Closed Christmas, New Year's Day, and 1 May.

Natives in the know frequent this large, chic and cosy café.

Les Goûters de Justine – 11 r. Pascal. ☏04 73 92 26 53. Mon–Fri noon-7pm, Sat 2.30pm–7pm. This unique tea room reminds you of a charmingly chaotic antique shop.

ROYAT

WHERE TO STAY

🛏 **Le Chalet Camille** – 21 bd Barrieu. ☏04 73 35 80 87. Closed Sun evening Nov–Mar. 🅿. 21 rms. 🍽6€. Restaurant🍽. Surrounded by a little garden, this family boarding house in a 1920s pavilion blends right in with the spirit of the nearby spa.

WHERE TO EAT

🍽🍽 **La Pépinière** – 11 av. Pasteur. ☏04 73 35 81 19. www.hotel-la-pepiniere. com. This venerable old building with a veranda attached houses a rustic dining room adorned with modern paintings.

Marcombes (north of the cathedral) which leads to place de la Poterne.

Fontaine d'Amboise★

This fountain erected in 1515 by Jacques d'Amboise, Bishop of Clermont, is a very fine piece of Renaissance architecture, carved in lava stone from Volvic. The basin is decorated with charming foliage in the Italian style. The central pyramid is adorned with small, naked figures with water pouring from their mouths, or from the part of the anatomy for which their cousin in Brussels is famous.

Rue du Port

No 21 *(right)* is a narrow old house with machicolations; on the right, at the corner of Rue Barnier, stands a 16C house with barbican. Note, on the left at no 38, the superb carriage entrance of the residence built in the early 18C for the financier Montlosier.

Basilique Notre-Dame-du-Port★★

Founded in the 6C by Bishop St Avit and burned down by the Vikings, the church was rebuilt with outstanding stylistic unity in the 11C and 12C. The bell-towers and lava, stone roof slabs that replaced

the tiles are 19C additions. The edifice is now on UNESCO's World Heritage List. The east end, restored during the 19C, is a consummate example of Romanesque architecture in the Auvergne.

The plain, robust design of Romanesque architecture as developed in the Auvergne is apparent from the entrance.

The raised **chancel**★★★, the most attractive part of the building, is strikingly beautiful. It is flanked by an ambulatory with four chapels.

Lighting is used to emphasize the details on the **capitals**★, which are among the most famous in the Auvergne.

The **crypt** dates from the 11C. Beneath the chancel, the "Underground," dear to the hearts of the local people, has the same layout as the east end.

▸ *Leave the church by the steps down to place Notre-Dame-du-Port.*

The bare, heavy west front forms a contrast with the remainder of the building; it is preceded by a 16C porch. The austerity and bareness of the old wall are tempered by a row of triple arching beneath the gable, itself consisting of a mosaic of multicoloured stonework.

Basilique Notre-Dame-du-Port – Detail of the west front

The square bell-tower above it was added in the 19C.

▸ *Follow rue du Port and turn left.*

Rue Pascal

"The streets climb up between careworn façades where gateways open, yawning, onto damp courtyards. In the depths of the iron-coloured shadow is the turret of a spiral staircase, a decorated gallery, a doorway with a lintel shaped like the point of a shield." (Henri Pourrat)

The old house at **no 22** has bosses on the ground floor and a wrought-iron balcony. **No 4** is M de Chazerat's residence; he was the last Intendant of the Auvergne and his mansion is a fine late-18C building. The **oval courtyard,** broken up by Ionic pilasters designed in accordance with the principles of the Colossal Order, conveys an impression of majesty.

▸ *Cross the tiny place du Terrail with its fountain (1664) and go down rue du Terrail. Turn right onto rue Fléchier, leading to rue des Grands-Jours which skirts the east end of the cathedral.*

Place de la Victoire

In the centre is a monument commemorating the Crusades, and a fountain with a statue of Pope Urban II. From this now pedestrian square, there is a general view of the cathedral.

Rue des Chaussetiers

Furniture and carpet shops fill the vaulted ground floors of old houses, and there is an abundance of doors and arches. At no 3, at the corner of rue Terrasse, is the **Maison de Savaron,** a mansion built in 1513. The **courtyard**★ contains a staircase turret linked to the main building by three floors of overhanging landings. The turret includes a superb carved doorway known as the "Door of the Wild Men." At **no 10** there is a Gothic doorway and mullioned windows. At the corner of rue des Petits-Gras are Romanesque arches (12C, the oldest examples of this style to be seen in vernacular buildings in Clermont).

Rue des Petits-Gras

At **nos 4–6** (windows with grotesque masks), in the second of the two buildings beyond the courtyard, there is a monumental three-storey **staircase**★ supported by corbels and oblique basket-handled arches. The straight flights of steps and landings are a particularly example of 18C architecture.

Sights

Cathédrale Notre-Dame-de-l'Assomption★★

🕐*Open mid-May–mid Sept daily 8am–6pm; rest of year, Mon–Sat, 8am–noon, 2pm–6pm, Sun, 9.30am–noon, 3pm–6pm.*

This is a lovely Gothic church with a design based on cathedrals in the Île de France. Its sombre colour is due to the lava used in its construction; it is the only major cathedral built of this particular type of stone. The church standing today was begun in 1248; a Romanesque church previously stood here, itself replacing one or two earlier churches.

Enter by the north door into the transept, beneath the Bayette Tower. Adjacent to the tower is the Guette Turret, once topped by a look-out post. The impression of lightness in the nave and, in particular, around the chancel shows the technical skills inherent in the Rayonnant Gothic style. The use of lava stone made it possible to reduce the width of the pillars, the arches of the vaulting, and the various sections of the openings. The scattering of the French fleur-de-lis motif and the towers of Castile visible on some of the windows would seem to suggest that they date from the days of St Louis; the King may have given them to the cathedral on the occasion of the marriage of his son (the future Philippe III) in the cathedral in 1262.

Set in the gallery of the north transept arm is a clock with a **jack o' the clock** which strikes the hours (**1**) dating from the 16C (the mechanism is 17C and 18C). Walk round the ambulatory. Note, above the doorway flanked by foliage into the vestry (**2**), three paintings from 13C-15C.

(**3**) **Chapelle St-Georges** – Stained-glass window illustrating the life and martyrdom of the saint.

(**4**) **Chapelle St-Austremoine** – To the right, Austremoine's arrival in the Auvergne where he was the first bishop. In the centre is an illustration of his martyrdom; to the left, the miracles accomplished after his death.

(**5**) **Mary Magdalene windows** – Stained glass illustrating the end of her life. 17C and 18C altar and Pietà. Statues of the Bishops of Clermont, St Arthème and St Alyre.

(**6**) **Apsidal chapel** – To the left is the life of John the Baptist; in the centre, the childhood of Christ and to the right the miracle worked by Theophilus.

(**7**) **St Bonnet windows** – St Bonnet was Bishop of Clermont in the 7C.

(**8**) **Funeral chapel of the bishops** – In the centre are 12C stained-glass windows from the former cathedral which illustrate the Life of Christ.

(**9**) **Chapelle Ste-Marguerite** – Altarpiece and Adoration of the Shepherds (17C).

(**10**) **St Agatha windows**.

(**11**) **Chapelle St-Arthème** – Endowed with an altarpiece which was rebuilt in 1840 using 17C statues. The **chancel**★★ is closed off by large but light arches. Above the triforium, the long 13C and 14C stained-glass windows (**12**) have a grisaille background and only one large figure per lancet. Set against the

Cathédrale Notre-Dame-de-l'Assomption: Virgin and Child in the first south aisle

S. Sauvignier/MICHELIN

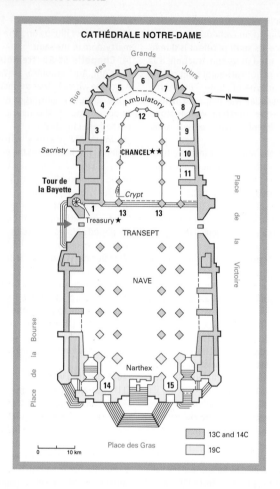

CATHÉDRALE NOTRE-DAME

Grands des Jours

Rue

←—N

5 6 7

4 Ambulatory 8

3 12 9

Sacristy 2 CHANCEL★★ 10

Tour de
la Bayette 11

Crypt

1 13 13

Treasury★

TRANSEPT

NAVE

Place de la Bourse

Place de la Victoire

Narthex

14 15

Place des Gras

13C and 14C

19C

0   10 km

pillars in the transept are two statues of the Virgin Mary and St John (**13**); they were originally part of the rood screen which was demolished during the Revolution.

At the west end of the inner north aisle note the 14C statue of Christ of the Last Judgement (**14**), once set against the tympanum of the north doorway. At the west end of the inner south aisle is a stained-glass window (1982) by Maka-raviez illustrating the Apocalypse of St John (**15**).

Musée d'Archéologie Bargoin★

🕐*Open daily except Mon 10am–noon, 1pm–5pm (Sun, 2pm–7pm).* 🕐*Closed 1 Jan, 1 May, 1 Nov, 25 Dec.* 🎫*4€, no charge 1st Sunday in the month.* ☎*04 73 91 37 31.*

This museum houses a sizeable **pre-historic** and **Gallo-Roman archaeo-logical collection**★ on the ground and basement floors, comprising artefacts discovered locally, particularly during recent excavations in the city of Cler-mont itself.

The Gallo-Roman period is the best rep-resented, with a marvellous collection of statuettes of animals, men, women and children in white terracotta, pottery from Lezoux with fine examples dating from the 2C, vestiges of the great temple of Mercury built on the summit of the Puy-de-Dôme at the beginning of the Imperial era.

The **Carpet Museum** includes over 80 carpets from the Middle and Far East: Turkey, the Caucasus, Iran, Afghanistan, Turkestan, Tibet, China etc.

Muséum d'histoire naturelle Henri-Lecoq

🕐*Open May–Sept, daily except Mon 10am–noon, 2pm–6pm (Oct–Apr 5pm).* 🕐*Closed Sun am, Mon and public holidays.* ✎5€. ☎04 73 91 93 78.

This museum is named after the naturalist Henri Lecoq (1802–71) whose wide-ranging collections of stuffed animals, rocks and regional flora make this a Natural History Museum very much centred on the Auvergne.

Parks

The attractive **Jardin Lecoq** stretches right in the town centre. Near the lake is a 14C entrance brought over from the Château de Bien-Assis, built for the Duc de Berry and owned, in the 17C, by Florin Périer, Blaise Pascal's brother-in-law.

Old Montferrand★★

Montferrand was founded by the counts of Auvergne who built a fortress on a rise that is now the site of place Marcel-Sembat, in order to counter the authority of the bishop, who was also Lord of Clermont. In the early 13C the town was rebuilt on the orders of a powerful woman named Countess Brayère and was turned into a bastide, a fortified hilltop town laid out to a strictly symmetrical geometric pattern. Montferrand was a commercial centre at the junction of several roads and, in the 15C, the wealthy middle classes began to commission town houses. The narrow plots of land made available by Countess Brayère's town plan, however, forced the architects to design houses that were deep rather than wide. Most of the houses were built with lava stone. Montferrand was so commercially successful that, in the 16C, the king set up law courts – known as the Cour des Aides – to try fiscal and criminal cases.

The proximity of Clermont caused rivalry and jealousy between the two towns. Montferrand eventually went into decline. In 1962 work was undertaken to renovate the old town of Montferrand, a project which involved some 80 old town houses and mansions that have retrieved their original façades, deco-

Aerial view of Old Montferrand

J. Damase/MICHELIN

rated with carved heads, balustrades, staircase turrets, cornerstones and lava stone arches contrasting with the honey-coloured "Montferrand roughcast."

▶ *Park in place de la Rodade.*

Place de la Rodade

This square was once known as place de Belregard because of the view over the Puys range. In the centre stands the Four Seasons fountain made of lava stone.

▶ *Enter the old town of Montferrand via rue de la Rodade.*

Hôtel Regin

At no 36. This 15C and 16C town house belonged to a family of magistrates and is typical of the mansions built in Montferrand.

Hôtel Doyac

At no 29. Late-15C mansion built for Jean de Doyac, Royal Bailiff of Montferrand and Minister to Louis XI. Huge, imposing Gothic doorway.

Hôtel du Bailliage

At no 20. Bailiwick House is the former Consuls' Residence. Its gargoyles and vaulted rooms are of interest.

After rue de la Rodade widens, a set of timbered houses with corbelling comes into view on the left in the renovated district. Their rounded doorways are

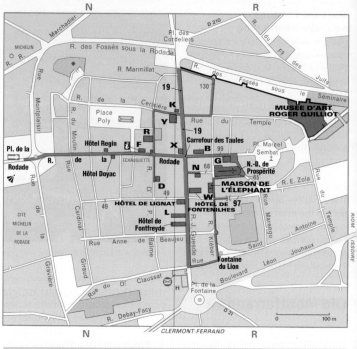

set out on high landings that show the original level of the roadway.

▶ *Turn back; right on rue Marmillat.*

Hôtel de la Porte

At no 5. In the courtyard of this mansion, also known as the Architect's House, there is a staircase turret decorated with a Renaissance sculpture from 1577.

▶ *Turn right onto rue de la Cerisière.*

Hôtel de la Faye des Forges

At no 2. A glass door protects a delightful inner door with a carved tympanum decorated with lions holding a phylactery. The house opposite has a double timber gallery, an unusual feature in Montferrand.

▶ *Turn left along rue des Cordeliers onto rue Waldeck-Rousseau.*

Rue Waldeck-Rousseau runs along the inside of the old ramparts, high above the road laid out along the moat which was once liable to flooding by the Tiretaine.

▶ *Turn right onto Rue du Temple, back to Rue des Cordeliers.*

Rue des Cordeliers

At no 11, note the Renaissance ground floor flanked by pilasters and the delightful little inner courtyard.

Carrefour des Taules

This is the central junction in the old town. Its name is a reminder that this was a butchers market.

Maison de l'Apothicaire

At no 1 rue des Cordeliers.
The old Apothecary's House dates from the 15C and has two timbered upper storeys. At the top of the house, the brackets on either side of the gable are decorated with an apothecary and the patient awaiting his operation.

▶ *Turn left onto rue du Séminaire.*

Halle aux Toiles

At no 3, the old cloth market, there is a long balcony supporting a fine row of four basket-handled arches and corresponding side doors.

Hôtel d'Étienne Pradal

At no 22. The ground floor of this mansion has superb semicircular and basket-handled arches. Its "Montferrand roughcast" and cornerstones made of lava stone are typical of the town's architecture.

Église Notre-Dame-de-Prospérité

The west front still has its north tower which was used as a watchtower. It is topped by a 16C lantern.

▶ *Continue along rue Kléber.*

Maison d'Adam et d'Eve

At no 4. In the courtyard on a balustrade is a 15C **bas-relief**★ of Adam and Eve.

▶ *Turn left onto rue Kléber.*

Maison de l'Éléphant★

At no 12. A 13C Romanesque house. The great arches on the ground floor support the twin bay windows on the first floor.

Maison de l'Ange

At no 14. In the courtyard is a small, triangular tympanum above a doorway representing an angel carrying a coat of arms.

Fontaine du Lion

The fountain comes from a square to which it had given its name. On the gable is a lion carrying the blazoned coat of arms of Montferrand.

▶ *Turn right twice onto rue R.J.-Guesde.*

Hôtel de Fontfreyde

At no 28. In the courtyard of this mansion, is a Madonna and Child on the Gothic doorway into the staircase turret. The balustrade on the gallery bears three fine Italianate medallions depicting Lucretia stabbing herself, torn between her husband and her seducer.

Hôtel Gaschier

At no 20. Three rows of galleries, one above the other, open onto the courtyard (15C-16C). The first floor is supported by superb pillars.

Hôtel de Lignat★

At no 18. This, the Lawyer's House, dates from the 16C. Gracious mullioned windows open onto the street. It opens onto Grande-Rue-du-Languedoc through an elegant door decorated with a garland of roses in the Italian Renaissance style.

Hôtel de Fontenilhes★

At no 13. The house, a fine residence dating from the late 16C, was built of lava stone from Volvic.

▶ *Start walking along rue Notre-Dame.*

Hôtel Mallet-de-Vandègre

At no 2. This building, with its austere courtyard, is said to have been the women's prison.

▶ *Cross carrefour des Taules, walk along rue de la Rodade and turn left onto rue du Dr-Balme.*

At no 5 is a Romanesque house with colonnettes and capitals on the front. At no 11 there is a second **Hôtel d'Albiat** dating from the 16C.

Musée d'Art Roger-Quilliot★★

&⏱Open daily except Mon 10am–6pm. ⏱Closed 1 Jan, 1 May, 1 Nov, 25 Dec. 4.50€, no charge 1st Sunday in the month. ☎04 73 16 11 30.

A change of use – The history of these premises reflects the history of Montferrand and Clermont, each in turn the seat of official bodies. The museum stands on the site of the Palais Vieux above the town walls. It was the seat of the royal bailiwick then of the Cour des Aides of the Auvergne, the Limousin and the Marches; the monumental gateway built in the early 17C in front of the courtyard that precedes the chapel is all that remains of this building.

When Montferrand and Clermont were combined, the Cour des Aides moved to Clermont and the Ursuline Order of nuns took over and reconstructed the buildings. The site was turned into a seminary after the Revolution, then into a military hospital from 1914 to 1918, and into barracks for riot police and *gendarmerie*, before being transformed into a museum. The buildings and their surroundings are a reflection of Montferrand. They constitute the old "Gateway of the Rising Sun" and open the historic centre of the town to its suburbs.

Driving Tours

①Volcanoes★★
35km/21mi – allow half a day

▶ *Leave Clermont via place des Carmes-Déchaux and head N on boulevard J.-B. Dumas towards Limoges, then take rue de Blanzat on the right.*

The road rises along the ravine separating the Côtes de Clermont from the Chanturgue plateau.

▶ *1.2km/0.8mi after the intersection with boulevard Charcot, turn right and drive on for 300m/330yd until you reach a junction.*

🚶A gravel path wends its way up towards the site, running along the edge of the ravine to the left *(1hr return)*.

Plateau de Chanturgue★
The Chanturgue plateau constitutes the remains of a vast volcanic table which erosion has worn down into several sections. In the bases of drystone walls, covered with stubble or concealed by the undergrowth, archaeologists have found the remains of what may have been Caesar's lesser encampment.

L'Oppidum des Côtes de Clermont
Follow the road to the start of a lane on the left, level with a right-hand turn and walk to the ridge of the Côtes de Clermont plateau (1hr return).
🚶History lovers will enjoy these ruins, the vestiges of a former stronghold.

▶ *Go back towards Clermont and turn right onto boulevard Charcot, heading for Durtol. Go to avenue du Puy-de-Dôme (D 941A) via avenue de la Paix (D 941), then take côte de la Baraque.*

Puy de Dôme★★★
👣*see Monts DÔME.*

▶ *In La Font-de-l'Arbre, take D 68.*

Royat – 👣*see Excursions.*

Chamalières
Lying south-west of Clermont, Chamalières is an important residential and business centre and the headquarters for some of the tourist and spa amenities in Royat.

Église Notre-Dame
🕐*Open daily except Sun afternoon.* ☎04 73 37 36 06. Of the five churches that once stood in Chamalières, only one remains. Its nave embraces an early building, dating from before AD 1000.

Moulin de la Saigne
Beyond the church take rue de la Coifferie and rue du Languedoc.
The swift currents of the River Tiretaine have always favoured the installation of water-wheels: there have been flour mills along the river since the 10C and papermills from the 15C.

▶ *Cross place de Geretsried to no 3 avenue de Fontmaure, within the Carrefour-Europe residential and shopping complex.*

Galerie d'Art Contemporain
&⃝*Open daily except Sun 2.30pm–7pm.* ⃝*Closed public holidays.* ☎*04 73 30 97 22.*
Space is fairly limited in this Modern Art Gallery but the exhibitions are interesting and they attract all the latest names in modern painting and sculpture.

▶ *Take avenue de Royat, then rue Blatin to return to the town centre (place de Jaude).*

Parc Bargoin – &see Excursions.

2 The Country South of Clermont★

45km/28mi

▶ *Leave Clermont starting from place de Jaude and take rue Gonod to the S. Then take avenue de la Libération, which leads to N 89.*

Église de Beaumont
The former wine-growing village of Beaumont developed round the **Église St-Pierre**. Founded in the 7C, the church was attached to a Benedictine convent until 1792.

Ceyrat
At the junction with the road to Boissé-jour, on the left, you will notice the curious remains of a volcano.

▶ *Continue heading S.*

Gorges de Ceyrat
These high granite cliffs have been deeply eroded by the river.

▶ *Go back to N 89 and turn right. After 250m/270yd, turn left onto D 120. Follow the signposting to Château d'Opme.*

Château d'Opme
&⃝*Open Easter-Oct Sun and public holidays 2.30pm–7pm.* ⃝*Closed Nov–Easter.* ☞*4€.* ☎*04 73 87 54 85.*
This old fortress (11C) stands high above a mountain pass which was once the route taken by the Roman road from Clermont to Le Puy-en-Velay. It originally

Fountain, Château d'Opme

belonged to the counts of Auvergne and was converted into an elegant Renaissance château by Antoine de Ribeyre, Treasurer of France under Louis XIII. The upper terrace is laid out as a formal **French garden★** around an ornamental basin with a fountain, the entire area shaded by two avenues of lime trees.

▶ *Return to the intersection of D 3 and D 120 and turn right.*

The road climbs up to the Gergovie plateau, offering pretty views of Clermont, the Puys mountain range with the Monts Dore in the distance.

Plateau de Gergovie★
&see Excursions, below.

▶ *Drive along D 120 to La Roche-Blanche then head for Clermont along D 978. Drive 2km/1.2mi along N 9 and turn left onto D 777 (avenue R.-Maerte); 1.5km/0.9mi further on, turn right onto D 69 (avenue J.-Noellet).*

Aubière
This southern suburb of Clermont has an interesting **Musée de la Vigne et du Vin** (&⃝ open Easter-Nov daily, 10am–noon, 2pm–7pm; Dec–Easter, Sat, Sun, 2pm–6pm. ☞5€. ☎04 73 27 60 04) housed in former cellars. The visit ends with wine-tasting.

▷ *Continue along D 69, then turn left onto boulevard Louis-Loucheur. A little further on, boulevard C.-Bernard will take you back to place de Jaude.*

Excursions

Plateau de Gergovie★

14km/8.6mi S of Clermont-Ferrand.

The Gergovie plateau stands above the Allier valley and the Limagne plain.

The Battle of Gergovia – In the year 52 BC Caesar was carrying out his seventh military campaign in Gaul; he had just defeated the Gallic army in Bourges and the Gauls had retreated to the mountains of the Massif Central, pursued by six Roman legions. **Vercingétorix**, the leader of the Gallic coalition, had retreated to the Arverni's hillfort in Gergovia, which was defended by a dry stone wall. One night, Caesar captured the Roche-Blanche hill, by surprise, and set up a lesser encampment there, linking it to the main camp by a ditch along which he could move his troops.

Caesar then ordered his troops to implement a diversionary movement by night, along the Bédat valley that skirted the Arverni's hillfort, to give Vercingétorix the idea that his army might be attacked from the rear.

The next day, three Roman legions moved from the main camp up to the lesser camp, and shortly after midday, launched an attack. Vercingétorix, however, was a good strategist and had concealed troops behind the Puy de la Mouchette who put up fierce resistance against the Romans. Furthermore, the Gauls on the plateau – alerted by the shouts of the womenfolk – ran quickly back to the scene of the real battle and routed the Roman legions.

At the same time the Aedui, allies of the Romans, arrived from the plain but the Roman soldiers thought they were coming to the aid of the Gauls and Caesar ordered the retreat. Vercingétorix wisely brought his troops to a halt on the plain. The Gauls' success was short-lived, however: their chieftain was besieged in Alésia and finally surrendered to Caesar at the end of the summer.

Maison de Gergovie

⌖ ◷Open May–Oct 10am–12.30pm, 2pm–6.30pm (Jul–Aug 10am–7pm); Mar–Apr and Nov Sat–Sun and public holidays 2pm–6pm. ◷Closed mid-Dec–end Jan. ⌱4€. ☏04 73 79 42 98.

The Information Centre on the plateau has exhibitions on geology and local flora, archaeology (grave containing the skeleton of a young woman), and on the history of this important site. A diorama retraces the various stages in the battle between the Romans and the Gauls.

Château de la Batisse★

12km/7.5mi – allow 2 hr.

Leave the plateau de Gergovie and head for Opme, then drive towards Chanonat. At the entrance to the village, turn right for La Batisse.

This **château** (◷open mid-Jun–Aug, daily except Sat, 2pm–7pm; Apr–mid Jun, Sept–Oct, Sun and public holidays, 2.30pm–6pm; ⌱6€) built of pale stone exudes an atmosphere of tranquillity and gracious living which forms a stark contrast to the feudal fortresses of Auvergne.

It is flanked by a pepper-pot tower and two corner towers crowned with red-tiled domes and lantern turrets, all that remain of the original 15C castle.

▷ *Return to Chanonat and turn right onto D 3 for Le Crest.*

Le Crest

This wine-growers' village at the very tip of the Serre mountain range has a 13C church. There is a superb **view**★from the old tower – northwards over the Gergovie and Limagne plateaux around Clermont.

▷ *Go back down towards D 213 and A 75, pass beneath them, and then take the small narrow road that climbs up around the Butte de Monton.*

Monton

This village has its houses spread out over the southern slopes of a mound. Not far from Monton are a series of **troglodyte caves,** affording views of the surrounding countryside.

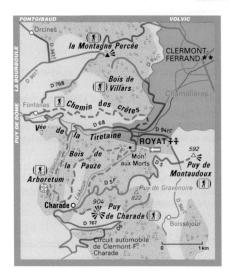

▶ Go back to Gergovie via La Roche-Blanche.

▶ At the end of the park.

Royat ‡‡

1km W of Clermont-Ferrand.

1 av. Auguste-Rouzaud, 63130 ROYAT. 04 73 29 74 70. www.ot-royat.com

Royat is a large, elegant thermal spa terraced on the slopes of the Tiretaine valley. The Tiretaine flows from the granite plateau at the base of the Dômes mountain range; until it leaves Royat, it is a torrent. The bottom of its bed was filled with lava from the Petit Puy de Dôme, the waters then cut gorges in it.

The **waters** of Royat were exploited by the Romans who built public baths here. Although the baths met with mixed success until the mid-19C, they have enjoyed popularity and fame ever since. A hydropathic establishment was built and the visit here by Empress Eugénie in 1862 launched Royat as a spa.

Parc Thermal

This spa garden, completed by the new English-style park through which flows the Tiretaine, contains the hydropathic establishment and the casino. The remains of the **Gallo-Roman public baths**, can be seen. One of the pools had mosaic-covered arches and marble-covered walls. Terracotta pipes brought the water into the pool in small, semicircular cascades.

Grotte des Laveuses

The "Washerwomen's Cave" is on the banks of the Tiretaine. Several springs gush from the volcanic walls before flowing into the Tiretaine.

Église St-Léger★

This fortified building resembles the churches of Provence.

Maison du Passé

Open daily except Sun and holidays 3pm–6pm. 3€. 04 73 29 98 18.

This museum offers a journey through the town's history.

Parc Bargoin

From Église St-Léger, follow avenue Jean-Jaurès then avenue Anatole-France.

This is a well laid out park on hilly land, and a botanical garden. It is home to the largest maple in France (250 years old).

Walks

See walks map.

Various walks depart explore the local countryside.

A map of the area on place Allard indicates a number of signposted trails for hikers leaving from Royat, including the **Bois de Villars**, **Puy de Montaudoux**, **Arboretum de Royat** and **Bois de la Pauze**, **Puy de Charade** and **Vallée de la Tiretaine**, and **Chemin des Crêtes**.

CONDAT

POPULATION 1,121

MICHELIN MAP 330: E-2

32KM/20MI SE OF BORT-LES-ORGUES – LOCAL MAP SEE LE CÉZALLIER

This pleasant holiday resort lies in the centre of a fertile basin into which flow the Rhue d'Égliseneuve, Bonjon and Santoire rivers. Its numerous, slate-roofed villas standing on the sunlit slopes of the Rhue valley were almost all built by local people who went elsewhere to seek their fortune, many of them as linen-drapers.

- **Information:** Le bourg, 15190 CONDAT, ☎04 71 78 66 63.
- **Orient Yourself:** At the heart of the Massif Central, SW of Clermont Ferrand.
- **Organising Your Time:** Condat does not take time, the Alpine Pastures do.
- **Also See:** CLERMONT FERRAND, Le MONT-DORE.

Alpine Pasture Tours

1 Rhue Gorge to Gentiane Country
80km/50mi – allow one day

- *Leave Condat to the W.*

The D 679 road follows the right bank of the Rhue. The road offers fine views of the gorge and Les Essarts lake-reservoir then enters the lovely Maubert Forest planted with pine and beech. In the middle of the forest, the Gabacut, having dug numerous cauldrons into the rock, drops down in two small waterfalls.

Cascade de Cornillou
30min on foot return. 50m/55yd before the exit from the hamlet of Cornillou, turn left on a cart track.
Just before reaching a deserted barn, turn right onto an uphill track that soon runs along the shores of a small lake-cum-reservoir. Turn left across a small bridge; further on, an overgrown path leads to the top of the waterfall.

Gorges de la Rhue★★
Upstream from Embort, the river flows through a gorge with sides covered in greenery. The ravine widens out at the confluence of the two Rhues. Between Sarran and Champs, the road follows a dry valley where the Rhue flowed.

Champs-sur-Tarentaine-Marchal
see BORT-LES-ORGUES.

- *Leave Champs E along D 679.*

Bort-les-Orgues
see BORT-LES-ORGUES.

- *Leave Bort on D 922 in the direction of Mauriac and after 5km/3mi turn left onto D 3 to Riom ès Montagnes. The D 678 takes you back to Condat, following the opposite side of the Rhue.*

2 Cheylade valleys and Gentiane Country★★
90km/56mi

- *Drive W along D 678.*

After crossing the dry Sapchat valley, once the bed of the Rhue, and the Rhue de Cheylade Valley, the road overlooks the wooded Véronne Valley and runs along its hillside. Riom-ès-Montagne appears in a pastoral setting.

- *Head S from Riom along D 3.*

Soon (4km/3mi from Riom), a superb **view** unfolds to the left over the Dore mountain range and the upper plateaux of the Cézallier area. Beyond lie the ruins of the Château d'Apchon and the mountains of Cantal.

Apchon
This is a typical Cantal village with its sturdy houses in volcanic stone. A footpath leads off from rue de la Porte-du-Barre to a viewing table and the **castle**

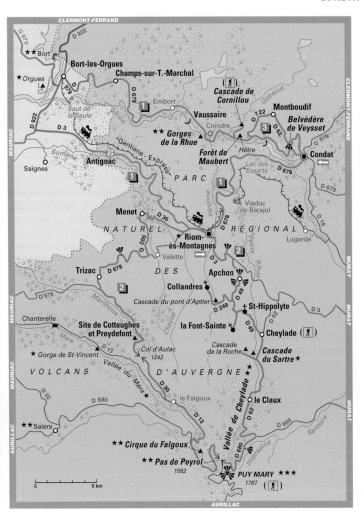

ruins *(access to the ruins could be dangerous for children)*. There is a good **view**★ of the surrounding countryside from the top of the rocky pinnacle where the ruins stand.

▸ *Leave Apchon S (D 249) then turn right onto D 63.*

Collandres

The Romanesque church of this tiny village stands on the site of a former look-out post which kept watch over the Véronne valley.

The road, which goes past the church, runs across high pastures where cattle graze in summer. Turn left at the first junction towards La Chatonnière. The road runs through woodland and pastureland dotted with *burons* (shepherds' huts) and farms.

▸ *Return to Collandres and leave the village S along D 263.*

Cascade du pont d'Aptier

This waterfall in its unspoilt setting is the ideal place for a picnic.

▸ *Beyond the bridge, turn left onto D 249.*

The Rhues

A number of streams and rivers on the north side of Cantal bear the name Rhue. The largest of them, the Grande Rhue, flows into the Dordogne below Bort-les-Orgues after crossing a bar of rock known as the Saut de la Saule (*see BORT-LES-ORGUES*), but an underground drainage channel takes some of its water into the Bort reservoir. The Grande Rhue rises in the south of the Dore mountain range near the Biche corrie. Once its waters have been swollen by the Rhue de Cheylade that flows down from the mountains of Cantal, the Grande Rhue flows through very picturesque wooded gorges.

Chapelle de la Font-Sainte

This 19C chapel, a popular place of pilgrimage, can be seen in the middle of the fields. The road *(D 49)* runs through St-Hippolyte and down to the Rhue de Cheylade. After crossing the river, the Puy Mary is visible to the right of a long ridge starting at the Puy de Peyre-Arse.

Cheylade

This resort above the Rhue is popular with anglers and is a good starting point for walks.

▶ *2.5km/1.5mi S of Cheylade, turn right on D 262. Park near a bridge and walk a further 100m/110yd to the right.*

Cascade du Sartre★

The waterfall is formed by the Rhue which flows down a drop of 30m/98ft. Continue along D 262 and, beyond another bridge, turn right on a path offering an attractive view of the **Cascade de la Roche**, a waterfall formed by a tributary of the Rhue which drops down over the rocks in a series of mini-cascades.

▶ *Turn back and continue along D 62.*

Le Claux

This small resort is ideal for the practice of a variety of outdoor activities: cross-country skiing and snowshoeing in winter, paragliding, climbing, riding and walking in summer.

Beyond Le Claux, the view of the Puy Mary and the Cheylade Valley with its forested floor becomes increasingly impressive. The road rises in a series of hairpin bends and continues through woods until it reaches the alpine pastures. It then crosses Col de Serres and arrives at the Impradine valley, hollowed into a bowl shape by ancient glaciers. During the final climb up to Pas de Peyrol, the road crosses the Eylac pass, clings to the sheer sides of the Puy Mary and provides a number of splendid **views**★.

Pas de Peyrol★★

See Monts du CANTAL.

▶ *Go back 3km/1.9mi along D 62, then turn right onto D 23, heading for Dienne.*

The road hugs the steep Impradine and Santoire valleys.

Puy Mary★★★

See Monts du CANTAL.

▶ *Leave Puy Mary along D 680 then turn right onto D 12 towards Le Falgoux. Beyond Col d'Aulac, turn left as you enter the Marihou woods.*

Trizac

This large village is renowned for its cattle markets. T
The road *(D 678)* running through pastures dotted with broom offers a fine view of the Artense plateau.

▶ *Turn right onto D 205.*

Menet

As the road runs down towards the village, it affords views of harmonious white buildings. The nearby lake offers relaxing water activities.

▶ *Leave Menet E; D 36 runs through woodland back to Riom.*

③ Belvédère de Veysset and Forêt de Maubert

20km/12.5mi – about 45min

▶ *Leave Condat via the steep, winding D 62 N.*

Belvédère de Veysset

The road leads to **Montboudif**, birthplace of **Georges Pompidou** (1911–74), who was the President of the French Republic from 1969 to 1974. A **museum** (🕐*open mid-Jun–mid Sept 10am–noon, 2pm–6pm; Apr–mid Jun and mid-Sept–Oct Sat–Sun and holidays 2pm–6pm; ⊜4€; ☎04 71 78 68 68)* is dedicated to his memory.

▶ *Turn left before the church onto D 622 and, a short distance further on, left again onto D 722.*

Forêt de Maubert

The beautiful state-owned Maubert et Gaulis Forest consists of landscaped woodland with a predominance of pines but also beech, lime and a few oaks.

▶ *At the junction with D 679 follow it back to Condat.*

Address Book

WHERE TO STAY

Ché Marissou – *Le Veysset, 15190 Condat, 3km/1.8mi N of Condat via D 62. ☎04 71 78 55 45. Closed Oct–Mar and open Fri, Sat and Sun except during school holidays. 🍴. Reservations required.* Typical Auvergnat decor, with box-bed, bread coffer and period knick-knacks.

Véronique Phelut Bed and Breakfast – *Le Veysset, 15190 Condat, 3km/1.8mi N of Condat via D 62. ☎04 71 78 62 96. Closed 1 Nov–Easter. 🍴. 4 rms.* A fine address in a gorgeous setting for nature lovers and hikers. The rooms are basic but comfortable.

LA CÔTE-ST-ANDRÉ

POPULATION 4,968
MICHELIN MAP 333: E-5

This small town, a liqueur-producing centre built in a semicircle on a hillside above the Bièvre plain, is the birthplace of *Hector Berlioz* (1803–69). The **Berlioz Festival** is held every year during the second fortnight in August in the covered market and parish church of La Côte-St-André.

🛈 **Information:** 38260 La Côte-St-André. ☎04 74 20 61 43. www.tourisme-bievre-liers.fr.

▶ **Orient Yourself:** Northwest of Grenoble via A 48.

🅿 **Parking:** There are numerous parking places in the centre of town.

👒 **Don't Miss:** The chateau Louis XI, and the Berlioz museum.

🕐 **Organising Your Time:** It isn't only the town that is attractive, the countryside is, too. So, expect to stay longer than you thought.

👣 **Also See:** VIENNE.

A Bit of History

A local lad – Hector Berlioz, the son of a wealthy local doctor, was born in La Côte-St-André in 1803. At the age of 17 he went to Paris to study medicine. He attended lectures but, at the same time, was a frequent visitor to the opera houses and the library in the Royal Music Academy where he later began learning composition. In 1830 he wrote his *Symphonie Fantastique* and won the Grand Prix de Rome.

Thereafter he worked as a music critic in order to earn a living, while at the same time continuing to compose works

©1990, Scala

Hector Berlioz

that brought him success and failure in turn. He seldom returned to La Côte-St-André. Having failed to win the fame he deserved during his lifetime, Berlioz died in Paris in 1869, but his genius earned him posthumous acclaim.

Sights

Musée Hector-Berlioz

⏱️*Open daily except Tue Jun–Sept 10am–7pm; Oct–May 10am–6pm.* ⏱️*Closed 1 Jan, 1 May and 25 Dec. Free.* ☎*04 74 20 24 88. www.musee-hector-berlioz.fr. Rue de la République.* This museum is housed in the composer's birthplace, a

handsome residence built in the late 17C and restored in 1969.

Château Louis XI

Built in the 13C for Philip of Savoy on a fine defensive site, this castle was designed as both fortress and residence; it suffered extensive damage during the wars in the 16C but was rebuilt thereafter.

Musée des Liqueurs

♿⏱️*Open Jul–Sept daily except Mon and public holidays, 3pm–6pm; rest of year Sun and public holidays, 3pm–6pm.* ⏱️*Closed Jan, Feb, 14 Jul, 15 Aug, 25 Dec.* 💶*2.50€.* ☎*04 74 93 38 10. www. cherryrocher.com.*
The Cherry Rocher company, which was set up in 1705 in a neo-Classical mansion, offers tours of its plant. The museum contains a collection of old machinery (fruit press, stills, infusers).

Excursions

Château de Bressieux

8km/3mi S on D 71, then on the narrow road to the left when you leave St-Siméon-de-Bressieux. In the centre of the village, when the road follows a bend, turn left into the small lane (15min on foot return). Perched high on a promontory overlooking Bressieux village, the castle ruins make an attractive, picturesque sight.

Roybon

17km/10.6mi S on D 71.
This small town boasts a charming group of buildings with traditional façades characteristic of the area: carved clay and wood decorated with pebbles. This architectural heritage is enhanced by the remains of a medieval rampart. A copy of the Statue of Liberty, which stands at the entrance to New York harbour, offers an unusual contrast.

COURPIÈRE

POPULATION 4,612

MICHELIN MAP 326: I-8 – LOCAL MAP SEE THIERS

The town lies at the entrance to a gorge formed by the River Dore. In addition to its picturesque houses, Courpière boasts a number of interesting castles in the vicinity and is the ideal starting point of excursions through Livradois country. During the summer season visitors can take the **Livradois-Forez Tourist Train** (*Livradois-Forez tourist railway – see AMBERT*), which runs along the Dore valley between Courpière and Ambert.

- **Information:** Place de la Cité Administrative, 63120 COURPIÈRE, ☎04 73 51 20 27. www.tourisme.pays-courpiere.fr.
- **Orient Yourself:** Under 50km/30mi east of Clermont Ferrand on A 72/D 319.
- **Organising Your Time:** This agreeable town will fill half a day or more.
- **Also See:** CLERMONT FERRAND, VICHY.

Old Town

Church★

This interesting Auvergne-style Romanesque building is topped by a Gothic bell-tower. Walk along the left side of the church to see the east end huddling between old houses.

Excursions

Château d'Aulteribe★

5km/3mi NW along D 223.

Open mid-May–mid Sept daily, 10am –noon, 2pm–6.30pm; mid-Sept–mid May daily except Mon 10am–noon, 2pm –5.30pm. Closed 1 Jan, 1 May, 1 and 11 Nov, 25 Dec. ✆6.50€. ☎04 73 53 14 55. This castle was rebuilt in the 19C in the Romantic style, on the site of an austere medieval construction. Originally the property of the **La Fayette** family, it

was purchased in 1775 by Jacques de Pierre. In the 19C, Henriette Onslow and Joseph de Pierre, who were avid collectors of furniture and 17C paintings, bequeathed the estate to the National Historic Monuments Trust.

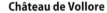The **Sentier du Bénitier du Diable**, starting from the château, is a footpath offering an insight into the history of the estate.

Château de La Barge

2km/1mi N on D 58 in the direction of Escoutoux.

Open Jul–Aug, Mon–Fri, 2pm, 3.30pm, 5pm. Closed May and Sept–Oct. ✆4€. ☎04 73 53 14 51.

This handsome residence is still circled by its moat. In the 16C the former citadel was converted into a Renaissance château. Two centuries later, it was graced with a terraced garden which its present owners are constantly refurbishing.

Château de Vollore

8km/5mi E along D7.

Open Jul–Aug daily, 2pm–7pm. ✆6€. ☎04 73 53 71 06.

This 17C building of pale granite stands on a spur, and is flanked to the south by a large 12C keep and to the north by a 14C tower. Inside, the rooms are sumptuously furnished with paintings, tapestries, furniture and decorative objects, and mementoes of **General La Fayette** and his involvement in the American War of Independence.

Château de Vollore

J. Damase/MICHELIN

CRÉMIEU★

POPULATION 3,169

MICHELIN MAP 333: E-3

Crémieu sits in a narrow valley between fairly rugged hillsides and was once a fortress standing guard over one of the gateways into the Dauphiné region; it was also a busy trading centre. Among the local gastronomic specialities are sabodets (a variety of sausage) and foyesse (a type of cake).

- **Information:** Pl. de la Nation. ☎04 74 90 45 13. www.ville-cremieu.fr.
- **Orient Yourself:** East of Lyon, and midway between the A 42 and A 43.
- **Parking:** There are a number of car parks around the edge of town, along the Cours Baron Raverat, for example, but limited parking in the centre.
- **Organising Your Time:** Half a day is sufficient; more if you take the tour.
- **Also See:** LYON.

Old Quarter Walk

▶ *Start from Porte de la Loi, which was part of the 14C town walls. Go through Porte des Augustins.*

Place de la Nation
The name of this square dates back to the French Revolution. In the NE corner is a lever-operated well built in 1823.

Hôtel de Ville
⛄◷*Open daily, 9am–noon, 1.30pm–5pm (Fri, 4pm, Sat 9am–noon, Sun, 2.30pm–5.30pm).* ◷*Closed public holidays, and Sat, Sun during winter months.* ☎04 74 90 45 13.
The town hall stands on place de la Nation and is housed in part of what was once an Augustinian friary founded in the 14C. The former cloisters *(cloître)* are entered from place de la Nation through a beautiful 18C wrought-iron gate.

▶ *Take rue Porcherie to the market.*

Halles★
The covered market was built in the 15C. The roof covered in lauzes is supported at each end by a thick wall comprising three arches. At the end on the right are the stone troughs over which corn measures were fitted.

▶ *Take rue Mulet then turn right onto rue du Four-Banal to Porte Neuve.*

Fortified Gateways
Porte Neuve was built in the 16C; **Porte de Quirieu,** which has steps and a central gutter, dates from the 14C.

▶ *Head along rue du Marché-Vieux.*

On the right, at **no 14**, note the 14C Window of the Three Hanged Men (Fenêtre des Trois Pendus).

▶ *Carry on up montée St-Laurent.*

Château Delphinal
This fortress on St-Laurent hill dates back to the 12C. On St-Hippolyte hill to the left are the remains of a 16C fortified Benedictine priory, including the old clock tower *(a footpath on the left leads to a viewing table).*

Address Book

WHERE TO STAY
▱ **Auberge de la Chaite** – *Pl. des Tilleuls.* ☎04 74 90 76 63. *Closed 22 Apr–11 May, 20 Dec–8 Jan, Tue lunch from Oct–Apr, Sun evening and Mon.* Facing the Porte de la Loi, this flowery inn has a big fireplace to warm the dining room in the winter.

▱ **Les Basses Portes** – *In Torjonas, 38118 St-Baudille-de-la-Tour.* ☎04 74 95 18 23. www.basses-portes.com. ▱. Meals ▱. This old farm has been extensively remodelled without detracting from its original, pastoral charm.

▶ *Return down montée St-Laurent; turn right at bottom; left on côte Faulchet.*

At the crossroads with rue du Four-Banal is a 16C house with mullioned windows, the **Maison du Colombier**.

▶ *Go down rue St-Jean, rue du Lieutenant-Colonel-Bel and, after skirting the south-west corner of the covered market, rue des Adobeurs.*

This street is lined with tiny low houses that used to contain craft workshops, including those of the town's tanners.

▶ *Passage Humbert on the left leads to cours Baron-Ravenat.*

Driving Tour

Île Crémieu: Land of Stone Roofs

60km/37mi.
With its cliffs, lakes, roofs covered in heavy stone slabs known as *lauzes*, fields bordered by standing stones, and country houses, the Île Crémieu region is quite unlike the countryside elsewhere in this area.

▶ *Leave Crémieu on D 52 NE and follow signs to Optevoz.*

As the road runs up the hill there is a view of Lake Ry and, further up the slope, of the large, modern **Château de St-Julien.**

▶ *Beyond the cool Optevoz basin, follow D 52 as far as Surbaix then turn left on a pleasant little road (D 52^B) which runs through a valley full of trees and meadows.*

St-Baudille-de-la-Tour

This charming village contains an attractive 15C fortified house, known as the **Maison des Dames,** with a tower covered in lauzes and a porch decorated with a coat of arms; it is the headquarters of Roulottes Dauphiné (see above).

▶ *Drive through Torjonas to D 65; turn right towards La Balme-les-Grottes.*

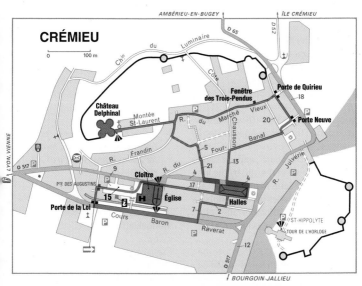

CRÉMIEU		Humbert Passage	7	Porcherie R.	17
		Loi R. de la	9	Porte Neuve Bd de la	18
Adobeurs R. des	2	Moulins Fg des	12	St-Antoine R.	20
Bel R. du Lt-Colonel	4	Mulet R.	13	St-Jean R.	21
Faulchet Côte	5	Nation Pl. de la	15		

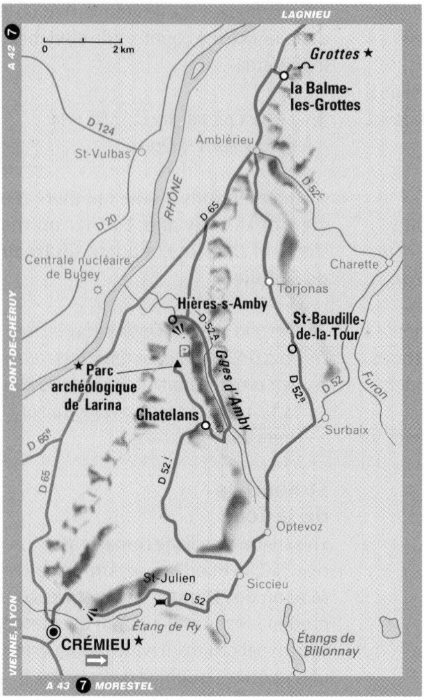

La Balme-les-Grottes★

Pleasant village especially known for its grottoes lying at the foot of a cliff marking the edge of the Île Crémieu plateau. The **Grottes de la Balme** *(270 steps –guided visits (1h15) ⊙Open May–Aug 10am–6pm; Apr and Sept daily except Mon, 11am, 2pm–5pm; Feb–Mar and Oct–Dec Sat, Sun and public holidays, 2pm–5.30pm. ⊙Closed Jan and 25 Dec. 6.50€. ☎04 74 90 67 03)* were discovered during the Middle Ages, visited by François I, described as one of the "seven Wonders of Dauphiné", and are said to have been used in the 18C by the infamous brigand Louis Mandrin. The Lake Gallery skirts a series of small **pools**★★ forming terraces of waterfalls before reaching the underground torrent.

▶ *Turn back along D 65 then take the first on the left, to Hières-sur-Amby.*

Hières-sur-Amby

This tiny village stands at the end of the Amby valley, at the foot of the Larina plateau. The former rectory is now the **Maison du Patrimoine** (*Guided visits (2h) Apr–Oct 2pm–6pm; Nov–Mar: 2pm–6pm, but closed Sat–Sun and public holidays. 4€. ☎04 74 95 19 10*). This modern museum houses objects discovered during archaeological digs at Larina *(see below)* including bones, tools, coins and jewellery, and includes a model of a Merovingian farm. Models, videos and a display retrace the origins of the people living in Île Crémieu, and present examples of popular arts, crafts and traditions.

▶ *Drive through Hières-sur-Amby; left onto D 52A.*

Gorges d'Amby

The river twists and turns between rocks covered with scrubby vegetation. There is a view of the 15C Brotel fortified house on the cliff.

▶ *A narrow road (right), opposite an old cement works, crosses the River Amby and runs up a hill to Chatelans.*

Chatelans

At the centre of the village is the **Musée de la Lauze** (*♿ ⊙open daily except Tue 9am–7pm. ⊙closed Jan*) which explains the traditional techniques in this region for cutting and fitting the stone slabs.

▶ *In the centre of the village, turn right onto a narrow road that runs for 2.5km/1.5mi to the tip of the plateau.*

Parc Archéologique de Larina★

The Larina site is bordered by the cliffs overlooking the Rhône plain and Amby valley.

The existence of human settlements on this site has been evidenced by objects dating from 5000 BP.

At the end of the Roman era and in the early days of the Dark Ages, two large farms existed in succession on this spot. The earlier one (4C and 5C) had a villa at its centre and included a number of farm buildings made of earth and timber over stone foundations that are still clearly visible. From the 6C to 8C a second farm developed around a large stonehouse with a stone roof and outbuildings.

Excursion

Morestel

21.8km/13.6mi. 🚹 *100 pl. des Halles, 38150 MORESTEL, ☎04 74 80 19 59.*

The lovely setting and exceptional luminosity here have attracted countless artists since the mid-19C, namely Corot, Daubigny and Turner; this has earned Morestel the nickname of "Painters' Town." **Auguste Ravier** (1814–95), who was a friend of Corot's, spent the latter part of his life in Morestel.

The D 517 road from Crémieu gives a delightful **view** of the village of Morestel, dominated by its Gothic church and the remains of a 12C square tower.

Maison Ravier

🕐 *Open Mar–Nov daily except Tue 2.30pm–6.30pm.* 🕐*Closed first fortnight in May.* ⊛*4€, free 1st Mon of month.* ☎*04 74 80 06 80. www.maisonravier.com.*

This handsome residence was home to Auguste Ravier between 1867 and 1895. The house has been bought by the municipality and hosts art exhibitions.

Tour Médiévale

🕐*Open Jul–Aug daily except Mon, 10am–noon, 2.30pm–7pm; mid-Mar–Jun and Sept–Nov daily except Mon, 2.30pm–6.30pm; Sun and public holidays, 10am–noon, 2.30pm–7pm.* 🕐*Closed Jan–mid-Mar.* ☎*04 74 33 04 51.*

This former keep is what remains of the 11C citadel overlooking the town. It offers lovely views of the surrounding region and will soon be converted into a cultural centre.

Parc d'Attractions Walibi Rhône-Alpes★

15km/9.5 mi S. Leave Morestel on N 75 towards Grenoble and in Veyrins turn left towards Les Avenières; D 40 on the right leads to the park (signposted). 🕐*Call for opening times.* ⊛*26€ (3–11-year-olds: 20.50€).* ☎ *04 74 33 71 80. www.walibi-rhone-alpes.fr.*

This is one of nine Walibi parks in Europe. Created in Belgium, France and the Netherlands, these parks are named after the Australian kangaroo. The Avenières Park is surrounded by lakes; with countless attractions and two shows, it has much to offer those who enjoy thrills.

LA DOMBES★

MICHELIN MAP 328: C-4 TO D-5

The Dombes plateau owes its unusual appearance and its charm to the presence of over 1 000 lakes dotted across its entire area. Here and there are low hills, formed by moraine, which were transformed in the Middle Ages into veritable earth fortresses surrounded by moats. Rural housing in the Dombes region is built mainly of cob (*pisé*) whereas the castles and outer walls are built of rough red bricks known as *carrons* (terracotta). The region's history, too, is somewhat out of the ordinary. Dombes was raised to the rank of a principality by François I following the confiscation of the property belonging to the Constable of Bourbon in 1523. A sovereign Parliament sat in Trévoux, its main town, and continued to sit until the mid-18C.

🚹 **Information:** 3, place de l'Hôtel de Ville, 01330 VILLARS-LES-DOMBES. ☎ 04 74 98 06 29. www.villars-les-dombes.com.

▸ **Orient Yourself:** The Dombes plateau is situated between Lyon and Bourg-en-Bresse and is bordered by the River Ain and the River Saône.

⊛ **Don't Miss:** A grand tour of the lakes.

🕐 **Organizing Your Time:** Allow a full day or two to explore the region.

⚸ **Also See:** LYON, VILLEFRANCHE.

A Bit of Geography

The impermeable soil encouraged local people very early on in their history to turn their fields into lakes enclosed by mud dikes. The **Grand Étang de Birieux,** one of the most extensive of the lakes, but now subdivided, dates from the 14C. In the 16C, Dombes boasted almost 2,000 lakes many filled with stagnant water, which led to an unhealthy climate. Most of the lakes are intermittent, one being emptied to fill another: they are filled with water and stocked with fish for a period of six or seven years; then drained and for one year turned over to agriculture.

Driving Tour

Tour of the Lakes ★
Round trip of 99km/61mi from Villars-les-Dombes – allow one day.

▶ *Leave Villars on D 2 heading W.*

Bouligneux
In a setting typical of this area stands a 14C brick-built **castle** that looks rather more like a fortress.

Sandrans
This village is known for its medieval fortress on which a large house was built in the 19C. Today a hillock remains, clearly visible, surrounded by a moat and crowned with a round tower.

Châtillon-sur-Chalaronne
– *see below.*

▶ *Leave Châtillon E on D 17 towards St-Paul-de-Varax.*

St-Paul-de-Varax
The Romanesque **church** dates back to the 12C.

▶ *Drive N along N 83 then turn right onto D64ᴬ.*

Lent
The village still boasts fine 16C monuments: the church belfry (restored in the 18C) and some timber houses.

Dompierre-sur-Veyle
This village grouped around a Romanesque church is near the largest lake in the area (100ha/247 acres): **Le Grand Marais.**

▶ *The D 70 road heading west to St-Nizier passes to the right of various stretches of water which are extensions of Le Grand Marais.*

St-Nizier-le-Désert
This pleasant village offers facilities for fishing and gentle rambles.

▶ *Follow D 90 which crosses N 83 and leads to Marlieux. Drive through the village and join D 7. Just after a bend, take a small road towards Beaumont.*

Beaumont
The **Chapelle Notre-Dame de Beaumont** stands on the lovely village square. This chapel was once a popular centre of pilgrimage, but subsequently fell into a state of disrepair. Restoration work has revealed 15C **frescoes** ★ which have been well preserved.

▶ *Turn back along the small road on which you arrived to the first intersection. The road branching off to the right goes through the hamlet of Villardières, crosses N 83 and leads to Le Plantay.*

Le Plantay
The village is surrounded by the waters of the Grand Châtel. The **tower** ★ here (⊶ *not open to the public*), of large red bricks and decorated with white stone around the machicolations, is a symbol for the region.

Abbaye Notre-Dame-des-Dombes
Monks from this abbey, founded by Cistercians in the 19C, helped to drain the area and cultivated those sections of land which are fertile.

Chalamont
This is the highest point in La Dombes. Rue des Halles is lined with a few old

houses (15C but restored) with overhanging storeys, and a wash-house.

▸ *Take D 61 to Joyeux.*

There is an attractive 19C house in Joyeux.

▸ *The castle at Le Montellier comes into view on the right.*

Le Montellier

The brick-built **castle** (⌖ *not open to the public*), the most impressive in La Dombes, is flanked at one end by a keep rising on its earth mound.

Cordieux

A handsome red-brick manor house stands here.

▸ *Rejoin D 4 and turn left (W) to St-André-de-Corcy; take D 82 to Monthieux.*

Monthieux

Breuil manor house (16C), just north of the village, has an interesting Saracen well.

▸ *Head towards Ambérieux-en-Dombes and turn right onto D 6.*

Lapeyrouse

From the war memorial there is a delightful view of the Alps and, in the foreground, the Grand Glareins lakes and the 15C Château de Glareins *(private)*.

▸ *Take D 904 back to Villars.*

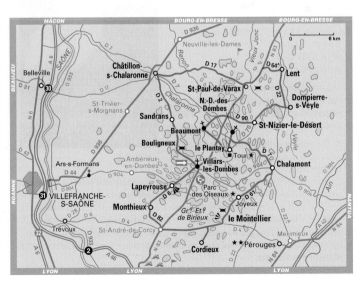

Town

Châtillon-Sur-Chalaronne

This pretty town in the shadow of its 11C castle on the border between the Bresse and Dombes areas, spreads along the Chalaronne Valley. Coming into Châtillon from the south-west on the road from Villefranche (D 936), there is a fine **view** over the town's red rooftops, dominated by the impressive bell-tower of the former almshouse. The half-timbered houses with cob or brick walls built in the style typical of the Dombes area are brightened up in summer with bunches of flowers arranged in wicker baskets called *nids-de-poule* (hens' nests).

Highlights include the **ramparts** of the Vieux Château (the remnants of one of the largest strongholds in Bresse) and the **Maison St-Vincent**, where St Vincent de Paul was lodged by a Protestant, M Beynier, for five months while he was the incumbent of Châtillon. A municipal **museum** along the path leading up to the castle, is devoted to rural life and ancient crafts, while the old **hospital**, commissioned by the Count of Châtelard in the 18C, now houses a regional arts centre.

CHÂTILLON SUR-CHALARONNE

0 _____ 200 m

A Bird's Paradise

Parc des oiseaux★   Kids

1km/0.6mi south of Villars-les-Dombes on N 83. ⟶⏱Open Apr–Sept 9.30am–7.30pm (Jul–Aug, 9.30am–9.30pm); Mar, Oct–Nov 9.30am–5.30pm. ⟶From 13€ (children 6–14, 10€). ☎04 74 98 05 54. www.parc-des-oiseaux.com.

This bird sanctuary, close to the Dombes Nature Reserve, lies along one of the main migration routes in Europe. Over 2,000 birds from five continents live in the park.

At the entrance, the **"Birds' House"** pro-vides a warm, humid atmosphere for a wonderful selection of brightly coloured

J. Damase/MICHELIN

Spoon-bill

exotic birds. Enjoy a walk round the park along the footpaths running round the lakes, which are the breeding ground of large birds such as common and night heron as well as rarer species in giant aviaries. Besides the spectacular **Vallée des rapaces**, the **Volière du Pantanal** and the **Cité des perroquets** are also fascinat-ing. The park is engaged in several conservation programmes aimed at endangered species. These are explained to children through various activities in the **Maison des enfants.**

MONTS DÔME★★★

MICHELIN MAP 326: D-8 TO E-9

The range of volcanic cones known as the *Chaine des Puys* **or Dôme mountain range rises to the west of Clermont-Ferrand and stands high above the Limagne plain. Some 80 extinct volcanoes, which look almost as they did when they were active, stretch in a line over a distance of some 40km/25mi** *(see Introduction: Volcanoes of the Auvergne).*

From the summit of the Puy de Dôme, the highest of the "cones" with an altitude of 1,465m/4,806ft, the view extends right across the range, over this extraordinary and magnificent landscape.

▸ **Orient Yourself:** The most splendid way of getting an idea of the landscape is to take the shuttle service from Clermont-Ferrand railway station to the Puy de Dôme (*see Address Book*), or you can simply drive the toll road to the summit.

🅿 **Parking:** Near the summit.

Especially for Kids: Vulcania theme park.

A Bit of Geology

The Dôme mountain range has the youngest volcanoes in the Auvergne. They came into being in the Quaternary Era and the earliest human settlers may have witnessed their eruptions. The cones, which rise up from the plain in a long string, stand on a plateau of crystalline rocks 900–1,000m/2,950–3,280ft high. Most of the volcanoes rise by only 200–300m/655–985ft above this plateau, with the exception of the Puy de Dôme which rises to 500m/1,640ft above it. These extinct volcanoes are not all the same shape. Several, such as the Puy de Dôme, are shaped like bells or domes; others contain a single or double crater, whereas a few have a breached crater. Areas of forest grew naturally, but much of it has been planted since the Count of Montlosier set the first example in the early 19C, showing that forests could be grown on land thought of as barren – he was initially taken for a fool. Long black lava flows known as *cheires* form heaps of rocks dotted with juniper and pines; they are scattered all across the plateau. One of these flows, created by the Puy de Lassolas and the Puy de la Vache, closed off the Veyre valley and created Lac d'Aydat.

Chaine des Puys, Puy de Dôme in the background

J. Damase/MICHELIN

Le Puy de Dôme

Volcano Hike

1 Le Puy de Dôme★★★

11km/7mi from Royat (⚲see CLERMONT-FERRAND).

🚶The ascent of the Puy de Dôme and the extraordinary panorama visible from the summit, best seen at sunset, are quite unforgettable. This former volcano is the oldest, highest and most famous of the Dôme mountain range, of which it is the centre.

It was only in 1751 that the volcanic origin of these mountains was recognised; until then, it was believed that they were part of gigantic fortifications built by the Romans.

Sacred Mountain – From the earliest times the solitude of this Puy, which is so difficult to get to, has been awe-inspiring. The Gauls made it a sanctuary for their god Lug. The Romans replaced it with the cult of "Mercury of the Dome". They built a magnificent temple to him, the foundations of which were discovered in 1872 during construction of the first observatory. This temple and all its treasures were destroyed by the Barbarian invasions.

According to popular superstition, all the sorcerers of the Auvergne meet on the deserted mountain top for blood-curdling midnight revels.

The weight of air – It is on the Puy de Dôme that **Blaise Pascal** carried out the experiment in 1648 which proved the theory about the weight of air. It had already been noted that mercury rises to about 76cm/30in in a tube in which a vacuum has been created. To explain this phenomenon, it was said that "nature hates vacuums". This axiom however did not satisfy Torricelli; he put forward the hypothesis that it is the weight of the air that pushes the mercury up.

Captivated by this idea, Pascal thought that, if this were the case, the weight of the air should be less at the top of a mountain. As Pascal was in Paris, he asked his brother-in-law to help. The latter chose a fine day, left a mercury barometer in Clermont and went with the Minimes Fathers to the top of the Puy de Dôme. He was overjoyed to see that the mercury rose 8.4cm/3.40in less than it did in Clermont. The theory about the weight of the air had been proven.

Puy-de-Dôme rather than Mont-Dore – In 1790, following the Revolution, administrative *départements* replaced the former provinces in France. There was talk of giving the name Mont-d'Or (Golden Mountain) – as Mont-Dore was then spelled – to the Lower Auvergne constituency, but the deputy for Clermont, Gaultier de Beauzat, was alarmed

Address Book

SHUTTLE SERVICE

There is a shuttle service between Clermont-Ferrand railway station and the Puy de Dôme or Vulcania (Parc européen du volcanisme): *6€ (5–16 year-olds: 3€)*. Another shuttle runs between the Puy de Dôme and Vulcania. *0 800 500 524 (toll free). Timetable available from the Tourist office in Clermont (see CLERMONT-FERRAND).*

WHERE TO STAY

Chambre d'hôte Chez Mme Gauthier Jocelyne – *Recoleine, 63210 Riom, 3km/1.8mi NW of Randanne via N 89. 04 73 87 10 34. Closed from 15 Nov–1 Feb. . Reservations required off-season. 3 rms.* A warm reception awaits you in this former barn neighbouring the Puy de Dôme mountain range and set in a tranquil and natural environment.

Chambre d'hôte Chez M. Bony – *Bravant, 63210 Olby, 2km/1.2mi N of Les Quatre-Routes dir. Ussel and secondary road. 04 73 87 12 28. Closed 15 Nov–15 Feb. . 5 rms.* This tastefully renovated farm is located in the heart of a charming village.

WHERE TO EAT

La Fourniale – *63210 Riom, 3km/1.8mi NW of Randanne via N 89. 04 73 87 16 63. Closed Mon–Tue Sept–Jun, 3 wks in Sept and 15 days early Jan. Reservations required off-season.* Aficionados of authentic Auvergnat cuisine frequent this inn housed in an ex-sheepfold. The setting is as rustic as can be, with wood tables and a stone trough protruding from the wall.

Le Village Auvergnat – *La Font-de-l'Arbre, at the base of the Puy de Dôme, 63870 Orcines. 04 73 62 25 34. Closed Mon–Thu evenings off-season. Reservations required.* Located at the foot of the Puy de Dôme, this restaurant serves regional specialities.

Auberge de la Moreno – *Col de la Moreno, 63122 St-Genès-Champanelle, intersection of D 941 and D 52, on the peak. 04 73 87 16 46. Closed first 2 wks of Jan and last 2 wks of Nov.* This small inn appeals to diners in search of authenticity, offering satisfying '100% regional' dishes.

---

that such a wealthy sounding name would give the wrong impression to outsiders. He asked for the less compromising name of Puy-de-Dôme, and it was accepted.

Ascent via the toll road

Open to traffic (depending on weather conditions): 7am–9.30pm (mid Jun–Aug, 7am–10pm). 6€ (cars). May–Sept: road reserved for cyclists Wed and Sun morning from 7am–8.30am (including the descent). Access is prohibited to pedestrians and two-wheeled vehicles with an engine capacity of less than 125cc. 04 73 62 12 18 (toll) – 04 73 62 21 46.

In 1926 this road replaced the tracks used by the miniature steam train which had operated for about 20 years. The road, which is well designed, has a constant slope of 12% for about 4km/2.5mi. As it spirals around the Dôme it offers a wonderful variety of views, becoming more extensive higher up. The first ascent on bicycle took place in 1891

in 28min; in 1913 a high-powered car reached the summit for the first time, in just 11min.

Ascent on foot via the Roman road *Allow 2hr there and back.*

Park at Ceyssat pass in a forest of fir trees. It was up this winding path (35–40% slopes) that chariots pulled by five to eight tandem-driven horses transported materials needed to build the Roman temple and subsequently, in the 19C, the observatory.

The Summit

Reception and Information Centre

Open Apr–Jun and Sept 10am–6pm, Sat–Sun and public holidays 10am–7pm; Jul–Aug 9am–7pm; Oct 10am–6pm. 04 73 62 21 46. This houses a display on volcanoes and exhibitions specifically on the Puy de Dôme and on various other sites of interest to be explored in the locality.

The Michelin Grand Prix

In 1908, when Henri Farman was making the first circular flight (1km/0.6mi) in the world, the Michelin brothers offered a Grand Prix of 100,000 francs to any aviator who could fly from Paris, with a 75kg/165lb passenger on board, to the top of the Puy de Dôme in less than 6hr, skirting the cathedral of Clermont by 1,500m/4,921ft on their right. Only three years later, on 7 March 1911, despite predictions that this feat could not possibly be achieved within less than a half a century, the aviator **Eugène Renaux**, with his passenger Senouque, successfully met the prescribed conditions in just 5hr 11min.

Panorama★★★

To the north and south, over a distance of about 30km/19mi, can be seen the 100 or so extinct volcanoes forming the Dôme mountain range, a marvellous museum of volcanic shapes, a lunar landscape unique in France and perhaps in the world.

To the north can be clearly distinguished volcanoes of the same origin as the Puy de Dôme which resemble enormous craterless molehills: Petit Suchet, Clierzou and Sarcouy. The others are all cones of debris topped with craters: Petit Puy de Dôme or Nid de la Poule ("Hen's Nest"), Grand Suchet, Puy de Côme, Pariou, Louchadière.

The view extends over 11 *départements*, one-eighth of the total surface area of France. Visibility varies almost from one minute to the next. The puys may be covered with grass or heath, with fir-groves or hazel copses. The chain itself is uninhabited as any rain which falls soaks into the volcanic rocks.

It is at sunset that the view is most spectacular. Fiery trails weave through the volcanic cones. The mountain throws its shadow to the east, covering first the Orcines plateau then suddenly reaching Clermont before gradually invading the plain: the extreme tip of its shadow goes right to Thiers.

Temple of Mercury

o━▪*No access.*

This Temple to the God Mercury (now a ruin) was built by the Romans. Originally it was twice the size of the famous Maison Carrée (1C AD) in Nîmes; 50 sorts of marble were used to decorate it. The television transmitter stands on the original site of a monumental bronze statue of Mercury by the Greek sculptor Zenodorus. It was, according to Pliny the Elder, one of the marvels of the ancient world.

The path winds around the ruins and passes in front of the monument recalling Renaux's exploit.

Driving Tour

2 Puys Mountains★★★

120km/75mi round trip – allow one day

Royat★★ – ℰ*see ST-FLOUR.*

▶ *Leave Royat on D 941C SE then turn right onto D 5.*

The road climbs above the plain until it reaches the granite base from which the volcanic cones rise.

Puy de Gravenoire

There are pozzolana quarries here. This old volcano, now clothed in pine forests, juts out from above the great Limagne fault. Its lava flowed down through the fault towards Royat and Beaumont, then the cone was formed from the materials thrown up during the eruption: ash, scoria and volcanic bombs.

At the top of the rise is the village of **Charade** at the foot of its own extinct volcano, the **Puy de Charade** (ℰ*see ST-FLOUR*).

The road then runs along the southern section of the **Clermont-Ferrand-Charade Racing Circuit.**

Follow the road through Thèdes and St-Genès-Champanelle and, in Theix, take N 89 which crosses the lava flow at Aydat.

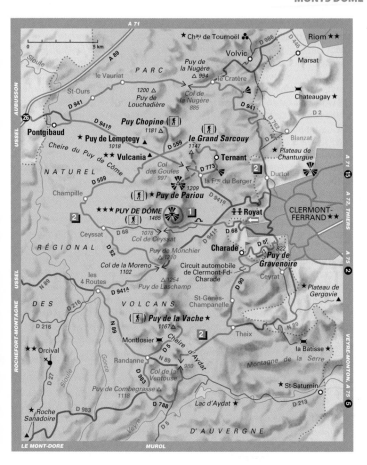

Cheire d'Aydat

This is a lava flow 6km/4mi long and 1,200m/3,937ft wide. It was thrown up by the Lassolas and La Vache volcanoes, and cooled to form a heap of blackened scoria. The desolation of this volcanic landscape is softened to some extent by juniper bushes, broom, birch trees and, on the shores of Lake Aydat for which the lava flow forms a dam, a forest of pines and spruces planted in the second half of the 19C.

▶ *Just beyond Col de la Ventouse, turn right onto D 5 towards Murol and right again along D 788. At the junction turn right towards Randanne.*

On the way to Randanne the road skirts the Puy de Combegrasse where the first gliding competition to be staged in France was held in 1922.

▶ *From Randanne, D 5 leads to the Puy de la Vache.*

Puy de la Vache

1hr on foot there and back.
This well-shaped volcano (alt 1,167m/ 3,828ft) offers, along with its neighbour, Puy de Lassolas, one of the most characteristic views of the Dôme chain.

Access – *3km/1.9mi from Randanne (situated along N 89 between Clermont-Ferrand and Le Mont-Dore) on D 5.*

Montlosier Castle

The **Comte de Montlosier,** a returned émigré in the early 19C, wanted to demonstrate that it was possible to make a

DISCOVERING THE AUVERGNE

forest grow in places which had previously been considered barren; the experiment was carried out on his property. Initially considered to be a madman, he eventually gained recognition when the results of his efforts became tangible. His work was taken up and extended by the Forestry Department.

The castle now houses the offices of the Parc Naturel Regional des Volcans d'Auvergne and organises exhibitions devoted to the region.

🚶 *The path leading to the breached crater of the Puy de la Vache (1hr on foot there and back) runs to the left off D 5. It follows the Cheire d'Aydat, a mass of solidified lava with a rough surface.*

The volcano

The crater first spewed ash and slag, which formed the cone, then the lava mounted, filling the crater. Under such enormous pressure the southern flank of the crater gave way, the volcano opened up and a real torrent of molten material poured out over the plateau, forming the present Cheire d'Aydat, 6km/3.7mi long which, by blocking off the Veyre Valley, formed Lake Aydat.

▶ *Return to Randanne and turn right on N 89.*

Near the village of Recoleine, the road crosses a landscape dotted with volcanic rocks just breaking the surface of the ground. At the crossroads of Les Quatre-Routes, D 941A on the right runs up towards the Puys until it reaches Col de la Moreno between the Puy de Laschamp (south) and the Puy de Monchier (north), both of which are covered in forest.

From Col de la Moreno the route runs along D 52 northwards to Ceyssat and Champille, providing interesting views of the numerous volcanic cones above the road.

The narrow D 559 (right) crosses the lava flow from the Puy de Côme, swathed in beech and conifer, then meets D 941B; turn right towards Col des Goules and La Fontaine du Berger.

This area is the site for the theme park **Vulcania**★★, which is devoted to volcanic activity in Auvergne (🕮 *see below*).

Le Grand Sarcouy

1hr 30min on foot there and back along a well-marked footpath leading off D 941B just after Col des Goules.

🚶 The Grand Sarcouy is still known as a "cauldron" because of its shape. In the south side of this gigantic mass of domite is a vast cavern.

Puy de Pariou★

Puy de Pariou is one of the most beautiful crater volcanoes in the Puys chain. It consists of two volcanoes one inside the other.

🚶 **Access** – *Take D 941B W of Clermont; beyond Orcines, 500m/550yd after the Shepherd's Fountain (Fontaine du Berger), park beside the road. Take a path off to the left (1hr 30min on foot there and back). Visitors should know that the Puy de Pariou was used for military training. So, it is forbidden cross the firing range and the trenches. Visitors are advised not to pick up any projectile or suspect device lying on the ground.*

The volcano

Step over the side wall of the first crater, which produced the still visible lava stretching across the road near Orcines. From here it is possible to climb to the second, far more impressive crater, a regular funnel with a depth of 96m/315ft. From the edge of this crater there are views of the Dôme mountain range, in particular, to the west, beyond the Clierzou and the Puy de Côme with its two craters that fit perfectly inside one another; to the north, over the Puy Chopine, the Puy de Chaumont and, behind the Puy des Goules, the Sarcouy; to the south, over the Puy de Dôme.

Ternant

Just before reaching Ternant, when on a level with the great cross in the village, the road *(D 773)* provides superb views over Clermont and the Limagne plain.

▶ *Take the path on the right, 300m/330yd before the junction with D 941B.*

Puy Chopine *2hr on foot return.*

🚶 In dry weather the path provides access to the volcanic cone's summit.

▶ *Carry on along D 559 to the junction with D 941B and turn right towards Pontgibaud.*

Puy de Lemptégy★

🔼☎*04 73 62 23 25. www.auvergne-vol-can.com.* This **open-topped volcano** is an old quarry hollowed out of a volcanic cone. The site is impressive, as visitors can go down into the very centre and see evidence of three successive phases of volcanic activity from 60,000 years ago.

▶ *Carry on along D 941⁸.*

Pontgibaud

This large peaceful village on the river was known in Gallo-Roman times for its silver-bearing lead mines. **Château Dauphin** (🔼*Easter-Oct guided tours (1hr) Sun and public holidays 2pm–6pm (Jul and Aug daily except Mon 2pm–7pm). ☎6.50€. ☎04 73 88 73 39. www.chateaudauphin.com*) is a lava stone fort which was built in the 12C.

Gorges and Site de Montfermy★

Leave Pontgibaud to the N on D 418 running alongside the Sioule gorges. In Montfermy, leave the car next to the bridge spanning the Sioule.

🔼 Take the path skirting the left bank of the River Sioule, leading to a waterfall and the ruins of an old mill.

On leaving Pontgibaud, D 941 begins to climb the west side of the mountain range. Beyond St-Ours and Le Vauriat the road provides stunning views of the **Puy de Louchadière,** one of the main extinct volcanoes in the range, and has a breached crater 150m/492ft deep.

Further on, to the left, is the easily recognisable outline of the **La Nugère**. Beyond Col de La Nugère and Le Cratère the road winds down to the Limagne plain.

Parc Européen du Volcanisme Vulcania★★

This gigantic theme park is devoted to the history of Auvergne and more specifically to its geological formation.

Puy de Lemptégy

Designed after plans by the architects **Hans Hollein** and **Philippe Tixier**, the park aims to spread knowledge about volcanoes and other earth sciences, while contributing towards the protection of natural sites in Auvergne.

Visit

15km/9.3mi W of Clermont-Ferrand along D 941B. 🕐 **Kids** *Open mid-Mar–mid Nov daily 10am–6pm (Jul–Aug 9.30am–7pm).* 🕐*Closed Mon, Tue Sept–Oct; 1 Apr. ☎21€ (children 13.50€). ☎0820 827 828. www. vulcania.com.*

The **Allée de la Grande Coulée,** an imposing 165m/542ft-long wall, leads to the **Caldera,** a circular area where the **Great Cone** is situated. The glowing crater marks the start of a fascinating journey to the centre of the Earth. You are invited to walk through a succession of wide spaces and galleries showing more or less spectacular aspects of volcanic activity, such as the **Rumbling Gallery,** which re-creates the conditions of an erupting volcano, complete with incandescent projections and formidable sound effects! You can either follow the suggested itinerary or travel as you please in a highly interactive way **"From the Cosmos to the Centre of the Earth"** then **"In the heart of a volcano"**; you can learn about the meaning of volcanoes in different cultures in **"Of volcanoes and men"** and end your visit with the **Volcanic Garden,** a huge, brightly lit greenhouse where a wide variety of plant species thrive on volcanic soil, or in the **Showroom,** where a giant screen projects impressive images of volcanic eruptions in countries all over the world.

VALLÉE DE L'EYRIEUX★

MICHELIN MAP 331: J-4 TO K-4/5

The River Eyrieux rises to the north of St-Agrève then tumbles down from the high plateaux of the Vivarais area and flows into the Rhône after a distance of 70km/44mi. The upper valley has a mountainous appearance, with steep slopes covered with chestnut and spruce; this is the area known as **Les Boutières.** Downstream from Le Cheylard the torrent flows into gorges, then less rugged basins and rocky narrows alternate down to the final plain and the Rhône valley.

- 🛈 **Information:** ☎04 72 59 21 59. www.rhonealpes-tourisme.com.
- 🕐 **Organising Your Time:** Allow a day for each of the Driving Tours.
- ♿ **Also See:** LE PUY-EN-VELAY.

A Bit of Geography

Fearsome spates – The Eyrieux flows swiftly. Because of the sloping ground on its upper course, autumn storms suddenly swell the main river and its tributaries. In September 1857, the waters in the Pontpierre narrow near St-Fortunat reached a height of 17.25m/56ft.

Old, isolated hamlets cling to the hillsides marked into strips by the low walls surrounding terraced fields. Larger villages and small towns grew up in the small inner basins in the valley, or at the mouth of tributaries. Some of them have industrial activity, but the dominant character of the valley derives from farming peaches. In the spring the peach trees turn this rugged valley into a carpet of pink-petalled blossom.

A model orchard - The widespread cultivation of orchards is due to favour-able natural conditions: light, warm soil which is easily drained; the valley's sheltered site from the Mistral and the winds from the south; spring frosts which are rare; and summers which begin early. The success story of the orchards is also due to the determination of the local people.

The first trees were planted in 1880, on an experimental basis. Production methods, improved since that time, have been copied in other regions.

Driving Tours

Orchards

In spring, the D 120 is the best route to follow to admire the sight of the peach trees in blossom. The season lasts for some time, beginning with the

Château de Pierre-Gourde

S. Sauvignier/MICHELIN

orchards in the lower valley, and creates an extraordinary blend of colours ranging from pale pink to carmine red and through to purple.

Beauchastel

Listed village at the foot of its castle ruins. A stroll through narrow alleys and streets takes you to the **Maison du Patrimoine** and the terrace offering a pretty view of St-Laurent-du-Pape and the nearby valley.

▶ *Rejoin D 21 and head towards St-Laurent-du-Pape.*

St-Laurent-du-Pape

Attractive town at the valley entrance, enhanced by its bridge over the Eyrieux.

▶ *Keep driving along the valley in the direction of Cheylard.*

St-Sauveur-de-Montagut

Dominated by the ruins of Montagut Château *(access by D 244 and a forest lane)*, the village stands at the confluence of the River Eyrieux and River Gluyère.

▶ *Just before the bridge take D 105 for St-Pierreville.*

The roads runs along the Gluyère valley, hugging the river banks almost up to St-Pierreville.

St-Pierreville

The **Maison du Châtaignier** (🕐*open Apr–Jun and Sept–Nov Wed, Sun and school holidays, 2pm–6pm; Jul–Aug daily, 11am–12.30pm, 2.30pm–6pm;* 🕐*closed Dec–Mar;* ☎*3.50€;* ☎ *04 75 66 64 33; www.chataignier.fr)* presents an exhibition on the chestnut production.

Musée Vivant de la Laine et du Mouton `Kids`

♿🕐*Guided tours (1h30) Jul–Aug 11am–5pm; Feb–Jun and Sept–Dec daily, 2pm–5pm.* 🕐*Closed Jan.* ☎*5.60€ (children: 4€).* ☎*04 75 66 63 08. www.ardelaine.fr.* The plateaux flanking the Eyrieux are perfect for sheep. This **Sheep and Wool Museum** presents the different breeds and the types of wool they produce.

Corniche de l'Eyrieux★★★

70km/43.5mi round trip

▶ *Leave St-Laurent-du-Pape on D 120; then right onto D 21 for Vernoux.*

As it winds up to Serre Mure pass, this road offers views of the Vivarois ridges, the upper basin of the Eyrieux and the Boutières region, as well as a view of the western slopes of Pierre-Gourde peak.

▶ *Turn left onto D 231, then D 331.*

St-Julien-le-Roux

From the church, mountains can be seen along the **horizon**★, above the ruins of Château de la Tourette.

▶ *D 331, D 231 and D 21 lead back to Vernoux.*

Vernoux-en-Vivarais

Vernoux stands on the Vivarais plateau, between the Eyrieux and the River Doux, in the centre of a large hollow.

Château de la Tourette

The ruins of this stronghold, which once marked the gateway to the States of Languedoc, lie in an unspoilt **setting**★ and are among the most evocative in the Vivarais.

▶ *Drive to Boffres situated 8.5km/5mi NE on D 14 and D 219.*

Boffres

The village of Boffres is built on a projection in a semicircle at the foot of its sim-

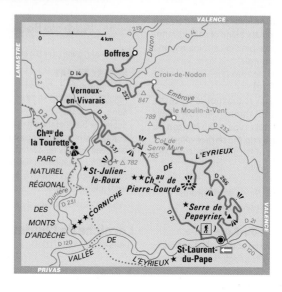

ple church and the remains of a fortified castle. Just outside the village, a bronze bust has been erected to the memory of **Vincent d'Indy,** the French composer and teacher (1851–1931), born in Paris, but descended from a family in the region. It was at **Château des Faugs**, west of Boffres, that d'Indy came to seek inspiration. He composed his third melody without words from a shepherd's song heard near Les Estables, and his opera Fervaal one misty morning on the peaks of Mont Mézenc.

▶ *Drive to the D 14; left onto D 232.*

The road runs along the hillside, offering views of Vernoux-en-Vivarais in the centre of the basin. Beyond Croix-de-Nodon, there are generous glimpses of the Rhône valley and clear views of the deep wooded Embroye valley.

▶ *At Le Moulin-à-Vent turn right onto D 266.*

After a long wooded section, the road runs along a spectacular stretch of ledge, opposite Pierre-Gourde peak, in front of the mountain ridges enclosing the Eyrieux valley.

▶ *A track, off D 286 to the right, leads to the Château de Pierre-Gourde. Park at a pass, in sight of the ruins.*

Panorama from the Château de Pierre-Gourde★★

This medieval castle, now in ruins, occupies a magnificent **site**★. At the foot of the peak on which the keep was built lie the ruins of the main building, parts of the curtain wall and the feudal village.

▶ *Walk left around the ruins to reach a rocky terrace.*

The **panorama** encompasses the Rhône and Trois-Becs, between the Vercors bar, the Baronnies and Mont Ventoux. Opposite, the backbone of Croix de Bauzon overlooks the Haut-Eyrieux gap. During the descent, two panoramic bends offer a view first of the Eyrieux valley, with its clearly delineated ridges, endlessly repeated, and then of the Rhône valley, on the left.

▶ *About 5km/3mi from Pierre-Gourde, a sign on the right indicates the Serre de Pepeyrier ridge.*

View from Serre de Pepeyrier★

There is a beautiful **view** from the ridge of the mouth of the Eyrieux valley with its vast peach orchards, the town of Beauchastel and the Rhône plain; in the background, Mont Ventoux.

MONTS DU FOREZ★★

MICHELIN MAPS 327: B-5/6, C-5/6, D-5/6

The granite mountains in the Forez area form a range some 45km/28mi long. Along the edge are parallel offshoots separating the picturesque valleys, some of which run down to the Dore whereas others head for the Loire. The eastern slopes stand high above the Forez plain; the slopes to the west, the only part of the range in the Auvergne, drop sharply down to the Dore basin and include some attractive beauty spots and magnificent views.

▶ **Orient Yourself:** The Monts du Forez are part of the Parc Naturel Régional Livradois-Forez, so a good place to start is at the Maison du Parc in St-Gervais-sous-Meymont.

▣ **Parking:** At the Maison du Parc.

◉ **Don't miss:** The panorama from the col du Bréal and from the balcon du Forez.

◐ **Organising your time:** Allow at least a day-and-a-half to explore the region fully.

◔ **Also see:** LYON, MONTBRISON.

A Bit of Geography

On the Heights – Up to altitudes of 800–1,000m/2,625–3,280ft, the mountainsides are covered with fields (rye, potatoes) and meadows – this is the zone in which villages have been built. The pure, abundant water supply that rushes down all the slopes of the Forez mountains is used to irrigate meadows where it is cool even in the height of the summer, and to turn the waterwheels in the mills, sawmills, and the last paper-mill in the Lagat Valley; it also supplies the cutlery works in Thiers. Above are the pine and beech forests covering the hillsides.

At altitudes above 1,200–1,300m/3,937–4,265ft lie the summer pastures, called "Hautes-Chaumes" (alpine pastures), of the Forez. On the mountain peaks a few spurs of rock jut out from scree slopes; Pierre sur Haute is the highest of them (alt 1,634m/5,360ft).

Parc Naturel Régional Livradois-Forez

The Forez mountains are part of the **Parc Naturel Régional Livradois-Forez** which was set up in 1984 and covers an area of almost 300,000ha/over 740,000 acres. Its aims are to revitalise a declin-

Hiking in Livradois-Forez park woods

© World Pictures/Photoshot

Address Book

For coin ranges, see the cover flap.

WHERE TO STAY

Les Genets – *63880 Le Brugeron.* ☎*04 73 72 60 36. Closed end Nov– mid-Feb.* 📶*. 10 rms.* ☐*6€.*
Guests can unwind in a pretty park hidden behind this stone house in the heart of the village. The spotless bedrooms sport modern furnishings. Dining room where simplicity is the rule and traditional fare is served.

WHERE TO EAT

Ferme-auberge du Mazet – *42990 St-Georges-en-Couzan.* ☎*04 77 24 80 95. Closed Dec, Jan and Sun evening.* If you've a taste for homemade delicatessen, you're bound to enjoy this farm-inn on the village heights. A convivial atmosphere reigns in the vast dining room where appetising farm-raised ham and pork dishes are served.

Ferme-auberge des Granges – *Les Granges, 42920 Chalmazel, 5km/3mi SW of Chalmazel dir. Le Col du Béal.* ☎*04 77 24 80 62. Closed Nov.* 📷*. Reservations recommended evenings.* This long chalet is a very convenient place to take it easy and re-energise after a hard day's skiing. The generous meals give healthful farm produce pride of place.

Gaudon – *63880 Le Brugeron, 6km/3.6mi S of La Chambonie via D 101 and D 37.* ☎*04 73 72 60 46. Closed Jan, Sun evening, Mon evening and Tue from 15 Sept–1 Jun.* In the bosom of the Monts du Forez, at the entrance of the village of Brugeron, this traditional house built in 1929 is a handy stopover.

---

ing rural environment and to present and promote local heritage, especially crafts and industry. The park also seeks to encourage rural holidays which do not disturb the environment.

The park's cultural programme includes the music festivals of La Chaise-Dieu and Thiers. The residents of the areas encompassed by the park are proud of their history and the craftsmanship they have practised over the centuries, reflected in various local museums: cutlery-making (Thiers); lacemaking (Arlanc); papermaking (Richard-de-Bas); agriculture and cheesemaking (Ambert).

There are a number of waymarked paths which cover the park, enabling visitors to explore it to the full. Those fond of sports will appreciate the facilities for water sports, riding and paragliding.

The **Maison du Parc** (⏱*May–Sept: 9am–12.30pm, 1.30pm–7pm (Sat, Sun, 3pm–7pm); rest of year: daily except Sat, Sun, 9am–12.30pm, 1.30pm–5.30pm (Fri, 1.30pm–4.30pm);* ⏱*closed 1 Jan, 1 and 11 Nov, 25 Dec;* ⏱*no charge;* ☎*04 73 95 57 57; www.parc-livradois-forez.org),* which is the park's information centre, is located in St-Gervais-sous-Meymont.

Driving Tours

1 Via Col de Béal★

Allow one day.

Boën

Boën (pronounced "Bowen"), situated high above the left bank of the Lignon, specialises in metalworking and mechanical engineering. Boën was the birthplace of Father Terray (1715–78), Comptroller-General of Finances at the end of Louis XV's reign. The unpopular measures he was forced to take in order to re-establish a balanced budget following the excessive spending of the royal court brought him the nickname "Emptier of Purses."

Musée de la vigne★

⏱*Open Jul–Aug, daily except Mon, 10am–noon, 2pm–6.30pm (Sun, 2pm–6.30pm); rest of year: daily except Mon, 2.30pm–6.30pm.* ⏱*Closed Dec–Jan and 1 May.* ☞*4€.* ☎*04 77 24 08 12. www.boen.fr.*
The elegant 18C Chateau Chabert houses a Winemaking Museum established with a real concern for authenticity, both in its reconstructions of traditional interiors and in its technical presentations of wine-growing.

▷ *Leave Boën on N 89 NW, 2.5km/1.5mi on from Boën, turn left onto D 6 to Sail-sous-Couzan.*

Sail-sous-Couzan

This peaceful village was suddenly thrown into the limelight on 12 July 1998, when the World Cup final between France and Brazil saw victory for the host country.

▷ *Turn right off D 6 onto a very steep tarmacked road leading to the castle ruins.*

Château de Couzan★

Park at the foot of the ruins; 15min on foot there and back. The ruins of this 11C fortress, one of the most important in the region, stand on a rocky promontory squeezed between the narrow valleys of the River Lignon and River Chagon. What remains of the curtain walls and towers still suggests the strength of the seigneurs of Couzan, the oldest barons of the Forez. There is a good view of the castle walls from a rocky promontory behind the fort, and panoramic **views**★ over the countryside from the ruins which are being restored.

▷ *Return to Sail-sous-Couzan and turn left onto D 97 towards St-Just-en-Bas.*

The road runs along the crest of the hill up above the Upper Lignon Valley overshadowed by Pierre sur Haute before reaching Jeansagnière. Continue on to the pass, **Col de la Loge**, where a curtain of pine trees opens onto a clearing carpeted with grass. Before La Chamba, the forest gives way to more pastoral scenery and the route, skirting a succession of corries filled with fine pastures, provides several outstanding views of the Dore basin and the Livradois area.

▷ *Continue 2km/1.2mi beyond La Chamba and turn left towards Le Brugeron.*

La Chambonie

A village nestling in a pastoral corrie.

▷ *Immediately beyond a sawmill turn right onto D 37.*

After a long climb up through the forest, there is a magnificent view over the Dômes mountain range. Beyond another stretch of road through the forest lie alpine pastures dotted with farmsteads *(jasseries)*.

Col du Béal★

From this pass there is a wide **panoramic view** over the mountains of the Auvergne and the Lyonnais area. The pass forms a threshold between the two sides of the Forez mountains.

Summer Pastures

The Monts du Forez feature a wide range of scenery, much of it covered by dark pine forests. Once above the tree line, the mountain summits, often shrouded in mist or cloud, are vast bleak stretches of moorland – the **Hautes-Chaumes**. This somewhat eerie landscape can look more like a moonscape in certain lights. The vast bare wastes are broken only by granite rocks, deep peat bogs or clumps of broom. Nonetheless, man – or rather, woman – has attempted to scratch a living from this unwelcoming environment. A matriarchal society evolved in the mountain farmsteads *(jasseries)* during the summer months; while the menfolk were down in the valley dealing with the harvesting, the women and children would be in charge of looking after the livestock in the summer pastures up in the mountains, where they would also make the famous local Fourme cheese and gather medicinal plants.

This harsh way of life gradually died out, and there are now no more working jasseries. However, some of them have been converted into open-air museums which inform visitors about the daily work and traditions of these "Amazons of the Mountains."

Pierre sur Haute★★

2hr 30min on foot there and back, recommended in clear weather.
Climb directly up to the summit across the alpine pastures and along the crest of the mountain or take the chair-lift.
🕐*Open Jul–mid-Sept: 2pm–6pm.* ✎*6€.* ☎*04 77 24 85 09.*

🏃 Pierre-sur-Haute, the highest peak in the Forez range is a dome-shaped granite mountain topped by military radar installations. The windswept moorland that carpets its slopes is gashed here and there by huge rockfalls. Small farmsteads dot the hillsides.

From the summit to the right of the military installations, the **panorama** stretches right across the Forez, the mountains in the Lyonnais area and Beaujolais, the Limagne, the Dômes and Dore mountain ranges, Cantal and the mountains in Velay and Vivarais.

Three types of scenery succeed each other during the rapid trip down from Col du Béal to Chalmazel – alpine pastures, then a superb pine forest and, finally, an area of pine trees and meadows.

▶ *About 7km/4mi from Col du Béal, a road cuts off to the right; it leads to the ski slopes and the Pierre-sur-Haute cable-car.*

Chalmazel✳

This mountain village, which clings to the hillside in the Lignon ravine, is a bustling place during the winter sports season. It is dominated by the old 13C **Château des Talaru-Marcilly** (🕐*open Jul–Aug 2pm–6pm; mid-May–Jun and Sept Sat, Sun and public holidays, 10am–6pm;* ✎*5.50€;* ☎*04 77 24 88 09; www. chateaudechalmazel.com*), a huge bastion flanked by corner towers which still has its parapet walkway. The chapel is decorated with 16C frescoes.

▶ *Take D 101 to Sauvain.*

Sauvain

The most notable feature of this village is the **Maison Sauvagnarde** (🕐*open Jul–Aug daily except Mon 2.30pm–6.30pm; Jun and Sept–Oct Sun 2.30pm–6.30pm;* ✎*3.50€;* ☎*04 77 76 82 18)*, an old 17C farmhouse that belonged to the inventor **Louis Lépine**, who founded a famous competition for the most innovative device or technique.

▶ *Continue along D 101 in the direction of Montbrison.*
Soon after crossing the Lignon at Pont-de-Pierre, turn left onto D 110, heading for Col de la Pelletière. Drive to Trelins via La Bruyère and Prélion (D 20) and take D 20A on the right.

Château de Goutelas

The château stands on a terrace high above the Forez plain; it is a late-16C residence which has been restored and is now used to host courses and seminars. The courtyard is open to visitors and it is possible to walk round the exterior.

▶ *Turn back and take D 8 back to Boën.*

2 Via Col des Supeyres★
70km/44mi – allow half a day.

Montbrison – *see MONTBRISON.*

▶ *Leave Montbrison to the W along D 101 which climbs up the bare, rocky Vizery ravine. A short detour leads to the village of Essertines.*

Essertines-en-Châtelneuf

From the village, with its small Gothic church with Flamboyant Gothic decoration, there is a view over the Forez plain from which emerges the rocky pinnacle of St-Romain-le-Puy.

▶ *Rejoin D 101 and continue up the valley before turning left on D 44^A. In Roche turn left onto D 44 and continue via D 113 to Col de Baracuchet.*

From the road there are several glimpses of the Forez plain. The road continues to climb through valleys filled with farms and fields and dominated by wooded peaks. Near the pass, the trees become gnarled and twisted until they eventually give way to a vast clearing from which there is a view of the Ance Valley

(left) and, opposite the road, the crest of the Forez mountains.

The road *(D 106)* climbs up to Col des Supeyres through alpine pastures, carpeted with heather and dotted with farmsteads, and past the Grand Génevrier farmsteads *(left)*.

Col des Supeyres

Alt 1,366m/4,481ft. This pass on the eastern edge of the Livradois-Forez Nature Park is surrounded by a landscape more reminiscent of steppes: poorly drained mountain pastures, without a soul in sight. The sense of ruggedness and isolation is particularly strong at the bottom of the road leading to Pierre-sur-Haute *(it becomes a dirt track 1km/0.6mi from the start)*. A viewing table on "La Montagne des Allebasses" and a themed footpath *(2hr 30min)* shed light on the way of life in this region (farmsteads, summer pasturing etc).

The route down from the pass towards St-Anthème passes the group of farmsteads known as **Les Jasseries du Grand Genévrier,** one of which is open to the public.

Jasserie du Coq Noir

A visit to this old farmstead (Black Cock Farm) used during the seasonal moving of livestock provides an insight into life in the mountains, into the art of thatching roofs and into the production of Fourme cheeses.

▶ *As the road runs down to St-Anthème there are views of the volcanic cones in the Velay area – Meygal, Lizieux, Mézenc and Gerbier-de-Jonc.*

St-Anthème

The red-roofed village nestles in the depths of the Ance valley.

▶ *Follow D 496 from St-Anthème to return to Montbrison.*

Beyond Col de la Croix de l'Homme Mort, the road provides some very attractive views of the Forez plain, the Monts du Lyonnais area, and Mont Pilat.

HAUTERIVES

POPULATION 1,333

MICHELIN MAP 332: D-2

The village of Hauterives, situated at the foot of a hillock bearing the ruins of the medieval castle which once belonged to the lords of Clermont, has an unusual tourist attraction – the "Ideal Palace."

- **Information:** R. du Palais-Idéal, 26390 HAUTERIVES. ☎04 75 68 86 82.
- **Orient Yourself:** E of a line S from Lyon to Valence, and accessible by A 7.
- **Also See:** LYON, VALENCE.

Sights

Palais Idéal★

&. ⏱Open daily 9.30am–12.30pm, and from 1.30pm until 7.30pm (Jul and Aug); 6.30pm (Apr–Jun and Sept); 5.30pm (Feb–Mar and Oct–Nov); 4.30pm (Jan and Dec). ⏱Closed 25 Dec, 1 Jan and mid–end Jan. ⊙5.30€. ☎04 75 68 81 19. www.facteur cheval.com.

In the late 19C the postman in Hauterives, **Ferdinand Cheval**, began bringing home strangely shaped stones every day that he picked up during his round. In the evenings he would add them to an unusual construction he was building in his garden, based on books and dreams, and possibly also inspired by the remains of petrified springs that were commonplace in this area of the Drôme. When he retired, Cheval continued his work, tirelessly bringing sand and stones back to his home in a wheelbarrow. After 33 years of relentless labour, he finished his weird and wonderful "Palace." Cheval then spent the last 10 years of his life building his own grave in the cemetery, in the same style. He died in 1924.

L'Art en marche

⏱Open Apr–Sept 10am–12.15pm, 1.30pm–6pm; Oct–Mar 10am–12.15pm, 1.30pm–5.30pm. ⏱Closed Mid-Jan–end-Jan, 1 Jan and 25 Dec. ⊙5€. ☎04 75 68 95 40.

This museum of "Art Brut" and "Neuve Invention" carries on in the spirit of Cheval's naïve innovations by presenting a large number of international works which cannot be classified.

Les Labyrinthes   [Kids]

3.5km/2.2mi. Follow D 51 towards Le Grand-Serre and turn left in St-Germain. &. ⏱Open May–Aug 11am–7pm; Sept: Sat, Sun, 11am–7pm). ⏱Closed Oct–Apr. ⊙5€. ☎04 75 68 96 27.

Four large mazes, occupying the top of a hill, combine their network of paths and hedges to offer young visitors a thrilling treasure hunt. The Maison des Enfants, located in a shaded position, organises activities involving mosaics.

Address Book

WHERE TO STAY

🛏 **Hôtel Le Relais** – ☎04 75 68 81 12. Closed mid-Jan–end Feb, Sun evening except Jul–Aug and Mon. 17 rms. ⊡6€. Restaurant🍽. This village hotel is set in a big old house with an exposed stone façade and white shutters.

WHERE TO EAT

🍽🍽🍽 **Yves Leydier** – 26330 Châteauneuf-de-Galaure, 6km/3.6mi SW of Hauterives via D 51. ☎04 75 68 68 02. Closed 17 Feb–12 Mar, 1–10 Jul, 28–31 Aug, Sun evening except Jul–Aug, Tue evening and Wed. Located on the village square, this pretty house built of round stones from the Galaure opens out back onto a large garden where children like to play in summer.

LAC D'ISSARLÈS ★

MICHELIN MAP 331:G-4 OR 239 FOLD 47
LOCAL MAP SEE GORGES DE LA LOIRE

The waters of this round and intensely blue-looking lake (alt 1,000m/3,281ft) are used to run the hydroelectric power plant at Montpezat, which can therefore affect the water level, though between 15 June and 15 September the lake is kept full to provide an attractive place for bathing.

▶ **Orient Yourself:** 40km/24.8mi S of Le Puy-en-Velay.
⚲ **Also See:** GORGES de la LOIRE, Le PUY-EN-VELAY.

Lake

The lake occupies an old volcanic crater 138m/452ft deep with a surface area of some 90ha/222 acres. It is possible to walk all the way round (5km/3mi), mostly through woodland, but do enquire before starting out as the woods are sometimes flooded owing to the hydroelectric power plant nearby.

Driving Tour

Lauze Country

▶ *Leave Lake Issarlès on D 16 heading for Béage and follow directions for Ste-Eulalie, then continue towards Lachamp-Raphaël until the D 378.*

Ferme de Bourlaties★ is a fine example of regional rural architecture with its lauze roof tiling, this stately farmhouse has been extensively restored in local tradition. Press on to **Gerbier-de-Jonc**★★, which looks like a giant haystack. Continue towards **Les Estables**, a small mountain village and a popular winter resort offering a choice of pistes for Alpine and cross-country skiing.

▶ *Cross the village heading N; turn right for Mont Mézenc via Peccata Cross.*

Mont Mézenc★★★

The volcanic Mézenc range (the final "c" is not pronounced) forms a natural barrier that divides the rivers flowing to the Atlantic from those flowing to the Mediterranean. A vast tract of land called the **Zone Nordique du Mézenc** is popular in the winter months for the cross-country skiing it offers; more than 100km/62mi of pistes are maintained around the towns and villages of Fay-sur-Lignon, Chaudeyrolles, Freycenet-la-Cuche, Les Estables and St-Front.

▶ *Rejoin D 274 to the N via the Peccata Cross. At the crossroads with D 39, turn right and follow directions to Fay-sur-Lignon.*

Fay-sur-Lignon

This mountain village (pronounced fa-yee), clinging to the slopes of a phonolithic cone, offers cross-country skiing facilities in winter.

▶ *Take D 39 to St-Front.*

St-Front

The ancient village lying at the foot of a mound offers excellent **views**★ of the northeast slopes of the Mézenc massif. Note the 11C church on the village square.

▶ *Return to Lake Issarlès.*

ISSOIRE★★

POPULATION 14,470

MICHELIN MAP 326: G-9

Issoire is located on the Couze River, near its junction with the Allier, south of Clermont-Ferrand and on the fertile plain of Limagne. The town is said to have been founded by the Arverni, a powerful Gallic tribe that inhabited the present-day region of Lyon. They gave their name to this region – Auvergne. During the 17th-century religious wars of the Reformation, Issoire suffered severely, and most of the old town was destroyed.

Architecturally, pride of place goes to the ornate 12C Abbatiale Saint-Austremoine, formerly the church of a Benedictine abbey, and one of the largest Romanesque churches in the Auvergne. But there is an agreeable, provincial ambiance about the place that rewards even the shortest break. Today, surrounded by boulevards, the town is bright, refreshing, and a delight to explore, not least its remarkable Renaissance clock tower, formerly the town belfry, from the top of which there is a fine panoramic view over the town, the Limagne landscape and the Monts Dore and Livradois mountain ranges.

- **Information:** Pl. du Gén.-de-Gaulle, 63500 ISSOIRE. ☎04 73 89 15 90. www.issoire.fr.
- ▶ **Orient Yourself:** Most shops, restaurants and bars cluster around the clock tower, and along the main street.
- P **Parking:** Ample car parking in the centre of town.
- **Don't Miss:** The clock tower.
- ◷ **Organising Your Time:** The town is amazingly compact, with many narrow streets; begin with the clock tower, which also houses a display of local life throughout the turbulent Renaissance period.

A Bit of History

High flyers – The **gliding club** at Issoire-le-Broc aerodrome to the south-east of the town attracts numerous French and foreign glider pilots who come to enjoy the strong thermal currents in the locality. These currents can lift gliders released at 800m/2,625ft up to an altitude of more than 10,000m/32,808ft.

Little Geneva – In 1540 a former Dominican monk arrived in Issoire from Germany and converted the Consuls to the Lutheran faith. He was burnt alive on the bailiff's orders but his death led, in fact, to numerous additional conversions. Issoire became a "Little Geneva," washed in the blood of the many martyrs to the new faith.

Walking Tour

The early-19C **corn-exchange,** situated next to the tourist office, has been turned into an entertainment centre.

Follow rue Ponteil which starts opposite and leads to the **Tour de l'Horloge** (clock tower, *see Sights below*). On reaching place de la République (the former Grande Place), where a busy market takes place on Saturday mornings, note the 15C **Maison Charrier** with its Gothic doorway and the **fountain** adorning the centre of the square, designed in 1823 by the architect Ledru.

Beyond, to the left, is the **Maison aux Arcades;** turn left onto rue des Fours and admire the 15C–17C **Hôtel Bohier** which houses a fine Renaissance staircase. Turn left at the end of the street to reach the **Centre Pomel** (*see Sights below*). Opposite, on the corner of square Cassin, the Maison de la Bascule (weights and measures building) houses the **Musée de la Pierre Philosophale** containing a col-

Address Book

⚭For coin ranges, see the cover flap.

WHERE TO STAY

⬭⬭**Chambre d'hôte Paul Gebrillat et Mireille de Saint Aubain** – *Chemin de Siorac, 63500 Perrier, 3km/1.8mi W of Issoire via D 996.* ☎*04 73 89 15 02. www.maison-gebrillat. com. Closed 1 Dec–31 Jan.* ⬭. *3 rms.* In a village right near the volcanoes, this pretty 18C house is inviting indeed. Breakfast is served under a trellis in the delightful courtyard planted with flowers. Charming rooms and reliable advice for adventuresome tourists.

⬭⬭⬭**Château de Grange Fort** – *63500 Les Pradeaux, 7km/4.2mi SE of Issoire, take A 75, exit 13, dir. Parentignat and D 34, rte d'Auzat-sur-Allier.* ☎*04 73 71 02 43. Closed Dec–Mar. 5 rms.* ⬭*10€. Meals*⬭⬭⬭. A 17C château with superb crenellated towers set in the bosom of a park encircled by mountains. The rooms, all unique, may feature a canopy bed, a sculpted door, a parquet floor or original mouldings. Splendid vaulted dining room.

⬭⬭**Chambre d'hôte Les Baudarts** – *63500 Varennes-sur-Usson, 6km/3.6mi E of Issoire via D 996 and D 123.* ☎*04 73 89 05 51. Closed 1 Oct–1 May.* ⬭. *3 rms.* Lost in the middle of the countryside, this Provencal-style house with pink walls and a Romanesque tiled roof is all elegance and sophistication. The spacious bedrooms are tastefully decorated and the living room is superb; the swimming pool and small park are lovely. Not to be missed!

WHERE TO EAT

⬭**Le Boudes La Vigne** – *63340 Boudes. 15km/9mi S of Issoire via D 909 and D 48.* ☎*04 73 96 55 66. Closed 2–22 Jan and 24 Aug–5 Sept.* Set in the heart of a quaint wine-making village, this basic hotel has small rooms that are modest but well-kept, and the restaurant, part of which is in the cellar, has its regular patrons.

⬭⬭**La Bergerie** – *63490 Sarpoil, 10km/6mi E of Issoire via D 999.* ☎*04 73 71 02 54. Closed Jan, Mon evening, Tue–Wed Sept–Jun. Reservations required.* A coaching inn and sheepfold in the olden days, this restaurant, featuring old stone walls in the vaulted dining room, has retained its old-fashioned charm. Classic cuisine.

⬭⬭**La Cour Carrée** – *63500 Perrier, 5km/3mi W of Issoire via D 996.* ☎*04 73 55 15 55. Closed Feb and Christmas holidays, Sun evening, Wed evening, Sat lunch Sept–Jun and Mon. Reservations recommended.* This former winemaker's abode is entered via the small square courtyard. In summertime, a terrace is set up here under the big horse chestnut, whereas in winter, you will be seated in the vaulted dining room. Traditional fare.

SHOPPING

Maison Chazal – *4 r. Gambetta. 04 73 89 20 11.* A handsome establishment with products divided into different sections. The 'roasting room' offers coffee beans from such illustrious provenances as the Galapagos Islands and a wide range of teas; the grocer's shelves are laden with preserves, foie gras, honey and the like; the vaulted wine cellar boasts about 350 different vintages, including 20 from outside of France, and 50-odd brands of whisky.

Pascale et Patrick Védrine – *8 r. du Ponteil.* ☎*04 73 55 28 18.* The unique decor and warm atmosphere set this baker's shop apart. Special breads are made according to traditional recipes and cooked in a wood-burning oven; pastries are also very popular, especially the Ponteil and the Sancy. We suggest you take the time to taste these treats on site – the decor is truly worth discovering.

lection of 1,000 minerals. Walk round the cathedral and back to place de la République. Turn right onto rue de la Berbiziale; on the corner, note the 15C **Maison du Chancelier Duprat** with its rectangular corbelled tower. Continue to place St-Avit; the 18C **Maison Bartin** on the left, has fine wrought-iron balconies.

Queen Margot (16C–17C)

This princess, popularised by the author Alexandre Dumas, was the sister of Charles IX who gave her in marriage to the King of Navarre (the future Henri IV), saying that, in doing so, he "had given her to all the Huguenots in the Kingdom"– a somewhat indiscreet allusion to the young queen's many love affairs. Her conduct was such that she was forced to seek asylum in Carlat, where her favourite was the young Lord of Aubiac. Fleeing Carlat when the king ordered her arrest, Marguerite took refuge in Ybois Castle, near Orbeil (northeast of Issoire). Her brother, Henri III sent the Marquis of Canillac to lay siege to the fortress. Canillac seized the queen and Aubiac; instructed by the court, he had her favourite executed. Marguerite was locked up in Usson under the guard of the marquis.

For 20 years Queen Margot led a life of passion, study and devotion. Her husband the king wanted her to agree to having the marriage dissolved. She would only agree, however, after the death of Gabrielle d'Estrées, the king's mistress, not wanting to be replaced (so she wrote to Sully), by "such an ill-esteemed piece of trash." After that, she was able to return to Paris.

Abbatiale St-Austremoine★★

St-Austremoine, once the church of a Benedictine abbey, was built in the 12C and dedicated to Austremoine, the first bishop of the Arverni people, martyred in the 3C; it is now the parish church, replacing the neighbouring Église St-Paul, which was destroyed shortly after the French Revolution.

Exterior

The **east end**★★ stands on a wide esplanade. This is the most perfect section of the building, a consummate example of Romanesque architecture as it developed in the Auvergne. No other church boasts such harmonious proportions, such purity of line and such restraint in its decoration. Its powerful, well-balanced design consists of various different elements; note the mosaics and sculptures representing signs of the Zodiac.

Interior

The two-storey **nave** is striking for its magnificent proportions; the painted decoration was added in the mid-19C. At the southern entrance to the ambulatory there is one of the finest, and most complete, views of the building as a whole. Walk round the chancel; it is particularly interesting for its superb narrative **capitals**★.

Crypt

This is one of the finest crypts in the Auvergne. The stocky columns supporting the vaulted roof give an impression of strength that is further emphasised by the total lack of decoration.

Sights

Centre Pomel

This houses the **Centre d'Art Roman Georges-Duby** (&⏱*open May–Sept daily except Mon morning 10am–noon, 2pm–6pm. ☎04 73 89 56 04. www.terres-romanes-auvergne.com*), which displays the vestiges of the Monastère St-Austremoine.

Tour de l'Horloge

&⏱*Open Jun–Sept daily except Mon 10am–1pm, 2pm–7pm, (last admission 45min before closing); Oct–May daily except Mon 2pm–6pm (Sat 7pm). ⏱Closed 1 Jan, 1 May, 25 Dec. ⚬5.50€. ☎04 73 89 07 70. www.issoire.fr.*
The chimes of the Renaissance belfry (15C) can still be heard throughout town. A lively 'Scenovision' presentation enlightens visitors on the rich and colourful past of Issoire and eight short documentary films retrace the impact of the Renaissance (printing and other great discoveries). Temporary exhibitions are also organised. From the top of the tower there is a lovely view of the town and surrounding countryside.

Excursion

Auzon★ *28km/17mi SE of Issoire*
Auzon's dramatic **setting**★ on a sheer-sided spur of rock overlooking the valley of the river that shares its name is best appreciated when seen from D 5, coming from the Allier Valley. This old fortified town still has many traces of its ramparts and castle and boasts a fine collegiate church.

Driving Tours

Approaching The Livradois

45km/28mi round trip

▷ *Leave Issoire on D 996 to the SE.*

Château de Parentignat★
🕐 *Open mid-May–Sept Sat–Sun and holidays 2.30pm–6pm (Jul and Aug daily).* 7€. ☎04 73 89 51 10. www.parentignat. com.
The château was built towards the end of Louis XIV's reign (early 18C) and has remained in the same family since. The main courtyard has formal grass parterres, contrasting with the English-style landscape gardens bordered by orange trees and roses. The ancestral treasures include furniture as well as paintings by Nicolas de Largillière, Mme Vigée-Lebrun, Rigaud and Van Loo.

▷ *Continue along D 996 towards Sauxillanges. After 6km/3.7mi, take D 709 on the right.*

Butte d'Usson
The basaltic rock of Usson was once the site of a formidable castle, of which nothing remains but the memory of Marguerite de Valois. "Usson is a town situated on a plain where there is a rock, and three towns one on top of the other in the shape of a Pope's mitre," says an ancient text. The castle was built by the Duc de Berry, and believed to be impregnable. On the door was written "Mind the traitor and the tooth!" meaning that only treason or famine could get the better of it.

View
From a viewing table off D 709 to the north of the town there is a beautiful view of the Limagne d'Issoire in the foreground and the Puys chain in the background. The Puy de la Vache and Puy de Dôme with its television tower can be seen on the extreme right.

Puy d'Usson
🔼A gentle path leads to the summit on which a chapel has been built with a colossal statue of the Virgin Mary; it provides a good **panorama**★ of the region. During the climb, a beautiful set of basalt columns can be seen in an old quarry.

▷ *Return to D 996.*

Sauxillanges
The 11C **church** with 15C alterations contains a mural depicting the Deposition and a 15C statue of Our Lady of the Woods. The Prior's Chapel, now a heritage centre, **Maison du Patrimoine** (🕐*Jul–mid-Sept: guided tours available (1hr 30min) 2.30pm–6.30pm;* 3€; ☎04 73 96 37 63), is part of the remains of a priory founded in 927 and attached to the Cluniac Order. The Gothic vaulting is decorated with interesting hanging keystones bearing the coats of arms of the various priors.
You can take the direct route (D 214) or choose to go the long way to St-Étienne-d'Usson on D 144, enjoying the drive down towards Sarpoil.

▷ *In Bansat, turn right onto D 24, then turn left in St-Martin-des-Plains, heading for Mailhat.*

Église de Mailhat
The small Romanesque church has a square belfry with double openings, and a five-sided apse.

▷ *D 123 leads to Orsonnette, then to Nonette.*

Nonette★
The village is built on a promontory overlooking the Allier. The half-Romanesque, half-Gothic **church**, once part of a priory, has a carved Romanesque

doorway and, inside, a superb late-14C bust of Christ (north chapel).

🚶 The ruins of the 14C **castle** *(45min on foot there and back via a steep path)* stand on a height offering a splendid **panorama**★.

Dauphiné d'Auvergne★
60km/37mi – allow half a day.

At the end of the 12C, the region to the southwest of Issoire between the Cézallier and the Allier valley, comprising rugged countryside scored by the various Couzes flowing between hilly outcrops and basalt plateaux, formed the Dauphiné d'Auvergne, a sort of local, royal fief whose lords and their entourage set up a glittering court in Champeix, Vodable and Mercœur successively.

▶ *Leave Issoire to the W on D 996, towards Champeix.*

Grottes artificielles de Perrier
The village of Perrier is overlooked by a plateau bristling with bizarre rocks, evidence of violent eruptions thousands of years ago in the Dore mountain region, which unleashed gigantic flows of mud mixed with boulders, or **lahars** (*see NATURE*). Erosion subsequently sculpted the fantastic rock formations known as "fairies' chimneys."

Artificial Caves
🚶 *1hr walk there and back. From the church in Perrier, take the footpath to the caves ("Chemin des Grottes"). These caves were hollowed out of the volcanic rock and used as troglodytic dwellings.*

▶ *From the caves, follow the route indicated as "vue panoramique."*

From the plateau there is a remarkable **view**★ of the surrounding rocks, the feudal keep, the village and the Couze de Pavin.

▶ *On leaving Perrier, take D 26 left (2km/1.2mi), then left onto D 23.*

Tourzel
Small wine-growers' houses in this village bear witness to a viticultural past,

specifically during the 18C and 19C when Tourzel's main source of income was wine. One of these lava-walled houses is home to a small museum on the pork butcher's trade. Further down, the **Maison de Pays** (*open May–mid Sept 10am–7pm;* ☎ *04 73 71 40 09),* another house typical of the region, contains a display evoking scenes from local history, as well as a wide variety of local farm produce.

▶ *Follow D 23 for another 1km/0.6mi, then turn left onto D 124.*

Ronzières
At the entrance to the village, a narrow track (*closed to traffic*) climbs up to a basalt plateau on which a pre-Romanesque church stands. In the graveyard, on the edge of the plateau, two viewing tables give information on the view of the surrounding countryside, which stretches over the Puy d'Ysson, the Couze de Pavin, Perrier plateau and Lembron plain. Examples of the two volcanic features so characteristic of the Dauphiné d'Auvergne region are easy to pick out.

▶ *Take D 124 as far as Vodable and turn left onto D 32 to Solignat.*

Puy d'Ysson★
This cone is formed by the chimney of a volcano; the plug of lava was laid bare by erosion. From the summit, there is a **panorama** of the Dore mountain range, the extinct volcanoes of the Comté region, the Limagne around Issoire, the Livradois mountains and the Cézallier.

▶ *Drive back down to Solignat and take D 32 back to Vodable.*

Église de Colamine-sous-Vodable
The church stands surrounded by its graveyard, on the side of a coomb. It boasts a Romanesque chancel and a group of wooden statues.

▶ *Rejoin D 32 and travel for 4km/3mi towards Dauzat-sur-Vodable, then turn left onto D 48.*

Boudes

Neatly sheltered by a range of hills to the north and by the Avoiron pinnacle to the west, this village was the only one in the entire region to escape the ravages of phylloxera. Thanks to the good soil here, local vines produce fine quality wine, including a particularly well regarded white wine. The layout of the vineyards, on a single slope, well-exposed to the sun, and the brightly coloured houses form a striking sight. Note the fine dovecots.

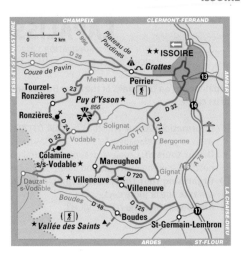

▶ *Leave Boudes to the S, crossing the Couzilloux, and take the track to the right which runs along the side of the graveyard.*

Vallée des Saints★

1hr walk return.

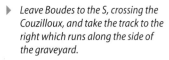 A waymarked path enables visitors to explore this area to the full, admiring the giant red and ochre pyramids with which it is populated. Their outlandish silhouettes, like gigantic statues, have earned the valley its name.

▶ *Return to Boudes and turn right at the church to rejoin D 48.*

St-Germain-Lembron

This small, once fortified village in the midst of an agricultural region still boasts some 18C houses with double-gabled roofs.

▶ *Take D 48 towards Boudes once again, then turn off to the right after 1km/0.6mi onto D 125.*

The road climbs towards Châlus, from where there are beautiful views of the volcanic necks and tables rising above the Limagne.

Villeneuve-Lembron

Narrow streets lined with old houses and wash-houses surround a 15C church.

Château de Villeneuve★

⏰*Open mid-May–mid Sept daily, 10am–noon, 2pm–6.30pm; mid-Sept–mid May daily except Mon 10am–noon, 2pm–5.30pm* ⏰*Closed 1 Jan, 1 May, 1 and 11 Nov, 25 Dec.* ⌾*5€.* ☎*04 73 96 41 64.*
This seigneurial castle was built for the Aureille family, one of whose members was the diplomat Rigault, who served under Louis XI, Charles VIII, Louis XII and François I and fought alongside Charles VIII in the Italian campaigns.
The castle has a square ground plan with a round tower at each corner and is surrounded by dry moats, for ornamental purposes only. The main building stands around a central courtyard with a covered gallery.

▶ *Carry on along D 125 and turn left onto D 720.*

Mareugheol

This is a typical example of a fortified village built during the Middle Ages in order to protect the inhabitants from the marauding bands of robbers that plagued the region. Old stone houses stand along narrow streets within a rectangular fortified wall of which only a few stretches of wall and a stump of corner tower remain.

▶ *Take D 720 as far as Gignat, then turn left onto D 719, which leads back to Issoire.*

LAPALISSE

POPULATION 3,332

MICHELIN MAP 326: I-5 – 23KM.14.3MI NE OF VICHY

Lapalisse lies on the banks of the River Besbre and is dominated by the outline of its castle.

- ℹ **Information:** 26, rue Winston Churchill, 03120 LAPALISSE. ☎04 70 99 08 39. www.cc-paysdelapalisse.fr.
- ▸ **Orient Yourself:** Lapalisse occupies a central position in France to the north-east of the Auvergne and 90km/56mi from Clermont Ferrand.
- 🕑 **Organising Your Time:** This is a complex area to explore, and to do so can take one or more days.
- 👖 **Also See:** MONTS du FOREZ, VICHY.

Sights

Château de La Palice★★ Kids

🕑 Open Apr–Oct: guided tours (1hr), daily, 9am–noon, 2pm–6pm. ⬟5.50€ (children: 2.50€). ☎04 70 99 37 58.

Little remains of the original medieval castle; the building standing today dates from 1527 and was designed by Florentines and is, as a result, an example of early Renaissance architecture.

The somewhat austere façade is relieved by diamond shapes and chequerboard pattern in multicoloured bricks.

Sandstone detailing emphasises the ridges of the towers and the window surrounds, in accordance with the fashion of the day.

The drawing room once had walls covered with leather from Cordoba; it contains the Chabannes family portraits.

The **Golden Salon★★** is decorated with a magnificent gilded coffered ceiling and two tapestries of knights, representing Godefroi de Bouillon and Hector. The tapestries, of 15C Flemish manufacture, come from a series of hangings 3.80m/12ft high and 4m/13ft wide, with a 30cm/12in border.

The chapel was rebuilt in the mid-15C but was pillaged during the Revolution. In the outbuildings (fine timber ceiling) there is a collection of standards and flags gathered by a priest from Doyet.

Musée de l'Art en marche

🕑 Open all year, daily, 10am–noon, 2pm–6pm (Sun, 2pm–6pm). ⬟5€. ☎04 70 99 21 78.

Occupying a former industrial site, this museum is devoted to "Art brut," i.e. work of artists who have escaped all

Château de La Palice

WHERE TO STAY

⊖⊖**Chambre d'hôte Les Vieux Chênes** – *Laprugne, 03120 Servilly, 6km/3.6mi W of Lapalisse via D 480 and D 32.* ☎*04 70 99 07 53. Closed 1 Nov–15 Mar.* ⌂. *5 rms. Meals*⊖⊖.
In this impeccably run country home, the very spacious rooms are downright basic, but we like it anyway. It is surrounded by nature.

WHERE TO EAT

⊖⊖**Auberge de l'Olive** – *Av. de la Gare, 03290 Dompierre-sur-Besbre.* ☎*04 70 34 51 87. www.auberge-olive.fr. Closed 20–29 Sept, Sun evening 1 Dec–15 Apr and Fri except Jul–Aug.*
This inn on a busy road is full of surprises. The light and airy veranda is a very inviting setting for a meal, as is the more rustic dining room with fine wooden beams and a lively blue theme.

forms of conditioning, either cultural or social.

Excursion

Neuilly-en-Donjon

27km/17mi NE along D 994 then right onto D 989.
This small village is mostly known for the delightful **porch**★ of its Romanesque church, characterised by painstaking detail and remarkable craftsmanship.

Driving Tour

Besbre valley★

60km/37mi – allow 4hr.

▶ *Leave Lapalisse to the NW on D 480, along the left bank of the Besbre.*

The Besbre valley contains a surprising variety and number of castles. Only a few are open to visitors, but they are all worth a close look.
This quiet little river, which rises in the Bois Noirs (Black Woods) at the foot of the Puy de Montoncel, flows into the Loire south of Bourbon-Lancy. There are many places where anglers can fish for tench, carp, pike and roach.

Chavroches

As it climbs towards the castle, the road gives a glimpse of the 15C main building. The gate and outer walls are 12C-13C.

▶ *Drive along the one-way street then turn right and follow D 163 then D 205.*

Jaligny-sur-Besbre

This little town is well known in France for being the adopted home of poet, journalist and novelist **René Fallet**. There is an **exhibition** (🕐*open Mon, Thu, Fri 2pm–6pm, Wed 9am–noon;* ⊖*no charge;* ☎*04 70 34 69 91*) about him in the old town hall. Jaligny is also an

Monsieur de La Palice

15C-16C – Jacques II de Chabannes, Lord of La Palice, Marshal of France, won renown for his valour during the campaign to capture the Milan region. He was killed at the Battle of Pavia in 1525. The French expression *une verité de La Palice* – meaning something that is so obviously true that it hardly bears pointing out – has its sources in a poem his officers wrote in his honour.

> *M. de La Palice est mort,*
> *Mort devant Pavie.*
> *Un quart d'heure avant sa mort*
> *Il était encore en vie.*

Although they meant to express that he had fought bravely up to the last instant, the words "A quarter hour before his death, he was still alive," have lost their meaning of courage in the face of battle and come to imply naïvety bordering on dim-wittedness.

agricultural centre famed for its fair. The **Château**★ (o━ *not open to the public*), visible from afar, consists of two sturdy towers with Renaissance windows.

▶ *Leave Jaligny heading NE along D 21.*

Châtelperron

Small, secluded village dominated by the rounded turrets of its **château** (o━ *not open to the public*).

Préhistorama   Kids

○*Open Apr–Sept daily except Tue 10am–noon, 2pm–6pm; Oct–Mar daily except Mon and Tue 2pm–5pm.* ◎*4€.* ☏*04 70 34 84 51.*

This museum is housed in the former railway station. It retraces the daily life of Neanderthal man.

▶ *Continue to St-Léon then turn left.*

Puy St-Ambroise

The **view**★ stretches over the entire Besbre Valley and, to the north and west, over the Sologne Bourbonnaise, a flat region studded with copses.

▶ *Return to St-Léon; follow D 53 to Vaumas to rejoin the Besbre Valley.*

Château de Beauvoir★

○*Open May–Oct: unaccompanied tour of the gardens 9am–7pm; Nov–Apr 10am–5pm.* ◎*No charge.* ☏*04 70 42 00 44.*

This ancient 13C stronghold shows traces of the 15C renovations carried out by the La Fin family. It differs from the other castles in the region because of its layout: the buildings are set at right-angles to each other. The old watchtower is a typical example of Bourbonnais architecture.

▶ *Continue along D 480, then turn left onto D 296.*

Château de Thoury★

&○*Open Apr–Oct 10am–noon, 2pm–6pm.* ◎*4€.* ☏*04 70 42 00 41.* This attractive 11C, 12C and 15C stronghold is surrounded by a park. High curtain walls link the two main buildings and the machicolated entrance gate which has two turrets with pepper-pot roofs; it is reached via a drawbridge over a moat. The **tour** takes in the inner courtyard (16C gallery), the guard-room, the dining room, the salon (fine Etruscan vase dating from 450 BC), the watchtower (family mementoes) and the vaulted 11C cellar.

▶ *On leaving the château, turn right.*

Map of the Besbre Valley region showing MOULINS, Sept-Fons, Dompierre-s-Besbre, ★ Le Pal, ★ Thoury, ★ Beauvoir, Vaumas, ★ Puy St-Ambroise, St-Léon, Châtelperron, Jaligny-sur-Besbre, Jaligny★, Chavroches, Trézelles, LAPALISSE★★, with roads N 79, N 1079, D 15, D 55, D 480, D 53, D 21, D 989, D 205, D 23, N 7, D 990, and directions to MONTLUÇON, DIGOIN, VARENNES-SUR-ALLIER, VICHY, ROANNE.

Parc Le Pal★

Kids &. ⊙ *Open at various dates Apr–Sept, check website for details.* ✐*19€ (children 16€; children under 1 metre: no charge).* ☎*04 70 42 03 60. www.lepal.com.*

The **amusement park** is laid out around place de la Gaîté, a copy of a Parisian square in the middle of the country-side. A dozen or so different attractions include a monorail, rafting, a water train, a caterpillar, a rollercoaster etc. The **zoo** is home to more than 500 species of ani-mals – including elephants, giraffes, big cats, monkeys, deer, waterfowl, parrots and birds of prey – which roam at semi-liberty in an environment reproducing their natural habitat.

▶ *From the park, turn left onto the road back up to D 480. Drive through Dompierre-sur-Besbre, then turn N onto D 55.*

Abbaye de Sept-Fons

This abbey is housed in 18C buildings; the church was rebuilt in 1955.
An audio-visual presentation describes monastic life. The monks make excellent organic food, including a wide range of delicious jams.

LAVAUDIEU★★

POPULATION 225
MICHELIN MAP 331: C-2 – 10KM/6.2MI SE OF BRIOUDE

This hamlet, established on the banks of the Sénouire, still has the remains of an abbey founded in the 11C by St Robert, the first abbot of La Chaise-Dieu. The Benedictines continued to live here until the French Revolution.

▤ **Information:** Le Bourg, 43100 LAVAUDIEU, ☎04 71 76 46 00.
▶ **Orient Yourself:** A peaceful setting mid-way between Clermont-Ferrand and Le Puy-en-Velay.
⊙ **Organising Your Time:** 2–3 hours will suffice.
&. **Also See:** BRIOUDE, LE PUY-EN-VELAY, CLERMONT FERRAND.

Sights

Abbey church

The octagonal belfry has two storeys of semicircular bays. Inside, the nave is dec-orated with fine 14C **frescoes**★ in the Italianate style: they represent scenes from the Passion and such calamities as the Black Death.

Cloisters★★

⊙*Open mid-Jun–mid Sept 10am–noon, 2pm–6.45pm (last admission 30min before closing); mid-Sept–Oct daily except Tue 10am–noon, 2pm–5pm.* ⊙*Closed 1 Jan, 1 Nov, 25 Dec.* ✐*4€ - tickets include the Maison des Arts et Traditions Popu-laires.* ☎*04 71 76 08 90.*

Little remains of the abbey buildings but there are particularly fine cloisters (restored), the only ones in the Auvergne to have escaped destruction. They include charming single or double col-onnettes, some of them twisted, some cylindrical or polygonal, with capitals decorated with carvings of foliage and animals.

The projecting upper storey is sup-ported by oak posts. In the refectory is a 12C **mural** (restored) which covers the entire end wall.

Lavaudieu

Maison des Arts et Traditions Populaires

ⒽOpen mid-Jun–mid Sept 10am–noon, 2pm–6.45pm (last admission 30min before closing); mid-Sept–Oct daily except Tue 10am–noon, 2pm–5pm. ⒽClosed 1 Jan, 1 Nov, 25 Dec. ⌨4€ - tickets include the Cloisters. ☎04 71 76 08 90.

This Traditional Arts and Crafts Museum is housed in an old peasant baker's house dating from the late 19C. The oven, well, bread trough and counter are still visible. On the ground floor, the living room contains a collection of everyday domestic items. The byre houses tools from old crafts (clogmaking, carpentry). Beside it is the *veillade*, the room where people gathered in the evening to chat, sing and tell stories. The cupboard contains an interesting collection of headdresses and nightcaps. On the first floor are three bedrooms. The so-called Lacemaker's Room contains superb samples of pillow, crochet and bobbin lace and several lengths of trimmings.

Carrefour du Vitrail★

♿ⒽOpen May–Oct 9.30am–noon, 2pm–6.30pm; Nov–Apr Mon–Fri (Sat–Sun, only by arrangement) 9.30am–noon, 2pm–6.30pm. ⌨5€. ☎04 71 76 46 11.

Housed in an elegant farmhouse, this exhibition area devoted to stained glass has been set up by an enthusiastic glass-blower who provides visitors with an insight into the thousand-year-old technique of stained-glass making. **Exhibition rooms** with suitable lighting present a history of this ancient craft through reproductions of famous stained-glass windows (rose-window of La Chaise-Dieu abbey) and house a display of contemporary stained glass.

Excursion

Frugières-le-Pin

3.5km/2.2mi E on D 20.

A museum devoted to the French Resistance and the deportation of many of its members was set up here as a tribute to Joseph Lhomenède, who was mayor of the municipality and who died in Buchenwald in 1944.

Musée de la Résistance, de la Déportation et de la Seconde Guerre Mondiale

ⒽOpen Jun–Oct 10am–noon, 2pm–7pm; Nov–May by appointment. ⌨5€. ☎04 71 76 42 15.

Located near the former station, the Second World War Museum contains numerous documents, posters, weapons and uniforms as well as moving photographs showing the sacrifices made by underground activists.

Vallée de la Sénouire

Ⓒsee BRIOUDE.

LE LIORAN ★

MICHELIN MAP 330: E-4 – LOCAL MAP SEE MONTS DU CANTAL

The winter and summer holiday resort of Le Lioran is encircled by the magnificent pine forests that cover the slopes of the Alagnon Valley above meadows dotted with old shepherds' huts (burons, used for cheesemaking).

- **Information:** Super-Lioran, 15300 Le LIORAN, ☎ 04 71 49 50 08. www.lelioran.com.
- ▶ **Orient Yourself:** Le Lioran lies to the west of St Flour, and is accessible from the A 75.
- P **Parking:** Limited parking in the village centre.
- **Don't Miss:** A trip up Plomb du Cantal, the highest peak in Cantal.
- **Organising Your Time:** This is the kind of place you can 'explore' in 30 minutes, or spend days here, using it as a base for wider exploration.
- **Also See:** ST FLOUR, AURILLAC, MURAT.

Super-Lioran ✱

Accessible via Le Lioran (N side of tunnel).
Situated opposite the high grassy Font-d'Alagnon corrie and closed off by pine woods, this modern **winter sports resort** stands in highly attractive surroundings. The resort is comprised of three separate sites: Font d'Alagnon, Font de Cère and Prairie des Sagnes. Most of the ski runs are on the north and east-facing slopes of Plomb du Cantal.

Excursion

Gorges de l'Alagnon★
3.5km/2.3mi NE towards Murat, then turn right (signpost) and follow a path 500m/550yd long down to the upper reaches of the river.
When the water level is low, it is possible to follow the river bed to the left over a distance of almost 200m/220yd. At the head of this very attractive ravine are piles of huge boulders.

Walks to the Peaks

Plomb du Cantal★★
45 min there and back by cable-car and on foot from Super-Lioran.
This is the highest peak in the Cantal range. From the summit there is a vast **panoramic view**★★. To the west, beyond the Cère valley, extend Cantal's great volcanic cones – Griou, Peyre-Arse, Mary, Violent and Chavaroche. A number of footpaths lead from the summit to the **Puy Gros** (view of the Cère valley at Thiézac) or to the Prat de Bouc via the Tombe du Père pass.

Puy Griou★★★
Head for the pastures in La Font d'Alagnon then turn left through the woods to a holiday camp; there, bear right.
The path rises towards the alpine pastures of Col de Rombière (superb **view**★ over the Jordanne valley and the great volcanic cones in Cantal) then turns left. For the summit, there is a strenuous climb over basalt rocks. From the top there is an exceptional **view**★★★ of the Puy Mary, the Puy de Peyre-Arse, and Plomb du Cantal barring the horizon to the north.

Le Puy Griou

J. Damase/MICHELIN

GORGES DE LA LOIRE★

MICHELIN MAP 327: C-8/9, D-8, E-7 OR 331: F-2/3, G-2/5, H-1/4

From the Gerbier-de-Jonc to Roanne, the Loire valley develops from a high, pastoral vale to a series of narrow channels and gorges, and wide basins; the result of a lively geological history. The course of the Loire follows an ancient marine ditch which felt the effects of the alpine uplift at the end of the Tertiary Era. The Puy, Forez and Roanne basins – veritable rift valleys – forced the river to carve a route for itself through the plateaux separating these basins. In the Velay region the river had to battle against the volcanic outpourings at the end of the Tertiary Era and at the beginning of the Quaternary: at Arlempdes the river managed to find a way through the basalt flows; in the Puy basin, however, the course of the river was forced to shift eastwards. In Forez, the Loire gorges, carved through the crystalline base, present a particularly wild appearance at Grangent Lake and around the meanders of St-Victor-sur-Loire.

A Bit of History

Man-made landscapes - In addition to the work of Nature, there are also attractive man-made landscapes: dams have flooded the former valley to produce La Palisse, Grangent and Villerest lakes.

Ancient castles and sanctuaries – Overlooking the river stand some fine ruined fortresses and a few old châteaux, perched on rocky spurs or on the side of the wider banks: Arlempdes, Bouzols, Lavoûte-Polignac, Rochebaron…

Driving Tours

1 Gerbier-de-Jonc to Le Puy-en-Velay
115km/71mi

Gerbier-de-Jonc★★
The Gerbier-de-Jonc, rising at an altitude of 1,551m/5,088ft on the crest of the range separating the Loire and Thône basins, looks like a giant haystack, or a huge heap of sheaves, when seen from a distance.
The route descends along the pastoral valley; houses with thatched roofs may still be seen at Ste-Eulalie and near Usclades-et-Rieutord. The road then runs beside Lake La Palisse and, further on, beside an attractive basalt flow.

Lac d'Issarlès★
⚭*see Lac d'ISSARLÈS.*

Arlempdes★
⚭*See Le PUY-EN-VELAY.*

Goudet
This small hamlet is dominated by the ruins of Beaufort Château.

St-Martin-de-Fugères
From D 49 above the village there is a fine panoramic **view**★.

Le Puy-en-Velay★★★
⚭*See Le PUY-EN-VELAY.*

2 Le Puy-en-Velay to Retournac
58km/36mi

▶ *Leave Le Puy-en-Velay to the N on D 103.*

Leaving the Puy basin the Loire enters into the Peyredeyre gorge.

▶ *At Peyredeyre turn right onto D 71.*

Chaspinhac
The small Romanesque **church**, built of red volcanic stone, contains interesting carved capitals.

Château de Lavoûte-Polignac
Open Jun–Sept guided tours (45min) 10am–1pm, 2pm–7pm; Apr–May and Oct 2pm–6pm. Closed from 1 Nov–Easter. ☎04 71 08 50 02.
The fortress owned by the Polignac family as early as the 13C, but was later

The Loire near Chamalières

B. Kaufmann/MICHELIN

transformed into a comfortable manor house as the castle at Polignac itself remained a powerful stronghold.

Chamalières-sur-Loire
The village stands at the foot of Mont Gerbizon; it is noted for its Romanesque **church**★, which once belonged to a Benedictine priory.

▶ *Shortly after leaving Chamalières, turn left onto D 35 which crosses the Loire and leads to Roche-en-Régnier.*

Roche-en-Régnier
This ancient village above the west bank of the river is overlooked by a volcanic stump crowned by an old defensive tower. From the foot of this tower there is a fine **panorama**★ over the mountains of Velay and Forez.

▶ *Follow D 29 to the right to St-André-de-Chalencon. In St-André, turn onto a minor road behind the east end of the church then continue along another road running below the cemetery, on the left; 1.8km/1.1mi further on, leave the car in the parking area near the ruins (15min on foot there and back).*

Château de Chalençon
The castle ruins stand proudly on a rocky outcrop, half-way between Le Puy-en-Velay and the Monts Forez.

Promenade de l'Ance
Retrace your steps and take the steep right-hand lane leading to a second stone bridge located upstream. This secluded **site**★ is the ideal backdrop for a pleasant stroll.

▶ *Go back to D 9 and drive on to Retournac.*

Retournac
The part-Romanesque church is of handsome ochre stone and has a sturdy belfry and a stone-slabbed roof.

Musée des manufactures de Dentelles
&.☉*Open Apr–Sept 2.30pm–6pm (Jul–Aug, 2.30pm–7pm).* ☞*5€.* ☎*04 71 59 41 55. www.ville-retournac.fr.*
This lacemaking museum, housed inside a former manufacture dating from 1913, recreates the atmosphere of a lace-making workshop.

③ **Retournac to Aurec**
35km/22mi – about 2hr

▶ *N of Retournac take D 46 which runs along the plateau W of the Loire.*

Beauzac
This small village has an interesting 12C–17C church.

Château de Rochebaron
Ruins of a 11C–13C medieval castle perched on a spur, with a **view**★ of the Loire.

Monistrol-sur-Loire –
&.*see MONISTROL-SUR-LOIRE.*

Address Book

⏴For coin ranges, see the cover flap.

WHERE TO STAY

⌨ **Chambre d'hôte Les Revers** –
*43130 Retournac, 8km/4.8mi SE of
Retournac, take D 103, and follow signs
to 'Les Revers'. ☎04 71 59 42 81. Closed
Oct–Mar.* ⏴. *4 rms.* Their love of nature
prompted these natives of St. Etienne
to retreat to this extraordinarily isolated
site between forest and fields.

WHERE TO EAT

⌨ **Ferme-auberge Les Granges** –
*43140 La Séauve-sur-Semène, 12km/7.2mi
E of Monistrol, take N 88 dir. St-Étienne,
then D 12 and follow signs. ☎04 71 61
00 82. Closed Jan–Feb, Sun evening and
Mon.* ⏴. *Reservations required.* Located
in a hamlet in the middle of the country.

Aurec-sur-Loire

This small town, nestling inside a
meander of the Loire, has retained a
harmonious ensemble of medieval
buildings recently restored: from the
church, built on foundations dating
back to before 1000 AD, walk through
the **castle grounds** (Guillaume de
la Roue Tower, 1466) and along the
ramparts overlooking the river, then
through the Porte David. The **Château
du Moine-Sacristain** and its 16C Burgundians' **Tower** house the **Musée de
la Vigne et de l'ancien vin des Côtes
d'Aurec** which has temporary exhibitions (◷*open May–Sept and Dec, daily,
2.30pm–6pm;* ◷*closed rest of the year;*
⏴*4€;* ☎*04 77 35 26 55).*

4 Aurec to St-Just-St-Rambert

30km/19mi – about 3hr

Aurec-sur-Loire stands at the edge of
the dammed **Lac de Grangent**★★. The
route★★ *(D 108 and D 32)* from Semène
to Grangent dam follows a steep ledge

View from Château d'Essalois

offering views over the wild, sometimes
submerged meanders of the river.

Cornillon

The **château** (⚬—*not open to the public)*
rising on a spur overlooking the gorges
was once the seat of one of the most
powerful baronies in Forez.

Chambles

The setting here is one of the loveliest
along the Loire gorges – beside a squat
church stands the tower of the old castle, on the edge of a high escarpment
overlooking the meanders of the Grangent. This tower is a typical example of
medieval fortifications with its entrance
half way up, accessible only up a collaps-
ible ladder.

▶ *Drive 2km/1.2mi beyond Chambles
and turn right onto a small road to
the ruins of the Château d'Essalois.*

Château d'Essalois

The sturdy outline of this castle overlooks a gorge and commands a superb
view★★ over Grangent reservoir.

Île de Grangent

This island was created when the man-
made lake isolated the tongue of a rocky
spine on which sit the ruins of Grangent
Castle (12C tower) and a small chapel
with a red-tiled roof.

St-Just-St-Rambert

This town was once a Gallo-Roman village clinging to a mound. The **Église St-
André**★ is a sturdy 11C and 12C building
crowned by an 11C fortified bell-tower
and the 12C main **bell-tower**★.

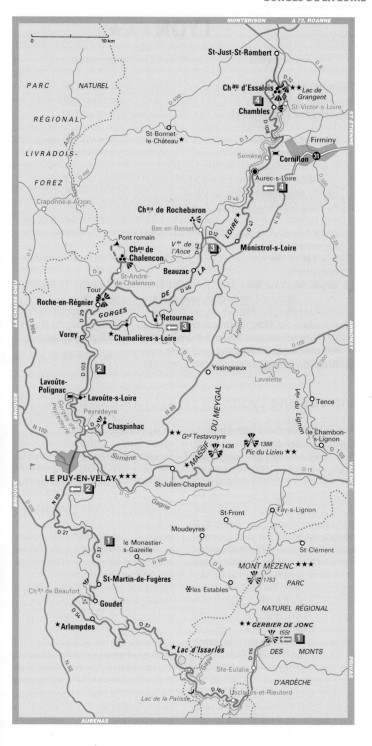

LYON

CONURBATION 1,348,832

MICHELIN MAP 327: H/I-5 – LOCAL MAP SEE MONTS DU LYONNAIS

Twenty centuries of history and a superb geographical situation at the confluence of the River Saône and the River Rhône give Lyon an appearance quite unlike any other city and justify its inclusion on UNESCO's World Heritage List.

- **Information:** Pl. Bellecour, 69002 LYON, ☎04 72 77 69 69. www.lyon-france.com.
- ▶ **Orient Yourself:** A pedestrian tour of La Presqu'île, sandwiched between the Rhône and the Saône, is the best way to get a feel for this massive, but hugely appealing, city; this is where you'll find most of the shops and restaurants; equally enlightening is the spectacular view from the Fourvière Basilica.
- **Parking:** Massive underground car park beneath place Bellecour, but be sure to make a note of exactly where you left the car – getting back to it can be confusing. Underground parking also at les Célestins, les Terreaux and la République.
- **Don't Miss:** The Fourvière district, but allow most of a day for a worthwhile exploration.
- **Organising Your Time:** Begin from place Bellecour, and wander the streets; this is no place to be methodical! Tours covering one, two or three days are detailed below, but a longer stay will gain the most from this magnificent city.
- **Especially for Kids:** Take a boat trip in a Bateau-Mouche, or visit the Musée de l'Automobile Henri-Malartre. A session with Guignol is popular; likewise visit the parc de la Tête d'Or.
- **Also See:** le MONT-DORE, La DOMBE, VIENNE.

Introducing Lyon

The rivers Rhône and Saône provide the magnificent sight of their very differing courses as they flow past the foot of the two famous hills, Fourvière and La Croix-Rousse, facing the low plain of Dauphiné. Flowing down from the north, the Saône skirts the small Mont-d'Or range and enters the Pierre-Scize gorge gouged out between Fourvière and La Croix-Rousse. The Rhône arrives from the Alps, a wide river that washes the lower slopes of La Croix-Rousse. During Roman times, the confluence lay at the foot of the hill. The alluvium built up by the Rhône gradually pushed the confluence further south and the resulting peninsula became the main centre of the city. The Fourvière and La Croix-Rousse hills have numerous terraces from which to admire the town; the views from some of these are famous, including the Fourvière Basilica viewing table, place Rouville and rue des Fantasques in La Croix-Rousse. Further

away but no less outstanding are the panoramic views from the Esplanade de Ste-Foy and Mont Thou.

Lyon's current prosperity serves as a reminder of the fact that the city's finest hours, during the Roman Empire and the Renaissance, were times when trade was of major importance and the city succeeded in taking full advantage of its outstanding geographical situation. It is, after all, on the road to Italy, between Central and Eastern France, and midway between Northern France and the southern provinces.

Lyon is not only an industrial city specialising in metalworking, chemistry and building trades, and famous for its silk and synthetic fabrics; it is also a university town and a world-famous centre in the field of medicine. It has a Court of Appeal and an Archbishopric (the Archbishop of Lyon bears the title "Primate of the Gauls"). The city is a popular tourist venue, famous for its cuisine: it is one of the best-known gastronomic centres in France.

Twenty Centuries of History

Capital of the Gauls – According to a Celtic legend two princes, Momoros and Atepomaros, stopped here one day at the confluence of the rivers and decided to build a town. While they were digging the foundations, a flock of crows flew down around them. Recognising the event as evidence of divine intervention, they decided to call their city **Lugdunum** (Crows' Hill).

Julius Caesar set up his base camp here during his relentless campaign to conquer Gaul. After his death, one of his lieutenants, Munatius Plancus, brought Roman settlers here (43 BC). Shortly afterwards Agrippa, who had been ordered by Caesar Augustus to organise Gaul, chose Lugdunum as his capital. The network of imperial roads began in Lyon and five major routes radiated out from the city towards Aquitaine, the Ocean, the Rhine, Arles and Italy. Caesar Augustus stayed in the town; Emperor Claudius was born here. In the 2C, aqueducts brought water to Fourvière from the surrounding mountains.

The city, governed by its council, held a monopoly in the trade of wine throughout Gaul. The mariners in its harbour were powerful shipowners; its potters were veritable industrialists. The wealthiest of the city's traders lived in a separate district, on the Île des Canabae, around where St-Martin-d'Ainay stands today. On the slopes of La Croix-Rousse was the Gallic town, Condate. The Amphitheatre of the Three Gauls (the votive inscription was uncovered in 1958) and the Temple of Rome and Caesar Augustus were the setting for the noisy Assembly of Gauls once a year.

Christianity in Lyon

– Lyon became the meeting-place for businessmen from all over the country. Soldiers, merchants and missionaries arrived from Asia Minor and began spreading the new gospel. Soon, a small Christian community developed in the town.

In AD 177 a popular revolt broke out and led to the famous martyrdom of St Pothin, St Blandine and their companions. Twenty years later when **Septimus Severus**, having defeated his competitor Albin (who enjoyed popular support from the locals), decided to set fire to the town, he found that there were still 18,000 Christians in Lyon. He had them massacred; among them featured St Irénée, St Pothin's successor.

This faith has continued through the ages. On 8 December each year, the **Feast of the Immaculate Conception** is celebrated in Lyon with a great deal of pomp and enthusiasm. In the evening, thousands of multicoloured lanterns can be seen in the windows of the city. The origins of this **"Festival of Lights"** date from the occasion of the consecration of the gilded Madonna of Fourvière in 1852. Floods had delayed the work of sculptor Fabish, who was not able to deliver the statue by the deadline of 8 September. Accordingly the ceremony was postponed until 8 December, the Feast of the Immaculate Conception. On the day itself, heavy rainfall resulted in cancellation of the evening festival. However, contrary to all expectations, the rain stopped at precisely the time the festivities had been scheduled to start.

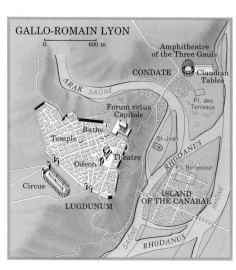

GALLO-ROMAIN LYON

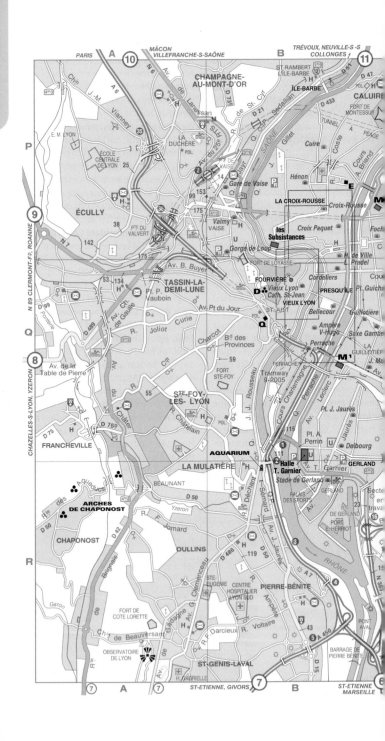

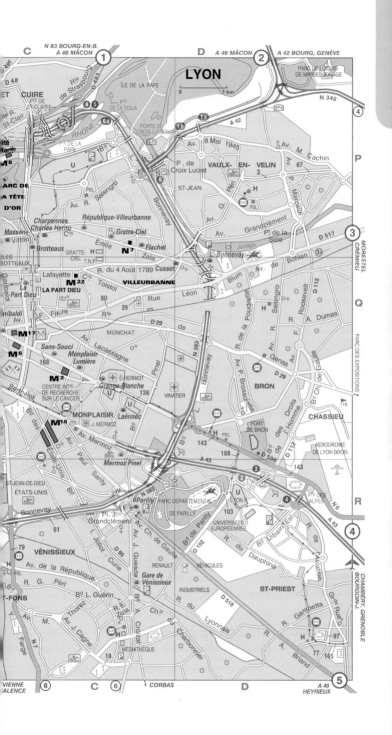

LYON

LYON

Address Book

🪙 *For coin ranges see the Legend on the cover flap.*

GETTING AROUND

Maps – In addition to the maps included in this guide, Michelin town plans 30 and 31 and Michelin map 110 (the surroundings of Lyon) will be useful.

Access – By road via motorways A 6, A 7, A 42, A 43. The city also boasts a regular 2hr link with Paris by TGV. Perrache and La Part-Dieu stations are close to the town centre by metro. There are flights to and from most major cities via Lyon-St-Exupéry airport, linked to the town centre by a shuttle service.

Parking – There are several underground car parks strategically placed for easy access to the town centre. Some of these are architectural gems, the most spectacular being the *Parc Célestins* by Buren, whose columns adorn the Jardins du Palais-Royal in central Paris.

Public transport – The underground train/subway *(Métro)* is the most convenient mode of public transport, and is especially well-adapted to the needs of tourists. The best-value ticket to buy is the **ticket-liberté,** valid for a day for unlimited travel on the Lyon urban transport network (métro, bus, funicular railway, trolley-bus). Details from TCL (Transports en Commun Lyonnais) kiosks or call ☏04 78 71 70 00.

Cultural Pass: You can buy a 1, 2 or 3-day **Lyon City Card: Pass Culturel et Touristique** which will gain you admission to museums, sights, transport, as well as reductions in theatres, on shopping, etc. Prices range from 1 day 18€, 2 days 27€, 3 days 36€, with a 10% discount if you buy online at www.lyon-france.com.

TOURING THE TOWN

Planning your visit – If you have only **one day** to spend in Lyon, then you must devote the morning to Old Lyon (on foot), to the Fourvière terrace and

PUBLIC TRANSPORT

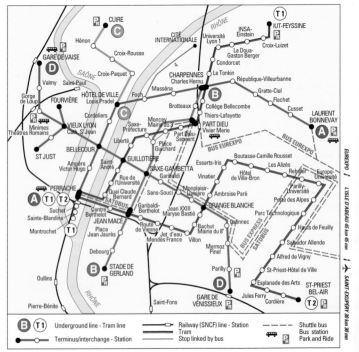

the Roman theatres (use the funicular), but you will not have time to visit the museums; the afternoon should be spent touring the Presqu'île with its Fabric Museum and, either visiting the Fine Arts Museum or an enjoyable walk around the Gros Caillou, on the slopes of the Croix-Rousse.

Two days will enable you to get better acquainted with Fourvière and the various museums and to stroll along the River Saône on the first day. The second day should be devoted to touring the Presqu'île on foot and to visiting its museums (fabrics, printing and hospice museums); you should even have time to take a stroll in the Croix-Rousse district.

Organised tours – Lyon, which is listed as a "Town of Art and history," offers discovery tours conducted by guide-lecturers approved by the Ministry of Culture and Communication. Information at the tourist office or on www.vpah.culture.fr. The Lyon tourist office offers tours of the city on foot, or by bus, boat, taxi or even helicopter.

Lecture tours are available around Old Lyon, the Croix-Rousse district and the Tony Garnier district.

Bateaux-mouches river trips – *13 bis quai Rambaud* – ☎*04 78 42 96 81 – www.naviginter.fr – departure from quai des Célestins.* These enable visitors to discover a different face of Lyon, seen from its four river banks: one trip explores the confluence of the Saône and Rhône; the other follows the Saône up to and round the Île-Barbe.

WHERE TO STAY

St-Pierre-des-Terreaux – *8 r. Paul-Chenavard.* ☎*04 78 28 24 61. Closed 15 days in Aug, and Christmas period. 16 rms.* ⌷*10€.* A very practical and affordable hotel in the city, opposite the St-Pierre museum and a few steps from the Opera. Pleasant welcome and practical, well-maintained rooms that benefit from efficient soundproofing.

Villages Hôtel – *93 cours Gambetta.* ☎*04 78 62 77 72. www.villages-hotel. com.* ▣. *114 rms.* ⌷*8€.* This chain hotel has a lot going for it, such as the central location, proximity to the train station and metro, and comfortable, spacious rooms with king-sized beds.

Élysée Hôtel – *92 r. du Prés.-Edouard-Herriot.* ☎*04 78 42 03 15. 29 rms.* ⌷*10€.* A small family-run hotel where one can enjoy the vitality of the Presqu'île at affordable prices.

Bellecordière – *18 r. Bellecordière.* ☎*04 78 42 27 78. www.hotel-bellecordiere.com. 45 rms.* Near the Rhône quayside and the Bellecour metro station, this hotel offers rooms that are smallish but quite suitable for a short stay.

Hôtel La Résidence – *18 r. Victor-Hugo.* ☎*04 78 42 63 28. 67 rms.* ⌷*10€.* Managed by the same family since 1954, this hotel borders on a pedestrian street quite near the Place Bellecour.

Savoies – *80 r. de la Charité.* ☎*04 78 37 66 94. 46 rms.* ⌷*12€.* Look for a façade decorated with the Savoie coat of arms in the Perrache train station quarter. The cleanliness of the standard rooms, with their simple furniture and pastel carpets, the convenient garage and reasonable prices make this a popular address with travellers.

Hôtel Ariana – *163 cours Émile-Zola, 69100 Villeurbanne.* ☎*04 78 85 32 33. www.ariana-hotel.fr.* ▣. *102 rms.* ⌷*12€.* This is a practical address for those who wish to stay amid the 1930s high-rises of Villeurbanne. Modern, it has air-conditioned, soundproofed rooms with a sober interior design of grey-tinted furniture.

La Villa du Rhône – *Chemin de la Lune, 01700 Miribel, 12km/7.2mi NE of Lyon. Take the A 42 dir. Genève, exit Parc de Miribel-Jonage, then dir. le Mas Rillier and la Madone Campanile.* ☎*04 78 55 54 16. www.lavilladurhone.com.* ◿. *3 rms.* ⌷*10€. Meals* ◿. Located just outside of Lyon, this is a peaceful residential home overlooking the Vallée du Rhône.

Hôtel Bleu Marine – *4 r. du Mortier.* ☎*04 78 60 03 09. 126 rms.* ⌷*12€.* This modern, glass-walled hotel on a small street in the Guillotière quarter, a five minute walk from the Place Bellecour, is worth mentioning.

WHERE TO EAT

Le Café 203 – *9 r. du Garet.* ☎*04 78 28 66 65. Closed 24 Dec–3 Jan.* Some customers come here for the fresh fare, slate menu and bistro setting.

Le Casse-Museau – *2 r. Chavanne.* ☎*04 72 00 20 52. Closed Tue and Wed evenings, Sun, Mon and public holidays. Reservations required.* Aunt Paulette's 'no chichi bistro' has been going strong since 1947. Her famous garlic chicken has given way to fresh pasta, mixed salads and other more modern fare, but the wine flows freely as ever and the ambience is still convivial.

Chez les Gones – *102 cours Lafayette, (Halle de Lyon).* ☎*04 74 88 98 24. www.chezlesgones.com. Closed Mon.* This tavern set in the bosom of the marketplace does not lack for customers, who come to enjoy the typical Lyon fare, smiling service and ambient good cheer.

Comptoir du Mail – *14 r. du Mail, (Croix-Rousse).* ☎*04 78 27 71 40. Closed 2–25 Aug.* The local population wasted no time in adopting this restaurant serving dishes straight from the marketplace.

Le Vieux Lyon – *44 r. St-Jean.* ☎*04 78 42 48 89.* Local epicureans are all familiar with this tavern, in operation since 1947, where good humour and hospitality reign. Home-made Lyonnais cooking.

Le Petit Carron – *48 av. Félix-Faure.* ☎*04 78 60 00 57. Closed 3 wks in Aug, Sat lunch and Sun. Reservations recommended.* The little puppet who inhabits the window of this attractive tavern beckons you into a muted dining room featuring a slate *menu du jour*, composed according to market availability.

Le Jura – *25 r. Tupin.* ☎*04 78 42 20 57. Closed 28 Jul–28 Aug, Mon from Sept–Apr, Sat from May–Sept, and Sun. Reservations requested.* Not far from the Rue de la République, this eatery seems to have been here forever! With its 1920s decor and aproned matron overseeing the stoves, it's as genuine as they come.

La Brasserie Georges – *30 cours de Verdun.* ☎*04 72 56 54 54.* Open since 1836, this brasserie near the Perrache train station is still a favourite Lyon haunt.

Le St-Florent – *106 cours Gambetta.* ☎*04 78 72 32 68. Closed 3 wks in Aug, 1 wk at Christmas, Sat lunch, Mon lunch and Sun. Reservations recommended.* Pluck and cluck: the interior design of

this restaurant – egg-yolk yellow, chair backs that look like feathers, etc – give diners a good hint of what to expect from the menu, essentially devoted to the poultry of Bresse.

L'Est – *14 pl. Jules-Ferry, Les Brotteaux station.* ☎*04 37 24 25 26.* The last of Bocuse's bastions in Lyon: the Brotteaux train station. The decor is that of a big, old-fashioned brasserie where electric trains circumnavigate the dining room.

Brunet – *23 r. Claudia.* ☎*04 78 37 44 31. Closed Sun-Mon. Reservations recommended.* An authentic Lyon bouchon (tavern), Brunet has a wood façade, elbow-to-elbow tables, Guignol-marked tableware, tasty little dishes enhanced by an enticing selection of wines by the carafe.

Restaurant des Deux Places – *5 pl. Fernand-Rey.* ☎*04 78 28 95 10. Closed 15 Jul–15 Aug, Sat–Mon.* A few steps from the Place Sathonay, this traditional little restaurant boasts a convivial atmosphere, a decor full of rural knick-knacks and time-honoured cuisine featuring a few house specialities, like warm lambs' tongues.

Le Mercière – *56 r. Mercière.* ☎*04 78 37 67 35. www.le-merciere.com. Reservations recommended.* Located in a passageway giving onto one of the most sought-after restaurant streets in town, here is a picturesque old house where authentic, traditional fare is served in a classic Lyonnais setting.

Lolo Quoi – *42 r. Mercière.* ☎*04 72 77 60 90.* In this pedestrian street where taverns and chain restaurants abound, those in the know go to Lolo. Minimalist furnishings and thoughtful lighting, modern Italian cuisine and innovative pasta – the Lyon crowd approves wholeheartedly!

Le Caro de Lyon – *25 r. du Bât-d'Argent.* ☎*04 78 39 58 58. Closed Sun.* This restaurant behind the Opera, designed to resemble a library, welcomes diners into an intimate atmosphere comprised of blond wood, Murano chandeliers, antique knick-knacks and coloured chairs.

La Table d'Hippolyte – *22 r. Hippolyte-Flandrin.* ☎*04 78 27 75 59. Closed Aug, 25 Dec, 1 Jan, Sat lunch, Sun-Mon.* Located in a small street near the Halles de la Martinière, here is a cosy address where curios, old mirrors, dried flowers and hefty objects coexist peacefully. It's the ideal setting for a candlelight supper.

SHOPPING

Two things stand out about shopping in Lyon – food and fashion. This is a gourmet's paradise, and the shopaholic will find numerous top designer stores and superb markets.

Markets *(Marchés)* – The Marché de la Création, Quai Romain-Rolland and the Marché de l'Artisanat, Quai Fulchiron are held Sunday mornings. These are no run-of-the-mill craft markets, as the workmanship is outstanding. Used book sellers line the Quai de la Pêcherie every afternoon. There are regional products and small taverns at the Halles de Lyon, 102 Cours Lafayette.

For food, head for the Quai Saint-Antoine, where food markets with producers from all over the region set up stall and sell their produce *(Tue–Sun, 7am–12.30pm)*. There is also a Farmers' Market twice a week in the Place Carnot *(Wed, 4–7pm; Sun, 5am–1.30pm)*, in front of the Gare Perrache.

Bonnard – *36 rue Grenette. ☎04 78 42 19 63. 8.30am–1.30pm, 3pm–7.30pm. Closed Aug and public holidays.* Come to this delicatessen founded in 1850 and stock up on Lyonnais specialities such as the celebrated *cervelas truffé* (truffled savaloy) and *quenelles de brochet* (pike dumplings). Note the Art Deco decor and glass-paned roof crowned by a splendid lion's head made of copper.

L'Atelier de Soierie – *33 r. Romarin. ☎04 72 07 97 83. Mon–Sat 9am–noon, 2pm–7pm. Closed public holidays.* Lyon became the silk capital of France in the 16C. Today, l'Atelier de Soierie continues this tradition of expertise, combining time-honoured methods with hand-painted decorations. Among other specialities, *la panne de velours,* made only in Lyon, is a silk and velvet hand-decorated muslin that is gorgeous.

Reynon – *13 rue des Archers. ☎04 78 37 39 08. Tue–Sat 8.30am–1.30pm, 3pm–7.30pm. Closed end Jul–mid-Aug, public holidays except Christmas and New Year's.* The Reynon family has run this delicatessen since its creation in 1937.

They specialise in carefully prepared sausages, rosettes, jésus and various ready-to-enjoy dishes. Francophones with a taste for homespun recipes and anecdotes will enjoy *Le fils du charcutier,* penned by Auguste Reynon.

Les Quenelles Giraudet – *2 r. du Col.-Chambonnet. ☎04 74 22 16 88. www. giraudet.fr. Daily except Sun, 9am–7pm (Mon, 11am–7pm). Closed 1–15 Aug.* Giraudet has been making their famous *quenelles* (dumplings) in the purest traditional manner since 1910. The shop also offers over 20 different quenelle-enhancing sauces concocted without artificial flavours or preservatives.

Pignol – *8 pl. Bellecour. ☎04 78 37 39 61. www.pignol.fr. Mon–Sat 8am–7.30pm; Aug: Tue–Sat.* This celebrated caterer has been delighting palates since 1954. Beginning with a back-kitchen debut that was an instant success, the Pignol family has added many feathers to their toques; today they own seven restaurants and two food-production units. For the Davis Cup finals and the Albertville Olympic Games, Pignol was entrusted with organising the meals.

Voisin – *28 r. de la République. ☎04 78 42 46 24. Mon 2pm–7pm; Tue–Sat 9am–7.30pm.* This confectioner concocts 50-odd kinds of chocolate, fruit jelly candies, candied fruit and other delicious Lyonnais specialities. It also supplies its 19 shops in the metropolitan area with freshly roasted coffees and gourmet teas.

Chez Disagn'Cardelli – Petit musée fantastique du Guignol – *6 r. St-Jean. ☎04 78 37 01 67. Mon 2.30pm–7pm, Tue–Sat 11am–1pm, 2.30pm–7pm, Sun 11am–1pm, 3pm–6pm. Closed Christmas and New Year's.* Marionettes, music boxes and masks. Downstairs, Guignol's Little Fantastic Museum reveals the fascinating world of the marionettes, robots and music boxes of Lyon.

ON THE TOWN

Rue Ste-Catherine – A very lively street featuring many establishments open until the far reaches of the night. *The Albion Public House* is the most British pub in town, *The Shamrock* the most Celtic. Rum fans convene at *La Taverne du Perroquet Bourré* (The Tavern of the Plastered Parrot), while *L'Abreuvoir* is highly recommended for those who fancy good French music.

BC Blues – *25 pl. Carnot.* ☎*04 78 37 11 24. Tue–Sat from noon and 10pm. Discotheque: Wed–Sat from 10.30pm.* Located on Place Carnot, a minute from the Perrache train station, this establishment operates on two different schedules. The pub opens at noon, then at around 10.30pm the club, rather more exclusive, gets going. Jazz concerts with professional musicians are organised several times a month here.

Café Léone – *8 r. de la Monnaie –* ☎*04 78 92 93 70. May–Oct: noon–2pm, 7pm–1am; Nov–Apr: Mon–Sat noon–2pm, 7pm–1am. Closed 31 Dec.* With its tapas served at the bar, just like in Barcelona, San Miguel beer and bullfights on TV, this café is a bona fide Iberian watering hole, lively and noisy as is befitting.

Hot Club de Lyon – *26 r. Lanterne.* ☎*04 78 39 54 74. www.hotclubjazz.com. Tue–Thu 9.30pm–1am, Fri 10pm–1am, Sat 4pm–1am. Closed end Jul–mid-Sept.* All jazz fans worth their salt frequent Lyon's Hot Club. Located in a cellar, just like its famous predecessors in Paris' Saint-Germain-des-Prés, every kind of jazz, from New Orleans to bossa nova and from Duke Ellington to fusion, is generously represented here.

La Cave des Voyageurs – *7 pl. St-Paul.* ☎*04 78 28 92 28. www.lacavedesvoyageurs.fr. Tue–Sat 2pm–midnight. Closed most of Aug.* An appealing little wine bar with a deliciously 'retro' decor. Burgundies, Mâconnais vintages and Beaujolais may be enjoyed with a plate of delicatessen or cheese.

Casino Le Lyon Vert – *200 av. du Casino, 69890 La Tour-de-Salvagny. 04 78 87 02 70. www.lyonvert.com. 10am–4am.* Tempted by the demon of gambling? Feel like spicing up your evening by trying your luck? Attracted to settings like those in the Scorsese film, Casino? Properly attired and over 18? If so, this is your address, with 400 slot machines, video poker, roulette and black jack, plus a restaurant and bar.

Bar de La Tour Rose – *22 r. du Bœuf.* ☎*04 78 37 25 90. 5pm–2am.* Molière himself gave a performance on the very site – formerly a Jeu de Paume court – where this bar belonging to a ritzy

hotel is now located. Known for its well-stocked cigar humidor, the establishment organises jazz concerts every Friday and Saturday. The drinks menu includes no fewer than 60 cocktails, of which 40 are house creations.

Eden Rock Café – *68 r. Mercière.* ☎*04 78 38 28 18. www.edenrockcafe.com. Tue noon–1am, Wed–Thu noon–2am, Fri–Sat noon–3am. Closed 3 wks in Aug.* In the heart of a pedestrian street that becomes very lively of an evening, this bar is located in a building classified as an historical monument. The decor is magnificent and the menu is worth perusing – if you've never tasted ostrich fillet, this is your chance! Blues, rock and funk concerts weekends.

Le Bartholdi – *6 pl. des Terreaux.* ☎*04 72 10 66 00. 8am–1am.* This is indubitably one of the biggest and loveliest terraces in Lyon, just across from the Fontaine Bartholdi, named after the very famous sculptor of the Statue of Liberty. The brasserie is open non-stop. Monthly debates on architecture, the sciences, Italy, international relations, politics and philosophy – public participation welcome – are held here.

THEATRE AND ENTERTAINMENT

Théâtre National Populaire – *8 pl. Lazare-Gougeon. 69627 Villeurbanne.* ☎*04 78 03 30 00. Tickets: on site Mon–Fri 11am–6pm; by phone Mon–Fri 10am–6pm.* Villeurbanne banks on its myriad cultural resources, including the Théâtre National Populaire (aka le TNP), one of the city's great successes.

Au Pied dans l'Plat – *18 r. Lainerie.* ☎*04 78 27 13 26. www.aupieddanslplat.fr. Mon–Sat from 8.30pm. Closed 26 Jul–26 Aug.* Lyonnais are very fond of this cabaret located in a handsome arched 15C cellar. Loosely translating as Foot in Mouth, the Pied dans l'Plat puts on dinner shows with a satirical bent in an unbridled, Rabelaisian ambience.

Le Guignol de Lyon – *Compagnie des Zonzons, 2 r. Louis-Carrand.* ☎*04 78 28 92 57. www.guignol-lyon.com. Wed and Sat: 3pm and 4.30pm, Sun 3pm; daily during school holidays.* La Compagnie des Zonzons stages children's performances that marry burlesque and fantasy, something like in Tex Avery cartoons, and give the rather conventional Guignol a second childhood. The shows for adults, inspired by aspects and events of life in Lyon, are more malicious.

Auditorium-Orchestre national de Lyon – 149 r. Garibaldi. ☎04 78 95 95 95. www.auditoriumlyon.com. Tickets: Mon–Fri 11am–6pm, concert Saturdays 2pm–6pm. Closed most of Aug. The Auditorium Maurice Ravel regularly hosts l'Orchestre National de Lyon.

Maison de la Danse – 8 av. Jean-Mermoz. ☎04 72 78 18 10. www.maisondeladanse.com. Tickets: Mon–Fri 11.45am–6.45pm. Closed mid-Jul–mid-Aug. From flamenco and tap dancing to ballet and the traditional dances of East and West, welcome to the citadel of the art.

Opéra national de Lyon – 1 pl. de la Comédie. ☎0826 305 325. www.opera-lyon.org. Tickets: Mon–Sat 11am–7pm. Closed late Jul–end Aug. In a perfect setting, this is one of the city's most beautiful monuments, thanks to the immense and splendid glass roof designed by Jean Nouvel. With a capacity of 1,100 seats, The Opéra includes an orchestra (60 musicians), a ballet (30 dancers), a choir (26 singers), a troupe and a solid expertise. With Ivan Fischer holding the baton, l'Opéra National de Lyon is an international class company. A 200-seat amphitheatre is the stage for a more varied programme, including classical, jazz and world musics.

Halle Tony-Garnier – 20 pl. Antonin-Perrin. ☎04 72 76 85 85. www.halle-tony-garnier.com. Visits following schedule; phone ahead. Since its restoration in 2000, this huge metallic structure presents a remarkable diversity of events from the Moscow State Circus to Lionel Richie and Johnny Halliday.

All over the city, thousands of balconies were lit up by tiny lights placed there in a spontaneous gesture by Lyon residents. This religious custom has become a traditional festival during which the city councillors and store owners inaugurate their Christmas displays.

Lyon in the Middle Ages – After Charlemagne's reign, Lyon passed from one family to another through legacies and dowries. Finally, the city was placed under the temporal authority of its archbishops. During this period a large number of major building projects were completed. Churches and abbeys sprang up in Lyon and the surrounding area. The Pont du Change (Exchange Bridge) was built over the River Saône; the Pont de la Guillotière, designed by the Pontiff Brothers, provided access to the other bank of the Rhône.

In the early 14C, Lyon was annexed to royal authority and obtained the right to elect 12 consuls. A municipal charter was proclaimed at Île Barbe in 1312. The consuls, all of them members of the rich *bourgeoisie*, raised taxes and ensured that there was law and order. The people of the working classes, who were quick to rebel and who had not hesitated in besieging the archbishop in his palace, discovered to their cost that the consuls were even more heavy-handed than the clergy had been.

A cultural centre – At the end of the 15C the setting up of fairs and the development of banking attracted traders from all over Europe. Social, intellectual and artistic life blossomed, stimulated by a visit from François I and his sister, Marguerite, who held the most dazzling court.

Famous "booksellers" took the fame of Lyon's printers far and wide. There were 100 printer's workshops in the town in 1515, and more than 400 by 1548.

Painters, sculptors and potters, all of them steeped in Italian culture, prepared the way for the French Renaissance.

Lyon boasted brilliant poets and storytellers such as **François Rabelais** (1494–1553). He was a doctor at the local hospital and, for the fairs in 1532 and 1534, published his works *Gargantua* and *Pantagruel*. It was, though, a woman, **Louise Labé**, who embodied the spirit of the day, not only for her grace and beauty but also for her skill in poetry. At the age of 20, Louise had developed comprehensive linguistic (Greek, Latin, Spanish and Italian) and musical talents. After a stint at the siege of Perpignan (not for

Lyon, City of Light

With the famous **Festival of Lights** held here on 8 December, when the city twinkles with the light of thousands of candles, Lyon was already predisposed to investing generously in street-lighting, and it has done just that in the shape of a project called "Plan Lumière" which places the emphasis on public safety and the highlighting of the city's architectural heritage. Over 100 monuments and locations have been selected for inclusion in a comprehensive and homogenous system of illumination which gives them a whole new dimension. Fourvière Basilica stands out like a lighthouse on the top of its hill; the opera house takes on a futuristic appearance with its huge glass superstructure glowing red; squares such as place des Terreaux or place de la Bourse and the banks of the Saône and the Rhône are lit up by subtle lighting in a variety of colours in warm or cold tones depending on the location. The Part-Dieu district with the distinctive Crédit Lyonnais tower soaring up from it, the Port St-Jean, the Hôtel-Dieu and many more of the city's famous monuments feature in this huge light show which weaves an atmosphere of fairy tale and magic. Along with the various events put on in the evenings, this invitation to explore "Lyon by night" proves irresistible.

A guide to the "Plan Lumière" is available from the tourist office. www.lyon.fr

the faint-hearted!), she eventually married a gentleman-ropemaker (*cordier* in French) from Lyon and opened a salon for poets, artists and men of learning, just as Madame de Sévigné was to do a century later.

"La Belle Cordière," as she was known, penned some pleasing verse herself, as well as encouraging others.

Scientific advances – Literature and the arts reigned in the Lyon of the 16C. Science became all the rage in the 18C, with the **Jussieu brothers**, famous botanists, and Bourgelat, who founded the first veterinary school in Europe in Lyon in 1762. In 1783 **Jouffroy** tested steam navigation on the Saône with his "Pyroscaphe," the first really viable steamboat; however, it brought him nothing but the ironic nickname of "Jouffroy the Pump."

In 1784 **Joseph Montgolfier** and **Pilâtre de Rozier** succeeded, at Les Brotteaux, in rising into the air on board a hot-air balloon. This was one of the first flights. A few years later, **André-Marie Ampère**, the great physicist, and **Joseph-Marie Jacquard**, who invented a weaving loom, showed their own form of inventive genius.

"Lyon is no more" – During the French Revolution, the residents of Lyon resisted the Convention. Retribution was harsh: on 12 October 1793 the Committee of Public Safety declared that "Lyon waged war on liberty. Lyon is no more." Houses were destroyed, countless local people died, and Lyon was renamed a "Free Commune."

Lyon's "Mr Punch" – Guignol, the popular wooden puppet who is well-known throughout France, his wife Madelon and his usual sparring partner, Gnafron, whose fine bass voice has coarsened somewhat through excessive consumption of Beaujolais, all embody the popular spirit of the local people in a way that provokes laughter without giving offence.

Laurent Mourguet (1769–1844), who created Guignol, was a local weaver. The few neighbours for whom he first performed his comedy shows were enthusiastic.

Soon, as his success grew, so did his public: he staged performances all over Lyon, in the Petit Tivoli, and in the main avenue in Les Brotteaux where, on Sundays, three rows of chairs were set out. After Mourguet's death his 16 children, all of whom had been trained by him, perpetuated his art form.

Nowadays, comedies based on current affairs are played out on the stage of the Guignol de Lyon theatre.

Threads of History

Silk, the fibre from cocoons produced by the caterpillars of the Bombyx moth, otherwise known as silkworms, was discovered in China, and was brought to France by Louis XI in 1466. The French silk industry did not really begin to evolve until the 16C; at this time Lyon was chosen as the central silk depot, and cultivation of the mulberry bushes on which silkworms feed was begun on a large scale. The industry's expansion continued under Louis XIV, with notable innovators such as Philippe de Lassalle playing a major role in its development, but was brought to an abrupt end by the outbreak of the French Revolution. It received a new lease of life under Napoleon's Empire, finally reaching its apogee in c 1850, shortly after which a devastating silkworm plague broke out, decimating French silkworm breeding centres. This was a blow from which the French silk industry never fully recovered. It also subsequently had to contend with strong foreign competition, the discovery of artificial fibres and mass industrialisation. Nonetheless, Lyon silk production has remained a standard of quality for the fashion world and among French luxury materials.

Sericulture, or the production of silk, involves raising silkworms in special silk-worm farms (in French, magnaneries) from the egg to cocoon stage. The silkworm chrysalides are suffocated in steam so that the cocoon can be unravelled as a single long filament of silk. The raw silk obtained at this stage is not strong enough to be woven and so undergoes a preparatory process – reeling, in which the silk fibres from several cocoons are wound together to form a single strand. Bobbins of this thread are arranged on a special frame, then unreeled in batches onto a warp frame. Next the warp is stretched on a draw loom to form parallel threads, across which the weft threads are drawn by a shuttle. To allow the shuttle to pass along with the weft, various mechanical systems for lifting the appropriate warp threads were developed, one of the most famous of which was Jacquard's (using punched cards). Various types of plain weave are possible using silk, to produce taffeta, silk serge and satin, for example. The manufacture of fancier, figured fabrics (with decorative motifs in coloured threads) requires a more complex system, however, using cords known – funnily enough – as simples. As for woven pile fabrics such as velvet, it is necessary to have a second set of warp threads which form the pile. Such fancy fabrics can be smooth (damask, lampas) or textured (brocade, brocatelle).

Silk can also be processed after it has been woven, for example in silkscreen printing, or the manufacture of figured or watered silks.

The silk industry – It was silk which, in the 16C, made Lyon a major industrial city; until then most of the silk fabrics in France had been imported from Italy. Two main figures dominate the history of this new industry. In 1536 **Étienne Turquet**, a man from Piedmont in Italy, offered to bring to Lyon silk and velvet weavers from Genoa and set up a factory in Lyon. François I, who was anxious to stem the flow of money out of the country as a result of purchases of foreign silks, accepted his offer. In 1804 **Joseph-Marie Jacquard** invented a loom which, by using a system of punched cards, enabled a single worker to do the work of six. The Croix-Rousse district was filled with its characteristic house-workshops – the upper storeys contained the looms on which the workers wove the silk provided by the manufacturer.

In 1875 a revolution occurred in the silk industry; the introduction of mechanical looms and the change in fashion away from figured fabrics and brocades quickly reduced the silk-workers to abject poverty. Only a few looms continued to exist in Lyon, capable of producing special fabrics at exorbitant prices. Ordinary silks were made by workers in rural areas where labour was less expensive.

J. Damase/MICHELIN

La Presqu'île

Today natural silk imported from Italy or Japan now represents only a minute proportion of the quantities of fabric processed here. It is subject to extremely meticulous care and attention in the silk-workers centre (Maison des Canuts, *see below*).

The so-called "silk-style" weaving, though, using all sorts of fibres (glass, carbon, borum, and aramide) remains one of Lyon's specialities.

The traditional know-how of the silk weavers has found direct applications in the production of highly sophisticated parts for the aeronautics, space and electronics industries.

Lyon Fair – In the Middle Ages, Lyon was "one of the keys to the kingdom," situated as it was on the frontiers of Savoy, Dauphiné, Italy and Germany on one side, and Beaujolais, Burgundy, Languedoc, Forez and the Auvergne on the other. In 1419 the heir to the French throne, the future Charles VII, having realised the value of this geographical situation in commercial terms, ordered two fairs to be held here every year; he made Lyon one of the largest warehouses in the world. Traders and merchants flocked here from every direction. From 1463 onwards, thanks to Louis XI, the fairs were held four times a year. Re-established in 1916 after a long break, the **Lyon International Fair** maintains the city's tradition as a major centre of international business. Running concurrently with the main fair are a number of specialist exhibitions.

A European crossroads – Lyon lies at the centre of a motorway network that links the city to Northern and Southern Europe in the north-south direction and to the Massif Central, Switzerland and Italy in the east-west direction, via St-Étienne, Clermont-Ferrand, Geneva, Annecy, Chambéry and Grenoble.

Since 1981, in addition to the many fast rail links with the rest of France, Lyon has enjoyed even more rapid communications due to the high-speed train (TGV) service. There is a busy international airport, **Lyon-St-Exupéry,** to the east of the town and the Édouard-Herriot harbour to the south of the Gerland district is full of heavy barges waiting to sail up to Auxonne on the Saône (*32km/20mi SE of Dijon*).

Lyon puts on a new face – There has been much development in Lyon since the "daring" tower blocks of the 1930s – including both new projects and restoration schemes in the old parts of the city. In order to ensure its success in the future, Lyon is developing a number of science and technology parks, which bring together scientific research, higher education and industry. The **Cité Internationale,** between the Rhône and the Tête d'Or park, is the site of an International Conference Centre (capacity 2,000), the head offices of Interpol (the International Criminal Investigation Organisation), a hotel complex and a Museum of Contemporary Art, all housed in a boldly innovative building. To the east, around the university campus, there are major technical research offices and, further out of town, the St-Exupéry TGV station, designed by Spanish architect Calatrava to resemble a bird taking flight, which provides a TGV link to the local airport.

La Presqu'île and its Squares

Allow one day; museums are discussed in detail under Sights below

Lyon's main city centre districts lie around place Bellecour. "La Presqu'île" – the Peninsula – has long been the setting of the Lyon trading centre, and until the 19C commerce centred on rue Mercière. Two main pedestrian precincts run across it linking place des Terreaux to Perrache railway station. They are rue de la République to the north and rue Victor-Hugo to the south.

La Presqu'île is the modern face of Lyon. The Rue de la République is bustling with department stores, shops, cinemas and bistros, and the street is lined with buildings typical of 19C Lyon. Their façades incorporate tall windows and lintels decorated with cut sheet-metal signs. The districts to the south of place Bellecour skirt the former Île des Canabae district, the site of Ainay Abbey.

Place Bellecour

This famous Lyon square, overlooked by the distinctive outline of Fourvière Basilica on its hill to the west, is one of the largest in France. The huge symmetrical Louis XVI façades lining the west and east sides of the square date from 1800.

The equestrian statue of Louis XIV is known to the locals as the "Bronze Horse." The pedestal is decorated with two bronzes by the Coustou brothers (17C-18C) representing the Rhône and the Saône, each facing in the direction of its respective river. On either side of the pedestal is the inscription: "Masterpiece by Lemot, Sculptor from Lyon." An earlier equestrian statue of the great King by Desjardins (1691) was erected on this spot in 1713. The symbol of royalty was overturned, smashed and melted down during the French Revolution. The present statue (1828) was itself threatened in 1848: it was about to be pulled down when the Commissary Extraordinary of the Republic saved it by suggesting that, if the pompous inscription in honour of Ludovicus Magnus were replaced by a homage to the talent of Lemot, this would constitute just as much of an attack on royalty.

To the south-east of the square, the bell-tower of the 17C former almshouse, the **Hôpital de la Charité**, stands on its own in front of the main post office.

To the north-east of the square, the Banque Nationale de Paris stands on the site of the cinema where the first films by the cinematographer **Lumière** were shown.

Place Louis-Pradel – The square is decorated with a fountain and sculptures by Ipoustéguy, and is an aesthetic combination of old and modern forms.

Opéra de Lyon

On the south side of the square, opposite the Hôtel de Ville, stands the new Lyon opera house, the result of a successful modernisation scheme. The façade of the old building has been preserved and the eight muses of the pediment appear to hold up the enormous glass semi-cylindrical roof, the design of the architect **Jean Nouvel**. Inside, beyond the original Rococo foyer is the concert hall itself, an Italianate chamber with a seating capacity of 1,300, and a restaurant under the glass roof. The building takes on a particularly impressive appearance during the evening illuminations, which floodlight it in predominantly red tones, throwing its architectural contours into sharp relief.

The successful restoration of the building was rewarded by Lyon Opera being promoted to the rank of a national opera company.

Opera house

Place des Jacobins

The main feature of the square is the majestic Dominicans' fountain, erected in 1886 in memory of four local artists: Philibert Delorme, Hippolyte Flandrin, Guillaume Coustou and Gérard Audran.

Exploring the Traboules

The traboules are private property and some are therefore kept closed by their owners. However, many of the most interesting are nonetheless open to visitors, under the terms of an agreement drawn up between the city of Lyon, the owners and the urban community. They can be accessed by pressing the entry button usually to be found above the interphone or entry code number pads by each main street door. Other traboules, not usually open to the public, can be visited as part of a guided tour organised by the Lyon tourist office. Before beginning a visit, it is advisable to ask at the tourist office for the list of passages that are open to visitors. The best time to explore many of the interior courtyards described in this section is in the morning.

Place des Terreaux

This square is the hub of city life. It derives its name from the filling in of a former bed of the Rhône by soil or leaf mould. The confluence of the rivers was situated nearby in Roman times. The famous monumental lead **fountain**✶ was made by the sculptor Bartholdi. Its four quivering horses symbolise the Rivers running towards the Ocean. The south side of the square is bordered by the 17C façade of the Palais St-Pierre. In 1994, D Buren was entrusted with the restoration of the square. He added an area of granite paving slabs in a harmonious pattern, 14 pillars and 69 water jets, and the whole installation is illuminated to great effect at night.

Hôtel de Ville

This remarkable city hall, part Louis XIII in style, was designed by Simon Maupin. It consists of a large rectangle of buildings flanked by pavilions. Inside is the main courtyard, an unusual construction on two levels separated by a semicircular porch.

The original façade of the Hôtel de Ville facing place des Terreaux was destroyed by fire in 1674. Jules Hardouin-Mansart and Robert de Cotte were commissioned to refurbish the building and they radically transformed the façade. The side pavilions and belfry were topped by a dome. In the centre, a large rounded tympanum supported by telamones is adorned with an equestrian statue of Henry IV.

Vieux Lyon★★★

Lyon old town, between Fourvière and the Saône, includes the **St-Jean district** in the centre, the **St-Paul district** to the north and the **St-Georges district** to the south. This was once the town centre and the seat of all the corporations, in particular those representing silk workers. Traders, bankers, clerks and royal dignitaries lived here, in magnificent town houses. Almost 300 of these mansions still stand, forming quite an exceptional example of Renaissance housing. Many of these 400-year-old houses originally had four floors; additional storeys were added very early on, in order to provide more light for the looms.

One of the main features of the old town is the numerous passages or alleyways known as **traboules** (from the Latin *trans ambulare* meaning "walking through") especially between rue St-Jean, rue des Trois-Maries and quai Romain-Rolland, rue St-Georges and quai Fulchiron. Since there was not enough space to build an extensive network of streets, these passageways, all perpendicular to the Saône, were built to link the buildings together.

The houses reflect their period of construction (15C-17C) and there are several architectural styles. The **Late Gothic houses** are distinguishable by the elegant decoration on the Flamboyant façades – multifoiled or ogee arches, flowerets, carved gables decorated with crockets. The windows are often set asymmetrically into the walls. A vaulted corridor leads to an inner courtyard where a corner turret contains a spiral staircase.

Most of the old houses, among them the most beautiful of all the mansions, are built in the **Renaissance style.** The basic structure remains unchanged but the buildings are bigger and include new decorative features of Italian inspiration. The staircase turrets are beautifully designed and built; each courtyard has its succession of galleries, one above the other, each with surbased arches.

The **French Renaissance houses** are fewer in number. There is a noticeable return to Antiquity with the inclusion of architectural orders. The famous architect **Philibert Delorme** (1515–70), a native of Lyon, launched the new fashion with the gallery on squinches at no 8 rue Juiverie. The main staircase, which was often rectangular, was set in the centre of the façade.

The **late-16C and pre-Classical houses** are distinguished by severe architectural lines. The decoration on the façade appears above the ground floor and includes triangular pediments with a central arch stone in relief, and rusticated bonding. The galleries overlooking the courtyard show Florentine influence with rounded arches supported by round columns.

While walking around the courtyards and passages, besides appreciating the *traboules* themselves, keep an eye open for attractive carved shop signs, wrought-iron imposts and railings, old wells, and amusing corbels supporting the spring ends of the diagonal ribs of the vaulted passageways.

St-Jean and St-Paul Districts

Place St-Jean
In the centre of the square is a fountain with four basins topped by a small openwork pavilion containing a sculpture of the Baptism of Christ. To the east of the

St-Jean Cathedral

©Jacques Croizer/istockphoto.com

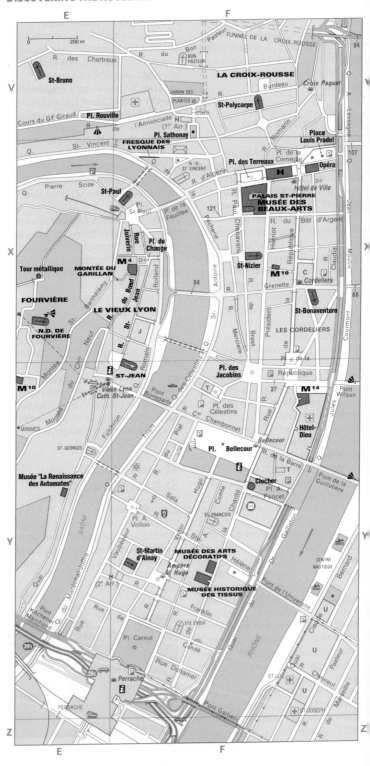

LA PRESQU'ÎLE		La-Fayette Pont	FX	88
		Lattre-de-Tassigny Pt de	FV	94
Childebert R.	FY 27	Morand Pont	FX	107
Juin Pont Alphonse	FX 84	Platière R. de la	FX	121

Hôtel de ville FX	H	Musée de l'Imprimerie	FX M¹⁶
Musée Gadagne		Musée de la Civilisation	
(Musée historique de Lyon		gallo-romaine	EY M¹⁰
et Musée international		Musée des Hospices civils FY M¹⁴	
de la Marionnette)	FX M⁴		

square is the cathedral of St-Jean and the choir school.

Manécanterie

To the right of the west front on place St-Jean is the 12C choir school. The front of the building, which lost 0.80m/2ft7ins of its overall height when the ground level was raised, is decorated with a blind storey topped by red-brick encrustations, colonnettes and niches containing statues of human figures. Despite alterations, it has retained its Romanesque appearance.

Primatiale St-Jean★

Dating originally from the 12C, St-Jean Cathedral is a Gothic building erected to complete a Romanesque apse. On the exterior the most notable features are the four towers, two on the west front and two over the arms of the transept. They are only slightly higher than the nave. In 1245 and 1274 the cathedral was the setting for the two Councils of Lyon. In the following century it was chosen for the consecration of Pope John XXII. In 1600 Henri IV married Marie de' Medici here. More recently, in 1943, the Sixth Grand Pardon was celebrated here. The event is celebrated approximately once every century, when Corpus Christi coincides, on 24 June, with the Feast Day of St John the Baptist, to whom the church is dedicated.

▶ *Skirt the cathedral to the right on rue St-Étienne and go to the archaeological gardens.*

Jardin Archéologique

In this archaeological park visitors can see the remains of several buildings that have occupied the former site of the church of St-Étienne to the north of the present cathedral, since the 4C. They include Gallo-Roman baths, a Palaeo-

Christian baptistery, and an arch from the 15C church of Ste-Croix.

▶ *The narrow rue Ste-Croix leads to rue St-Jean.*

Rue St-Jean★★

This was the main street in the old town of Lyon and, as such, royal corteges and religious processions passed along it. No 7 has a Flamboyant Gothic façade.

The old **Hôtel de la Chamarerie** at no 37 was built in the 16C for the cleric responsible for overseeing the cathedral cloisters, who was known as the chamarier. The façade, which was modified in the 19C, is in the Flamboyant Gothic style.

The arcading in the galleries of the **Maison des Avocats★** (Barristers' House) is supported on massive columns and the outbuildings have pink roughcast. Seen from rue de la Bombarde, the house presents a fine example of 16C architecture in the Italian style.

No **58** has an unusual feature in the shape of a well with a tripartite roof so that it is accessible from the courtyard, the staircase and the workshop.

At no **54**, the **longest traboule** in old Lyon crosses five courtyards before reaching no 27 rue du Bœuf. Walk past

Astronomical clock (14C), St-Jean Cathedral

©Jacques Croizer/istockphoto.com

the Palais de Justice to no **52**: the house of printer Guillaume Leroy (late 15C) has a spiral staircase in a round tower. The bays are supported on arches.

No **50** is a fine example of a renovated courtyard enhanced by galleries and a spiral staircase. The same features can be admired at no 42, which has retained its corbelled passageway resting on sculpted consoles.

At no **36**, a house dating from the late 15C, there is a polygonal tower containing a spiral staircase. The keystones in the galleries are decorated with coats of arms on the first two floors and the well is protected by a shell-shaped canopy embellished with pearls. The niche at the corner of rue St-Jean and place Neuve-St-Jean contains a statue of John the Baptist.

▸ *Take rue du Palais-de-Justice and turn left onto rue des Trois-Maries.*

Rue des Trois-Maries
The "Street of the Three Marys" derives its name from the niche on the pediment of no **7** containing a statue of the Virgin Mary flanked by two Holy Women. On the same side of the street, numerous traboules lead off downhill to the Saône; that from no **9**, for example, gives a view of no 17 quai Romain-Rolland.

At no **3** a handsome example of French Renaissance has a staircase surmounted by a tower in the centre of its façade; this feature is repeated in the house at no 5 place du Gouvernement.

The façade of no **4** is adorned with a regular arrangement of fluted pilasters and, in the courtyard, a tower in which the spiral staircase is clearly visible through the openwork.

▸ *Retrace your steps to no 6, and cross the traboule leading across two restored courtyards to no 27 rue St-Jean.*

The façade at no **27** has mullioned windows framed by fluted pilasters.

No **28** conceals a magnificent **courtyard**★★ with an imposing tower with a spiral staircase inside it.

The **Hôtel Laurencin** at no **24** has a crenellated octagonal tower containing a spiral staircase. The loggias on the superimposed galleries feature ribbed vaults.

▸ *Cross place de la Baleine and go to place du Gouvernement.*

Place du Gouvernement
The façade of no **5**, its doorways topped by wrought-iron imposts and a stone balcony, dates from the early 17C.

Hôtel du Gouvernement (16C) stands at no **2**. The upper courtyard lies at the end of a long passageway roofed with ribbed vaulting. All that remains of the well to the right is the shell-shaped top (note the traboule at no 10 quai Romain-Rolland).

▸ *Rejoin rue St-Jean and walk on until you reach place du Change.*

Place du Change
This square, originally called place de la Draperie, was frequented by money-lenders in the 15C and 16C. The **Loge du Change** was designed mainly by Soufflot, the architect who altered the original design between 1747 and 1750. On the upper storey are engaged columns topped by Ionic capitals and carved entablatures.

Since 1803 the building has been used as a Protestant church.

Opposite, at no **2**, is the **Maison Thomassin** which has a 15C façade built in the 14C style. On the second floor the mullioned ogee bays rising to trefoiled arches are set into Gothic arches decorated with coats of arms.

▸ *Continue along rue Lainerie.*

Rue Lainerie
Note the vaulted corridor of no **18**. The **Maison de Claude de Bourg** at no **14** has a 15C flower-decked façade which is typical of Lyon, with ornately carved accolades.

▸ *To the right is rue Louis-Garrand and the Guignol puppet theatre.*

Rue Lainerie opens onto place St-Paul, where you can glimpse the train station and, further back, the **church**.

▶ *Turn left onto rue Juiverie.*

Rue Juiverie★

The Jews were expelled from this street in the late 14C and the Italian bankers who replaced them had luxurious mansions built.

The **Hôtel Paterin,** also known as "Henri IV's House," at no **4** is an outstanding example of Renaissance architecture. The **staircase** in the courtyard, with its three tiers of arches, one above the other, supported on massive columns, is particularly impressive. To the right is a niche containing a statue of Henri IV.

At no **8**, the second courtyard in the **Hôtel Bullioud** contains the famous **gallery**★★ designed by **Philibert Delorme,** a gem of French Renaissance architecture in Lyon. Delorme built it in 1536 on his return from Rome. Note the squinches supporting the corner pavilions decorated in the Antique style; Doric frieze with an entablature on the lower level including metopes and triglyphs and pilasters with Ionic volutes on the upper level.

The Renaissance façade on the **Maison Antoine Groslier de Servières** (no **10**) has five arches on the ground floor topped by triangular or broken pediments of black marble. In the courtyard is a round tower with mullioned windows containing a spiral staircase. The corbels on the balcony on the first floor are carved with human figures.

The house at no **21** has ogee windows with rounded frontons. There is a Gallo-Roman cellar in its basement. Between nos **16** and **18** rises the picturesque, steep **ruelle Punaise**, which leads onto montée St-Barthélémy. In the Middle Ages it served as an open sewer.

The mansion at no **20** was built by a wealthy 15C gentleman, E Grolier. The façade is decorated with mullioned windows flanked by colonnettes. Note in the courtyard a tower with a spiral staircase inside and the rib-vaulted galleries.

At no **22** is the **Maison Baronat**, which has a corbelled corner turret overlooking montée du Change.

At no **23**, at the corner of rue de la Loge, is the **Maison Dugas** whose long façade is decorated with bosses and lions' heads.

Gallery, Hôtel Bullioud

▶ *Turn left onto rue de la Loge, then right into rue de Gadagne.*

Musée Gadagne★

This mansion stretches from no 10 to no 14 rue de Gadagne and is the largest Renaissance building in the old town. In 1545 it was purchased by the **Gadagne Brothers**, bankers of Italian origin who had amassed a colossal fortune. Indeed, the expression "as rich as Gadagne" became a local figure of speech. On the façade set slightly back from the street, note the cant-walled tower and, to the left, the wrought-iron grid of the cellar window, a masterpiece of ironwork. In the inner courtyard, the two main buildings with large mullioned windows are linked by three storeys of galleries. The well, which is topped by a dome covered with scales, was brought here from the Maison du Chamarier (no 37 rue St-Jean); it is said to have been designed by Philibert Delorme.

Musée Historique de Lyon★

In the Local History Museum the rooms on the ground floor have been laid out with **religious sculpture**★, including bas-relief sculptures from old churches or abbeys in Lyon, in particular from Ainay, St-Pierre and Île Barbe (Annunciation bas-relief, a mantelpiece known as "Charlemagne's Crown").

Musée International de la Marionnette★

The exhibits of this museum include not only Guignol and a number of glove

La Tour Rose

J. Damase/MICHELIN

puppets but also an outstanding collection of string and rod puppets and shadow figures from France, England, Belgium, Holland, Venice, Turkey, Russia and the Far East. South of the Hôtel de Gadagne is montée du Garillan.

▶ *Walk across place du Petit-Collège and along rue du Bœuf.*

Rue du Bœuf

This street owes its name to the statue of an ox (or more precisely a bull) at the corner of place Neuve-St-Jean, a work attributed to M Hendricy. The street

contains some lovely examples of Renaissance architecture, some of which are occupied by luxury hotels.

At no **6**, "La Cour des Loges" Hotel occupies a fine set of four restored houses. It is possible, with discretion or perhaps stopping for refreshment, to have a look at the beautiful courtyard with its U-shaped galleries on three floors.

No **14** leads into a pretty courtyard with a polygonal tower and galleries supported on arches surmounted by a frieze of Greek motifs.

The **Maison du Crible**★ at no **16** dates from the 17C. It has an ornate doorway with bosses and ringed columns topped by a pediment decorated with a small carving of the Adoration of the Magi said to have been the work of Giambologna. An alleyway with ogival vaulting supported on carved corbels leads to an inner courtyard in which the elegant round tower, with staggered openings, owes its name, **Tour Rose** (Pink Tower), to the colour of its famous roughcast. *Do not go up to the terraced gardens.* "Tour Rose" is also the name of the famous hotel complex which has moved to no **22**.

Place Neuve-St-Jean

This old street was transformed into a square under the Consulat. At one end is the sign signalling the beginning of rue du Boeuf, and at the other a niche housing a statue of John the Baptist. At

Le Guignol de Lyon – Compagnie des Zonzons

Guignol, the satirical puppet, is characterised by his black cap under which he has a short plait which he calls his *sarsifis*. His naïvety and waggish banter make him a perfect example of the "urchins" of Lyon. His wife, Madelon, with whom he has frequent arguments, is a model wife, if somewhat prone to grumbling. His inseparable friend is Gnafron whose most notable features are his tall stature

Guignol and Gnafron

J. Damase/MICHELIN

and his ruddy nose, an indication of his marked liking for Beaujolais. If anybody asks him what he does for a living, he answers, "Educated people call us cobblers or botchers; the uneducated call us gowks" *("gnafres")*.

Shows at this Guignol theatre are now a blend of tradition and modern innovation, influenced by contemporary authors and even films.

no **4** is a vast building set slightly back from the others which features a superb staircase over arches corresponding to galleries with surbased arches.

▶ *Return to rue du Bœuf.*

The **Maison de l'Outarde d'Or** (House of the Golden Bustard) stands out at no **19** because of its carved stone sign. The courtyard is particularly interesting for its two turrets. One of them is round and built over a squinch; the other, corbelled turret is a rectangle built on an upturned pyramid. Another building of interest can be seen at no **27** (the longest *traboule* in Lyon, leading to no 54 rue St-Jean) with an elegant 16C spiral staircase preceding a succession of three courtyards.

No **36** opens onto a pretty courtyard decorated with restored galleries. It is interesting to compare these *(turn round)* with those of no **38**, which are largely sealed up by additional structures. Most of the galleries were closed off when the district's fortunes sank to make more space and to keep in heat.

▶ *No 31 opens onto rue de la Bombarde (on the right). Almost opposite, take rue des Antonins, which leads back to place St-Jean.*

From St-Jean metro station it is possible to take the funicular railway up to the top of Fourvière hill and come back down the same way after visiting the Basilica, Gallo-Roman Museum, and Roman theatres.

St-Georges District

▶ *Go to rue Mourguet and walk on until you reach place de la Trinité.*

Place de la Trinité
The **Maison du Soleil** (Sun House), which became famous after inspiring the backcloth for the Guignol puppet theatre, lends an old-fashioned touch to the square.

Montée du Gourguillon
Set on the hillside in the Fourvière district, this was the usual route taken by carriages heading for the Auvergne in the Middle Ages. It is difficult to imagine the heavy loads climbing such a steep slope. It was also the direct route between the cloisters of St-Jean belonging to the Canon-Counts, and St-Just, the fortified town of the Canon-Barons. At no **2** stands a Renaissance house. Slightly further up the hill is the **Impasse Turquet**, a picturesque passageway with old timber galleries.

Rue St-Georges
The ground floor of no **3** has basket-handled arches and the springer of the door is decorated with two rampant wrought-iron lions. At no **3 bis** the springer is decorated with a phoenix rising from the flames. At no **6**, the 16C house has a fine interior courtyard (art gallery). The spiral staircase is set in a round tower with sloping windows.

▶ *Continue to no 100 if you want to visit the Automata Museum.*

Musée
"La Renaissance des Automates"
100 rue St-Georges. 🧸 ♿ 🕐 *Open all year, daily, 2.30pm–6pm.* 🕐 *Closed 25 Dec.* 💳 *7€ (children: 5€).* ☎ *04 72 77 75 20. www.museeautomates.com.*
Seven rooms house 250 automata in perfect working order, displayed according to cultural, traditional and regional themes.

▶ *Turn right when you reach the Église St-Georges and come back via quai Fulchiron.*

Fourvière Hill

The Fourvière district of Lyon stands on a hill of the same name; the term **Fourvière** is said to come from the Latin *forum vetus*, relating to the forum situated in the heart of the Roman colony established in 43 BC; its theatre, odeon and aqueducts have survived to this day. The forum, which stood on the site now occupied by the esplanade in front of the basilica, is said to have collapsed in AD 840. In the 3C people moved from the side of the hill and the stones were

Fourvière hill

A. de Valroger/MICHELIN

reused to rebuild the town at the bottom of the slope. In the Middle Ages the hill was largely given over to farming (in particular vineyards). In the 17C numerous religious orders set up monasteries and convents here, which inspired the historian, Michelet, to make his famous comment about Fourvière, "the hill that prays," opposite La Croix-Rousse, "the hill that works." Nowadays Fourvière, with its basilica, Roman monuments and museum is, with the old town below, one of the most popular tourist venues in Lyon.

The Montées

The *montées,* or rises, consist of winding flights of steps or steeply sloping streets that climb the Fourvière hill, providing superb views down over the old town. Each of them has its own charm.

Montée des Carmes-Déchaussés and Montée Nicolas-de-Lange

The former derives its name (Rise of the Barefoot Carmelites) from the monastery founded in the early 17C which now houses the Regional Archives; it has 238 steps. The second has 560 steps which means that there is a total of 798 steps down to place St-Paul from the metal tower *(Tour Métallique)* on Fourvière.

Montée du Change

This links rue de la Loge to montée St-Barthélemy. On the way down, there are interesting views of the spires on the

church of St-Nizier which rises from the buildings on the banks of the Saône.

Montée du Garillan★

This is a remarkable series of zigzag flights of steps (224 steps).

Montée des Chazeaux

With its 228 very steep steps, it leads onto montée St-Barthélémy.

Montée du Chemin-Neuf and Montée St-Barthélémy

From these steps there is an extensive view over the rooftops of the old town and St-Jean Cathedral.

Montée du Gourguillon

See St-Georges District, opposite.

Montée des Épies

This rise climbs up above the St-Georges district, high above the church dedicated to St George, a Neo-Gothic building designed by Bossan, the architect also responsible for Fourvière Basilica.

Fourviere Sanctuary

The history of the religious buildings erected in honour of the Virgin Mary on the site of the Roman forum spans almost eight centuries. The massive basilica standing today at the top of Fourvière hill is an integral part of the Lyon landscape.

Basilique Notre-Dame★

The basilica is a famous place of pilgrimage built to designs by an architect named Bossan after the Franco-Prussian War (1870) in fulfilment of a vow taken by Monsignor de Genouilhac, the Archbishop of Lyon, who undertook to build a church if the enemy did not approach the city.

Crenellated walls with machicolations, flanked by octagonal towers, form an odd blend of Byzantine and medieval features. The abundance of decoration inside (nave and crypt) is no less unusual.

Ancienne Chapelle de la Vierge

To the right of the basilica stands the real pilgrimage chapel dating from the

VIEUX LYON-FOURVIÈRE

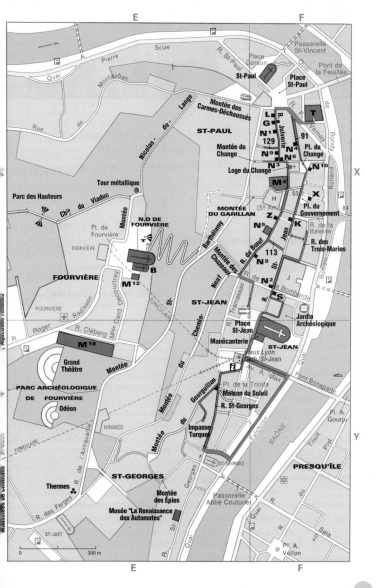

Basilique Notre-Dame

18C: the former Lady Chapel containing a statue of the Virgin Mary (16C).

Musée de Fourvière

🕐 *Open daily 10am–12.30pm, 2pm–5.30pm.* 🎫*6€.* ☎*04 78 25 13 01. www.fourviere.org.*

This museum, housed in the chapel and buildings once belonging to the Jesuit Order, contains a collection of polychrome wooden statues (12C-19C), various projects designed for the basilica in the 19C, and votive offerings.

Viewpoints

For a 360° **panoramic view★★**, climb to the foot of the basilica's observatory; from there the hillsides of the Lyonnais area, Mont Pilat and Mont-d'Or are visible and, in good weather, also the Alps and Mont Blanc to the west and the Puy de Dôme to the east.

Parc des Hauteurs

Follow a path to the left, just before the Tour Métallique.

This ambitious project was set up to enhance visitors' appreciation of Fourvière hill by laying out panoramic walks. The most original construction is that of the "Chemin du Viaduc," a footbridge that gives a breathtaking **view★** down onto Lyon and La Croix-Rousse.

Parc Archéologique de Fourvière★

🕐*Open 7am–7pm.* 🕐*Closed 1 Jan, 1 May, 1 Nov, 25 Dec.* 🎫*4€.* ☎*04 72 38 49 30.*

Fourvière archaeological site was opened in 1933 and has brought to light ancient and medieval public buildings in the district: Gallo-Roman baths in rue des Farges, remains of early basilicas in rue des Macchabées and quai Fulchiron (montée de Choulans).

Musée de la Civilisation Gallo-Romaine★★

17 rue Cléberg.

♿🕐*Open daily Tue–Sun 10am–6pm.* 🕐*Closed 1 Jan, 1 May, 1 Nov, 25 Dec.* 🎫*6€, free Thu.* ☎*04 72 38 49 30. www.musees-gallo-romains.com.*

This museum stands on the hill at Fourvière, at the heart of the district that was once the plateau of the ancient town of Lugdunum. The museum displays thematic exhibitions of its mainly Gallo-Roman collections.

Théâtres Romains

The group of buildings uncovered near rue de l'Antiquaille includes a theatre built during the reign of Caesar Augustus (1C BC) and extended during the reign of Hadrian (2C AD) and an odeum.

Life at the Crossroads

As the "Gateway to the south of France," where the better qualities of the north of France can be found in a more Mediterranean context embodied not least by the red pantile roofs, Lyon enjoys not only the reputation of being a hard-working, major city, but also of having an outstanding standard of living in which good food plays a leading role. Life in Lyon is characterised above all by its lack of stress or complication. The Lyonnais are creatures of habit, and some of their favourite pastimes can be appreciated by visitors to the city as well, such as watching (perhaps even playing!) the odd game of boules, especially during the boules tournament at Whitsun, taking a quiet stroll along the banks of the Saône or Rhône, or a gentle wander around the sloping streets of La Croix-Rousse, or indulging in a little shopping spree on the peninsula or in the Part-Dieu district. Then there is the pleasure of drinking in the sumptuous Renaissance architecture in the old town, or the peacefulness of the Tête d'Or park early in the morning, not forgetting the rose garden which is an absolute must in June; lengthy conversations over a bottle of Beaujolais in one of Lyon's cafés, the somewhat noisier delights of local festivals, convivial lunches in a crowded Lyon bistro, or bouchon, surrounded by the delicious rich smell of Lyonnais cuisine; and finally, for those who are young at heart, a Sunday afternoon spent watching the antics of the Guignol puppets.

Grand Théâtre

This is the oldest theatre in France. It is similar in size to those in Arles and Orange (108m/354ft in diameter) but smaller than the one in Vienne.

The initial construction dates from the pre-Christian era. The number of tiers of seats was later increased by building on top of the promenades. The paving in the orchestra pit has been reconstructed. The outer circular wall of the theatre shows substructures in which archaeologists have noted the particular attention paid by the builders to exits via underground corridors and to ground drainage through a system of pipes and sewers.

The stage curtain machinery, housed in the orchestra pit, is some of the best preserved of its kind in the Roman world. A model of how it worked is on display in the museum.

▶ *Climb the staircase leading to the top of the tiers of seats.*

From here, the full size of the theatre can be appreciated. It is possible to walk round the upper section by following the Roman road of large granite slabs.

▶ *Walk down the Roman road to the odeum.*

Area overlooking the theatre

Beyond the paved road behind the theatre, recent excavations have revealed the existence of an impressive residence and not, as was thought at one time, a temple dedicated to Cybele.

From the late 1C BC there stood on this huge rectangular esplanade a vast and magnificent house, bordered on one side by shops sheltered by a portico. Early in the 1C AD it was replaced by a large public building. To the east, above the theatre, lie the powerful foundations of an extended platform. At an indeterminate date an enormous cistern was installed here which was no doubt linked to Gier aqueduct.

Aqueducs Romains

On either side of the start of rue Roger-Radisson (once the road west to Aquitaine) are the interesting remains of one of the four aqueducts which provided the town's water supply.

Mausolées de Choulans

In the centre of place Wernert are three mausoleums that serve as reminders of the Gallo-Roman burial ground situated outside the town walls. The one in the centre, the oldest of the three (1C BC), bears an inscription on one of the sides indicating that the monument was built by emancipated slaves once belonging to Calvius Turpin.

La Croix-Rousse

La Croix-Rousse (literally "The Russet Cross") owes its name to a coloured stone Cross which stood at one of the district's crossroads in the days before the French Revolution. The district still has all the character and flavour of a small village community and today remains the last bastion of true Lyon traditionalism. The most fiercely proud inhabitants of La Croix-Rousse are deeply attached to the "Plateau" and look down from a distance on the hustle and bustle below. They might even spend months on end without going down the hill. Each autumn, the air is filled with the smell of roasted chestnuts and the local crêpes *(matefaim)* as the bustling boulevard de La Croix-Rousse plays host to the "Vogue" fun-fair, an annual event since 1865.

The invention of new looms by **Joseph-Marie Jacquard** (1752–1834) led the "canuts" or silk workers to abandon the low cottages in the St-Jean district and move to larger austere buildings with wide windows that let in the light. In the 19C the streets echoed with the rattle of the hand looms operated by some 30,000 silk workers.

The *traboules* in La Croix-Rousse follow the lie of the land and include a large number of steps. They were used to move bolts of silk about the district without any risk of damage from inclement weather. In 1831, and again in 1834, they were the scene of bloody uprisings when the silk workers waved black flags symbolising poverty and bearing the famous motto: "Life through work or death through conflict."

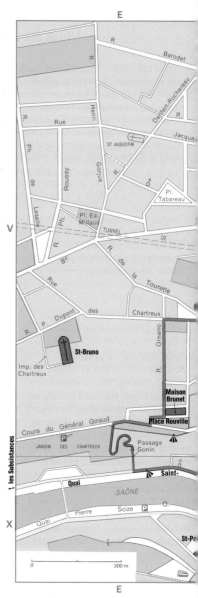

Historic Textile Workers District

▶ *Round tour starting from place des Terreaux. Go to no 6 (near the fountain), which communicates with rue Ste-Catherine. Turn right and walk down rue Romarin until you reach rue St-Polycarpe. Keep on walking towards the church.*

The **"Condition Publique des Soies"** (Public Silk Packing Works) at no 7 has a porch in which the upper arch is decorated with a majestic lion's head and mulberry leaves (the food of the silkworm). The building now houses a cultural and social centre but it was on these premises during the 19C that the hygrometric packing of silk cloth was monitored since, due to the fact that silk can absorb up to 15% of its weight in

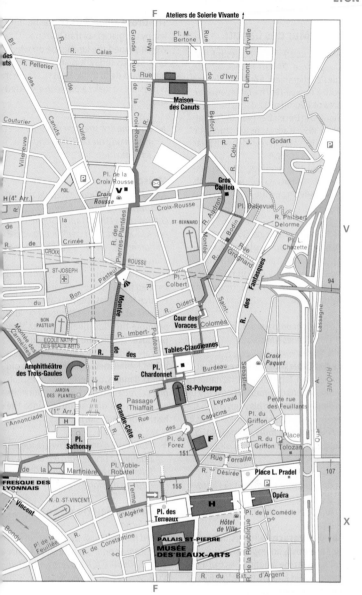

water, checks had to be made to ensure that the weight of the fabric actually complied with the official norms.

▶ *Walk up rue de l'Abbé-Rozier.*

At the end stands the church of **St-Polycarpe** dating from the 17C and 18C. From no 19 rue Leynaud (opposite no 14), the passage Thiaffait (derelict) leads up a double flight of steps to rue

Mur des Canuts

At the junction of boulevard des Canuts, rue Denfert-Rochereau and rue Pelletier stands a tall wall adorned with a *trompe-l'œil* mural covering an area of 1,200sq m/12,840sq ft.

Painted in December 1987 and updated in 1997, it serves as a picturesque reminder of life in one of the districts in La Croix-Rousse.

Note, in the windows, the puppet-theatre characters of Guignol, his wife Madelon and the Bailiff.

Burdeau. Opposite no 36 montée du Perron climbs up to **place Chardonnet**, on which stands the monument erected in memory of Count Hilaire de Chardonnet (1839–1924), the inventor of artificial silk.

▶ *Turn right onto rue des Tables-Claudiennes (steps).*

Rue des Tables-Claudiennes (street of the Claudian Tablets) owes its name to the inscriptions on bronze discovered by the draper Gribaud in his vineyard (*see Musée de la Civilisation Gallo-Romaine, in the Fourviere Sanctuary section*). No 55 is linked to no 20 rue Imbert-Colomès.

▶ *Take no 29 opposite, which communicates with cour des Voraces (steps and lane on the right, then turn left level with a street lamp).*

Cour des Voraces with its imposing flight of steps is an impressive sight. In the 19C it was the meeting place of a silk workers' guild known as the Voraces or Dévorants ("The Ravenous").

▶ *Take rue Bodin to place Bellevue.*

True to its name, this square commands a fine panorama of the surrounding town.

▶ *Follow the steps rising above the square and continue straight on along a steep path that crosses a garden. It will take you to the Gros Caillou.*

The **Gros Caillou** is an erratic boulder left by the glaciers of the Quaternary Era which shaped the landscape on which Lyon stands today. It marks the end of boulevard de la Croix-Rousse where it is possible to make a pause in a shaded spot.

▶ *Take the first street on the right, walk along rue de Belfort and turn left onto rue d'Ivry.*

Maison des Canuts

10 r. d'Ivry. &. ⊙Daily except Mon, Sun and public holidays, 10am–6.30pm. Guided tours (1hr): 11am, 3.30pm. ⊙1st week in Jan and 2nd week in Aug. ⊕5€ (children: 3€). ☎04 78 28 62 04. www.maisondescanuts.com.

At no 10 and no 12, craftsmen and women from the home workers cooperative (Cooptiss) perpetuate the traditions of the Lyon silk workers' and promote the high-quality fabrics they produce. During the guided tour visitors are shown how a draw loom and a velvet loom work. An exhibition of old fabrics (lampas, damasks, brocades, cutpile velvets) and pictures and portraits woven on silk give an insight into the history of Lyon's silk industry.

▶ *Walk back along rue d'Ivry to rue Dumont-d'Urville, turn left and follow it up to rue Richan (fifth on the right).*

Ateliers de Soierie Vivante★

21 rue Richan.

Guided tours (30m) daily except Sun and Mon 9am–noon, 2pm–6.30pm (Tue 2pm–6.30pm). ⊙Closed Aug and public holidays. ⊕3€ (children: 2€). ☎04 78 27 17 13. www.soierie-vivante.asso.fr.

This association was founded in 1993 to protect and promote the heritage of the Croix-Rousse silk working industry. It organises a number of tours of authentic family-run silk workshops, leaving from the Atelier Municipal de Passementerie, the municipal furniture trimmings workshop (where techniques involved in the manufacture of braid and other trimmings are explained at the start of the tour). Other workshops included in the tour are hand-loom weaving (with some very rare extra wide draw looms exhibited upstairs), machine-loom weaving, velvet weaving, making silk-wrapped thread and trimmings (gimping) and hand painting on silk.

> ▶ *Return to rue d'Ivry and walk past the Maison des Canuts to rue du Mail which leads to place de la Croix-Rousse.*

On place de la Croix-Rousse is a statue of Jacquard.
The second part of this itinerary is easier since it is often downhill.

> ▶ *Walk across the square and along rue des Pierres-Plantées to the junction with rue du Bon-Pasteur.*

From the square there is a fine view of the town and Fourvière hill.

> ▶ *Walk down the steps (montée de la Grande-Côte lower down) to rue des Tables-Claudiennes. Turn right towards the Amphithéâtre des Trois-Gaules.*

Amphithéâtre des Trois Gaules

According to the dedication discovered at the bottom of a well in 1958, this venerable spot was built in 19 BC by Rufus as a meeting place for delegates from the 60 Gallic tribes. Extended during the reign of Emperor Hadrian, it became sadly notorious during the days of Marcus Aurelius as the place where followers of the new Christian faith were tortured. Among them was St Blandine who perished here in 177 (a post in the arena marks the site of her martyrdom).

> ▶ *Via montée des Carmélites, place Morel and rue des Chartreux, walk to rue Ornano. It is possible to reach Église St-Bruno (Baroque church) by continuing along rue des Chartreux, turning left onto rue Dupont then left again.*

> ▶ *Rue Ornano leads to place Rouville.*

Place Rouville

From the square there is a fine **view**★ over Lyon. Jutting out from above the

seemingly endless sea of red rooftops on the peninsula is the belfry of the Hôtel de Ville and the Part-Dieu district overlooked by the tower of the Crédit Lyonnais bank on the left, and on the right, the spires of the church of St-Nizier. The final meander of the Saône flows past the hill at Fourvière; the belfry of the church of St-Paul can be seen at the foot of the hill. On the north side of the square, nos 5 and 6 house the **Maison Brunet** with its 365 windows, a typical silk worker's dwelling.

> ▶ *Head down toward the quaysides of the Saône via passage Gonin.*

To the west, the shaded terraces of the Chartreux gardens overlook the river. Note the games areas reserved for playing boules.

Quai St-Vincent

From the quay there are views over the meander in the Saône overlooked by a row of buildings with Art Nouveau façades (caryatids, floral patterns).
Upriver is a vast architectural complex, known as **Les Subsistances**, consisting of an early-17C cloister, later turned into an army supply-storage space and extended by the addition of a large square building with two mills in the centre. The restored complex is now occupied by artists *(visits: information available at the mill).*

> ▶ *Turn back and walk along quai St-Vincent as far as rue de la Martinière.*

At the beginning of the street, on the right, there is a fine painted wall known as the **Fresque des Lyonnais;** it is the work of the Cité de la Création.

> ▶ *Rue du Sergent to place Sathonay.*

Place Sathonay

On the north side of the square are the monumental steps of montée de l'Amphithéâtre, flanked by two lion-shaped fountains.

> ▶ *Rue Vittet to place Tobie-Robatel.*

The **École La Martinière des Jeunes Filles** (finishing school for young ladies), built at the turn of the 20C, is a fine example of the architecture of this period, with its polychrome mosaics and wrought-iron entrance.

▸ *Rue Terme and rue d'Algérie lead back to place des Terreaux.*

Sights

La Presqu'île

Église St-Bonaventure

St Bonaventura's Church, which the people of Lyon cherish, has retained its original Franciscan layout. The bareness and simplicity of the architecture are a reminder of the Franciscans' respect for all forms of poverty.

Église St-Nizier

Tradition has it that the present church of St-Nizier, much of which dates from the 15C, was built on the site of Lyon's very first church. On the outside, the nave is supported by double flying buttresses which can be seen clearly from rue de la Fromagerie. The spires on the bell-towers of the church of St-Nizier are one of the outstanding features of Lyon's urban landscape.

Musée de l'Imprimerie ★★

13 rue de la Poulaillerie (metro Cordeliers). Open daily except Mon and Tue 9.30am –noon, 2pm–6pm. Closed public holidays. 4€. 04 78 37 65 98. www.imprimerie.lyon.fr.

The splendid late-15C Hôtel de la Couronne, once the property of a rich merchant, houses this printing museum. The collections retrace the glorious history of printing, from the invention of the printing press in the 15C.

Musée des Hospices civils

1 place de l'Hôpital *(Bellecour metro station).* Open Jul–Sept daily except Sat–Sun, 10am–noon, 1.30pm–5.30pm (Mon, 10am–5.30pm); rest of year 1st and 3rd Sun in each month, 1.30pm–5.30pm. Closed public holidays. 04 72 41 30 42.

This museum is housed in the 17C building of the Hôtel-Dieu extended by Soufflot in the 18C. It contains an important collection of old ceramics used in pharmacies, a considerable amount of furniture including fine chests of drawers, objects made of pewter, objets d'art, in particular a bust by Coustou. Also on display are instrument cases once used by dentists, surgeons and doctors.

Palais St-Pierre★

Pl. des Terreaux.

This 17C and 18C building was formerly the abbey of the Ladies of St Peter, one of the oldest Benedictine abbeys in Lyon, whose nuns were recruited among the highest ranks of French aristocracy. Inside, the buildings have retained part of their original Italianate decor, particularly in the refectory and main staircase. The building fell into disuse during the Revolution and was turned into a museum in the 19C. In 1884 the artist Puvis de Chavannes painted the "Sacred Wood" in the staircase at the entrance to the Fine Arts Gallery.

Ancienne Église St-Pierre

Next to no 23 rue Paul-Chenavard.

Note the narrow 12C façade of the former church of St-Pierre and the austere Romanesque doorway flanking superb 18C wooden doors.

Musée des Beaux-Arts★★★

20 pl. des Terreaux *(Métro Hotel-de-Ville-L.-Pradel)* Open daily except Tue, 10am–6pm (Fri, 10.30am–8pm). Closed public holidays. 04 72 10 17 40.

From place des Terreaux, enter the gardens in the former cloisters, where the galleries are surmounted by terraces. Tall loggias crown the corner pavilions on the south side. The statues here include *The Shadow* by Rodin and *Carpeaux at Work* by Bourdelle.

The Musée des Beaux-Arts ranks among the finest museums in France. Its splendid collections, carefully displayed, have been further enriched by the donation of 35 famous Impressionist and modern paintings of Jacqueline Delubac's private collection. The Fine Arts Gallery presents an exceptional overview of art through the centuries, throughout the world. Its collections are organised into five separate departments: painting, sculpture, antiquities, objets d'art and medals.

Paintings

The rooms contain a selection of works from the great periods in European painting.

Sculpture

There are works from the Romanesque to the Gothic and Renaissance periods. Among the 17C to early-20C works, the most outstanding are busts by Coysevox and Lemoyne, and marble and bronze statues by Etex, Pradier, Bourdelle, Maillol and Rodin.

Antiquities

This department consists of three sections organised by theme. The **Egyptian section** contains the most extensive collections covering art from all the Ancient Egyptian periods. In the **Near and Middle East section,** note the "priest's head" from Assyria, heads of statues from Cyprus and lead sarcophagi from Roman Syria (3C-6C). The final section covers art from **Ancient Greece and Rome,** and includes an exceptional Korah (statue of a young girl) from the Acropolis illustrating the degree of skill attained by the sculptors of Ancient Greece.

Objets d'art

This section of the museum comprises a huge variety of exhibits from all ages and all continents.

Basilique St-Martin-d'Ainay

This church consecrated by Pope Pascal II in 1107 has undergone major alterations. The porch-belfry is topped by a pyramid roof, surrounded by unusual corner acroteria which give it its characteristic outline. Note the animal frieze beneath the cornice between the second and third levels, and the decoration of inlaid bricks.

Musée des Tissus★★★

34 rue de la Charité (metro Ampère–Victor-Hugo). ○*Open daily except Mon: Textile Museum 10am–5.30pm.* ○*Closed public holidays.* ◎*5€.* ☎*04 78 38 42 00. www.musee-des-tissus.com.*

The Textile Museum, founded by the Lyon Chamber of Commerce over a century ago and housed in the Hôtel de Villeroy (1730), former residence of the governor of the province, is the pride of the Lyon people, and a veritable "repository" of decorative fabrics.

The prestigious collections come from the most influential Western and Eastern countries as regards fabric design and production.

Musée des Arts Décoratifs★★

30–34 rue de la Charité.
○*Open daily except Mon 10am–noon, 2pm–5.30pm.* ○*Closed public holidays.* ◎*5€.* ☎*04 78 38 42 00. www.musee-des-tissus.com.*

This museum is housed in a mansion built in 1739 and is mainly devoted to 18C furnishings. The collection includes pieces of furniture, objets d'art, musical instruments, tapestries, porcelain and faience. Among the sections devoted to Medieval and Renaissance art, the gallery containing over 200 examples of 15C and 16C Italian majolica is of special interest.

Left Bank

Musée d'Art Contemporain★

81 Cité Internationale – Quai Charles-de-Gaulle.
&○*Open Wed, Sat, Sun 10am–7pm, Thu, Fri noon-7pm.* ◎*8€.* ○*Closed 1 May, 25 Dec.* ☎*04 72 69 17 17. www.moca-lyon.org.*

This new cultural focus in the Cité Internationale complex is built around the atrium of the old market hall.

Its modern structure allows for great flexibility of display and for works of art to be exhibited to their best advantage.

The museum collection is presented as a standing exhibition presented alongside "display areas" designed for temporary shows.

The collection is very varied, as since its first acquisition (*Ambiente Spaziale* by Fontana) the museum has been a "production centre" with works by Baldessari, Brecht, Filliou, Kosuth, Yvonnet and numerous other artists.

Musée Lumière

Jacques Croizer/istockphoto.com

Muséum d'Histoire Naturelle★★

Entrance on boulevard des Belges.
&⚿Open daily except Mon 10am–6pm.
Closed 1 Jan, 1 May, 1 Nov and 25 Dec.
≈4€. ☎04 72 69 05 00. www.museedes
confluences.fr.
This Natural History Museum, founded in 1879 by the industrialist and scientist **Émile Guimet** (founder of another museum, of the same name, in Paris), is being entirely renovated.

Centre d'Histoire de la Résistance et de la Déportation★

14 avenue Berthelot (metro Jean-Macé).
⚿Open daily except Mon and Tue.
9am–5.30pm (Sat, Sun, 9.30am–6pm).
⚿Closed Christmas school holidays and
public holidays except 8 May. ≈4€. ☎04
78 72 23 11. www.lyon.fr.
The museum is set up in part of buildings that from 1882 to the early 1970s were the Military Medical School and which, from 1942 to 1944, housed the headquarters of the Gestapo in this region. The aim of the museum is to keep alive the memory of the events relating to the Resistance, the Deportation of its members and of the Jews,

in France and in Lyon in particular and the Liberation.

Musée des Moulages

3 rue Rachais (metro Garibaldi).
⚿open mid-Sept–Jun Tue, Thu 2pm–6pm.
⚿Closed school and public holidays. ☎04
72 84 81 12.
This fascinating museum, housed in a renovated ready-made clothes workshop, is devoted to the history of sculpture from archaic Greece to the 19C.

Musée Africain

150 cours Gambetta (metro Garibaldi).
⚿Open Wed–Sun 2pm–6pm (last admission 5pm). ⚿Closed Aug, 1 Jan, Easter,
1 May, 24, 25 and 31 Dec. ≈8€. ☎04 78
61 60 98. www.musee-africain-lyon.org.
This museum has three floors exhibiting over 2,500 objects from West Africa, particularly Benin and Côte d'Ivoire.

Musée Lumière

*25 rue du Premier-Film, Lyon-Monplaisir
(metro Monplaisir-Lumière).*
⚿Open daily except Mon 11am–6.30pm.
⚿Closed 1 Jan, 1 May, 25 Dec. ≈6€. ☎04
78 78 18 95. www.institut-lumiere.org.
Antoine Lumière, the father of Auguste and Louis who invented the cinema and the autochrome plate had this residence built between 1889 and 1901 in the majestic style favoured by the wealthy bourgeoisie during the transitional period between the Second Empire and Art Nouveau. The interior houses the **Institut Lumière** and hosts events based on still and moving pictures. An exhibition retraces the life of the Lumière family and explains the early stages of the cinema.

Musée urbain Tony-Garnier

*On both sides of boulevard des
États-Unis, between rue Paul-Cazeneuve
and rue Jean-Sarrazin; public entrance:
4 rue des Serpollières.*
&⚿Open daily Tue–Sun 2pm–6pm
(Mar–Oct Sat 11am–7pm). ⚿Closed public holidays and school holidays in Dec).
≈6€ (children: 4€). ☎04 78 75 16 75.
www.museeurbaintonygarnier.com.
This group of buildings was built in the 1930s by the urban architect **Tony Garnier**, a native of Lyon whose most

famous landmark in Lyon is the great covered market. Since 1991 many of the blind walls of these large buildings have been decorated with murals painted by a group of artists calling themselves **"The City of Creation."**

Walking Tours

Cité Internationale to La Part-Dieu

Cité Internationale
This vast complex, comprising an imposing Conference Centre (Palais des Congrès), cinemas (14 screens), hotels and a Museum of Contemporary Art, was installed between the Tête d'Or Park and the Rhône.

Parc de la Tête d'Or★
♿ ◷ *Open mid-Apr–mid Oct 6.30am–10.30pm; mid-Oct–mid Apr 6.30am–8.30pm. ☎04 72 10 30 30. www.lyon.fr.*
The name of the English-style gardens surrounding the Conference Centre derives from local folklore, which claims that a golden head of Christ is buried here. The entrance is marked by huge wrought-iron gates. The park is an ideal place to go walking and cycling and there is also a narrow-gauge railway. A subway leads to the **Île du Souvenir,** a small island rising from the lake.

Serres★ and Jardin Botanique
◷ Open: *Gardens: Oct–Mar 8am–5pm; Apr–Sept 8am–6pm; Alpine garden: Mar–Oct: 8am–11.30am; Serres: Oct–Mar 9am–4.30pm; Apr–Sept 9am–5.30pm, except the garden of Madagascar, which is closed 11.30am–1.30pm. ☎04 72 82 35 02. www.jardin-botanique-lyon.com.*
The **botanical gardens** are laid out to the south-east end of the park and consist of acres of outdoor plants, great glasshouses containing tropical vegetation including numerous palm trees, and an Alpine garden where you are taken on a miniature tour of the world's mountainous areas and their plant life.

Jardin Zoologique
◷ Open: *Zoo: 9am–5pm (8pm in summer); Cat and Reptile Houses: 1pm–5pm (Sat–Sun 2pm–5pm).*
The **zoological park** located north of the botanical gardens is one of the oldest in Europe (1858). It has 1,100 animals including numerous wild animals from outside Europe. West of the zoo lies the deer park. Between the two, on **place** de Guignol, children's activities (merry-go-round, games) and Guignol shows are organised by the **Véritable Guignol du Vieux Lyon** team (☎04 78 28 60 41. www.theatre-guignol.com).

Grande Roseraie★
◷ *Open mid-Apr–mid Oct 6am–11pm; mid-Oct–mid Apr 6am–9pm. ☎04 72 69 47 60.*
The **great rose gardens** are laid out between the lake and quai Achille-Lignon, and boast 70,000 plants representing 350 varieties which are a stunning sight between June and October.

La Part-Dieu district
The name of the district ("God's Area"), suggests that it was once placed under divine protection by a landowner during the Middle Ages. A vast complex spread out over what was once Army land, it is built around a pedestrian precinct (raised 6m/20ft above ground level) and consists of a large number of buildings and towers, including government offices, a hotel, the shopping centre, the radio studios and the library.
The **Crédit Lyonnais Tower,** affectionately known as "The Pencil" by locals, has now become the second most famous landmark in the city after the Fourvière Towers, and its brick-red colour blends in well with the rooftops of the old urban districts. To the east is the new **La Part-Dieu** station built to accommodate the TGV high-speed train. Hotel facilities and residential apartments complete this new development. Modern sculptures and gardens enhance the esplanades.

Quaysides along the Rhône
Quai Augagneur, by the Hôtel-Dieu, is lined with imposing bourgeois houses built in the late 19C. This wonderful esplanade beneath the plane trees is

enhanced by the lively atmosphere of an open-air market *(except Mondays)*, and is particularly attractive in misty weather, when the river is turbulent and fast-flowing. The district of Les Brotteaux, with its geometrically laid out streets, stretches to the east; it lies on the site of sandbanks *("brotteaux")* once deposited by the Rhône, hence its name.

From Wilson bridge the **view**★ extends to the heights of La Croix-Rousse on the other bank, where the tall houses of the former silk workers rise one above the other.

Gerland district

This district sits opposite the confluence of the Rhône and the Saône and with a covered meat market at its centre. The area is one large "Science and Technology Park" and incorporates a high-level technical college, the Institut Pasteur, the Institut Mérieux and a sports centre. The International School, built to designs by the architects Jourda and Perraudin, is a glass construction overlooking the Parc Gerland.

Tony Garnier created the huge meat market or abattoir in 1914. Its restored gigantic metal framework is now the setting for cultural and commercial events.

Outskirts

La Mulatière

Grand aquarium de Lyon ★
7 rue S.-Déchant (Bastéro bus stop).
Take bus 63 from Perrache towards Oullins. ⊞ *Large car park.* ⊙*Open Wed–Sun 11am–7pm (school holidays, daily, 11am–7pm).* ⊙*Closed 1 Jan, 1 May, 24 and 25 Dec.* ⊛*13€ (children up to 12, 9€, children under 1 metre, free).* ☎*04 72 66 65 66. www.aquariumlyon.fr.*
Kids This new, rather unobtrusive building on the banks of the Saône offers you a journey to the different rivers and oceans of the world: impressive fish reign supreme in rivers of temperate climates; nearby, sharks swim round a wreck inside a huge pool on two levels; a myriad of small brightly coloured fish of all shapes feel quite at home in tropical waters.

Villeurbanne

Adjacent to the Part-Dieu district, the municipality of Villeurbanne owes its name to the Villa Urbana, an important agricultural complex established by the Romans on the Cusset hill. The development of the town is relatively recent and it is interesting to note how it has always made a point of being independent from Lyon. After the first wave of silk manufacturers at the end of the 19C, the expansion of the town increased during the 20C and in the 1930s Villeurbanne asserted its specificity by building the spectacular skyscraper district. Today, the town is continuing to develop, concentrating its efforts on culture: a popular national theatre (TNP), an ultra-modern reference library, a museum of contemporary art, the antique-dealers' hall (boulevard de Stalingrad) where no fewer than 150 antique shops can be found.

Skyscrapers
Metro Gratte-Ciel.
Around 1930, at the height of the economic crisis, the housing facilities in Villeurbanne were totally inadequate in view of the town's fast-growing population. The mayor, Lazare Goujon, launched his city into a daring development programme: the town centre, which was the first project to be completed, was soon nicknamed **"Skyscraper City"** as its unique architectural style was more reminiscent of North-American buildings than of French suburbia. Avenue Barbusse ends with the imposing and austere **town hall** designed by R Giroud: a belfry towers over the façade decorated with fluted columns.

▸ *Walk down cours de la République towards cours Tolstoï and cross over.*

Nouveau Musée (Institut d'Art Contemporain)
11 rue du Docteur-Dolard (metro République).
&⊙*Open Jun–Sept Wed–Sun 1pm–7pm (Thu 1pm–8pm); Oct–May daily except*

Belfry tower of the town hall, Villeurbanne

Mon and Tue, 1pm–6pm (Thu 1pm–8pm). ⊙Closed 1 Jan, 1 May, 25 Dec. ⊜4€. ☎04 78 03 47 00. www.i-art-c.org.
Created in 1978, the Association Nouveau Musée moved into this space a few years ago; there is an information section and an area presenting themed exhibitions on contemporary art.

Maison du Livre, de l'Image et du Son

247 cours Émile-Zola (metro Flachet). &⊙Open daily except Sun, 11am–7pm (Sat 10am–6pm). ⊙Closed public holidays. ☎04 78 68 04 04. www.bm.villeur banne.fr.
This reference library, designed in 1988 by the famous architect Mario Botta, is spread over five storeys round a central light shaft.

West of Lyon

Île Barbe

From the mass of greenery on Île Barbe peeks the tip of a Romanesque bell-tower. The island, now a quiet residential area, was once the site of one of the region's most influential abbeys.

▷ *Leave Lyon to the NW (towards Mâcon), then follow D 7 towards Charbonnières.*

The vast **Lacroix-Laval Park** (⊙open May–Sept 6am–10pm; Oct–Apr 7am–8pm) in Marcy-l'Étoile is one of the "lungs" of Lyon. A small tourist train, **Le Furet** takes you on a tour of the château and park.

Château de la Poupée★

Kids &⊙Open daily except Mon, 10am–5pm. ⊙Closed 1 Jan, 1 May, 1 Nov, 25 Dec. ⊜4€. ☎04 78 87 87 00.
At the eastern end of Lacroix-Laval Park stands an elegant 18C château which houses an exceptional private collection of dolls dating from the 18C to the present day.

Charbonnières-les-Bains

10km/6mi to the NW, heading towards Mâcon, then N 7.
Set in woodland formerly worked by the charcoal burners, the Vale of Charbonnières is a traditional holiday resort popular with the people of Lyon. The ferruginous spring here was officially discovered by a priest in 1778. Pump rooms and a casino were soon opened. In 1900, people flocked to the spa, which quickly gained a reputation for excellence. The baths were closed down and demolished a few years ago.

Banks of the Saône★
38km/24mi round tour – allow 3hr

▶ *Leave Lyon to the N, in the direction of Trévoux. The pleasant D 433 follows the east bank of the river, bordered by vegetation, as far as La Rochetaillée.*

The river banks are a favourite weekend destination with Lyon residents, who come to stroll along the towpath, or to indulge in a light lunch of fried fish washed down with a bottle of Beaujolais in one of the many riverside restaurants.

Musée de l'Automobile Henri-Malartre★★

🕐*Open daily except Mon 9am–6pm; Jul–Aug 10am–7pm).* 🕐*Closed last week in Jan, 1 Jan and 25 Dec.* ⊛*6€* ☏*04 78 22 18 80. www.musee-malartre.com.*
This restored 15C castle and its terraced grounds overlooking the Saône, contain remarkable collections of motor cars (1890–1986), cycles (1818–1960), motorcycles (1904–64) and public transport vehicles (1886–1935), all in full working order. Of the 150 **cars** on show, 50 date from before 1914, and 18 were built in Lyon, a reminder of the fact that there were over 100 manufacturers in the region in the adventurous early days of the motor car. Some of the exhibits are unique, such as the Rochet-Schneider (1895), the Gobron-Brillié (1898), the Luc Court (1901) and the Thieulin (1908).
The collection of cycles ranges from the hobby horse to Anquetil's bicycle, not forgetting the amazing "Penny Farthings." Over 50 **motorcycles** are on show, including a Herdtlé-Bruneau (1904), the Koehler-Escoffier (1935) ridden by Georges Monneret, side-cars and a Zundapp (1937) used by the German Army in Africa and Russia.

▶ *Drive on towards D 433 and turn right.*

Neuville-sur-Saône
The town lies in a picturesque setting on a bend of the Saône. The church, topped by twin bell-towers dating from the 17C, contains a set of wood panelling by Perrache, a sculptor from Lyon (18C).

Trévoux
🕐*See VILLEFRANCHE-SUR-SAÔNE.*

▶ *Take D 933 and turn left onto D 504 towards Villefranche.*

Villefranche-sur-Saône
🕐*See VILLEFRANCHE-SUR-SAÔNE.*

▶ *Return to Lyon on N 6.*

Monts du Lyonnais★

This attractive mountainous region lying to the south-west of Lyon has a pastoral appearance with chestnut groves and oakwoods.
Land in low-lying valleys is given over to market gardening, vineyards and orchards, whereas pastures extend over the higher ground.
This is essentially cattle breeding country, where traditional rural housing is still very prominent and industrial activity confined to towns.
The best way to experience the Monts du Lyonnais is to drive to St-Étienne, and then do a slightly different return journey the next day.

Landscape of Monts du Lyonnais

⒈Lyon to St-Étienne
128km/80mi – allow one day

This tour heads first for the Col de la Luère, a pleasant forest pass. Half way between Col de la Luère and Col de Malval, close to St-Bonnet-le-Froid Château, the road affords a nice **view**★ of the Brévenne valley.

Zoos seem to abound here: first at Courzieu (**Parc Animalier de Courzieu** Kids ⏱*Open Mar–Oct 10am–7pm. Falconry displays: 2.30pm and 4.30pm.* ✆*12.50€ (children: 8.90€).* ☎*04 74 70 96 10. www.parc-de-courzieu.fr)*, and then at St-Martin-la-Plaine (**Parc Zoologique de St-Martin-la-Plaine** Kids ⏱*Apr–Sept: 9am–6pm; Oct, Nov, Feb, Mar: 10am–5pm.* ⏱*Dec–Jan.* ✆*12€ (3–10-year-olds: 8€).* ☎*04 77 75 18 68. www. espace-zoologique.com.*

⒉St-Étienne to Lyon
108km/67mi – allow one day

The return journey visits the lovely village of **Veauche**, on the edge of a plateau overlooking the Loire, and popular among archaeologists and art lovers.

The village of **St-Galmier** may not be well known, but its product is: although the spring coming from this town was known to the Romans, it was only in the early 19C that it was marketed on a large scale, thanks to the enterprising spirit of **Augustin Saturnin Badoit**, who decided to bottle this naturally sparkling water. Backed by an aggressive promotional campaign both in France and abroad, sales of Badoit rapidly reached record figures.

Further on, **Chazelles-sur-Lyon** in the foothills of the Lyonnais area, owes its fame to the production of high quality felt hats, commemorated in the **Musée du Chapeau** (☎*04 77 94 23 29; www. museeduchapeau.com*).

The route continues through the fortified village of **St-Symphorien-sur-Coise**, followed by the peaceful Notre-Dame de la Neylière, views of **St-Foy-l'Argentière** (seen from just north of **Aveize**) and views of the **Brévenne Valley** as you approach Col de la Croix-de-Part on the D 25..

MAURIAC★

POPULATION 4,019

MICHELIN MAP 330: B-3 – 19KM/11.8MI NW OF SALERS

Situated between the River Dordogne and Puy Mary, this small town, which is an important agricultural trading centre, consists of black, lava stone houses on the edge of a vast basalt plateau.

- **Information:** 1 r. Chappe-d'Auteroche, 15200 MAURIAC ☎04 71 67 30 26.
- **Orient Yourself:** 20km/12mi NW from Salers, 50km/31mi north of Aurillac.
- **Organising Your Time:** 2–3 hours will suffice to wander around Mauriac.
- **Also See:** SALERS, AURILLAC, ST-FLOUR.

Basilique Notre-Dame-des-Miracles★

This is the most important Romanesque building in upper Auvergne, erected between the 12C and the 14C. The elegant east end has three chapels. The vast main doorway at the west front is the best piece of Romanesque carving in the area.

Around place Georges-Pompidou are a few old houses including one with double Romanesque bays.

Additional Sights

Note the old houses with twinned Romanesque openings surrounding place Georges-Pompidou:

Monastère St-Pierre

Open daily, 10am–noon, 2pm–6pm. Closed Tue during Oct–Mar, l and 8 May. 3€. ☎04 71 68 07 24. This monastery was once a daughter-house of Église St-Pierre-le-Vif in Sens. It is possible to see a few Gallo-Roman remains, some of the foundations of the Carolingian church (early 9C), the 11C **chapter house** (columns made with local marble) and part of the **cloisters** (14C-15C) separated from the chapter-house by an arch with double columns.

- Follow rue du Collège.

Hôtel d'Orcet

Currently the Sous-Préfecture. This 16C-18C building incorporates the 12C tympanum that decorated the doorway into the monastery refectory: the carving depicts Samson slaying the lion. On the other side of the street stands the monumental gateway to the former Jesuit college.

- Continue along rue du Dr-E.-Chavialle; the first left leads to the museum.

Musée des arts et traditions populaires

Same admission times and charges as the Monastère St-Pierre. ☎04 71 68 07 24. Housed in a former prison, this museum has a range of collections: Gallo-Roman ceramics, religious artefacts etc. There are temporary exhibitions of regional arts and crafts (leather-working, cheese-making etc).

Excursions

Puy St-Mary

Climb up to the chapel at the top of the grassy hill known as Puy St-Mary. From here there is a panoramic view of Mauriac and the mountains of Cantal on one side and the plateaux bordering the Auvergne and the Limousin on the other.

Château de la Vigne

Open mid-Jun–mid Sept 2pm–7pm. Chateau only: 5€. ☎04 71 69 00 20. This 15C castle is flanked by two round towers topped by pepper-pot roofs, and a square tower that served as a keep and to which, in the 18C, a second building was attached; a watch-path runs around the top. Inside, there are 16C **frescoes** on the walls and ceiling of the Salle de Justice; other rooms are also tastefully appointed (panelling; canopy bed with barley-twist columns; coffered ceiling).

Driving Tour

Churches of the northern plateaux

Round trip of 70km/44mi – allow a day

▶ *Head NE from Mauriac on D 922 and turn right onto D 678.*

Église du Vigean

In the small church is a **reliquary**★ made of 13C Limousin enamelwork.

▶ *Follow D 678. About 2km/1mi before reaching Moussages, take D 12.*

Moussages

Overlooking a square decorated with an old fountain and surrounded by old houses is the **church**, whose Romanesque east end has carved modillions.

▶ *Leave N on D 22 then turn right.*

Château d'Auzers★

○ *Open Easter-Oct: guided tours (1hr) 2pm–6.30pm.* ⊛*5€.* ☎*04 71 78 62 59. www.auzers.com.*
This 14C and 16C castle comprises a central building flanked by two high turrets crowned by pepper-pot roofs. The terrace running along the southern façade offers a sweeping **view** of the vast meadows extending to the steep Marilhoux Valley and the Cantal summits in the distance.

▶ *2km/1mi after leaving Auzers, turn right onto D 22, heading to Saignes.*

Saignes

This small but appealing summer resort perched above the Sumène valley has a Romanesque church built in typical Auvergnat tradition and several quaint 15C **houses**. The rocky promontory still carries vestiges of the former castle and the tiny Chapelle Notre-Dame.

Château d'Auzers

▶ *Turn right towards Le Monteil then left onto D 36.*

Chastel-Merlhac

Its circular shape makes this eroded lava flow look like a basalt fortress.

▶ *Return to Saignes and turn NE onto D 236 towards Riom; turn right onto D 15 then right again onto D 3.*

Antignac

The **Jardins ethnobotaniques** (○*open daily except Sat at 3pm;* ○*closed 1 Jan and 25 Dec;* ⊛*5€, no charge 1 May;* ☎*04 71 40 23 76)* grow plants of medieval origin found on archaeological sites.

▶ *Leave Antignac on D 3 to Bort-les-Orgues; turn left on D 15, then D 315.*

Ydes-Bourg

The exhibition called **Insectes du Monde** *(entrance behind the town hall.* Kids ᕫ ○*open Jul-Aug 2pm–7pm.* ⊛*3€.* ☎*04 71 40 82 51)* is mainly devoted to butterflies and moths, many of which come from Hungary, Mexico and Pakistan.

▶ *Rejoin D 922; right to Bassignac.*

Bassignac

Kids The **Jardin botanique textile** *(*○*open mid-Jun–mid Sept 10am–noon, 2pm–7pm;* ⊛*4€ (children: 2.50€);* ☎*04 71 67 32 50)* is devoted to textiles and weaving. The garden grows more than 150 species of textile plants as well as plants used in dyeing.

▶ *Rejoin D 922 to return to Mauriac.*

LE MONASTIER-SUR-GAZEILLE

POPULATION 1,734

MICHELIN MAP 331: G-4

This large village in Haute-Loire derives its name from the largest Benedictine monastery in the Velay area, founded in the late 7C. St Calmin, Count of Auvergne, founded the monastery and became its first abbot. In AD 728 St Théofrède, his successor, was murdered during a Saracen raid. The monastery was raised from the ruins and for several centuries enjoyed an extraordinarily wide-ranging influence. In the late 12C the abbey boasted 235 daughter-houses or priories.

- **Information:** Mairie, 43150 Le MONASTIER-SUR-GAZEILLE. ☎04 71 08 37 76.
- ▶ **Orient Yourself:** The village is 17km/11mi south-east from Le Puy-en-Velay.
- ⏱ **Organising Your Time:** Allow one hour to visit the church.
- ⚑ **Also See:** Le PUY-EN-VELAY, MONISTROL-SUR-LOIRE, ST-FLOUR.

A Bit of History

Stevenson's travels - In front of the post office is a memorial commemorating the travels undertaken across the Cévennes, in the autumn of 1878, by the Scottish writer **Robert Louis Stevenson**, author of *Treasure Island.* As much to satisfy his wish to travel as to try and retrace the spirit that once fired the *Camisards,* or Protestant rebels, Stevenson, then aged 28, decided to cross the Cévennes on foot from Le Monastier to Alès, accompanied only by a somewhat capricious donkey. Sleeping outdoors or in any inns he happened to come across (with one menu for all, and all visitors sleeping in the one room), he took 12 days to reach Alès. His travel notebook is a mine of humorous and penetrating observations on the wonderful countryside he discovered and the people he met on his way. His travels were full of comic incidents, which he recounts with glee.

To carry the strange sleeping bag that he had made, Stevenson acquired the donkey which he immediately christened Modestine. The conflict between the obstinacy of the Scottish novelist and the strong will of the donkey from the Velay lasted for the entire trip: "Modestine's pace is quite beyond description. It was something much slower than a stroll, when a stroll is much slower than a walk. She held back each hoof for an incredibly long time…"

Sights

Abbey Church

The Romanesque church built in the 11C underwent extensive alterations in the 15C. The abbey's treasures include a stone Pietà dating from the 15C, and two lengths of Byzantine silk used to shroud the bodies of the founding saints.

Musée Municipal

♿ ⏱ *Open Jul–Aug daily except Tue 10.30am–noon, 2pm–6pm; Sept daily except Mon, 10.30am–noon, 2.30pm–5pm; Jun and Oct daily except Mon, 2.30pm–5pm.* 🚫*Closed Nov–May.* ☎04 71 03 80 01.

The local museum is housed in the vaulted chambers of the **abbey castle**. The collections illustrate the history of regional life (lace, traditional costumes), and the prehistoric period in the Upper Loire Valley. One of the rooms deals solely with **Robert Louis Stevenson**.

Nave of the abbey church

J. Damase/MICHELIN

MONISTROL-SUR-LOIRE

POPULATION 7,451
MICHELIN MAP 331: H-2

The town has a surprisingly Mediterranean feel about it, both in its appearance and its climate.

Information: 4 bis r. du Château, 43120 MONISTROL-SUR-LOIRE
☎04 71 66 03 14. www.ot-monistrol.com.

Orient Yourself: Monistrol lies 45km/28mi north-east of Le Puy-en-Velay, and 30km/19mi south-west of St-Étienne.

Parking: Limited parking in the town centre.

Organising Your Time: Relax over a coffee and spend a few hours here.

Also See: ST-ÉTIENNE, LE PUY-EN-VELAY.

The Old Quarter

Château des Evêques

Open Jul–Aug 9am–noon, 2.30pm–6pm (Mon, 9am–noon); rest of year 9am–noon, 2pm–5.30pm (Mon, 9am–noon) Closed holidays except 14 Jul. ☎04 71 66 03 14.

An avenue of lime trees leads to the large round towers of the old **Bishop's Palace** (14C-18C), which now houses the tourist office and hosts temporary exhibitions.

Follow path round château on right.

From the church, take rue du Commerce then the first street on the right.
Take a stroll along the network of narrow **alleyways** and travel back in time, from the Middle Ages to the 17C (Classical façades of the Couvent des Ursulines and Couvent des Capucins).

Excursions

Château de Rochebaron

in Bas-en-Basset (7km/4mi W): 330m/330yd above place des Marronniers, take the path running to the left of the rampart.

The ruins of this medieval castle (11C-13C), perched on a spur overlooking the Loire, are preceded by three rows of protective walls.

Château de Valprivas

In Valprivas, 16 km/ 10mi W.

Open Apr–Sept for guided visits (45min) daily except Mon 10.30am–noon, 3.30pm–6pm. ☎04 71 66 71 33. www.val privas.com.

In the court of honour, the round tower features an unusual spiral staircase entirely sculpted in oak and a porch framed by caryatids and crowned by a coat of arms.

Address Book

For coin ranges, see the Legend on the cover flap.

WHERE TO EAT

L'Air du Temps – *43590 Confolent. 4km/2.4mi E of Beauzac via D 461.* ☎04 71 61 49 05. *Closed Jan, Sun evening and Mon.* This hamlet nestling in the countryside is a good place to stop for a meal, as one of its houses is also a gourmand restaurant run by a former baker-pastry chef.

Table du Barret – *Bransac, 43590 Beauzac. 3km/1.8mi S of Beauzac via D 42.* ☎04 71 61 47 74. *Closed Feb, 10–23 Nov, 24–30 Dec, Tue evening, Sun evening and Wed.* A restaurant set in a house dating from the 1920s in the heart of a peaceful hamlet near the Loire. Owned by a former jeweller and his son, it serves appetising traditional cuisine.

MONTBRISON

POPULATION 14,589
MICHELIN MAP 327: D-6

The town is built around a volcanic mound and dominated by the 18C dome of the old Convent of the Visitation (today the law courts), and by the imposing belfry of its Gothic **church**, Notre-Dame-d'Espérance, which was founded in 1226 (restored 1970). The town was fortified following the attacks by the English army at the start of the Hundred Years War. During the Religious Wars, Montbrison was captured and pillaged by the protestant forces of François de Beaumont in 1562, with the town's garrison thrown from the ramparts.

- **Information:** Cloître des Cordeliers, 42600 MONTBRISON ☎04 77 96 08 69.
- ▶ **Orient Yourself:** 44km/27mi north-west of St-Étienne, via the A 72.
- ⏰ **Organising Your Time:** Allow half a day.
- **Also See:** ST-ÉTIENNE, LYON.

Town Centre

Opposite the church stands **La Diana** (⏰guided tours (1hr) Tue 2pm–5pm, Wed and Sat 9am–noon, 2pm–5pm; ⏰closed public holidays; ⊙5€; ☎04 77 96 01 10; www.ladiana.com), built in 1296.
The **Musée d'Allard** (⏰open daily except Tue 2pm–6pm; guided tours (1h30) on request; ⏰closed 1 Jan and 25 Dec; ⊙3€; ☎04 77 96 39 15) contains a fine collection of minerals and stuffed birds. The town also features several splendid **hôtels particuliers**, notably on rue St-Pierre and rue Puy-de-la-Bâtie.

Old houses
The town features several splendid **hôtels particuliers**, notably on rue St-Pierre (nos 1, 7, 10, 11, 13 and 17) and rue Puy-de-la-Bâtie (nos 5, 9, 11, 14, 18, 19 and 20).

Excursions

Moingt
3km/1.8mi. Leave Montbrison S on D 8. This former Roman city has retained its medieval appearance and narrow winding streets. Note **Église St-Julien** (⏰open during services) and its 11C capitals with interlacing ornamentation.

Église de Champdieu★
4.5km/2.8mi N on D 8.
Champdieu lies on the edge of the Forez plain and hills. It has a remark-

La Diana

J. Damase/MICHELIN

Address Book

&*For coin ranges, see the cover flap.*

WHERE TO STAY

⊜ **Camping Le Bigi** – *42600 Bard. 2km/1.2mi SW of Montbrison via D 113 dir. Lérigneux.* ☎04 77 58 06 39. *Open 15 Apr–15 Oct.* 🕮. *Reservations recommended. 46 sites.* On land formerly used as a nursery, this campground within reach of the Monts du Forez is simple and very well maintained. In addition to the usual features, there are a children's playground and a small pool.

⊜⊜ **Marytel** – *95 rte de Lyon, 42600 Savigneux, 1.5km/1mi E of Montbrison via D 496.* ☎04 77 58 72 00. 🅿. *33 rms.* 🖙*8€.* This modern edifice by the side of the road is protected from road noise by efficient double-glazed windows. The basic, functional rooms are neat and tidy. Above all, a convenient stopover.

WHERE TO EAT

⊜⊜ **Le Vieux Logis** – *4 rte de Lyon, 42210 Montrond-les-Bains.* ☎04 77 54 42 71. *Closed 1–15 Mar, 1–15 Sept, Sun evening and Mon.* In the heart of this little spa town, a family restaurant established in a modern building offering simple, generous cuisine. The 'main dish and dessert' lunch menu and the most basic fixed-price menu are reasonably priced. Terrace in summer.

CHEESE

The cylindrical Fourme de Montbrison, a blue cheese prepared in the Hautes-Chaumes that is creamier than its cousin, La Fourme d'Ambert, has a delicate, distinctive flavour and a velvety, blue-speckled body. Come fill up your shopping basket at the Saturday market and the Journées Annuelles de la Fourme that honour this cheese.

ON THE TOWN

Casino de Montrond-les-Bains – *Le Saxo, Rte de Roanne, 42210 Montrond-les-Bains.* ☎04 77 52 70 70. *10am–4am; discotheque: weekends 10.30pm–4am.* Feel like bucking the odds? Come try your luck at the Montrond-les-Bains Casino, with its 180 slot machines and traditional games (roulette, black jack, etc.). You can celebrate your good fortune at the locally renowned disco, the Saxo, or by popping open a bottle of bubbly at the La Montgolfière Restaurant.

---

able Romanesque **church** which was built for a Benedictine priory. In the 14C the church and priory buildings were heavily fortified.

The most surprising feature of this church is the extent of its system of defence. High arcading forms machicolations on the south side and the south arm of the transept. A similar system of arcading runs along the walls of the priory built on four sides of a quadrangle, with the church forming the south side. The church has two bell-towers, the more outstanding being the one over the transept, which dates from the Romanesque period and has fine semicircular openings.

The second bell-tower, by the west front, dates from the 15C; its base forms the narthex. Note, to the left of the west front's portal, the capital depicting a mermaid with two tails.

St-Romain-le-Puy

7km/4.3mi S of Montbrison.

The church of the former priory of St-Romain-le-Puy which, at the end of the 10C, belonged to the abbey of St-Martin-d'Ainay in Lyon rises on a volcanic peak emerging from the Forez plain, dominating a St-Gobain glassworks at the foot of the peak. Water is bottled from a mineral spring (Source Parot) north-east of the village near D 8.

Église du Prieuré★

◷*Open Apr–Oct daily except Tue, 2.30pm –5pm (Sun, 10.30am–7pm).* ☎04 77 76 92 10.

From the plateau in front of the church, the panorama encompasses a vast circle of mountains: those of Forez to the west, the Monts d'Uzore to the north, the Tarare mountains and those of the

Lyonnais from the north-east to the south-east.

Chalain-d'Uzore
7km N, off the D8.

The 14C-16C **château** (🕐 *open mid-Jul–Aug guided tours at 2.30pm, 3.30pm and 4.30pm;* ⊜ *4€;* ☏ *04 77 97 13 12)* is notable for its former courtroom, converted into a village hall during the Renaissance (imposing fireplace) and for its gallery with sculpted doors.

Montrond-les-Bains ⚓
14km NE on D496.

This spa resort, recommended for obesity and diabetes, has kept its **château** (Kids 🕐 *open Apr–Jun, daily except Tue, 2pm–6pm; Jul–Sept daily except Tue, 2pm–8pm; Oct Sat, Sun, 2pm–6pm;* 🕐 *closed Nov–Easter;* ⊜ *4€;* ☏ *04 77 94 50 31; www.montrond-les-bains.com)*, whose ruins stand proudly on top of a hill near the River Loire.

Although the castle was damaged by fire in the 18C, the outer walls have survived. Beyond the vast porch, decorated with fluted pilasters and capitals, stand the remains of the 14C and 15C building where the lord of the castle lived with his family.

Sury-le-Comtal
13kmSE on D8.

This small town's 17C **château** (📷 ☏ *04 77 52 05 14)* features lavish **ornamentation**★ consisting of sculpted ceilings and intricate wainscoting. There are also several fine fireplaces with carved panels.

Château de la Bastie-d'Urfé★
19km N on D8 and N89.

🐾 *Guided tour (45m): Apr–Jun and Sept–Oct 10am–noon, 2.30pm–6pm (Jul and Aug 10am–noon, 1pm–6pm); Nov–Mar Wed, Fri, Sat, Sun, 2pm–5pm.* 🕐 *Closed 25 Dec–1 Jan.* ⊜ *5€.* ☏ *04 77 97 54 68. http://labastie.chez-alice.fr.*

In the 15C, the rough lords of Urfé built a manor on the banks of the River Lignon. The family's rise to power was rapid. During the Italian Wars Claude d'Urfé spent several years in Rome as an ambassador, and on his return to France he converted Bastie manor into a Renaissance château.

Neptune in Château de la Bastie-d'Urfé's Rockwork Grotto

Honoré d'Urfé (1567–1625), grandson of the ambassador and author of the first French novel, *L'Astrée*, grew up in these refined surroundings.

The original manor (14C-15C) was enlarged in the 16C by Claude d'Urfé, who brought artists from Italy to help with the decoration.

After graduating from Tournon College, Honoré d'Urfé returned to Bastie, where he stayed as the guest of his elder brother. The latter's wife, the beautiful Diane de Châteaumorand, a passionate woman disappointed by her husband, aroused burning passion in the young man. After obtaining the annulment of her first marriage, which had never been consummated, Diane wed her former brother-in-law in 1600. The couple moved to her castle in Châteaumorand, north-west of La Pacaudière. This second marriage was no more successful than the first.

Honoré d'Urfé fled from Châteaumorand and started writing L'Astrée, for which he had already begun to draft a few ideas on his return from Tournon. Published between 1607 and 1628, this extraordinarily popular saga 5,000 pages long set the fashion in France for the novel and all things pastoral.

The interminable love affair of a shepherd, Céladon, and his shepherdess, Astrée, became a bible for the 17C "honest man."

LE MONT-DORE⚜⚜

POPULATION 1,682
MICHELIN MAP 326: D-9 – 45KM/28MI SW OF CLERMONT-FERRAND

Le Mont-Dore stretches out along the banks of the upper reaches of the River Dordogne in a magnificent corrie in the shadow of the Puy de Sancy; it is a spa town (the season lasts from mid-May–early October) and a remarkably well-equipped winter sports resort. The ski area *(see below)* covers the north face of the Puy de Sancy and the slopes of Le Capucin. Paths that are waymarked in winter provide an opportunity to discover the unexpected beauty of the volcanic landscape under snow. In summer the resort offers a wide range of leisure facilities and is an ideal base for ramblers or those touring by car.

- **Information:** Av. de la Libération, 63240 Le MONT-DORE ☎04 73 65 20 21. www.mont-dore.com.
- **Orient Yourself:** Le Mont Dore lies 45km/28 mi to the south-west of Clermont-Ferrand.
- **Don't Miss:** A ride in the ancient funicular.
- **Organising Your Time:** Half a day is sufficient to look around the spa town.
- **Also See:** La BOURBOULE, ORCIVAL, MASSIF DU SANCY, ST-NECTAIRE.

The Spa Town

The waters were used by the Gauls in swimming pools, the remains of which have been discovered beneath the Roman baths. The latter were a splendid sight and much larger than the present establishment. It was not until Louis XIV's reign that the "Mont d'Or," as Mme de Sévigné wrote, regained its clientele – in spite of the fact that there was no road to the resort. The road was not built until the 18C, and the fashion for "taking the waters" emerged in the 19C.

Établissement Thermal

Open May–mid-Oct. Guided tours (45min) daily except Sun at 2pm, 3pm, 4pm and 5pm; mid-Oct–Apr: daily except Sat–Sun at 3pm. Closed 1 Jan, 1 May, 25 Dec. 3.50€. ☎04 73 65 05 10.

The pump rooms were built between 1817 and 1823 and later extended and modernised. The most remarkable rooms are the **Hall des Sources,** the **Salle des Gaz Thermaux**, the **Galerie César**★ and the main foyer (**Salle des Pas Perdus**★).

Inside the spa – Salle des Gaz Thermaux

S. Sauvignier/MICHELIN

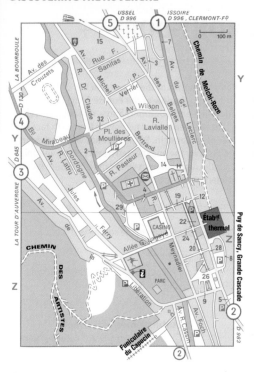

LE MONT-DORE

Apollinaire R. S.	Y	2
Banc R. Jean	Y	3
Chazotte R. Capitaine	Y	4
Clemenceau Av.	Z	5
Clermont Av. de	Y	7
Déportés R. des	Z	8
Duchâtel R.	Z	9
Favart R.	Y	12
Gaulle Pl. Ch.-de	Y	14
Guyot-Dessaigne Av.	Y	15
Montlosier R.	Y	19
Moulin R. Jean	Z	20
Panthéon Pl. du	Z	22
Ramond R.	Z	24
République Pl. de la	Z	26
Rigny R.	Z	28
Sand Allée G.	YZ	29
19-Mars-1962 R. du	Y	32

The Resort

Le Mont-Dore was one of the earliest winter resorts in France, dating from 1907. Situated south of the town, it takes advantage of the elaborate equipment and activities designed for visitors taking the waters (accommodation, skating rink, swimming pool, entertainment). During the winter season there is alpine skiing, monoskiing, snowboarding, cross-country skiing, snowshoeing and climbing frozen waterfalls.

Ski area

Alpine ski runs are on the north slopes of the Sancy, which enjoy good snow cover. In winter, a free shuttle service operates between the town and the slopes. The **ski pass,** which can be bought in Le Mont-Dore, entitles holders to ski on the Super-Besse skiing area (*see BESSE-EN-CHANDESSE*). For **cross-country skiing,** there are marked tracks starting west of Le Mont-Dore (below Le Capucin).

Walks

Chemin de Melchi-Roze

About 1hr on foot. This flat path overlooking the town is a delightful place for a stroll in the late afternoon or in cool weather.

Chemin des Artistes★

About 1hr on foot along the path running down to the tennis courts. This walk leads through the woods and offers attractive views of the resort. It is also possible to reach this path by taking the funicular to Le Capucin *(see below).*

Funiculaire du Capucin★

Open May–Oct 10am–noon, 2pm–6pm (Jul and Aug 9.30am–6.45pm). 5€. ☎04 73 65 01 25.

When this elegant 100 year-old funicular was inaugurated in 1898, it was electrically powered, although the resort itself was not yet enjoying the benefits of electricity. The funicular has two beautiful wooden carriages, which shuttle to the Salon du Capucin.

Address Book

For coin ranges, see the Legend on the cover flap.

WHERE TO STAY

Chambre d'hôte La Closerie de Manou – *Au Genestoux - 3km/1.8mi W of Mont-Dore via D 996, towards Murat-le-Quaire.* 04 73 65 26 81. *Closed 1 Nov–1 Mar.* 5 rms. Nestling in verdure, this 18C Auvergnat house is simply enchanting! Its comfortable bedrooms are harmoniously and tastefully decorated, the reception is delightful and breakfast is succulent.

WHERE TO EAT

Mon Clocher – *5 r. Sauvagnat.* 04 73 65 05 41. Mon Clocher is ideally located in the heart of Mont Dore's pedestrian and shopping zone between the church, the casino and the spa. The dining room's decor is unabashedly countrified: old farming implements, shining copper pots hanging from the walls etc.

Le Bougnat – *23 r. Georges-Clemenceau.* 04 73 65 28 19. *Closed 10 Nov–15 Dec. Reservations required.* The furnishings chosen to decorate this old restored *buron* are faithful to tradition.

Salon du Capucin

10min by funicular then 8min on foot.
This pleasant clearing, a highly popular destination during the peak season, is reached by a picturesque funicular railway dating from the Edwardian era.

Pic du Capucin★

1hr walk from Salon du Capucin.
The path runs for some distance through woodland. From the summit of Le Capucin there is a particularly fine view of the Massif du Sancy.

Excursions

Fontaine Pétrifiante

3km/2mi NW along D 996.

Waterfalls

3km/2mi NE via Le Queureuilh and Prends-toi-Garde hamlets. About 3hr on foot.
The most outstanding of the three cascades (Saut du Loup, Queureuilh and Rossignolet) is the **Queureuilh**★ which drops down in a very attractive natural setting.

Puy de la Tache

5km/3mi E then 1hr 30min on foot there and back. The

road rises in a series of hairpin bends up to **Col de la Croix-Morand** where the landscape becomes increasingly rugged and bare. From here it is possible to walk to the summit of the Puy de la Tache.

Grande Cascade★

3.5km SE along D 36. About 1hr 30min on foot. Beware: the access path can be slippery.
At the waterfall's foot, a footbridge leads to steps to the Plateau de Durbise.

Puy de Sancy★★★

Sancy station situated 4km/2.5mi along D 983. Cable-car ride (3min) then 20min on foot to the summit (see Massif du SANCY).

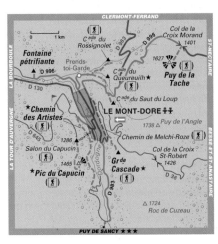

MONTÉLIMAR

POPULATION 31,344

MICHELIN MAP 332: B-6

The name Montélimar derives from a feudal fortress, "Mont-Adhémar," built in the 12C by the powerful Adhémar family. The last member of the family was the Comte de Grignan who lived in the 17C and was the son-in-law of **Madame de Sévigné,** the lady of letters. Of the nine gates that were once part of the town walls, only the **Porte St-Martin** to the north of the town, still stands. The diversion of the Rhône towards Montélimar feeds the **Châteauneuf Power Plant.**

The nearby town of Privas occupies an unusual **site**★ in the Ouvèze basin, at the foot of Mont Toulon. Business concentrates on small industry (milling, sprung bed bases) and *marrons glacés* (candied sweet chestnuts), of which it is the capital.

- **Information:** Allées Provençales, 26200 MONTÉLIMAR ☎04 75 01 00 20. www.montelimar.net.
- ▶ **Orient Yourself:** On the banks of the Rhône, between Valence and Orange.
- **Parking:** There are numerous car parks in and around the centre of town.
- ⊙ **Organising Your Time:** Take it easy and spend a whole day here.
- **Especially for Kids:** Château and Musée de la Miniature.
- ⚭ **Also See:** VALENCE, PRIVAS, VIVIERS.

Old Town

In the centre, around the 15C **Collégiale Ste-Croix,** most of the streets have overhanging eaves. **Place du Marché,** lined with arcades surmounted by façades and wrought-iron balconies, has a southern feel about it. On Place Émile-Loubet is **Diane de Poitiers' house** with its fine façade.

Sights

Château

⊙Open Jul–Aug 9.30am–11.30am, 2pm –6pm; rest of year 9.30am–11.30am, 2pm–5.30pm. ⊙Closed Tue from Nov–Mar, 1 Jan, 25 Dec). ☞4€ (under-11s free). ☎04 75 00 62 30.

The original fortress (12C) to the east of the town was extended in the 14C by order of the Pope. Only the seigneur's lodgings (main apartments) and the watch-path are open to the public.

Allées provençales★

The shaded pavements of these wide half-pedestrianised avenues are the hub of the town's activity and their boutiques offer a wide choice of regional products.

Musée de la Miniature

⊙Open Jul–Aug 10am–6pm; Sept–Jun daily except Mon and Tue. 2pm–6pm. ⊙Closed Jan, 1 Nov, 25 Dec. ☞5€ (children: 3.50€). ☎04 75 53 79 24. www.ville-montelimar.com.

The success of the International Miniature Festival led to the exhibition housed inside the chapel of the Hôtel-Dieu (19C). The miniatures have to meet certain criteria such as the use of the original material and a scale of 1:12.

Excursions

Château de Rochemaure★

7km/4.5mi via D 11 NW – allow 45min. Near Rochemaure Church (follow signs to: Château) take the minor road right of the Mairie.

⊙Open mid-Jul–mid Aug daily except Tue, 10am–noon, 3pm–7pm. ⊙Closed rest of year. ☞3€. ☎04 75 49 08 07.

The ruins of Rochemaure Castle stand on an impressive **site**★★ on the southern edge of the Coiron plateau. The castle (12C-14C) was besieged by the Huguenots in the 16C and 17C and abandoned in the 18C.

Address Book

MONTÉLIMAR

WHERE TO STAY

🛏 **Provence** – *118 av. Jean-Jaurès. ☎04 75 01 11 67. Closed 15 Jan–15 Feb and Sat from Nov–Feb.* 🅿. *16 rms.* 🍽*7€.* Managed by a couple from Alsace and their daughter, this hotel is modest but spick-and-span.

🛏🛏🛏 **Hôtel Les Hospitaliers** – *26160 Poët-Laval, 5km/3mi W of Dieulefit via D 540. ☎04 75 46 22 32. www.hotel-les-hospitaliers.com. Closed 10 Nov–14 Mar.* 🅿. *22 rms.* 🍽*10€. Restaurant*🛏🛏🛏. Enjoying a select location in the village, this hotel occupies a cluster of stone houses with a superb view of the valleys and mountains.

WHERE TO EAT

🍽 **Le Grillon** – *40 r. Cuiraterie. ☎04 75 01 79 02. Closed 12 Jul–2 Aug, Thu, Sun evening and Mon.* Located on a little street in the old town, this restaurant has an inconspicuous façade that leads to a big dining room at the end of a corridor.

ON THE TOWN

Café Cantante – *18 r. Roger-Poyol. ☎04 75 00 01 30. Mon–Sat 6pm–2am.* This unusually alluring, original nightspot is in a class of its own. The fine house, built in 1906, is worth discovering, as are the works of the painters who come to exhibit their works here year-round.

THEATRE

Théâtre Municipal – *1 pl. du Théâtre. ☎04 75 00 79 01. Tickets: Tue–Fri 10am–12.30pm, 3.30pm–6.30pm. Closed Jul–Aug and public holidays.* Built in 1885 in the pure neo-Classical style popular during the Third Republic, the municipal theatre is a symbol of Montélimar's 'Golden Age'. The programmes generally includes popular theatre, dance and classical music concerts.

HOW SWEET IT IS

Nougat Chabert and Guillot – *9 rue Charles-Chabert. ☎04 75 00 82 00. Mon–Sat 8am–12.30pm, 2pm–7pm; Tue–Fri 8am–7.15pm. Closed public holidays.* For nougat aficionados, pros and amateurs alike, this establishment founded in 1913 makes the quintessential Montélimar nougat.

Au Rucher de Provence – *35 bd Desmarais. ☎04 75 52 01 59. Shop: daily 8am–7.30pm; confectionery: tours Mon–Fri 8am–11.30am, by appointment weekends.* The Bonnieu family makes high-quality nougat under two brand names: Stoupany, the oldest (since 1787), and Le Rucher de Provence, launched in 1938.

Escobar Patissier-Confiseur-Chocolatier-Glacier – *2 pl. Léopold-Blanc. ☎04 75 01 25 53. www.nougats-escobar.com. Mon 9.30am–12.30pm, 2pm–7pm; Tue–Sat 8am–12.30pm, 2pm–7.30pm; Sun and public holidays 8am–1pm, 3pm–6.30pm. Closed Sun and public holidays Jun through Aug.* This pastry and chocolate chef belongs to the elite set of genuine Montélimar artisans. His nougat recipe is, of course, a house secret.

PRIVAS (EXCURSION)

WHERE TO STAY

🛏🛏 **Hôtel Chaumette** – *Av. Vanel. ☎04 75 64 30 66. www.hotelchaumette. fr.* 🅿. *36 rms.* 🍽*12€. Restaurant*🛏🛏. Pleasant dining room with contemporary furniture and a wood parquet. Summer terrace and pool.

🛏🛏🛏 **Chambre d'hôte Château de Fontblachère** – *07210 St-Lager-Bressac. 15km/9mi SE of Privas. Take D 22, then D 2 and left onto D 322 opposite the village of St-Lager-Bressac, and follow signs. ☎04 75 65 15 02. www.chateau-fontblachere.com. Closed Nov–Feb; open weekends off-season. 5 rms.* Nestling in the hills of the Ardèche, this gorgeous home promises a peaceful stopover in a simple, elegant setting.

WHERE TO EAT

🍽🍽 **Le Corentin** – *2 pl. de la République - ☎04 75 64 75 75 - closed 1–15 May, 15–30 Sept, 22 Dec–6 Jan, Wed evening and Sun.* This crêperie also serves bistro fare and a regional menu called 'Goûter l'Ardèche'.

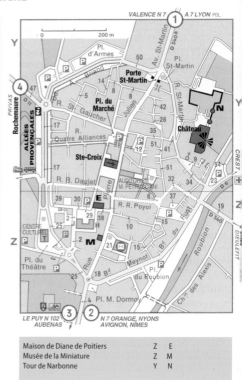

MONTÉLIMAR

▶ *Turn left as you reach the plateau and park below the castle walls. A road veering to the left leads to the ruins.*

The 12C square **keep** is surmounted by a pentagonal tower which enabled the archers to vary their angle of fire.

The old village
On your way back, take rue du Faubourg in front of the town hall (Mairie), then take rue de la Violle. The streets are lined with medieval houses.

Pic de Chenavari★★
4.5km/2.8mi N of Rochemaure Castle. ⚡*At the foot of the Chapelle St-Laurent, take the road on the right, heading for Les Videaux. Then turn left onto Chemin des Freydières and keep on climbing. Ignore the right-hand lane leading to a farmhouse and take the dirt track to the plateau with electric pylons. From here you can easily reach the summit (45min on foot there and back).* From the top there is a **view** of Rochemaure Castle and the Rhône, of the Vercors and the Barronies and of the Lower Ardèche.

Le Teil
6km/4mi W on N 102.
This industrial town owes its prosperity to its chalk cliffs. In the early 19C, small local businesses had already begun working the open-air quarries to produce cement and lime.

Notre-Dame-d'Aiguebelle
20km/12.5mi S of Montélimar on D 56.
The abbey was founded in 1137 at the instigation of St Bernard, Abbot of Clairvaux. Today the lives of the monks are governed by strict rules and they devote themselves to prayer, manual work and intellectual pursuits, as well as making a famous liquor.

Privas
30km/19mi from Aubenas (SW) and Montélimar (SE). ⚡ *Pl. du Gén.-de-Gaulle, 07000 PRIVAS ☎04 75 64 33 35.*
Privas played a key role in the Wars of Religion which earned it the title of

"Boulevard de la Réforme." Right in the throes of religious dissent, the town was one of the strongholds conceded to the Protestants under the Edict of Nantes in 1598. Richelieu's unification policy and the undying hatred of the people revived the religious conflict. In 1629 the Royal Army, under the command of Schomberg and Biron, set up camp near Privas. Cardinal Richelieu took up lodgings in Entrevaux Castle while Louis XIII was housed south of the town. The townspeople were no match for the 20,000 strong Royal Army. After 16 days of siege, the town was taken by storm, pillaged, burnt and massacred.

Mont-Toulon

🚶 *Park near the museum and walk up boulevard du Montoulon.*

A signpost marks the path to the right that goes to the hilltop, where there is a monumental **calvary** (three crosses) and a good **view**★ over the town, the Ouvèze Valley, the Rhône and the Alps.

Pont Louis-XIII

South of the town centre.

The bridge spanning the River Ouvèze has preserved its coping of rough stone corbels and offers a good view of Privas.

Le Bouschet de Pranles

15km/9.3mi N of Privas along D 2 and D 344.

A small **Protestant Museum** (⏱open *Jul–Aug 10am–noon, 2pm–6pm; May–Jun Sat, Sun and public holidays, 2pm–6pm; Sept 2pm–6pm;* ⏱*closed Oct–Apr, and Mondays;* ✆*4€;* ✆*04 75 64 22 74)* has been set up in the birthplace of Pierre Durand and his sister Marie Durand. This Huguenot heroine was locked up in the tower of Constance d'Aigues-Mortes for 38 years (1730–68).

Driving Tours

Medieval Towns★

Round tour of 78km/48.5mi. Allow 3hr 30min. Leave Montélimar on D 540. After 2km/1mi, on the right, stands a former factory where you can park the car.

Inside the Musée de la Soie

Montboucher-sur-Jabron

Set up in a former mill, the **Musée de la Soie** evokes the silk industry that was once the area's main source of income.

▸ *Just after the underpass beneath the motorway, turn right to Puygiron.*

Puygiron

Dominated by its castle (13C-16C), this village is remarkable for its attractive **site**★, offering views of Les Trois-Becs, Marsanne and the Coiron plateau.

▸ *Rejoin D 540 and turn right.*

La Bégude-de-Mazenc★

Turn left on D 9 in the modern village and take the small road to the fortified gateway.

This medieval hanging village, partly-ruined, is a particularly good example of the old villages of this type in the area around Montélimar.

▸ *D 540 follows the Jabron Valley upstream, towards Dieulefit.*

Almonds and honey

The nougat industry is fairly recent; originally the sweetmeat was made by artisans. In the 16C almond trees were brought to France from Asia. The popularity of almond-growing across the Gras plateau, and the ready supply of honey from Provence and the Alps, were behind the growth of the nougat industry in Montélimar.

Le Poët-Laval

The village has kept some of its medieval belfry, a 12C keep and sections of the old ramparts. The old temple houses the public library and the **Musée du Protestantisme Dauphinois** (⏱open Apr–Nov 11am–noon, 3pm–6.30pm (Jul–Aug 11am–noon, 3.30–7pm); ⏱closed Fri and Sun mornings; ✆4€; ✆04 75 46 46 33; www.museeduprotestantisme dauphinois.org), devoted to Protestant religion in the Dauphiné region.

Dieulefit

Cosily nestled in a stretch of the Jabron valley, this small town of Protestant tradition is an important tourism centre. D 538 follows the Lez valley downstream, amid the medieval ruins of Béconne and the 14C Blacon keep.

▶ *Return to Montélimar on D4.*

There are lovely **views** of the Vercors foothills and the Roubion basin. As you drive down towards Fraysse, you will catch a glimpse of the impressive ruins of the **Château de Rochefort-en-Valdaine,** overlooking the wooded valley of La Citelles.

Plateau du Coiron★★

77km/48mi from Privas

▶ *Head S from Privas along D 7, following signs to Villeneuve-de-Berg.*

The deeply-eroded volcanic bar that forms the Coiron plateau marks the limit of the Lower Vivarais area. Its black basalt rocks cut across the line of hills from the Escrinet pass to the Rhône. The upper part of the Coiron plateau takes the form of a vast, bare *planèze* rising from the banks of the Rhône.
The road crosses the Ouvèze basin then enters the sun-baked Bayonne gorge. As the road climbs the hillside, there is a succession of views of Privas and the surrounding area.

▶ *At the junction with the road to Freyssenet, turn left towards Taverne.*

The **planèze** is undulating moorland dotted with juniper bushes, box and broom, a landscape that would be bereft of human habitation were it not for the hamlet of Taverne.

▶ *In Taverne, take D 213.*

Between the Col de Fontenelle and Les Molières, a gap in the hills provides a view of the Rhône. The road then runs down to Les Molières along a ravine. Before arriving in St-Martin-le-Supérieur, the road gives a view of its little Romanesque church with its belfry-wall.

▶ *Beyond St-Martin-l'Inférieur turn right along the Lower Lavézon valley. The river bed is covered with large, rounded, black and white boulders.*

Meysse

The old village can be discerned beneath a façade of modern housing. Around the Romanesque church is a network of narrow streets and vaulted passages.

▶ *Leave Meysse on N 86 S.*

On the right of the road on the village's outskirts stands a basalt pinnacle. Beyond are Rochemaure Castle's ruins.

Château de Rochemaure★
⏱see MONTÉLIMAR.

Pic de Chenavari★★
⏱see MONTÉLIMAR.

▶ *Return to Meysse and follow D 2 up the Lower Lavézon Valley; turn right towards St-Vincent-de-Barrès.*

The road runs through the vast **Barrès** basin with its fertile farmland. It then follows a tributary valley of the Rhône which separates the limestone uplands of Cruas to the east from the volcanic Coiron plateau to the west.

St-Vincent-de-Barrès

This village perches on a basalt neck jutting out above the Barrès plain, dwarfed by the basalt towers of its old fortress.

▶ *Return to Privas via Chomérac.*

MONTLUÇON

POPULATION 41,362

MICHELIN MAP 326: C-4

The economic capital of the Bourbonnais area, facing the first outcrops of the Combraille hills, mostly huddles round the castle that once belonged to the dukes of Bourbon but its industrial suburbs stretch over a long distance northwards, up the Cher Valley.

- **Information:** 67ter boulevard de Courtais, 03110 MONTLUÇON. ☎04 70 05 11 44. www.montlucontourisme.com.
- ▶ **Orient Yourself:** Montluçon lies north-west of Clermont-Ferrand and is easily accessed using the A 71 autoroute.
- **Parking:** There are several car parks in the centre of town.
- **Don't Miss:** the Château des Ducs de Bourbon.
- **Organising Your Time:** Montluçon is a bustling place; you may find it useful to allow a full day to explore.
- **Also See:** Hérisson, the gorges de la Sioule, the forest of Tronçais.

A Bit of History

Successful rebirth – The completion of the Berry Canal in 1841 linked the iron seams of Berry and the coalfields of Commentry. Because of this, throughout the Second Empire when the steel industry began to develop, Montluçon enjoyed rapid expansion. It became the centre of a major railway network and its functions as a trading and administrative centre spilled over into the surrounding countryside.

By the turn of the 20C, the iron seams and coal faces had been exhausted and the death knell sounded for the smelting works. A serious crisis, with vast social repercussions, hit the region.

The current industrial activity is fairly diverse and includes electro-mechanics, tyre making, mechanical engineering, chemistry, furniture etc.

Musical Son – André Messager (1853–1929), the composer, first became known as a conductor in Covent Garden in London, then in the opera house in Paris. However, he quickly gained a reputation as a brilliant composer of operettas containing a large number of popular and elegant airs, refrains and ballets. One of his most famous performances was in 1902 when he directed and conducted Claude Debussy's opera *Pelléas and Mélisande*.

Old Town★

▶ *Start from avenue Marx-Dormoy and head for the castle.*

Château des Ducs de Bourbon

The castle was built during the Hundred Years War (14C-15C) by Louis II de Bourbon and his successors, Jean I and Charles I. Banks of flowers climb the old walls, and the castle itself consists of a vast rectangular building flanked, on the town side, by a turret and a large rectangular tower with crenellations.

▶ *Turn right onto rue des Serruriers and continue along Grand-Rue.*

This old street is lined with 15C houses (nos 42, 39 and 27). Continue to place Notre-Dame with its 18C buildings. Stroll through **passage du Doyenné** which leads to place de la Comédie. On Saturday mornings this part of the old town is filled with colour and bustle thanks to its flower market.

Église Notre-Dame

The church, never completed, was built on the orders of Louis II de Bourbon in the 15C; it stands on the site of a Romanesque sanctuary of which one apsidal chapel still remains.

▶ *Turn left along rue du Château.*

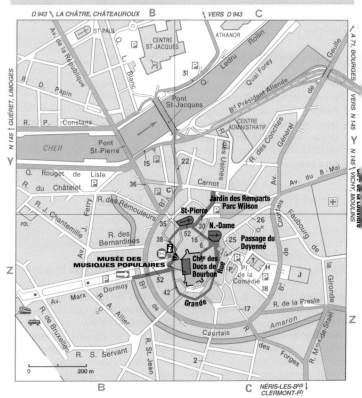

Castle esplanade

This is a pleasant spot for a stroll. From here there is a **view**★ over the entire town, the industrial estates beyond and, in the distance, the first outcrops of the Massif Central, the peaceful Cher valley and the Berry region. On this side, the castle stands in the shadow of the clock tower and its first floor is decorated with a timbered gallery including red and black surbedded brick hoardings.

▸ *Return to place Notre-Dame and turn left onto rue de la Fontaine.*

Rue Pierre-Petit leads to the **Président-Wilson Gardens**; rue des Cinq-Piliers on the left leads to the picturesque place St-Pierre.

Église St-Pierre

The church of St-Pierre, built in the 12C and 13C, is hidden by houses, some of which date from the 15C. The impressive cylindrical pillars at the transept crossing give the **interior**★ a simplicity and nobility that are totally unexpected.

▸ *Rue St-Roch and rue des Serruriers lead back to the foot of the castle opposite the statue of Marx Dormoy, former Mayor of Montluçon.*

Sights

Musée des Musiques Populaires

○*Open daily except Tue 2pm–7pm (Oct–Mar: 2pm–6pm).* ○*Closed 1 Jan,*

Address Book

♨ *For coin ranges, see the cover flap.*

WHERE TO STAY

▣ 🍴🍴 **Château St-Jean** – *Near the Hippodrome.* ☎04 70 02 71 71. www. chateaustjean.net. 🅿. *20 rms.* ⌑10€. *Restaurant* ▣🍴🍴. The stone walls of this lovely 15C manor by a park contribute to its timeless appeal. The pretty, spacious rooms are soothingly quiet. Medieval ambience in the dining room under the vaulted ceiling of a 12C chapel. Covered pool.

WHERE TO EAT

▣ **L'Eau à la Bouche** – *26 r. Grande.* ☎04 70 03 82 92. Very popular when the lunch hour strikes, this establishment serves meals centred around sandwiches, fondues, grilled titbits and *tartiflette*, made from high quality local ingredients. Countrified decor with exposed beams, enjoyable atmosphere and friendly welcome.

A LEISURELY MEAL

▣ **La Vie en Rose** – *7 r. de la Fontaine.* ☎04 70 03 88 79. Closed Sun lunch. Outside, a pretty pink façade; inside, orange-toned walls, old photos and advertising posters round out this restaurant's bistro-style decor. The menu offers Bourbon specialities, featuring famous Charolais beef, served with soft jazz in the background.

▣🍴 **Le Grenier à Sel** – *Pl. des Toiles.* ☎04 70 05 53 79. Restaurant closed Feb school holidays, 27 Oct–2 Nov, Sat lunch in winter, Mon lunch in Jul–Aug, Sun evening and Mon rest of year. This attractive, ivy-covered manor in the old quarter of Montluçon is surrounded by a walled garden. The contemporary fare is flavoursome and the spacious, pleasantly furnished rooms are conducive to a good night's sleep.

ON THE TOWN

Le Perceval – *3 pl. Ste-Anne.* ☎04 70 28 38 28. Mon–Thu 2pm–2am, Fri–Sat 2pm–3am. Repose and well-being define this luxurious, yet relaxed, bar. Curled up in a leather booth or taking it easy on a comfy chair, you'll enjoy sipping champagnes, whiskies or exotic cocktails in the velvety atmosphere.

SHOWTIME

Le Guingois – *3 r. Ernest-Montusès.* ☎04 70 05 88 18. Tickets from 8.30pm. Closed Jul–Aug. Dedicated to contemporary music of all genres, Le Guingois gives new talents space to perform and be heard. Music of the world, modern jazz and French compositions are in the spotlight weekly in this dynamic and original nightclub-café.

SHOPPING

Baujard – *73 bd de Courtais.* ☎04 70 05 05 86. Having manned the ovens for the past 30 years, this pastry-chef is a pastmaster in the confection of chocolate delicacies, traditional pastries and iced desserts that delight the refined sweet tooth. The fresh, elegant decor – pastel shades, crown moulding and high ceiling – invite lingering and it's just as well, given that Baujard is also a tearoom.

La Ferme St-Pierre – *3 Pl. de la Poterie.* ☎04 70 28 89 00. Three farmers joined forces to create this shop selling produce straight from the farm. The result is a very nice choice of poultry and related products, such as foie gras, magret and confits, plus milk and goat cheese. Also available are preserved pork, delicatessen, jam, honey and mustard from Charroux.

---

and 8 May, 14 Jul, 11 Nov, 25 Dec. ⊜4€. ☎04 70 02 56 57.
This museum housed in the former **château des ducs de Bourbon** has recently undergone extensive renovation. Today there are 711 instruments in the collections and six workshops making and repairing stringed instruments as well as hurdy-gurdies, bagpipes and brasses. There is a good library of documents relating to instruments of all the families, including electric instruments and percussion.

Château de la Louvière

Leave Montluçon to the E on N 145 towards Montmarault. 500m/547yd past the hospital, turn right onto avenue du Cimetière de l'Est.

Ⓛ*Open Jul–mid Sept daily except Tue 2pm–7pm; mid-Sept–Jun daily except Tue 2pm–6pm.* Ⓛ*Closed 1 Jan, 1 May, 8 May, 14 Jul, 25 Dec.* ☞*3€.* ☎*04 70 05 04 91. Gardens open all year.*

In 1926, **François Joseph Troubat-le-Houx**, an art enthusiast, had this château built, based on the design of the façades of the Petit Trianon in Versailles. The interior features furniture, tapestries and objets d'art from the 17C, 18C and 19C. The castle grounds combine French and English style gardens.

Excursions

Hérisson

24km/14mi N of Montluçon.

🛈 *Mairie, 2 av. Marcellin-Simonnet, 03190 HÉRISSON,* ☎*04 70 06 82 23.*

The artist **Henri-Joseph Harpignies** (1819–1916) often stayed in Hérisson and this region provided him with the inspiration for some of his finest landscapes, strongly influenced by the Barbizon School. Two 15C fortified gateways and old houses including the "Mousse House" (15C-18C) are to be seen in the village.

The town has kept several old houses (15C-18C) and two fortified gateways from the 15C, Porte de la Rivière and Porte de la Varenne. The 22 turrets running along the ramparts are no longer standing.

Musée du Terroir

Ⓛ*Open Jul–Aug Wed–Mon 2.30pm–6.30pm.* ☞*3€.* ☎*04 70 06 89 40.*

The museum presents an exhibition of farming tools and various artefacts uncovered on excavation sites.

Castle

The impressive mass of beautiful russet-coloured ruins stands high above the village. The castle was built in the 13C, with fortifications added to it under Louis de Bourbon in the 14C.

View★

South bank of the River Aumance; access via rue du Calvaire.

From the Calvary chapel on the hillside, the **view** extends over the entire village with its porch-belfry, all that remains of the former collegiate church of St-Sauveur (12C-17C), the castle and the Aumance Valley.

Ainay-le-Château

44km/27mi N of Montluçon. 3km/1.9mi N of the Forêt de Tronçais on D 953.

Formerly part of Berry and old Aquitaine, Ainay became a Bourbonnais stronghold in the late 12C. The castle has not survived, but vestiges of the ramparts remain. The 12C Porte de l'Horloge in the main street was once used as a guard-room and prison.

Driving Tours

Canal de Berry

65km/40.5mi – allow 3hr.

This round trip, running west and north of Montluçon, offers an interesting insight into the local cultural heritage.

▶ *Leave Montluçon to the NW on D 916, heading for Boussac.*

Domérat

The Romanesque **church** has kept its east end and its chancel. In one of the castle's outbuildings, the **Musée de la Vigne** (☞Ⓛ*open Apr–Sept Sat–Sun and public holidays 3pm–6pm.* ☎*04 70 64 20 01*) illustrates the techniques of wine-growing and winemaking in the Allier département★.

Huriel

12km/7mi NW on D 916.

12C **keep** (Ⓛ*open Jul and Aug daily except Mon 10am–noon, 2.30pm–6.30pm; Jun and Sept–Dec daily except Sat–Sun by request; apply to the town hall; Museum* ☞*3€*) and church.

▶ *Leave Huriel to the N and take D 40 to La Chapelaude, then take D 943 on the left for 11km/6.8mi. At the locality called Goëlat, turn right.*

Église de St-Désiré★

This remarkable Romanesque construction was once an 11C priory.

▶ *Take D 479 N of St-Désiré, then follow D 30.*

Vallon-en-Sully

A charming village in local pink sandstone, set alongside the Berry canal.

▶ *Return towards Montluçon on D 301, running along the River Cher and the Berry Canal. Stop at Magnette; from there cross the canal.*

Musée du Canal de Berry

⏱*Open Jul–Sept: guided tours (1hr30min) 2.30pm–8pm (last admission 1hr before closing).* ⊛*3€.* ☎*04 70 06 70 92.*
The museum will enlighten visitors on the history of the canal and the successive stages of its construction.
🚶The towpath along the canal offers good opportunities for jogging and mountain biking.

Former Mining Country

50km/31mi – allow 3hr

▶ *Leave Montluçon to the SE on N 144 in the direction of Clermont-Ferrand.*

Néris-les-Bains ⊹

🛈*Av. Max-Dormoy, 03310 NÉRIS-LES-BAINS* ☎*04 70 03 11 03.*
This peaceful health resort was once a thriving Gallo-Roman city. You can visit the church, the Merovingian necropolis, the amphitheatre, the ancient baths and the **Maison du Patrimoine** (⏱*open Apr–Oct: guided tours (1hr) daily except Mon and Tue 3pm–6pm;* ⏱*closed 1 May.* ⊛*4€;* ☎*04 70 03 42 11),* which displays Gallo-Roman artefacts discovered in Néris: ceramic pieces, coins, jewellery, and sculptures in bronze and other materials.
🚶Rambling can be enjoyed along the old railroad between Néris and Montluçon. Contact tourist office for information.

Scuplture in St-Désiré church

J. Damase/MICHELIN

▶ *Leave Néris to the E on D 998.*

Commentry

Until the end of the First World War, Commentry was at the heart of an area devoted to mining. Today this activity has been replaced by chemical, mechanical and other industries.

▶ *Leave Commentry to the SE and continue along D 998.*

Église de Colombier

Crowned by an elegant 12C belfry, the church and its nearby priory, defended by a citadel, form a harmonious architectural ensemble.

▶ *Leave Colombier to the N on D 200.*

Malicorne

Jardin-Verger (⏱*open Jun–Sept: 10am–noon, 3pm–6pm;* ⊛*5€ (children: 3€);* ☎*04 70 64 87 39),* is a dazzling garden-orchard bursting with colour: the rose garden alone boasts several hundred varieties blossoming between June and September.

▶ *Leave Malicorne to the N on D 69. In Doyet, turn right onto N 145, heading for Moulins. After 2km/1mi, turn left onto D 438.*

Donjon de la Souche

⌒*Not open to the public.* This superbly restored square 13C and 14C keep is surrounded by multifoil machicolations.

▶ *Continue along D 438 towards D 38. Turn right. Cross the railway tracks,*

Address Book

&For coin ranges, see the cover flap.

WHERE TO STAY

⊜⊜ **Chambre d'hôte l'Ombre de Goziniere** – 03350 Theneuille. ☎04 70 67 59 17. ⌒. Reservations required. 3 rms. Meals⊜⊜. Formerly an outbuilding belonging to the neighbouring manor house, this attractive 17C edifice has been very nicely renovated.

WHERE TO EAT

⊜ **Le Tronçais** – 03360 Tronçais. ☎04 70 06 11 95. Closed 16 Nov–14 Mar, Sun evening, Mon and Tue off-season. ☐. 12 rms. ☐8€. Restaurant⊜⊜. Calm, spacious bedrooms. Bright dining room with bay windows opening out onto the countryside.

---

then the motorway and turn left onto D 157. At Deneuille-les-Mines take D 33 on the left. After St-Angel, skirt the roundabout and continue along D 33, which will soon take you back to Montluçon via N 145.

Forêt de Tronçais★★★

30km/18.6mi N of Montluçon.
🅿 Pl. du Champ-de-Foire, 03350 CÉRILLY, ☎04 70 67 55 89. www.onf.fr/foret/dossier/troncais.

Tronçais Forest is located at the junction of the Berry and Bourbonnais regions; it has a total surface area of over 10,000ha/24,711 acres and contains a remarkable plantation of trees. Its many pools and beauty spots make it a popular recreational area.

🚶**"Discovering the forest"** – The forest offers walkers additional attractions besides the contemplation of its oak trees. Mushroom pickers will find boletus, hydnum, russula and chanterelles. There is also quite a large population of red deer, roe deer and wild boar. Great crested grebes can often be glimpsed on Pirot Lake. In season, **guided tours** (🅿 ☎04 70 46 82 00) of the forest are organised.

① **Eastern Sologne Region★★★**
20km/12.5mi

Cérilly

This was **Charles-Louis Philippe**'s (1874–1909), home, writer of semi-autobiographical novels based on his memories. His **birthplace** (◷open May–Oct: Sat–Sun and public holidays 3pm–6pm; ◷closed Nov–Apr; ⊛3€; ☎04 70 67 52 00), at no 5 in the street that bears his name, is open to the public.

▶ Leave Cérilly to the N on D 111 which leads through the eastern part of the forest. Cross over Rond de Brot roundabout and D 978A, then take the first tarmacked road on the left, Ligne de Cros-Chaud.

Étang de Pirot★

Rond des Pêcheurs offers a lovely overall **view** of the vast Lake Pirot.

▶ Take Ligne des Pêcheurs, then turn right on D 978A.

Fontaine Viljot

Oaks and conifers form a charming decor around the crystal clear water of this spring. Legend has it that, if a maiden wishes to marry, she must throw a pin into the spring; if the pin pricks the bottom, the maiden has "pricked a heart." Nowadays, small change appears to have replaced pins.

Émile-Guillaumin and Charles-Louis-Philippe Oak Trees

These two trees close to the roadside to the north commemorate two novelists from the region.

▶ At Rond Gardien, turn sharp right onto the Planchegross forest road (one-way) up to the car park.

Rond de la Cave

30min on foot there and back.
🚶This large, sheltered picnic area lies at the very heart of the forest.
Return to **Rond Gardien** (viewing table) and continue to Tronçais.

▶ Take D 250 on the right.

Étang de St-Bonnet★

The lake, to the left of the road, sits in a very attractive setting.

Futaie Colbert★

There is a marked trail which begins and ends at Rond du Vieux-Morat. Beautiful plantation of 300-year-old oaks in a cool, undulating setting.

Rond de Buffévent

2km/1mi from Rond du Vieux-Morat.
Short walks south-west along the forest road lead to magnificent 300-year-old oaks: **Jacques-Chevalier, Jumeaux** (the Twins) and **Sentinelle** (the Sentry).

2 Western Sologne Region★

30km/19mi

St-Bonnet-Tronçais

A pleasant place to stay on the edge of the forest. Guided tours of the surrounding area are organised by the **Centre permanent d'initiatives pour l'environnement** (CPIE – *Avenue Nicolas-Rambourg, Tronçais, 03360 St-Bonnet-Tronçais*, ☎04 70 06 14 69).

▶ *From St-Bonnet-Tronçais take D 250 S; beyond Tronçais factory turn right; at Rond du Chêne Aragon turn right on D 145.*

Étang de Saloup★

The road bisects the lake.

▶ *Turn left on D 39, then follow route Forestière des Lurons. From the car park, take the footpath (past a no-entry sign).*

The path ends at **St-Mayeul Chapel** overlooking a ravine.

▶ *From the car park turn right onto the narrow route Forestière des Vauves winding through the ravine and right to Rond de Meneser.*

Rond de Meneser

Various paths provide pleasant walks *(30min on foot there and back)*.

▶ *Continue on the forest road; turn left on D 110; in Le Breton turn left on D 312. The road runs through the forest to **Meaulne** in the Aumance valley.*

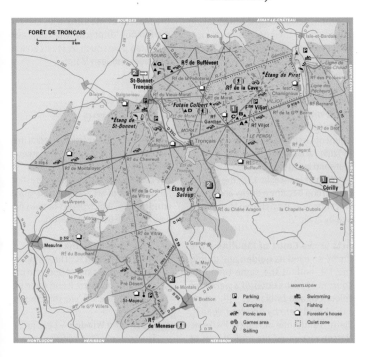

MOULINS ★

POPULATION 21,892

MICHELIN MAP 326: H-3

Moulins lies on the banks of the River Allier and is the quietly charming main town of the Bourbonnais area. It boasts a range of economic and industrial activities linked to the rich farmland of the Moulins region, with food industries, shoe factories and machine tool production. The wide avenues and streets of the old town are an ideal place for a stroll.

- 🛈 **Information:** 11 r. François-Péron, 03000 MOULINS, ☎04 70 44 14 14. www.ville-moulins.fr.
- ▸ **Orient Yourself:** Moulins lies roughly mid-way between Nevers and Clermont-Ferrand, and is accessible from the A 71.
- 🅿 **Parking:** Park around the edge of the town centre rather than in it.
- 👁 **Don't Miss:** Take a tour around the lovely streets of the cathedral district.
- 🕐 **Organising Your Time:** The heritage here merits a three day visit.
- 🧒 **Especially for Kids:** Visit the Val d'Allier nature reserve.
- 👣 **Also See:** BOURBON-l'ARCHAMBAULT, LAPALISSE, SOUVIGNY.

A Bit of History

The Duchy of Bourbonnais – Bourbon lands first appeared in history books in the early 10C, but it took more than three centuries for the lords and, later, the counts of Bourbon to create a State capable of rivalling its powerful neighbours, Berry and Burgundy. The Bourbons achieved their aim by taking advantage of their geographical location between the kingdom of France and the duchies of Auvergne and Aquitaine, placing their troops at the service of the crown.

This alliance with royal authority, combined with a skilful policy of marriage (Béatrice de Bourbon married Robert, Count of Clermont, St Louis' sixth child, in 1265), facilitated the building of a vast State and led to eight Bourbons becoming King of France. In 1327 the Barony of Bourbon became a duchy and, in the following year, it was raised to the peerage by Philip VI.

Arts at the Court of Moulins – The duchy enjoyed its golden age during the 15C and, at the same time, the court in Moulins entered a period of splendour and brilliance, with artists summoned here by Charles I, Jean II, Pierre II and Anne of France. Pierre de Nesson recounted the misfortunes of Jean I; the Flemish musician Jean Ockeghem sang for Charles I before moving on to the king's chapel. Sculpture flourished under Jean II, firstly with Jacques Morel, then with Michel Colombe and his followers, Jean de Rouen and Jean de Chartres. It is, however, the painters who produced the finest works, with Jean Perréal, Jean Richer and above all the **Master of Moulins** who created the famous "Triptych." The court also attracted poets such as Jean Lemaire de Belges and Jean Marot.

Cathédrale Notre-Dame

A good overall view of the cathedral may be had from the old covered market, a 17C arcaded building.

The cathedral is particularly interesting for its works of art and **stained-glass windows★★**, which depict famous figures from the Bourbons' Court.

1) **St Catherine's or the Dukes' Window** – Late 15C. The window shows the Cardinal of Bourbon on the right and Pierre II and Anne of France on the left, worshipping St Catherine.
2) **Crucifixion Window** – Late 15C. The bottom of the window shows

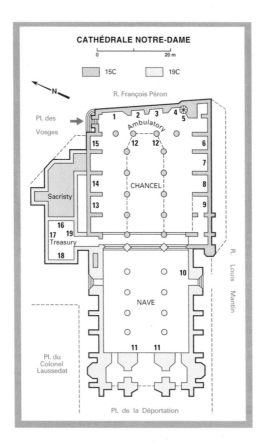

CATHÉDRALE NOTRE-DAME

0 — 20 m

▨ 15C   ☐ 19C

N ↖

R. François Péron

Pl. des Vosges →

Ambulatory

CHANCEL

Sacristy

Treasury

NAVE

R. Louis Mantin

Pl. du Colonel Laussedat

Pl. de la Déportation

The Entombment of Christ★ (16C).

3) **Window of the Virgin Mary Enthroned** – Late 15C.

4) **Tree of Jesse Window** – 16C.

5) **Elegant spiral staircase.**

6) **Window of the Suffering and Triumphant Church** – Early 16C.

7) **Window of the Church Militant** – 16C. The Crown of Thorns is handed over to the King.

8) **Chapel of the Black Virgin** – The Black Virgin, a replica of the one in Le Puy-en-Velay, serves as a reminder that Moulins was one of the stopovers used by pilgrims on their way to Le Puy-en-Velay and Santiago de Compostela.

9) **Chapter Chapel** – The centre of the stained-glass window depicts the martyrdom of St Barbara.

10) **Classical Painting** – Two Carthusian monks.

11) **The Annunciation** – 18C painting on each side of the doorway.

12) **Window depicting the life of the Virgin Mary.**

13) **St Mary Magdalene Window** – 16C.

14) **Window of Christ on the Cross** – Late 15C.

15) **St Elizabeth of Hungary's Window** – Early 16C.

16) **Triptych by the Master of Moulins** ★★★ – ○*Open Apr–Sept: guided tours (20min) 9.30am–noon, 2pm–6pm; Oct–Mar daily except Tue 10–noon, 2pm–5pm (last admission 30min before closing).* ○*Closed Sun morning, 1 Jan, 25 Dec. Free admission.* ☎*04 70 20 89 65.* This splendid painting on wood, probably completed in 1498, is considered to be one of the last masterpieces of Gothic painting in France.

Triptych by the Master of Moulins

The room also contains a 17C ivory crucifix reliquary (**17**) mounted on an ebony stand, the Aubery Triptych (**18**) and the Bethlehem Triptych (**19**) attributed to 16C Flemish painter Joos van Cleve.

Walking Tour

Cathedral District

▶ *Leave the cathedral by the north door, walk round the east end of the church and go down rue Grenier, then rue des Orfèvres.*

Jacquemart★

The belfry, topped by a timber-framed roof and a campanile housing the bells and automata, was once the symbol of the town's privileges as a borough. Today, the Jacquemart family announce the time of day for those working in, or visiting, the city. The clock tower was burnt down in 1655 and was once again ravaged by fire in 1946. in 1947 it was rebuilt by public subscription.

Musée Bourbonnais
See Sights below.

Donjon de la Mal Coiffée

All that remains of the old castle is a massive keep restored in the 15C and named the "Dishevelled" because of its roof; this was originally the angle tower in the north-west corner of the old ducal palace – *see Sights below.*

Pavillon dit d' Anne de Beaujeu

The so-called Anne de Beaujeu Pavilion is the only remaining part of the extension to the ducal palace commissioned by the princess around 1495.
This elegant construction is one of the earliest examples of Renaissance architecture in France and was used in later years by King Charles VIII.
A porch tower stands in front of the Italianate façade, which presents six arcades decorated with the initials of Peter and Anne of Beaujeu and the emblems of the Bourbons, the belt of hope, thistle and stag beetle. The pavilion houses the Musée d'Art et d'Archéologie (*see Musée Anne de Beaujeu in Sights below*).

Quartier des Mariniers

While you are visiting the historical heart of Moulins, you can explore the neighbourhood formerly occupied by the town's community of bargemen, starting from the Église du Sacré-Cœur.

Sights

Musée Bourbonnais

Open Apr–Sept: Mon, Tue, 9.30am–11.30am, 3pm–6.30pm, Wed–Sun, 3pm–6.30pm; Oct–Mar: Mon, Tue, 9.30am–11.30am, 2pm–5.30pm, Wed–Sun, 2pm

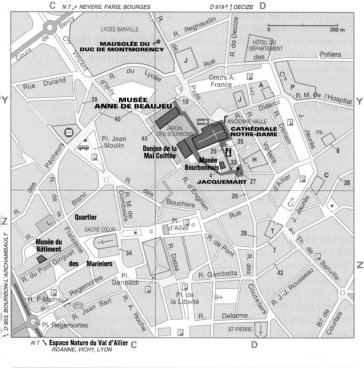

–5.30pm. ◷Closed 1 Jan, 1 May, 25 Dec. ⊜5€. ☏04 70 44 39 03.

The museum, housed in several 15C-17C buildings linked by 17C galleries, is devoted to four main themes:

Religious art

Abbé Déret's collections are displayed on the ground floor (statues, liturgical objects etc). The history of the Order of the Visitation whose founder, St Jeanne de Chantal, died in Moulins in 1641, is also evoked.

Salles Ethnographiques

Several rooms contain reconstructions of workshops illustrating ancient crafts and a 19C farmhouse interior. Fine collections of headdresses, hats and regional costumes as well as musical instruments and objects of daily life.

Collection d'orfèvrerie française et européenne

This collection of French and European gold plate includes some unique items such as a 17C ewer in gilded silver.

Collection de Jouets, Poupées et Fers à Repasser

A fine collection of antique dolls was gathered by the founder of the museum during the course of her travels. In addition, two rooms display some 160 irons, the oldest dating from the 16C.

Musée des Moulins

Exhibition devoted to French and foreign mills.

▶ Take rue de l'Ancien-Palais.

Donjon de la Mal Coiffée

Closed for restoration.

This recently restored keep will become one of the area's most attractive sights. Used as a prison until 1986, its walls still bear the inscriptions of past prisoners.

Musée Anne de Beaujeu★★

Open daily except Tue 10am–noon, 2pm–6pm (Jul–Aug daily except Tue 10am–6pm). Closed 1 Jan, 1 May, 25 Dec. 5€. 04 70 20 48 47.

This museum occupies the so-called Anne de Beaujeu Pavilion, the only remaining part of the extension to the ducal palace.

Musée du Bâtiment

18 rue du Pont-Guinguet.

Open daily except Mon and Tue 2pm–6pm. Closed 1 Jan, 1 May, 1 Nov, 25 Dec. 4€. 04 70 34 23 69. http://musee-batiment.pays-allier.com.

Tools, building materials, techniques but also fixtures and fittings of bygone days are displayed in this unusual and interesting museum housed in a fine 18C building.

Mausolée du Duc de Montmorency★

Open Jul–Aug: guided tours (45min) Sat 3pm–5pm. 3€. 04 70 48 51 18.

The mausoleum, completed in 1653, is the work of Parisian artists, the Anguier Brothers, and was commissioned by the wife of Henri II of Montmorency after she was widowed by Richelieu in 1632 and sent to the Convent of the Visitation in Moulins (now the high school). It was transported in pieces by road from Paris to Montargis and then by waterway.

Espace Nature du Val d'Allier

6 boulevard de Nomazy.

Kids Open Apr–Oct daily except Mon and Tue. 2pm–6pm (Jul and Aug daily). 5€. 04 70 44 46 29.

The **Val d'Allier nature reserve** extends along both banks of the River Allier, between Moulins and St-Pourçain-sur-Sioule. Information about guided nature rambles organised by the Ligue pour la Protection des Oiseaux (LPO, society for the protection of birds) is available from the Espace Nature.

Driving Tour

Châteaux in the Bourbonnais Area

100km/62mi – allow one day

▶ *Leave Moulins to the NE heading towards N 7, then turn right onto D 12.*

Yzeure

The village of Yzeure is older than Moulins, and was the seat of the parish until the Hundred Years War.

Château de Seganges

Closed to the public.

Small château built at the same time as the Anne de Beaujeu Pavilion.

▶ *Continue on D 29D; right nto D 29.*

The road wends its way through Munet Forest, offering pretty glimpses of both coniferous and broad-leaved trees.

▶ *Leaving the forest, take D 133 on the left. At the entrance to Auroüer, continue along D 133 on the left.*

Château du Riau

Apr–Sept: guided tours daily except Tue 2.30pm–6.30pm (last admission 6pm). 5€. 04 70 43 34 47.

The Riau estate comprises several buildings dating from the 15C to the 18C which lie in a lovely green setting on the border of the Allier and Nièvre regions. The most remarkable building is the **tithe barn★** built in 1584, with its stables on the lower ground floor and grain storage on the three upper floors; the top floor, with its beautiful timber roof, provides an attractive view of the castle, moat, **fortified gatehouse** and dovecote. The gatehouse contains the chapel and the guard-room. In the square tower, a 15C staircase with a wooden balustrade leads to **bedrooms** decorated in Louis XV, Louis XVI and Empire styles.

▶ *Continue along D 133 until you reach Villeneuve-sur-Allier. On leaving the village, turn right onto D 433.*

Address Book

For coin ranges, see the cover flap.

WHERE TO STAY

Parc – *31 av. du Gén.-Leclerc.* *04 70 44 12 25. www.hotel-moulins. com. Closed 11–26 Jul, 26 Sept–4 Oct and 23 Dec–4 Jan.* *28 rms.* *7€. Restaurant* *. A few steps from a verdant park and the train station. Modest, well-kept bedrooms and two dining rooms, rustic and contemporary.*

WHERE TO EAT

Restaurant des Cours – *36 cours Jean-Jaurès.* *04 70 44 25 66. http://restaurant-des-cours.com. Closed 9–18 Feb, 14–31 Jul and Wed.* This fetching bourgeois house in the heart of the city is embellished by a lacework of Virginia creeper. Fixed-price menus.

Logis Henri IV – *03340 Neuilly-le-Réal. 16km/9.6mi SE of Moulins via N 7 and D 989.* *04 70 43 87 64. Closed 17 Feb–7 Mar, 2–5 Sept, Sun evening and Mon.* The logis was a hunting lodge back in the 16C. You'll enter the half-timbered dining room with its pretty tiled floor via the perron. Fixed-price menus featuring classic fare.

ON THE TOWN

La Bodega – *12 r. du Four.* *04 70 20 59 55. Tue–Thu 10am–1am, Fri–Sat 11am–2am, Sun 2pm–1am. Closed 3 wks in Aug.* Definitively the most appealing venue in Moulins. Overflowing with anachronistic charm.

Le Grand Café – *49 pl. d'Allier.* *04 70 44 00 05. Summer: daily 8am–1am; rest of the year: closed Sun, Tue, 1 Jan and 25 Dec.* Built in 1899, this café is classified as an historic monument. An imposing fresco honouring Gambrinus, the god of ale, surrounds customers whereas enormous mirrors copy their images ad infinitum.

Le Vieux Moulins – *2 r. de l'Ancien-Palais.* *04 70 20 67 81. Summer: Mon–Sat noon–4pm, 7.30pm–11.30pm, Sun 7pm–11.30pm. Rest of the year: closed lunch, Sundays, public holidays and 2 wks in Nov.* Contrary to what some locals used to believe, this eminently agreeable establishment has always been a *crêperie*. Moreover, the bar now has a terrace on the pedestrian street, the pavement of which is used by the owner to organise her concerts and other original goings-on.

RECREATION

Poneys et nature en Bourbonnais – *La Solée, 5km/3mi E of Moulins via D12 dir. Aérodrome Dompierre and road on left, 03400 Yzeure.* *04 70 34 68 94. 9.30am–7.30pm.* As an introduction to outdoor riding, the 'Poney et Nature' association offers excursions on horseback with a guide schooled in equestrian tourism.

SHOPPING

Fossey – *10 r. François-Péron.* *04 70 44 08 70.* Frédérick Fossey creates mouth-watering confections, the most sought-after of which are chocolate-based. The tearoom also offers the *Moulinois*, a luscious pastry starring hazelnuts and praline, sans chocolate.

Les Palets d'Or – *11 r. de Paris.* *04 70 44 02 71. Tue–Sat 9.30am–12.15pm, 2pm–7.15pm, Sun and public holidays 9.30am–12.30pm.* Palets d'or are cream and coffee-filled chocolates originally created in this very shop in…1898! The current owner, who studied at the ever-famous Lenôtre, continues the palet tradition and adds sweetmeats of his own inventions.

HORSE RIDING

Nature Rides: Poneys et nature en Bourbonnais – *03400 Yzeure -* *04 70 34 68 94 - 9.30am–7.30pm.* The "Poney et Nature" association organises riding tours led by a qualified guide/instructor.

Arboretum de Balaine★

Open Mar–Nov 9am–noon, 2pm–7pm. *8€.* *04 70 43 30 07.* This botanical garden founded in 1804 is landscaped in the English style and includes numerous species: various types of fir (Caucasian, Spanish, Douglas), giant sequoias, oaks, Cedar of Lebanon and locally grown varieties. The trees are pleasantly set amid beautiful shrubs of rhododendron, azalea, bamboo and dogwood.

Sequoia tree in Arboretum de Balaine

J. Damase/MICHELIN

▶ *Return to Villeneuve-sur-Allier and take D 133 to Bourbon-l'Archambault on the right. After leaving Bagneux, D 133, then D 13 cut across the forest of Les Prieurés Bagnolet. Leave D 13 at the end of a straight section and turn right onto D 54. Soon afterwards, proceed straight ahead on C 3.*

St-Menoux★

🔼 *see BOURBON-L'ARCHAMBAULT.*

▶ *Leave St-Menoux to the S on D 253.*

Souvigny★★ – 🔼 *see SOUVIGNY.*

▶ *Leave Souvigny to the E on D 945, heading for Moulins. On leaving the village, turn right onto D 34, which crosses the railway line.*

Besson

This village has an interesting Roman-esque church with a single nave. Note the Château de Rochefort, whose ruins overlook the Guèze valley.

▶ *Leave Besson to the SW on D 34.*

Château du Vieux Bostz

🕒 *Open May–Sept 2.30pm–6.30pm.* ☎04 70 42 80 84.

This castle, dating from the 15C and 16C, is curious because of its many square and round turrets crowned by delicate belfries.

▶ *Continue along D 34. At the crossroads, turn left onto D 291, then take D 292 on the right.*

Château de Fourchaud

Huge, imposing castle featuring two massive towers with pepper-pot roofs and a sturdy-looking keep. Originally erected in the 14C, the stronghold was heavily restored during the following century.

▶ *Continue along D 292. In Bresnay, take D 34 for 4km/2.5mi, then turn left onto D 33.*

Châtel-de-Neuvre

Pretty village with a Romanesque church built on a promontory dominating the Allier Valley. Enjoy the **view**★ extending over the nearby river and landscape.

▶ *Leave Châtel-de-Neuvre to the E on D 32, crossing the Allier, then turn left onto D 300.*

Toulon-sur-Allier

This hamlet used to be an important centre for the production of pottery back in Gallo-Roman times.

▶ *Leave Toulon-sur-Allier to the S on N 7, then take N 79 on the right. After crossing the Allier, take N 9 to Moulins on the right.*

Bressolles

Small village situated north-east of the charming **Prieurés Moladier Forest**.

▶ *Rejoin N 9, leading back to Moulins.*

MURAT ★

POPULATION 2,153

MICHELIN MAP 330: F-4

25KM/15.5MI NW OF ST-FLOUR – LOCAL MAP SEE MONTS DU CANTAL

Murat lies in the pleasant Alagnon Valley, in a scenic **setting**★★. Its grey houses with stone-slabbed roofs rise picturesquely on terraces up the slopes of the basaltic Bonnevie hill. Two other steep peaks overlook the small town: Chastel rock to the north-west and Bredons rock to the south-east topped by an interesting Romanesque church. Murat is an ideal centre from which to tour the volcanoes of Cantal and enjoy rambling in the surrounding State-owned forest. In August there is a large influx of music lovers who come to enjoy the International Festival of World Music and Dance.

- **Information:** r. du fg-Notre-Dame, 15300 MURAT, ☎04 71 20 09 47. www.murat.com.
- ▶ **Orient Yourself:** Murat lies in the Alagnon valley, west of St Flour, along the road to Aurillac.
- **Parking:** There is ample parking near the tourist information centre.
- **Don't Miss:** Take time to wander the streets and take a coffee.
- **Organising Your Time:** Murat is not large; a couple of hours will suffice.
- **Also See:** ST FLOUR, MONTS DU CANTAL, MONTS DU CÉZALLIER.

A Bit of History

Nothing is impregnable to the French – The **Count of Anterroches,** who was born near Murat, is remembered for his reply to the proposal by the English, at Fontenoy, to fire first: "Gentlemen, we never fire first. Fire yourselves." This was not simply a gesture of courtesy but rather an application of the tactic by which troops would come under fire first and then march on the enemy while the latter were reloading their muskets. Anterroches is also credited with another famous saying: as he stood before Maastricht, someone declared that the town was impregnable; "Nothing", replied Anterroches, "is impregnable to the French."

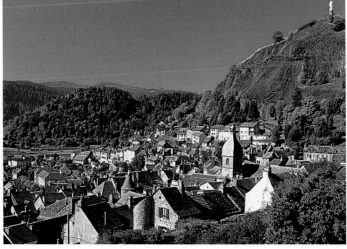

Murat

WHERE TO EAT

⊜⊜ **Le Jarrousset** – *3km/1.8mi E of Murat via N 122 dir. Clermont-Ferrand.* ☎*04 71 20 10 69. www. restaurant-le-jarrousset.com. Closed 12 Nov–15 Jan, Tue except Jul–Aug and Mon.* This rural restaurant in a pavilion set back a bit from the road has a contemporary-style dining room with a veranda giving onto the garden and a terrace in summer. Fine dining without the pretensions of haute cuisine; a peaceful place for a relaxing evening meal.

Town Walk

A brochure to this town of steep, narrow streets is available from the tourist office.

Église Notre-Dame-des-Oliviers

The church dates from the late Gothic period but has a modern west front.

Halle

This covered market is a fine example of 19C ironwork architecture.

Former Bailiff's Court

The building dates from the 16C and opens onto rue de l'Argenterie through a doorway decorated with moulding.

Maison Rodier

This elegant Renaissance style building has some attractive bonding in trachyte (a type of volcanic rock) and a corbelled watchtower.

Consul's Residence

Faubourg Notre-Dame.
The late-15C stone façade has two storeys with narrow windows topped by an ornament. Note the two carved angels above the door, part of which consists of linenfold panels.

Rocher de Bonnevie

The sides of this hill feature strange basalt columns which are remarkable for the uniformity and length of their prisms. A castle once stood on the hill but it was razed to the ground on the orders of Richelieu; it did, however, take six months and six hundredweight of gunpowder to complete the task.

There is a fine view over Murat, the Alagnon valley, the mountains of Cantal and the Chevade valley.

Additional Sight

Maison de la Faune

⏲*Open school holidays 10am–noon, 2pm–6pm; outside school holidays 10am–noon, 2pm–5pm, Sun 2pm–5pm (Jul–Aug 10am–noon, 3pm–7pm); guided tours available (1hr30min).* ⏲*Closed mid-Nov–late Dec, Christmas and New Year's Day.* ⬤*5€ (children 3€).* ☎*04 71 20 00 52.*

This former mansion has retained a late-15C turret. Inside, a large collection of beetles and butterflies, stuffed birds and animals are displayed in reconstructions of their natural environment.

Excursions

Église de Bredons★

SE along D 926. Contact the town hall for information. ☎*04 71 20 02 80.*
The small fortified 11C church is all that remains of the Benedictine priory. The doorway on the south side has billet moulding. Inside, note the monumental giltwood altarpiece completed in 1710 for the High Altar; the intricate detail and abundance of gold and polychrome make this a grandiose piece of decoration. The Resurrection is depicted in the centre. Other giltwood altar screens decorate the chapels.

Albepierre-Bredons★

5km/3mi SW on D 39.
This tiny village built on a volcanic hill overlooks the Alagnon valley. Underground houses were once built into the caves in the rock. From the top of the village, there is an interesting view of Murat below and of the Rocher de Bonnevie in the distance.

ORCIVAL★★

POPULATION 244

MICHELIN MAP 326: E-8 – 27KM/16.8MI SW OF CLERMONT-FERRAND

Orcival, a small town in a cool valley watered by the River Sioulet, has a superb Romanesque church founded by monks from La Chaise-Dieu.

- **Information:** Le Bourg, 63210 ORCIVAL.
  ☎04 73 65 89 77. www.terresdomes-sancy.com.
- ▶ **Orient Yourself:** Tucked into the Massif Central south of west from Clermont Ferrance.
- ○ **Organising Your Time:** Allow half a day, and take a relaxing coffee.
- ◔ **Also See:** La BOURBOULE, Le MONT-DORE, Massif du SANCY, ST-NECTAIRE.

Basilique Notre-Dame★★

This grey mass of volcanic andesite was probably erected during the first half of the 12C and, judging by its remarkable stylistic unity, was the result of uninterrupted construction.

Exterior

The very beautiful, although sparsely decorated, east end has four radiating apsidal chapels; one of these, on the south side, encompasses the crypt level.

The panels of the three doors still have their Romanesque hinges and ironwork; the most elaborate, with ornamental foliage and human heads, are on the south door (known as St John's door). In thanksgiving for released prisoners, chains have been hung from the blind arcades in the southern part of the transept, next to the entrance. A high gable wall forms the west façade.

Interior

The most striking features are the slender pillars and the way the light disperses through the church, through an increasing number of windows from the nave to the transept, culminating in the chancel where most of the light is concentrated.

Excursion

Château de Cordès

2.5km/1.5mi N along D 27.
○ *Guided tours (30min) 10am–noon, 2pm–6pm. Unaccompanied tours of the gardens.* ◔5€. ☎04 73 65 81 34.
An avenue lined with hedgerows enclosing two beautiful formal flowerbeds designed by André Le Nôtre (17C) leads up to this charming 13C-15C manor house, restored in the 17C.

J. Damase/MICHELIN

Basilique Notre-Dame

AVEN D'ORGNAC★★★

MICHELIN MAP 331: I-8 – LOCAL MAP SEE GORGES DE L'ARDÈCHE

Until 19 August 1935 the people of Orgnac-l'Aven had paid little attention to the swallow-hole known to them as "Le Bertras." **Robert de Joly** (1887–1968), President of the Speleology Society of France, who explored it at that time, then described its wealth of interesting features to them. He was an engineer with the College of Electricity in Paris and an enthusiastic potholer. He was also a daring explorer of this area of the Cévennes, where he lived, and he played a vital role in the development of equipment and techniques used in underground explorations. The huge chambers in the swallow-hole were formed by the action of underground water from infiltrations in the cracked limestone rocks. The first concretions, some of which were 10m/33ft in diameter, were broken by an earthquake at the end of the Tertiary Era. These truncated or overturned columns then became the base for more recent stalagmites.

- **Information:** 1 pl. de l'Ancienne-Gare - 07150 Vallon-Pont d'Arc. ☎04 75 88 04 01. www.vallon-pont-darc.com.
- ▶ **Orient Yourself:** Located 15km/10 miles from Vallon-Pont d'Arc, the Aven d'Orgnac is at the southernmost edge of the Ardèche. The location is well sign-posted, 25km/16 miles west of the Rhône valley.
- **Organising Your Time:** You will need at least half a day for the cave and area.
- **Also See:** Gorges de l'ARDÈCHE, VIVIERS.

Underground Maze

Temperature below earth 13°C/55°F.
Guided tours (1hr30) Feb–Mar and Christmas school holidays 10.30am–4.45pm; Apr–Jun and Sept 10am–5.30pm; Jul–Aug every 20 minutes from 10am; Oct–mid Nov 10am–4.30pm. closed mid-Nov–Jan. Cave and museum: 10€ (children: 6€). ☎04 75 38 65 10. www.orgnac.com.

This fabulous cave system, discovered in 1935, is now a major tourist attraction and hugely popular. The development of the caves was a difficult task, and today the paths are at the bottom of the cave system up to 120m/390ft below the surface.

The system is entered through a long tunnel leading down to the entrance hall. The various tours descend by walking from chamber to chamber, which collectively cover 5km/3 miles and over 30,000 sq metres. In June 2004, the cave system was listed as a Grand Site de France. Anyone contemplating

Cave of Aven d'Orgnac

© Guillaume Buffet/Fotolia.com

Address Book

♿ *For coin ranges, see the Legend on the cover flap.*

WHERE TO STAY

🍽🍽 **Domain de la Sérénité** – *Pl. de la Mairie, 30430 Barjac, 6km/3.6mi W of the Aven d'Orgnac via D 317 and D 176.* ☎04 66 24 54 63. *Closed Dec–Easter.* 🚫. *3 rms.* Located in the heart of the village, a 17C residence sporting blue shutters and covered with Virginia creeper. Old furniture, odds and ends, patined walls, ceramic wall tiles and earthen floor tiles give each room a personal touch. The scrumptious breakfast is served by the fireplace or on the flowered terrace when the sun shines. A gem!

WHERE TO EAT

🍽 **Les Stalagmites** – *07150 Org-nac-l'Aven.* ☎04 75 38 60 67. *Closed 16 Nov–28 Feb.* A simple, very inexpensive family boarding house with a warm welcome, located right in the village. In summer, the generous, traditional cuisine is served on the tree-shaded terrace. Children's menu. Rooms and studios to let.

🍽 **L'Esplanade** – *Pl. de l'Église, 30430 Barjac.* ☎04 66 24 58 42. *Closed 30 Sept–15 Jan and Tue except Jul–Aug.* A small stone house dating from the 18C. The flowery terrace offers a lovely view of the countryside; the vaulted dining room is decorated with old farm tools and miscellaneous bric-a-brac.

---

touring the caves need to be tolerably fit and agile.

The **Upper Chamber** (Salle Supérieure) is amazing for its sheer size (height :17–40m/56–131ft; length: 250m/ 820ft; width: 125m/410ft) and the views in and around it.

The dim light from the natural mouth of the swallow-hole gives it a bluish tinge that appears somewhat unreal. It contains a number of magnificent stalagmites, in an incredible variety of shapes. The largest (in the centre) have the appearance of pine cones. For the most part, the height of the gallery roof has prevented stalagmites from joining up with the stalactites overhead to form columns; instead they have thickened at their base until some reach quite impressive dimensions. Other, more slender stalagmites look like piles of plates, as a result of the slow oozing of water through the high, thin roof.

Beneath the lower sections of cave roof are slim **candle-like formations**, with straight or tapering sides.

In the niche of a huge formation of draperies and stalagmites like organ pipes is an urn containing the heart of Robert de Joly.

In the **Rockfall Chamber** (Salle du Chaos), filled with concretions from the Upper Chamber, there are magnificent "drapes" of various colours – white, red and brown – hanging from a crack in the cave roof.

The **Red Chamber** (Salle Rouge) has a fantastic decor centred around colossal pillars of calcite. It owes its name to the layer of clay, the residue of the dissolving calcite, which covers floor, walls and concretions alike.

The climax of the tour is the **Grand Theatre** viewpoint overlooking a huge chamber which, at first, is in total darkness; however, music gradually fills the cave and, combined with light effects underlining details round the rock walls, creates a spellbinding atmosphere.

Rando' souterraine

🕐 *Available Jul–Aug: by appointment. Groups of 4–8 persons over 10 years of age.* 💶*From 40€.* ☎04 75 38 65 10. www. orgnac.com.

Cave enthusiasts may like to take part in this 3-hour underground ramble, available to groups of restricted size only, through the red chambers, a magnificent part of the cavern which has been left as it was when discovered apart from the installation of electric lighting.

This walk is an ideal compromise between standard guided tours of caves and full-blown potholing "in the raw," and is not unduly problematic or physically taxing, although you will need to be reasonably agile.

Musée de Préhistoire

&⊙*Same times and charges as the cave (see above).* ☎*04 75 38 65 10. www.orgnac.com.*

The rooms, laid out around a patio, contain the finds from archaeological digs in Ardèche and the north of Gard. They date from the Lower Palaeolithic to the Iron Age (from 350,000 to 600 years BC). Reconstructions, including an Acheulian hut from Orgnac 3, a flint workshop and a cave decorated with a Lion's Head provide an insight into the everyday life of prehistoric man.

Driving Tours

1 Gorges de l'Ardèche, Route panoramique★★★

38km/24mi itinerary.
&*see Gorges de l'ARDÈCHE.*

2 Plateau d'Orgnac

45km/28mi itinerary starting from Aven d'Orgnac; local map &*see Gorges de l'ARDÈCHE.*

Barjac

The narrow streets of the upper town, lined with fine 18C houses surround the castle now a cultural centre (cinema and multimedia library).

From the esplanade overlooking the valley, there is a fine view of the Cévennes mountains.

Twice a year (Easter weekend and around 15 August), Barjac holds an antique fair which attracts enthusiasts and specialists from all over the region.

▸ *Follow D 979 N; in Vagnas, turn right onto D 355.*

Labastide-de-Virac

This fortified village on the boundary between the Languedoc and Vivarais regions is an ideal departure point for outings to the Aveyron gorge or the Orgnac plateau.

Just north of the village stands a 15C castle, the **Château des Roure** (⊙*open mid-Apr–Jun and Sept daily except Wed 2pm–6pm (Jul–Aug daily 10am–7pm);* ⊛*6€ (ticket including Musée de la Soie:*

8€); ☎*04 75 38 61 13; www.chateaudesroure.com),* which guarded the passage through the gorge at the Pont-d'Arc.

The two round towers were pulled down in 1629 during the Wars of Religion. Since 1825, the castle has belonged to the family of sculptor James Pradier (1795–1825) whose forebears were tenant farmers to the counts of Roure; he carved the statues representing Lille and Strasbourg on place de la Concorde in Paris.

The tour takes in the Florentine courtyard, a spiral staircase and the great hall with its fine chimney-piece.

The castle watch-path overlooks the Ardèche and Gras plateaux, and in fine weather Mont Lozère and Mont Mézenc can be seen to the north.

The tour ends with an exhibition of handmade silk goods. A working silkworm farm illustrates traditional methods of silkworm breeding.

▸ *Beyond Labastide, turn left off D 217.*

The road runs through **Les Crottes**, a ruined village *(partly restored)* destroyed during the Second World War.

A stele commemorates the inhabitants who were shot by the Nazis on 3 March 1944.

Continue to the **Belvédère du Méandre de Gaud**. This promontory commands an excellent **view**★★ of the Ardèche and the Gaud cirque.

▸ *Drive back to D 217 and turn left; a minor road on the right leads to Aven de la Forestière.*

Aven de la Forestière★

⊙*Open Apr–Sept: guided tours (1hr) 10am–7pm.* ⊛*6€.* ☎*04 75 38 63 08. www.laforestiere.net.*

This cavern, first explored by A Sonzogni in 1966, was opened to tourists in 1968. It is not far below ground and is easily accessible.

The cleverly lit chambers contain a wealth of fine concretions in interesting shapes and subtle colours.

A small underground zoo is home to a variety of fish, shellfish, frogs, toads and insects.

LAC DE PALADRU ★

MICHELIN MAP 333: G-5

Lake Paladru lies in a depression originally formed by a glacier. The lake, mainly supplied by rain and snow, has a tributary at its southern end; the Fure, which flows down to the River Isère. Its beautiful emerald waters form a lovely stretch 6km/4mi long which, during summer months, attracts many watersports enthusiasts and ramblers from Lyon and the Dauphiné region. Anglers will find a wide variety of fish to test their skill, including char and freshwater crayfish.

The hillside farms overlooking the lake and Upper Bourbre Valley will appeal to those interested in traditional rural architecture: these houses are remarkable for their imposing eaves, sometimes reaching over the barn almost right down to the ground. The walls are made of mud, sometimes combined with shingle.

- **Information:** rue des Bains, 38850 Charavines. ☎04 76 06 60 31. www.paysvoironnais.info.
- ▶ **Orient Yourself:** Just over 20km/12½ miles to the east of Côte-St-André.
- **Don't Miss:** Take a walk around the lake.
- **Organising Your Time:** Allow around 2 hours.
- **Also See:** La CÔTE-ST-ANDRÉ, La DOMBES.

Wood Civilisation

The discovery of a large number of piles emerging at low water level proves the existence of houses built directly on chalk shoals. The variety and abundance of the remains discovered as well as an analysis of pollen contained in the sediment have helped define the nature of the surrounding forest mantle and the daily activities of the inhabitants, who were mostly woodlanders.

"Les Baigneurs"

This farming village underwent two successive phases of occupation around 4700 years ago, both connected with the Saône-Rhône civilisation. Axe handles, wooden spoons, flint stones, spindle-whorls and charred debris indicate the practice of several crafts as well as burn-beating after deforestation in preparation for cropping (wheat, poppies, flax).

Colletière

This site to the south reveals a fortified village set up towards the end of the 10C, following a considerable drop in the level of the lake as a result of the climate warming up. The inhabitants were farmers, stock-breeders and fishermen. The discovery of riding equipment, lances and heavier weapons would indicate that there were knights with regular military duties whose task was to protect the community. This pre-feudal society was governed by laws concerning work and seems to have been more than able to provide for all its needs. The good condition of the dwellings has enabled specialists to reconstruct the original dwellings with accuracy, using a model to represent the three buildings identified. The lakeside

Emerald waters of Lac Paladru

Address Book

For coin categories, see the cover flap.

WHERE TO STAY

⊜ **Chambre d'hôte Mme Ferrard** – 145 chemin de Béluran, lieu-dit Vers-Ars, 38730 Le Pin, 1km/0.6mi SW of the Lac de Paladru via D 50. ☎04 76 06 68 82. 5 rms. Meals⊜. This old farm looks out over the Lac de Paladru. Nearly all of the bedrooms enjoy a view of the emerald-coloured waters.

WHERE TO EAT

⊜ **Hôtel les Bains** – 345 r. Principale, 38850 Charavines, 1km/0.6mi S of Lac de Paladru via D 50. ☎04 76 06 60 20. Closed 1 Jan–14 Feb. This restaurant's appealing, old-fashioned decor – parquet, bistro furnishings, flowered plates – is most enjoyable. Traditional cuisine with one speciality: la friture, tiny fish fried whole.

---

environment has preserved numerous everyday objects, such as leather shoes, textiles, rare wooden musical instruments, games (a complete chess set) and even toy weapons (crossbow).

Around The Lake

Musée du Lac de Paladru

Open Jul–Aug daily except Mon, 3pm–7pm; May: Sat, Sun and public holidays, 2pm–6pm; Jun and Sept daily except Mon, 2pm–6pm. 3€ (12–18s, 2€). ☎04 76 55 77 47. www.museelacdepaladru.com. This museum displays the finds of underwater archaeological excavations of the drowned Neolithic and medieval villages.

Tour of lake★

It is possible to walk all round the lake (for details ask at the tourist office in Paladru). The Maison du Pays d'Art et d'Histoire de Paladru organises **heritage trails (visites-découvertes du patrimoine** – Information at the Musée du lac de Paladru in Charavines). Two scenic roads – D 50 and D 50^D (which become D 90) – encircle the lake (15km/9.5mi). They connect the lively resort of **Charavines** on the southern point of the lake to the village of **Paladru** at the other end.

Excursions

Tour de Clermont

From Charavines, take the footpath along the Fure as far as the D 50 bridge, then the trail waymarked in yellow which goes uphill through fields. After the hamlet of La Grangière, take the path on the left up to the Tour de Clermont.

This 13C pentagonal keep is all that remains of the powerful stronghold of Clermont. The top of the tower has disappeared, and the doorway was knocked out after the original date of construction. This was the residence of one of the oldest families of the Dauphiné, which married into Burgundy to give rise to the Clermont-Tonnerre branch of the family.

La Croix des Cochettes

Steeper than the above, but better signposted. From the car park in Colletière, take the footpath uphill, waymarked in orange, towards Louisias. Where the land levels out, turn E along the hillside to join a footpath waymarked in blue which leads to the Cochettes Cross. Admire the panoramic view of the lake.

Château de Virieu★

7.5km/5mi NW on D 17.

Open mid-Apr–Oct: guided tours (45m) Sat–Sun and public holidays 2pm–6pm (Jul–Aug daily except Mon). 6€. ☎04 74 88 27 32. www.chateau-de-virieu.com.

The castle overlooking the Upper Bourbre valley dates from the 11C to 18C, and was restored at the beginning of the 20C; it still looks like a fortress.

PÉROUGES★★

POPULATION 1,103

MICHELIN MAP 328: E-5 – LOCAL MAP SEE LA DOMBES

Pérouges is perched on a hilltop and surrounded by ramparts; it remains a model of medieval architecture, with narrow winding streets and ancient houses, making it very popular with visitors. Pérouges has such an authentic historical flavour that it is often used as the setting for period films by French directors.

- **Information:** Entrée de la Cité, 01800 PÉROUGES. ☎04 74 46 70 84. www.perouges.org.
- ▶ **Orient yourself:** Pérouge lies 34km/21 miles north-east of Lyon, and 38km/23½ miles from Broug-en-Bresse.
- **Don't miss:** the place de la Halle.
- **Parking:** There is limited parking, but you will find a car park near the church.
- **Organising you time:** allow 2h to explore the town.
- **Also see:** CRÉMIEU, La DOMBES.

A Bit of History

During the Middle Ages and up to the French annexation (1601) the town was disputed many times by the sovereigns of Dauphiné and Savoy. In the rich and active town centre, hundreds of craftsmen wove fabric from hemp grown in the surrounding fields.

In the 19C the town's prosperity waned: Pérouges was too far from the railway line and local craftsmen could no longer compete with industry.

In 1909–10 the town nearly disappeared altogether: many of the owners turned to mass destruction and entire blocks of old houses were pulled down. Fortunately, an historical society from Lyon and a few artists from Pérouges stepped in, helped by the School of Arts. The most interesting houses were bought, restored, and classified as historical monuments.

Most of the houses in Pérouges mark the transition between the Gothic and Renaissance styles. The houses of the gentry and richer townsfolk have large dimensions and luxurious interiors. Those of the merchants were more modest, with semicircular openings to light the workshop or serve as counters to display their goods. The streets have barely changed since the Middle Ages. Narrow and winding, they had double-sloping paving with a drainage channel in the middle.

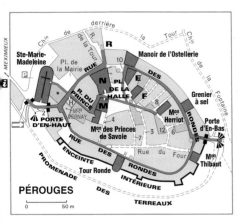

PÉROUGES	
Boulevard	2
Brune R. de la	3
Contreforts R. des	4
Filaterie R. de la	6
Halle-au-Four R.	7
Herriot R. É.	8
Place R. de la	10
Tambour R. du	12

Maison Cazin	E
Maison du Vieux-St-Georges	F
Musée du Vieux-Pérouges	M
Ostellerie	N
Puits de la Tour	R

Place de la Halle

Walking Tour★★

Porte d'En-Haut★

This gateway, the main entrance to Pérouges, was also the most exposed. Its defence was reinforced by the fortress-church and a barbican.

Rue du Prince★

Butchers, basket-makers, drapers, the armourer and apothecary held shop here. At one end stands the **Maison des Princes de Savoie**, which presently houses a museum.

Place de la Halle★★

This market square is one of the prettiest in France. It derives its name from the covered markets or **Halles**, which stood here and were razed in 1839.

Ostellerie

This inn has a sign bearing the town's coat of arms. The half-timbered east façade is 13C whereas the south front is Renaissance.

Musée du Vieux-Pérouges

◔*Guided visit (45m): Apr–Sept 10am–noon, 2pm–6pm.* ⊛*4€.* ☎*04 74 61 00 88.* This museum is housed partly in the Maison des Princes de Savoie and in the Maison Heer which opens onto place de la Halle.

Maison du Vieux-St-Georges

A shell-shaped niche on the façade houses an unusual wooden 15C statue of St George, patron saint of Pérouges, mounted on a horse.

▶ *Take the narrow street which goes downhill from the corner of the square.*

Maison Herriot

This is a sumptuous-looking house with semicircular and mullioned windows.

▶ *Return to the square and take rue de la Place, to the N.*

Maison Cazin

This lovely house has projecting upper floors and half-timbering.

▶ *Turn right onto rue des Rondes.*

Rue des Rondes★

This street still has most of its ancient paving and central drainage channel. The old houses on either side are protected by wide eaves.

Porte d'En-Bas

The Lower Gateway is older than the Upper Gateway. On the outside there is an inscription referring to a siege in 1468, which can be translated as:

"Pérouges of the Pérougians! Impregnable town! Those rascally Dauphinois wanted to take it but they could not. So they went off with the doors, the hinges and the locks instead. May the devil take them!"

▶ *Rue des Rondes leads round to place de l'Église.*

Église Ste-Marie-Madeleine

This 15C church looks like a fortress with its north-western wall incorporating crenellations, arrow slits and very high, narrow openings.

▶ *Rejoin rue des Rondes which leads to rue de la Tour.*

Puits de la Tour

For a long time this well supplied water to the entire town. The tower built by the Romans was destroyed in 1749. A lantern in the upper part of the tower was used to send light signals to similar towers forming a relay right to Lyon.

The two curtain walls

The path uphill from the Upper Gateway leads to **Promenade des Terreaux**★ in the moat of the outer curtain wall of which only vestiges remains. The **Round Tower,** against which the house of the Sergeant of Justice is built, was formerly used as a prison.

Excursions

Montuel

Leave Pérouges on N 84 towards Lyon.
Montuel has retained several interesting buildings worth admiring. Take a stroll through the flower-decked town starting from the collegiate church of Notre-Dame-du-Marais (16C-17C) past the chapel of the former Visitation Convent then the 12C St-Stephen's porch, note the carved wood decoration of the **apothecary's shop** (🕐*open May–Oct Wed and Sat 3pm–6pm; Nov–Apr Sat 3pm–6pm;* 🕐 *closed public holidays;* ☞*3€;* ☎*04 78 06 06 23*).

St-Maurice-de-Gourdans

12km/6.6mi S on D 65B.
This village lies on the edge of a plateau dominating the confluence of the River Ain and the River Rhône. The 12C **church** has been restored to reveal its original masonry: limestone and stone chippings taken from the bed of the Rhône, with alternating layers of small bricks and flat pebbles.

Centre Nucléaire de Production d'Electricité du Bugey

11km/6.8mi. Leave St-Maurice-de-Gourdans E along D 84; turn right onto D 65 towards Loyettes then left onto D 20 shortly before Loyettes.
Overlooked by the Île Crémieu, this nuclear power plant is located in **St-Vulbas,** on the right bank of the Rhône. The visit consists in a technical presentation of the plant, followed by a tour of some of its installations: cooling tower, turbine and condenser hall. The visit ends with an explanation of the control room simulator. The information centre provides documents on the production and consumption of energy, on nuclear technology and on the different types of power plants.

LE PILAT★★

MICHELIN MAP 327: F-7 TO G-8

The influence of the Mediterranean to the east and the Atlantic to the west makes it something of a watershed, particularly at Chaubouret Pass; it also acts as a water tower for the St-Étienne region. The coolness of its fir plantations, swift streams and high pastures contrasts with the industrial aspect of the Ondaine, Janon and Gier valleys. Formation of the massif goes back to the Hercynian fold: it was then a high mountain with its folds lying in a south-west-north-east direction. During the Secondary Era, erosion reduced it to a plateau, sloping down towards the present-day Rhône valley; the plateau was then covered with water leaving several layers of sediment. During the Tertiary Era, the water withdrew. The Alpine fold then caused subsidence of the Rhône valley and tilting of the massif. Le Pilat, having been "rejuvenated," rose to an altitude of 1,500m/4,921ft while the rivers – the Gier in the north and the Limony in the south – slid to the foot of the faults. During the Quaternary Era, erosion took its toll once again.

- **Information:** 16 av. de la Libération, 42000 St-Étienne. ☎0892 700 542. www.tourisme-st-etienne.com.
- ▶ **Orient Yourself:** The Massif du Pilat lies to the east of St-Étienne, between the Loire basin and the Rhône valley.
- **Don't Miss:** The panorama of the valley from the Crêt de l'Œillon.
- **Organising Your Time:** Allow a whole day to explore; more if you can.
- **Also See:** ANNONAY, VIENNE.

A Bit of Geography

Grassy Heights - Crêt de la Perdrix at 1,432m/4,698ft and Crêt de l'Œillon at 1,370m/4,495ft – bristle with strange piles of granite blocks called **chirats**, resulting from complete erosion of the summits.

Many rivers rise near the summits and flow rapidly down towards the Gier, the Rhône or the Loire along steep-sided valleys. The Gier itself, close to its source, crosses a *chirat* at the **Saut du Gier** falls.

😊 A Bit of Advice 😊

Regional parks are different from national parks in their concept and purpose. They are inhabited areas selected for development of the local economy through specific activities (the creation of cooperatives, promotion of crafts), the preservation of the natural and cultural heritage (museums, architecture) and the appreciation of the distinctive character of the region.

A Tribute To Nature

Parc Naturel Régional du Pilat

Created in 1974, the park contains about 50 towns and villages in the Rhône and Loire *départements*. The countryside is diverse: forests of beech and fir at high altitude, pastureland on the plateaux, orchards and vineyards along the banks of the Rhône. Committed to preserving nature and the environment, Pilat Park promotes rural, craft, tourist and cultural activities.

Maison du Parc

Moulin de Virieu in Pélussin.

Open Easter–mid Nov 9.30am–12.30pm, 2pm–6pm (Sat–Sun and public holidays 9.30am–12.30pm, 2pm–6.30pm); mid-Nov–Easter daily except Sun 10am–12.30pm, 2pm–6pm (Fri 5pm, Tue 2pm–6pm). Reserve centre and tourist office, Moulin de Virieu 42410 Pélussin. ☎04 74 87 52 00. www.parc-naturel-pilat.fr.

The park's main information centre also organises exhibitions, special activities and walks. To facilitate an introduction to flora and fauna within the regional park there are 500km/310mi of marked

The rolling landscape of the Pilat hills

footpaths (brown and white stripes), including sections of GR7 and GR42 (Grande Randonnée long-distance footpaths, marked with red and white stripes), three nature trails and eight special themed trails each identified by a number.

The **Jean-Jacques Rousseau trail,** from Condrieu to La Jasserie ① is a reminder that the philosopher and writer came to Mont Pilat in 1769 for botanical reasons; the **flora trail** ⑨ takes the rambler from the almost Mediterranean vegetation of the Malleval region to the subalpine formation of Perdrix ridge, from prickly pear to mountain tobacco. The **ornithological trail,** between St-Pierre-de-Bœuf and St-Sabin Chapel features up to 90 registered species of birds (particularly from mid-May–mid-June).

To promote traditional activities and revive near-forgotten crafts, the park has opened the **Maison des Arts et Traditions Populaires La Béate** (◷open Jul–Sept Sun and public holidays, 2.30pm–6.30pm; ⊕no charge; ☎04 77 51 24 70) in Marlhes, the **Maison de la Passementerie** (◷open early May–mid Oct Sat–Sun 2.30pm–6.30pm; other days by appointment; ⊕2€; ☎04 77 39 93 38) in Jonzieux and the **Maison des Tresses et Lacets** (♿◷open Jul–Aug daily except Tue 2.30pm–6pm; Feb–Jun and Sept–Dec daily except Tue and Sat 2.30pm–6pm; ⊕4€; ☎04 77 20 91 06) in La Terrasse-sur-Dorlay.

Tourist and sporting facilities include the St-Pierre-de-Bœuf Leisure Park which has an artificial river for canoeing and kayaking; the canoe base at Terrasse-sur-Dorlay; downhill skiing resorts at La Jasserie and Graix, and cross-country ski clubs at Le Bessat, Burdignes, St-Régis-du-Coin and St-Genest-Malifaux. Other sites are suitable for climbing, hang-gliding, cycling and orienteering. **Mountain-biking** facilities are being developed, with numerous waymarked tracks categorised by degree of difficulty. **Festivals:** Apple Day on 11 November at Pélussin, the Farm Produce Fair in Bourg-Argental in June, the Wine Fair in Chavanay (second weekend in December) and the Cheese and Wine Fair in Condrieu (1 May) provide an introduction to local produce.

Driving Tour

St-Étienne to Condrieu

89km/56mi – about 6hr, not including St-Étienne.

▸ *Leave St-Étienne on D 8 SE.*

Rochetaillée

This is a small village perched on a narrow rocky channel between two ravines, below the ruins of a feudal castle.

Gouffre d'Enfer★★

1hr on foot there and back.

To the right of the inn, Auberge de la Cascade, a path follows the bed of the old torrent to the foot of the dam. The site is impressive: the heavily gouged walls of rock come together to form a dark, narrow gully, dramatically named **"Chasm of Hell."** The dam was built in 1866 to supply water to St-Étienne; steps lead up to the top of it.

▸ *To get back to the car, turn left and follow the path on the right running past the Maison des Ponts et Chaussées.*

Beyond Rochetaillée, there are attractive views (right) over the dams of Gouffre d'Enfer and Pas-du-Riot.

Le Bessat✵

Small summer and winter resort.

▸ *Beyond Le Bessat, take D 63 towards La Croix-de-Chaubouret.*

Crêt de la Perdrix★

Just after La Croix-de-Chaubouret turn left onto D 8ᴬ towards La Jasserie. The road winds past spruce, mountain pastures and heathland.

▸ *After about 5km/3mi, at the top of the climb, park near the path leading to Perdrix ridge (15min on foot there and back) which is crowned with a chirat (granite rock).*

The **panorama** from the viewing table takes in the peaks of Mézenc, Lizieux, Meygal and Gerbier-de-Jonc.

▸ *Rejoin D 8 and follow D 63 to Crêt de l'Œillon.*

The road meanders alternately through fir trees and moorland covered in broom.

Crêt de l'Œillon★★★

15min on foot there and back. At the Croix de l'Œillon pass, take the road on the left leading to the turn-off to the

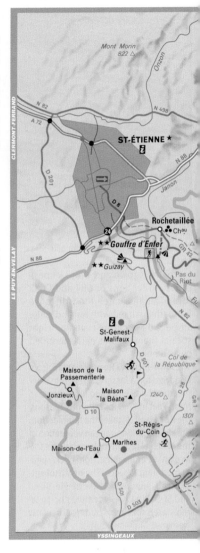

private road ending at the television relay station. Park in the car park. At the top, walk to the left around the fence; the viewing table is on the eastern end of the promontory, at the foot of a monumental cross.

The **panorama** is one of the most spectacular in the Rhône valley. In the foreground, beyond the rocks of the Pic des Trois Dents (Three Teeth Peak), there is a view of the Rhône valley.

▸ *Continue to Pélussin.*

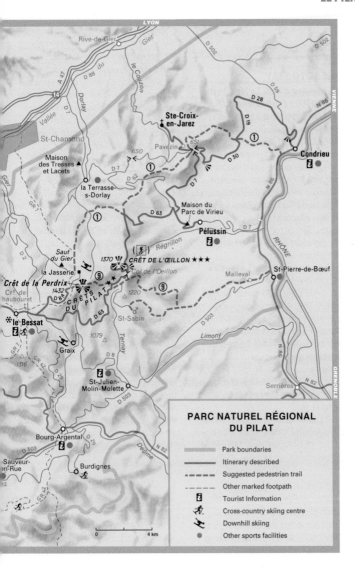

PARC NATUREL RÉGIONAL DU PILAT

Park boundaries
Itinerary described
Suggested pedestrian trail
Other marked footpath
Tourist Information
Cross-country skiing centre
Downhill skiing
Other sports facilities

0 ____ 4 km

Pélussin

Park on place Abbé-Vincent in front of the hospital. Walk down rue Dr-Soubeyran and take rue de la Halle on the left.

The old covered market provides a view of the Rhône plain and the town of Pélussin. Go through a fortified gatehouse and turn left. Note the ancient chapel and castle.

▶ *Turn back the way you came and take D 7 right to Pavezin Pass. Continue to Ste-Croix-en-Jarez.*

Ste-Croix-en-Jarez

The Carthusian monastery of Ste-Croix (Holy Cross) was founded in 1280 by Béatrix Roussillon. During the Revolution the monks were forced to leave; the monastery was then split up, the cloisters demolished in 1840 and, in 1888, Ste-Croix became a municipality.

Address Book

For coin ranges, see the cover flap

WHERE TO STAY

Chambre d'hôte Le Moulin du Bost – *42131 La Valla-en-Gier, 13km/8mi N of Le Bessat. Take D 2, then D 76 after La Valla-en-Gier dir. Doizieux.* ☎*04 77 20 06 62. Closed 1 Nov–Easter.* ☑. *3 rms. Meals*. An impassioned trekker and member of the 'relais randonneurs' (lodgings for hikers), the owner of this house located in the Parc Naturel Régional du Pilat can recommend rambles adapted to your capacity and desires. Simple rooms and generous fare. An address for communing with nature.

Chambre d'hôte La Rivoire – *42220 St-Julien-Molin-Molette, 5km/3mi E of Bourg-Argental via N 82.* ☎*04 77 39 65 44. info@larivoire.net.* ☑. *Reservations required in winter. 5 rms. Meals*. What a charming house, with its round tower and generous vegetable garden! It dominates the Vallée de la Déôme - an ideal vantage point with a splendid view that can be admired from all the bedrooms and the terrace.

Castel-Guéret – *42220 St-Julien-Molin-Molette. 1km/0.6mi N of St-Julien via D 8, dir. Le Bessat.* ☎*04 77 51 56 04.*

☑. *Reservations required. 5 rms. Meals*. A noble 19C manor framed by a vast park. Carefully restored in the spirit of the era, the interior still has its original parquet floor. Bedrooms are furnished in Louis XV and Louis XVI styles; bathrooms have been allowed to join the present day.

WHERE TO EAT

Auberge Vernollon – *42220 Colombier-sous-Pilat, 8km/4.8mi E of Le Bessat. Take D 8, then D 63 towards Le Col de l'Œillon.* ☎*04 77 51 56 58. Closed 1 Dec–28 Feb, Mon in summer and Mon–Fri lunch off-season. Reservations required.* The patronne's able cuisine is delectable – to be enjoyed under the magnificent wood frame ceiling in the barn or on the terrace with a panoramic view. Dinner shows are organised in the spring.

Chanterelle – *Sagnemorte, 42520 Roisey.* ☎*04 74 87 47 27. Closed Jan–Feb, Sun evening and Mon. Reservations required.* Located in a wooded, well-landscaped park, this stylish chalet looks out over a superb panorama of the Rhône valley and the peaks of the Pilat. Classic cuisine with a special touch served in a contemporary setting.

▶ *Return to Pavezin Pass, turn left onto D 30 which, as it begins its descent, offers a beautiful view of the Rhône Valley. Continue along D 19 and D 28 to Condrieu.*

Just before arriving, in a bend with a Calvary overlooking the town, there is a panoramic **view**★ of the Condrieu basin and the bend in the Rhône below.

Condrieu

One of the largest markets in the region is held here, specialising in fruit and early vegetables.
The town is also famed for its excellent white wine, made from the *viognier* grape The **church** has a Gothic doorway with a tympanum bearing fragments of a Romanesque bas-relief. Next to it stands **Maison de la Gabelle,** a house with an attractive 16C façade. The port – the town was once renowned for its sailors – is a pleasant place for a stroll, with its slightly Mediterranean feel.

Excursion

Bourg-Argental

This small busy town lying at the foot of the Pilat massif has specialised in local craft and industrial activities. The church, rebuilt in the Romanesque style in the 19C, presents a sculpted **doorway** (12C).

LE PUY-EN-VELAY ★★★

POPULATION 20,490

MICHELIN MAP 331: F-3

The **site**★★★ of Le Puy-en-Velay is one of the most extraordinary in France. Out of a rich plain set in a depression rise enormous peaks of volcanic origin: the steepest, the St-Michel rock (or Mont d'Aiguilhe) is surmounted by a Romanesque chapel, making it even higher; the largest, Corneille rock (or Mont d'Anis) is crowned by a monumental statue of the Virgin Mary. This strange and splendid vision is complemented by a visit to the church of Notre-Dame du Puy, no less strange, almost oriental, which houses the Black Virgin still venerated by numerous pilgrims. On Saturday, market day, the town is a striking sight: place du Breuil and the old streets between the square and the market become incredibly busy. In autumn, the **Festival of the Bird King** (Fêtes du roi de l'Oiseau) is held, in commemoration of an age-old local custom to discern the town's best archer, celebrated in a Renaissance atmosphere that pervades the upper end of the town during festivities.

- **Information:** 2 pl du Clauzel, 43000, Le Puy-en-Velay. ☎04 71 09 38 41. www.ot-lepuyenvelay.fr.
- ▶ **Orient Yourself:** Le Puy-en-Velay is situated south-west of Lyon and St-Etienne, and accessible from the A 75.
- **Parking:** There are plenty of car parks around the southern ring road, but precious few within the town itself.
- **Don't Miss:** St Michel-d'Aiguilhe.
- **Organising Your Time:** Head for the cathedral area first, and then wander the streets, or follow one of the Town Walks. Allow a full day to explore.
- **Also See:** GORGES de la LOIRE, ST FLOUR.

The Puy Basin

The Puy Basin owes its formation to the collapse of the Vellave plateau, an after-effect of the Alpine folding during the Tertiary period. Sediment stripped from the hills partly filled the basin, which was then cut by the River Loire. At the end of the Tertiary Era a series of volcanic eruptions convulsed the region; the bed of the Loire was shifted east.

During the Quaternary Era the erosion began again, forming spurs from the most resistant of the volcanic reefs, of various origins; these include basalt tables, the remains of lava flows (Polignac rock), volcanic chimneys (St-Michel rock, Espaly and Arbousset peaks) and parts of eruptive cones (Corneille and Ceyssac rocks, Denise volcano). As the lava flow cooled, combinations of prismatic columns were formed, such as those at Espaly. It is to these volcanic phenomena that the basin owes its highly original physiognomy.

A Bit of History

City of the Virgin Mary – The site of Le Puy seems to have been an ancient place of pagan worship (remains of a 1C sanctuary among the cathedral foundations), evangelised in the 3C. Apparitions of the Virgin Mary and miraculous cures near a dolmen capstone (since known as the "Fever Stone") encouraged the first bishops to come and settle here, probably at the end of the 5C. A basilica was erected, then a cathedral, around which a town soon developed, the old Ruessium having been deposed.

In the Middle Ages, pilgrimages to Le Puy were popular since it was also a point of departure for the pilgrimage to Santiago de Compostela in Spain. Along with Chartres, Le Puy is the oldest site of Marian worship in France. Kings, princes and crowds of humble origin flocked here to invoke the mother of God.

In the 12C the havoc wrought by a group of privateers, known as **Les Cotereaux**,

Lacemaking

posed a serious threat to the pilgrimages and all they contributed to the town in terms of prosperity and renown.

The **Black Virgin** brought even greater fame to Le Puy. The present statue, dating from 1856 replaces the original one mutilated and burnt during the French Revolution.

City of lace – In Le Puy and the Velay, as well as in the region of Arlanc, handmade lace was an important part of the local economy. It probably originated in the 17C and soon began to develop so that a special organisation was established. In all the villages, women worked at home for merchants in the neighbouring towns. "Collectors" who provided the lacemakers with thread and cartoons (patterns), served as intermediaries.

Originally reserved for the gentry, lace became so popular that, in 1640, the Toulouse Parliament outlawed its use as clothing. A Jesuit priest, moved by the distress of the lacemakers who suddenly found themselves out of work, managed to have the ban lifted.

Moreover, he invited his fellow missionaries to make Le Puy lace known throughout the world. This benefactor from Le Puy later became the patron saint of lacemakers. The lace trade retained its religious overtones for a long time: the art was passed on not only from mother to daughter but also by religious women known as "the beatified" who also taught catechism and cared for the sick.

A Perched Chapel

St-Michel-d'Aiguilhe★★

🕓*Open May–Sept 9am–6.30pm (mid Jul–Aug, 6.45pm); mid-Mar–Apr and Oct–mid Nov: 9.30am–noon, 2pm–5.30pm; Feb–mid-Mar and Christmas period: 2pm–5pm.* 🕓*Closed 1 Jan and 25 Dec.* ⊜*3€.* ☎*04 71 09 50 03.*

St-Michel Chapel crowns St-Michel rock, a gigantic needle of lava which rises up in a single shaft to a height of 80m/262ft above ground level. Its slender belfry, in the form of a minaret, looks like a pointed finger of rock.

St-Michel-d'Aiguilhe

Address Book

For coin ranges, see the cover flap.

WHERE TO STAY

Dyke Hôtel – *37 bd du Mar.-Fayolle.*
04 71 09 05 30. Closed Christmas week,
1 Jan. 15 rms. *6€. The contemporary*
rooms are small but tidy. Breakfast is
served in the bar room, in the company
of local regulars.

Chambre d'hôte La Paravent –
43700 Chaspinhac, 10km/6mi NE of Le
Puy via D 103 dir. Retournac, then D 71.
04 71 03 54 75. *5 rms. Meals.*
The decor is authentic and the cosy
bedrooms are very welcoming.

WHERE TO EAT

Lapierre – *6 r. des Capucins.*
04 71 09 08 44. Closed Dec–Jan, week-
ends and public holidays. A little family
restaurant off the beaten path serving
flavoursome traditional fare.

La Renouée – *In Cheyrac, 43800*
St-Vincent. 16km/10mi N of Le Puy via
D 103 and secondary road. *04 71 08*
55 94. Closed Jan, Feb, Tue, Wed and Thu
evenings from 12 Nov–31 Dec. Country-
style dining room with a stone fireplace
featuring tasty regional cuisine that
won't break the bank.

SHOPPING

Market – *Pl. du Plot. Sat morning.*
On the public square with a water
fountain, the country comes to pay
its respects to the city in the form of
baskets overflowing with the finest
farm produce; berries and mushrooms
in season.

Marché aux puces (Flea market) –
Pl. du Clauzel. Sat and fair days. Bargain
hunters, second-hand buffs and bric-a-
brac enthusiasts take note should visit
the Place du Clauzel.

**Centre d'enseignement de la den-
telle (lace making centre)**– *38/40 r.*
Raphaël. *04 71 02 01 68. www.ladent*
elledupuy.com. Mid–Jun–mid Sept:
Mon–Fri 9pm–11.30am, 1.30pm–5pm,
Sat 9.30am–5pm; rest of year: Mon–Fri
9.30pm–11.30am, 1.30pm–5pm. Closed
public holidays. 2€. We can thank St.
François-Régis, patron saint of lace
workers, for inspiring the creation
of this establishment allowing us to
discover lace in an original manner!

**Maison de la Lentille verte
du Puy** – *R. des Tables.* *04 71 02 60 44.*
www.lalentillevertedupuy.com. Jul–mid
Sept 10am–12.30pm, 2pm–7pm. Emblem
of the region, the Le Puy green lentil
was the first vegetable in France to
receive an AOC (Appellation d'Origine
Controllée) label.

**Distillerie de la Verveine du
Velay-Pagès** – *ZI de Blavozy, approx.*
6km/3.6mi E of Le Puy via N 88, exit
ZI de Blavozy, dir. St-Étienne, 43700
St-Germain-Laprade. *04 71 03 04 11.*
All year: Mar–Dec: Tue–Sat 10am–noon,
1.30pm–6.30pm (Jul–Aug: daily);
Jan–Feb: Tue–Sat, 1.30pm–4.30pm.
Closed public holidays. The Pagès distillery takes visitors on a discovery tour
of the production of Verveine du Velay
liqueur. The recipe, invented in 1859
by J. Rumillet-Charretier and still used
today, requires no fewer than 32 plants.

Sabarot – *Z.A. Lacombe, 43320*
Chaspuzac. *04 71 08 09 10. www.*
sabarot-wassner.fr. Mon–Thu 9am–noon,
2pm–5pm, Fri 9am–noon, 2pm–4pm.
Closed Wed and Fri afternoons in sum-
mer. Founded in 1819, Sabarot was
originally a flourmill. A century later,
the company branched out into the Le
Puy lentil, followed by other pulses and
mushrooms.

ON THE TOWN

Le Michelet – *5 bis pl. Michelet -* *04 71*
09 02 74. Mon–Wed 7.30am–1am, Thu
7.30am–2am, Fri–Sat 9am–4am. 1960s
America and its symbols (a petrol
pump, licence plates, photos of actors
and movie posters) seem to attract the
young people of Le Puy.

Le Bistrot – *7 pl. de la Halle.* *04 71 02*
27 08. Tue–Fri 5pm–1am; Sat 10am–
12.30pm, 5pm–2am. Closed Sun-Mon
and last 2 wks of Aug. The terrace is calm
despite its proximity to the old town.

The King's Head English Pub –
Pl. du Marché-couvert. *04 71 02 50*
35. Mon–Fri 5pm–1am, Sat 10am–1am.
Closed 1st week of Jul. The decor is
rustic, the choice of beers and whiskies
inspired and the atmosphere as English
as can be. Light meals include the Le
Puy version of fish and chips.

> *Walk up montée de Gouteyron linking the Aiguilhe rock and the upper town. Alternatively, you can reach the foot of the rock by car and park nearby.*

This chapel probably replaced a temple dedicated to Mercury. The building standing today, which dates from the 10C-12C, shows Oriental inspiration in its trefoil portal, its decoration of arabesques and its black, white, grey and red stone **mosaics**. Inside, the highly irregular ground plan follows the contours of the rock. The complexity of the vaulting testifies to the architects' ability to make the most of the site. The small columns, which form a sort of ambulatory around a short nave, are surmounted by carved capitals.

The vaulting above the small apse is decorated with 10C **paintings.** On the right, objets d'art found under the altar in 1955 are on display; note in particular a small 11C wooden reliquary Christ and a 13C Byzantine ivory cask.

A covered watch-path goes around the chapel, overlooking **Vieux Pont,** the old cusp bridge that spans the Borne.

Walking Tours

1 The Treasure Trail★★★

The cathedral dominates the upper part of the town, which is one large conservation area.

Start from place des Tables with its graceful Chorister Fountain (15C) and walk up to the cathedral via the picturesque **rue des Tables** lined with stone steps bordered by several old houses.

Cathédrale Notre-Dame★★★

This marvellous Romanesque building, now a World Heritage Site, owes its unusual appearance to the influence of the Orient; Byzantine influence, a result of the crusades, can also be seen in the octagonal domes over the nave.

The original church corresponds to the present east end. When work was begun to extend it in the 12C, shortage of space quickly became a problem. The last bays of the nave (built two by two, in two stages), together with the

west porch, were built virtually above a sheer drop, with the tall arcades serving as open piling. At the end of the 12C, the For Porch and St-Jean Porch were added. Extensive restoration was carried out on the cathedral in the 19C.

Route under the cathedral

Steps lead to the main door under the four bays built in the 12C. At the level of the second bay, two 12C **panelled doors**★ close off two side chapels; their faint decoration in relief recounts the life of Christ. Go through the main door, framed by two red columns.

Straight ahead, the main staircase leads right into the cathedral, opposite the High Altar, which led to the saying that "One enters Notre-Dame du Puy through the navel and leaves through the ears."

> *Take the central staircase or, if it is closed, the right-hand one which leads to a door in the side aisle.*

Interior

The most unusual feature of the church is the series of domes which cover the nave (that over the transept crossing is modern). Note the pulpit (**1**) and the beautiful high altar (**2**), which supports the wooden statue replacing the original Black Virgin burnt during the Revolution. The Baroque organ, recently restored, is located at the west end of the nave. Bishop Jean de Bourbon's 15C fleur-de-lis tapestry hangs at the end of the chancel.

In the north aisle hangs a large painting by Jean Solvain known as the "Vow of the Plague" (1630) (**3**) illustrating a thanksgiving procession held in place du For.

In the north arm of the transept are beautiful Romanesque frescoes: the Holy Women at the tomb (**4**) and the Martyrdom of St Catherine of Alexandria (**5**).

A gallery on the left contains a **fresco of St Michael**★ (late 11C-early 12C), the largest known painting in France depicting the Archangel Michael.

The famous stone known as the **"Pierre des fièvres"** (**12**) is in the chapel next to St-Jean Porch.

For Porch

This porch with highly elaborate capitals dates back to the late 12C. The smallest door is known as the "Papal Door" because of the inscription above it. From the small place du For there is an attractive overall view of the site and a particularly good view of the belfry.

▶ *Walk around the east end via rue de la Manécanterie.*

St-Jean Porch

This porch preceded by a large flattened arcade was designed for sovereigns to pass through; it connects the cathedral to the 10C and 11C baptistery, whose entrance is flanked by two stone lions. The leather-covered doors have beautiful 12C strap hinges (wrought-iron brackets).

▶ *Pass under the belfry to the small courtyard adjoining the east end of the cathedral.*

On the way, note the tombs of abbots and canons, and in the courtyard (**6**), behind the Romanesque well, the Gallo-Roman low-relief sculptures incorporated into the base of the east end and the frieze above: they depict hunting scenes.

Cloisters★★

The beautiful cloisters abut the north face of the cathedral; each gallery is from a different period; the oldest, to the south, is Romanesque. The **historiated** capitals in the west gallery include one (**7**) depicting a dispute about an abbot's crook, and another (**8**) showing a centaur.

A remarkable **Romanesque railing**★ (**9**) closes the west gallery. From the south-west corner of the cloisters, a Romanesque chimney can be seen rising above the altar boys' house.

Around the cloisters, above the arcades, is a delicately decorated **cornice** illustrating a medieval bestiary. The polychrome arch stones and the quoins with their black, white, red and ochre lozenges form a decor reminiscent of Islamic art.

Chapel of Relics

The Chapel of Relics or Winter Chapel derives its name from the beautiful gold altarpiece which, until the Revolution, housed relics brought to Notre-Dame du Puy.

Religious Art Treasury★★

The Treasury, displayed in the former **Velay State Room** above the Chapel of Relics, contains a large number of works of art, including an 11C silk cope, a 13C engraved enamel reliquary, a polychrome-stone 15C nursing Virgin, a magnificent 16C embroidered cloak for the Black Virgin, and a piece of 15C **parchment** showing the Genesis of the World to the Resurrection.

Cloisters of Notre-Dame Cathedral

J. Damase/MICHELIN

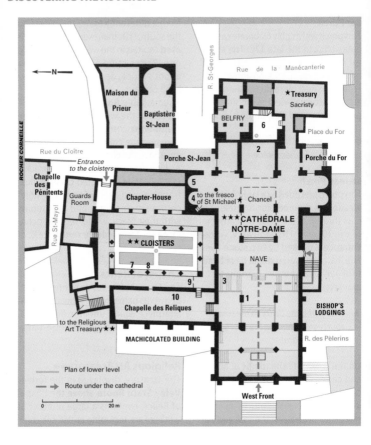

Penitents' Chapel

🕐*Open Jul–Aug 2pm–6pm.* ☏*04 71 09 38 41.*

The entrance is through a panelled wooden door carved in the Renaissance style and flanked by two groups of wreathed columns.

Inside, the paintings decorating the gallery, the panelled walls of the nave and, in particular, the beautiful coffered ceiling, recount the Life of the Virgin Mary.

St-Jean Baptistery

This building, dating back to the 10C and 11C, and connected to the cathedral by the porch of the same name, served as a baptistery for all the parishes in the town during the Revolution.

Prior's Lodgings

🕐*Open Jul–mid Sept: 10am–noon, 2pm–6pm.* ☏*04 71 05 62 75.*

Adjoining St-Jean Baptistery, the vaulted rooms of the former residence of the administrator of baptisms house an historical exhibition on Velay, and a remarkable collection of rural and craftsmen's tools.

Rocher Corneille

🕐*Open May–Sept 9am–7pm (Jul–Aug 7.30pm); mid-Mar–Apr 9am–6pm; Oct–mid Mar and Christmas school holidays: 10am–5pm; Dec–Jan Sun 2pm–5pm.* ⊕*3€.* ☏*04 71 04 11 33.*

This is the remainder of a cone, no doubt belonging to the volcano of which St-Michel rock is the chimney.

The rock is surmounted by a monumental **statue of Notre-Dame-de-France** erected in 1860 by national subscription. This cast iron statue is 16m/52ft high and weighs 110t. An outstanding 213 cannon from among the trophies from the capture of Sebastopol given to contractors by Napoleon III were melted down to cast it. It is possible to go up inside the statue to neck level.

▶ *Return to place des Tables.*

2 The Old Quarter★

The tall, red-roofed houses of the old town cluster around Corneille rock, while the circular boulevards mark the beginning of the lower, more modern town.

▶ *Turn left onto Rue Raphaël.*

Prominent citizens and members of the middle class once lived in this street. At no 38 is the Lace Centre; no 56 is a handsome 16C building on five levels, known as the **Logis des Alix Selliers.**

▶ *At the end of this street turn left onto rue Saulnerie then left again onto rue Roche-Taillade.*

On the corner with rue Cardinal de Polignac is the 15C **Hôtel du Lac de Fugères** and, further to the right at no 8, the **Hôtel de Polignac,** the Polignac family mansion with its 15C polygonal tower.

Back beyond rue Roche-Taillade, at no 3 rue Vaneau, rises the **Hôtel des Laval d'Arlempdes.**

▶ *Walk back down rue Roche-Taillade which runs onto rue Chênebouterie.*

Note, at no 8, the courtyard with a 15C turret, and opposite at no 9, the birthplace (16C) of Marshal Payolle. The road leads to **place du Plot** which, at the end of the week, bustles with a colourful market around **La Bidoire fountain,** dated 1246. Nearby, at no 8 **rue Courrerie** there remains an interesting 16C façade next to the Hôtel de Marminhac with arched windows bearing keystones carved with masks. Continue to place du Martouret – the site of many executions during the Revolution – where the Hôtel de Ville stands.

▶ *Return to place du Plot and follow rue Pannessac.*

This part-pedestrianised street is bordered by elegant 16C and 17C Renaissance houses with overhanging fronts, sometimes flanked by a tower or watchturret (nos 16, 18, 23).

To the right, some of the alleys – **rue Philibert, rue du Chamarlenc** – retain a medieval character.

The façade of no 16 rue Chamarlenc, known as the Demeure des Cornards (the Cornards were companions whose prerogative it was to poke fun at the town's burghers) is adorned with two horned heads, one laughing, the other sticking out its tongue, surmounted by satirical inscriptions.

At no 42 Rue Pannessac, the **Logis des André,** and at no 46 the 17C **Logis des Frères Michel** decorated on the ground floor with masks and carved quoins, and on the upper storeys with masks, garlands and scrolls, both reveal the opulence of the wealthy merchant who lived in this district. At the end of the street, the 14C **Pannessac Tower** retains a level of trefoiled machicolations. It is the last remaining trace of the original 18 fortified gateways, with twinned towers which allowed access through the town walls.

Sights

Musée Crozatier

◷Open May–Sept daily except Tue 10am –noon, 2pm–6pm (mid Jun–mid Sept daily); Sept–Apr daily except Tue 10am– noon, 2pm–4pm (Sun 2pm–4pm). ◷Closed Dec–Jan, 1 May and 11 Nov. ☎04 71 06 62 40. The museum collections are housed in an imposing building (1865) erected at the bottom of the Henri Vinay garden, which includes, among other

A French berline coach, Musée Crozatier

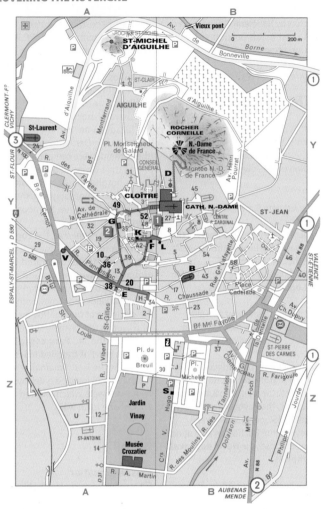

monuments, the beautiful portal from Vorey Priory.

Église St-Laurent

The church of St-Laurent is a rare example of Gothic art in Velay; it dates from the 14C and was part of a Dominican convent.

Église du Collège

At the beginning of the 17C, a Jesuit priest named Martellange built a building in the new Italian Baroque style for the order's newly founded college.

Driving Tours

Vallée de la Borne

Round trip of 60km/37mi – allow half a day.

▶ *Leave Le Puy SW on D 590 to Espaly-St-Marcel.*

Espaly-St-Marcel

Shortly before reaching the railway, turn right towards the car park.

Piton d'Espaly

This peak was formerly crowned with a castle which, after serving as a residence for the bishops of Le Puy (Charles VII, while dauphin then subsequently king of France, was given hospitality here during his frequent pilgrimages), was ruined during battles involving the Catholic League *(private)*.

Rocher St-Joseph

🕑*Sanctuary: Open Apr–Oct except Mon 8am–7pm.* 🕑*Closed Nov–Mar.* ☎*04 71 09 16 71.* The upper terrace, built at the foot of the statue, offers a **view**★ of the old town of Le Puy-en-Velay.

▶ *Rejoin D 590 and continue towards Chaspuzac. Turn right onto D 113 then right again onto D 112.*

Château de St-Vidal

🕑*Open mid-Jul–Aug: guided tours (30min) 2pm–6.30pm.* ⊘*4€.* ☎*04 71 08 03 68.* This castle, its massive towers dominating the village which clusters below around a rise in the Borne valley, was the fief of Baron Antoine de la Tour, governor of Velay in the 16C. The castle has retained from its feudal days the vaulted cellars and Gothic kitchen with its immense fireplaces. Gothic and Renaissance decorative elements from the alterations carried out in the 15C and 16C still remain, including the galleries with ribbed vaulting lining three sides of the inner courtyard, the beamed ceiling and carved stone doorway of the State Room, and the southern façade.

▶ *Return to D 113, turn right towards Clazelle then left onto N 102 and right again onto D 25. When the castle appears in the distance, turn left.*

Château de Rochelambert

🕑*Open Apr–Sept daily except Thu 10am–noon, 2pm–6pm (last admission 30min before closing); Oct–Mar by appointment.* 🕑*Closed 1 Jan, 25 Dec.* ⊘*4€.* ☎*04 71 00 48 99.* Built on the banks of the River Borne, this 15C-16C castle set in pastoral surroundings was the setting of one of George Sand's novels, Jean de la Roche.

▶ *Continue along the minor road for 2km/1.2mi then turn left onto D 131.*

Allègre

This village nestles round the ruins of a feudal castle built on the southern edge of the Boury volcano. Once through the Porte de Monsieur, you see the Chapelle de Notre-Dame de l'Oratoire standing in the centre of the square.

Tourbière du Mont Bar

This Stromboli-type volcano is the only one of its kind in France for its crater

Atelier du peintre Chaleyé	BY	B	Hôtel des Laval			Rocher Corneille	BY
Cathédrale Notre-Dame	BY		d'Arlempdes	AY	K	St-Michel-d'Aiguilhe	AY
Chapelle des Pénitents	BY	D	Hôtel du Lac de Fugères	AY	F	Statue N.-D. de France	BY
Cloître	BY		Jardin Vinay	AZ		Tour Pannessac	AY	V
Fontaine de la Bidoire	AZ	E	Musée Crozatier	AZ		Vieux pont	BY
Hôtel de Polignac	BY	L	Portail du Prieuré de Vorey	BZ	S	Église St-Laurent	AY

Polignac

is filled with a peat bog. A marked footpath leads to the bog and enables visitors to walk all the way round. (↖*2hr there and back*). The climb is rather steep, but shaded by fir trees.

▶ *Leave Allègre S along D 13.*

St-Paulien
Once the capital of the Velay region, this village was a bishopric until the 6C. The church is a fine example of Romanesque style from Auvergne.

▶ *Leave St-Paulien S along D 906 then follow N 102.*

Polignac★
Rising on its basalt hillock, the fortress of Polignac still has imposing remains of its powerful martial past from both Antiquity and the Middle Ages. The view of the site, from N 102, is superb.

Church
This is a beautiful Romanesque building with a Gothic porch and a 12C Romanesque-Byzantine dome.

Château
○━*Closed for restoration.*
The building, which could house 800 soldiers as well as the family and servants, is perched on an enormous basalt platform, the remaining fragment of a lava flow; the platform sits on a softer strata of rock which has been protected from erosion as a consequence.

▶ *Return to N 102 which leads back to Le Puy.*

Allier Gorges to the Devès

Round tour of 105km/65.2mi. Departs from Saugues, a small town favoured by anglers, 44km/27mi SW of Le-Puy-en-Velay.

▶ *Leave Saugues to the N on D 585.*

St-Arcons-d'Allier
⟵*See BRIOUDE.*

▶ *Take D 48 which runs along the east bank of the Allier.*

Chapelle Ste-Marie-des-Chazes
This chapel on the east bank of the Allier stands at the foot of a basalt rock.

▶ *Cross the Allier again before going through St-Julien-des-Chazes and on along D 48.*

Prades
Small village hemmed in by the valley sides. After dropping downhill a little, the road runs along the foot of the ruins of the **Château de Rochegude.**

Monistrol-d'Allier
This village lies in a fine **setting**★ in the Allier valley.

> *Leave Monistrol E on D 589, and turn right in St-Privat-d'Allier onto D 40.*

St-Didier-d'Allier

This small village occupies a precarious site on a steep-sided rock.

> *Take D 40 as far as Le Pont-d'Alleyras, then turn left onto D 33.*

Lac du Bouchet★

This lake lies at the bottom of an old crater which explains its circular shape. No river or stream is known to feed the lake, nor any overflow channel, yet the clarity and freshness of the lake's waters show that they are being constantly renewed.

St-Haon

The village built on the edge of the plateau has a church with a late-12C apse.

> *Follow D 31.*

Chapeauroux

This hamlet lies at the confluence of the Allier and the Chapeauroux.

> *On leaving Chapeauroux, turn right onto D 321.*

St-Christophe-d'Allier

From the road leading up the steep slope to this village there is a broad view of the Allier gorge.

> *Follow D 32 and just before it crosses the Ance, turn right onto D 34.*

St-Préjet-d'Allier

This village on the Margeride has two dams spanning the Ance.

> *Take D 33 alongside the graveyard. It leads back to Saugues.*

B. Kaufmann/MICHELIN

Ste-Marie-des-Chazes Chapel

Excursion

Arlempdes★

28km/17.5mi S of
Le-Puy-en-Velay via N 88.
Arlempdes occupies one of the most striking **sites**★★ in the Velay area. Perched on a spur of volcanic rock, the ruins of a medieval castle overlook the Loire gorge from a height of 80m/260ft.

Village

The village huddling below the castle boasts a fortified 11C gate and a charming church. On the small square in front

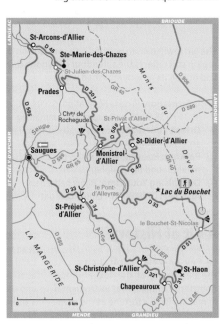

Arlempdes

of the church stands a beautiful 15C cross decorated with figures.

Castle

🕐*Open Jul–Aug: guided tours (30min) 2pm–5.30pm; Mar–Jun and Sept–Oct 8am–6pm. ☞3€. ☎04 71 57 19 47.*
The castle was built by the lords of Montlaur in the 13C and, despite its impregnable position, has been sacked on numerous occasions.

The north wall overlooks magnificent basalt lava flows on the opposite bank.

Volcanic Plateaux★

Various local villages are built on or of volcanic stone. A half-day tour *(56km/35mi)* of this region would take in **St-Paul-de-Tartas** *(S via D 54 and D 500)* with its Romanesque church built of purplish volcanic rock; the attractive, once-fortified village of **Pradelles** *(S)*, with a **local museum** in one of the houses with Renaissance windows on the market square, and the **Musée Vivant du Cheval de Trait** (Draught-Horse Museum – ♿🕐*Open Apr–Aug Sat–Sun and school holidays 10am–7pm. ☞8€. ☎04 71 00 87 87)* housed in a 19C inn (including reconstructed workshops and a collection of carriages dating from the end of the 19C as well as various breeds of donkeys).

▸ *Return to Arlempdes along D 298 then turn right onto D 500 and immediately left onto D 54.*

RIOM★★

POPULATION 18,548

MICHELIN MAP 326: F-7 – 15KM/9.5MI N OF CLERMONT-FERRAND

The old town of Riom perched on a small hill on the western edge of the Limagne region still reflects the splendour of bygone days within the ring of boulevards laid out on its now demolished walls.

- 🛈 **Information:** Pl de la Fédération, 63204 RIOM.
  ☎04 73 38 59 45. www.tourisme-riomlimagne.fr.
- ▸ **Orient Yourself:** Riom is situated 15km/9 miles north of Clermont-Ferrand, accessible from the A 71.
- 🅿 **Parking:** Rge centre of Riom is pedestrianised, but there are a number of car parks around the periphery.
- 🕐 **Organising Your Time:** Allow half a day.
- 👣 **Also See:** CLERMONT-FERRAND, Monts DÔME, VOLVIC.

A Bit of History

Le Puy-en-Velay capital city – At the beginning of the 13C Philippe Auguste's campaign was instrumental in making Riom's fortune as the monarchy decided to base the officers of its administration here.

In 1360 Duc **Jean de Berry**, the son of Jean le Bon (the Good), was given the Land of Auvergne, elevated to a duchy, as an apanage. The Duke, ostentatious and extravagant, was surrounded by a brilliant court of artists and chose Riom as one of his favourite places of residence. He ordered extensive work

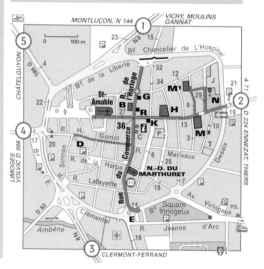

to be carried out on the old castle which he had converted by the architect Gui de Dammartin.

After the Duke's death, Riom and the Duchy of Auvergne passed to the Bourbon family. The town remained very much attached to the king; when **Joan of Arc** needed powder and arrows for the siege of La Charité-sur-Loire, she appealed to the people of Riom, who were reputed for their wealth. They pledged 60 gold écus but were slow to send them. In 1430 the townspeople received a letter of reminder; the priceless letter has been preserved at the town hall, though the saint's hair, caught in the wax seal on the letter, has now disappeared.

Walking Tour

▶ Start from place des Martyrs-de-la-Résistance.

Sainte-Chapelle★
In the Palais de Justice.
Open Jul–Aug: guided tours (30min) daily except Sat–Sun 10am–noon, 2.30pm–5.30pm (last admission 30min before closing); Jun and Sep daily except Sat–Sun 3pm–5pm; Apr–May Wed 3pm–5pm. Closed 1 Jan, 8 May, 14 Jul, 15 Aug, 25 Dec. 2€. 04 73 38 99 94.

The chapel (14C), the only remainder of the Duke of Berry's castle, has some remarkable late-15C **stained-glass windows**★ in the chancel.

▶ Walk along rue de l'Hôtel-de-Ville to the town hall.

Hôtel de Ville
Tours of the courtyard, Apr–Sept 8am–7pm; Oct–Mar 8am–5pm. Closed 1 Jan, 1 May and 25 Dec. 04 73 38 99 94.

In the vestibule is an enamelled stone plaque reproducing the letter from Joan of Arc to the people of Riom.

The lovely 16C **courtyard**★ is enclosed by two buildings decorated with vaulted arcades; note the basket-handled arches and a staircase turret with a carved door. Beneath the arcades stand two bronze sculptures by Rodin, including Gallia Victrix (modelled on Camille Claudel) and a marble sculpture by Rivoire (the Kiss of Glory).

Address Book

For coin ranges, see the Legend on the cover flap.

WHERE TO STAY

⊜⊜ **Chambre d'hôte Mme Beaujeard** – 8 r. de la Limagne, lieu-dit Chaptes, 63460 Beauregard-Vendon, 9km/5.4mi N of Riom via N 144 and D 122. ☎04 73 63 35 62. Closed 1 Nov–1 Mar except by advance booking. ⌂. 3 rms. This bucolic, bourgeois home is encircled by a pretty garden that comes into its own in the summer.

⊜⊜ **Honnorat Nicole et Stéphan** – 25 r. de l'Église, 63200 Davayat, 7km/4.2mi N of Riom via N 144. ☎04 73 63 58 20. ⌂. 4 rms. A handsome bourgeois residence (c 1810) designed along the lines of Italian neo-Classicism. Guests stay in the orangerie, an elegant outbuilding surrounded by a superb garden; each smart, well-kept room has its own decoration scheme.

WHERE TO EAT

⊜⊜ **Le Flamboyant** – 21 bis r. de l'Horloge. ☎04 73 63 07 97. Closed 15–28 Sept, Tue lunch and Mon. Located in an historical edifice of the old town that used to be a girls' school, this restaurant welcomes diners in three small rooms decorated with watercolours and flowery curtains. Several fixed-price menus.

Maison des Consuls★

Fine 16C residence. The ground floor of the Consuls' House has five archways. The first-floor windows support an elegant frieze crowned by two busts of women and two busts of Roman emperors. The wooden house opposite dates from the 15C.

Carrefour des Taules

Near this crossroads (taule is an old word for stall) which forms the intersection of the main streets of old Riom stand some of the town's most interesting old houses.

There are façades with carved windows at the corner of rue de l'Hôtel-de-Ville and rue de l'Horloge.

Rue de l'Horloge

The street is lined with old mansions with remarkable courtyards (see below) and beautiful windows such as those of no 4 and above all no 12. The town's belfry, with its gilt clock face, stands at the beginning of the street.

Tour de l'Horloge★

🕐 Open Apr–Sept 10am–noon, 2pm–6pm; Oct–Mar 10am–noon, 2pm–5pm. 🕐 Closed 1 Jan, 25 Dec and days when the fair is held. ☎04 73 38 99 94.

Surmounted by a 17C dome, this octagonal Renaissance tower rests on a square medieval base. It houses an exhibition retracing the history of the town (Riom, Ville d'Art et d'Histoire d'Hier à Aujourd'hui).

Hôtel Arnoux-de-Maison-Rouge

7 rue de l'Horloge. The corridor, lit with oval windows, leads to a delightful early-17C courtyard (guided tour only).

Cour de l'Hôtel Guimoneau★

12 rue de l'Horloge. 16C door. Go through the corridor into the attractive courtyard. The staircase is decorated with delicate carvings including an Annunciation. On the left, the gallery incorporates four statuettes representing, from left to right, Fortitude, Justice, Prudence and Temperance.

▶ Return to carrefour des Taules and turn right onto rue St-Amable.

Basilique St-Amable

Only the nave and part of the transept remain from the original 12C church. The chancel, from the early 13C, is a combination of Romanesque and Gothic (capitals with full-face figures and large crockets). The northern side chapels, with their fine ribbing on carved figure bases, date from the 15C; the southern side chapels and the west front are 18C. The sacristy features fine wood panelling (1687) around the chapter's chancel, and an interesting collection of silks.

▶ *Follow rue du Commerce, turn right onto rue Hyppolyte-Gomot and walk to the intersection with rue Sirmon.*

The numerous **fountains** that were erected in Riom in the 17C and 18C make strolling through the town very pleasant. One of the most famous is the 17C **Adam and Eve Fountain,** decorated with caryatids, by the Riom sculptor Languille.

▶ *Return to the crossroads and take rue du Commerce.*

Rue du Commerce

The modern sculptures of lava stone contrast with older works of the same material, at no 36, note the caryatids of the Hôtel Valette de Rochevert.

Église Notre-Dame-du-Marthuret★

This church was built in the Languedoc style; it dates from the 14C and 15C. The west front was extensively damaged during the French Revolution; a copy of the Virgin with a Bird stands against the pier.

On place J.-B.-Laurent, the fountain recalls the Hero of the Battle of Marengo, **General Desaix** (1768–1800), who was born in Ayat-sur-Sioule.

Additional Sights

Musée Régional d'Auvergne★

🕐*Open Jun–Sept daily except Tue 10am –noon, 2.30pm–6pm; Oct–May 10am–noon, 2pm–5.30pm.* 🕐*Closed on some public holidays.* ⌘5€, no charge Wed. ☎04 73 38 17 31.

This Regional Museum of Arts, Crafts and Traditions, laid out on three floors, houses a remarkable collection of farming implements, rural and craft tools, furniture, games, domestic items and costumes which, with the reconstruction of typical Auvergne interiors, reflect the physiognomy of the province prior to the Industrial Revolution.

The collection of headdresses and the room of religious statuary (13C-18C) are particularly interesting.

Musée Mandet★

🕐*Open Jun–Sept daily except Tue 10am–noon, 2.30pm–6pm; Oct–May daily except Tue 10am–noon, 2pm–5.30pm.* 🕐*Closed on certain public holidays.* ⌘5€, no charge Wed. ☎04 73 38 18 53.

This museum is arranged into two private mansions: one, Hôtel Dufraisse (built 1740), houses the painting collections; the other, Hôtel Desaix, houses the Richard Bequest. The first rooms display the **painting collection.** On the first floor, rooms decorated with delicate woodwork present a series of paintings from the 17C Flemish and Dutch Schools and the 17C and 18C French Schools. The second floor is given over to 19C painting, particularly the works of Alphonse Cornet, an artist from Riom.

The **Richard Bequest** includes interesting collections of ornamental objets d'art.

Driving Tour

Les Combrailles

Round trip of 75km/46.6mi – half a day.

▶ *Leave Riom W on D 986 towards Pontgibaud.*

Mozac★★

This town lies at the gateway to Riom and is famous for the capitals and treasure in its church. An abbey was founded here by St Calmin in the 7C.

Church★

The church was built in the 12C to a design inspired by the great churches of the Auvergne, but underwent major reconstruction in the 15C following an earthquake. During the French Revolution the cloisters and part of the abbey buildings were demolished.

Remains from the Romanesque period include a series of fine **capitals★★** in the nave and north side aisle which are renowned for their importance in the history of Romanesque sculpture. At the end of the nave are two of these very beautiful 12C capitals; they were originally part of the ambulatory, which no longer exists.

On the approach to the chancel there is a rich Romanesque bestiary visible, with griffins, men astride goats, dragons, a corded monkey (third pillar on the left), centaurs, birds of paradise, masks etc.

On the floor of the chancel is a third capital depicting four angels closing the mouths of four other characters; this is an illustration of a passage from St John's Book of Revelations. The chancel also contains 15C stalls. A 15C wood carving of the Madonna with a Bird stands near the baptistery.

The right aisle leads off to the former cloisters where the old tympanum (12C) may be seen.

Treasury★★

The most priceless object is the enamel **reliquary of St Calmin**★★, said to date back to 1168. It is displayed in a glass case in the right arm of the transept.

▶ *Rejoin D 986 and follow it towards Pontgibaud.*

Volvic – *see VOLVIC.*

▶ *N of Volvic, before the D 15-D 83 junction, turn left.*

Château de Tournoël★★ –
See VOLVIC.

▶ *Return to Volvic and take D 15 left alongside the graveyard. At the D 15 exit to Enval, leave the car just before the bridge spanning the Ambène.*

Gorges d'Enval★

Having crossed the bridge, take a path uphill to the left along the shaded banks of the river. After a few minutes of occasionally strenuous walking, cross the ford over the mountain stream, which forms a waterfall here that drops down into a picturesque gorge.

▶ *Continue to Charbonnières-les-Varennes then turn left onto D 16 towards Paugnat.*

Manoir de Veygoux

Open Jul–Aug 10am–noon, 2pm–7pm (last admission 1hr before closing); May–Jun daily except Thu 10am–noon, 2pm–6pm; Feb–Apr and Sept–mid-Nov daily except Mon 2pm–6pm. 7€. 04 73 33 83 00.

The manor, where General Desaix spent his childhood, is partly concealed by a building recently added. Walk round the building to see the restored façade. Inside, there is a modern illustration of the life of this general who won fame during the Revolution and later in Bonaparte's army.

▶ *Return to Charbonnières-les-Varennes then drive to Châtelguyon.*

Châtelguyon – *see Excursion.*

▶ *Leave Châtelguyon on D 415 towards Manzat.*

Château de Chazeron

Open May–Jun, Sept: 3pm–6pm. Jul–Aug, 2.30pm–6.30pm. 7€. 04 73 86 59 46.

This medieval castle was altered in the 17C by the architect Mansart. A staircase was built on the site of the former east tower, three of the outer walls were also demolished and the moat filled in, then two wings were built, one of them containing the servants' kitchen (south wing).

The tour provides a lively insight into the history of the castle. The château is now a cultural centre, with exhibitions of drawings and avant-garde furniture.

▶ *Follow D 415 to the junction with D 227. Turn right at Pont de la Ganne on D 19 towards Combronde.*

Gour de Tazenat★

A footpath leads around the lake: leave from the refreshment stand in an anticlockwise direction. The first part of the footpath is flat but becomes steep in places along the second part. The green waters of Lake Tazenat lie in a volcanic crater, or maar. The lake marks the northern boundary of the Puys range.

▶ *In Charbonnières-les-Vieilles, take D 408 NE to Montcel then turn left to St-Hilaire-la-Croix.*

Église St-Hilaire-la-Croix

This attractive building stands on the shores of the "Red Lake," whose waters once mingled with the blood of martyrs, or so says local tradition. The lofty late-12C church shows strong Limousin influence (capitals decorated with palmettes and foliage motifs).

▶ *Take N 144 to Combronde, then S of the village take D 412.*

Sources Pétrifiantes de Gimeaux

&. ⏱ *Open all year except Jan, daily: guided tours (45min) 9.30am–noon, 2pm–6.30pm.* ⏱ *Closed Christmas period and Jan.* ⊜*3€.* ☎*04 73 63 57 59.*
These natural thermal mineral springs are a geological phenomenon known locally as the "volcano." The industry of encrusting objects with lime dates back to the early 19C and uses tried and trusted techniques.

▶ *Carry on along D 17 on the banks of the Danade.*

Château de Davayat

&. ⏱ *Open mid-Jul–Aug: guided tours (45min) daily except Sat 2.30pm–6pm.* ⊜*5€.* ☎*04 73 63 30 27.*
A fine avenue of chestnut trees leads to this Louis XIII manor built by Blaise Roze, a wealthy merchant from Riom. The ambitious plans for the house and gardens were curtailed at Roze's death.

▶ *Return to Riom via St-Bonnet along N 144.*

Excursion

Châtelguyon ⚓

5km/3mi NW. 🛈*Av. de l'Europe, 63140 CHÂTELGUYON,* ☎*04 73 86 01 17. www.ot-chatel-guyon.com.*

Gour de Tazenat

J. Damase/MICHELIN

Châtelguyon is situated on the edge of a regional park (Parc Naturel Régional des Volcans d'Auvergne).
The Calvary stands on a hilltop overlooking the centre of town, on the site once occupied by the castle of Count Guy II of Auvergne, after whom the town was named.

The Spa Resort

The resort enjoyed a massive boom in the 19C. Pipes bring water from 12 springs up to the park on the banks of the River Sardon. The main feature of the springs is their magnesium content, the highest in Europe; their temperature varies from 27.5°C to 38°C/81°F to 100°F. The spa itself includes the **Grand Spa** (1st class) and the **Henry Spa** (2nd class) which was completely rebuilt in 1983. The resort specialises in the treatment of digestive and gynaecological disorders. Today, life in the resort centres on the casino-theatre, the park at the foot of Mont Chalusset containing the Grands Thermes, and avenue Baraduc which is lined with cafés and souvenir gift shops.

Église Ste-Anne

The church is decorated in a modern style. The stained-glass windows made of Baccarat crystal distil light onto **Byzantine-style frescoes** painted by the Estonian artist Nicolas Greschny.

ROANNE

CONURBATION 80,272
MICHELIN MAP 327: D-3

Rodumna, as the town was called in ancient times, dates to more than a century before the birth of Christ. In the 11C the lords of Roanne built a fortress. The Seignieury of Roanne belonged in turn to the counts of Forez, Jacques Cœur, the dukes of Bourbon and the dukes of Roanne. The inauguration of the Roanne-Digoin canal in 1838 brought intense activity to the port of Roanne, thereby determining the town's industrial vocation.

- **Information:** 8 place Maréchal de Lattre de Tassigny, 42300 ROANNE. ☎04 77 71 51 77. www.leroannais.com.
- ▶ **Orient Yourself:** Roanne lies 85km/52 miles north-west of Lyon, accessible by the A 72.
- **Parking:** There are a number of car parks in the centre.
- **Don't Miss:** You will be delighted by a visit to the Musée des Beaux-Arts.
- **Organising Your Time:** You should allow a full day to explore fully.
- **Especially for Kids:** Visit to the Parc des Canaux.
- **Also See:** BEAUJOLAIS.

Modern Roanne

Roanne is one of the best-known French textile centres for ready-made garments, hosiery and knitted goods (second in France) and towelling.

Its other economic activities are highly diversified: food processing, metallurgy, armoured tanks, tools, boiler making, tanning, dyes, paper mills, plastics and tyres. A Michelin tyre production unit has been operating in the north-east of the town since 1974.

The local gastronomy has earned a well-deserved reputation for excellence and the town boasts several fine restaurants, including one of the most famous establishments in France.

Sights

Musée des Beaux-Arts et d'archéologie Joseph-Déchelette

Open daily except Tue 10am–noon, 2pm–6pm (Sat 10am–6pm, Sun 2pm–6pm). Closed public holidays. 4€, no charge Wed afternoon. ☎04 77 23 68 77.

This eclectic museum, housed in an early-18C mansion, was founded by the archaeologist **Joseph Déchelette** (1862–1914), a native of the town. He gathered the rich **archaeological collections** which include many Gallo-Roman artefacts found during the course of excavations in the region.

The museum is also known for its fine collections of faience including items of 16C and 17C Italian **majolica**.

Place de-Lattre-de-Tassigny

The site of the old castle (part of its keep still stands) is flanked by the church of **St-Étienne** with its 15C stained-glass window.

A popular marina

Traffic on the canal from Roanne to Digoin and in the port of Roanne, which was important until 1945, declined rapidly from 1970 onwards and came to a halt in 1992.

This has been offset by an increase in pleasure boating with the opening of locks on Sundays during the summer months.

Barge trips (Several types of trip are proposed (1/2 day, 1 day or more) from or to Roanne aboard the barge "L'Infatigable". Groups take priority. Marins d'Eau Douce, Port de plaisance de Briennon. ☎04 77 69 92 92) are also organised on the canal.

Parc des Canaux   Kids
In Briennon.

🕐*Open Jul–Aug: guided tours (45min) 10am–noon, 2pm–7pm; Easter–May and Sept–early Nov 2pm–6pm.* ☞*6€ (3–12-year-olds: 3€).* ☎*04 77 60 75 79 or 04 77 69 92 92.*

This park, located along the canal between Roanne and Digoin, has a lot to offer children interested in inland navigation: a real barge turned into a museum and a hands-on system of miniatures locks and barge.

Chapelle St-Nicolas-du-Port
The small chapel can be seen near the wharfs of the port. The date on the pediment – 1630 – marks the year the bargemen made a vow to erect a chapel to their patron saint if they were spared the death throes of the plague.

Excursions

Montagny
14km/8.7mi E along D 504.
On leaving Montagny, follow the signpost indicating "La Roseraie."

Roseraie Dorieux
🕐*Open Jul–Sept: free access to the rose garden; rest of the year, enquire for opening hours.* ☎*04 77 66 11 46.*
This colourful and fragrant rose garden and nursery is freely accessible from July to September.

Plateau de la Verrerie
Leave Roanne W along D 9 to Renaison then follow D 47 to La Grand'Borne and turn right onto D 478 which leads to La Tourbière. To get back, follow D 39 from Col de la Rivière then D 9 to Roanne or D 4 if you fancy a detour via Briennon.
🚶 The solitary road climbs through the forest before reaching the Plateau de la Verrerie which offers a pleasant ramble and a view of the Roanne plain.

Le Crozet
25km/15.5km NW on N 7. Leave the car at the entrance to Le Crozet.
The flower-decked houses of this small medieval town are spread out along the foothills of the Madeleine mountains.

You enter the old main square by the **Grand-Porte,** flanked by two round towers that are truncated and partly concealed by houses.

Maison du Connétable
Fine front with pretty wooden panels. The adjoining house with walled-in arcades used to be a cobbler's workshop (15C).

Maison Dauphin
A former meat market, a restored late-15C house with Renaissance windows.

Maison Papon★
Enter the courtyard to appreciate the Renaissance façade made with enamelled ceramics and with mullioned windows.

Tour de guet
The 12C keep standing near the 19C church has lost its machicolated crown.

Maison des Amis du Vieux Crozet
🕐*Open Jun–Sept daily except Mon and Tue 3pm–7pm; rest of the year by appointment,* ☞*2€.* ☎*04 77 64 11 06.*
A peasant's interior has been carefully reconstructed in this 15C residence, alongside an old-fashioned smithy and a clog-maker's workshop.

Driving Tours

Côte Roannaise★

A line of vineyard-covered slopes running north-south, known as the "Côte," dominates the Roanne basin to the west. Contrasting with the harshness of the Madeleine mountains, the Côte is gentle and colourful, with rectangular houses, often roughcast with green shutters and red-tiled double pitched roofs, reddish soil, and vineyards that produce reputed AOC *(Appellation d'Origine Contrôlée)* red wines, as well as rosés and whites.

▶   *Leave Roanne on D 9 W and turn left onto D 51 to St-André-d'Apchon.*

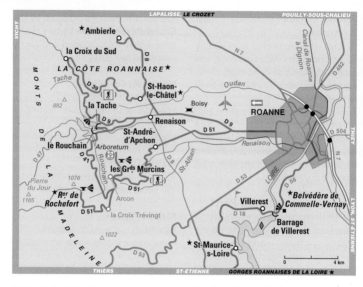

St-André-d'Apchon

At the centre of the town, in a secluded setting, stands a 16C château built for the Marshal of St-André.

▶ *From the War Memorial, walk up the street with the Lion d'Or Hotel on the corner, then along the covered passageway 30m/33yd on the right, next to a butcher's shop.*

The **church** in Flamboyant Gothic style, is decorated with 16C stained-glass windows.

▶ *Continue along D 51 to Arcon.*

The road twisting uphill above St-André offers a series of vistas of the Roanne plain.

▶ *Leave Arcon to the N, to Les Grands-Murcins and its arboretum.*

Les Grands-Murcins

The arboretum, created in 1936–37 at the heart of a national forest is particularly rich in coniferous trees, including Himalayan weeping pines.

▶ *Return to Arcon and head S to La Croix-Trévingt. Turn right onto D 51 towards St-Priest.*

Rocher de Rochefort★

The Rochefort Rock is equipped with a viewing table: **views** of the Roanne plain, the Beaujolais and Lyonnais hills.

▶ *Return to La Croix-Trévingt. Turn left onto D 51 and left again onto D 41 along the Rouchain Valley to the dam.*

Barrage du Rouchain

Duplicating the Tache dam to supply Roanne with drinking water, this dam (1977), made of rockfill, is equipped with a spillway on the River Rouchain, and occupies three valleys.

Barrage de la Tache

This dam was built between 1888 and 1892. It is a gravity dam, that is, the sheer mass of the dam resists the pressure of the water.

Renaison

This is the economic heart of the Côte Roannaise. Its neo-Gothic church houses a Romantic organ by John Abbey.

▶ *Turn back then follow D 9 to La Croix-du-Sud.*

On the way, a **look-out rock**★ on the left offers an attractive view of the Tache reservoir. The road up to the pass looks over the Madeleine mountain range.

Address Book

&For coin ranges, see the Legend
on the cover flap.

WHERE TO STAY

⊝⊝ **Grand Hôtel** – *18 cours de la
République, opposite the train station.
☎04 77 71 48 82. Closed 2–25 Aug and
20 Dec–5 Jan.* 🅿 *. 31 rms.* ⊂*9€. Just
across from the Roanne train station,
this well-maintained hotel dates from
the early 20C.*

⊝⊝⊜ **Chambre d'hôte Domaine
de Champfleury** – *Le Bourg, 42155 Len-
tigny, 8km/4.8mi SW of Roanne via D 53.
☎04 77 63 31 43. Closed 15 Nov–15 Mar.*
🍴*. Reservations recommended in winter.
3 rms.* *A 19C bourgeois house surrounded by century-old trees in a handsome
park. Perfect for a thorough rest.*

WHERE TO EAT

⊝⊝ **Le Central** – *20 cours de la République (opposite the train station).* ☎*04 77
67 72 72. Closed 2 wks in Aug, 24 Dec–
5 Jan, Sun-Mon. Reservations requested.*

Right next to the Troisgros brothers'
restaurant, this bistro-grocery also
belongs to the famous family. Simple,
contemporary cuisine is served here.

⊝⊝⊜ **Le Marcassin** – *Rte de St-Alban-
les-Eaux, 42153 Riorges, 3km/1.8mi W of
Roanne via D 31.* ☎*04 77 71 30 18. Closed
Feb school holidays, 2 wks in Aug, Sun
evening, Fri evening and Sat.* After visiting the Maille museum in Riorges, you
might try this family restaurant offering
modern fare in fixed-price menus and
à la carte.

⊝⊝⊜⊜ **Troisgros** - *Pl. de la Gare.*
☎*04 77 71 66 97. www.troisgros.fr.
Closed Feb school holidays, 2 wks in Aug,
Tue–Wed. Reservations essential.* With
three Michelin stars, this is a veritable
institution that sets the standard for
French gastronomy. The Troisgros family receives its guests in a setting where
modernism, quality, luxury and sobriety
intermingle in perfect elegance.

La Croix-du-Sud

This pass is a major intersection on the
rise separating the Madeleine mountain
range from the Côte, and the valley of
the Teyssonne from that of the Tache.

St-Haon-le-Châtel★

The **fortified village**★ has preserved
its medieval appearance and some of
its ramparts. The restored **church** (12C-
17C) is a modest building, with typical
furniture from the Forez region.

▶ *Take D 8 N to Ambierle.*

Ambierle★

This pretty town, exposed to the morning sun, is set amid vineyards that yield
a pleasant rosé wine. There is an old
Cluniac priory in the upper part of the
village.

The **Musée Alice-Taverne** (🕐 *open
Feb–Nov 10am–noon, 2pm–6pm;* ⊛*4€;*
☎*04 77 65 60 99*) focuses on traditional
home life in the region – games, costumes, superstitions of local life – and
has recreations of various interiors
(workshop, inn etc).

▶ *Take D 8 and D 9 back to Roanne.*

On the left is an attractive view of the
large round tower of **Château de Boisy**
(⊶ *not open to the public*). This castle
(14C-16C) belonged successively to the
Couzan family, Jacques Cœur, and the
Gouffier family, and occupies an important position in the history of Roanne.

Gorges Roannaises
de la Loire★

Round trip of 139km/87mi

▶ *Leave Roanne to the S along
avenue de la Libération.
Turn right by the station onto
D 43 and then right again onto
D 56 to Commelle-Vernay
viewpoint (signposted).*

Construction of the Villerest dam
upstream of Roanne created a new
"Loire Lake," 33km/20.5mi long, which
attracts numerous sailing enthusiasts
in the summer.

Belvédère de Commelle-Vernay★

The **view** encompasses Roanne and its outskirts and the Vernay bridge to the north, the town and dam of Villerest and the modern installations of the Villerest paper mills to the west. A small **tourist train** (*Reservations required: Mar–Oct 9.30am, 11am, 3pm, 4.30pm and 6pm. 6€ (children: 5€). 04 77 68 58 12. www.le-petit-train-touristique.net)* offers a 7km/4.3mi ride along the shores of Lake Villerest.

Barrage de Villerest

Designed to combat low water levels and floods on the Loire, this is a solid concrete arch gravity dam with a crown length of 469m/1,538ft. Its curved shape reinforces its stability. The variable-level reservoir is 30km/19mi long and has an average width of 250m/820ft.

▶ *Cross over the dam to Villerest.*

Villerest

The old **medieval town**★ is a pleasant place to visit; there are many houses with corbelled construction or timber-framed walls, and the remains of ramparts. The 13C **Porte de Bise** is the starting point for a tour on foot; points of particular interest are highlighted on information boards. During the summer, crafts are sold from the traditional street stalls.

Musée de l'Heure et du Feu

Open Apr–Jun and Sept–Oct Sat–Sun and public holidays 2.30pm–6.30pm (Jul–Sept daily). 5€. 04 77 69 71 97. This unusual museum is divided into two parts, the **Section on Fire**★ traces the history of the creation and the upkeep of domestic fire since Antiquity and across different countries.

▶ *Leave to the W and head for St-Jean-St-Maurice-sur-Loire.*

St-Maurice-sur-Loire★

This town occupies a **site**★ overlooking the river. The old houses cling to a spur crowned by the ruins of a medieval castle.

▶ *Drive towards Bully, down the hill towards the Loire and over the bridge at Presle. Turn right onto D 56 and along the east bank of the river.*

Château de la Roche

Open Jul–Aug 10.30am–noon, 2pm–7pm; Apr–Jun daily except Wed 2pm–7pm; Nov–Mar Thu–Sun, 2pm–6pm; Sept–Oct daily except Wed, 2pm–6pm (Sat, Sun, 7pm). 5.50€. 04 77 64 97 68. www.lechateaudelaroche.fr. This medieval manor presents the history of the Gorges de la Loire area and a model of the gorge in a refined 17C decor (painted panels on the walls and ceilings).

▶ *Shortly after the Chessieux viaduct the road meets N 82 near Balbigny; turn left towards Neulise. After 6km/4mi turn right onto D 5.*

St-Marcel-de-Félines

This peaceful village facing the Forez mountains has a 12C fortified house altered in the 16C into a **château** (*open Easter-Oct Sun and public holidays 2pm–6pm. 5€. 04 77 63 54 98).* A bridge over the old moat leads to an inner courtyard of Italian inspiration. Inside, the decoration of the reception rooms is unified by the 17C wall and ceiling **paintings**★.

▶ *Rejoin N 82 and continue to Neulise; turn right onto D 38. At Croizet turn right, cross the River Gand and take the path to the right.*

Château de l'Aubépin

Open daily except Tue and Wed 10am–noon, 2pm–5pm. Closed 15 Aug. This lovely old château (16C-18C), flanked by corner pavilions is topped with a watch-turret set back from an avant-corps decorated with masks.

▶ *Return to Roanne on N 82.*

ROMANS-SUR-ISÈRE

POPULATION 32,667

MICHELIN MAP 332: D-3

The town is built on a hillside opposite Bourg-de-Péage, whose name is a reminder of the toll once collected by the Chapter of St Barnard to cross the bridge linking the two towns. Romans, a flourishing trade centre in the Middle Ages, was once the capital of footwear. Lovers of good food will appreciate the local *pogne,* which is a type of *brioche* or sweet bread flavoured with orange blossom, *saint-genis* (praline *pogne*) and goats' cheese, *Tomme,* which is also used to make the local dish *ravioles*).

- **Information:** Pl. Jean-Jaurès, 26100 ROMANS-SUR-ISÈRE, ☎04 75 02 28 72. www.ville-romans.com.
- **Orient Yourself:** 17km/10 miles E of Tournon, 13km/8mi NE of Valence.
- **Parking:** There are a number of central parking areas.
- **Don't Miss:** It's all about shoes; visit the shoe museum.
- **Organising Your Time:** Allow at least half a day.
- **Especially for Kids:** Goblins and trolls at Le Monde Merveilleux des Lutins.
- **Also See:** VALENCE, HAUTERIVES, TOURNON-sur-RHÔNE, VALENCE.

A Bit of History

Dauphiné joins France – From the 11C on, the counts of Albon, natives of Vienne, gradually took over the region from the Rhône Valley to the Alps that eventually formed Dauphiné. The origin of the name "Dau-phin," given to members of the dynasty which then reigned over Dauphiné, remains uncertain.

The last of the Vienne dauphins, Humbert II, lived mostly at Beauvoir Castle, opposite St-Marcellin. After the death of his son, which left him without an heir, he sold Dauphiné to the French crown. It was in St-Barnard Collegiate Church that the treaty unifying the Dauphiné region, formerly part of the Holy Roman Empire, to France, was solemnly signed on 30 March 1349. This province was to become the attribute of the oldest sons of the kings of France, who subsequently bore the title of Dauphin.

Old Town

▶ *Start from place du Pont.*

A maze of picturesque streets surrounds St-Barnard Collegiate Church and, half way down the hill from the church, place de la Presle and place Jacquemart.

Collégiale St-Barnard

Quai U.-Chevalier.

♿🕐*Open mid-Jun–mid Sept: guided tours (1hr), daily, 10am–noon, 2.30pm–6pm, Sun and public holidays 2.30pm–6pm; rest of year by arrangement.* ◉*3€.* ☎*04 75 72 43 58.*

In the 9C St Barnard, archbishop of Vienne, founded a monastery here. It was destroyed in the 12C and replaced by a Romanesque church of which the western porch, the northern portal and lower parts of the nave still remain. Towards the middle of the 13C the chancel and transept were rebuilt in Gothic style. Largely destroyed by the Protestants in the 16C, the church was completely restored in the 18C.

▶ *Take rue Pêcherie, opposite the west end of the church.*

Escalier Josaphat

These **steps** go down from rue Pêcherie towards the houses with their wooden balconies on place de la Presle.

The stairway is part of the "Great Journey" or Way of the Cross which attracts a large crowd of people on Good Friday.

▶ *Rue du Fuseau runs straight onto rue de l'Armillerie.*

At no 15 rue du Mouton, off to the right, the Gothic windows on the first floor are now mullioned windows; above, the outline of a sheep's head carved in a projecting stone can just be made out.

▶ *Continue towards place Fontaine-Couverte.*

Place Fontaine-Couverte

This square in the heart of the old town is decorated with a modern fountain representing a flautist.

Côte Jacquemart

The hill is lined with 13C and 14C houses.

Le Jacquemart

This is an old square tower from the outer curtain wall of Romans, converted into a belfry in the 15C and given a Jack-o'-the-clock, which since 1830 has proudly sported the costume of a 1792 volunteer.

▶ *Facing towards the river, turn left to côte des Cordeliers; walk down to rue Fontaine-des-Cordeliers and rue St-Nicolas.*

Hôtel Thomé

This fine town house presents a Renaissance façade with beautiful mullioned windows on the upper floors.

▶ *Continue towards the river via rue Sabaton and turn right onto rue des Clercs.*

Rue des Clercs

The street is very picturesque with rounded cobblestones. Notice, opposite the town's archives, the portal decorated with fine chiselling.

Rue des Trois-Carreaux

This is an extension of rue des Clercs. At its intersection with **place aux Herbes** there is a monumental door, surmounted by an unusual corbelled construction with machicolations.

Place Maurice-Faure

Beside St-Barnard, to the right of the St-Jean door on the north side of the church, is a beautiful house with a corner tower.

On the north-west corner of the square is **rue de l'Écosserie,** in which the first houses are joined by an arch.

Sights

Musée International de la Chaussure

🕐Open Jan–Apr and Oct–Dec Tue–Sat 10am–5pm; May–Sept Tue–Sat 10am–6pm (Jul–Aug Mon–Sat); Sun and public holidays all year 2.30pm–6pm. 🕐Closed 1 Jan, 1 May, 1 Nov, 25 Dec. ☜4.50€. ☎04 75 05 51 81. www.ville-romans.com.

The Shoe Museum is located to the east of town and reached through the gateway in rue Bistour, across terraced gardens in front of the building, which is adorned with an elegant colonnade.

Shoe Collection★

The museum aims to present the technical, ethnographic and aesthetic aspects of footwear. Numerous documents and other material trace the evolution of the shoemaker's craft and associated activities in the town of Romans (dressing and tanning leather etc).

In the old nuns' cells, the collections of footwear are displayed in chronological and thematic order from Antiquity to 1900. Some of them are extremely comprehensive, such as that of Paris designer Victor Guillen.

The Jacquemart collection and Harms' original collection of buckles are also interesting. These sumptuous, amusing and enigmatic shoes reveal the ingenuity of their creators and evoke the customs of their country of origin and fashion throughout the ages: Roman sandals, cracowes whose length varied with social rank, pattens inlaid with tortoise-shell and pearl from Mauritania, Indian moccasins from North America, shoes from Ardèche used to open chestnuts and ankle boots from the Belle Epoque. The collections are displayed in rotation in temporary exhibitions.

The 18C and 19C paintings on the theme of shoes and shoemaking add another angle of interest to the museum visit.

Excursions

Mours-St-Eusèbe

4km/2.5mi N. Leave Romans on D 538 then turn right onto D 608.
The village church has kept only its bell-tower, at the west end, and the south wall of the nave from the 11C.
It houses an interesting **Musée Diocésain d'Art Sacré★** (⏱*open May–Oct: guided tours (1hr30min) daily except Sat 2.30pm–6.30pm;* ✆*4€;* ☎*04 75 02 36 16)* with rich collections of sacred art (15C-20C) arranged according to a new theme each year.

Hostun

Leave Romans E towards St-Nazaire-en-Royans. Shortly beyond L'Écancière, turn right onto D 125C to Hostun.

Kids An old farm (at Les Guerbys) has been turned into **Le Monde Merveilleux des Lutins** (the wonderful world of elves – ⏱*open Apr–May and Dec and school holidays daily 2pm–6pm; Jun–Aug daily 10am–6.30pm; Sept Sun 2pm–6pm.* ⏱*closed Jan–Mar, Sept and Oct.* ✆*7€ (children: 5.50€).* ☎*04 75 48 89 79. www.mondedeslutins.com)*, a fantasy realm where children can meet trolls, gnomes, sprites, gremlins and other goblins.

Driving Tour

Les Collines

▶ *Leave Romans to the NW by D 53 (towards the swimming-pool).*

St-Donat-sur-l'Herbasse

This old Drôme village is a popular haunt among music lovers. The 12C-16C **collegiate church** houses modern organs designed after plans made by the famous Silbermann Brothers (3 keyboards, 3 sets of pipes). Every year the church hosts a prestigious **John Sebastian Bach Festival.** ☎ 04 75 45 10 29.

▶ *Leave St-Donat on D 584 and head N for Bathernay.*

Bathernay

This pretty village enjoys a charming setting in the midst of the lush countryside. West of Bathernay a narrow road leads to the octagonal tower of **Ratières.**

▶ *Take D 207 to the S, then D 53 for 1.3km/0.9mi; A path to the right will take you to the Chapelle St-Andéol.*

Chapelle St-Andéol

The small chapel commands a superb **panorama** over the Isère valley, the Galaure Basin and Mont Pilat.

▶ *A small, picturesque road to the S rejoins D 112. Turn left in Bren and return to St-Donat, where D 53 leads back to Romans.*

ST-ANTOINE-L'ABBAYE ★

POPULATION 910

MICHELIN MAP 333: E-2

Nestling in an undulation of the Chambaran plateau north of the River Isère is the old village of St-Antoine-l'Abbaye, which is dominated by an imposing Gothic abbey church.

- **Information:** Pl. Ferdinand-Gilibert, 38160 ST-ANTOINE-L'ABBAYE, ☎ 04 76 36 44 46. www.sainteantoineabbeye.fr.
- **Orient Yourself:** St-Antoine l'Abbaye is 24km/15 miles north-east of Romans-sur-Isère.
- **Organising Your Time:** Allow a day to visit the abbey and the village.
- **Also See:** La CÔTE-ST-ANDRÉ, HAUTERIVES, ROMANS-sur-ISÈRE.

The Abbey Church

St Anthony's fire – In the 11C a noble-man from Vienne, Jocelyn de Châteauneuf, made a pilgrimage to the Holy Land. On his return he brought back from Constantinople the bones of Anthony the Great, the original "desert father," who lived in the Upper Nile Valley. In the Middle Ages this saint owed his popularity as much to the pig who was the daily companion of his hermetic life as to his battles with the devil.

The relics in the church of La Motte-St-Didier, which took the name of St-Antoine, were entrusted by the Bishop of Vienne to Benedictines from Montmajour Abbey. A first monastery was built. Not long after, in 1089, a dreadful epidemic broke out in Dauphiné – erysipelas, or St Anthony's fire. It was a sort of gangrene which burnt away the limbs.

The saint's relics drew a large crowd of sick and poor people; to help and care for them, a group of young nobles created the Brotherhood of Charity.

A powerful order – In the 13C the brothers managed to supplant the Benedictines. In 1297 the brotherhood became the Hospital Brothers of St Anthony; the Antonine monks founded hospices all over Europe.

The great abbey church of St-Antoine, which took from the 13C to the 15C to build, was visited by popes, emperors from Germany, and kings of France who came to kneel before the relics.

Abbey

& ⏰*Open: guided visits (1h): mid-Jun–mid Sept: daily except Tue, 3pm–6pm, Sun and public holidays, 2pm–5pm; Mar–mid Jun, and mid-Sept–Oct, Wed, Fri and Sat, 3pm–6pm, Sun and public holidays, 2pm–*

St-Antoine-l'Abbaye

B. Kaufmann/MICHELIN

7pm. Closed Nov–Mar. 4€. 04 76
36 44 46.

The entrance to the abbey church is
at the top of the village, through the
17C **main entrance gate** (Entrée d'Hon-
neur), now the town hall (Hôtel de Ville),
with its glazed mosaic tiles.

Musée Départemental

Open Jul–Aug daily except Tue,
*11am–12.30pm, 1.30pm–6pm; Mar–Jun
and Sept–Oct, daily except Tue, 2pm–
6pm.* Closed 1 May. 04 76 36 40 68.
www.musee-saint-antoine.fr.

This museum, located in the monastery's
old novitiate, contains works by Jean
Vinay (1907–78), a landscape artist from
Dauphiné, and thematic exhibitions by
his friends from the Paris School, and
exhibitions on the Middle Ages or the
Antonine Order.

Excursions

St-Marcellin

*10km/6.2mi to the E on D 27,
then D 20 on the right.*

This town, where the last Viennese dauphin Humbert II set up his Parliament
in the 14C, was badly hit by the Wars of
Religion: besieged twice by the Baron
des Adrets, it was subsequently recovered by the Catholics in 1568.

The colourful Saturday market and
annual fairs attract a great many locals
from Bas-Grésivaudan; the area is known
for *Saint-Marcellin*, a small, round cheese
made with cow's milk that has a soft and
moulded rind. The **Promenade de Joud**
affords pretty views of the Isère valley
and the Royans, overlooked by the Vercors ramparts.

Chatte

8km/5mi to the SE on D 27.

The most interesting sight in this
small village is its **Jardin Ferroviaire**
(open Apr–Aug 10am–7pm (Jul–
Aug 8pm); Mar and Sept–Oct Sat, Sun,
public and school holidays, 10am–7pm.
7€ (children: 5€).* Closed Nov–Feb.
04 76 38 54 55. www.jardin-ferroviaire.
com*) a miniature park complete with
paths and 200 plant varieties, cut across
by 1km/0.6mi of tiny tracks served by 30

trains. A charming outing for children
and parents alike.

La Sône

6km/3.7mi to the S on D 20, then on D 71.
This village stands in a lush, peaceful
setting along the banks of the Isère.
Do not miss the **Jardin des Fontaines
Pétrifiantes** (open Jun–Aug 10am–
6.30pm (last entry, 5.45pm); May and
Sept–Oct daily except Mon, 10am–6pm
(last entry, 5.15pm); 6€; 04 76 64 43
42; www.jardin-des-fontaines.com), set
up in a niche where petrified water concretions have coated the surrounding
relief and objects with glittering crys-
tals. The leafy grounds, featuring around
15,000 plant species, are enhanced by a
series of basins and small waterfalls.

The most picturesque way to visit
the region is to go on a **boat ride**
(Kids open Jul–Aug: cruise with com-
mentaries (1hr 30) daily at 10.30am, 2pm
and 4pm from St Nazaire en Royans, and
11.30am, 3pm from La Sône; Apr–Jun and
Sept–mid-Oct: inquire about departure
times. 9€ (children: 6€). 04 76 64 43
42) on board the Royans-Vercors paddle-
boat, which will enlighten you on the
local fauna and flora lying at the foot
of the Vercors.

ST-ÉTIENNE★

CONURBATION 291,960
MICHELIN MAP 327: F-7 – LOCAL MAP SEE LE PILAT

St-Étienne lies in the Furan depression, close to the Massif du Pilat, Grangent Lake and the Forez plain. The town is located at the centre of a coal basin which supplied over 500 million tonnes of coal until the mines were closed in the 1980s. Since then St-Étienne has adopted a new image: the façades of its buildings have been cleaned, its gardens and parks renovated. The busiest area lies along a north-south axis: place Jean-Jaurès, place de l'Hôtel-de-Ville. The 15C and 16C main church of St-Étienne, popularly known as the "**Grand'Église**," remains dear to the hearts of the local people. The home town of the composer **Jules Émile Frédéric Massenet** (1842–1912), has an intellectual and artistic life which extends over the whole of Forez.

- **Information:** 16 av. de la Libération. 42000 ST-ÉTIENNE. ☎0 892 700 542. www.tourisme-st-etienne.com.
- ▶ **Orient Yourself:** Close to the Massif du Pilatm south-west of Lyon.
- **P Parking:** The centre of St Etienne is a difficult place to drive and park, but there are parking areas at stages along the tram line.
- **Don't Miss:** The Museum of Modern Art and the Old Town.
- **Organising Your Time:** You will need at least a whole day, maybe more.
- **Kids Especially for Kids:** Go star gazing at the Planetarium.
- **Also See:** GORGES de la LOIRE, LYON.

A Bit of History

In the 12C St-Étienne was a village on the banks of the Furan, by-passed by major communication routes. Local coal, and the enterprising spirit of the inhabitants, brought about an extraordinary development; the population shot up from 3,700 in 1515 to 45,000 in 1826, then 146,000 in 1901, while the industrial estate spread west, east and north.

Armeville – In 1296 the people of St-Étienne started working coal quarries for domestic needs, then to feed the forges which produced the first knives, followed by cutting and thrusting weapons, crossbows and finally, firearms – St-Étienne was quick to make this change in direction in the manufacture of arms.
In 1570 the Arms Manufacturers' Lodge consisted of 40 trades. Mass production was already being practised. In 1746 the Royal Arms Factory was founded. During the Revolution this activity was to earn the town the name of Armeville.

From St-Étienne to Andrézieux – In May 1827 the first French railway, built to plans by Beaunier, was inaugurated: it ran between St-Étienne and Andrézieux over a distance of 21km/13mi and was used to transport coal; the wagons were pulled by horses. This ancestor of modern means of transport, perfected in 1829 thanks to the tube boiler developed by Marc Seguin, led to a revolution in transport and a prodigious boom in industry.

The town that made everything – To the ribbon industry, imported from Italy, was added shirred fabric at the end of the 19C.
To escape the Depression, the region of St-Étienne had already specialised in quality steels, tools, hunting guns, bicycles and automobile parts.

Industrial redeployment – The mines, saw their coal production decrease regularly between 1960 and 1980. This gradual closing was planned, allowing the metallurgical and textile industries time to restructure themselves; they now operate in conjunction with diversified activities such as precision mechanics, electronics, food processing, plastics and cardboard manufacturing.

Musée D'Art Moderne★★

*4.5km/3mi from the city centre.
Leave St-Étienne N via rue Bergson
towards La Terrasse and follow signs
to the Musée d'Art Moderne.*

♿⏱*Open daily except Tue 10am–6pm
(visit 2 hrs).* 🚫*Closed 1 Jan, 1 May, 14 Jul,
15 Aug, 1 Nov, 25 Dec.* 💶*5€, no charge 1st
Sun in the month.* ☎*04 77 79 52 52. www.
st-etienne-metropole.com.*

This vast art gallery located in the town of St-Priest-en-Jarez was designed by the architect D Guichard; it is devoted to 20C art, of which it provides an interesting retrospective owing to its policy of continual acquisition. The sober, functional building looks like an industrial structure from the outside. Its walls, covered with black ceramic panels, are a reminder of the important role of coal.

Old Town★ Tour

Start out from **place du Peuple,** which used to be the market square in the Middle Ages. On the corner of rue Mercière a 16C tower rises above an arcade; a timber-framed house stands opposite.

Cross the avenue used by the trams to reach rue Denis-Escoffier, which marks the entrance to the old Outre-Furan district. At the junction of rue des Martyrs-de-Vingré is an unusual mid-18C house, adorned with a statue and eaves with four rows of tiles and large, visible beams, typical of the urban architecture

to be found in Forez. On the left at no 3 rue Georges-Dupré a massive façade includes imposing lintels in one piece. Turn back and follow rue des Martyrs-de-Vingré; nos 19 and 30 are examples of 18C houses incorporating weaving lofts or workshops.

▶ *After reaching place Neuve, turn right onto rue Nautin, which leads to rue Michelet.*

Rue Michelet

This artery, pierced along the north-south axis parallel to rue Gambetta, contains some examples of innovative architecture from the 1930s (nos 34, 36, 42 and in particular no 44, an imposing building in reinforced concrete).

▶ *Continue along rue Nautin and rejoin rue Gambetta, to get to place W.-Rousseau. Skirt the square dominated by the castle. Rue du Théâtre leads to place Boivin.*

Place Boivin

This marks the site of the former 15C north rampart. Walk down rue Émile-Loubet; there is a fine façade adorned with five caryatids at no 12, the 16C **Maison de "Marcellin-Allard."**
Return to the square, one corner of which is occupied by the Grand'Église. To the right of the church, at the beginning of rue de la Ville, note the two handsome façades (15C and 16C): no 5, known as the **Maison François I** is decorated with five Renaissance medallions.

Musée D'Art Moderne

© Philippe Hervouet/Saint-Etienne Office of Tourism

Address Book

For coin ranges, see the Legend on the cover flap.

TRAMWAY

The tramway is the best way to get around town. You can buy a one-day pass and rent an audio tape to serve as a guide to help you discover St-Étienne. Information at the Office de tourisme, ☎04 77 49 39 00.

WHERE TO STAY

Hôtel Carnot – *11 bd Jules-Janin. ☎04 77 74 27 16. Closed 2–24 Aug. 24 rms. ☞8€.* This hotel near the Carnot train station has a steady flow of regular customers who appreciate the warm reception and reasonable prices.

Hôtel Ténor – *12 r. Blanqui. ☎04 77 33 79 88. www.hoteltenor.com. 64 rms. ☞8€.* A hotel in a modern residential building a minute's walk from the Place de l'Hôtel-de-Ville.

WHERE TO EAT

L'Escargot d'Or – *5 cours Victor-Hugo. ☎04 77 41 24 04. Closed 1–10 Mar, 29 Jul–26 Aug, Sun evening and Mon.* A restaurant above a bar near the *Musée d'Art et d'Industrie.* Traditional cuisine.

Corne d'Aurochs – *18 r. Michel-Servet. ☎04 77 32 27 27. Closed 1–4 May, 27 Jul–25 Aug, Mon lunch, Sat lunch and Sun.* Just a short walk from the *hôtel de ville,* here's a bistro serving cuisine of the Lyon tavern genre.

La Nouvelle – *30 r. St-Jean. ☎04 77 32 32 60. Closed 2–12 Jan, 10–25 Aug, Sun and Mon.* This restaurant in a pedestrian street. The refined setting is in perfect harmony with the inventive cuisine concocted by the young owner-chef.

ON THE TOWN

Place Jean-Jaurès – Opposite the St-Charles church, not far from the heart of the city, this big square is where natives of St-Étienne rendezvous.

Square du Temps Passé – This square is a reminder that St-Étienne is a green city boasting many parks. On one side, la Rue Richelandière is currently a hot spot of Stéphanois nightlife.

THEATRE AND ENTERTAINMENT

Comédie de St-Étienne, Centre Dramatique National – *7 av. du Prés.-Émile-Loubet. ☎04 77 25 01 24. www.comédie-de-saint-etienne.fr. Tickets: Mon–Fri 2pm–7pm. Closed end Jul–end Aug and public holidays.* This centre was founded in 1947 in order to initiate and promote drama outside of the capital. Today it orchestrates a permanent troupe of actors, a stage set workshop and a costumes atelier, as well as four different performance halls.

L'Esplanade - Opéra Théâtre de St-Étienne – *Allée Shakespeare, Jardin des Plantes, BP 237. ☎04 77 47 83 47. www.saint-etienne.fr. Tickets: Mon–Fri 2pm–7pm. Closed mid-Jul–Aug.* The focal point of cultural animation in St-Etienne offering theatre, ballet and operetta.

Le Triomphe - *4 sq. Violette. ☎04 77 32 22 16. Tickets: Tue–Sat, 2pm–8pm. Closed Jul–Aug.* This café-theatre in a converted cinema cultivates in its shows the spirit, the culture, the accents, and the language of the region.

Le Tamora – *15 r. Dormoy. ☎04 77 32 36 97. Wed, 10pm–3am, Thu 7pm–3am, Fri–Sat 7pm–4am. Closed 2 wks in Aug.* Known in St-Étienne for its karaoke evenings, this club has hosted the popular French songsters Gilbert Montagné, Zouk Machine, and Larusso, who used their visits to promote newcomers on the music scene.

Nouvel Espace Culturel – *9 r. Claudius-Cottier, 42270 St-Priest-en-Jarez. ☎04 77 74 41 81. Tickets: Mon–Fri, 8.30am–4.30pm. Closed Aug and weekends.* The Nouvel Espace Culturel was created in 1991 in a suburb close to Saint-Étienne. Many professional and amateur theatre troupes from all over France appear here performing new works or repertory pieces. Each year, the NEC organises a dance festival called 'Les mais de la danse'.

Grand'Église

The church of St-Étienne is the town's only example of Gothic architecture; its parish is the oldest in the city.

▸ *On leaving the church, turn right and rejoin rue Ste-Catherine, leading down to rue du Général-Foy. Turn left towards place Jean-Jaurès.*

Place de l'Hôtel-de-Ville, the main town square, and place Jean-Jaurès form the hub of city life in St-Étienne.

Place Jean-Jaurès

In the summer this square is a delight with its pretty bandstand and plane trees offering shade.

▸ *Rue Gérentet leads to place Dorian, then rue Alsace-Lorraine will take you back to place du Peuple.*

Sights

Musée du Vieux St-Étienne

Open daily except Sun, Mon and public hols, 2.30pm–6pm. 3€. 04 77 25 74 32. www.vieux-saint-etienne.com.
An 18C toll marker, from the old Outre-Furan district, signals the entrance to the Hôtel de Villeneuve (18C). The City Museum inside is arranged on the first floor, in a series of rooms with fine moulded and coffered ceilings. The first charter mentioning St-Étienne (1258) is on display, together with maps and engravings illustrating the expansion of the city.

Musée d'Art et d'Industrie

Open daily except Tue 10am–6pm, Mon 10am–12.30pm and 1.30pm–6pm (last admission 30min before closing). Closed 1 Jan, 1 May, 14 Jul, 15 Aug, 1 Nov and 25 Dec. 4.50€. 04 77 49 73 00.
This Art and Industry Museum located in the former Palais des Arts is a real repository of local and regional know-how relating to toolmaking and the evolution of equipment and machinery from the 16C up to the present day.

Site of the old Manufacture des Armes et Cycles de St-Étienne

Cours Fauriel.
Laid out under the Second Empire to be, together with Avenue de la Libération, one of the showcases of the industrial expansion in St-Étienne, cours Fauriel was occupied by the buildings of the Arms Factory which were built by Léon Lamaizière in 1893, and which were in use until 1985.

Planetarium

Espace Fauriel, 28 rue P.-et-D.-Ponchardier. Kids *Open: Call or check website for times of shows and visits. Closed Sept, 1 Jan, 1 May, 25 Dec. 6.60€ (children: 5.50€). 04 77 33 43 01. www. astronef.fr.*

Planetarium

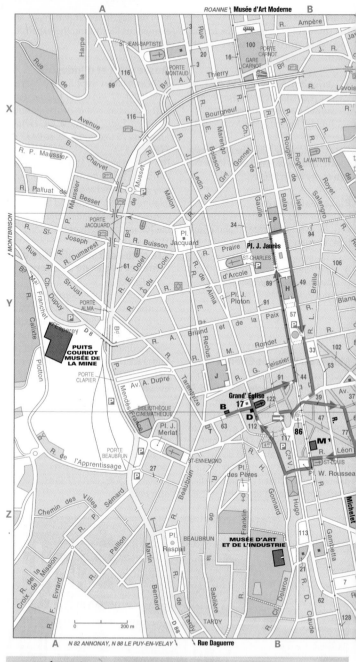

Crowned by a hemispherical dome, this planetarium is fitted with highly sophisticated equipment which enhances the appeal of its shows about the universe. Most impressive is the astronomical simulator, able to calculate and project onto the screen the movements of the planets and of some 3,000 stars.

Puits Couriot, Musée de la Mine★

Guided tours (1hr30min) daily except Tue at 10.30am, 3.30pm, Sat–Sun at 2.15pm. Audio-guided tours daily except Tue 3.45pm–5.30pm (departure every 10min), Sat–Sun 2.45pm–5.30pm. Closed 1 Jan, 1 May, 14 Jul, 15 Aug, 1 Nov, 25 Dec. Guided tour: 6€ (children: 4.50€), audio-guided tour: 5€

Puits Couriot

(children: 4€), no charge 1st Sunday in the month. ☎04 77 43 83 26.

The visit begins in the **Salle des Pendus★,** a vast locker room where, as space was limited, miners' clothes were hung from the ceiling to dry. The adjoining shower is evidence of the collective life they led. Visitors are taken to the lower galleries in the cages used by miners for accessing the mines, bringing up coal and sometimes the injured.

Excursions

Firminy

11km/6.8mi. Leave S on D 88.

Firminy lies in the Ondaine valley, half way between the mountains and the St-Étienne plain. The town is known for its urban appearance stamped by the famous architect **Le Corbusier** – housing complex, arts centre, stadium and St-Peter's Church (unfinished) – making it the second **"Le Corbusier site"★** in the world after Chandigarh in India.

Château des Bruneaux   Kids

Château: daily Tues–Sun 2pm–6pm. Mine: guided tours Sun and public holidays 2pm–6pm. Closed 1 Jan, 1 Nov, 25 Dec. Château 3.50€ (children: 2€); château and mine: 5€ (children: 3.50€). ☎04 77 89 38 46. www.multitex.fr/bruneaux.

The castle features a nailer's workshop and a collection of toys. The outbuildings house a reconstructed mine showing the different types of support structures.

Le Pertuiset

15km/9.3mi. Leave SW on D 25.
This hanging bridge marking the transition between the industrial city and the wild Loire gorges provides access to the driving tours.

St-Didier-en-Velay

25km/15.5mi S via N 88 and D 500.
A small town in the heart of the Semène Valley with an old quarter, Romanesque church and 19C corn exchange.

Vallée du Gier

The Gier valley canyon from Terrenoire to Givors has verdant flanking slopes.

St-Chamond

7km/4.3mi to the W on N 88.
This is the industrial cradle of the area, bringing together a wide variety of factories (iron, steel, plastics, dyes, mechanics, synthetics etc). It is also the birthplace of former racing driver **Alain Prost**, affectionately nicknamed "Professor of the Track," who became famous by winning the Formula 1 World Championship four times (1985, 1986, 1989, 1993).

Rive-de-Gier

20km/12.5mi W on N 88, then on D 88.
An industrial town, dating back to the early 18C.

Givors

30km/18.6mi to the W on N 88, then A 47.
The vestiges of Château St-Gérald command a view of the town hall, the two churches in Givors and the Rhône.

Driving Tours

The Belvederes

▶ *Leave St-Étienne to the S along Cours Fauriel (D 8). N 82 makes its way along the Furet ravine, dotted with schist outcrops.*

Col du Grand-Bois

Charming forest site.

▶ *Turn around and drive to Planfoy. There, turn left and rejoin Guizay.*

View from Guizay★★

From the foot of the Sacré-Cœur statue there is a fine extensive view over the town. The village of **Rochetaillée** can be seen, to the far right, perched on its crest. To the left unfolds the Ondaine corridor: Le Chambon-Feugerolles, Firminy and the hills of Forez.

▶ *D 88 takes you back to St-Étienne.*

Grangent Dam

▶ *Leave St-Étienne on D 8 and drive to Roche-la-Molière. There, take D 3A towards St-Victor.*
In Le Berlan, turn left onto D 25. After 1km/0.6mi turn right onto the road to Quéret. Drive past Trémas village (on the right) and after 400m/400yd, turn right. On leaving Quéret, on the square, take the steep road going downhill.

Plateau de la Danse

Leave the car in the car park and follow the path signposted "Point de Vue" that disappears into the woods.
This region, steeped in local history and legends, has a rocky belvedere commanding a lovely **view**★ of Grangent Dam and Island, St-Victor promontory, Essalois Château, and medieval tower in Chambles.

▶ *Return to the car and drive to St-Victor.*

St-Victor-sur-Loire

This pretty village adorned with roses overlooks the artificial lake formed by the Loire upstream of Grangent. The **sailing base** is a popular meeting-place in summer and there are facilities for many other sports and leisure activities.
The open-air theatre and the **castle** (◐ open 9am–noon, 2.30pm–5.30pm, Sat–Sun 2.30pm–5.30pm; ◑ closed Aug, 1 Jan, 25 Dec; ⊜ no charge; ☎ 04 77 90 49 29; www.chateau-saint-victor.fr) sporting its 11C towers are perched on top of the hill.

ST-FLOUR★★

POPULATION 6,625

MICHELIN MAP 330: G-4

St-Flour is perched on the end of the *planèze* which bears its name, at an altitude of 881m/2,890ft on a basaltic table 100m/330ft above the River Ander. The beauty of its site★★ can be best appreciated from an eastern approach which reveals a line of houses dominated by the massive towers of the cathedral, looming above rocky escarpments. The town developed around the tomb of St Flour, one of the Evangelists preaching in the Auvergne in the 4C. During the Middle Ages, under the administration of three elected consuls, it had a population of 7,000 people. In 1317 the Pope made it a cathedral town.

- **Information:** Cours Spy-des-Ternes, 15100 ST-FLOUR, ☎04 71 60 22 50. www.saint-flour.com.
- ▶ **Orient Yourself:** There are two towns, one, a modern, busy place on the plain, the other, perched imperiously on a huge rocky upthrust overlooking the Ander and Lescure valleys, a network of old streets and cranky buildings, wherein lies all the interest.
- **Parking:** There are ample parking areas in both the upper and lower town; beware the *priorité à droite* in some of the upper town streets.
- **Don't Miss:** The view from the town walls, or the museum in the Hotel de Ville.
- **Organizing Your Time:** Half a day to explore the upper town.

A Bit of History

Revolt of the Tuchins - During the Hundred Years War St-Flour was close to the battlefield. The Treaty of Brétigny (1360) made St-Flour a frontier town, "France's key to Guienne" (Aquitaine). Fear of the English grew but it was the mercenaries, more than the English, who controlled the country from the fortresses of Saillant and Alleuze. The town was often attacked, its outlying districts burnt and pillaged. The consuls made pacts with the enemy who, in return for a fee, agreed to leave the people of St-Flour in peace. However, the truce was endangered by some of the inhabitants, nicknamed the *Tuchins,* who saw it as tantamount to capitulation, and who were seen as patriots by the lower classes. Formed secretly into a band, they waged implacable guerilla warfare on the occupant. After 1384 the *Tuchins* also attacked the rich and privi-

View of St-Flour

Address Book

For coin ranges, see the cover flap.

WHERE TO STAY

Grand Hôtel de l'Étape – *18 av. de la République, ville basse. ☎04 71 60 13 03. Closed Sun evening Sept–Jun. 8€. Restaurant*. The whole family teams up to run this traditional hotel of the lower town, built in the 1970s and offering modern bedrooms. The tasty cuisine is made from regional recipes; most of the vegetables come straight from the garden.

Chambre d'hôte et ferme-auberge Ruisselet – *15100 Roffiac. 3km/1.8mi W of St-Flour via D 926. ☎04 71 60 11 33. 5 rms.* Stop at this hospitable farm-inn and sample local dishes made with ingredients from their cattle farm. Pretty, comfortable and spacious bedrooms for a half-board holiday. Good tips for discovering the region given with pleasure.

La Pagnoune – *Valadour, 15320 Loubaresse. ☎04 71 73 74 69. auberge-lapagnoune.com. Closed Feb, 1–15 Oct and Mon. 7 rms. 5.50€.* Built in 1877, this farm is a halt with a personality of its own. The rustic bedrooms are decorated with flair and the dining room is well worth a glimpse: exposed stones, two granite fireplaces, rustic furniture, an alcoved bed and farm tools contribute to its unabashedly pastoral flavour. Local produce on the dinner plate.

WHERE TO EAT

Chez Geneviève – *25 r. des Lacs, ville haute. ☎04 71 60 17 97. Closed 1 wk in Feb, 1 wk in Jun, 15 Oct–5 Nov, Mon evening, Tue evening and Sun except 2 Jul–8 Sept.* On a pedestrian street in the city centre, this small, no-frills restaurant is very convivial. Seated between beams and wainscot, diners come savour local specialities, such as the *tripoux de St-Flour*, made fresh. Quite affordable.

SHOPPING

Le Manoir des Saveurs – *54 av. du Lioran. ☎04 71 60 47 24.* Make sure you visit this grand shop housing a grocer's and a bakery. The former's shelves are laden with cheeses (including raw milk Cantal from Chez Charrade, *Ecir d'Aubrac* and *Gaperon*) tripoux, pounti, Valette foie gras and sweets. The latter offers a selection of 25 different kinds of baked bread. Enjoy it all here or take your purchases on a picnic!

leged orders, and became outright robbers. Having become dangerous to local authorities, they were overcome by the troops of the Duc de Berry.

Cathedral★

Built in late-Gothic style, it stands on the vast place des Armes and is a reminder of the town's vocation as a stronghold. Its construction, begun after the collapse in 1396 of the Romanesque basilica which preceded it, was not completed until the late 15C.

The architect had previously worked for the Duc de Berry, which explains why the construction is not in the usual style of the region. On the west front, the right-hand tower is pierced with square mullioned windows letting daylight into two rooms once used as a prison.

Inside, the lines of the five aisles are strikingly sober. Under the organ loft, a 15C mural depicts **Purgatory and Hell.** Note, against the left pillar at the entrance to the chancel, the large wooden **Crucifix★** (13C or 15C) known as the "Beautiful Black God"; the 15C *Pietà* in the chapel of the Holy Sacrament and, in the Tomb Chapel, a gilded bronze shrine containing the relics of St Flour.

Town Walk

Old streets

From place d'Armes, lined with arcades and old façades (particularly at the corner of rue de Belloy), walk to rue Sorel and the church of St-Vincent, a former Dominican convent.

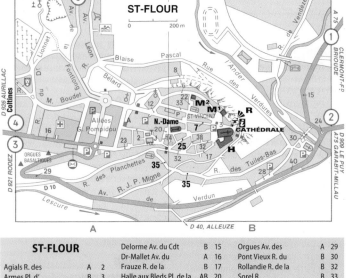

Follow rue des Jacobins on the left, then rue de la Collégiale named after a disused 14C church: **Notre-Dame collegiate church** whose apse has Flamboyant windows. **rue Marchande** has a few interesting old houses, including no 31, the governor's house, a 15C mansion whose façade and courtyard can be seen, and at no 15, Hôtel Brisson with a 16C courtyard, its original windows separated by columns with rope moulding.

Other interesting streets include **rue du Breuil** (15C house at no 8), and **rue des Tuiles-Haut** (old houses).

Ancienne Maison Consulaire

The façade of this former consul's residence dates from the 16C. The courtyard (enter through no 17 bis), from which can be seen three houses successively bought by consuls in the 14C and 15C to serve as their consular establishment, has an old well, a 15C staircase turret and various painted inscriptions. It houses the Musée d'Art et d'Histoire Alfred-Douët (see Museums below).

Terrasse des Roches

Behind the east end of the cathedral. From this square on the old ramparts there is a lovely view of the lower part of the town, the Ander Valley and the Margeride mountains.

Museums

St-Flour prides itself on its rich cultural heritage and its many museums, which will enlighten you on local art and history.

Musée de la Haute-Auvergne

Place d'Armes. Open mid-Apr–mid-Oct 10am–noon, 2pm–6pm; mid-Oct–mid Apr daily except Sun and public holidays, 10am–noon, 2pm–6pm. Closed 1 Jan, Easter, 1 May, and 11 Nov, 25 Dec. 4€. 04 71 60 22 32.

This museum is located in the former bishop's palace rebuilt in the 17C. Displays in the low 15C vaulted rooms explain how blue-veined Fourme cheese is made (including Cantal and Salers varieties) and the different facets of pastoral life, particularly the shepherd's huts or *burons* where the cheese is made.

On the ground floor, in the former chapel, note a 12C polychrome wooden statue of St Peter from the church at Albepierre-Bredons, a 14C statue of St Flour, nine 16C carved wooden panels and a lovely set of Marian statues from the 12C to the 18C. The next room leads to the chapter-house, the only vestige of the Cluniac priory, where the treasure of the cathedral of St-Pierre and portraits of bishops are displayed.

The exhibits on the first floor concentrate on Auvergne folklore: popular music and its traditional instruments, hats and headdresses, a collection of regional carved-wood pieces, Cantal furniture (chests, cupboards, dressers, wooden bed panelling).

The contents of the archaeological section mainly come from the digs at Mons and also from Laurie, near Massiac. A beautiful bronze **brassard**★ consisting of six rings attached with a bar, and bracelets and swords are the main items displayed.

Musée d'Art et d'Histoire Alfred-Douët

○*Open mid-Apr–mid Oct: guided tours (45min), Mon–Fri, 9am–noon, 2pm–6pm, Sat–Sun and public holidays 10am–noon, 2pm–6pm; mid-Oct–mid Apr Mon–Fri, 9am–noon, 2pm–6pm, Sat, 10am–noon, 2pm–6pm.* ○*Closed 1 May.* ✆*3.50€.* ☎*04 71 60 44 99. www.musee-douet.com.*

Beyond the entrance hall with its collection of ancient weapons is the library which boasts Diderot's Encyclopaedia; the guard-room with its monumental fireplace, and the Consul Room where fine tapestries hang, contain Renaissance furniture; the Louis XVI bedroom with painted wood panelling displays 18C furniture and the gallery is exclusively decorated with 17C paintings and furniture.

In addition, you will see fine Limousin enamels, glassware as well as a collection of pewter and copper.

In a small oratory, note a *Pietà* and a 15C Christ with His hands bound.

Musée Postal d'Auvergne

♿○*Open Jun–Oct 10am–noon, 2pm–7pm.* ✆*3.50€.* ☎*04 71 60 38 03.*

This Postal Museum, occupying an old monastery, contains a collection of 6,000 items retracing the history of postal services since the 17C. The local postal service is given special emphasis, with the reconstruction of Ytrac post office (1900), and a horse-drawn sledge used until 1950 to enable mail to be delivered in the Margeride mountain region even when it was under a thick covering of snow.

Excursions

Roffiac

2km/1.2mi W along D 40.

An old restored mill, **Moulin du Blaud** (♿○*hours variable, ring tourist office for information, or* ☎*04 71 60 75 75),* houses a trout information centre: all you want to know about this freshwater fish which you can catch *(no licence required; fishing tackle hiring facilities)* in the lake.

The museum, which illustrates fishing in the past, includes an observation laboratory, aquariums and a model of a dam. A nature-discovery trail runs round the lake.

Coltines

12km/7.5mi W. Leave St-Flour along D 926 towards Murat then turn right onto D 14 to Coltines.

Musée de l'Agriculture

Kids ♿○*Open Jul–Aug 10am–noon, 2pm–6.30pm; Feb–Jun and Sept–Nov 10am–noon, 2pm–5.30pm, Sun 2pm–5.30pm; Dec–Jan 2pm–5pm, Sat by appointment.* ○*Closed 1 Jan, 25 Dec.* ✆*4.50€ (children 2.50€).* ☎*04 71 73 27 30. www.coltines.com.*

Located in a 17C house, this interactive museum is devoted to agriculture in the Auvergne region from the beginning of the 20C to the 1950s.

Massiac

28km/17.3mi N of St-Flour on E 11.
🛈*24 r. du Dr.-Mallet, 15500 MASSIAC,* ☎*04 71 23 07 76.*

This old village, in an excellent setting by the River Alagnon, is enlivened by a traditional weekly market (Tuesday mornings) and two picturesque annual fairs (Jun and Oct). The town's glorious past is evidenced by the **old château** (which currently houses the town hall), a fine 17C **wooden house** or a round **stone tower** belonging to the former ramparts.

Musée Municipal Élise-Rieuf

♿🕐*Open Jul–Sept: daily except Mon 2.30pm–7pm.* 🕐*Closed Oct–Apr.* ⊚*4€.* ☏*04 71 23 03 95.*

The museum displays portraits of people from the Auvergne and China, Provençal and Scandinavian landscapes and Italian towns painted by **Élise Rieuf**, a native of Massiac (1897–1990).

Driving Tours

Vallée de l'Ander

40km/25mi – allow 4hr.

▶ *Leave St-Flour E onto D 990. After crossing the River Ander, turn right onto D 250.*

Gorges de l'Ander

Continue along the edge of the river which runs between both rocky and wooded slopes. The path ends in a very picturesque meander, at the hamlet of Le Bout du Monde ("World's End").

▶ *Turn around and at the crossroads take D 250 on the left, then left again onto a small road leading to Grizols. After the village, turn left onto D 40.*

Ste-Madeleine Chapel

Site du Château d'Alleuze★★

ⓒ*see Gorges de la Truyère driving tour.*

▶ *Leave Alleuze to the N on D 116.*

Villedieu

The **church,** half-Romanesque, half-Gothic, has an attractive door with a wrought-iron knocker. In the chancel, notice the beautiful High Altar, the staffs and finely carved lectern.

▶ *Continue along D 116. At the intersection turn right onto D 921, then onto D 926, heading for Murat.*

Église de Roffiac

The church is a little Romanesque building from the beginning of the 12C.

▶ *Leave Roffiac to the N on D 104. Park in the hamlet of Le Sailhant.*

Cascade du Sailhant

15min on foot there and back.

🚶The path to Le Sailhant (or Le Babory) waterfall weaves among the houses bordering the beautiful volcanic rocks on which Château du Sailhant is built.

The tiny cascade falls into a semicircle of tall cliffs; in the hollow lies a small lake. It is also possible to park at the entrance to the château and walk the short distance to the edge of the cliff, which offers a bird's-eye view of the cascade and the lake in its rocky surrounds.

▶ *Leave Le Sailhant S along D 40. Further on, D 979 leads back to St-Flour.*

Gorges de l'Alagnon★

70km/43.5mi round tour.

▶ *Leave Massiac (28km/17.3mi N of St-Flour on E 11, ⓒsee Excursions) towards Clermont-Ferrand. At the roundabout follow D 909.*

The road alongside the lower reaches of the River Alagnon, as it cuts its way between Le Babory-de-Blesle and Lempdes-sur-Allagnon, makes a most appealing drive. Before long you reach the small 11C **chapel of Ste-Madeleine** at the south-eastern extremity of the Chalet plateau.

Further on, **Blesle** developed around a once-powerful Benedictine abbey. To the north, the ruins of Léotoing castle can be seen on a high ground to the right.

The castle at **St-Gervazy** is the setting of visits presented by members of the association "La Vie de château," which have been in charge of restoration work for the past many years.

The chapel located at the entrance to the village of **Léotoing** houses a model of the site and several panels providing information on local history, architecture and traditions. The fine view (viewing table) encompasses the Alagnon gorge, the Cézallier, the Brioude plain, the Livradois, the Plateau de la Chaise-Dieu and the Monts du Velay.

Gorges de la Truyère★★

Laval, 15320 CHALIERS.
☎04 71 73 72 21.

South of St-Flour, the River Truyère has carved narrow, deep and sinuous gorges, often wooded and rugged, through the granite plateaux of Upper Auvergne. These are among the most attractive natural sites in central France. Dams, built to serve the needs of hydroelectric power stations, have transformed them into one long lake without affecting their picturesque aspect, except when the waters are low.

1 Grandval Reservoir★★

60km/37mi tour.

▶ *From the 165m/541ft-long Garabit bridge there is a view of the viaduct. The bridge is 13km/8mi SE via A 75 from St-Flour.*

Viaduc de Garabit★★

The Garabit viaduct is an elegant, and very bold, construction designed by an engineer named **Léon Boyer** and built (1882–84) by **Gustave Eiffel**. It has an overall length of 564m/1,850ft and stretches across the River Truyère at a height of 123m/403ft. Its 448m/1,470ft superstructure is supported by a bold metal arch.

▶ *At the southern end of the bridge turn right to Faverolles.*

The route crosses the rocky Arcomie ravine and the Arling stream and continues to Faverolles where the Cantal, Margeride and Aubrac mountains come successively into view.

Château du Chassan

🕐*Open end Jun–early Sept: tours (30min) 2pm–6.30pm.* 🕐*Closed Nov–Easter.* ⊜*4€.* ☎*04 71 23 42 20 or 04 71 23 43 91.* In a region where medieval fortresses abound, this château provides a more peaceful addition to the landscape. In the 18C Jean-François de Ponsonnaille demolished the feudal castle of Faverolles in order to build the present house, which has remained in the family ever since.

Belvédère de Mallet★★

From here, there is a splendid view over Grandval reservoir. From D 13 turn right on D 40 through Fridefont, and down along a twisting route to the ridge of the dam itself.

Barrage de Grandval★

The central arch of the dam houses a circular power station beneath a metal dome which produces 144 million kWh per year. **Boat trips** (☎*04 71 23 49 40)* are organised on the lake during the spring and summer seasons.

Château d'Alleuze★★

The fortress was built in the 13C by the Constables of the Auvergne but belonged to the Bishops of Clermont.

▶ *In Alleuze turn back and take D 48 towards Lavastrie, then D 921 left to Chaudes-Aigues.*

2 The Planèze★

40km/25mi tour. The tour departs from Chaudes-Aigues, which is 26.5km/16.5mi S of St-Flour via D 921.

At the foot of the Plomb du Cantal, the St-Flour *planèze* unfolds to the east and south-east; a vast plateau on which few trees thrive, but where fields of crops stretch as far as the eye can see, earning the region its reputation as the agricultural heart of Upper Auvergne.

S. Sauvignier/MICHELIN

Source du Par

Chaudes-Aigues ⚜

🛈 *1 av. Georges-Pompidou, 15110 CHAUDES-AIGUES, ☎04 71 23 52 75. www.chaudes aigues.com.*

Chaudes-Aigues is ideally situated in the picturesque Remontalou gorge. As its name suggests, there are hot springs here, which have made it not only a spa resort but also a town where hot running water has been piped to houses since ancient times. Today, 32 of the springs are tapped (they are said to be the hottest in Europe), yielding water at temperatures from 45 to 82˚C/113 to 179˚F. The springs were slow to find widespread popularity, largely because of the difficult access and problems with communications. However, they now seem to be on the verge of a massive boom, firstly due to the opening of the A 75 motorway and secondly thanks to the ongoing renovation work undertaken to turn the spa into a modern, functional place for the treatment of rheumatism, arthritis, sciatica and gout.

At the **Source Du Par** the spring alone daily gushes out water at a temperature that can be as high as 82ºC/179ºF. It provides the water supply for the spa centre, but its waters are also used to heat the school, the swimming pool and local houses. Tourists planning a picnic may like to test the spring's properties for themselves – it can reputedly hard-boil an egg in eight minutes! Three hundred out of the 450 houses in the village benefit from the heat supplied by the water, which, in places, still runs through pinewood pipes.

The Gothic and Renaissance periods are evident in the **Église St-Martin-et-St-Blaise**, while in the streets of the town, there are several glazed alcoves containing statues of patron saints. Dominating the town on the south side is the **Tour du Couffour**, which offers a sweeping panorama of the nearby countryside and still features its circular medieval keep.

The **Musée Géothermia** (♿ 🕐 *open Apr–Oct and school holidays: daily except Tue 10am–noon, 2pm–6.30pm (Jul and Aug daily 10am–6.30pm);* 🕐 *closed Nov–Mar;* ✺*5€;* ☎*04 71 23 58 76),* located behind the Source du Par, unveils secrets of subterranean Chaudes-Aigues.

West from Chaudes-Aigues

▷ *The route on the map briefly follows the west bank of the Remontalou, then turns right onto the planèze.*

Espinasse

From this small village there are plunging views of the River Truyère.

From Auzolles on, the road clings to the steep sides of the **Lévandes valley**. A long, vertiginous descent into the valley follows, with breathtaking views of the valley floor and southern slopes.

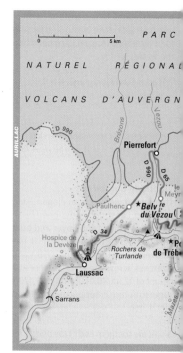

Pont de Tréboul★

This suspension bridge is a stunning piece of modern engineering. It replaced a Gothic bridge, built by the English in the 14C, which was submerged, together with the village of Tréboul, when the valley was flooded.

▶ *Cross the bridge; left to Pierrefort.*

Belvédère du Vézou★

A path leads through broom and ferns up to a rocky height overlooking the confluence of the Vézou and Truyère. The scenic D 65 climbs the initially deep and wooded Vézou valley which is covered with moorland and pastures higher up. Beyond Le Meynial volcanic rocks can be seen on either side of the road. After **Pierrefort** the road runs across a plateau and then returns to the Truyère valley, dropping almost to the level of the water and offering splendid views over the lake.

Laussac

Built on a promontory; flooding of the valley turned it into a peninsula.

South from Chaudes-Aigues

▶ *The D 989 and D 13 south from Chaudes-Aigues towards Aubrac takes you away from the Gorges de la Truyère to La Chaldette and St-Urcize (not marked on the map).*

Beyond Chaudes-Aigues, the road offers scenic views over the Remontalou valley, then over the mountains in Cantal. It then climbs up through the Bès valley in a landscape of granite that, in most places, is harsh and rugged.

La Chaldette

This tiny old spa resort, where the water is warm with a high sulphur content, nestles in the Bès valley.

St-Urcize

This locality can be found nestling at the foot of a rock crowned by medieval ruins. It is known both as a winter resort and a popular market town.

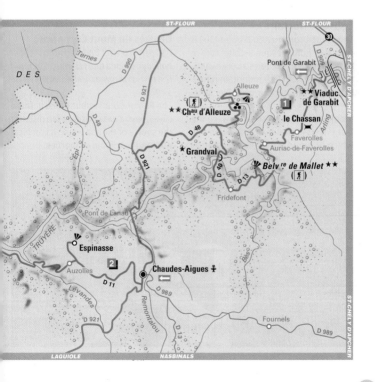

ST-NECTAIRE★

POPULATION 675
MICHELIN MAP 326: E-9
25KM/15.5MI W OF ISSOIRE

Two villages are grouped together under this name: the thermal spa of St-Nectaire-le-Bas (Lower St-Nectaire), which spreads out over 2km/1mi in a green valley, and the old village of St-Nectaire-le-Haut (Upper St-Nectaire) dominated by its **church**. In the Middle Ages a Benedictine priory was established as an offshoot of La Chaise-Dieu Abbey; a castle, no trace of which remains, was also built on the hill. It was inhabited by the glorious St-Nectaire family whose most famous member was **Madeleine de St-Nectaire** – young, beautiful and virtuous, widowed early, always followed by 60 men on horseback; she sided with the Protestants in the Wars of Religion, defeated the king's lieutenant in Upper Auvergne and ended up killing him by her own hand. The name "St-Nectaire" is also given to a well-known cheese, made with pasteurised or unpasteurised milk which has been produced for centuries in a well-defined area within the Cantal and Puy-de-Dôme *départements*.

- **Information:** Les Grands Thermes, 63710 ST-NECTAIRE ☎04 73 88 50 86. www.ville-saint-nectaire.fr.
- ▶ **Orient Yourself:** St-Nectaire lies 25km/15½ miles to the west of Issoire, on the D 996.
- ◔ **Organising Your Time:** A splendid and relaxing area; allow one or two days.
- ◔ **Also See:** Le MONT-DORE, Massif du SANCY, BESSE-EN-CHANDESSE, ORCIVAL.

St-Nectaire-le-Haut

Église St-Nectaire★★

This church constructed around 1160 is typical of Romanesque architecture in the Auvergne; it occupies a very beautiful site near the Dore mountain range. It was built in honour of St Nectaire, the companion of St Austremoine and monks from La Chaise-Dieu were the first priests in charge of it. The damage which occurred during the Revolution required extensive renovation work in 1875 (belfry, towers, west front).

Grottes du Mont Cornadore

◔*Open Feb–Oct and Christmas school holidays: guided tours (35min).* ◔*Closed the rest of the year.* ☞*6€.* ☎*04 73 88 57 97.*

The Romans built public baths in these caves, where today visitors can discover the source of the spa water, its medical uses and petrifying properties.

St-Nectaire

Maison du Saint-Nectaire

Open May–Sept daily 10am–noon, 2pm–6pm (Jul–Aug 10am–7pm). Closed the rest of the year. 5€. ☎04 73 88 57 96.
A video show *(in French)* explains the origin of farmhouse St-Nectaire cheese, how it is made and matured. There is a demonstration cellar and a sampling at the end of the visit.

The Spa Resort ✚

The thermal spa, with smart shops lining D 996, has more than 40 springs. Their waters issues at temperatures ranging from 8–56°C/46–133°F. Its treatment installations are grouped together in the modern Gravières spa establishment; the waters are used to treat kidney and metabolic complaints.

Fontaines Pétrifiantes

Open Jun–Sept 9am–noon, 2pm–7pm; rest of year daily except Mon 9am–noon, 2pm–5.30pm. Closed 1 Jan, 25 Dec. 5€. ☎04 73 88 50 80. www.fontaines-petrifiantes.fr.
The water gushes forth at more than 50°C/122°F from volcanic faults. Since 1821, seven generations of the same family have developed the technique of petrification, turning it into a real art form.

Dolmen

A fine granite slab on four stones in the upper part of the park, east of the river.

Walking Tours

Puy de Châteauneuf

30min on foot there and back. Fairly steep climb. Follow the street climbing up from the north-east end of the church, then take a rocky path on the left.

🚶 The path leads to the top of the Puy (alt 934m/3,064ft) from where there is an attractive view of the Dore mountain range. The side of the mountain is hollowed out by nine caves which, like the Jonas caves (*see BESSE*), were probably inhabited in prehistoric times, then used again in the Middle Ages.

Puy d'Éraigne

30min on foot there and back. Follow a rocky and very difficult path branching off to the left from the road to Sapchat, D 150.

🚶 From the summit there is a stunning vista of the Dore mountain range.

Cascade de Saillant

2km/1.2mi E of St-Nectaire-le-Bas.
see BESSE-EN-CHANDESSE, Exploring the Couze valleys.

ST-SATURNIN★

POPULATION 964

MICHELIN MAP 326: F-9 – 18KM/11.2MI S OF CLERMONT-FERRAND

This village in the Monne valley was the home of the barons of La Tour d'Auvergne who later became the counts of Auvergne. This is the family that produced Catherine de' Medici – daughter of Lorenzo de' Medici and Madeleine de La Tour d'Auvergne – who became Queen of France after marrying Henri II. St-Saturnin attracted a colony of painters and several writers, including novelist and critic **Paul Bourget** (1852–1935). The location of St-Saturnin near the Monts Dômes and the Couzes and Comté valleys, its picturesque streets, its castle and its little square with a charming 16C fountain, make this an attractive tourist destination.

- **Information:** pl. du 8 Mai, 63450 Saint-Saturnin. ☎04 73 39 61 14.
- ▶ **Orient Yourself:** St-Saturnin lies 18km/10 miles S of Clermont Ferrand.
- **Parking:** Use the car park on the pl. du 8 mai.
- **Don't Miss:** A visit to the chateau.
- **Organising Your Time:** Allow 1–2 hours.
- **Also See:** MONTS DÔME, CLERMONT-FERRAND, ISSOIRE.

Sights

Church★★

The church was built in the 12C and is very simple. Despite the lack of apsidal chapels, the **east end** is nonetheless quite attractive. The radiating transept chapels, the wide ambulatory around the semicircular chancel, and the powerful mass of the transept, which has the best-preserved octagonal bell tower in the Auvergne, form a remarkable architectural whole. The external decoration is elaborate, with its strings of billet-moulding, its modillions and its set of arches, some of them remarkable just for the alternate colouring of their basalt and arkose archstones. In contrast to this lavish decoration, the side buttresses and simple end-wall of the west front are striking in their lack of ornamentation.

Inside, note the high barrel-vault of the nave, the galleries above the side aisles with their groined vaulting, the elevation of the transept crossing with its supporting diaphragm arches and the crypt resting on powerful pillars.

Next to the church is the small 11C **Ste-Madeleine Chapel** fortified in the 14C.

Château

☙Open Jul–mid-Sept: guided tours (50min) 10am–7pm. ☙5€. ☎04 73 39 39 64. www.chateaudesaintsaturnin.com.
This imposing fortress, which has undergone extensive restoration, is typical of the military architecture of the Middle Ages: triple curtain wall, ramparts, towers with machicolations and crenellations. The main part of the building, with a massive, late-15C roof, is flanked by two wings (14C and 15C). The keep, the watch-path (views of the village and its surroundings) and formal gardens are open to visitors.

Medieval village of St-Saturnin

J. Damase/MICHELIN

SALERS★★

POPULATION 359
MICHELIN MAP 330: C-4
20KM/12.4MI SE OF MAURIAC – LOCAL MAP SEE MONTS DU CANTAL

Salers is one of the prettiest little towns in Upper Auvergne and has a very distinctive character. It stands at an altitude of 951m/3,120ft on its planèze and has retained, from its military and judicial past, a rare set of ramparts and old houses, grouped together on a pinnacle giving a magnificent view of the confluence of the River Aspre and River Maronne. Salers is also a tasty farmhouse cheese made from unpasteurized full-cream milk.

- **Information:** Pl. Tyssandier-d'Escous, 15140 SALERS ☎04 71 40 70 68. www.pays-de-salers.com.
- **Orient Yourself:** Salers lies 20km/12½ miles SE of Mauriac, and 45km/ 28 miles from Aurillac, via the D 680.
- **Parking:** There is generous parking around the centre.
- **Don't Miss:** A walk through the old streets.
- **Organising Your Time:** Salers is the sort of place you come back to; allow half a day and enjoy a relaxing lunch.
- **Also See:** MAURIAC, AURILLAC, TOURNEMIRE.

A Bit of History

Arms and the gown (15C-16C) – The twofold character of the buildings in Salers can be explained by the town's history. Initially unwalled, it suffered cruelly at the hands of the English and the mercenaries "free companions" who roamed the highways; as a result the ramparts were built, and still stand today. In the 16C Salers became the seat of the bailiwick of the Upper Mountains of the Auvergne and the established *bourgeois* families, from which the judges were selected, started building their impressive turreted houses.

Walking Tour

Eglise St-Mathieu★

12C porch still remains from the Romanesque church which pre-dated the present church, begun in the 15C. The bell tower, which was struck by lightning, was rebuilt in the 19C.

At home in Salers

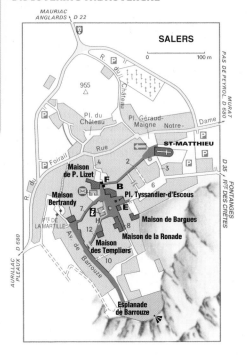

SALERS

SALERS	
Beffroi R. du	2
Courbière R.	3
Coustil R. du	4
Couvent R. du	6
Martille R. de la	7
Nobles R. des	8
Ste-Barbe R.	10
Templiers R. des	12

Maison d'un Bailli dite ancien Bailliage	B
Maison de Flojeac	E
Tour de l'Horloge	F

> *On leaving the church, pass a fountain on the left and follow rue du Beffroi uphill.*

Go under the Tour de l'Horloge (clock tower also known as Belfry Gate), flanked by a round tower with machicolations. Just beyond the gate, on the right, is the house of Pierre Lizet with its Gothic window and Renaissance portal.

Place Tyssandier-d'Escous
The old houses of dark lavastone with their clean, sober lines, flanked by corbelled round or polygonal turrets, and their pepperpot or many-sided roofs, look like a stage-set; the scene is completed by a fountain in the centre.
On the main square a monument has been raised to Tyssandier d'Escous who improved the region's breed of cattle in the 19C and made it famous.

Ancien Baillage
This Renaissance building, the former Bailiff's Court, stands at the corner of rue du Beffroi.
It is a vast residence of fine architectural design, flanked by two corner towers. Inside are several rooms open to view,

one of which has a beautiful Renaissance fireplace.

Maison de Flojeac
Opposite the tourist office. The house has a turret with canted corners.

Maison de la Ronade
Guided tours (40min). 3€. 04 71 40 76 18.
This building has a tower rising five storeys high. It has been converted into a guesthouse and tearoom.

> *At the entrance to rue du Couvent, on the right, a wooden door leads to a large courtyard.*

Maison des Templiers – Musée de Salers
Rue des Templiers, on the left of the tourist office. Open Apr–mid Nov daily except Tue 10.30am–noon, 2.30pm–5.30pm (Jul–Aug daily 10.30am–noon, 2.30pm–6.30pm). 3€. 04 71 40 75 97.
The 15C building houses an exhibition on the town's folklore and past: reconstruction of Auvergne interiors, cheesemaking, chemist's shop dating from 1890, religious objects and garments.

Address Book

🐚 *For coin ranges, see the Legend on the cover flap.*

WHERE TO STAY

🍽 **Chambre d'hôte M. et Mme Prudent** – *R. des Nobles.* ☎04 71 40 75 36. 6 rms. In the heart of Salers, this stunning 17C house has a charm all its own. The simple rooms are comfortable, the pretty garden looks out towards the volcanoes, and breakfast is served either outdoors or in a handsome room typical of the region, unless you'd rather be served in bed.

WHERE TO EAT

🍽🍽 **La Diligence** – *R. du Beffroi.* ☎04 71 40 75 39. Closed 12 Nov–1 Apr. Don't be fooled by the modern look of this establishment – the dishes served here are traditional local fare. If the crêpes won't satisfy your appetite, the *truffade, tripoux, pounti,* or *potée auvergnate* will, especially when washed down with a native wine. Convivial atmosphere around big farm tables.

🍽🍽 **Les Sorbiers** – *Le Bourg, 15380 Anglars-de-Salers, 9km/5.4mi N of Salers via D 22.* ☎04 71 40 02 87. Open evenings Apr–end Sept, Sat lunch and Sun lunch Jul–Sept. 🍴. Reservations required. Stuffed cabbage, truffade, delicatessen - everything on the menu is home-made from farm fresh products. Once you've settled into the dining room with exposed stone walls and wood tables, take the time to savour the plentiful family cuisine served within. Six B&B guestrooms.

🍽🍽 **Auberge de l'Aspre** – *15140 Fontanges, 6km/3.6mi S of Salers via D 35.* ☎04 71 40 75 76. www.auberge-aspre.com. Closed Dec–Jan, Sun evening, Wed evening and Mon Oct–May. A hearty welcome awaits you in this old country house with a pleasant garden. A lawn chair on the grass or a cocktail on the terrace: what more could one desire? Modern decor in the bedrooms; fireplace in the dining room and veranda.

▶ *Turn left onto avenue de Barrouze.*

Esplanade de Barrouze

The small, shaded park here offers an impressive **view**★ of the Maronne, Rat and Aspre valleys and the Puy Violent massif.

▶ *Retrace your steps and turn right onto rue de la Martille.*

Maison Bertrandy

The house has a round tower and an attractive door.

▶ *Return to Grande-Place, then take rue du Beffroi back to the church.*

Excursions

Maison du Fromage, de la Vache Salers et de la gentiane

4km/2.5mi from Salers on the road to Puy Mary. 🕐Open early Apr–Oct 10am–7pm. 🎫4€. ☎04 71 40 70 71.

Appropriately located in a restored *buron* (shepherd's hut), this "cheese house" retraces the history of the Salers breed of cattle and of the local cheese-making tradition; fine collection of tools. Another *buron* presents the history of the "Salers," a liqueur made from the gentian plant.

Anglards-de-Salers

10km/6.2mi N on D 22.

The Auvergne-style church with its octagonal belfry is built in a fairly pure style. Below it stands the **Château de la Trémolière** (15C – 🕐open Jun–Sept 2pm–7pm (Jul–Aug, 10.30am–12.30pm, 2pm–7pm); 🕐closed Mon morning; 🎫4€; ☎04 71 40 00 02) which houses a collection of 16C Aubusson **tapestries**.

▶ *You can extend your tour by pressing on to Mauriac (🐚see MAURIAC).*

MASSIF DU SANCY★★★

MICHELIN MAP 326: D-9

The Massif du Sancy, which forms part of the Dore mountain range, consists of a set of extinct volcanoes. It is one of the most picturesque areas in the Auvergne thanks to the dramatic power of some of the peaks, the depth of its valleys, its waterfalls and its lakes. The highest peak in the range, Puy de Sancy, rises to an altitude of 1,885m/6,184ft and is the highest summit in central France.

- **Information:** Office du Tourisme du MOnt-Dore, Av. de la Libération, 63240 Le MOnt-Dore. ☎04 73 65 20 21. www.sancy.com.
- ▸ **Orient Yourself:** Just 30 miles SW of Clermont Ferrand, within the Parc Naturel Régional Volcans d'Auvergne.
- **Don't Miss:** The Puy de Sancy panorama, the highest peak in central France.
- **Organising Your Time:** Allow a full day for a driving tour of the area, and much longer to explore on foot.
- **Also See:** Le MONT-DORE.

A Bit of History

Three huge volcanoes – The mighty system of volcanoes, of which the last remains form the Dore mountain range, evolved at the end of the Tertiary era. At its zenith, it covered an area three times larger than that of Vesuvius and consisted of three large cones in juxta-position (Sancy, Banne d'Ordanche and Aiguiller) whose craters opened at an altitude of almost 2,500m/8,202ft. Volcanic lakes add a touch of beauty to the landscape which is covered with forests of pine, spruce and beech. Lower down the slopes are valleys with meadows and hedgerows.

Rhinoceros in the Auvergne – Between the periods when the volcanoes were active, life returned to the Dore area. Footprints and bones found among the

Sancy mountain massif

J. Damase/MICHELIN

volcanic ash prove that laurel, bamboo and other plants which are now found only in hotter climes once grew on the slopes of the volcanoes, whereas rhinoceros, elephants and sabre-toothed tigers roamed the countryside.

Former glaciers –The great period of glaciation which spread across Europe at the beginning of the Quaternary Era covered the Dore mountain range with an ice cap more than 100m/328ft thick. This considerable mass dug out corries and deep valleys, created the scarp slopes down which the waterfalls cascade, and threw into relief the most resistant sections of mountain, the peaks and enormous rocks that add to the picturesque beauty of the Dore mountain range.

Final throes – Decapitated and dismantled by the glaciers and by the surging melt waters that accompanied the fusion of the ice flows, the central area of the range looked very much as it does today when the first human settlers arrived. It was then that a new volcanic upthrust occurred along the edges: secondary volcanoes erupted, closing off valleys with their cones and lava flows, gouging out craters and creating a number of lakes.

Driving Tours

1 Puy de Sancy★★★

Le Mont-Dore⚐⚐
⚓ *see Le MONT-DORE.*

🚶 *From Le Mont-Dore, drive to the upper part of the winter resort (4km/2.5mi) in order to reach the* **cable-car station***. After a 3min ride, allow 45min on foot to the summit.*

Panorama★★★
Rising to an altitude of 1,885m/6,184ft, Puy de Sancy in the Dore mountain range is the highest peak in central France.

2 Northern Slopes★★★

A round trip of 85km/53mi.
It is also possible to start this trip from La BOURBOULE.

Le Mont-Dore⚐⚐
⚓ *see Le MONT-DORE.*

▶ *Leave Le Mont-Dore N along D 983; 3km/1.9mi further on, turn right onto D 996.*

Col de la Croix-Morand
Alt 1,404m/4,606ft. This pass is also known as **Col de Diane,** although the real pass of this name is set away from the road. It used to have a bad reputation, for according to a local saying, "The Col de la Croix-Morand claims one man every year."

▶ *Return to D 983 and turn right (beware: in winter, this road is sometimes blocked by snow).*

After driving through the forest then through a valley with hillsides covered

Lac de Guéry

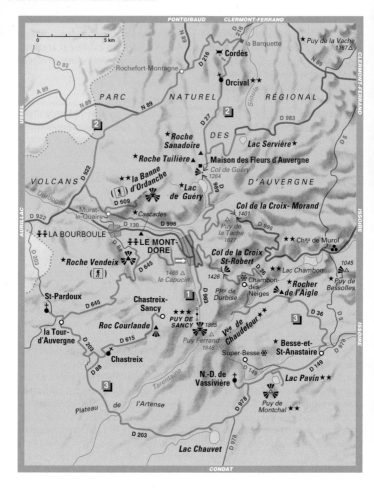

with basalt rock falls, the road reaches Lake Guéry (**view** of the Sancy massif).

Lac de Guéry★

The lake was formed by a basalt flow which arrived from a south-easterly direction, closing off the end of the valley. The pastures are studded with black rocks and the surrounding pine forests create a rather austere environment lightened in the springtime by great expanses of snow.

Maison des Fleurs d'Auvergne

🕒Open mid-Jun–mid Sept 10am–7pm; May–mid Jun Sat–Sun and public holidays 10am– 6pm. ∞4€. ☎04 73 65 20 09. http://maisondesfleurs.free.fr.
Located at Col de Guéry, this centre belonging to the Parc Naturel Régional des Volcans d'Auvergne, proposes an introduction to the local flora. In summer, the Maison de la Flore d'Auvergne organises themed walks.

Roches Tuilière et Sanadoire★

From Col de Guéry there is a fine **view** ★★ over the deep, wooded Chausse corrie from which the rocks of Tuilière and Sanadoire stand out.

To the left is **Tuilière rock**★, once the chimney of a ruined volcano. **Sanadoire rock**★ to the right is all that remains of a volcanic cone. Near the junction of D 27 and D 983, a path off D 983 leads to a rocky promontory.

▶ Continue along D 983.

Lac Servière★

This lake is a former crater with gently sloping sides, except to the south where it cuts into the Puy de Combe-Perret. A round lake as unruffled as a mirror, its shores are lined with pines and firs, and meadows.

▶ *Turn back and follow D 27 on the right.*

Orcival★★ – *see ORCIVAL.*

▶ *Leave Orcival N along D 27.*

Château de Cordès – *see ORCIVAL.*

▶ *In La Baraquette turn left towards Rochefort-Montagne and Murat-le-Quaire. Turn left onto D 609.*

La Banne d'Ordanche★★
see La BOURBOULE.

▶ *Beyond Murat-le-Quaire, return either to La Bourboule on D 609 or to Le Mont-Dore on D 996.*

As well as the long-distance footpaths (Grande Randonnée), marked with red and white stripes, and the local paths (Pays Balisé), marked in red and yellow, there are many other interesting footpaths.

③ **The Sancy Range**★★
85km/53mi

Some of the roads may be blocked by snow from November to April. The trip can also start from La BOURBOULE.

Le Mont-Dore‡‡
see Le MONT-DORE.

▶ *Leave Le Mont-Dore E on D 983 and turn left onto D 36.*

Col de la Croix-St-Robert

From the pass there is a superb **panoramic view**★★ to the west over the Millevaches plateau, to the east over Lake Chambon, Murol plateau and castle and, in the distance, the mountains in the Forez and Livradois areas.

The road runs down beyond the pass towards Besse-en-Chandesse across the

Durbise plateau with its vast expanse of pasture where the winter sports resort of **Chambon-des-Neiges** has been built.

▶ *Continue along D 36 and leave the car in the parking area at the entrance of the site.*

Vallée de Chaudefour★★

This interesting valley was gouged out of the granite and lava by the glaciers of the Quaternary Era, which covered the slopes of the Dore mountain range, and by the River Couze which flowed through the area after the glaciers had melted.

The valley floor and lower slopes boast abundant plant life. Some of the upper slopes and peaks are gashed by ravines, others bristle with rocks which have been laid bare and carved into strange shapes by erosion.

Vallée de Chaudefour

J. Damase/MICHELIN

Geology enthusiasts will discover examples of volcanic rock, and there are many good climbs for those interested in mountaineering.

Viewpoint

From a small bridge spanning the Couze, a spring can be seen and there is a picturesque view over the valley floor forming a majestic amphitheatre. When facing Puy Ferrand, with the Roc de la Perdrix to the left and, opposite, the sharp pointed pyramid of the Aiguille standing out against its slopes.

To the right of Puy Ferrand stand some interesting rock formations, the Crête de Coq and the Dent de la Rancune.

▶ *Return to the car park and continue along D 36.*

Rocher de l'Aigle★

From "Eagle's Rock" there is a striking view of the Chaudefour Valley and the Dore mountain range.

▶ *Keep driving along D 36.*

Besse-en-Chandesse★

♿ *see BESSE-EN-CHANDESSE.*

▶ *Leave Besse SW along D 149.*

Lac Pavin★★

♿ *see BESSE-EN-CHANDESSE.*

▶ *Return to D 978 and turn left.*

Chapelle de Vassivière

During the summer, this 16C pilgramage chapel, standing in a beautiful rural setting, houses the statue of Our Lady of Vassivière.

▶ *Turn round and then turn right onto D 978 towards La Tour-d'Auvergne.*

Lac Chauvet

Lake Chauvet is surrounded by woods and pastures, and was formed by a series of volcanic eruptions which caused soil subsidence.

▶ *Return to D 203 and turn left; 12km/7.5mi further on, turn right onto D 88.*

Chastreix

Winter sports in Chastreix-Sancy. The **church** is a fine building with a nave but no side aisles.

▶ *Leave Chastreix N on D 615.*

Roc de Courlande

The road leads to the winter sports resort of **Chastreix-Sancy** then to Courlande rock on the west side of the Puy de Sancy.

▶ *Turn back to rejoin D 203 and turn right.*

La Tour-d'Auvergne

This is a small town in a delightful, rustic setting crisscrossed by streams forming waterfalls. It lies on a basalt plateau ending in prismatic columnar basalt rock that can be seen near the church. The market place laid out on the top of these prisms seems to be made of gigantic cobblestones.

▶ *Continue NW along D 203.*

Église de St-Pardoux

Interesting Gothic **church** which still has 13C strap hinges on its doors and a fine gilt-wood altarpiece.

▶ *Return to La Tour-d'Auvergne and drive NE on D 645.*

Roche Vendeix★

♿ *see La BOURBOULE.*

▶ *Return either to La Bourboule by continuing along D 88 beyond Vendeix rock, or to Le Mont-Dore by turning right onto D 645.*

GORGES DE LA SIOULE★★

MICHELIN MAP 326: C-5 TO E-7 – 30KM/18.6MI NW OF RIOM

The upper course of the River Sioule has a winding, undulating character as it flows down the Dômes mountain range, contrasting with the lower course, which is flat with numerous islands in the Limagne basin. As erosion brought down the level of this calcareous basin, the Sioule, flowing at an increasing speed, cut into the granitic plateau upstream, thereby hollowing out a gorge between the outlying areas of Ébreuil and Châteauneuf-les-Bains. An intricate network of footpaths and bridlepaths enable visitors to discover the attractions of the area, which is also ideal for fishing and canoeing.

- **Information:** R. du Gén. Desaix, 63390 St Gervais d'Auvergne. ☎04 73 85 80 94. www.ot-couer-de-combrailles.com.
- **Orient Yourself:** Access to the gorges is effected to the NW of Riom, by the N 144 (direction Montluçon).
- **Don't Miss:** The gorges de Chouvigny, and the Méandre de Queuille.
- **Organising Your Time:** You will need a whole day to do the gorges justice.
- **Especially for Kids:** Visit the château de Chouvigny.
- **Also See:** AIGUEPERSE, CHARROUX, MONTS DÔME, VOLVIC.

Driving Tours

1 Gorges and Castles
40km/25mi – about 3hr.

Ébreuil

The small town lies on the banks of the Sioule which, having crossed the famous gorge of the same name, flows through a wide, fertile valley. The **Église St-Léger**★, built in the 10C and 13C, was part of a Benedictine abbey whose buildings were replaced in the 18C by the present hospice (to the right of the west front) and by an abbot's palace (behind the east end) that is now a retirement home.

The belfry-porch, remarkable for the purity of its architectural design, was added to the 11C west front around 1125.

The interior includes **frescoes**★ dating from the 12C and 15C. The 12C paintings decorating the gallery depict St Austremoine, first Bishop of Clermont, the martyrdom of St Valery and St Pancras, and the three archangels, Michael, Gabriel and Raphael.

The 15C fresco on a pillar to the right of the nave shows St George slaying the Dragon. Behind the High Altar on a stone column is the superb **reliquary of St Léger**★ (16C) made of wood cov-ered with silver-gilt. In one of the apsidal chapels is a 16C statue of the Virgin Mary seated.

- *Leave Ébreuil to the W on D 915.*

The corniche road, 4km/2.5mi after Ébreuil, overlooks the Sioule. On the steeper and more rugged slope on the right, bare granite alternates with heather. Beyond Péraclos, the road descends down to the river's edge.

Detail of a fresco in the Église St-Léger

J. Damase/MICHELIN

Address Book

For coin ranges, see the cover flap.

WHERE TO STAY

Montarlet – *63390 St. Gervais d'Auvergne, 3km/1.8mi W of St-Gervais-d'Auvergne via D 532, dir. Espinasse then turn left.* ☎04 73 85 87 10. *3 rms.* Located in a lovely, natural environment, this old farm is a most pleasant stopover. The restored bedrooms are delightful, with their sponge-painted walls, antiques and carefully chosen fabrics. Park with a view of the hills of Auvergne.

Castel Hôtel 1904 – *63390 St-Gervais-d'Auvergne.* ☎04 73 85 70 42. *Closed 12 Nov–14 Mar.* ▣. *17 rms.* ⏤9€. *Restaurant* ⏢⏢⏢. This handsome, flowery 17C manor became a hotel in 1904. The inviting interior is a reminder of centuries past with its period furniture, waxed parquets, grandfather clocks and statuettes. You'll discover appetizing, innovative cuisine in the more formal restaurant, whereas meals at the bistro, Le Comtoir à Moustaches, are of good value.

WHERE TO EAT

Restaurant Vindrié – *Gorges de la Sioule, 63560 Servant.* ☎04 73 85 51 48. ⏤. This family restaurant is set right in the heart of the Gorges de la Sioule area, just next to the river. Tasty food with a nice choice of fish dishes and a very impressive wine list with over 45,000 bottles waiting patiently in the cellar! Pleasant summer terrace under an ivy cover.

RECREATION

Sioule Loisirs – *Pont de Menat, 63560 Menat.* ☎04 73 85 52 87. www.val-de-sioule.com/loisire.html. *May–Sept: from 9am. Reservations required.* Canoe and kayak rentals for trips down the Sioule. All-day and half-day itineraries possible.

Château de Chouvigny

🕐 *Open May–Sept Sat–Sun and public holidays 2.30pm–5.30pm (Jul and Aug daily 10am–noon, 2.30pm–6.30pm).* ⏤5€. ☎04 70 90 44 95.

This Bourbonnais-style fortress is built on a spur of rock in a delightful **setting**★ in a valley, its impressive crenellated silhouette towering high above the gorge of the Sioule flowing below.

Gorges de Chouvigny★★

At the entrance to the gorge the road cuts through a rocky headland, the left part of which, detached from the rest, is called **Roc Armand.**

The summit can be reached by a staircase cut out of the rock.

Upstream, there is a beautiful view of the gorge – wooded slopes spiked with granite tips – whereas downstream, Chouvigny Castle can be seen. Beyond Armand rock, the gorge becomes very picturesque.

At the entrance to a tunnel there is a **viewpoint** on the left, over a bend in the Sioule dominated by high cliffs. Upstream, the Sioule flows silently and smoothly down. Below the viewpoint, however, it flows quickly and noisily through a mass of pebbles; it is gradually wearing down a shelf which interrupts the natural slope. The picturesque valley unfolds a succession of wild-looking gorges and green narrow stretches.

Menat

This small village was once home to a Benedictine monastery founded in the 6C. Today there remain the 12C abbey church, vestiges of the 15C cloisters, along with the buildings housing the town hall and the Museum of Paleontology.

Musée de Paléontologie: "Le Gîte à Fossiles"

🕐 *Open Jun–Sept daily except Tue 10.30am–noon, 2pm–6.30pm; Apr–May Sat–Sun and public holidays 10am–noon, 2pm–6.30pm.* ⏤3.50€. ☎04 73 85 54 22.

The museum is chiefly devoted to the small geological basin of Menat, dating from the end of the Secondary Era. The exhibition "La Marche vers l'Homme" illustrates the evolution of life on earth from the first cell up to modern Man.

Pont-de-Menat

This is an ideal point of departure for canoeing and kayaking. Crossing the river, there is an attractive view *(right)* of the old humpback bridge. Soon, on the edge of a cliff ahead, the romantic ruins of **Château-Rocher** (13C) loom into sight. Immediately below the ruins is an attractive view of a bend in the Sioule, a typical example of an incised meander: the concave bank *(this side)*, excavated by the direct attack of the current, is steep; the convex bank *(opposite)*, which receives the alluvial deposits, is low and cultivated.

The road then rises, providing greater views of the river; it reaches its culmination just before the intersection with D 99 from St-Rémy-de-Blot. Forming a ledge above a small, still-active mill, it offers a remarkable view of the entire valley.

Lisseuil

Here the road reaches the bottom of the valley. The village church has a beautiful Romanesque Virgin (13C) in its restored chancel.

Ayat-sur-Sioule

An attractive road leads to this village, once the home of General Desaix (1768–1800), one of Napoleon's officers.

Châteauneuf-les-Bains

This thermal spa actually consists of several hamlets. Twenty-two springs are tapped here, providing cold water for bottling and hot water (ranging from 28–36°C/82–96°F) for the baths treating rheumatism and nervous disorders.

②Queuille Meander

60km/38mi – about 3hr 30min

Châteauneuf-les-Bains

see above.

▶ *Take D 227 W.*

St-Gervais-d'Auvergne

The village is built on a knoll. Its Gothic church still has some Romanesque features: a portal in the transept and, on the left side, a watchtower with a curious gargoyle. Beautiful lime trees shade

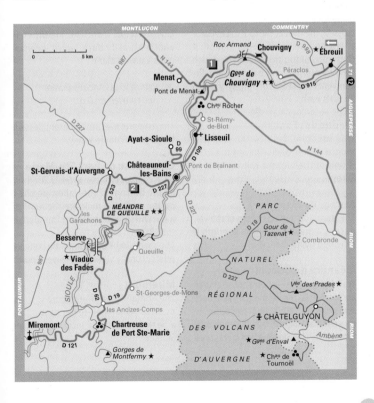

J. Damase/MICHELIN

Méandre de Queuille

the terrace by the church. The **Maison des Combrailles** *(Place R-Gauvin, BP 25, 63390 St-Gervais d'Auvergne. Information: ☎04 73 85 82 08)* provides information on the area.

South of St-Gervais the road winds through the middle of a wood, offering some lovely views of the Sioule before crossing the river at the foot of Les Gara-chons hydroelectric power station. It then runs along the east bank which follows numerous meanders and cir-cumvents the seams of porphyry which lie in its path.

Viaduc des Fades★

This structure, built by the engineer Vidard at the beginning of the 20C, is one of the highest rail viaducts in Europe.

Barrage de Besserve

The **dam,** located upstream of the via-duct, is a gravity dam – its strength is provided by its sheer mass.

Méandre de Queuille★★

Walk behind the east end of the church and continue through undergrowth to a viewpoint at the end of the promon-tory overlooking the Queuille meander, formed by the Sioule after it was wid-ened by a dam. This side, the concave bank of the loop, is high and spiked with rocks; opposite, on the convex side, the river forms a tight circle around the Murat "peninsula," a long wooded headland.

Barrage de Queuille

Downstream from the meander is another gravity **dam**, which incorpo-rates a power plant.

▶ *Return to Les Ancizes-Comps and turn left on D 61.*

The road provides a magnificent descent through the Sioule Valley.

Chartreuse de Port-Ste-Marie

Visits by appointment. ☎04 73 26 68 44. At the bottom of the valley, perched on the edge of a rock, are the ruins of a **Carthusian monastery** founded in the 13C.

The road climbs back up to the plateau, offering pretty views of the River Sioulet.

Miremont

The Romanesque church here with its massive square bell-tower rises up on a peak dominating a loop in the River Sioulet.

SOUVIGNY★★

POPULATION 1,952

MICHELIN MAP 326: G-3 – 13KM/8MI W OF MOULINS

Souvigny, which lies in the middle of a rich farming area, retains the most beautiful sanctuary in the Bourbonnais region, a reminder of the town's past splendour.

▐ **Information:** Musée de Souvigny, 03210 SOUVIGNY ☎04 70 43 99 75. www.ville-souvigny.com.

▶ **Orient Yourself:** Lying 13km/8 miles west of Moulins along the D 945, Souvigny is equally accessible from Bourbon-l'Archambault.

☺ **Don't Miss:** A visit to the museum.

⏱ **Organising Your Time:** To make the most of Souvigny and the surrounding area, allow a full day.

⚓ **Also See:** BOURBON-L'ARCHAMBAULT, MOULINS, MONTLUÇON.

A Bit of History

Resting place of the Dukes of Bourbon – In 916 Aymard, lieutenant of the Duke of Aquitaine, sold his land at Souvigny to the monks of Cluny; in doing so he bestowed an uncommon destiny upon the former Carolingian villa here. Two famous abbots from the powerful Burgundian abbey died in the monastery founded here: St Mayeul in 994 and St Odilon in 1049. The saintliness of the two men, soon united in the same tomb, drew numerous pilgrims to Souvigny, and the oldest of the Cluny priories, showered with gifts, developed dramatically.

The lords of Bourbon, descendants of Aymard, created a state around Souvigny which was to become the Duchy of the Bourbonnais. In the 14C and 15C the monastery underwent further alterations when Duke Louis II and Duke Charles I decided to make the sanctuary their necropolis.

Abbey

Église Prieurale St-Pierre-et-St-Paul★★

The **west front** of the original Romanesque edifice, of which only the left door remains, was preceded in the 15C by an avant-corps with a portal and a wide Flamboyant opening. Two Romanesque bell-towers, connected since the 15C by a gable with a rose window, dominate the priory. The three Romanesque bays in the centre of the façade belonged to the original building consecrated in 1064. The north side shows the church's different stages of construction: the towers, the second aisle and the ambulatory are 12C whereas the upper part of the nave and the transept are 15C.

Nave and aisles

The interior has surprisingly large dimensions: 87m/285ft by 28m/92ft. The double side aisles flanking the nave, and the double transept are evidence of Cluniac influence.

The inner aisles, built in the 11C, are very narrow with barrel vaulting whereas the outer aisles, which are later, have groined or pointed vaulting.

Chapelle Vieille★

The old chapel has a beautiful stone screen in Flamboyant Gothic style.

♦ Tomb of **Louis II of Bourbon,** known as Louis the Good, and his wife, Anne of Auvergne. The two marble recumbent figures are still extremely realistic, despite the defacements.

♦ 15C **Entombment**.

Chapelle Neuve★★

The new chapel is larger than the old chapel and has a very fine enclosure.

♦ Tomb of Charles I and his wife, Agnes of Burgundy by Jacques

Morel. The recumbent figures, clothed in flowing cloaks, rest on a black marble slab.

- A graceful Mary Magdalene from the late 15C.
- The Virgin, Child and St John (16C).
- Small 15C *Pietà*.

Cloisters

Only one side of these 15C cloisters remains, with groined vaulting because of the arrangement of the pillars. French-style gardens have been laid out on the site of the former priory buildings.

Sights

Musée de Souvigny

🕐 *Open daily except Tue 9am–noon, 2pm–6pm (7pm in Jul–Aug).* ≈4€. ☎04 70 43 99 75.

This museum to the right of the priory church houses local history collections, as well as a glassworking exhibition. Next to the sarcophagi, recumbent figures and capitals stands a 12C **calendar**★★, the most striking piece in the collection. This 1.80m/5ft 9in octagonal pillar, weighing 840kg/1,848lb (over 0.75t), is carved on two sides with scenes showing the labours of the months and the corresponding signs of the Zodiac; symbols of strange peoples and fabulous animals adorn the other faces.

Local history is recalled in the Souvigny glassworks founded in 1755: the master glassmakers' tools and examples of glassware (carafe stoppers, pharmacy bottles, champagne glasses) on show are reminiscent of this ancient craft.

Detail from a 12C calendar

Driving Tour

Combraille Bourbonnaise 65km/40.5mi

This lush *bocage* countryside with its pretty churches will charm all visitors.

▶ *Leave Souvigny to the SW on D 945, heading for Le Montet.*

Noyant-d'Allier

The most striking feature of this former miners' town is its **pagoda**, surrounded by Buddha statues.

▶ *Continue N on D 18.*

Église de Meillers

The church is crowned by an unusual belfry. The chapel to the left of the chancel houses a late-12C Virgin.

▶ *Leave Meillers to the S on D 18, then turn right onto D 106.*

The **Côtes-Matras** command an enjoyable vista of the Allier plain.

Le Montet

The 12C Église St-Gervais-et-St-Protais was fortified in the 14C, but today only the nave and the side aisles have survived.

▶ *Leave Le Montet to the W on D 22, heading towards Cosne-d'Allier. After 9km/5.6mi, turn right onto D 68.*

Buxières-les-Mines

This locality features the very last open-air coal mine in the area.

Église St-Maurice

This church has a curious two-tier bell tower and a blind nave crowned by barrel vaulting.

▶ *Return to Souvigny via D 289, then D 11, driving along the Gros-Bois and Messarges oak forests.*

MASSIF DU TANARGUE★★

MICHELIN MAP 331: G/H-6

At the southern end of the high volcanic lands of the Velay and Vivarais rises the Tanargue, a crystalline range made up of granite, gneiss and micaschist. Its shredded appearance is due to the upheavals of the Tertiary and Quaternary Eras. This is one of the wildest regions in the Vivarais.

The storms in Tanargue are famous, especially for their violence in autumn. Sudden spates, given added power by the steepness of the terrain, transform local mountain rivers into raging torrents, which nonetheless subside as quickly as they swell.

▶ **Orient Yourself:** To the south of the Ardèche, the massif du Tanargue is easily accessible from the N102, although the minor roads are rather tortuous.

🕭 **Don't Miss:** The view from the cols de Meyrans and the Croix-de-Bauzon.

🕓 **Organizing Your Time:** Allow three hours or more for a tour of the massif by car, and much longer for exploration on foot, of course.

🕭 **Also See:** AUBENAS, AUBENAS, GORGES DE L'ARDÈCHE.

Driving Tour

Vals-les-Bains–Valgorge
80km/50mi – about 3hr.

Vals-les-Bains✝✝
🕭*see VALS-LES-BAINS.*

▶ *Leave Vals-les-Bains on N 102 S towards Le Puy-en-Velay. At Pont-de-Labeaume take D 5 to Jaujac.*

The route passes the basalt flows of the Lignon Valley; 2km/1mi beyond Pont-de-Labeaume, at a signpost, park and walk up to the edge of the volcanic platform on which the road runs; here and there the **basalt flow**★ takes on a striking appearance of perfectly vertical tube-like sections, some of a blue-grey colour.

Jaujac
This village has attractive 15C and 16C houses, especially in the Chastelas district on the west bank, and the ruins of its old fortified castle. To the south-east rises the "Jaujac dish," an ancient volcano from which the flows of the Lignon emerged, and where mineral springs emanate.

Leaving Jaujac, the small 15C **Château de Bruget** comes into sight on the right.

From La Souche the road becomes more mountainous; the tip of Abraham's Rock stands ahead to the right, dark slopes covered in pines lie to the left;

Col de la Croix de Bauzon★
From this pass the view extends over the valleys of the Borne and the Masméjean to the mountains of the Margeride; to the east, the Lignon basin continues into the Aubenas depression. A small ski resort has been created at the foot of the Tanargue slopes, between La Souche and St-Étienne-de-Ludgarès *(information available from the tourist office in St-Étienne-de-Ludgarès).*

▶ *Follow D 19 towards St-Étienne-de-Lugdarès and turn left on D 301 (narrow road).*

Basalt flow in Jaujac

J. Damase/MICHELIN

Gorges de la Borne★

Beyond a stretch of route across broom-covered moorland, the descent to Borne offers plunging views over the gorge. To the west is the profile of Le Goulet mountain. **Borne**★ itself is a village in a secluded site, on a ledge above the deeply embanked torrent.

Within a rocky corrie on a spur lie the ruins of a castle, overlooking the waters. A small road leads to the tiny hamlet of **Mas-de-Truc**, seemingly lost in the mountains.

▶ *Continue to Col de Meyrand, via Loubaresse. As far as the village the road is narrow and sometimes impassable due to rockfalls.*

Col de Meyrand★★

From this pass a splendid ledge is suddenly revealed. An extensive panorama is visible, from left to right, over the summit of the Tanargue, the Valgorge Valley, the Ardèche depression overlooked by the Dent de Rez, the Valgorge ridge opposite and, to the right, the back of Mont Lozère.

▶ *Turn back.*

Beyond Loubaresse there are views along the channel down to Valgorge, then of stretches shaded by chestnut trees. The road drops downhill, twisting along the upper valley of the Beaume.

Valgorge

This small village is situated within a lush setting of vineyards and orchards.

▶ *Continue on D 24 until you reach Roche and take D 5 on the left.*

The road follows the Ligne valley up to Col de la Croix-de-Millet.

▶ *D 5 leads back to Jaujac and Pont-de-Labeaume. There, take N 102 on the right, heading for Vals.*

Excursion

Thines★★

20km/12.5mi N of Les Vans, on the edge of the Cévennes national park.

This small village sits on a spectacular **site**★★ perched above the Thines torrent and its ravine. It boasts old houses clinging to the rock, narrow alleyways and a fine Romanesque **church**: the doorway has four staTue–columns and a lintel bearing a frieze of small figures.

The **east end**★ is particularly attractive, with a cornice adorned with fanciful motifs below which is a blind arcade resting on carved consoles and engaged columns.

The alternating colour of the stonework – pink sandstone, grey granite and white limestone – adds to the charm of the building.

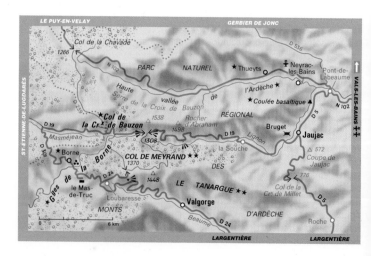

THIERS★★

POPULATION 13,338

MICHELIN MAP 326: I-7 – 37KM/23MI E OF CLERMONT-FERRAND

The town's **site**★★ – on the side of a ravine through which the River Durolle flows – has a magnificent view over the Limagne and the Dômes mountain range. This and the town's historic district, make Thiers an attractive tourist destination. It is the waters of the Durolle which made Thiers' fortune: paper and knives have been made here since the 15C and although papermaking has nearly disappeared, cutlery-making continues to contribute to the town's renown. The town was first founded on the south bank of the Durolle, around the original church of Le Moutier. Thiers was pillaged and razed to the ground by the Franks in 532 but rose from its ruins when the Bishop of Clermont, Avitus, built a sanctuary on the opposite bank, around the tomb of the martyr St Genès. Later, a fortified castle was built near the new church and the town started to develop on the north bank. Thiers subsequently became the seat of a barony.

- **Information:** Château du Pirou, 63300 THIERS, ☎04 73 80 65 65. www.auvergne-centrefrance.com.
- **Orient Yourself:** Thiers lies within the Parc Naturel Régional du Livradois-Forez, just 40km/25ml east of Clermont-Ferrand.
- **Parking:** Beside the Eglise St Genès, and at the northern end of town.
- **Don't Miss:** The view from the Terrasse du Rempart; Maison des Couteliers.
- **Organising Your Time:** Allow half a day to explore this lovely town.
- **Also See:** CLERMONT-FERRAND, MONTS DU FOREZ.

A Bit of History

Thiers Cutlery Trade

For many centuries Thiers has been the largest French cutlery manufacturing centre. The origin of the town's specialisation dates back to the Middle Ages: legend has it that Auvergne knights from the first crusade (1096–99) brought back the secret of cutlery manufacture; in fact, the Thiers metallurgical industry dates back to the 14C. By the 16C the town's cutlery trade had developed sufficiently for it to start exporting its products to Spain, The Netherlands and Lombardy.

Blades of all types were sharpened on grinding wheels powered by the waters of the Durolle. Cutlery production has subsequently been modernised, leaving the traditional figure of the knife-grinder lying face down over his grinding-wheel with his dog lying on his legs to keep him warm as but an image of the past. Developments in technology and electricity have led to enormous factories. Today Thiers still has nearly 300 manufacturers or craftsmen.

The Cradle of Cutlery

Maison des Couteliers

21 and 23 rue de la Coutellerie.

Open Jul–Aug 10am–6.30pm; rest of the year daily except Mon 10am–noon, 2pm–6pm. Guided tours of the workshops (20min). Closed Jan, 1 May, 1 Nov, 25 Dec. 5€. ☎04 73 80 58 86. www.musee-coutellerie-thiers.com.

Five rooms are devoted to the history of the cutlery industry in Thiers: history and origins, crafts and techniques, working conditions, leisure, commercialisation and advertising etc. Exhibits include documents, photos, tools and machinery, huge knifes and miniature ones, and various hallmarks from 1591 to 1857. Part of the exhibition space is devoted to sharpeners (model of a workshop).

A passage leads to no 21 where visitors can see a sharpener at work, lying down with his dog on his legs.

Musée de la Coutellerie

58 rue de la Coutellerie.

Open Jul–Aug 10am–6.30pm; rest of the year daily except Mon 10am

Thiers cutlery

J. Damase/MICHELIN

–noon, 2pm–6pm. ⊘*Closed Jan, 1 May, 1 Nov, 25 Dec.* ⊕*5€.* ☎*04 73 80 58 86. www.musee-coutellerie-thiers.com.*
Here, craftsmen may be watched working on the different phases of the manufacture of a knife. Workshops on the ground floor specialise in the polishing, shaping, mounting and carving of top-quality knives in limited numbers. In the basement *a son et lumière* show evokes the deafening world of the forge (power-hammer, furnace etc).

Walking Tours

1 The Old City★

A number of 15C, 16C and 17C half-timbered houses have been restored in the centre of the old town (Vieux Thiers). These picturesque houses line narrow, winding streets known as *peddes*, many of them reserved for pedestrians.

▷ *Start from place de la Mutualité and walk down rue Prosper-Marilhat leading onto rue Terrasse.*

Terrasse du Rempart★
The terrace offers a beautiful **panorama**★ of the Limagne, the Dore mountain range and the Dômes mountain range. The view of the sunset can be magnificent from here. The viewing table is made of enamelled lava stone.

▷ *50m/55yd further on, turn right onto rue du Bourg.*

Rue du Bourg
At nos 10 and 14 note the 15C Volvic-stone doorways; no 20 is a 16C house.

Place du Pirou
This square is dominated by the early-15C **Maison du Pirou**★. The house, with its pointed gables and timbered façade, is a handsome example of civil architecture of the Middle Ages. It houses the tourist office.

Rue Grenette
No 8 is a 16C and 17C house (Maison dite de Lauzun).

Rue de la Coutellerie
Note the unusual houses at no 12 and 14, the latter with wooden corbels carved in a somewhat free and vigorous style. No 21, the **Maison de l'Homme des Bois** (15C), is decorated with an enigmatic ape-like figure. This house and the ancient alderman's house at no 58 contain the Cutlers' Centre and the Cutlery Museum.

▷ *Follow rue Chabot on the left and take the first street on the left leading to the steps; turn left then first right onto impasse Jean-Brugière.*

Église St-Genès
This Romanesque church has undergone many alterations. The west front and the bell-tower have been rebuilt but the south transept retains the interesting decoration on its gable and graceful windows.

▷ *Walk through the public gardens surrounding the east end of the church of St-Genès.*

The north door, which gives onto place du Palais, is preceded by an 18C porch, in the wall of which an elegantly carved 14C recess has been incorporated.

▷ *Turn right onto rue du Palais and leave place du Pirou to the right.*

Rue du Pirou
At no 11 stands the Maison des Sept Péchés Capitaux, named after the decoration (Seven Deadly Sins) on the seven

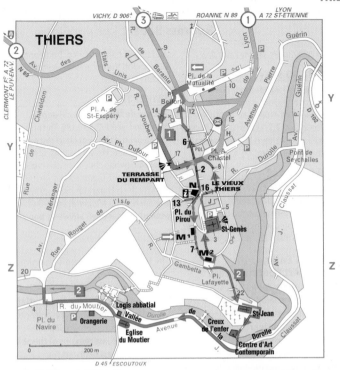

beams supporting the first floor; at no 9, note a corbelled construction.
Further along is the "Coin des Hasards," an intersection dominated by the tower of Maître Raymond (15C), one of the ancient towers from the Thiers castle.

▶ *Continue along rue Alexandre-Dumas and place Antonin-Chastel. Take a few steps to the left and follow rue Conchette.*

Rue Conchette

In the courtyard at no 4 there is a 16C staircase; at no 10, a beautiful inner façade on pillars. At no 18, in the small courtyard with its turret, two 16C medallions. This was the wealthy district.

▶ *Return to place de la Mutualité.*

▨ The Old Manufacturing Valley

🚶 This is a walking tour, starting from the Maison des Couteliers. The return journey is by local bus (TUT).

▶ *Walk down rue du Quatre-Septembre, heading towards the Creux de l'Enfer (signposted itinerary). You will reach place St-Jean and its church.*

Église St-Jean

This 15C church occupies a picturesque site overlooking the Durolle.

▶ *A path to the right as you leave the church runs round the church and leads to Creux de l'Enfer.*

Address Book

For coin ranges, see the cover flap.

WHERE TO STAY

Éliotel – *Rte de Maringues, 63920 Pont-de-Dore, 6km/4.8mi W of Thiers via N 89. ☎04 73 80 10 14. Closed 26 Dec–20 Jan.* 🅿️. *13 rms.* ⊠*7€. Restaurant*. Bed, board and a cyber-café are to be found here.

WHERE TO EAT

Moulin Bleu – *Le Courty. ☎04 73 80 06 22.* This establishment set in a wooded garden has a spacious dining room decorated with rustic furnishings and bright, happy fabrics. Traditional dishes with the occasional regional touch are served.

SWEET TREATS

Pâtisserie Museur – *15 r. François-Mitterand. ☎04 73 80 00 89.* The noble cocoa bean is this chocolate and pastry-chef's passion. His specialities, the Chabriou (white chocolate and crushed nougatine), the *Grêlons du Sancy* (milk chocolate and hazelnut mousse) and the *Rochers des Margerides* (tea-flavoured soft caramel) are wildly popular.

Creux de l'Enfer, Centre d'Art Contemporain

♿ Open daily 2pm–7pm. Closed 1 Jan and 25 Dec. ☎04 73 80 26 56. www.creuxdelenfer.net.

This contemporary arts centre is set up on the premises of a former factory facing the impressive Durolle waterfall. Exhibitions focus on unusual aspects of modern art that draw inspiration from the nearby landscape. The site is also used as an artists workshop for experimental projects.

▶ *Walk along avenue Joseph-Claussat.*

Vallée de la Durolle

The route follows the Durolle. The river's many waterfalls once operated numerous cutlery works. There were at least 140 falls over a distance of 3km/2mi. The most picturesque are those known as the **Creux de l'Enfer** ("Hell-Hole") falls, just before St-Jean bridge, and the **Creux du Salien** falls, just after Seychalles bridge (15C).

Legend has it that St Genès, tracked by soldiers, made his mule jump across the valley near the Creux de l'Enfer falls. The spot where the saint came down with his mule is called **Saut du Moine** ("Monk's Jump").

Église du Moutier

⊶ Closed for restoration.

The church was part of the powerful Benedictine abbey founded in the 7C. In 1882 it was reduced in height and badly disfigured.

At the corner of avenue Joseph-Claussat stands the fortified **Logis abbatial du Moutier** (Open Jul–Aug: daily except Mon and Tue 2.30pm–6.30pm; ☎04 73 80 59 08), the last remains of the abbey, which has been restored.

Orangerie

Open all year Tue–Fri, 9am–noon, 2pm –5.30pm, Sat–Sun 2pm–5.30pm. Closed 1 Jan, 1 May, and 11 Nov, 25 Dec. ☎04 73 80 53 53.

Located in Moutier park, the orangery has been turned into an information centre on the environment. The large hothouse is landscaped: pool, walls made of plants and exotic species contrast with a desert environment.

▶ *Continue along rue du Moutier to place du Navire (note the Pont du Navire, listed as a historic monument) then travel back to the town centre by public transport (from the church of Moutier).*

Excursions

Château et Jardins de la Chassaigne

Leave Thiers N towards Vichy.
Beyond the tunnel, turn left onto D 94C, and follow signposts to the castle.
Visitors enter through the gardens.

🕐 *Open Jun–Aug daily except Tue 2.30pm–6pm.* 🎟️*5€.* ☎️*04 73 80 59 08.*
The 15C manor, which had already suffered during the Revolution, was dismantled at the beginning of the 20C; its trees were also felled with the exception of the lime tree in the main courtyard. Although the castle was still inhabited, its upkeep was totally neglected until it acquired new owners in 1986.

ILOA "Les Rives de Thiers"
12km/7.5mi. At the large roundabout at the entrance to Thiers, head for Vichy. Take the fork at the toll-check and at the next roundabout turn left. Follow signs to ILOA.
This large leisure park offers facilities for a great many sports: rambling, cycling, riding, swimming, tennis and golf.

St-Rémy-sur-Durolle
9km/6mi N on N 89 and a small road on the left.
The scenic road winds through woodland before reaching St-Rémy. This cutlery-making centre is built on the southern flank of "Thiers mountain," an extension of the Bois Noirs massif.

▶ *In St-Rémy, take a road uphill on the left to the wayside cross. Leave the car near the sports ground and walk to the top of the cliff (🚶 15min there and back).*

From the wayside cross, the **panorama**★ includes the Forez mountains, the Margerides, the Plomb du Cantal and the Dômes mountain range. North-east of St-Rémy, on the right of D 201, a large lake offers various watersports, swimming, sailing, rowing.

Lezoux
15km/9.3mi W of Thiers. Population 4,957. 🏛️ *Mairie, le Bourg, 63190 LEZOUX,* ☎️*04 73 73 01 00.*
In the 2C Lezoux was a major centre of the ceramics industry, which was fuelled by the plastic clay quarried in the Limagne. Within a radius of 3km/2mi, the remains of more than 200 potters' kilns have been uncovered, and pottery made in Lezoux has been found as far away as England and Prussia. The town,

in which there is now a large oil-making plant, still has a 15C belfry topped by a tower. It stands adjacent to one of the old town gates.
The **Musée de la Céramique** (⛔ *temporarily closed*) contains collections of sigillated pottery (marked with a seal) dating from the 1C to the 4C AD – vases, cups, dishes, goblets, bowls etc – brick-red in colour, with rough but varied decorations in relief (animals, figures, floral motifs).

Moissat
5km/3mi S of Lezoux along D 229.
The Romanesque **church** at **Moissat-Bas** has retained its very early dome on squinches, its modest triumphal arch, its paintings and old gilt-wood statues. The restoration work undertaken in the chancel has revealed Romanesque arcading with columns and capitals, and paintings dating from the 14C and 15C.

Ravel
6km/3.7mi SE of Lezoux along D 223.
This village, set among the pasture and woodland of the Limagne, is easily identified by the **château**★ (*access is either from Ravel by a street, with several very steep sections, which leads off a small square opposite the church, or by a road running through the undergrowth, which branches off D 223 SE of Lezoux;* 🕐*May–Jun: guided tours (1hr) 2pm–6pm (Sun, 10am–noon, 2pm–6pm); Jul–Sept: 10am–noon, 2pm–6pm;* 🎟️*6€;* ☎️*04 73 68 44 63; www.chateauderavel.com*) which overlooks its houses and its church. In 1294, the castle was given by Philip the Fair to his chancellor Pierre Flotte and passed by inheritance and marriage to the D'Estaing family, who had it renovated in the 17C. The most beautiful and best preserved part of its decoration dates from the 18C.

Church
The building, in very pure Gothic style, has two 14C stained-glass windows in the nave and another (late 13C) in the sacristy. A strange Romanesque capital acts as a support for a 12C stone stoup. A 14C carved wooden staircase-door is protected by a second door.

Driving Tours

1 Les Margerides★

5km-9.5mi

▷ *Leave Thiers NE along N 89 towards Lyon.*

From the look-out point by the turn-off to St-Rémy, there is an attractive view over to the right of the Durolle gorge, Thiers and the Limagne.

▷ *In Château-Gaillard, take the first turning to the right.*

Vallée des Rouets

🚶 *Sturdy shoes required.* 🕑 *Open Jun–Sept Tue-Sun noon-6pm (last tour 5pm); Jul– Aug noon–6.30pm.* ☎*04 73 80 58 86.* The various paths formerly used by craftsmen have been restored and are now clearly signposted, offering interesting views of both architectural features and natural sites. There used to be 27 cutlery workshops in the valley; the last one in operation was the Rouet Lyonnet (1816) which closed in 1976.

▷ *Beyond Château-Gaillard and Bellevue turn right on D 320.*

The road crosses the river and winds through green and fertile countryside.

▷ *On leaving Vernières there is a view of the Durolle valley, and the village of St-Rémy on the mountainside; D 102 descends to Thiers and makes a right-hand bend near Borbes rock.*

Rocher de Borbes

From the rock there is an extensive **view★** of the Limagne, the Dômes and the Dore mountain ranges, the Livradois and, in clear weather, the Cantal mountains.

▷ *Continue on D 102 to return to Thiers.*

2 La Dore to Monts Forez★★

130km/81mi

This Dore is a tributary on the right bank of the Allier, rising in the mountains of the Livradois area. It flows down in a

south-easterly direction into deep, granite gorges then turns northwards to cross, at a leisurely pace, the Ambert plateau, a small gully lined by the mountains of Forez.

▷ *Leave Thiers to the W and drive up to Pont-de-Dore. Follow D 906, Then D 44 on the right.*

Château d'Aulteribe★

🕑 *See COURPIÈRE.*

▷ *Take D 223 then turn right onto D 906.*

Courpière – 🕑 *see COURPIÈRE.*

▷ *Beyond Courpière, continue to Ambert on D 906; right onto D 315.*

Sauviat

This village, situated on a spur of rock, stands high above a meander of the River Dore as it flows through a narrow valley.

▷ *Drive down on D 316 and rejoin D 906 on the right.*

Olliergues

Pleasantly situated on the north bank of the Dore, over which there is a pretty 15C bridge, Olliergues has terraces of houses rising up the hillside and features a castle (restored) that once belonged to Marshal Turenne's family.

▷ *Continue towards Ambert and 3km/2mi before reaching Ambert, turn right onto D 66 and right again onto a road leading to Volpie rock.*

Rocher de la Volpie★

🚶 From the rocky Volpie peak the **view★** stretches over the Livradois mountains with the Ambert plain in the foreground. Those reluctant to tackle the climb can take a path to the right beyond the farm, which leads across the meadows to the foot of the rock *(20min there and back).*

▷ *Rejoin D 66 and turn right.*

Église de Job

Superb 15C **church** topped by a large square belfry.

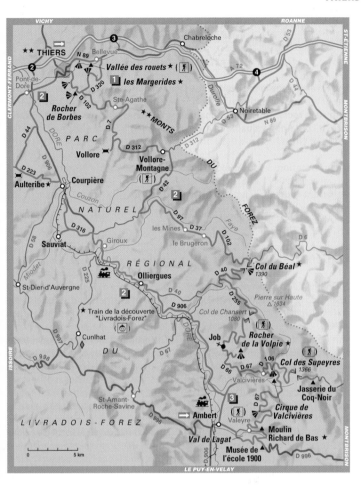

▶ *D 255 to the right then D 40*
lead to Col du Béal.

Col du Béal★

From this pass there is a wide **panoramic view** over the mountains of the Auvergne and the Lyonnais area.

▶ *Leave Col du Béal on D 102.*

The road crosses vast expanses of pasture and soon provides a superb view of the mountains of the Livradois area.

▶ *In Brugeron, take D 37 towards*
Olliergues and, when you reach the
hamlet of Les Mines, turn right
onto D 97.

The road follows the Faye Valley.

▶ *Shortly after crossing the River Faye,*
turn right onto D 42.

Vollore-Montagne

This mountain village is an ideal centre for walkers. The forests, the landscapes of woodland and meadow, and local beauty spots make this part of the journey most enjoyable.

▶ *Drive W on D 312.*

Château de Vollore–&COURPIÈRE.

▶ *N along D 7; 7km/4mi beyond Ste-*
Agathe, the road begins its descent
to Thiers via the Margerides route.

3 Le Val Lagat
&*see AMBERT.*

TOURNEMIRE★

POPULATION 145

MICHELIN MAPS 330: C-4 – LOCAL MAP SEE MONTS DU CANTAL

This lovely village in the heart of the Cantal mountains has been recognised as one of the most beautiful villages in France. The lava-stone houses are covered with slate roofs. The small, Romanesque **church** is built of coloured volcanic tufa. It contains a valuable reliquary containing a thorn allegedly from the Crown of Christ.

- **Information:** Seasonal information office at entrance to village; times variable. ☎04 71 47 61 34.
- ▶ **Orient Yourself:** This peaceful village lies 22km/14mi N of Aurillac along country lanes.
- **Also See:** SALERS, AURILLAC, MAURIAC.

Château d'Anjony★

🕒 *Open mid-Feb–mid Nov: guided tours (45min) daily, 2pm–6.30pm (Jul–Aug 11 and 11.30, 2pm–6.30pm, daily except Sun).* ⚏7€.

This castle of reddish basalt is one of the most remarkable in Auvergne. Strategically located on the tip of the Tournemire promontory, it dominates the lush landscape of the Doire valley with its four tall towers.

The castle was built in the 15C by Louis II of Anjony, the companion of Dunois and Joan of Arc, near the towers of Tournemire which had been held in joint fief by his family and the Tournemires since 1351. This dual ownership led to three centuries of bloody rivalry between the families, one of old feudal stock, the other having prospered through business and service to the royal family. The feud ended around 1650.

The main hall on the first floor boasts a coffered ceiling with three tiers of beams, and throughout the castle there are some fine furnishings and furniture: a vast fireplace, tapestries from Aubusson and Flanders, a tester bed, a reclining seat. The Knights' Hall on the second floor has **frescoes**★ of Michel of Anjony and his wife Germaine of Foix in late-16C dress, and scenes illustrating the legend of the Nine Valiant Knights from a medieval poem.

Knights' Hall in the château d'Anjony

TOURNON-SUR-RHÔNE★

POPULATION 9,946
MICHELIN MAP 331: L-3

This busy town on the Rhône overlooks **Tain-l'Hermitage** on the opposite bank, which is famed for its fine wines.

Information: Hôtel de la Tourette BP 47, 07301 TOURNON-SUR-RHÔNE ☎04 75 08 10 23. www.ville-tournon.com.

▶ **Orient Yourself:** Tournon is not far from Romans-sur-Isère (20km/12.5 miles to the east) and Valence, about the same distance to the south.

Parking: There are car parks on the north (left) bank of the Rhône, and around the Place de la République on the south.

🕐 **Organising Your Time:** Allow half a day, at least. Arrive in time for lunch, and then amble leisurely.

Also See: ANNONAY, ROMANS-sur-ISÈRE, VALENCE.

Town

Tournon-sur-Rhône boasts a 15C-16C **château** containing a museum about bargemen on the Rhône, set in a charming **terraced garden**★. The **Lycée Gabriel-Fauré** has an attractive Renaissance doorway, and a collection of busts and tapestries.

Excursions

Pierre-Aiguille Belvedere★
Leave Tain in the direction of Larnage, then follow directions.
The far-reaching views from here encompass Tain-l'Hermitage and its vineyard; the town of Tournon across the river and the foothills of Vercors with the Alps in the background.

Chantemerle-les-Blés
Leave Tain as if for Romans and turn left onto D 109, and under the autoroute. Park behind the post office. Then take the path to the right of the memorial. This hamlet has kept its humble and sober church, enhanced by a number of ornamental features.

Driving Tours

Panoramic Route★★★

▶ *Leave Tournon-sur-Rhône to the S via rue du Dr-Cadet and rue Greffieux towards St-Romain-de-Lerps.*

Tournon, set on the banks of the Rhone

J. Damase/MICHELIN

From Tournon to Valence the **panoramic road**★★★ along the hillside offers magnificent views. The road out of town climbs steeply in a series of hairpin bends, giving breathtaking views.

▶ *In Plats turn left by the War Memorial onto GR 42.*

St-Romain-de-Lerps★★★

The **panorama** from here is immense, covering 13 *départements*. This is one of the most impressive views along the Rhône: to the east, above the Valence plain, rises the Vercors bar, dominated by the Moucherolle needle and the dome of the Grand Veymont; beyond lie the Alps and Mont Blanc. Westwards lie the plateaux and the greenhouses of the Vivarais.

▶ *From St-Romain-de-Lerps take D 287 down to St-Péray; the road offers wonderful views over the Valence basin. Return to Tournonsur-Rhône on N 86.*

Gorges du Doux via the Corniche Road★ 50km/31mi

▶ *Leave Tournon-sur-Rhône on the road to Lamastre.*

The road runs along the pretty orchards of the Doux basin. The **corniche road**★ dominates the Doux gorges, planted with oak, broom, ferns, boxwood and pine trees.

▶ *Take D 209 on the right, heading for Boucieu-le-Roi.*

Boucieu-le-Roi

This village was once the seat of the old royal bailiwick in the Upper Vivarais area.

▶ *Return to Tournon-sur-Rhône via Colombier-le-Vieux and D 234, running on the opposite side of the gorges, through wild vegetation.*

Défilé de St-Vallier★

▶ *Leave Tournon-sur-Rhône to the N on N 86.*

Vion

The **church**, partly Romanesque, has a transept crossing with capitals.

▶ *In Vion, take the narrow road that leads to D 532. At Croix de Fraysse, head for St-Jeure-d'Ay, then turn right onto D 6. About 7km/4.3mi further on, take D 506 on the right, leading to Ozon.*

The steep descent to Ozon offers **views**★★ over **St-Vallier Gorges**★ and the orchards and vineyards along the river.

▶ *Return to Sarras and St-Vallier, then take N 7 to Tain-l'Hermitage along the east bank of the Rhône.*

This section of the valley, which narrows into a corridor again, is the most evocative of the Rhône in medieval times: ruins of feudal strongholds and old defensive towers and watchtowers line the escarpments.

The entrance to **Serves-sur-Rhône** is preceded by a superb **view,** ahead, of the impressive remains of its castle. On the west bank stands the rival tower of **Arras-sur-Rhône**.

LE TRICASTIN★

MICHELIN MAP 332: B-8

The Tricastin plain, with **Pierrelatte** at the centre, is encircled by three mountainous ranges, in which veins of iron and lignite have been found, which were first mined as long ago as the 4C BC by the Celts. The area marks the transition between the north and the south of France, with a climate and vegetation not unlike Provence. There is major industry here, most of it linked to the production of nuclear energy, though a zone has been set aside for agricultural use.

Information: Office de Tourisme de Saint Paul Trois Châteaux, Place Chausy - 26130 SAINT PAUL TROIS CHATEAUX. ☎04 75 96 59 60. www.office-tourisme-tricastin.com.

▶ **Orient Yourself:** Le Tricastin is situated between Viviers and Pont-St-Esprit to the east of the Rhône.

Don't Miss: The truffle museum.

Organising Your Time: Allow half a day.

Kids **Especially for Kids:** Get snappy at the crocodile farm near Pierrelatte.

Also See: GORGES DE L'ARDÈCHE, MONTÉIMAR, AVEN d'ORGNAC, VIVIERS.

Villages Excursion

St-Paul-Trois-Châteaux

The old town is surrounded by the remains of ramparts but has never had the three castles that its name – St-Paul-Three-Castles – would suggest. It was appointed capital of the region during Roman times, under the name "Augusta Tricastinorum." During the second half of the 4C, the first part of its Roman name was replaced by the name Paul, commemorating one of the town's first bishops. The name of the old capital of "Tricastini" may possibly have been Frenchified by a clerk in the 16C to "Trois Châteaux," though there is no evidence for this theory. The town was a bishopric until the Revolution.

Modern St-Paul sits at the heart of the main truffle region of France.

Cathedral★

This imposing building, begun in the 11C and completed in the 12C, is a remarkable example of Provençal Romanesque architecture. Most striking is the exceptional height of the transept walls and the powerful aspect of the nave.

Maison de la Truffe et du Tricastin

⏱*Open Jun–Sept 9am–noon, 3pm–7pm (Sun, 10am–noon, 3pm–7pm; Mon, 3pm–7pm); Mar–May and Oct–Nov daily except Sun 9am–noon, 2pm–6pm (Mon, 2pm–6pm); Dec–Feb: daily except Mon, 9am–noon, 2pm–6pm, Sun 10am–noon, 2pm–6pm. ⏱Closed public holidays. ◉3.50€. ☎04 75 96 61 29.*

The Truffle Centre, located inside the tourist centre, houses an exhibition with posters, showcases and a video projection on the cultivation and marketing of what is known as the "black diamond" of the Tricastin region, and an ingredient in many tasty local dishes.

St-Restitut

The village **church**★ in Provençal Romanesque style has wonderful **carved decoration**★.

Route des Carrières

Leaving St-Restitut along D 59A, turn right onto a twisting road running across the limestone plateau.

Quarries were worked here between the 18C and the early 20C.

La Garde-Adhémar

This old village is signalled from some distance away by its church, perched on a rise. It is an ideal spot for a stroll, with its picturesque limestone houses, its vaulted alleyways and its narrow, winding streets with their arches. In the Middle Ages this village was a major fortress belonging to the Adhémar family.

In the 16C a Renaissance château was built for **Antoine Escalin**, Baron de la Garde, who started life as a mere shepherd then became a soldier; he ended his career as one of François I's ambassadors and as General in charge of the French galleys. Old town walls can be seen on the north side; to the south of the village is a fortified gate and a few ruins, not far from the huge Cross erected on a Roman base.

The Romanesque church is remarkable for its two apses and the attractive outline of its two-storey octagonal belfry topped by a stocky pyramid. Thanks to the writer **Prosper Mérimée** (1830–70), at the time Inspector of Historic Monuments, it underwent major restoration in the mid-19C.

Chapelle du Val-des-Nymphes

2km/1.2mi E on D 472. In a valley kept cool by many little waterfalls and which, as its name suggests, was once a place of pagan worship, stand the ruins of a 12C chapel. For a long while a ruin, this Romanesque chapel was restored from 1991 and an elegant timber ceiling now covers the nave.

Clansayes★

Park the car and head for the far end of the promontory.
From here there is an extensive **view**★★ over the Tricastin area and its peaks carved by erosion.

Barry★

Backing onto a cliff into which several of its houses are carved, this troglodytic village has been inhabited from prehistoric times to the Second World War; though now abandoned, it is undergoing restoration.

Farm

La Ferme aux Crocodiles★

Pierrelatte. 🅺🅺🅳🅷 ⏱Open daily Mar–Sept: 9.30am–7pm; Oct–Feb 9.30am–5pm. ⊛11€ (children: 7€). ☎04 75 04 33 73. www.lafermauxcrocodiles.com.
This crocodile farm is stocked with a great many species from countries all over the world (Cuba, America, Egypt), installed in large basins. Further on, visitors can discover a vast hothouse containing tropical vegetation and superb exotic birds. From the many footbridges, visitors can watch some 300 crocodiles from the Nile region basking in the sun or swimming in dark waters.

J. Damase/MICHELIN

La Ferme aux Crocodiles

VALENCE★

CONURBATION 117,448
MICHELIN MAP 332: C-4

This ancient Gaulish city, named Colonia Julia Valentia by the Romans at the beginning of the 2C BC, owes its development to its location on the Rhône, near the meeting of the tributary valleys of the Doux, Eyrieux, Isère and Drôme which mark out a vast internal basin and where the flora and fauna of Mediterranean France begin. The city, dominated by St-Apollinaire Cathedral, is built on a series of terraces going down to the river. Old Valence, surrounded by boulevards built in the 19C on the site of the old ramparts, has a network of shopping streets and picturesque sloping lanes, animated in season by the "Summer Festivals" *(see Calendar of events)*.

- **Information:** Parvis de la Gare, 26000 VALENCE ☎0892 707 099. www.tourisme-valence.co`m.
- ▶ **Orient Yourself:** Valence is 103km/64 miles south of Lyon, and accessible from the A 7.
- **Parking:** Parking is difficult in the centre, but there are ample car parks within walking distance.
- **Don't Miss:** Try to be there for either sunset or sunrise from the Esplanade.
- **Organising Your Time:** Half a day is probably enough, but you can easily be distracted.
- **Also See:** ROMANS-sur-ISÈRE, TOURNON-SUR-RHÔNE.

A Bit of History

A regional hub – The city, which is served by a large network of communications (A 7 motorway, N 7 national highway, River Rhône, airport), is the true centre of the Middle Rhône Valley and a focal point for entertainment and other attractions within the Drôme and Ardèche *départements*.

The population of Greater Valence, including the outlying suburbs spread out on either side of the Rhône – Bourg-lès-Valence, St-Péray, Portes-lès-Valence, Granges – is over 100,000, including numerous students enrolled at the Law Faculty and engineering schools.

Rabelaisian studies – In 1452 the dauphin Louis, who was to begin his reign a few years later under the name of Louis XI and who, at the time, was preparing for his kingly role in his princedom of Dauphiné, founded a university in Valence consisting of five faculties, including an Arts Faculty. Among the students was **François Rabelais**. He was to recall his student days here in his tales of the adventures of Pantagruel.

Courses were given by reputed masters, including the lawyer Cujas. Besides studying under this strict academic taskmaster, Rabelais is said to have had a love affair with his daughter.

Bonaparte in Valence – In 1785 Napoleon Bonaparte, a 16-year-old military cadet, arrived in Valence to improve his knowledge of warfare at the School of Artillery. Every morning, he went to the Polygon to direct his bombardiers' tactical exercises.

He lived almost directly opposite the Maison des Têtes (*see Old Town Tour*) which was occupied by a bookseller named Marc Aurel. Bonaparte soon befriended him, and in less than a year had read his entire stock. The future emperor had already embarked on a voyage of self-discovery. In a letter to a friend, he used a striking image to describe himself: "the southern blood which runs through my veins flows with the rapidity of the Rhône…"

Aurel's son was to publish the famous Souper de Beaucaire, in which Bonaparte set forth his ideas about the Revolution, a few years later in Avignon.

Old Town Tour

▶ *Leave from Peynet kiosk.*

Kiosque Peynet

This structure, built in 1880, owes its name to the artist **Raymond Peynet** (1908–99) who once drew a sketch of a pair of lovers seated beside it.

Champ-de-Mars

This vast esplanade, built on a hillside opposite the Rhône, overlooks Jouvet Park. From the belvedere there is a beautiful **view**★ of Crussol mountains. The sunsets visible from here, which throw the mountain range into relief, are famous, although it is at sunrise that the view of Crussol is the most striking.

▶ *Take the staircase below the belvedere and cross avenue Gambetta. The narrow rue des Repenties and côte St-Estève lead round the cathedral and onto place du Pendentif.*

Pendentif

This small monument was built in 1548, in the Antique style. The structure is completely open with a semicircular arch on each side, and has lovely proportions. It draws its name from the shape of its vault, reminiscent of the pendentives of a dome.

Cathédrale St-Apollinaire

This vast Romanesque construction was largely rebuilt during the 17C in the primitive style.

▶ *Enter the cathedral through the north door.*

Under the porch, on the left, notice the lintel from the original portal; its carved compartments represent the Annunciation, the Nativity, the Adoration of the Magi and the Magi before Herod.

Interior★

The influence of Auvergne Romanesque architecture is evident; the nave, with its barrel vaulting and transverse arches, is lit by the aisle windows. An arcade separates the chancel from the ambulatory. Note the depth of the transept arms,

unusual in Rhône buildings. Behind the chancel stalls is a cenotaph-bust of Pope Pius VI, who died in Valence in 1799.

▶ *Leave through the south door.*

Under the porch *(left)*, on the carved tympanum of the original portal, is Christ giving benediction, and on the lintel Christ multiplying the loaves.

▶ *Walk around the east end.*

Note the elegant billet-moulding above the arcades of the apse and the transept arms.

Musée des Beaux-Arts

The Fine Arts Museum is in the former bishop's palace, but is closed until 2011 (see Museum).

▶ *Take rue du Lieutenant-Bonaparte, then rue Pérollerie to reach the Maison Dupré-Latour.*

Maison Dupré-Latour

The interior courtyard of no 7 has a Renaissance staircase turret with a door surrounded by a remarkable carved frame.

▶ *From place de la Pierre, take rue St-James on the left then follow rue Sabaterie and rue Malizard.*

On the left stands the former St-Ruf temple. As you reach the public gardens, you will get a good view of Crussol in the distance.

▶ *Head for place St-Jean via côte des Chapeliers.*

Église St-Jean

This church was rebuilt in the 19C. The porch features some interesting original Romanesque capitals.

▶ *Walk along Grande-Rue.*

Maison des Têtes★

The "House of Heads" at no 57 is recognisable by the abundance and originality of the sculptures on its façade. Note two standing figures (Eve is on the left) and,

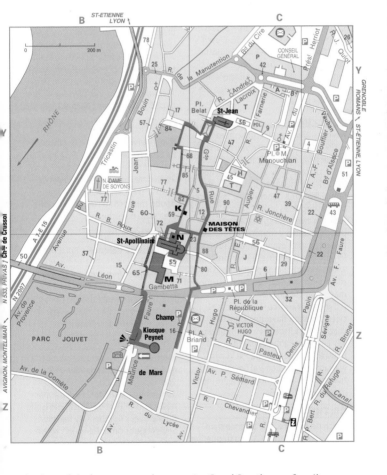

under the roof, the four enormous haut-relief heads symbolising the winds, after which this Renaissance house (1532) was named.

▶ *Grand-Rue, then rue Saunière, lead back to place du Champ-de-Mars.*

Address Book

For coin ranges, see the cover flap.

WHERE TO STAY

Hôtel St-Jacques – *9 fg St-Jacques.* 04 75 78 26 16. *29 rms.* *6€.* Not too far from the centre of town, this is a practical, modern hotel. The restaurant has several menus.

Chambre d'hôte La Mare – *Rte de Montmeyran, 26800 Étoile-sur-Rhône, 15km/9mi SE of Valence via D 111 and D 111B.* 04 75 59 33 79. *4 rms.* This family farm is the right place to become acquainted with the local savoir-vivre and the charm of the Drômois.

WHERE TO EAT

L'Auberge du Pin – *285 bis av. Victor-Hugo.* 04 75 44 53 86. *Closed Wed from Oct–May.* What a delightful Provençal bistro! Treat yourself to a slice of the good life, inside or under the shade of the century-old trees on the summer terrace.

SHOPPING

Nivon – *17 avenue Pierre-Semard.* 04 75 44 03 37. *www.nivon.com. Daily except Mon, 6am–7.30pm. Closed last wk in Jan and 3 wks in Jul.* Established in 1852 and managed by the Maurin family for three generations, the Nivon pastryshop does an exceptionally good job with two local specialities: the pogne, a buttery sourdough brioche flavoured with orange flower, rum or lemon; and the *Suisse,* a shortbread with candied orange peel packed into the dough and flavoured in the same manner as the pogne.

A Swiss in Valence – *Le Suisse* is a sweet, orange-flavoured brioche shaped like a little person. Traditionally eaten on Palm Sunday, it is said to owe its name to Pope Pie VI who was arrested by Général Berthier and transported to Valence where he died, imprisoned, in 1799.

ON THE TOWN

Place de la Gare. The Valence train station, serving the TGV and frequented by scores of tourists in transit, may well be the hub of the city.

Place des Clercs. This elegant square in the city centre is lined with bars and restaurants. Saturdays - market days -

it is overwhelmed with highly colourful fruit and vegetable stands.

Le Djam – *11 Grand-Rue.* 04 75 43 32 32. *Jul–Aug: 6pm–2am; Sept–Jun: Mon–Thu 6pm–1am, Fri–Sat 6pm–2am.* An original decoration scheme reigns in this small neighbourhood bar reminiscent of Alice in Wonderland. Sink into a chair shaped like a spade, heart, diamond or club before ordering an excellent glass of punch while listening to jazz, blues or ballads. Terrace on the street.

Café Victor-Hugo – *30 av. Victor-Hugo.* 04 75 40 18 11. *Mon–Sat 7am–2am.* Valence's chic literary café - chic but vivacious! Lunchtime, it is a noisy brasserie, and then in the afternoon ladies gossip over their hot cocoas while students play billiards upstairs.

Le Malvern – *27 r. Denis-Papin.* 04 75 44 10 07. *Jul–Aug: 9.30am–2am; Sept–Jun: Sun–Thu 7am–1am, Fri–Sat 'til 2am. Closed 1 wk Aug and Christmas.* With its 100 beers (16 on tap), 80 whiskies and rather rustic decor of the Irish pub ilk, this convivial, trendy bar is a favourite.

Le Blue Note – *Quartier des Fontaines, 26120 Chabeuil.* 04 75 85 24 77. *www. lebluenote.com. Thu–Sat and public holiday eves from 10.30pm.* Without a doubt, this techno stronghold is the area's top discotheque.

THEATRE

Comédie de Valence – *1 pl. Charles-Huguerel.* 04 75 78 41 70. *Tickets: Tue–Fri 1pm–7pm, Sat from 1pm on performance days. Closed Aug.* This handsome 873-seat theatre has a nice bar that is open for drinks before the show and during intermissions.

RECREATION

Marina – *Chemin de l'Épervière.* 04 75 81 18 93. *Apr–Oct: daily 9am–noon, 2pm–8pm; Nov–Mar: Mon–Sat 8am–noon, 2pm–6pm. Closed public holidays.* The Port de l'Épervière is the Rhône river's number one harbour. Several clubs organise sports activities here, including wind-surfing, water-skiing, para-skiing. There are also a bowling lane, a tennis facility, a pool, a campground, a hotel and several restaurants.

Detail of the façade, Maison des Têtes

Museum

Musée des Beaux-Arts

○*Closed until 2011.* ☎*04 75 79 20 80.*
www.musee-valence.org.
The Fine Arts Museum, located in the former bishop's palace is currently undergoing renovation, and will be closed until 2011.

Excursions

Crussol★★

5km/3mi W along N 532, via St-Péray.
On the top of Crussol Mountain stand the ruins of **Château de Crussol**, at one of the valley's best **beauty spots**★★★. The smooth grain of the white Crussol stone makes it ideal for building.
In the 12C, Bastet de Crussol chose this site for his fortress. The ambition of the "insignificant lords of Crussol" took them to the highest-ranking offices in the kingdom. One of the Crussols was Chamberlain to Louis XI, another became heir to the County of Uzès through marriage.
His son, Seneschal of Beaucaire and Nîmes, took part in the Italian Campaigns with Charles VIII and Louis XII. Their official duties took the Crussols away from the uncomfortable ancestral home and it was partially demolished in

the 17C. Bonaparte is supposed to have scaled the cliff at Crussol in a particularly death-defying feat of bravado with one of his brothers in 1785 while garrisoned in Valence.

▶ *In St-Péray take the road past the Château de Beauregard. There is a car park at the end of the road. Then take the path to the ruins. It is highly recommended to take care in rain, when the stones become slippery.*

🚶After passing the fortified north gateway in the old castle walls, follow the path on the left. It climbs through the remains of the **"villette,"** where the

Crest keep

Fr. Isler/MICHELIN

people who lived on the plain sought refuge in times of danger.

Take the path on the left which runs inside the walls then head for the squire's living quarters. Perched on a rocky promontory, the castle towers above the Rhône. Inside the keep, a belvedere offers a view of the Valence plain, the Bourg-lès-Valence dam, and the confluence of the Rhône and Isère.

Soyons

3.5km/2.2mi S on N 86.

This village is on the west bank of the Rhône, on the site of important prehistoric and medieval settlements. It derives its name from "Soïo," a local god revered by the Gauls in the 7C BC. Excavations carried out in the surrounding hills are gradually revealing a wealth of information spanning 150,000 years. The **Musée Archéologique** (&open *Jul–Aug: 10am–7pm (last admission 1hr before closing); Apr–Jun and Sept–Oct Wed–Sun, 2pm–6pm; closed Nov–Jan. 4€; 04 75 60 88 86)* displays a collection of Gallo-Roman finds and finds about prehistoric man and his environment.

Grottoes★

After leaving Soyons S on N 86, turn right towards a parking area. A botanical trail runs up the side of the hill and leads to the grottoes. Open Jul–Aug: guided tours (1hr) 10am–7pm (last admission 1hr before closing); Apr–Jun and Sept–Oct: 2pm–6pm. 7€. 04 75 60 88 86.

These caves are important for the study of Neanderthal man. The network of underground galleries starts from the **Trou du Renard.** The grottoes were occupied at an early date by men and cave animals. Over the centuries, bones from bears, wolves and lions have been uncovered here.

Crest

28km/17mi S. Pl. du Dr-Maurice-Rozier, 26400 CREST, 04 75 25 11 38. www. crest-tourisme.com.

The town of Crest, situated at the spot where the River Drôme flows into the Valence plain, is particularly proud of its castle keep. The town has grown up around it, with a dual role as market town and a community specialising in food processing. Among the many local gastronomic specialities are *défarde*, a stew made with lamb's feet and tripe, and *picodons*, small goats' cheeses.

Keep★

184 steps to the upper terrace.

Open *May–mid Sept 10am–7pm; Feb–Apr and mid-Sept–Oct: 2pm–6pm; rest of year Sat–Sun, 2pm–6pm.* Closed *January and 25 Dec.* 5€. 04 75 25 32 53.

The keep in Crest, also known as the "Tower", is all that remains of a fortress which was dismantled in 1633 on the orders of Louis XIII. The keep was erected over Roman foundations on a spur of rock, in various stages between the 11C and the 15C. The north wall, the tallest of the four, reaches a height of almost 52m/169ft; the base of the tower lies at an altitude of 263m/855ft.

From the upper terrace there is a view over the rooftops of Crest and beyond, in a superb **panoramic view★** to the north-east over Glandasse Mountain and the outcrops of the Vercors, and to the south over the Roche-Courbe range with the Trois-Becs, and Roche Colombe further in the distance. To the west the horizon is broken up by the long narrow ridge of the Vivarais area rising to the Gerbier-de-Jonc and Mézenc, both of which are visible in clear weather.

Further down the hill, on the left, are a few steps leading to a vaulted alleyway. This is the five-arched **Portique**

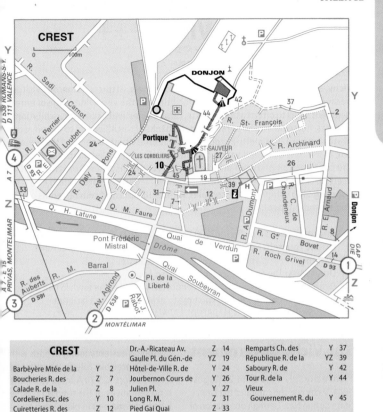

des Cordeliers which opens onto the monumental **Escalier des Cordeliers**.

Old houses

Along the main thoroughfare and the picturesque neighbouring streets are some of the vast mansions built for the wealthy bourgeoisie in Crest in the 16C and 17C.

Jardin des Oiseaux   Kids

In Upie, 11km/6.7mi N. Leave Crest on D 538 towards Chabeuil, then take D 142 to the left.
 Open Jul–Aug: 10am–7pm; Sept–Jun: 10am–dusk. 10€ (children: 6€). 04 75 84 45 90. www.jardin-aux-oiseaux.com.
This superb **Bird Sanctuary** is home to over 200 different European and exotic species: humming-birds, crested grebes, flamingoes, pelicans, ostriches, parrots etc.

The Hills of Drôme★

Past Crest, 43km/26mi SE of Valence.
Exploring the hills of Drôme, head first for the forest of Saoû, planted with beech, oak and pine trees. **Saoû** itself *is a* small village famous for its *picodon* goat's cheese, which has now entered the AOC category.
The village of **Soyans** is dominated by the imposing ruins of its castle, burned during the French Revolution.
The drive down offers pretty views of the valley and the outskirts of Marsanne, home town of **Émile Loubet,** President of France between 1899 and 1906.
The pretty houses of **Mirmande** spread out over the slopes of a hill. Towards 1930, the painter **André Lhote** (1885–1962) came to settle here and many contemporary artists followed.

VICHY

POPULATION 26,528

MICHELIN MAP 326: H-6

Vichy, a world famous spa resort and holiday town, attracts numerous visitors because of its high quality shopping facilities and the very wide range of entertainment it has to offer: casino-theatre, cabarets, festivals, concerts, exhibitions, lectures, horse races. The parks along the banks of the Allier add to the pleasure of staying here. The multi-purpose sports centre, situated north of the town, is one of the best designed sports complexes in Europe. Lake Allier, created after the construction of a dam bridge on the river downstream from the town, is used for international competitions (rowing, regattas, water-skiing etc). The Sporting Club completes the complex with its 18-hole golf course, tennis courts and swimming pool.

- **Information:** 19 r. du Parc, 03200 VICHY ☎04 70 98 71 94. www.ville-vichy.fr.
- **Orient Yourself:** North-east of Clermont-Ferrand, set on the River Allier.
- **Parking:** There is ample parking in the town centre.
- **Don't Miss:** The Spa district (*see Walking Tours*).
- **Organizing Your Time:** You can comfortably explore the town in half a day, but a longer period will give you time to experience its spa facilities.
- **Also See:** AIGUEPERSE, CHARROUX, LAPALISSE.

The Vichy Government

From early July 1940 until 20 August 1944, Vichy was the capital of the French State during Nazi German occupation of the north of France. Vichy, with a direct railway line to Paris (the "Thermal-Express"), relatively modern telephone links, and many hotels which could be requisitioned for government offices, was chosen in preference to cities such as Clermont-Ferrand, Marseille or Toulouse. It had the added advantage of being quite close to the line of demarcation between occupied and unoccupied France. Maréchal Pétain, hero of Verdun during the First World War, was granted full executive powers by the French parliament. He and his Cabinet had their headquarters in the Pavillon Sévigné.

The disproportionate centralisation of government power in this city was accompanied by a strictly monitored exercise of power and the laying aside of the fundamental principles of democracy. During the dark days of the Vichy regime, the city was subject to a permanent police presence, with the oppressive atmosphere further heightened by furtive and unexplained comings and goings, cowed public apathy and an overriding austerity totally at odds with the city's previous role as a health and leisure resort. On 20 August 1944, the representatives of the toppled regime who had remained in place were taken back to Germany by the Nazis as they retreated. Six days later the Free French Forces entered the city.

The Spa Resort

The healing properties of Vichy water were appreciated by the Romans, who built a small spa town here – Vicus Calidus. After a long period of relative obscurity, Vichy's vocation as a spa was resurrected in the 17C.

A day in the life of a 17C bather – This is an account by Madame de Sévigné, who came here for her rheumatism: "I took the waters this morning, my dear. Oh! How awful they are! At 6am we go to the spring; everyone is there; we drink and pull the most awful faces – just imagine, the water is boiling hot, with a most unpleasant taste of saltpetre. We walk back and forth, we come and go, we stroll about. Finally, we have luncheon. After eating, we go visiting. At 5pm we go walking in the most delightful places. At 7pm we have a light supper. We go to bed at 10pm. Today, I began taking showers. What an excellent preparation for purgatory! Then we get into a warm bed – and that is what makes you better."

Famous bathers – During the 18C the daughters of Louis XV, Mesdames Adelaide and Victoire, came to spend the season here. One of the springs now bears their name (Source Mesdames). In 1799 Maria-Letizia Bonaparte, Napoleon's mother, came here. In 1810 the Emperor himself created the Parc des Sources. In 1821 the Duchess of Angoulême laid the first stone of the thermal establishment. Napoleon III came on several occasions to take the waters at Vichy and the spa became extremely fashionable. A series of chalets was built alongside the new Allier park, with their façades all facing the gardens, at the Emperor's request, in order to avoid the obsessive ovations. Since the Second Empire, countless celebrities have come to spend a pleasant holiday here while tending their health. The local facilities are remarkable and the town is constantly improving them.

The Vichy Springs

Vichy's mineral and thermal springs contain mainly bicarbonate of soda and carbonic acid. The main springs belong to the State and are operated by a contracting company founded in 1853. The waters here are used to treat conditions of the liver, gall-bladder and stomach, diabetes, migraines, nutritional and digestive disorders, and also rheumatological complaints.
Waters from the Grande Grille, Hôpital and, in particular, Célestins springs, are bottled and exported the world over.

Hot springs – These are the basis of the Vichy drinking cures. The **Grande Grille** is named after the grille which used to protect it from thirsty animals. The bubbling water (temperature 40°C/104°F) comes up from a depth of 1,000–1,200m/3,280–4,028ft. The **Chomel**

Taste the natural spring water

(temperature 41°C/106°F) is named after the doctor who captured the spring in 1750 and managed the waters. A third hot spring, the **Hôpital** (temperature 33°C/91.4°F), rises in a rotunda-shaped pavilion behind the Casino.

Cold springs – Part of the regimen includes drinking the water. The **Parc** (temperature 24°C/75°F) gushes forth in the Parc des Sources. The **Lucas** (temperature 24°C/75°F) is named after the doctor and inspector who bought the spring at the beginning of the 19C on behalf of the State. The **Célestins** has a temperature of 21.5°C/71°F.

Thermal establishments – The Centre Thermal des Dômes can provide up to 2,500 people with thermal and related treatment each morning. The Callou pump room, like that of the Célestins, boasts the latest technical innovations.

Walking Tours
1 The Spa District★

The "spa resort" architecture of the late 19C and early 20C, the period when Vichy, the "Queen of Spa Towns," was at its most popular, is well worth a closer look. The buildings of the Vichy spa complex have been carefully restored and listed as protected for some years now,

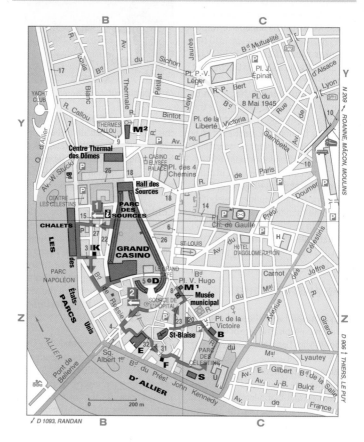

and make up a rich and unique part of France's architectural heritage.

Parc des Sources★

This beautiful park planted with chestnut and plane trees was laid out on the orders of Napoleon I and links a number of springs. The spa district effectively grew up around it, and it has remained the centre of the town's spa industry and leisure facilities.

In the morning the district is permeated with the peculiar atmosphere of the spa, punctuated by the comings and goings of people taking the waters, gathering in clusters around the springs as they await their "glass of water."

In the afternoon and on gala evenings, fashionable society comes to life, going for an evening stroll, having a drink on the terrace of the Grand Café or attending some glittering function.

Hall des Sources

Fed by the waters of Vichy's six thermal springs, the **Pump Room** is built of glass and metal, and its very transparency and the fluidity of its design bring to mind the element which is dispensed within.

Centre Thermal des Dômes

The luxury assembly rooms in a neo-Moorish style were designed by Charles Lecoeur, architect of the Grand Casino, and inaugurated in 1903. The central dome and corner cupolas are covered in gold enamelled roof tiles.

Grand Casino★

The Grand Casino, which opened in 1865, represents the influence of general good spirits on people's health. The first of its kind in France, it housed various assembly rooms and gaming halls beneath a single roof. From 1900 to 1903, it was renovated and extended with the addition of an opera house under the direction of architect Charles Lecoeur. Inside, the superb Art Nouveau decor is the work of wrought-iron worker Émile Robert and master glass-artist François Chigot.

Covered arcades

These are beautifully delicate Art Nouveau creations in wrought iron, crafted by Émile Robert for the 1889 World Exhibition in Paris and transferred to Vichy in 1900.

The balustrade of the **bandstand,** also the work of Robert, forms a garland of musical motifs *(several concerts a week are given here in season).*

Hotels, chalets and villas

Despite the demolition of the prestigious Queen's Hotel, most of the grand hotels on which Vichy's reputation is based have survived intact. The Hôtel du Parc is among the most impressive neo-Baroque buildings in town. Walk along rue du Parc and turn onto rue Prunelle *(first on the right)* where the mansion at no 8 is a pastiche of an English cottage. Take a glimpse along rue Alquié *(on the right)* which looks like an English street. The row of **chalets**★ lining avenue des États-Unis (nos 101 to 109bis) was built from 1862 to house Napoleon III and his entourage, who used to come regularly to take the waters at Vichy. Turn onto rue de Belgique *(second on the left)* to admire the Venitian-style villa with St Mark's lions at no 7 and the **Castel Flamand**★ at nos 2–2bis. Retrace your steps and turn left onto rue Alquié leading to boulevard de Russie. The Palais des Parcs (the old Ruhl) at no 15 is another neo-Baroque hotel. It was after the fall of the Empire that architects unleashed the full power of their imagination to create truly eccentric buildings. There are some remarkable examples of florid design along boulevard de Russie (neo-Classical at nos 17, 19 and **21**★, Art Deco at no 29).

2 Old Vichy

▶ *Start from the Source de l'Hôpital. Follow avenue A.-Briand to reach square Albert-1er (signposting).*

Note the Ermitage du Pont-Neuf Hotel, which exemplifies Art Deco style. The **Maison de Madame de Sévigné,** constructed during the time of Louis XIII, has been extensively restored and converted into a hotel (Pavillon Sévigny). The Marquise of Sévigné would stay here when she came to spend the season at Vichy.

▶ *Continue along rue de la Tour (on the right) then rue Verrier (on the right) and walk past the 16C Castel Franc, remodelled in the 19C when it became the town hall.*

Source des Célestins

The water from this spring now flows as far as the Pump Room, but it is worth taking the short walk to have a look at the elegant Louis XV pavillion which houses the spring itself.

The Célestins Park contains some magnificent evergreen trees, as well as traces of the old convent after which the spring and the park are named.

▶ *Head for rue du Mar.-Lyautey.*

Médiathèque Valéry-Larbaud★

♿⏱*Guided tours (1hr) Sat at 11am, 3pm.* ✉*No charge.* ☎*04 70 58 42 50.*

Address Book

For coin ranges, see the Legend on the cover flap.

WHERE TO STAY

Atlanta – 23 r. Pasteur. ☎04 70 98 42 95. Closed 13 Dec–13 Jan. 13 rms. ⌷6€. Here's a small, inexpensive hotel near the train station. The simple rooms are spic-and-span and well-soundproofed.

Arverna Hôtel – 12 r. Desbrest. ☎04 70 31 31 19. Closed 17–26 Oct, 17 Dec–5 Jan and Sun Dec–Feb. 26 rms. ⌷6€. A family hotel in a shady street between the train station and the spas. Bedrooms are small, functional and clean; those on the top floor have sloping ceilings.

Aletti Palace Hôtel – 3 pl. Joseph-Aletti. ☎04 70 30 20 20. 126 rms. ⌷12€. Belle Epoque architecture and ambience in this palatial former spa near the Parcs d'Allier. The rooms, of varying sizes, are furnished in the Art Deco style. Elegant dining room and traditional cuisine in the restaurant.

Sofitel Les Célestins – 111 bd des États-Unis. ☎04 70 30 82 00. Closed 7–25 Dec. 131 rms. ⌷16€. A big, modern and very chic hotel on the banks of the Lac d'Allier, with a complete fitness centre geared towards pampering your body and mind. Bright, sizeable rooms.

WHERE TO EAT

Brasserie du Casino – 4 r. du Casino. ☎04 70 98 23 06. Closed 16 Feb–3 Mar, 20 Oct–13 Nov, Tue–Wed. Come experience an authentic brasserie from the 1930s! It's all here: the old-fashioned atmosphere, the ambient gaiety, and tables so close to one another that you can eavesdrop on your neighbour. Menu featuring fish and traditional brasserie fare.

La Colombière – 03200 Abrest, 5km/3mi SE of Vichy via D 906. ☎04 70 98 69 15. Closed mid-Jan to mid-Feb, 6–21 Oct, Sun evening and Mon. This 1950s villa with a dovecote by the side of the road is rather imposing. Bountiful cuisine with a good choice of fixed-price menus.

La Fontaine – 03300 Vichy-Rhue. ☎04 70 31 37 45. Closed 15–30 Oct, 17 Dec–7 Jan, Mon evening, Tue evening and Wed. 'The Fountain' is a wellspring of well-being in all seasons. Traditional and regional cuisine.

Chez Mémère – R. Claude-Decloitre, 03700 Bellerive-sur-Allier. ☎04 70 59 89 00. Closed Feb school holidays, 15 days in Oct–Nov and Christmas wk. Reservations recommended weekends. The façade is nothing special, but customers line up to dine at Chez Mémère. The highly enthusiastic, self-taught chef whips up tasty, well-prepared dishes that are served on the bucolic shaded terrace along the Allier, or indoors in the wood-panelled dining room.

ON THE TOWN

L'Ascot Bar – 3 pl. Joseph-Aletti. ☎04 70 30 20 20. From 11am. With its Art Deco and posh interior, this Vichy bar is a classic. Come have a drink here in a fine musical setting.

Le Blue Note – 111 bd des États-Unis. ☎04 70 30 82 00. Noon–midnight. Closed 8–25 Dec. An inviting piano-bar frequented by spa-goers and celebrities visiting Vichy. Live music from 7pm onwards Fri, Sat and Sun. When the weather allows it, the musicians go out and play on the terrace.

Le Grand Café – 7 r. du Casino. ☎04 70 97 16 45. 10am–3am. Its location right in the middle of the thermal park and the high quality of its bar, snack and traditional restaurants, casino, discotheque and dance hall, make this the most popular of the spa establishments.

Le Samoa – 13 sq. de la Source-de-l'Hôpital. ☎04 70 59 94 46. Opens at 8.30am. Closed Sun morning in winter. Under the shady arcades lining the square, this Vichy institution is jam-packed whenever there's an event on at the music kiosk. At other moments, tourists and spa-goers can take their time and enjoy home-made ice cream on the peaceful terrace.

Casino de Vichy 'Élysée Palace' – Passage de la Comédie. ☎04 70 97 93 37. Mon–Fri 10am–3am, weekends until 4am; disco: Thu–Sat; roulette, black-jack: Wed–Sun. Slot machines and traditional games (boule, blackjack, French and English roulette) vie for the favours of enthusiasts. The Élysée Club discotheque and a theatre round out the casino complex.

SHOWTIME

Palais des Congrès - *Opéra de Vichy, 5 r. du Casino, BP 2805.* ☎*04 70 30 50 30/04 70 30 50 56. Tickets: Tue–Sat 1.30pm–6.30pm; phone reservations: Tue–Fri 10am–12.30pm. Closed Sun-Mon except performance days.* A citadel of Vichy culture, this handsome Art Nouveau-style opera house has opted for an exacting programme alternating opera, theatre, dance and even pop music.

SHOPPING

Aux Marocains – *32 r. Georges-Clemenceau.* ☎*04 70 98 30 33.* Red marble from Italy, a gigantic bronze chandelier, woodwork decorated with gold leaf: this is one very chic confectioner's! The laboratory in the basement guards the secret of the *Marocain,* a hard caramel

with a soft caramel centre, created in the 1920s. Other tempting specialities include candied fruit and barley sugar.
Calondre – *Passage de l'Amirauté.* ☎*04 70 98 40 57.* Although it has been restored, this pastry shop founded in 1880 has kept its wonderfully old-fashioned character. The Napoleon III decor – painted ceiling, cream-coloured walls – sets the scene for a display of appetizing pastries such as the *Tranche de Vienne.*
Pastillerie de Vichy – *94 allée des Ailes.* ☎*04 70 30 94 70. Mon–Thu 9am–noon, 2pm–6pm, Fri 9am–11am. Closed 29 Jul–18 Aug, Sat–Sun and public holidays.* After having visited the packaging workshop and seen the slide show, you'll know everything there is to know about the production of the legendary *Pastille de Vichy.*

The local multimedia library presents an exhibition on the author **Valéry Larbaud,** who was born in Vichy in 1881. Around 14,000 books, 180 manuscripts, 8,800 letters and many other documents are displayed on antique furniture.

▶ *From place de la Victoire, turn left onto rue d'Allier. Look to your right along rue Besse; no 2 was the birthplace of the famous reporter Albert Londres (1884–1932).*

Église St-Blaise

The old church, altered many times over, has a highly venerated Black Virgin, known as Our Lady of the Sick and Suffering; only the statue's head is original (12C).

▶ *On leaving the church, follow rue Hubert-Colombier lined with villas illustrating a variety of styles. Turn left onto rue du Mar.-Foch.*

The Source des Celestins in Vichy

S. Sauvignier/MICHELIN

Musée Municipal

🕐*Open daily except Mon 2pm–6pm, Sat 2pm–5pm.*🕐*Closed Sun and public holidays (Oct–Apr) and during Christmas holidays.* ✆*No charge.* ☎*04 70 32 12 97.*
Set up in the Centre Culturel Valéry-Larbaud, this small museum is devoted to local archaeology, contemporary painting, as well as coins and medals from Vichy. There is a collection of modern painting and sculpture with works by Gustave Moreau and Picasso.

▶ *The Opera Museum is opposite.*

Musée de l'Opéra de Vichy

🕐*Open daily except Mon and public holidays 3pm–6pm.* ✆*3€.* ☎*04 70 58 48 20.*
http://opera.vichy.musee.free.fr/
This museum presents in rotation the archives of the Grand Casino Theatre which were faithfully kept until the 1960s: costumes, accessories, posters, stage documents, programmes of all the operas performed from 1901 onwards… and some 10,000 photographs of artists, of famous people who visited the town, illustrating life in the spa resort.

Additional Sights

Musée des Arts d'Afrique et d'Asie

16 avenue Thermale (opposite Thermes Callou). 🕐*Open Apr–Oct daily except Mon 2pm–6pm.* ✆*4€.* ☎*04 70 97 76 40.*
www.musee-aaa.com.
The former Musée du Missionnaire contains exhibits collected by missionaries and private donations now entered in a catalogue for the first time since the foundation of the museum in 1923. A quarter of the collection is displayed in eight rooms, inside a 19C house.

Parcs d'Allier★

These beautiful landscape gardens created at the request of Emperor Napoleon III are built on land reclaimed from the river. They are graced with trees of various species, lakes with swans and ducks, rock gardens, rose gardens and flowerbeds, and are ideal for long, peaceful strolls. The Parc du Soleil provides all sorts of attractions for children.

Excursion

St-Pourçain-sur-Sioule★

30km/18.6mi S of Moulins.
🏛*29, Rue Marcellin Berthelot, 03500 St-Pourçain-sur-Sioule.* ☎*04 70 45 32 73. www.tourismesaintpourcinois.com.*

This small market town, which is an important crossroads on the River Sioule, is popular with trout fishermen and hiking enthusiasts. It owes its name to St Pourçain (died c 532), a former slave, turned monk, who defended the Auvergne from the ravages of Thierry, son of Clovis, the king of the Franks.

One of the oldest vineyards in France – Tradition has it that grapevine first appeared on the hillsides of the Bouble and the Sioule valleys a little before the Christian era. The stony ground of this region is ideal for vine growing, which developed rapidly during Roman times, and later at the demand of the monasteries and local squires.

Walking Tour

From St-Pourçain-sur-Sioule's place Maréchal-Foch, with its attractive fountain dominated by the **belfry** of the ancient monastery, walk through the covered passageway to the carefully restored courtyard, cours des Bénédictins, which offers a beautiful view of the bell-tower and imposing roof of the church of Ste-Croix.

▶ *Enter the church, flanked by houses on each side, through the door leading into cours des Bénédictins.*

Église Ste-Croix★

This vast, former abbey church was constructed in several stages from the 11C to the 15C. The chancel, built fairly late, is not in the axis of the nave, which has Gothic arches surmounted by a false triforium. Whimsical, humorous carvings decorate the 15 stalls' misericords.

▶ *For a good view of the east end, leave by the main portal and turn right towards place Clemenceau.*

Musée de la Vigne et du Terroir★
1 cours des Bénédictains.

🕐 *Open Mar–Dec, daily except Mon, 2pm–6pm (Jul–Sept daily 10am–noon, 2.30pm–6.30pm).* 🕐 *Closed mid-Nov–end Mar.* ✆4€. ☎04 70 45 32 73 or 04 70 45 62 07.

Great care has been taken in presenting the history of the region's main agricultural activity. A spiral staircase in the clock tower (15C) leads to rooms with attractive beams and stonework. Here a large number of items show the different aspects of vine-growing and winemaking.

Palais de la Miniature   Kids
Gare de St-Pourçain. ♿ 🕐*Open mi Apr–mid Nov daily except Tue, 3pm–7pm; mid-Jun–Aug, 10am–noon, 3pm–7pm.* ✆5€ *(children: 3€).* ☎04 70 45 99 01.

A railway network comprising trains and carriages on a scale of 1:87 runs through Bourbonnais landscapes. Light and sound effects bring life to a panoramic setting representing Venezy, an imaginary village, but typical of the area.

Driving Tours

Around Vichy *75km/46.6mi*

▶ *Leave Vichy to the SE on D 906. Before entering Abrest turn left onto D 126, heading for Cusset, then right onto D 270 to Vernet. At the entrance to the village, on the right, a narrow road leads to a platform especially laid out as a site.*

Site des Hurlements
The view extends over the Vichy basin, the Allier Valley, the Limagne, the Monts Dôme and Bois Noirs.

▶ *Rejoin D 906 and continue until you reach the entrance to St-Yorre.*

St-Yorre
This small town famed for its numerous springs of mineral water has become an important centre for glassmaking and bottling.

▶ *Leave St-Yorre to the E on D 121.*

Château de Busset

Château de Busset
🕐*Open Jun–Sept: guided tours (45min) daily except Wed 2.30pm–6.30pm; Apr–May and Oct Sat–Sun and public holidays 2pm–6pm.* ✆5€. ☎04 70 59 13 97. www. busset.com.

Erected on a granite promontory overlooking the Allier valley, this elegant castle has belonged to the same family for 14 generations. Although considerably remodelled since it was built in the 13C, the edifice has retained a drawbridge and four defensive towers including the fine **Tour d'Orion** topped by an octagonal roof.

▶ *On leaving Busset, turn left onto D 121 running by the cemetery, then take D 995 on the left. D 995 crosses the River Sichon, offering pleasant views of the lower valley.*

Cusset
This town on the outskirts of Vichy is circled by wide avenues lined with century-old trees. **Place Victor-Hugo** has several gabled houses, notably the Taverne Louis XI.

The door and window of the **Maison Barathon** are embellished with fine late-16C sculptures. Set up in Tour Prisonnière, the only vestiges of the 15C curtain wall, the **Musée Municipal** (🕐*open Jun–Oct daily except Mon 2pm–7pm (guided tours of the underground passages);* ✆4€; ☎04 70 96 29 17) presents an exhibition on local history through an extensive collection of documents, weapons, costumes and headdresses, drawings, paintings, old implements and street plaques.

▶ *Leave Cusset to the NE on D 906B.*

St-Étienne-de-Vicq

This hamlet has a Romanesque church with unusual architectural features. Note the historiated capitals at the entrance to the chancel.

▶ *Rejoin D 906^B. In Bost, turn right onto D 190. At the church cross-roads, take D 558, then turn right onto D 907. In Les Gadons, take D 174 on the right.*

Pastillerie Vichy

⊙*Open daily except Sat–Sun 9am–noon, 2pm–6pm, Fri 2pm–6pm. Slide show (15min).* ⊙*Closed public holidays, end Jul –mid-Aug.* ✎*No charge.* ☎*04 70 30 94 70.* A gangway overlooking the workshop will introduce visitors to the art of making and packaging **Pastilles de Vichy,** a type of boiled sweet made with Vichy water that became popular in the days of Empress Eugénie.

▶ *Bear right towards St-Germain-des-Fossés, then turn left onto D 27. In Vendat, take D 279 running along the railway tracks.*

Cognat

300m/330yd beyond the village, turn left onto a lane leading to the church. This unusual 12C building stands on a knoll commanding a pretty **view** of the Limagne and Monts Dôme.

▶ *Return to Cognat and turn right onto D 117.*

The road cuts across Montpensier Forest (⟲*see AIGUEPERSE).*

Brugheas

⚑Lying on the banks of the Sarmon, half way between the forests of Boucharde and Montpensier, this village is an ideal starting-point for country walks and bicycles rides.

▶ *Leave Brugheas to the SE on D 221, heading for Hauterive. Before reaching the area known as "La Tour," turn left onto the narrow lane bordered by meadows and small ponds.*

Source du Dôme

This bubbling spring, the hottest in the Vichy basin, yields algae that are used in the preparation of mineral mud baths.

▶ *The path runs through a small wood then across pastoral countryside. On reaching the surfaced road, turn left onto D 131 which leads back to Vichy via Bellerive bridge.*

Limagne Bourbonnaise
75km/46.6mi

Leave St-Pourçain to the W on D 46, heading for Montmarault. Just before Venteuil village, turn right onto D 1 and head for **Saulcet** (church frescoes). Continue to the medieval village of **Verneuil-en-Bourbonnais** (Musée du Lavage et du Repassage). Leave Verneuil to the NE until you reach Varennes-sur-Allier.

Frescoes in the church in Saulcet

On leaving the town, turn left onto D 21, heading for **Jaligny**, and the Hospice de Gayette, an impressive sight in which a 15C keep has been incorporated into a set of classical buildings. Further exploration leads to the **Château du Méage**, an elegant 15C and 18C manor house, and on to the village of Bill, overlooking the Allier valley to the south, and an ideal starting point of walks through the surrounding area.

VIC-LE-COMTE ★

POPULATION 4,404
MICHELIN MAP 326: G-9 – 16KM/10MI N OF ISSOIRE

Vic-le-Comte lies in the middle of **Comté**, a region made up of a series of volcanoes that appeared in the Limagne at the end of the Tertiary Era, forming a transition between the plain and the Livradois mountains. Most of the volcanoes have been eroded and only their chimneys remain, sometimes combined with outliers of lava flow. There are more than 50 eruptive pinnacles, now covered in woodland; in the past, grape vines grew on the more exposed slopes. In the 8C a priory was established in the village (vicus in Latin) – which was probably of Gallo-Roman origin – by the Benedictine monks of Manglieu.

At the beginning of the 13C the Count of Auvergne, Gui II, after being defeated by King Philippe Auguste, saw his estate reduced to the Vic-le-Comte region, which was well protected by a ring of fortresses (Buron, Busséol etc). During the same period, the Cistercian abbey of Le Bouchet, near Yronde, became the necropolis of the regional lords. From 1651 up to the time of the French Revolution, the earldom of Auvergne belonged to the dukes of Bouillon. Today, Vic-le-Comte has a papermill owned by the Bank of France, which makes the watermarked paper used for bank notes printed in Chamalières.

- **Information:** Les Pradets, 63114 MONTPEYROUX ☎04 73 96 68 80. www.vic-le-comte.fr.
- **Orient Yourself:** Vic-le-Comte is 25km/q5.5mi from Clermont Ferrand, and 16km/10mi from Issoire, and well served by the A 75 autoroute.
- **Parking:** There are a number of car parks both in the centre and just outside.
- **Don't Miss:** The fortified village of Montpeyroux.
- **Organising Your Time:** Allow half a day for a leisurely walking tour.
- **Also See:** CLERMONT-FERRAND, ISSOIRE.

Walking Tour

Sainte-Chapelle ★

This, the Holy Chapel, is a beautiful Gothic building heralding the Renaissance. The cornice is decorated with sculptures of mythical beasts, crockets, thistles and human figures.

The richly coloured **stained-glass windows ★**, depict scenes from the Old and New Testaments. The very fine stone **altarpiece ★** (1520) is the work of the Florentine artists who made the balustrade.

Old houses

Rue Porte-Robin (north-east of the Sainte-Chapelle) has several buildings with 15C and 16C façades. From the north-western end of the chapel go round to the right as far as the old town gate, **Porte Robin,** the only remains of the fortified curtain wall. Place du Vieux-Marché has a 16C fountain. Continue straight ahead towards rue du Palais, at the entrance to which are two corbelled houses.

- *Take the covered passage on the right, rue des Farges, then rue de Coulogne beyond; turn back.*

Stained glass window in the Sainte-Chapelle

Driving Tour

Castles and Wine-Growing Villages 45km/28mi

▶ *Drive S out of town along D 49. In Yronde, take D 136.*

Yronde

This is where Le Bouchet Abbey once stood. Note the lovely small church.

Buron

The road runs round the village, overlooked by the ruins of a castle perched on a peak of basalt rock.

▶ *Cross the River Allier; take D 229 left.*

Coudes

This ancient wine-growing village situated at the confluence of the Allier and Couze de Chambon once thrived on an important river traffic of wine.

▶ *Continue along D 229, across the A 75 motorway, then turn right on D 797.*

Montpeyroux★

This fortified hillside village overlooks the Allier to the east. A medieval gateway gives access to narrow twisting lanes leading to the three-storey 13C **keep**. Some of the old houses in the village have been restored and their cellars are a reminder of the wine-growing past of the village which now welcomes a colony of artists and craftsmen.

▶ *Continue along D 797.*
In Authezat, turn left on D 96.

View of Montpeyroux

La Sauvetat

This once fortified village has retained part of an ancient commander's residence belonging to the Order of St John and some houses (12C-14C).

▶ *Leave La Sauvetat NE along D 630, cross the A 75 and rejoin D 96.*

Corent

This village overlooking the River Allier clings to the north-eastern slopes of the Puy de Corent; it is known for its high-quality wine, one of the five vintages making up the Côtes d'Auvergne *appellation.*

▶ *Continue along D 786 then follow D 751 and cross the River Allier.*

The road follows the east bank of the river, jotted with wine-growing villages such as Mirefleurs *(D 1)*, La Roche-Noire and St-Georges-sur-Allier *(D 118)*.

▶ *On leaving St-Georges-sur-Allier, turn right on D 759.*

Château de Bosséol★

🕘*Open mid-Jun–mid Sept: guided tours (45min) 10am–noon, 2.30pm–6.30pm; rest of year Sat–Sun and public holidays 2.30pm–5.30pm.* ⊗6€. ☎04 73 69 00 84. The main façade collapsed in 1963 but has since been rebuilt with Romanesque-style windows.

▶ *Leave Bosséol S and follow D 4 then continue on D 229. In Benaud hamlet, turn right on D 116 then take D 81. Park in St-Maurice; continue on foot.*

Puy de St-Romain★

45min on foot there and back.

🚶The setting of the puy is striking; the summit, an ancient place of worship, offers a **panorama**★ encompassing the Comté *Puys*, the Forez mountains, the Livradois mountains, the Vic-le-Comte basin, the Allier Valley, the Cézallier and Cantal mountains, the Dore and Dôme mountain ranges, Clermont-Ferrand and the Limagne.

▶ *Go to Longues on D 758 then follow D 1 and D 225 back to Vic-le-Comte.*

VIC-SUR-CÈRE ★

POPULATION 1,890

MICHELIN MAP 330: D-5

20KM/12.4MI NE OF AURILLAC – LOCAL MAP SEE MONTS DU CANTAL

The old town of Vic in the Cère valley, with its picturesque houses clustered around the church, is a spa town with a mineral spring (pump room).

- **Information:** Av. André-Mercier, 15800 VIC-SUR-CÈRE ☎04 71 47 50 68. www.vicsurcere.com.
- ▶ **Orient Yourself:** Vic-sur-Cère lies along the Aurillac/Murat road.
- ☺ **Don't Miss:** The Château de Pesteils.
- ◔ **Organising Your Time:** Allow half a day to explore the area.
- ☝ **Also See:** AURILLAC, MURAT, ST-FLOUR, Monts du CANTAL.

A Bit of History

The "mad monk" – In the 12C Pierre de Vic, the youngest son of a local family who had been forced to enter the church despite not having a religious vocation, was put in charge of a rich priory when he was still very young; he turned it into a pleasure-dome, composing drinking songs and love ballads there. He gradually wearied of his sedentary life and began to travel and sing ballads at the courts of Philippe Auguste, Richard the Lionheart and the King of Aragon. The "mad monk," as he called himself, carried off first prize at the Courts of Love Literary Tournament and won the Golden Hawk at a contest at Le Puy.

Winning barrels (16C) – During the Wars of Religion **Captain Merle** was escorting a convoy of supplies for the Huguenots when the Roman Catholics ambushed him in a gorge. Merle ordered the men to cut the mules' traces and flee. After they had gone some distance, he stopped the stampeding men, having calculated that the Catholics would fall upon the casks of wine instead of pursuing his men. He proved to be right; after rallying his men, he counter-attacked, wiping out his drunken adversaries.

Old Town

Turreted houses still grace the town centre, testifying to the city's former prosperity.

▶ *For a tour of the old city, allow 20–30min. Leave from place de l'Hôtel-de-Ville. Turn left towards place de Monaco.*

Note the elegant turreted house at no 4 passage du Chevalier-des-Huttes.

▶ *Turn left towards place de Monaco.*

Maison des Princes de Monaco

South of the church, off rue Coffinhal. This 15C house *(no 4)* served as a residence on several occasions for the princes of Monaco, to whom Louis XIII had given the Carladez region in 1642, the capital of which was Vic, and which remained in their possession until the Revolution. The house has a turret with a mullioned window and a door surmounted by a badly damaged bas-relief depicting the Annunciation.

▶ *Continue on rue Coffinhal.*

Maison Dejou

At no 5, there is a small *hôtel particulier* from the late 17C with a semicircular pediment.

Retrace your steps. On the left, note the tower adjoining the façade of the École St-Antoine on rue du Moine-de-Montaudon.

▶ *Walk down to place de l'Église, pass behind the east end and follow the path to the waterfall.*

Lou Cap Del Liou

Pretty old mill spanning the Iraliot.

▶ *Walk up to the church.*

Église St-Pierre

This partly Romanesque building has undergone many alterations. Note the graceful apse and the curious modillions on the south façade. Opposite the church, the former bailiwick is now private property. Walk up to the calvary along rue du Dr-Civiale. From the chapel there is a fine panoramic view of the town.

Hikes

Cascade du Trou de la Conche and Rocher de Maisonne

Behind the church, take the street leading to a footbridge over the Iraliot. On the other side of the torrent, walk up a very steep path.
🚶At the top of the rise the road divides: *(left)* to Trou de la Conche cascade; *(right)* to the top of Maisonne rock, giving a fine view of Vic and the valley below.

Grotte des Anglais

Leave Vic on N 122 towards Murat and immediately turn onto the road to La Prade. Park on the platform.
🚶A small knoll commands a nice view of the spa, with Curebourse plateau and wood in the background.

▶ *Go to Fournol village (vestiges of a Roman bridge down below). Bear left to rejoin and cross RN 122.*

Opposite, slightly to the right, a sign-posted trail leads to the **Grotte des Anglais,** a cave that gave shelter to bandits and highway robbers during the Hundred Years War.

Excursions

Thiézac

9km.5.6mi NE along N 122.
This is a sunny summer resort with a Gothic church (Église St-Martin) and a chapel (Chapelle Notre-Dame-de-Consolation) which overlooks the village – it

was after undertaking a pilgrimage here that Anne of Austria conceived, after 22 childless years of marriage, the future Louis XIV.

Cascade de Faillitoux

5km/3.1mi to the W. Leave Thiézac on the road to Vic and, soon after the graveyard, turn right onto D 59.
Around 3km/2.1mi further on, the road goes through Lasmolineries village, offering views of the Faillitoux waterfall flowing from its basalt ledge.

Driving Tour

Upper Goul Valley and Carladès 80km/50mi

▶ *Leave Vic to the SE on D 54, heading for Raulhac and Mur-de-Barrez.*

Rocher des Pendus

Leave the car near Col de Curebourse and take the path on the right, opposite Auberge des Monts.
🚶From this rock there is an extensive **panorama**★★ over the Cère valley, the Cantal mountain range, Carladès rock, the Châtaigneraie and the Aurillac basin.

▶ *Continue along D 54.*

Église de Jou-sous-Monjou

Interesting Romanesque church with a fine belfry and a porch resting on a slender column.

▶ *Take D 59, then D 600 until you reach Raulhac.*

On the way, note the Château de Cropières (🔒 *not open to the public*), a typical manor from the Cantal region.

▶ *Continue along D 600 towards Mur-de-Barrez.*

Château de Messilhac

🕐 *Open mid-Jun–Aug: guided tours (50min) 2.30pm–6.30pm.* 👓*4€.* ☎*04 71 49 55 55.*
At the end of a beaten track, this former fortress stands proudly in a delightful

Rocher de Carlat

bucolic setting. The Renaissance façade, flanked by two square towers crowned by pointed roofs, is pierced with mullioned windows.

▸ *On leaving Mur-de-Barrez, D 990 and D 459 (right) lead to Ronesque rock.*

Rocher de Ronesque★★

This basalt rock forms a plateau dominating the entire countryside. It was formed in the same way as Carlat rock; first covered by volcano activity then deeply gashed by large valleys.

The picturesque **hamlet** at the foot of the rock is typical of the Cantal where the houses often have roofs of stone slabs called lauzes.

Rocher de Carlat★

The scenery here is typical of the Carlat area. The region was covered with basalt by lava flows from the volcanoes of Cantal; erosion fragmented the coating of rock, isolating a few flows which now stand, sheer-sided, at the top of steep hillsides. With its delightful valleys and its houses with steeply sloping hipped roofs of stone slabs surrounded by gardens and orchards, the Carlat region is a pleasant place to stay or travel around.

▸ *Cross the breach and skirt, to the left, the north side of the rock.*

Climb the Escalier de la Reine (Queen's Staircase) carved out of the rock to reach the northern edge of the plateau; there is a wonderful **view**★ of the mountains of Cantal. Then climb Murgat rock, topped by a statue of the Virgin Mary: the view stretches southwards beyond the village, to the Carlat region. In the distance, to the left, is the rock and chapel at Ronesque.

▸ *Continue on D 990 to Vézac. D 208 on the right leads to Polminhac.*

Château de Pesteils★

🕓 *Open Apr–Sept 2pm–6.30pm (Jul and Aug 10am–7pm). ⊛7€. ☎04 71 47 44 36. www.chateau-pesteils-cantal.com.*

This beautiful medieval castle, built on a rocky promontory on the north bank of the Cère overlooking the town of Polminhac was one of the strongholds designed to defend the valley. The imposing 13C square keep, is crowned with a machicolated watch-path.

▸ *Visits by candlelight are organised in summer.*

Grand Salon, Château de Pesteils

VIENNE★★

POPULATION 29,975

MICHELIN MAP 333: C-4

Vienne, "perched like an altar on the buttresses of the noble Dauphiné", to quote a local poet, is a town of exceptional interest. In a delightful **setting**★ basking in sunlight reflected from the Rhône, a Gothic cathedral stands next to a Roman temple, while Romanesque cloisters and several ancient churches rub shoulders with an Antique theatre. The charm of "Vienne the Beautiful" of Roman times is enhanced by the charm of "Vienne the Holy," the Christian city. The flower-filled pedestrian precinct, along cours Brillier and around the Hôtel de Ville, is a popular place for a leisurely stroll. Two bridges connect Vienne to the west bank of the Rhône. The old suspension bridge is now used as a footbridge; the modern bridge (1949) has a remarkable central arch. A 15C humpbacked bridge spans the Gère.

- **Information:** Cours Brillier, 38200 VIENNE, ☎04 74 53 80 30. www.vienne-tourisme.com.
- ▶ **Orient Yourself:** Situated 38km/24ml to the south of Lyon, and 52km/32ml east of St Étienne.
- **Parking:** There are ample parking areas to the south of the town.
- **Don't Miss:** The important Gallo-Roman city of St-Romain-en-Gal; the cathedral of St Maurice, and the Temple of Augustus ad Livia.
- **Organising Your Time:** Allow half a day to explore Vienne; maybe an hour to visit St Romain.
- **Also See:** LYON.

A Bit of History

Vienne the Beautiful – More than 50 years before Julius Caesar conquered Gaul, the stomping ground of the Allobroges tribe – of which Vienne became the capital in the 1C BC – was subjugated by the Roman legions. In the absence of a more open site, the town was chosen for its geographical location which was easier to manage than that of Lyon as there was only one river to cross.

Public monuments were erected at the foot of Mont Pipet, with private residences and trade and craft establishments on both banks. Vienne soon extended its suburbs beyond the Rhône to the present-day villages of Ste-Colombe and St-Romain-en-Gal. Drapers, leather workers and potters had flourishing businesses and the poet Martial described the town as "Vienne the Beautiful."

Joys and sorrows of "Greater Burgundy" – After the Western Roman Empire was dissolved in 476 and despite political confusion, Vienne remained a centre of artistic achievement: the construction of the church and necropolis of St-Pierre was continued; the foundations were laid for the abbey of St-André-le-Bas. The incessant in-fighting between the Carolingians for Charlemagne's heritage enabled Boson, Count of Vienne, Arles and Provence to proclaim himself "King of Burgundy" at Mantaille Castle in 879. His palace was in Vienne.

Vienne, the Holy City – As the distant Holy Roman Emperor only exercised nominal suzerainty, the temporal authority of the bishops, who were also the counts of Viennois, held sway over the city and over an area of land on the east bank of the Rhône. Around the abbey of St-André-le-Bas, which was at the height of its power, a large Jewish community plied a thriving trade. Two famous prelates sat on the throne of the "primate of the primates of the Gauls – **Gui de Bourgogne** (1088–1119), crowned Pope in his own cathedral under the name of Calixtus II, and **Jean**

Address Book

For coin ranges, see the Legend on the cover flap.

WHERE TO STAY

Camping Bontemps – 38150 Vernioz. 19km/12mi S of Vienne via N 7, D 131 and D 37. ☎04 74 57 83 52. Open Apr–Sept. Reservations recommended. 100 sites. Food service. Tourism and sports are on this campground's programme. Set off walking or sightseeing to discover the region – unless you'd rather stay put and take advantage of the on-site sports facilities to go horseback riding, mountain biking or swimming.

Hôtel Central – 7 r. de l'Archevêché. ☎04 74 85 18 38. www.hotel-central-vienne.com. Closed 9–14 Aug and 6 Dec–18 Jan. 25 rms. 7€. In the heart of the city, as its name implies, this simple hotel's best feature is its central location.

WHERE TO EAT

La Chamade – 24 r. Juiverie. ☎04 74 85 30 34. Closed mid-Aug. The decor of white walls, yellow tablecloths and indirect lighting is simple, the service efficient and the prices quite affordable.

L'Estancot – 4 r. de la Table-Ronde. ☎04 74 85 12 09. Closed 1–15 Sept, Christmas to mid-Jan, Sun-Mon and public holidays. Interested in trying some *criques*, the delicious, Ardéchois potato pancake dish? Then take a seat in this restaurant. Featured for dinner daily, they can be ordered with vegetables, foie gras or prawns.

ON THE TOWN

Canicule – 5 r. Cornemuse. ☎04 74 85 40 22. Tue–Thu, Sun 8pm–1am, (Fri–Sat –3am). 'La canicule' means 'the dog days' - will this new cocktail bar succeed in turning up the heat in the rather complacent city of Vienne? In a pretty, exotic setting, you can order sizeable cocktails spiked with varying (generally generous) quantities of alcohol.

Bar du Temple – 5 pl. du Gén.-de-Gaulle. ☎04 74 31 94 19. Summer: 7am–midnight; rest of the year: Mon–Sat. Closed public holidays. This is THE café that everyone who's anyone in Vienne knows about. Its best feature is the superb terrace at the foot of the Temple d'Auguste and de Livie. In spite of the influx of tourists, it has retained its convivial ambience and regular clientele.

O'Donoghue's Pub – 45 r. Francisque-Bonnier. ☎04 74 53 67 08. 4pm–3am. All year round, this Little Brittany in Vienne holds Celtic music concerts attended by a cluster of Breton 'ex-pats'. If you've never tasted a Coreff, typical Breton beer, this is your chance.

SHOPPING

Markets – On Saturday mornings, the streets of centre city, from the banks of the Rhône to the Jardin de Cybèle, overflow with enticing market displays. This is the perfect time to shop for a few bottles of Côte-Rôtie, a delicious Côte-du-Rhône wine made in the region.

Ets Patissier Jean-Guy – 16 place de Miremont. ☎04 74 85 08 77. Tue–Sun 8am–7.30pm. Closed last wk of Jan and Jun. Founded in the 1970s and remodelled in 2000, this pastry shop-cum-tearoom's fine reputation has spread throughout the province. Its chocolate, made with the finest cocoa beans, pastries made with grade AA butter, ice cream and cakes are devilishly delicious.

THEATRE

Théâtre de Vienne – 4 r. Chantelouve. ☎04 74 85 00 05. Mid-Sept–Jul: Mon–Fri 10am–noon, 2pm–6.30pm, Sat 3pm–6pm performance days. Built in the early 18C, when Marivaux, Goldoni and Beaumarchais prevailed, this theatre, whose façade was renovated in 1930, exudes history and charm. Events of all genres are staged here, including drama, classical and pop music, dance, opera and children's shows.

de Bernin (1218–66), who directed the extensions to the cathedral of St-Maurice based on Gothic principles, ordered restoration of the Roman bridge over the Rhône, and built a hospital and the Château de la Bâtie.

Modern times – During the centuries of the Renaissance and the absolute monarchy, Vienne's decline offers a painful contrast with the prosperity of Lyon – commercial activity collapsed and the population dropped by one-fifth between 1650 and the beginning of the 18C. Even the bridge over the Rhône, swept away by flooding in 1651, was not rebuilt until the 19C. A certain industrial rebirth occurred once the Revolution had swept away the Ancien Régime.

Walking Tour

Roman and Christian Vienne★★

▶ *Leave from place St-Maurice.*

Cathédrale St-Maurice★★
Built from the 12C to 16C, the cathedral combines both Romanesque and Gothic. The patronage of St Maurice is a reminder of the veneration given to martyrs of the Theban Legion in the Burgundian kingdoms.

Doorways
The west front with its three doorways is adorned with fine Flamboyant ornamentation. Although the Wars of Religion deprived it of the statues decorating the niches of the engaged piers and tympana, the delightful decoration of the covings has fortunately remained intact. The late-14C **south doorway** has two covings: the inner row depicts the prophets seated under canopies; the outer row has pairs of musician angels.

Cathédrale St-Maurice

The **central doorway,** with its cut-off gable, dates from the late 15C. It has three covings with sculptures which are to be read horizontally.
The **north doorway**, from the second half of the 15C, is devoted to the Virgin. At the top of the central niche two angels with folded wings are carrying the Virgin's crown.

Interior
The vast nave, with no transept, reflects a surprising harmony despite its construction over a period of four centuries. The far seven bays enclosing the Gothic nave are Romanesque. Reminiscent of Roman times, the piers are flanked with antique-style pilasters and fluted half-columns; this stage of construction, from the early 12C, is contemporary with or slightly later than the pontificate of Gui de Bourgogne.
The four bays of the nave nearest the west front were built in the 15C in pure Gothic style, their engaged columns rising in an unbroken line to the base of the ribbing.
The **Romanesque capitals** form a decorative whole, closely inspired by Antiquity. They feature narrative scenes (right aisle) or whimsical subjects.
In the apse, on the right of the High Altar, stands the **mausoleum** of archbishops Arnaud de Montmorin and Henri-Oswald de La Tour d'Auvergne (1747), by **Michel-Ange Slodtz;** it is one of the finest 18C works in Dauphiné.
A splendid Renaissance stained-glass window, the **Adoration of the Magi,** throws light from the east into the chancel from the right aisle. The stained-glass clerestory windows in the chancel date from the 16C; the central window depicts St Maurice, in armour, with St Peter.
The north aisle has interesting sculptures: between the sixth and seventh chapel a large 13C bas-relief depicting the meeting of Herod and the Magi is striking for the very noble poses; an amusing detail is the two grotesque heads on either side of Herod, symbolizing his two-facedness – one, turned towards the kings, appears to listen to them attentively while the other, unseen by them, is laughing maliciously.

B. Kaufmann/MICHELIN

A covered passageway (north aisle) once connected the cathedral to the ancient cloisters, which no longer exist.

▶ *Leave the cathedral along the covered passageway (north aisle).*

Outside, the decoration on the door of the north wall combines Romanesque and Gothic elements with Roman fragments. Beneath the pointed arch, delicate griffons and leaves decorate the lintel.

▶ *Walk to place du Palais.*

You will be taken aback by the beauty of the Roman temple standing in the centre of the square, pleasantly contrasting with the 18C façades of the houses framing place du Palais.

Temple of Augustus and Livia★★

This is a rectangular building of agreeable proportions. Its dimensions are approximately the same as those of the Maison Carrée, the well-known Roman temple in Nîmes. A row of six Corinthian columns supports the entablature on the façade and the sides; the carved ornamentation is better preserved on the north side. The rear part, which is the oldest, probably dates from the end of the 1C BC.

The façade, facing east, overlooked the forum. It was rebuilt under the reign of Augustus, perhaps after a fire. Its triangular pediment bore a bronze inscription to the glory of Augustus and Livia, his wife.

▶ *Rue des Clercs leads to the church of St-André-le-Bas.*

Église and Cloître St-André-le-Bas★

👟*See Additional Sights.*

▶ *Take rue de la Table-Ronde to rue Marchande.*

At no 32, there is a beautiful portal with coving and a carved arch stone.

▶ *Continue to rue des Orfèvres.*

No 11 has a 15C-16C inner courtyard whereas no 9 has a beautiful Renaissance façade.

▶ *Turn around and take rue du Collège on the right.*

Église St-André-le-Haut

This church was once a Jesuit College chapel but was consecrated to St Louis in 1725.

Théâtre Romain★

👟*See Additional Sights.*

▶ *Take rue des Célestes, then walk down montée St-Marcel to rue Victor-Hugo and the archaeological gardens.*

Jardin Archéologique

A white-stone double archway is the only remaining part of a **portico,** thought in the past to be part of some Roman baths; note the fine decorative frieze on the inside.

On the right of the portico is a wall which formed the northern side of a **theatre** said to have been reserved for performances of the Mysteries of Cybele.

▶ *Take rue Chantelouve, then rue Ponsard to the Musée des Beaux-Arts.*

Musée des Beaux-Arts et d'Archéologie

👟*See Additional Sights.*

▶ *Cours Romestang, then boulevard de la République, lead to place St-Pierre.*

Additional Sights

Église St-André-le-Bas★

Same admission times as for the cloister (see below). ☎*04 74 85 50 42.*

Apart from the lower parts of the east end, the apse, a large part of the southern wall and a few later additions, the church is mainly 12C. The large freestone gable wall provides an unusual decorative effect. The whole of the decoration is remarkable: piers and colonnettes on the twin openings, small festooned

Cloisters, St-André-le-Bas

arches ending in consoles bearing expressive masks.

The Salle du Patrimoine (Heritage Gallery) hosts a **standing exhibition** on the theme "The Many Faces of Vienne."

▶ *Walk into the southern courtyard flanked by the base of the bell-tower.*

The first mask to be seen is poking out an enormous tongue.

The nave was originally covered with timber framing; the restoration in 1152 consisted of raising and vaulting it, which required the construction of outside flying buttresses and reinforcement of the walls by arches and piers.

The decoration of the fluted pilasters is attributed to Guillaume Martin who signed and dated his work (1152) on the base of the second pier from the right; the most beautiful capitals depict Samson overwhelming the Lion (second pier from the left). The two superb Corinthian capitals at the entrance to the apse are from a Roman monument.

▶ *Leave the church through the north door.*

Cloître St-André-le-Bas★

🕐 *Open Apr–Oct daily except Mon 9.30am–1pm, 2pm–6pm; Nov–Mar daily except Mon 9.30am–12.30pm, 2pm–5pm (Sat, Sun, 1.30pm–5.30pm).* 🕐 *Closed*

1 Jan, 1 May, and 11 Nov, 25 Dec. ☞2.50€. ☎04 74 85 50 42.

These small, trapezoidal cloisters date from the 12C. They have a series of blind arcades, resting alternatively on twinned colonnettes and the piers marking the bays. The colonnettes in the south gallery show an element of fantasy: spiral or zigzag fluting, strings of beads or palm leaves with knotted stems.

Théâtre Romain★

The Roman theatre had been abandoned since the time of Emperor Constantine, in the early 4C, and was one of the largest theatres in Roman Gaul; its diameter is greater than that of the Roman theatre at Orange in Provence and is only 1m/3ft less than that of the great theatre of Marcellus in Rome.

Backing onto Mont Pipet, it had 46 tiers over a series of well-preserved vaulted passageways; the dressed masonry stone of the tiers was entirely faced with white stone slabs.

Musée des Beaux-Arts et d'Archéologie

The Fine Arts and Archaeology Museum is housed in a 19C covered market and comprises several collections: prehistoric and Gallo-Roman antiquities; 18C French earthenware (Moustiers, Lyon, Roanne, Marseille, Rouen, Nevers); paintings from the 17C and 18C European Schools and the Lyon, Vienne and

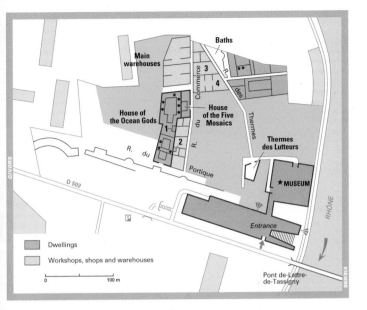

Dauphiné Schools; works by the Vienne sculptor, J Bernard (1866–1931).

Ancienne Église St-Pierre★

The church of St-Pierre, now a museum, is the oldest building of Christian Vienne, dating to the 5C. The church was the burial place of the bishops of Vienne. St-Pierre, built "outside the walls," was to suffer from the devastations of the Saracens in about 725, followed by those of the Carolingian princes in 882.

St-Romain-en-Gal, Ste-Colombe

St-Romain-en-Gal and Ste-Colombe, on the west bank of the Rhône, are located in the Rhône administrative *département* whereas Vienne, opposite, is in the Isère *département*. In Ancient times, these three towns formed a single urban centre.

Gallo-Roman City of St-Romain-en-Gal★★

Excavations of the site since 1967 have unearthed an urban district including not only sumptuous villas but also businesses, workshops and thermae (hot baths).

Museum★

&⏰Open all year, daily except Mon 10am–6pm. ⏰Closed 1 Jan, 1 May, 1 Nov, 25 Dec. ✎4€; no charge on Thu. ☎04 74 38 49 32. www.musees-gallo-romains.com. This on-site museum was designed as a showcase which presents the archaeological site on the one hand and the Rhône and Vienne of today on the other hand.

A staircase, situated just before the entrance, leads to a terrace offering a panoramic view of the town, the river and the excavations. The site includes a wealth of workshops and sumptuous residences, the most splendid of all

Roman temple

VIENNE

STE-COLOMBE (Rhône)

being the **Maison des Dieux Océan** (House of the Ocean Gods).

The **Dieux Océan mosaic**★ invites visitors to discover works of art of the Gallo-Roman period. Vienne was a thriving city under Roman occupation; the Rhône, which played a key role in the town's prosperity, separated the city itself from the more residential district of St-Romain-en-Gal.

The main asset of the site are the magnificent floor mosaics which are as beautiful as the *opus sectile* pavings, made with much larger marble slabs. Motifs were often inspired by mythological subjects.

Archaeological site★

The remains found in the area so far indicate occupation from the end of the 1C BC to the 3C AD, though the structure of the area does not correspond to the grid layout usually adopted by the Romans. A portico runs along the side of **rue du Portique,** from east to west. **Rue du Commerce** and **rue des Thermes,** which run approximately north-south, converge in the northern part of the site.

Dwellings

At the entrance to the site is a vast residence, the **House of the Ocean**

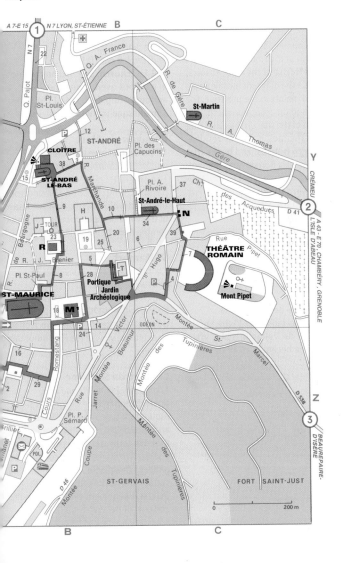

Example of mosaic, St-Romain-en-Gal

Gods; its southern entrance is its only connection with the outside. The vestibule had a mosaic floor depicting ocean gods with bearded heads and long flowing hair, and marine motifs. To the north of the House of the Ocean Gods is the **House of the Five Mosaics,** named after the different mosaic floors discovered mainly in the peristyle, the *triclinium* and the reception room.

North-east of the site, on the other side of rue des Thermes, is another residential area with **houses,** and **baths** that follow a typically Roman arrangement: hypocaust, *caldarium* (hot room), *tepidarium* (warm room) and *frigidarium* (cold room).

Sainte-Colombe

During Roman times this suburb was filled with luxurious residences decorated with works of art and immense mosaics.

Tour Philippe-de-Valois

The tower was built next to the Rhône by Philippe de Valois in 1343, after Ste-Colombe became part of the royal domain.

Excursions

La Pyramide

Leave Vienne S on cours de Verdun and turn right onto boulevard F-Point.

The monument rests on a small square portico and used to adorn the central forecourt of the vast Vienne amphitheatre in the 4C. During the Middle Ages it was thought to be the tomb of Pontius Pilate; according to legend, after leaving Jerusalem for Vienne, the Roman procurator, struck with remorse, threw himself into the Rhône. Pilat mountain range is said to be named after this event (there is a similar legend attached to Mount Pilate near Lucerne in Switzerland).

Ternay

13km/8mi N. Leave Vienne N on N 7 and turn left onto D 150^E.

The 12C **church,** perched on the edge of a hillock overlooking the Rhône, is an interesting example of the Rhône Romanesque School.

Beauvoir-de-Marc

19km/12mi E. Leave Vienne on D 502 and, at La Détourbe, turn left onto D 53^B.

The small 11C-14C **church** with its painted ceiling stands on a hillside from the top of which there is a **panorama**★ of the Viennois hills, dominated by the sombre mass of Mont Pilat.

St-Mamert

13km/8mi S. Leave Vienne on N 7 S and turn left onto D 131^A.

The **chapel of St-Mamert,** with its 11C belfry-wall and 17C restored interior, is built on a terrace of pebbles which offers an extensive view of the Pilat mountain range.

Château de Septème

12km/7.5mi E on D 502 and D 75.

Not far from Septème village, this picturesque castle was built in the 14C and 15C and remodelled in the 16C; overlooking the inner courtyard are Renaissance loggias on two storeys and a colonnaded gallery. The castle is surrounded by curtain walls dating from an earlier age that have kept many of their loopholes and part of the watch-path.

VILLEFRANCHE-SUR-SAÔNE

POPULATION 59,261

MICHELIN MAP 327: H-4 – LOCAL MAPS SEE BEAUJOLAIS AND LA DOMBES

This busy industrial and commercial city is the capital of the **Beaujolais** region. It was founded in 1140 by the lords of Beaujeu, to match the Anse fortress belonging to the Archbishops of Lyon. The settlement sprang up quickly, and in 1260 Guichard IV de Beaujeu granted the town a charter, which earned it the name of *Ville Franche,* meaning free town.

- **Information:** 96 r. de la Sous-Préfecture, 69400 VILLEFRANCHE-SUR-SAÔNE, ☎04 74 07 27 40. www.villefranche.net.
- **Orient Yourself:** The A 6 and D 306 link the town to Lyon, 34km/21mi to the south. The numbering of houses in Villefranche is based on a metric system, calculating the distance of each house from the beginning of the street. Street numbers run from rue Nationale east and west, and south from the north of town.
- **Parking:** There are numerous spacious car parks in the centre of town.
- **Don't Miss:** The lovely old houses along the rue Nationale.
- **Organising Your Time:** Normally allow 2 hours, but you can be side-tracked.
- **Also See:** BEAUJOLAIS, La DOMBES, LYON.

A Bit of History

La Vague – Every year, on the last Sunday in January, local conscripts celebrate the **Fête des Conscrits.** Those eligible to take part are men between the ages of 20 and 80.

Dress code for the occasion is a black suit and top hat, decorated with a coloured ribbon (different colour for each decade: 20s, 30s etc).

At 11am the participants form a procession, link arms and, clutching colourful bouquets of mimosa and carnations, make their way along rue Nationale close on each others' heels, in what is known as the Friendship Wave (*La Vague de l'Amitié*).

"La Vague"

J. Damase/MICHELIN

Modern Villefranche – In addition to its historical role as a wine trading centre, Villefranche now earns its living from the manufacture of sports and work wear (Joannès Sabot founded an overalls factory here in 1887), shirts and hosiery. The metallurgy, mechanical and food-processing industries are also represented here.

Sights

Old houses

Guided tour of the town: mid-Jun–mid-Sept: Sat, 9.30am, 3pm. ☞8€. ☎04 74 07 27 40. www.villefranche.net. Most of the town's oldest houses built between the 15C and 18C are to be found along **rue Nationale.** They have relatively narrow façades, because of a tax imposed on the width of house façades in 1260, to make up for the exemption from taxes and the other privileges which had been granted to the town in its charter.

Odd-numbered side of the road

Note nos 375 (vaulted passageway), 401 (16C openwork spiral staircase in the courtyard) and, at no 17 rue Grenette the turret staircase with skylights. In the courtyard of no 507 the well is

VILLEFRANCHE-SUR-SAÔNE				
		Nationale R.		
		République R. de la	AZ	41
		Savigny R. J.-M.	AZ	47
Carnot Pl.	BZ	9	Sous-Préfecture Pl.	AZ	49
Faucon R. du	BY	19	Sous-Préfecture R.	AZ	50
Fayettes R. des	BZ	20	Stalingrad R. de	BZ	52
Grange-Blazet R.	BZ	23			

Ancien hôtel de ville	BZ	B
Auberge de la Coupe d'Or	BY	D
Hôtel Mignot de Bussy	BY	E
Maison Eymin	BZ	F
Niche du Pélican	AZ	K

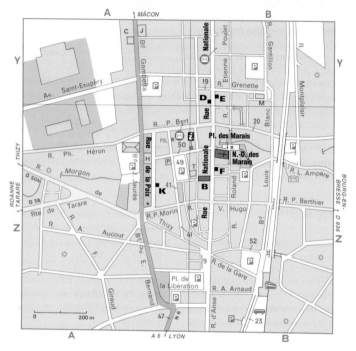

surmounted by a shell-shaped canopy in the courtyard. At no 523, the **Hôtel de Mignot de Bussy** is a lovely Renaissance building with a spiral staircase, mullion windows and shell-shaped niche containing an elegant statue. Behind the splendid 1760 façade of no 561, a vaulted passageway with sculpted supports leads to a 16C courtyard surrounded by pink-walled buildings.

The **Maison Eymin** at no 761 has an 18C façade with four levels of arches in the courtyard, hammer-wrought coats of arms (damaged) and an elegant turret housing a spiral staircase. No 793, once the residence of the Roland de la Platière family, is indicated by a medallion and a commemorative plaque and features a monumental staircase with a beautiful wrought-iron bannister.

Even-numbered side of the road - From no 400, there is a good view of the polygonal tower and sculpted stone balustrade of the Italian Renaissance house at no 407 opposite. A 15C half-timbered house stands on the corner of rue du Faucon and rue Nationale (no 476). At no 486, at the back of the alley on the right, a Renaissance bas-relief depicts two cherubs with chubby cheeks holding coats of arms with the date 1537.

The **Auberge de la Coupe d'Or** at no 528 was the oldest inn in Villefranche (late 14C) before it was transformed in the 17C. On the corner of rue Paul-Bert, the façade on the right (no 596) with crocket gables dates from the late 15C, and that on the left with moulded mullioned windows and medallions is Renaissance. Note the Gothic corner niche at no 706. A passage at no 810 leads to a restored courtyard.

Address Book

ⓒ*For coin ranges see the cover flap.*

WHERE TO STAY

🍴 **Emile Job** – *01190 Montmerle-sur-Saône, 13km/8mi N of Villefranche. Take N 6 to St-Georges-de-Reneins, then D 20.* ☎*04 74 69 33 92. www.hoteldurivage. com. Closed 1–15 Mar, 22 Oct–14 Nov, Sun evening from Oct–May, Tue lunch from Jun–Sept and Mon. 22 rms.* ☐*8€. Restaurant*🍴. Located just before the bridge crossing the Saône, here is a hotel-restaurant with a lovely terrace surrounded by linden trees. The rooms are bourgeois and clean, the renovated dining room is rather elegant, the menus are varied and the reception is hospitable: most enjoyable.

🍴🍴 **Hôtel Plaisance** – *96 av. de la Libération.* ☎*04 74 65 33 52. www.beau jolais-hotel.com. Closed 24 Dec–1 Jan.* 🅿. *68 rms.* ☐*9€*. An impeccably managed family hotel across from l'Esplanade de la Libération. True, the decor in the lounge is somewhat dated, but the recently renovated rooms, each with its own style, are clean and nicely furnished.

WHERE TO EAT

🍴 **Ferme-auberge La Bicheronne** – *Le Bicheron, 01480 Fareins, 10km/6mi NE of Villefranche. Take D 44, then at Beauregard take dir. Château de Fléchères via D 933 and 2nd road on right towards 'Le Bicheron'.* ☎*04 74 67 81 01. Closed Jan, Mon and Thu. Reservations recommended.* Wielding her saucepans and whisks, the owner of this farm has been delighting well-fed guests for over twenty years. Her farm chickens and guinea fowl, generally accompanied by a *gratin dauphinois*, are popular.

The old **town hall** at no 816 was completed in 1660. The façade is built of beautiful warm golden Jarnioux stone and has a solid oak door decorated with cast-iron nails. The house at no 834 was built in the late 15C and has a charming courtyard with a staircase turret. The coat of arms is that of Pierre II de Bourbon and Anne de Beaujeu.

Rue de la Paix

The façade of the building to the south of the post office features a "pelican niche," a Gothic sculpture decorated with finials and pinnacles. Next to it, set slightly further back, is a pretty Renaissance well.

Place des Marais

This pretty square to the north-east of the church contains a fountain and is enclosed by modern houses with arcades, painted in shades of pink and ochre. On the corner with rue Nationale, a ceramic plaque depicts Pierre II de Bourbon and Anne de Beaujeu in the same pose as that on the famous triptych by the Master of Moulins.

Notre-Dame-des-Marais

In the 13C a chapel was built in honour of a statue of the Virgin Mary which had been found in a nearby marsh (marais); all that now remains of it is the small Romanesque tower above the chancel. The magnificent Late Gothic (16C) façade of the church was donated by Pierre de Bourbon and Anne de Beaujeu.

Inside, the nave is surprisingly high and has pretty vaulting decorated with sculpture and pendant keystones. The organ was made by J Callinet in 1835. Note the gargoyles on the north façade; one of them represents lust.

Excursions

Ars-sur-Formans

6km/3.7mi E along D 904.

This tiny Dombes village was once the spiritual charge of the priest **Jean-Marie Vianney** (1786–1859), who was canonised in 1925. The "priest of Ars" subsequently became the patron saint of parish priests and the village has therefore become a popular place of pilgrimage.

Pilgrimage

The small village church is now abutted by a basilica built in 1862 to plans by Pierre Bossan. Inside, the saint's body reposes in a magnificent shrine. The bare concrete crypt, built half underground and 55m/179ft long, is the work of one of the architects of the basilica dedicated to St Pius X in Lourdes.

The old presbytery has been kept as it was when the priest of Ars died. Visitors can see the kitchen, the priest's bedroom and the "relics room," containing mementoes of the priest. An audio-visual show in a room by the presbytery gives an insight into the saint's personality. The **Chapelle du Coeur** houses a repository which contains the priest's heart, and a marble statue by the sculptor Émilien Cabuchet (1819–1902) showing the priest at prayer. The largest annual pilgrimage takes place on 4 August, the anniversary of the priest's death.

L'Historial

Walk down the high street.

&🕑*Open Mar daily except Mon 2pm–6pm; Apr–Oct 10am–noon, 2pm–6pm (Jul–Aug daily except Monday am); rest of year weekends and public holidays 2pm–6pm.* ⌾*5€.* ☎*04 74 00 70 22. www.musee-ars.org.*

Thirty-five waxworks figures, made by the workshops of the Musée Grévin (Paris' answer to Madame Tussaud's), are displayed in a series of 17 tableaux illustrating scenes from the life of the saintly priest.

Château de Fléchères★

6km/3.7mi NE along D 933.

The early-17C château stands in a shaded 30ha/74-acre park offering pleasant strolls. Built by a wealthy Protestant from Lyon, the edifice included a *temple* (Protestant church) on the third floor of the central building.

The huge hall beneath the church was used for gatherings of the local Protestant community. The owner's living quarters were confined to the wings, which were lower than the central building. The interior is decorated with superb Italian frescoes (1632) believed to be the work of Pietro Ricchi.

Trévoux

10km/0.6mi SE via D 933.

This town is built on different levels along the steep bank of the Saône, its colourful façades and flower-filled gardens all facing southwards. Trévoux stands at the intersection of three Roman roads; it was once the capital of the Principality of Dombes, the seat of a sovereign Parliament, and was independent until 1762. After the Duke of Maine decreed that the town's magistrates and members of Parliament must also be residents here, a number of mansions were built in the 18C, along the alleyways of the old districts. In the 17C and 18C the town was one of the most brilliant intellectual centres in France. Its printing house, founded in 1603, was famous. In 1704 the Jesuits published the first edition of the famous Trévoux Dictionary; under their supervision, the Trévoux Journal fought a relentless campaign against Voltaire and the "Encyclopædic" philosophers for 30 years. 🛈*Pl. du Pont BP 108, 01600 TRÉVOUX,* ☎*04 74 00 36 32.*

Old Town Tour

Park in boulevard des Combattants. Walk to place de la Terrasse which overlooks the Saône. The Palais du Parlement is on the other side of rue du Palais.

Palais du Parlement

🕑*Open May–Sept: (guided tours, 45m), Sat, Sun and public holidays. Ask at tourist office for the hours.* 🕑*Closed Sat–Sun (Oct–Apr), 1 Jan and 25 Dec.* ⌾*2€.* ☎*04 74 00 36 32.*

Parliament House was built at the end of the 17C; the Dombes Parliament sat from 1697 to 1771.

The hall leads into the courtroom with its beautiful beamed ceiling with painted decoration.

Rue du Gouvernement

On either side of the street, just below the church, the Trévoux Dictionary and Journal were written and printed. The Jesuits who lived on the right, in the tall, spacious Maison des Pères had only to cross the street to take their manuscripts to the printers opposite.

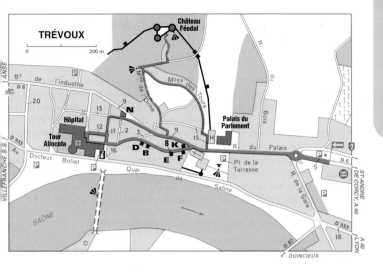

Further down are a number of old houses: the house of the Governor of Dombes, that of the Grande Mademoiselle and the Mint, their austere façades concealing terraces overlooking the Saône.

▶ Take Rue des Halles to the hospital.

Hôpital

🕐 Open May–Sept: guided tours (30min) of the Apothecary's dispensary: from the tourist office at 3pm and 4.30pm. ✎2€. ☎04 74 00 36 32.

The hospital was founded in 1686 by La Grande Mademoiselle; it still has the original wood-panelled pharmacy and a beautiful collection of pottery from Gien and Nevers.

▶ Return to rue des Halles and turn left onto rue du Port. Turn right onto rue de l'Herberie.

This street was once reserved for Jews. The intersection of rue de l'Herberie and Grande-Rue forms a triangle dominated by the square-shaped Arsenal tower of 1405, later converted into a belfry.

▶ Walk up montée de l'Orme to the castle.

Château Féodal

🕐 Open Jul–Aug daily except Thu; May–Jun and Sept Sat, Sun and public holidays; Mar–Apr and from Oct–mid Nov Sun and public holidays: enquire at tourist office for times. ✎2€. ☎04 74 00 36 32.

Remains of the medieval castle (14C); from the top of the octagonal tower there is a view of the Saône.

▶ Walk down montée des Tours, then return along rue du Palais back to boulevard des Combattants.

VIVIERS

POPULATION 3,413

MICHELIN MAP 331: K-7

It was this episcopal town – created in the 5C – that gave its name to the province of Vivarais. Its location, boxed in between Jouannade hill and the rocky peak on which the upper town is built, meant that it remained almost untouched by the Industrial Revolution. Only the quarries, originally opened in about 1750 by the Pavin brothers in the hamlet of Lafarge north of the town to produce cement, are witness to the conversion of a small Ardèche business into a firm of international rank. The ecclesiastical town, built at the foot of the cathedral, commands a view of the Rhône as it enters Donzère gorge. The contrast between the cliffs on either side of the river, the isolated peaks in the middle of the gap and the stately flowing river upstream of Châteauneuf power plant form a picturesque sight.

- **Information:** 5 Pl. Riquet, 07220 VIVIERS, ☎04 75 52 77 00. www.viviers-tourisme.com.
- ▶ **Orient Yourself:** Viviers is easily reached from the A 7 and N 7; Montélimar is 17km/11mi to the N, Bourg-St-Andéol, 14km/9mi to the S.
- **Parking:** Limited centre parking; park near the Hotel de Ville (see local map).
- **Don't Miss:** Take a tour of the Old Town.
- **Organising Your Time:** Allow 1–2 hours.
- **Also See:** GORGES DE L'ARDÈCHE, AVEN d'ORGANC, MONTÉLIMAR.

A Bit of History

After Alba-la-Romaine, the Roman capital of the Helvia people, fell into ruins, Bishop Ausonne went to live in Vivarium, at the confluence of the Escoutay and the Rhône where the city had its port. In the 5C the upper town was fortified.

Numerous donations and skilful politics gradually turned the Vivier bishops into overlords of an immense domain east of the Rhône – the Vivarais. They fiercely defended its independence against the counts of Toulouse, sharing ownership with them of the Largentière mines and minting their own coins.

At the end of the 13C the French monarchy wanted to expand its territory into the Rhône valley. The Bishop of Viviers finally recognised the suzerainty of the King of France in 1308; a large part of the Vivarais became "Crown" land, whereas the west bank of the Rhône remained "Empire" land, under the distant control of the Holy Roman Emperor.

Inside a second set of ramparts, a medieval city began to develop. All that remains of the defence towers and the main doors is a clock tower, the **Tour de l'Horloge,** extensively refurbished

in the 19C. In 1498 Claude de Tournon, became Bishop of Viviers; he had the Romanesque cathedral destroyed and a Flamboyant Gothic chancel built.

Noël Albert, a nouveau-riche entrepreneur who had made his fortune in the salt trade and tax collection, had the Renaissance façade of the Maison des Chevaliers built. After becoming head of the Protestants, he captured the ecclesiastical city. As a result, the cathedral was partly ruined and the cloisters and canon's buildings destroyed. Albert was arrested and beheaded, but the bishop had already fled Viviers and did not return until 1731. That year, François Reynaud de Villeneuve began construction of the current bishop's palace according to the drawings of the Avignon architect J-B Franque.

Old Town★

The ecclesiastical town is distinct from the lower town. They communicated via the **Porte de la Gâche** to the west and **Porte de l'Abri** to the south. The houses in the lower town, in a tight cluster, are roofed with Roman tiles. They generally consist of two upper storeys and a ground floor housing a high cellar or a shop. Most of them have kept their medieval appearance despite many alterations over the centuries. The houses in the ecclesiastical town hide their gardens and courtyards behind bare walls with semicircular openings, sometimes surmounted by a coat of arms.

▸ *Park on place de la Roubine. Follow rue J.-B.-Serre and Grande-Rue as far as place de la République.*

From the eastern corner of the square there is a view of the ruins of Château-vieux Tower.

Maison des Chevaliers

The "Knights' House," also called the house of Noël Albert, was built in 1546. The ornate window-frames on the first

Maison des Chevaliers

floor consist of columns and fluted pilasters with Ionic capitals; rams' heads and garlands of leaves have been carved on the lintels, between the modillions. Above are two bas-reliefs: on the left, a cavalcade of knights on horseback and on the right, a jousting tournament.

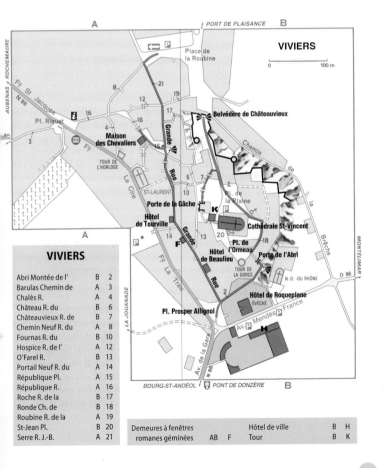

VIVIERS

Grande-Rue

This street is lined with meticulously dressed façades, some with ornate portals surmounted by wrought-iron balconies such as **Hôtel de Tourville** and **Hôtel de Beaulieu** (18C).

Grande-Rue leads to a series of little cross-streets, narrow, stepped and often spanned by arches.

Place Prosper-Allignol

The square is flanked by two buildings erected between 1732 and 1738 by Franque. Their Classical symmetry and neat stonework makes them beautiful examples of 18C Viviers architecture.

▷ *Walk up the steep montée de l'Abri, which passes under Porte de l'Abri and leads to place de l'Ormeau.*

The street offers a fine view over the chapel of Notre-Dame du Rhône, rebuilt by Franque, and the mouth of the Donzère gorge.

Place de l'Ormeau

The square, lined with old canons' houses (17C) owes its name to a centuries-old elm tree *(ormeau)* which perished in 1976; a new tree has been planted.

▷ *Take the parapet walk (Chemin de Ronde) around the cathedral; from place de la Plaine, a passageway north leads to a vast terrace.*

Belvédère de Châteauvieux

This belvedere, built on a natural acropolis at one time washed by the Rhône during floods, stands above place de la Roubine. The **view** embraces the old roofs of the city, the clock tower, the enormous cutting formed by the Lafarge quarries, the cooling towers of Cruas power station and the factory at Châteauneuf.

▷ *Turn round and go downhill via rue de Châteauvieux (on the right) to Porte de la Gâche.*

With its smooth cobblestones, covered passageways and arches, rue de Châteauvieux has a picturesque medieval air.

▷ *Climb the steps to the tower.*

Tower

In the 12C, this tower was the entrance to the upper town. Only the square part of the building existed at the time, with a Romanesque chapel dedicated to St Michael on the first floor.

Cathédrale St-Vincent

The only remains of the 12C Romanesque building are the porch, the west front and the lower part of the nave walls. The chancel is remarkable for its Flamboyant **ribbed vaulting★** and the fenestration of its stained-glass windows.

Excursions

Chapelle Notre-Dame-de-Montcham Viewpoint★

The belvedere to the right of the chapel commands a lovely panorama of Mont Ventoux.

Défilé de Donzère★★

14km/9mi S on D 73 and D 144 to Donzère and then D 486 to the river.
This is a very picturesque canyon through which the Rhône flows. The vertical wall of the west bank contrasts with the isolated peaks lining the east bank. This point is traditionally considered to be the gateway into Provence. The bridges upstream and downstream of the canyon offer attractive views of it.

▷ *Do not stop on the bridges. Park the car after crossing the first bridge, within sight of Viviers, and walk down to the Rhône along the path leading to the camp site.*

Donzère

About 5km/3mi S on N 86 and D 486.
The terraced village is spread out over the slopes of a hill, at the foot of a 15C castle. Of the medieval fortifications, there remain several vaulted streets, ramparts pierced by gates, and a 12C church built in the Provençal Romanesque style and remodelled in the 19C.

PARC NATUREL RÉGIONAL DES VOLCANS D'AUVERGNE

MICHELIN MAPS 326: E-6 TO F-9 AND 330: E-1 TO F-5

This park is the largest of all France's regional nature parks; it encompasses 153 localities in the *départements* of Puy-de-Dôme and Cantal and has a resident population of 91,000. Five main natural regions make up the park: the **Dôme** mountain range of volcanic hills *(puys)*; the **Dore** massif, the vast grass-covered basalt plains of **Cézallier**; the **Artense** with its granite hills, moorland and valleys dotted with lakes and peat bogs; and the **Cantal** mountains.

The main aim of the park is to protect the region's exceptional natural and architectural heritage, which it does by running nature reserves and making good any sites that have fallen into disrepair. It is also involved in boosting the local rural economy – based largely on agriculture and handicrafts – and developing tourism in the region (information centres, lodging for ramblers, marked footpaths and itineraries, cross-country skiing).

- **Information:** www.parc-volcans-auvergne.com.
- **Don't Miss:** Puy-de-Dôme, Puy de Sancy, Monts du Cantal.
- **Also See:** MONTS DU CÉZALLIER, SALERS, AURILLAC, MURAT.

Maisons du Parc

There are eight excellent Maisons du Parc dotted around, to inform visitors about activities within the park and present the local flora and fauna as well as typical local products: Maison des Fromages, Égliseneuve d'Entraigues; Maison du Buronnier, Belles-Aigues near Laveissière; Maison de la Pierre, Volvic; Maison de l'Eau et de la Pêche, Besse-en-Chandesse; Maison de la Faune, Murat; Maison des Fleurs d'Auvergne, Lac de Guéry; Maison des Tourbières, St-Alyre-ès-Montagne; La Chaumière de Granier, Thiézac.

Fauna and Flora

The region's varied flora includes 2,000 different species, including gentian, Alpine anemone, bilberry, valerian. The mountainous areas are the natural habitat of moufflon, chamois and marmot. Wild boar, roe deer, fox, marten and genet (rarer) live in forests. There are numerous birds of prey including eagle owl, short-toed eagle, kite and goshawk.

VOLVIC
POPULATION 4,202
MICHELIN MAP 326: F-7 – 14KM/8.7MI N OF CLERMONT-FERRAND

Volvic is built on the edge of the solidified lava flow from Nugère volcano. The village is not only famous for the extremely pure water of its spring, filtered through thick layers of volcanic rock and now exported throughout the world, but also for the quarrying and processing of its lava.

- **Information:** Pl. de l'Église, 63530 VOLVIC ☎04 73 33 58 73. www.volvic-tourisme.com.
- **Orient Yourself:** Volvic is 14km/9mi N of Clermont Ferrand and 10km/6mi from Riom; it is reached using the D 986.
- **Organising Your Time:** Allow 2 hours.
- **Also See:** RIOM, CLERMONT-FERRAND, MONTS DÔME.

A Bit of History

Volvic lava – Andesite, extracted from open quarries, is both solid and light; this pale-grey rock has been used as building stone since the 13C and the fact that many buildings in the Auvergne are black is due to atmospheric pollution and not to the stone's original colour. Volvic cemetery is full of extraordinary monuments cut from this stone.

The hardness of the lava and the fact that it can be enamelled at high temperatures have made it popular, for more than a century, for signs and plaques that have to stand up to the weather: clock faces, street signs, level gauges etc. As a result of its exceptional qualities, this rock was chosen by Michelin's road sign department to make enam-elled lava corner-posts, signposts, wall plaques etc from 1920 to 1970. Andesite is also used to make apparatus used in the chemical industry, because of its excellent resistance to acids.

Sights

Church

This was part of the old priory of Mozat; its nave and façade were rebuilt during the 19C. The vast 12C chancel is surrounded by an ambulatory opening onto three radiating chapels; a beautiful wrought-iron grille, from the Romanesque period, closes the axial chapel. There are interesting historiated capitals. At the entrance to the chancel, on the left, note the 14C Virgin with a Bird.

Château de Tournoël

J. Damase/MICHELIN

Musée Municipal Marcel-Sahut

♿ ◷*Open mid-Feb–mid Jun and mid-Sept–Nov Wed–Sun 2pm–5pm; mid-Jun–mid Sept daily except Mon, 2pm–6pm.* ◷*Closed Dec–Jan, 1 May.* ✎*3€, no charge on Wed.* ☎*04 73 33 57 33.*

The museum displays many works by Sahut, a native of this region, including charcoals, watercolours and paintings *(View of Nantes, The Tumbler).*

Maison de la Pierre de Volvic

◷*Open Mar–mid-Nov: guided tours (1hr) 10am–noon, 2pm–6pm.* ◷*Closed 1 May.* ✎*5€.* ☎*04 73 33 56 92.*

A former underground quarry has been used to create the House of Stone, a centre focusing on lava and lava quarrying. Visitors travel to the heart of a **lava flow**★ from the Puy de la Nugère, while a soundtrack reproduces the noises during different phases of an eruption.

Volvic Springs

◷*Open Apr–Oct: Mon–Fri, 9am–noon, 2pm–6pm.* ◷*Closed 1 May.* ✎*No charge.* ☎*04 73 64 51 24.*

In the **Information Centre** there is a presentation of the hydrologic characteristics of the Volvic area and of the bottling of its mineral water; there are also audio-visual shows about the Auvergne and its volcanoes. A network of footpaths provides visitors with walking opportunities *(15min to 1hr 45min).*

Driving Tour

Monts Dôme *25km/15.5mi*

▶ *Leave N on D 15 towards Châtelguyon; left before the cemetery.*

Château de Tournoël★

◷*Open Jul–Aug 10am–12.30pm, 2pm–7pm.* ✎*6€.* ☎*04 73 33 53 06.* www.tournoel.com.

Tournoël Castle, on the crest of a rocky spur overlooking the whole of the Limagne, was owned by the counts of Auvergne, captured and almost entirely destroyed it in 1213.

In the 14C, however, it was rebuilt by Hugues de la Roche, who widened the bases of the towers.

▶ *Rejoin D 15; continue towards Enval.*

Châtelguyon ✚

◷*see CHÂTELGUYON.*

▶ *Leave Châtelguyon SW on D 227.*

Mozac★★ – ◷*see RIOM.*

Riom★★ – ◷*see RIOM.*

▶ *Leave Riom to the SW on D 83.*

Église de Marsat

Built in the 11C and 12C, the church consists of two, heavily restored adjoining naves. Note the curious wheel hanging from the vaulted ceiling, around which a wax thread has been wound in accordance with local tradition.

▶ *Leave Marsat on D 446, heading for Riom. It joins up with N 9 at the entrance to the town. Drive for 3km/1.9mi towards Clermont-Ferrand, then turn right onto D 402.*

Châteaugay

The town lies on the edge of a basaltic plateau and is overlooked by the squat outline of its castle. Châteaugay was built in the 14C by Pierre de Giac, Chancellor of France, and its history is a tragic one. It was in the keep that the grandson of the Chancellor poisoned his wife, Jeanne de Giac, who had won over the heart of John the Fearless, Duke of Burgundy, before becoming one of his murderers' accomplices. After being appointed minister to Charles VII, Giac himself was arrested, tortured, sewn into a sack and drowned.

Keep★

◷*Open Jul–mid Sept: guided tours (45min) 2pm–6pm;* ✎*2€. Apply to the town hall.* ☎*04 73 87 24 35.*

The square keep built in lava stone is the most interesting part of the castle; it is almost the only one in the Auvergne to have remained intact.

Richelieu did not include it in his demolition orders, and during the French Revolution, Couthon, a member of the National Convention, was unable to raze it to the ground.

INDEX

INDEX

INDEX

INDEX

WHERE TO STAY

WHERE TO EAT

MAPS AND PLANS

LIST OF MAPS

COMPANION PUBLICATIONS

Motorists who plan ahead will always have the appropriate maps at hand. Michelin products complement each of the sites listed in The Green Guide; map references are given to help you find your location on our range of maps.

- The regional maps at a scale of 1:200 000 nos 519, 522, 523 and 526, which cover the main roads and secondary roads, include useful indications for finding tourist attractions. In addition to identifying the nature of the road ways, the maps show castles, churches and other religious edifices, scenic view points, megalithic monuments, swimming beaches on lakes and rivers, swimming pools, golf courses, race-courses, air fields, and more.

- The Local Maps maps at a scale of 1:150 000 and 1:175 000 are the latest maps in our collection. They include useful symbols for identifying tourist attractions, town plans and an index. The map diagram below indicates which maps you need to travel in Auvergne and the Rhône Valley.

- Remember to travel with the latest edition of the map of France no 721 (1:1 000 000), which gives an overall view of the region, and the main access roadsthat connect it to the rest of France. Convenient Atlas formats (spiral, hard cover and "mini") are also available.

Michelin offers travellers a route-planning service on the internet: **www.ViaMichelin.com.**
Choose the shortest route, a route without tolls, or the Michelin recommended route to your destination; you can also access information about hotels and restaurants from the *Michelin Guide France.*

Bon voyage!

LEGEND

	Sight	Seaside resort	Winter sports resort	Spa
Highly recommended ★★★		≗≗≗	❋❋❋	⧾⧾⧾
Recommended	★★	≗≗	❋❋	⧾⧾
Interesting	★	≗	❋	⧾

Additional symbols

🛈	Tourist information
═══ ═══	Motorway or other primary route
❶ ❶	Junction: complete, limited
⊨⊨ ═══	Pedestrian street
⌁⌁⌁⌁⌁	Unsuitable for traffic, street subject to restrictions
▭▭▭ ----	Steps – Footpath
🚂 🚉	Train station – Auto-train station
🚌 🚍	Coach (bus) station
━━━━	Tram
Ⓜ	Metro, underground
🅿	Park-and-Ride
♿	Access for the disabled
✉	Post office
☎	Telephone
✉	Covered market
⨉⨉⨉	Barracks
△	Drawbridge
∪	Quarry
✕	Mine
Ⓑ Ⓕ	Car ferry (river or lake)
⛴	Ferry service: cars and passengers
⛵	Foot passengers only
③	Access route number common to Michelin maps and town plans
Bert (R.)...	Main shopping street
AZ B	Map co-ordinates

Sports and recreation

🏇	Racecourse
⛸	Skating rink
≗ ⌇	Outdoor, indoor swimming pool
🎥	Multiplex Cinema
⛵	Marina, sailing centre
⛺	Trail refuge hut
□━■━■━□	Cable cars, gondolas
□━┿━┿━□	Funicular, rack railway
🚂	Tourist train
◆	Recreation area, park
🎭	Theme, amusement park
⚘	Wildlife park, zoo
❀	Gardens, park, arboretum
❀	Bird sanctuary, aviary
🚶	Walking tour, footpath
☻	Of special interest to children

Abbreviations

A	Agricultural office (Chambre d'agriculture)
C	Chamber of Commerce (Chambre de commerce)
H	Town hall (Hôtel de ville)
J	Law courts (Palais de justice)
M	Museum (Musée)
P	Local authority offices (Préfecture, sous-préfecture)
POL.	Police station (Police)
🏚	Police station (Gendarmerie)
T	Theatre (Théâtre)
U	University (Université)

Selected monuments and sights

◉ ⇒	Tour - Departure point
🏛 ✝	Catholic church
🏛 ✝	Protestant church, other temple
◙ ◘ ⛓	Synagogue - Mosque
▬	Building
■	Statue, small building
✝	Calvary, wayside cross
◎	Fountain
●▬►	Rampart - Tower - Gate
✕	Château, castle, historic house
⁘	Ruins
◡	Dam
✿	Factory, power plant
☆	Fort
⌒	Cave
▭	Troglodyte dwelling
⛏	Prehistoric site
▼	Viewing table
☇	Viewpoint
▲	Other place of interest

Michelin Apa Publications Ltd

A joint venture between Michelin and Langenscheidt

Suite 6, Tulip House, 70 Borough High Street, London SE1 1XF, United Kingdom

© 2009 Michelin Apa Publications Ltd
ISBN 978-1-906261-52-8
Printed: September 2008
Printed and bound: Himmer, Germany

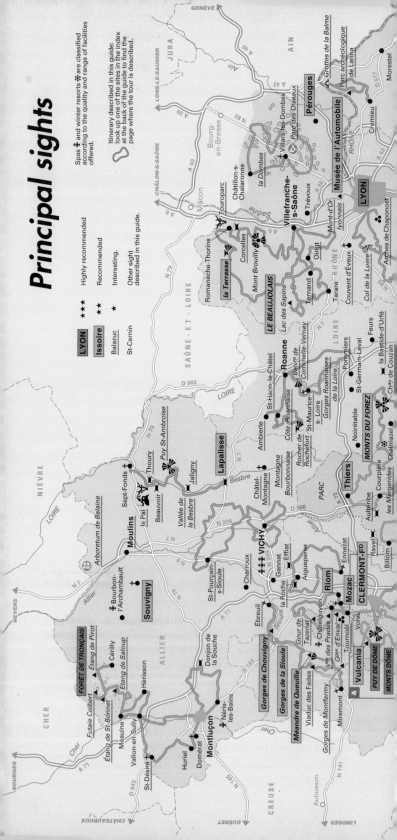

Principal sights

LYON	Highly recommended
Issoire	Recommended
Balazuc	Interesting.
St-Cernin	Other sight described in this guide.

★★★ Highly recommended
★★ Recommended
★ Interesting.

Spas ‡ and winter resorts ❄ are classified according to the quality and range of facilities offered.

Itinerary described in this guide: look up one of the sites in the index at the back of the guide to find the page where the tour is described.